Family Portraits

WestBow Press books may be ordered through booksellers or by contacting:

WestBow Press
A Division of Thomas Nelson
1663 Liberty Drive
Bloomington, IN 47403
www.westbowpress.com
1 (866) 928-1240

ISBN: 978-1-4908-1174-1 (sc)
ISBN: 978-1-4908-1173-4 (hc)
ISBN: 978-1-4908-1175-8 (e)

Library of Congress Control Number: 2013921686

Printed in the United States of America.

WestBow Press rev. date: 12/3/2013

Family Portraits

Character Studies in 1 and 2 Samuel

Randy McCracken

WestBow
PRESS
A DIVISION OF THOMAS NELSON

To Paul and Helen Walton
(Dad & Mom)
With much love and appreciation

Table of Contents

Abbreviations

Textual

4QSam^a	The first Samuel manuscript found in Qumran Cave 4
K	Kethibh (the written Hebrew text)
LXX	Septuagint
LXX^A	Septuagint as found in Codex Alexandrinus
MT	Masoretic Text (the standard Hebrew text)
Q	Qere (the Hebrew text to be read out)

Miscellaneous

ANE	Ancient Near East
BC	Before Christ
cf.	*confer*, compare
chap(s).	chapter(s)
contra	against
ed(s).	edited by; editor(s); edition
esp.	especially
e.g.	*exempli gratia*, for example
ESV	English Standard Version
et al.	*et alii*, and others
ff.	following (verses, pages, etc.)
ibid.	*ibidem*, in the same place
i.e.	*id est*, that is
n.	note, footnote
NASB	New American Standard Bible
NIV	New International Version
NRSV	New Revised Standard Version
NT	New Testament
OT	Old Testament
p., pp.	page(s)
rev.	revised
trans.	translated by
v., vv.	verse(s)
vis-à-vis	opposite to; compared with
vol(s).	volume(s)

Commentaries, Journals, Reference Works

AB	Anchor Bible
AOTC	Apollos Old Testament Commentary

BAR	*Biblical Archaeology Review*
BDB	F. Brown, S. R. Driver, and C. A. Briggs, *A Hebrew and English Lexicon of the Old Testament*, Oxford: Clarendon, 1907
Bib	*Biblica*
BibInt	*Biblical Interpretation*
BSac	*Bibliotheca Sacra*
BTCB	Brazos Theological Commentary on the Bible
CBC	Cambridge Bible Commentary
CBQ	*Catholic Biblical Quarterly*
DSB	Daily Study Bible
DOTHB	Dictionary of the Old Testament Historical Books
EBC	The Expositor's Bible Commentary
EWCS	Enduring Word Commentary Series
GCK	*Gesenius' Hebrew Grammar*, ed. E. Kautzch, rev. and trans. A. E. Cowley, Oxford: Clarendon, 1910
HUCA	*Hebrew Union College Annual*
IBC	Interpretation Bible Commentary
IDB	*The Interpreter's Dictionary of the Bible*, G. A. Buttrick, et al., eds., 4 vols. Nashville: Abingdon, 1962. *Supplementary Volume*, ed. K. Crim, et al., 1976
Int	*Interpretation*
JBL	*Journal of Biblical Literature*
JESOT	*Journal for the Evangelical Study of the Old Testament*
JSOT	*Journal for the Study of the Old Testament*
LWC	The Living Word Commentary
MTOT	Mastering the Old Testament
NAC	The New American Commentary
NBC	The New Bible Commentary
NCBC	The New Century Bible Commentary
NIB	The New Interpreter's Bible
NIBC	The New International Bible Commentary
NICOT	The New International Commentary on the Old Testament
NIDOTTE	*New International Dictionary of Old Testament Theology & Exegesis*, ed. W. A. VanGemeren, 5 vols., Carlisle: Paternoster; Grand Rapids: Zondervan, 1996
OTL	Old Testament Library
TBC	Torch Bible Commentary
TDNT	*Theological Dictionary of the New Testament*, ed. Gerhard Kittel, trans. Geoffrey W. Bromiley, vol. VIII, Grand Rapids: Wm. B. Eerdmans, 1971
TOTC	Tyndale Old Testament Commentaries
TynB	*Tyndale Bulletin*
USQR	*Union Seminary Quarterly Review*

VT	*Vetus Testamentum*
WBC	Word Biblical Commentary
WTJ	*Westminster Theological Journal*
ZAW	*Zeitschrift für die alttestamentliche Wissenschaft*

Preface

Although character studies abound on Saul, and especially, David, there has been no attempt (that I am aware of) to focus on the other characters who people the pages of 1 and 2 Samuel in one volume. This book is a modest attempt in that direction and seeks to illuminate these lesser known figures.

How one attempts a character study is of great importance. Being too narrow in focus is a mistake commonly made by interpreters. Biblical characters appear in a story that is part of a larger narrative, which has its own themes and agenda. To isolate a character by not considering the larger purpose of the narrative does an injustice to the message that the biblical author wanted to convey. Therefore, the character studies contained in this book seek to keep the overall purposes of the biblical author in mind.

Since this book includes the word "portrait" in its title, allow me to draw an analogy from the art world. A painting may have as its central focus a particular person or structure, but that central object (or person) is enhanced and most appreciated by noting the context in which it appears. Various colors, objects, or people, provide background and contrast that give the painting's focus its definition. For example, while Christ is the main character in Leonardo da Vinci's The Last Supper, the painting is greatly enhanced by the portraits of the twelve disciples, whose expressions and demeanor contribute to the overall effect of the painting. The portraits of the disciples tell a small part of the story but the painting is constructed in a way that uses all of them to point to Christ. Similarly, to truly appreciate the main themes of the books of Samuel, and to better understand the main characters, it is important that we examine those who interact with them. For example, the author purposely contrasts Eli and his sons with Samuel, and Jonathan with Saul. The author's portrait of these "minor" characters gives us a better understanding of the "major" characters, which, in turn, helps us to discern the author's overall purpose(s).

I have written this book with three convictions: 1) consulting the original languages of the Bible significantly enhances one's understanding. Therefore, I have examined the text of 1 and 2 Samuel in Hebrew and have referred to it (and, at times, provided my own translation of it) where appropriate. 2) It is a lack of wisdom or a mark of arrogance to ignore the studious labors of others. Therefore, I have sought, and frequently noted, the insights of others throughout this book. I have also made my own presuppositions clear by noting those with whom I disagree, believing that dialogue is a key to learning. Accordingly, I decided to use footnotes rather than endnotes, so that the interested reader may have immediate access to any references or additional discussion. 3) God intended the biblical message to change our lives. Therefore, it is important not only to interpret the Word, but also to apply it.

I am aware that these three convictions run the risk of alienating some readers. Some will find reference to the Hebrew, or the many footnotes cited, too "scholarly" (to use a nice word) for their taste. Others of a more academic bent may find the applications suggested too "devotional," or "moralistic" in nature. Yet I am not only convinced that scholarship and application *should* go together; I believe they *must* go together. Therefore, it is my hope that both the academic and non-academic reader will proceed with an open mind.

The target audience of this book includes pastors, Bible College (University) students, and the average Christian who seeks to grow in his or her understanding of 1 and 2 Samuel. Keeping this broad range of audience in mind, I have sought to be as non-technical as possible. I refer to the Hebrew only when it is necessary to illuminate a point, and I have sought to explain terminology that might be unfamiliar to a layperson. At times I have used the footnotes as a way of pursuing a thought or discussion a little further, but the reader who is not interested in the "small print" can overlook them without harm of losing the essence of the book. I have chosen to use the NKJV except in those places where I have used my own translation. When I use italics in a biblical quote, it is for the purpose of emphasis.

I have had the pleasure of teaching 1 and 2 Samuel to the students at Calvary Chapel Bible College in York, England for the past ten years, as well as to students at Calvary Chapel Bible College Mallorca in the winter of 2006 and Calvary Chapel Bible College Jerusalem in the summer of 2009. I would like to thank them for the opportunity of making that pilgrimage together, and for the many insights they have added to my understanding of the characters and of the books of Samuel. Additionally, I am indebted to the many Christians who have heard me teach some of these character studies over the years, especially those in the Calvary Chapels of York, Bridlington, Mansfield, and Hastings in England, as well as the Calvary Chapels in Stone Mountain (Ga.), Heartland (Fort Valley, Ga.), Aiken (SC.), and Greeneville (Tn.) in the USA.

A special thank you is due to those who helped with the editing of this manuscript. This includes my teaching assistants, Hannah Siler, and Megan Holando, who spent many hours reading, editing, and offering helpful suggestions. I would also like to thank Matthew Ward, another teaching assistant, who compiled an early version of the indexes, and James Siler who checked portions of the Scripture index and made many helpful corrections. Tasha and Lindsay Kennedy were of great help with the family tree and triangle diagrams, and a source of encouragement as I neared the end of this project. My friend Polly Williams read portions of this manuscript and offered insights and encouragement, as did my good friend Alan Manchester whose insights and suggestions have greatly improved the readability of this book. My colleague Christian Nowraty has been a Godsend by answering my many computer questions as I have neared the end of preparing this manuscript and Caelen Weber was generous in offering his photography skills for the author photo that accompanies this book.

I want to say a special "thank you" to two of my former professors: the late Gerald Vinther, who first gave me a love for the Old Testament and the God revealed in its pages; and John T. Willis, who fueled that passion and inspired a particular love for the books of Samuel. I would like to thank all those at WestBow Press who were involved in the various stages of designing, publishing, and making this book available. Without their expertise, this manuscript would only be available on my computer! I would especially like to thank Paul and Helen Walton, my father and mother, to whom this volume is dedicated, for their love, encouragement, and support over the years, and for the image of Christ I see reflected in their lives. I also want to thank Gloria my dear wife and partner in the ministry for these past 37 years. Thank you for your love, support, and for unselfishly allowing me the time necessary to complete this book. Finally, all thanks and praise be to God who has given his only Son so that "whoever will" can experience his grace, love, and forgiveness, and an eternal home with him.

Randy McCracken
York, June 2013

Introduction: The Importance of Families in 1 and 2 Samuel

Indeed we are your bone and your flesh (2 Sam. 5:1).

Power and Family

If you were asked to name the major theme of the books of Samuel in one word perhaps the best word would be *power*. After all, what word better describes books that speak about the establishment of a monarchy, the slaying of giants, the killing of Philistines and other enemies, and the struggle to maintain control over the throne of Israel? Power—its use and abuse and the question of who ultimately is in control of the events described, is certainly a main theme of 1 and 2 Samuel.[1]

Hannah's song at the beginning of 1 Samuel clearly announces this theme, as it speaks of the One who is in control of all things. Her song includes statements such as, "I smile at my enemies, because I rejoice in your salvation" (1 Sam. 2:1). This sounds more like the declaration of an exultant warrior than a barren woman who has been blessed with a son! The same is true when she says, "The bows of the mighty men are broken, and those who stumbled are girded with strength" (2:4). This military imagery suggests that Hannah's song of praise is about more than just her own situation. Her final words, "He will give strength to His *king*, and exalt the horn of his *anointed*" (2:10), confirm this. There is a futuristic ring to these words, as the reader is aware that there was not yet a king in Israel.

While this fighting imagery suggests the theme of power, Hannah's song is specific about where power ultimately comes from. In 1 Samuel 2:6–8 she declares,

> The LORD kills and makes alive; He brings down to the grave and brings up. The LORD makes poor and makes rich; He brings low and lifts up. He raises the poor from the dust and lifts the beggar from the ash heap, to set them among princes and make them inherit the throne of glory.

---

[1] Mary J. Evans, in *The Message of Samuel*, (Leicester: Inter-Varsity Press, 2004), p. 21, writes, "One of the main concepts that links all the stories in these books and all the other interests of the writers is that of power." Bruce C. Birch, in *The First and Second Books of Samuel*, NIB, Vol. II (Nashville: Abingdon Press, 1998), p. 949, states, "On the surface, these stories may seem preoccupied with political power, but we will discover that these narratives testify to the true power of the Lord, acting in and through personalities and events to bring Israel to a new future in keeping with God's purposes."

1

The stunning reversal Hannah mentions in the previous verse, of the hungry ceasing to hunger and the barren giving birth to seven (2:5), is the result of this powerful God who "kills and makes alive" and who "brings low and lifts up." This is the same powerful God who will later dispense with the terrifying military "machine" named Goliath, clothed head to foot with impregnable armor and wielding fearsome weapons, with only a sling and stone in the hands of a shepherd boy. It shows, as David so eloquently states, that, "the LORD does not save with sword and spear; for the battle is the LORD's" (1 Sam. 17:47). This story leaves no doubt about who is in control and where real power resides.

The theme of power in the books of Samuel[2] works itself out, not only in the stories of military battles and kings, but also within another context: *family*. It is sadly true that many families today can relate to their homes being a battleground. Husbands and wives fight things out at home or in the courts, children turn on their parents, and brother harms brother (or sister). These are all too common occurrences in our world.

The books of Samuel thus remind us that human nature and strife have not changed much. The events sound like any modern newscast. These books have it all: children disrespecting parental authority (Hophni and Phinehas—1 Sam. 2), a young man seeking to kill the father that gave him life (Absalom—2 Sam. 17), adultery and murder (David—2 Sam. 11), and the rape of a young woman by her brother (Amnon and Tamar—2 Sam. 13).

Besides family scandal and violence, in almost every modern newscast there are other stories of national interest. Once again, 1 and 2 Samuel are no different. There are foes who threaten and invade (the Philistines—1 Sam. 4), and foes who show no respect for treaties or cordial relations between nations (the Ammonites—2 Sam. 10). Trouble also manifests itself from within when a political tyrant imposes his own will to the detriment of those he is governing (Saul). My point in mentioning these stories, which reflect power struggles on a national level, is that political instability also threatens life at the family level. Perhaps this is most clearly illustrated in Saul's slaughter of the priests of Nob, when he wipes out the entire priestly family of Ahimelech, the great grandson of Eli except for Abiathar who escapes (1 Sam. 22).

---

[2] While I refer to the "books" of Samuel, originally they were one book. The division into 1 and 2 Samuel originally took place when the Hebrew text was translated into Greek in the third century BC. The Greek version of the Hebrew Scriptures (known as the Septuagint and abbreviated as LXX) divided Samuel and Kings into the books of 1 and 2 Kingdoms (our 1 and 2 Samuel) and 3 and 4 Kingdoms (our 1 and 2 Kings). Peter R. Ackroyd, in *The First Book of Samuel*, CBC (Cambridge: Cambridge University Press, 1977), p. 3, argues that this shows "...the division between Samuel and Kings is artificial." For more information, see P. Kyle McCarter, *1 Samuel*, AB (Garden City: Doubleday & Company, Inc., 1980), p. 3.

It may seem at first glance that all the news about families in 1 and 2 Samuel is bad news, but this would be a misconception. There are children who respect authority, love the Lord, and grow up to be influential leaders (Samuel—1 Sam. 3). There is the love of loyal friends that goes deeper than family ties (Jonathan and David—1 Sam. 20). There is wisdom in words and action that turns away wrath and saves a family from potential destruction (Abigail—1 Sam. 25). And there is mercy for the weak and helpless when promises are kept (Mephibosheth—2 Sam. 9).

The overriding reason for this good news is that, despite human failings and imperfections, there is an all-powerful, all-wise, and all-loving God who ultimately is in control of all the affairs of men and women. God is even powerful enough to use the actions of the wicked and the errors of his own people to bring about his own good purposes. This is one of the reasons that Hannah's prophetic song opens the books of Samuel.[3] God certainly deals with the unrepentant and rebellious sinner, but he also delights in showing mercy and grace. We shall observe this principle frequently as we examine the various lives found in 1 and 2 Samuel.

The Families and Family Language of 1 and 2 Samuel

The majority of the characters mentioned in 1 and 2 Samuel come from just four families: the families of Samuel, Eli, Saul, and David.[4] However, the appearance of characters that are not blood-related to one of these families (e.g., Doeg, Achish, Uriah and Ittai), also usually incorporates the family motif.[5]

Another interesting observation contributing to the idea of "family portraits," is the regular use of familial terms throughout 1 and 2 Samuel. For example, the words son(s), house, father(s), brother(s), wife/wives, daugh-

---

[3] Many have noted that the books of Samuel are framed by two important poems with similar themes. Hannah's prayer/song and David's psalm (2 Sam. 22) share common words and motifs. See, for example, Raymond B. Dillard and Tremper Longman III, *An Introduction to the Old Testament* (Leicester: APOLLOS, 1995), p. 141.

[4] See the family trees included at the beginning of each main section of this book.

[5] For example, Doeg is responsible for the destruction of an entire priestly family (1 Sam. 22:9–19). The most obvious connection between family and foreigner is Uriah the Hittite. David's adultery with Bathsheba and murder of Uriah is certainly a disruption of his family life, not to mention the story of how Bathsheba later becomes incorporated into David's family. Other characters, such as Nabal (1 Sam. 25), Ziba (2 Sam. 16:1–4), the wise woman of Tekoa (2 Sam. 14:1–21), and the wise woman of Abel Beth Maachah (2 Sam. 20:15–22) could be cited as further examples that incorporate family language and motifs.

ter(s), and family/families occur with such frequency that their use can hardly be accidental.[6]

These words occur in different contexts and sometimes describe more than immediate family relationships. At times they have a nationalistic sense and refer to the relationship among the tribes of Israel. Notice how David's return to Jerusalem after Absalom's revolt is recounted in terms of a family squabble:

> Just then all the men of Israel came to the king, and said to the king, "Why have our *brethren*, the men of Judah, stolen you away and brought the king, his *household*, and all David's men with him across the Jordan?" So all the men of Judah answered the men of Israel, "Because the king is a *close relative* of ours. Why then are you angry over this matter?" (2 Sam. 19:41–42).

The language bears resemblance to the question Abner directs to Joab during the civil war between the houses of David and Saul: "How long will it be then until you tell the people to return from pursuing their *brethren?*" (2 Sam. 2:26).

"You are my bone and my flesh" is another expression used to show the family connection of all the people of Israel. These words, similar to those first spoken by Adam concerning the most intimate relationship of

---

[6] The word "son(s)" is used several ways in the narrative, but its frequency cannot be ignored. "Son(s)" occurs 141 times in 1 Samuel and 209 times in 2 Samuel. This does not include its occurrence in the proper name, *"Benjamin"* (*ben* is the Hebrew word for son), a name that occurs in these books 13 times, and 11 times, respectively, and which, on a few occasions (e.g., 1 Sam. 22:7), has special relational significance. See comments on this verse in J.P. Fokkelman, *Narrative Art and Poetry in the Books of Samuel, Vol. II: The Crossing Fates,* (Assen/Maastricht & Dover: Van Gorcum, 1986), p. 381. I have made no attempt to distinguish the idiomatic use of "son(s) of" which is found in a number of expressions such as, "son of 40 years" = 40 years old, "son of death" = "dead man," or the common usage in tribal or national identities such as "sons of Ammon," or "sons of Judah," etc. Even if these are excluded, the count remains significantly high.

Other words include: "house," 61 times in 1 Samuel and 115 times in 2 Samuel; "Father(s)," 54 times in 1 Samuel and 28 times in 2 Samuel; "Brother(s)," 12 times in 1 Samuel and 34 times in 2 Samuel; and "Daughters," 16 times in 1 Samuel and 20 times in 2 Samuel. "Wife/wives " is more difficult since the same word also means "woman/women." Based on context the translation "wife/wives " occurs approximately 23 times in 1 Samuel and 18 times in 2 Samuel. Other family terms that appear in 1 and 2 Samuel include "husband" (13 times), "sister" (10 times), "family/families" (9 times), "concubine(s)" (9 times), "son-in-law" (7 times), "mother" (7 times), "father-in-law" (2 times), and "daughter-in-law" (1 time).

all—that of a husband and wife (Gen. 1:23), are used several times in 2 Samuel. When David is anointed king over all Israel, the tribes respond: "Indeed we are your bone and your flesh" (2 Sam. 5:1). David rebukes Judah for being the last tribe to return him to his throne in Jerusalem using this same expression (2 Sam. 19:12). In the next verse, he uses it again in a literal way referring to Amasa his nephew, promising to make him commander of his army. This repeated use of "my bone and my flesh" demonstrates how familial terms can refer to the nation of Israel or be used in a more intimate sense.[7]

The close connection between familial language and the fate of a nation is illustrated in the judgment pronounced against Eli's house:[8] "For I have told him that I will judge *his house* forever for the iniquity which he knows, because *his sons* made themselves vile, and he did not restrain them" (1 Sam. 3:13). The resulting judgment on Eli's house also leads to a devastating defeat of the entire nation of Israel (1 Sam. 4).

David Jobling points out a pattern of surrogate fatherhood and sonship among the four leaders mentioned in 1 Samuel. "Through three transitions in leadership we see the following pattern. The leader has natural sons who play a significant role in the story, but he adopts the next leader as a surrogate son."[9] Saul and David call each other "father" and "son" (1 Sam. 24:11, 16), and a similar relationship is implied between Eli and Samuel, and Samuel and Saul.

One of the best examples of 1 and 2 Samuel's "focus on the family" occurs in the introductory story of 1 Samuel. These books about *"power"* begin perhaps surprisingly with the story of a family from the mountains of Ephraim. It is the family of Elkanah, experiencing a crisis that leads eventually to the story of kingship told in the rest of 1 and 2 Samuel. Another exam-

---

[7] This is not to overlook Brueggemann's assertion that the terms "brother" and "bone and flesh" do not necessarily refer to blood ties but to the sharing of covenant oaths. See Walter Brueggemann, "Of the Same Flesh and Bone," *CBQ* 32/4, 1970, pp. 532-542 (esp. p. 536). Such "family" language is known to be a part of covenant terminology in the Ancient Near East. My contention is that the author of the books of Samuel purposely exploits this family terminology to demonstrate the abusive use of power. One cannot give a more devastating critique of the misuse of power than to show how it destroys "families," whether political or personal in nature.

[8] The word "house" has many shades of meaning in 1 and 2 Samuel: 1. a physical building, as when David has a house built for himself (2 Sam. 5:11); 2. the Lord's sanctuary, whether the tabernacle (1 Sam. 1:7, 24), or the future temple (2 Sam. 7:5ff.); and 3. a family and the generations that follow (as in the case of Eli) and, thus, a dynasty (as in the case of David—2 Sam. 7:11). See the excellent treatment of this topic in Joel Rosenberg, *King and Kin: Political Allegory in the Hebrew Bible*, (Bloomington & Indianapolis: Indiana University Press, 1986), pp. 113-123.

[9] David Jobling, in *1 Samuel*, Berit Olam: Studies in Hebrew Narrative & Poetry (Collegeville: The Liturgical Press, 1998), p. 112. See his extended discussion on pp. 111-125.

ple is the account of how the wickedness of Eli's sons eventually leads to a new line of high priests in Israel (1 Sam. 2:34–35).

Israel's first king is also not without family conflict. When Saul perceives Jonathan's loyalty to David as a threat to his kingship, their disagreement erupts into a dispute that threatens Jonathan's life (1 Sam. 20:31–33). Saul's jealousy of David, not only divides his family, it divides the nation.

The books of Samuel continually show how Israel's national history intersects with family life.[10] This may explain why the story of David alternates between events in his public and private life.[11] The pivotal event which greatly affects the life of the whole nation is his adultery with Bathsheba and murder of her husband (2 Sam. 11). What seems like a private act between "consenting adults" becomes a scandal that leads to death within David's own family (2 Sam. 12:10–14; chap. 13) and civil war (2 Sam. 15–18).[12] David's "secret" adultery is re-enacted publicly by his son Absalom (16:22), just as Nathan prophesied (12:11). Absalom's rebellion leads to indescribable personal pain for David who, in one of the most moving passages in 1 and 2 Samuel, cries out, "O my son Absalom—my son, my son Absalom—if only I had died in your place! O Absalom my son, my son!" (2 Sam. 18:33).[13] David calls Absalom "my son" a total of eight times in this verse and in 19:4. This highlights the connection between national life (Absalom's revolt) and personal pain within a family (a father mourning the death of his son). Power struggles on a national level can devastate families, and power struggles within families can wreak havoc in a community, tribe or even an entire nation.[14]

---

[10] David M. Gunn, in *The Story of King David: Genre and Interpretation*, JSOT Supp. 6 (Sheffield: JSOT Press, 1978), pp. 88-89, makes this point concerning David's life. He writes, "In sum it is possible to describe the story as one of accession, rebellion and succession. It is a story about David as king." He continues, "The pattern of intrigue, sex and violence in the Bathsheba episode is played out at length in the subsequent story within David's own family. The story of David then, is also a story about David the man, about David and his family, about David's own personal or private life."

[11] Kenneth R. R. Gros Louis, "King David of Israel," *Literary Interpretations of Biblical Narratives*, Vol. II, ed. Kenneth R. R. Gros Louis (Nashville: Abingdon, 1982), pp. 204-219, has written an excellent article on this topic.

[12] Regina M. Schwartz, in "Adultery in the House of David: The Metanarrative of Biblical Scholarship and the Narratives of the Bible," *Semeia* 54, 1991, pp. 45-46, argues for an even more direct connection. "These are not separate spheres, public and private, that have impact on one another…instead, politics and sexuality are so deeply and complexly integrated as to be one, and it is anachronistic to even understand them as two different spheres of life."

[13] On occasion, verses in the Hebrew Bible are numbered differently from modern English versions. For example, 2 Sam. 18:33 is 19:1 in the Hebrew Bible. For the sake of familiarity, the verse notations used in this book will follow the English versions.

[14] Michael J. Smith, "The Failure of the Family in Judges, Part 1: Jephthah," *BSac.* 162, 2005, pp. 279-298 and "The Failure of the Family in Judges, Part 2: Samson,"

A Literary Approach to the Bible

The Bible is the bestselling book of all time. It is also considered by many to contain the greatest literature of all time. This implies that it was written with artistry. For example, the first five books of the Bible are known as "The Law of Moses" or in Hebrew "The Torah." Yet these books are not just a collection of dry laws devoid of context. Instead "the Law" occurs within the context of a story that reaches back to the Creation itself, contains the promises given to the patriarchs (Abraham, Isaac and Jacob), includes the people of Israel's Exodus from Egypt and wanderings in the wilderness, and looks forward to the conquest of the land of Canaan. In other words, the meaning of the Law is rooted in the story of Israel's origin and development.

A person's initial encounter with the God of the Bible is thus not an abstract meeting. It is through the medium of narrative that readers first learn what God is like, what life is about, how life is to be lived, and how God and people interact.[15] Like any good story, the biblical story has a plot, characters, setting, and a narrator. To say that much of the Bible is written in narrative form and contains the elements of a good story is not to suggest it is unhistorical, but simply to affirm that the biblical authors wrote the history of Israel with (a high level of) literary skill.[16]

There are many good books that explore the art of biblical narrative.[17] It is not my purpose to repeat what others have done. However, because the topic of this book is character studies, it is important to explain how one determines a biblical character's portrait.

BSac. 162, 2005, pp. 424-436, not only points to the significance of the family theme in the Book of Judges but sees a similar dynamic expressed (see esp. Part 1, p. 298—"What happened in his own family [i.e., Jephthah's] in the episode with his daughter reflects what happened in the larger family of the nation at the end of the story").

[15] This narrative, however, consists of many different genres: poems, genealogies, and legal material, to name a few.

[16] For a defense of the literary but historical nature of the Hebrew Bible see, Eugene H. Merrill, "Old Testament History: A Theological Perspective," and V. Philips Long, "Old Testament History: A Hermeneutical Perspective," in *NIDOTTE*, vol. 1, ed. Willem A. VanGemeren (Grand Rapids: Zondervan, 1996), pp. 68-85, and 86-102 respectively. Also see, Iain Provan, V. Philips Long, & Temper Longman III, *A Biblical History of Israel*, (Louisville: Westminster John Knox Press, 2003), esp. chap. 4, "Narrative and History: Stories About the Past," pp. 75-96.

[17] The following are considered the standard classic treatments of this approach: Robert Alter, *The Art of Biblical Narrative*, (New York: Basic Books, Inc., 1981); Adele Berlin, *Poetics and Interpretation of Biblical Narrative*, (Sheffield: Almond Press, 1983); Meir Sternberg, *The Poetics of Biblical Narrative: Ideological Literature and the Drama of Reading*, (Bloomington: Indiana University Press, 1985); and Shimon Bar-Efrat, *Narrative Art in the Bible*, (Sheffield: JSOT Press, 1989).

The Biblical Author's Purpose

Understanding that the inspired author[18] of 1 and 2 Samuel had specific messages that he wished to communicate is an important guideline for our character studies.[19] The theological themes of the author determine which characters and events are highlighted. From our modern standpoint we might like to know more about certain characters and situations. However, all authors must be selective.[20] As House states, "Readers must remember…that prophetic narrative has certain points it wants to make. The author presents characters in ways that will highlight those particular ideas."[21]

The stories in the books of Samuel are not isolated short stories, but must be interpreted in a larger context. Chisholm states, "Old Testament narratives do exhibit a **macroplot**—a larger plot that encompasses but also transcends the individual stories. Each individual story must be viewed within the context of this macroplot" (author's emphasis).[22] Therefore, the larger

---

[18] A detailed discussion of the authorship of the books of Samuel is beyond the scope of this work. By "inspired author" I mean the person or persons God chose to put these books into writing. For a comprehensive treatment on the authorship of 1 and 2 Samuel see David Toshio Tsumura, *The First Book of Samuel*, NICOT (Grand Rapids: Wm. B. Eerdmans, 2007), pp. 11-32.

[19] Some argue that 1 and 2 Samuel is part of a larger work called the "Deuteronomic (or, Deuteronomistic) History." The seminal work on this was done by Martin Noth, *The Deuteronomistic History*, JSOT Supp. 15 (Sheffield: JSOT Press, 1981), originally published in 1943. This expression has evolved to mean different things to different scholars. The main point is that the books of Joshua to 2 Kings are heavily influenced by Deuteronomy and are often treated as one work. I am in agreement that the book of Deuteronomy has an important influence on these books and that they are related to one another, nonetheless, each of these books has its own focus. While 1 and 2 Samuel may be part of a larger prophetic history, I would argue that it has its own special themes and emphases. For a similar assessment see, David G. Firth, *1&2 Samuel*, AOTC (Downers Grove: InterVaristy Press, 2009), p. 20. Having said this, there is obviously a strong connection between Samuel and Kings (see n. 2 above), as the story of kingship begun in Samuel continues, and finds its conclusion in Kings.

[20] Raymond B. Dillard and Tremper Longman III, *An Introduction to the Old Testament*, p. 23, observe, "No history can tell everything about its subject. It would take longer to write about an event than it does to experience it if the historian's goal were to be comprehensive. Thus all history writing involves selectivity."

[21] Paul R. House, in *1, 2 Kings*, NAC (Nashville: Broadman & Holman, 1995), p. 65. In the Hebrew canon the books of Samuel are included with Joshua, Judges, and 1–2 Kings, in a section known as the Former Prophets. This title suggests that prophets wrote these books and that the prophetic word is a key theme of these books. By prophetic word I mean the declaring of God's truth. This can be described as both, "forth-telling" (proclamation), and "foretelling" of events yet in the future.

[22] Robert B. Chisholm Jr., *Interpreting the Historical Books: An Exegetical Handbook* (Grand Rapids: Kregel, 2006), p. 77.

context, and important themes (such as power) provide the framework for our character studies.[23]

The author achieves his purpose by using techniques that include: the narrator's point of view, characterization and typology. On some occasions, omissions (gaps) and even ambiguities help to convey his message. We will now take a closer look at each of these.

Narrator's Point of View

In some forms of literature the author of a book may be distinguished from the narrator. In biblical literature they are one and the same and thus I will use the terms interchangeably. The narrator is the one who introduces the story. For example, 1 Samuel 1:1 begins, "Now there was a certain man of Ramathaim Zophim." The narrator provides the setting by giving geographical details ("came to their house at Ramah"—1 Sam. 1:19), and details of time ("So Samuel lay down until morning"—1 Sam. 3:15). The narrator controls the plot of the story, the description of characters, and the interaction between characters. As Longman observes, "The narrator is a device used by authors to shape and guide how the reader responds to the characters and events of the story."[24] Usually the narrator tells the story in the third person, meaning the narrator does not figure in the story himself.[25] The narrator of the Bible "gives the impression of an all-knowing mind…a mind that in the context of the canon must be associated with God himself."[26] This means that any observation or statement made by the narrator is reliable. As Meir Sternberg has observed, "The Bible always tells the truth in that its narrator is absolutely and straightforwardly reliable."[27] Thus any statement made by the narrator about a character or event should be accepted as factual. If it stands in contradiction to a statement made by another character, then we can know that this character is lying, deceived or misinformed.[28]

---

[23] Gordon J. Wenham, in *Story as Torah* (Grand Rapids: Baker Academic, 2000), p. 17, notes the importance of understanding the overall message of a biblical book, and the author's purpose for including a given story, if we are to interpret it accurately.

[24] Tremper Longman III, in "Biblical Narrative," *A Complete Literary Guide to the Bible*, eds. Leland Ryken and Tremper Longman III (Grand Rapids: Zondervan, 1993), p. 75.

[25] Ibid. The only exceptions to this in the Bible are the Books of Ezra, Nehemiah, and the "we" sections of Acts.

[26] Ibid.

[27] Sternberg, *Poetics*, p. 51. See also pp. 130-131 for a discussion of point of view and the authority of the biblical narrator. For an alternative view see Jobling, *1 Samuel*, pp. 141-142. While Jobling offers some great insights, I have a fundamental disagreement with the presuppositions that underlie his approach.

[28] Bar Efrat, in *Narrative Art in the Bible*, pp. 13-45, has an excellent in-depth treatment on the role of the biblical narrator.

Characterization

What are the criteria for evaluating a biblical character? The most obvious is any explicit description of the character by the narrator: such as when we are told that Eli's sons are "worthless men" or that Abigail was "a woman of good understanding and beautiful appearance; but the man [her husband] was harsh and evil in his doings" (1 Sam. 25:3).[29] However, such descriptions are rare, and this is part of the art of the biblical narrator. It seems most often he would rather lead his reader on a journey of discovery. Leo Perdue differentiates these two approaches as "telling" and "showing," with "showing" being the preferred method of the author of 1 and 2 Samuel.[30] Similarly, Long states, "The portrayal of character is most often achieved through a variety of implicit, or indirect, means."[31] Robert Alter lists the following ways (in ascending order of importance) in which the Bible reveals a person's character:

> Character can be revealed through the report of actions; through appearance, gestures, posture, costume; through one character's comments on another; through direct speech by the character; through inward speech, either summarized or quoted as interior monologue; or through statements by the narrator about the attitudes and intentions of the personages, which may come either as flat assertions or motivated explanations.[32]

Adele Berlin has identified three main categories for classifying characters: 1) full-fledged (some use the term "round" character); 2) types (some use the term "flat" character); and 3) agents. The most obvious examples of *full-fledged* characters in the Books of Samuel are Saul and David. A *flat* character would be someone like Peninnah, where only one aspect of personality is emphasized. Sometimes the function of a flat character is to serve as a "foil" to another character. For example, Peninnah's actions contrast sharply with Hannah's. In 2 Samuel 11, Bathsheba is an example of an *agent*. Her main function is to highlight David's sin, although later she appears as a full-fledged character in 1 Kings 1–2.[33] Therefore, certain characters (Peninnah,

---

[29] V. Philips Long, "First and Second Samuel," *A Complete Literary Guide to the Bible*, p. 173.

[30] Leo G. Perdue, " 'Is There Anyone Left of the House of Saul...' Ambiguity and Characterization of David in the Succession Narrative," *JSOT* 30, 1984, p. 70.

[31] Long, "First and Second Samuel," p. 173.

[32] Alter, *The Art of Biblical Narrative*, pp. 116-117.

[33] Adele Berlin, *Poetics*, pp. 23-32. However, Bar-Efrat, *Narrative Art*, p. 86 cautions, "It is not always possible to make a clear and unequivocal distinction between a primary and a secondary character."

Eliab., etc.) seem one-dimensional, because the writer has little to say about them.[34]

Typology

One way in which Scripture comments on its characters is by the use of analogy, or typology. "Typology means that earlier characters and events are understood as figures of later characters and events, and the text is written in a way that brings out the connection."[35] Biblical authors frequently use the descriptions, actions, words, and circumstances, of one character and situation to remind the reader of a similar biblical character or situation.[36] By this technique, the author is able to make comparisons (demonstrating either similarities or contrasts) with the present character or situation he is describing. This is a more interesting and effective way of writing than the author simply telling the reader what he thinks of a given character or situation.

> Analogies thus provide clues and signposts to show the attentive reader the point of the story and to help him form the judgments that the writer intended. Readers who fail to catch the significance of these analogies will be misled about who's the villain and who's the hero.[37]

The books of Samuel are full of this literary technique and, thus, typology and analogy will frequently be a reliable guide in our evaluation of the characters we examine.

Gaps and Ambiguities

Since an author cannot possibly say everything about a character or situation, there are inevitably "gaps" in the story.[38] These intentional gaps

---

[34] For a fuller discussion, and helpful chart, on characterization see Chisholm, *Interpreting the Historical Books*, pp. 28-32. David W. Cotter also has a helpful discussion on characters and characterization in *Genesis*, Berit Olam: Studies in Hebrew Narrative & Poetry (Collegeville: The Liturgical Press, 2003), pp. xxix-xxxvii.

[35] Peter Leithart, in *A Son to Me: An Exposition of 1&2 Samuel*, (Moscow: Canon Press, 2003), p. 13.

[36] Ibid., p. 14, states, "The analogies between different characters can be brought out by names, quotations, allusions, physical details, actions, and so forth. The analogies between different events can be brought out by location, similar sequences of events, repetition of key words or phrases, and so on."

[37] Ibid., p. 15. In the following pages, we will often find interpreter's confusing biblical heroes and villains.

[38] David J.A. Clines, in "An Introduction to Reading Her Story," *Telling Queen Michal's Story: An Experiment in Comparative Interpretation*, JSOT Supp. 119, David J.A. Clines and Tamara C. Eskenazi eds. (Sheffield: Sheffield Academic Press, 1991), p. 61,

may have one of several purposes. For example, Samuel disappears from the narrative of 1 Samuel 4–6, for which there are two possible reasons.[39] First, it demonstrates that Israel did not rely on the prophetic word of Samuel with which the author concluded the previous section of narrative (1 Sam. 3:19–4:1a). Second, Israel's destruction cannot be associated with Samuel, since he appears nowhere in the account. The blame lies solely with Israel and with the priesthood of Eli and his sons. The author may also withhold information to cause the reader to jump to wrong conclusions as with Mephibosheth (2 Sam. 16:1–4; 19:24–30), or to surprise the reader later (David's handing over of seven of Saul's descendants to the Gibeonites—2 Sam. 21:1–14).

Some gaps occur because the author has no interest to explain them. Perhaps the Bible's most (in)famous gap provokes the question, "Where did Cain get his wife?" Various explanations have been offered, including that she must be one of Cain's sisters, but the author has no interest in explaining her identity. In the books we are studying Samuel is, again, an excellent example. As noted above, he disappears from the narrative at the end of 1 Samuel 3 (technically 4:1a) and does not reappear until 1 Samuel 7. In 1 Samuel 3, he is a young man, but by 1 Samuel 7 he is much older. The reader may wonder what Samuel was doing all those years and how he managed to escape the destruction at Shiloh, but such questions are not a concern of the author.

Chisholm notes yet another possibility for gaps. He writes,

> Sometimes the gaps remain due to the fact that we as readers are so far removed temporally, linguistically, and culturally from the world of the text. Many of the gaps we perceive in a story would not have been present for an ancient Israelite audience, for ancient readers would have intuitively understood nuances of their language and aspects of their culture better than we do.[40]

The obvious problem with "gapping" is that it can create ambiguity. Why does Jonathan not know that Saul has broken his promise and tried several more times to kill David (1 Sam. 20:2)? Was there really a prophecy that

---

writes, "No text can spell out all that is implicit in its story-line or in its characterization; any interpretation of the story, any telling of it that is not a mere verbal repetition of it, is bound to fill gaps in the original."

[39] Some would add a third reason I do not find convincing: the author's combination of various source materials.

[40] Chisholm, *Interpreting the Historical Books*, p. 69. Similarly, Moises Silva, in *God, Language and Scripture: Reading the Bible in the Light of General Linguistics* (Grand Rapids: Zondervan Publishing House, 1990), p. 94, states, "Ambiguity arises more frequently when we read literature distant in time and culture from us, since we are less familiar with the whole context in which the writing originated."

said, "By the hand of My servant David, I will save My people Israel from the hand of the Philistines and the hand of all their enemies" (2 Sam. 3:18), or were these just the politically expedient words of Abner?

Some gaps create questions that cannot be answered (Where was Samuel all those years?). However, explanations can be provided for other gaps, if the reader pays close attention to the narrative. In these instances the reader must be careful to adhere to the text, and to what is known about the language and cultural world of ancient Israel. We certainly do enter a subjective area here, but that does not mean we should avoid filling in the gaps. Again, Chisholm states,

> Sometimes an author gives us enough information to attempt to resolve ambiguity. In such cases it is valid to read the textual clues, connect the dots, as it were, and propose reasonable explanations that are consistent with what the author tells us in the context and with the dictates of common sense.[41]

Sternberg encourages gap-filling, but also offers words of caution:

> Of course, gap-filling may nevertheless be performed in a wild or misguided or tendentious fashion, and there is no lack of evidence for this in criticism ancient and modern. But to gain cogency, a hypothesis must be legitimated by the text.[42]

As Chisholm and Sternberg make clear, any attempt at gap-filling must involve close scrutiny of the text. There is an important difference between legitimate gap-filling and mere speculation. Gap-filling involves examining clues *anchored in the text.* Speculation is simply an imaginative effort to fill in details *without any basis in the text.* David J. A. Clines makes the following important observation:

> It is worth distinguishing between gap-filling and speculation. While we are gap-filling we are engaged in interpretation; when we speculate, about events or motives, we have stopped interpreting. For interpretation is interpretation of the given text; when we speculate, we are speculating about the characters as people or about events the text might allow

---

[41] Chisholm, *Interpreting the Historical Books*, p. 70.
[42] Sternberg, *Poetics*, p. 188.

but does not require, and we have loosened our attachment to the text.[43]

In the pages that follow it will be necessary at times to engage in some gap-filling. Sometimes the solution will seem more obvious than at other times. On those less obvious occasions I will attempt to suggest what I think is the most likely scenario without, I hope, wandering too far from the intent of the biblical author. I will endeavor to engage in *interpretation* of the text rather than *speculation* (although, I must admit, in a few instances I cannot resist a little speculation). In the end, it will be up to the reader to decide how successful I have been.

I hope that taking into account these principles (considering the wider context, and the author's purposes and writing methods) will prevent our character studies from falling into the trap that Dale Ralph Davis warns of: "The focus on biblical characters in biblical narrative usually leads biblical interpretation astray."[44] In summary, we do not have complete biographies, but rather snapshots, or portraits,[45] of certain incidents and people that contribute to the overall message. Our task is to extract as full a portrait of each character as the text and context allow, and establish the author's (and God's) message and lessons for us.

Purpose and Method

The purpose of this book is to examine people who are introduced to us in the books of Samuel and to learn from their lives. We will sketch the main outline of each character, based on the information given in Scripture. Some lessons will be positive and others negative.[46] Some profiles will be

---

[43] Clines, "Introduction," *Telling Queen Michal's Story*, p. 61.

[44] Dale Ralph Davis, *2 Samuel: Out of Every Adversity* (Ross-shire: Christian Focus, 1999), p. 166. On the other hand, Michael A. Eschelbach, in *Has Joab Foiled David? A Literary Study of the Importance of Joab's Character in Relation to David*, Studies in Biblical Literature 76, (New York: Peter Lang Publishing, 2005), p. 17, laments the fact that, "while literary approaches have proliferated in recent years and been fruitful, studies concerning characterization have been lacking."

[45] Tremper Longman III, in "Biblical Narrative," in *A Complete Literary Guide to the Bible*, p. 73 writes, "Characters are like real people in that we can know them only partially and never exhaustively." Long, "Old Testament History: A Hermeneutical Perspective," p. 87, compares historiography with portraiture. He writes, "It is perhaps not too far off the mark to characterize *historiography* as a kind of *verbal representational art*, analogous in significant respects to, say, portraiture, which is itself a kind of *visual* representational art" (author's emphasis).

[46] Chisholm, *Interpreting the Historical Books*, pp. 34-35, characterizes these as "negative example stories" and "admiration stories." Unfortunately, there are more "negative example stories" than there are "admiration stories" in the books of Samuel! Regard-

short and some more detailed, depending on the amount of material provided by the biblical text.

Our journey through the books of Samuel will not be a smooth one. Examining the characters of these four families will necessitate moving back and forth in the text. A number of characters are embedded in a certain chapter or section, but others are spread throughout the narrative (e.g., Michal and Joab). Therefore this may seem to be a liability, but the strength of this approach lies in the sustained reflection on a given character, which a commentary approach is unable to provide. I hope that this book will demonstrate that an intense focus on character development can lead to insights that otherwise pass undetected.

While our main focus will be the books of Samuel, the approach chosen necessitates extending the scope of our study, since several characters introduced in the books of Samuel reappear in the first two chapters of 1 Kings.[47] Due to the significance of family in 1 and 2 Samuel, this book is arranged according to the four main families listed above. Not every character in the books of Samuel is physically related to one of these four families; so to keep the present book at a reasonable length I have decided to omit treatment of these individuals.

Three glaring omissions will be obvious—Samuel, Saul and David. Apart from God himself, these three are of course the most prominent and important characters. An examination of Samuel, Saul and David, therefore, deserves separate treatment.[48] Despite that, however, many observations and

---

ing the characters of the Hebrew Bible, Wenham, *Story as Torah*, p. 15, writes, "It deals with a world where there are few perfect saints and few unredeemable sinners: most of its heroes and heroines have both virtues and vices, they mix obedience and unbelief."

[47] This includes Abiathar and Jonathan (his son), Shimei, Joab, Bathsheba and Adonijah. While I have argued above that each book extending from Joshua to Kings has its own theological emphasis (and I might add, conclusion), I have also noted the close connection between them, especially the books of Samuel and Kings (see n. 19 above), which, hopefully justifies including the opening chapters of Kings in this study. Many have noted the obvious connection of 1 Kings 1–2 with the narratives in 2 Samuel beginning with the influential work by Leonhard Rost, *The Succession to the Throne of David* (Sheffield: Almond Press, 1982), first published in 1926, here after cited as *"Succession."* While I am not in full agreement with this work, completing certain character studies necessitates looking at 1 Kings 1–2 and is justified by the narrative flow between Samuel and Kings which will hopefully become obvious from the character studies. Joel Rosenberg, *King and Kin*, p. 110, notes the many different contexts in which it is possible to read the David story, ranging from the story itself, or some smaller component of it, all the way to its context within the Hebrew Bible or canonical Christian Bible.

[48] This also means that certain chapters of 1 and 2 Samuel will not be explored in any detail (e.g., 1 Sam. 5–7, as well as other chapters, receive only a cursory mention).

comments are made about each of them as we examine their families and the people closely associated with them.

I have not incorporated the biblical text itself. Therefore as you read this book I encourage you to follow along in your Bible. I have chosen the New King James Version for my quotations, except where I have used my own translation of the Hebrew text to illuminate a particular point. It is my hope and prayer that as you follow along with the text, God will speak to you in a fresh way. As the writer of Hebrews says, "the word of God is living and powerful and sharper than any two-edged sword" (Heb. 4:12). Therefore, while these are stories of people in the past, they still speak a relevant message to us, if we have "ears to hear." While my intention is to remain true to the biblical context and to be sensitive to the cultural context of ancient Israel, I will also seek to communicate that message to contemporary concerns. The writers of the Bible (both Old and New Testament) set the precedent for this, as they often applied the timeless Word of God to their particular situation.[49]

As I have studied 1 and 2 Samuel over the years I have been greatly blessed by their message. Each time I read these books I approach them with a renewed sense of excitement and anticipation about what God will teach me. These books are deep and rich with God's truth. They abound with insight into the human soul and the personality of God. We are introduced to many unforgettable people and to a classic, timeless story that speaks as powerfully today as it did when it was first written.

---

[49] Leland Ryken and Tremper Longman III, "Introduction," A *Complete Literary Guide to the Bible*, pp. 20-21 state, "*The Bible invites both approaches*, but biblical scholars do not find it natural to discuss the universal experiences portrayed in a biblical text. They are generally content to discuss the events and characters in the Bible as data of the ancient world, and not to worry about modern applications. To literary critics, *biblical literature is a mirror in which we see ourselves*" (emphasis mine). Speaking of the historical-critical method which most modern commentaries are based on, Cotter, *Genesis*, p. xix, states, "Essential to this method, despite what some of its skeptical critics think, is the application of the text to the contemporary situation."

Section 1

The Family of Samuel

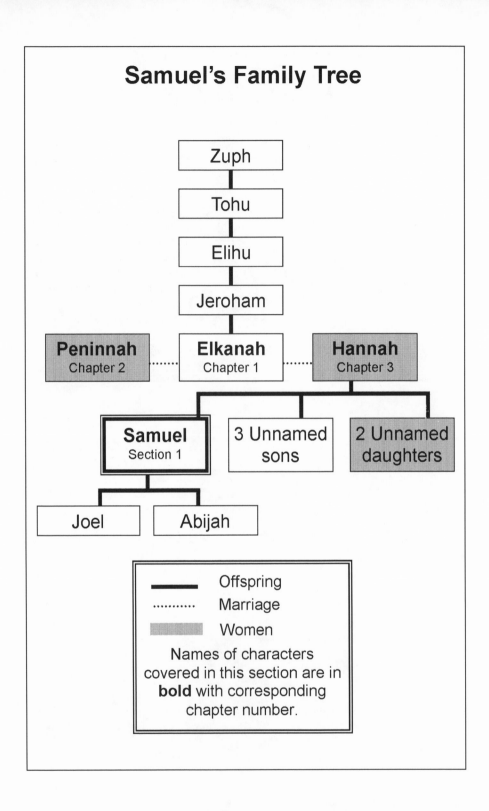

Samuel's Family Tree

Zuph

Tohu

Elihu

Jeroham

Peninnah
Chapter 2

Elkanah
Chapter 1

Hannah
Chapter 3

Samuel
Section 1

3 Unnamed sons

2 Unnamed daughters

Joel

Abijah

——— Offspring

·········· Marriage

Women

Names of characters covered in this section are in **bold** with corresponding chapter number.

Introduction to Samuel's Family

And all Israel from Dan to Beersheba knew that Samuel had been established as a prophet of the LORD (1 Sam. 3:20)

Although these books are named after the prophet Samuel, his family members play the smallest role in the story. This does not detract from the importance of people like Elkanah or, especially, Hannah. For without their piety, the history of Israel might have been very different. It is only to say that, after the initial story of Samuel's birth, none of his family has a significant role in the story that follows. Not only do Elkanah, Hannah and Peninnah disappear after chapter 2, no other relatives of Samuel are mentioned in 1 and 2 Samuel except his two sons. Furthermore, the brief mention of his sons (1 Sam. 8:1–5; 12:2) does not provide enough material for a character study. All we are told is that they did not follow the example of their godly father: "But his sons did not walk in his ways; they turned aside after dishonest gain, took bribes, and perverted justice" (1 Sam. 8:3). Besides this, we only know their names (Joel and Abijah),[1] and that Samuel appointed them as judges over Israel in Beersheba (8:2). Their disobedience disqualified them from having an important role among God's people, for the elders of Israel were disenchanted with them (8:5). Their corrupt practices, however, provided an opportunity for the elders to put forward a demand that would change the course of Israel's history—their request for a king!

It is somewhat surprising that Samuel's descendants play such a minor role, given that he is such an imposing figure in 1 Samuel. However, the books of Samuel show that a consistently ungodly lifestyle leads to ineffectiveness in ministry and public office. God is abundantly patient with sinful, imperfect people; but when selfishness and pride lead to lives of wanton rebellion, God looks elsewhere for a heart that desires to serve him (1 Sam. 3:10). Eli's sons are an example of this same truth (1 Sam. 2:27–36), as is Saul (1 Sam. 13:13–14).

One of the sad storylines of these books is godly parents begetting ungodly offspring (Samuel and David). The stories stand as an admonition to us to "Train up a child in the way he should go" (Prov. 22:6). We do not know what caused Samuel's sons to depart from his ways, but in the case of Eli's sons we are told that "he did not restrain" them (1 Sam. 3:13). In the case of David his sin clearly influenced the behavior of his children (2 Sam. 13). Nevertheless, 1 and 2 Samuel does not place all the responsibility on par-

---

[1] "Joel" means "Yahweh is God" and "Abijah," "My father is Yah." Tsumura, *The First Book of Samuel*, pp. 245-246, states, "Since the name designates the personality which should characterize the holder, one might see irony here. Samuel's sons did not deserve their good names."

ents' shoulders. Children are responsible for the choices they make. In contrast, Saul's son Jonathan represents someone who made godly choices in spite of his father's disobedience. On the other hand, Samuel's example demonstrates that godly parents can produce a godly son. Ultimately each of us stands before the throne of God and must give an account of the things done in the body, whether good or bad (2 Cor. 5:10).

It is encouraging to note that while Samuel's sons may have been corrupt, his grandson Heman was appointed as one of the leading singers in the tabernacle during the time of David (1 Chron. 6:31–33). However, Samuel's story begins with Elkanah, the first character introduced in the books of Samuel and it is to him that we now turn.

Chapter 1

Elkanah: Pious and Imperfect (Samuel's father)

"Only let the LORD establish His word"
(Elkanah speaking to Hannah—1 Sam. 1:23)

Elkanah's Pedigree (1 Sam. 1:1)

Having established that family ties are important in these books, we should not be surprised that 1 Samuel begins with a four-generation genealogy of Elkanah, Samuel's father.

As Ronald Youngblood notes, Elkanah's name means, "God has created [a son]," "tantalizingly prophetic of what was soon to occur in Hannah's womb."[1] But the word *qanah* also means, "to buy," or "acquire," and thus the name *'el-qanah* (spelled "Elkanah" in English translations) could suggest the meaning, "God redeemed."[2] We know nothing about the spiritual walk of Elkanah's ancestors. All we have are their names. It could be that Elkanah had a rich spiritual heritage (see below) but, whatever the case may be, the following verses demonstrate that at some point God gained a hold of this man's life. While at times we can read more into a biblical name than the author may have intended, nonetheless, biblical names are often important within the context of a story.[3] In fact, sometimes context suggests more than one meaning for a name.[4] This may be the case with Elkanah's name as the succeeding verses show him to be a very pious and devout man.

We are told that Elkanah's home is in Ramathaim Zophim in the mountains of Ephraim. Most people are proud to tell others where they are from. The mention of Elkanah's home is important and worth investigating. Ramathaim, better known as "Ramah" (1 Sam. 1:19), means "double height," or "two hills." The town was located somewhere in the mountainous area around the border of Ephraim and Benjamin. The name may suggest the town was associated with two hills, its name referring simultaneously to the hill on which the city was built and the location of the local high place.[5] A reference to Ramah in 1 Samuel 9:11–12 does mention the hill the city is on

---

[1] Ronald F. Youngblood, *1, 2 Samuel*, EBC 3:553-1104 (Grand Rapids: Zondervan, 1992), p. 571.

[2] Elkanah's name consists of two parts: 1. *'el* which is the singular form of the word *ᵉlōhîm* (God); and 2. *qānāh*, which means "to buy, purchase," or "acquire" (sometimes used in the sense of "redeem"—Exod. 15:16; Ps. 74:2). See *NIDOTTE*, vol. 3, pp. 940-942.

[3] The character studies which follow will lend weight to this contention.

[4] The naming of Samuel in 1:20 is another example from this chapter.

[5] Tsumura, *The First Book of Samuel*, p. 107, makes this suggestion.

plus a high place. It has been suggested that Ramathaim is the same place as the "Arimathea" of the New Testament (Matt. 27:57), but this is questionable.[6]

The second part of this place name (Zophim) comes from the name "Zuph," one of Elkanah's ancestors mentioned in this verse. Perhaps a better translation for this phrase is "one of the Zuphites from Ramathaim." We can ascertain that Zuph was a very prominent person, as the area around Ramah was named for him. When Saul searches for his father's lost donkeys the author informs us that he reaches the land of Zuph (1 Sam. 9:5) and is told that there is a prophet there (Samuel) who might be able to help him.

For our purposes, the importance of the name Zuph is that it is part of a Levitical genealogy recorded in 1 Chronicles 6:33–35. There we learn that Zuph, and those descended from him (including Elkanah), are from the family of Kohath one of the sons of Levi. This means that Ramathaim (or Ramah) was a city in the mountains of Ephraim inhabited by the family of Zuph, a Levitical family descended from Kohath.

It is well known that the Levites had no tribal territory of their own. Instead they were given Levitical cities throughout the territories of all the other tribes of Israel. Joshua 21:5 states: "The rest of the *children of Kohath* had ten cities by lot from the families of the *tribe of Ephraim*, from the tribe of Dan, and from the half-tribe of Manasseh." While Ramah is not listed as one of these cities (cf. Joshua 21:20–22), there is evidence that Levites were mobile (e.g., Judg. 17:7–8, 19–20; 19:1). Tantalizingly, Auld suggests that Zuph's name may be a pun on the word for "scout,"[7] which could suggest a change in locality for his family and descendants. Thus Elkanah and his family had two identities: they were Levites and they were Ephraimites. This information is not only important in understanding why Samuel is qualified to serve in the tabernacle, but it is also important in our evaluation of Elkanah later. Just as certain information about our family and where we are from may help others understand us better, so the writer provides us with this important background about Elkanah.

Elkanah's Polygamy (1 Sam. 1:2)

The emphasis on family continues as the writer gives us an intimate glimpse into the family of Elkanah in the following verses. We have discussed Elkanah's ancestry, his home, and the meaning of his name, but the next

---

[6] This may be due to the fact that the Greek text of 1 Sam. 1:1 reads, "Armathaim." On the reading of the Greek text see, A. Graeme Auld, *I&II Samuel*, OTL (Louisville: Westminster John Knox Press, 2011), p. 27.

[7] Ibid. Auld suggests another reason for the pun: "...the family's place of origin was already pregnant with special 'seeing.'"

piece of information is disconcerting. We are bluntly told, "And he had two wives."

While it is true that the Hebrew Scriptures do not contain a commandment saying, "Thou shalt not marry more than one person," there is not a single example of polygamy in the Bible without problems. There are two ways to teach a truth. One way is to make an authoritative statement about what is right and what is wrong ("Thou shalt!" or "Thou shalt not!"). The other way is to tell a story which illustrates right or wrong actions and their consequences. Both ways are used in Scripture and both are valuable; but a story has an emotional impact that usually goes deeper than a mere statement. The fact that Elkanah has two wives, alerts readers to suspect problems.

Next, the author informs us that one wife has children and the other does not. Such information is designed to recall similar stories in Scripture. The stories of Abraham, Sarah, and Hagar, and Jacob, Leah, and Rachel immediately come to mind. These allusions to the patriarchs suggest there is bound to be trouble in Elkanah's family, and reading the next few verses confirms this suspicion.

The mention of bigamy casts an element of doubt over Elkanah's character. He has only done what the fathers of the Israelite nation had done, and bigamy was certainly an acceptable practice of his time, but it raises questions concerning his good judgment. Sometimes society offers solutions to certain problems that are perfectly acceptable within that culture, but these might not be God's best choice for our lives. We only need to recall the problems encountered by Abraham and Jacob to be reminded that following cultural norms does not always bring happiness and fulfillment.

The fact that Hannah is introduced first suggests that Elkanah only married Peninnah because he was unable to have children with Hannah.[8] Peninnah thus became a constant reminder to Hannah that she was not enough for Elkanah. On the other hand, the fact that Peninnah was second-choice, and was apparently chosen for procreation, easily explains her bitterness toward Hannah (and perhaps toward Elkanah also).

When we read the family problems that develop as a result of Elkanah's bigamy we are prompted to ask, "What if Elkanah had chosen to wait on God's timing, and accept God's will whatever the outcome?" In other

---

[8] J.P. Fokkelman, *Narrative Art and Poetry in the Books of Samuel*, vol. IV: *Vow and Desire* (Assen/Maastricht & Dover: Van Gorcum, 1993), pp. 16-17 points out that the word used in Hebrew to describe Hannah (one) is a cardinal number, while the number used to describe Peninnah (second) is an ordinal number. Certainly, however, this expression considers Hannah to be the "first" wife, just as in Genesis 1:5, "day one" means "first day." Fokkelman's point is that "one" here has the connotation of "unique" which may well be true. See also, Tsumura, *The First Book of Samuel*, p. 108 who defends the translation, "first."

words, what if he would have persistently sought God for his barren wife rather than take another wife?

We are faced with similar decisions today. Our society offers many culturally-acceptable "answers," but are they God's will for our lives? If we have an "unwanted" pregnancy our culture says that abortion is an acceptable alternative. If we think we have married the "wrong person" we divorce and continue our search for the "right one." If we have Hannah's problem our culture offers an array of solutions for infertility. Some involve important moral choices.

The question that confronted Elkanah also confronts us. Are we willing to wait on God and accept his will no matter what the outcome might be? For the believer, God's will may result in something other than what we had hoped for, but we know that it is for our good (Rom. 8:28). If we believe in a loving, all-wise God, then we are assured that his will is better for our lives than our own will. If we believe in the all-powerful God spoken about in 1 and 2 Samuel, then we also know that he is able to work in miraculous ways in even the most difficult situations. The believer's response is to wait, trust, and allow God to work things out in his way and his time.

Elkanah's Piety (1 Sam. 1:3)

Verse 3 contains good news and begins to give us another perspective on Elkanah: "This man went up from his city yearly to worship and sacrifice to the LORD of hosts in Shiloh." Elkanah is not only a worshipper of the Lord; he is a committed and dedicated worshipper. "Yearly" (NKJV) is literally "year by year" and shows a consistency in his life. Elkanah's commitment to worship is emphasized throughout the story (1:7, 21; 2:19). According to 1:22, Hannah missed a few of these annual trips to Shiloh while she weaned Samuel, but Elkanah continued to go.

Elkanah's commitment to worship is commendable, but a seemingly innocent statement, which at first seems a little out of place, makes this commitment all the more praiseworthy. After mentioning Elkanah's practice, verse 3 ends with the statement, "Also the two sons of Eli, Hophni and Phinehas, the priests of the LORD, were there." The writer says nothing else about them and in verse 4 returns to Elkanah and the subject of his worship.

It is characteristic of the author of 1 and 2 Samuel to briefly mention a detail that will be important to the story later.[9] In chapter 2 we learn that

---

[9] This literary device is known as "prolepsis." For example, in 1 Sam. 21:7 the mention of Doeg the Edomite seems almost incidental. But in the very next chapter (22:9ff.), Doeg's presence becomes an integral part of the story. Another example is found in 2 Sam. 4:4. In the middle of a story about Ish-bosheth, Mephibosheth is suddenly introduced but then the narrative returns to Ish-bosheth. The purpose,

Hophni and Phinehas are scoundrels who pervert the worship of the Lord at the tabernacle in Shiloh. Once this information is digested, Elkanah's faithfulness in going year by year to worship at Shiloh is much more remarkable. Following the description of Hophni and Phinehas's sin in 2:12–17, the writer reminds us again of Elkanah's yearly visit (2:19).

The reader may also surmise from verse 1 that Elkanah is from a priestly family.[10] This fact, in addition to the mention of the "mountains of Ephraim," provides echoes with the ending of the Book of Judges, which concludes with two stories concerning Levites who live in the mountains of Ephraim (Judg. 17–19).[11] The story in Judges 17 is particularly interesting. A Levite in Judges 17–18 comes to the home of Micah in the mountains of Ephraim and becomes his personal priest. He proceeds to establish a house of false worship there. Later he is enticed by the tribe of Dan to leave Micah's house and become a priest for them, where he continues his idolatrous practices. This Levite reminds us that it is within Elkanah's power, were he so disposed, to cease going up to the Tabernacle and develop his own homemade religion. After all, others were doing that very thing! In contrast, Elkanah is faithful to go year by year to Shiloh in obedience to God's word and in spite of a wicked priesthood (1 Sam. 2:17).

Elkanah's piety and commitment speak loud and clear to a world that shows little loyalty to family or church. When difficulties develop with relationships in our modern world, the popular thing is to sever ties and move on. Rather than work on our marriages, we seek divorces. Rather than salvage a friendship, we hold a grudge. And rather than stay in our church and work

---

however, is to prepare the reader for the events of 2 Sam. 9. For further examples and explanation see, Sternberg, *Poetics*, pp. 337-341.

[10] The modern reader has the advantage of consulting 1 Chronicles which connects Elkanah with the Levitical family of Kohath (1 Chron. 6:22, 27). However, this information was probably evident to the original readers of 1 Samuel also since genealogies were often memorized and passed on orally, as well as written down (1 Sam. 1:1 being one small example). A genealogy would have been of particular importance for a Levitical family, as it would validate their eligibility to serve at the tabernacle. It may also plausibly be argued that since Zuph was prominent enough to give his name to an area (1 Sam. 9:5), the author felt no need to mention Elkanah's Levitical connection. In cultures built on honor and shame (such as ancient Israel) being able to demonstrate that one was from an honorable family was important. Thus the keeping, and knowledge, of genealogies was very significant. See for example, David A. deSilva, *Honor, Patronage, Kinship & Purity* (Downers Grove: IVP Academic, 2000), p. 28. All of this suggests that ancient readers were much more familiar with genealogies than we moderns are, and thus, may have been aware of facts that are less obvious to us.

[11] In the Hebrew Bible 1 Samuel is immediately preceded by the Book of Judges, providing a flow in the story between these two books. In our English Bible the Book of Ruth interrupts this continuity.

out our differences, we shop around for a new one. Our society needs the type of commitment that Elkanah exhibits. We need to recognize the value of worship and the importance of being committed to the fellowship of believers that God has led us to.[12] As we look at the various people in 1 Samuel 1 we will notice that none of them are perfect, yet Elkanah and his imperfect family were committed to worshipping God with other imperfect people. His example stands as an exhortation to us.

Elkanah's Imperfection (1 Sam. 1:4–8)

The first character to speak in 1 Samuel is Elkanah, who asks: "Hannah, why do you weep? Why do you not eat? And why is your heart grieved? Am I not better to you than ten sons?" (v. 8). In these four questions we gain some insight into the personality of Elkanah, which includes some of his shortcomings. First, we can see evidence of soft heartedness as he tries to cheer Hannah up with a mild rebuke. The author has already told us of Elkanah's love for Hannah (1:5). But as we listen to his words we may also notice a sense of exasperation and aggravation.[13] The language of verses 4–7 speak of habitual actions. Elkanah and his family not only make the pilgrimage to Shiloh year after year, there is also continual friction and contention between his wives. Like a broken record playing, Elkanah listens every year to the taunts of Peninnah and the tears of Hannah.

These words, however, not only reveal Elkanah's concern and frustration, they may also reveal his obtuseness. Mary J. Evans writes,

> As for Elkanah, he could observe the pain but did not really understand it. Because Peninnah had many children including several sons, Hannah's childlessness, to her an unbearable tragedy, was for him simply a minor inconvenience. It did not matter to him that she was childless, so why should it matter so much to her...? Perhaps if he had said 'Don't

---

[12] This is not to say that there is no legitimate reason for seeking another church home at certain times. For example, if a pastor does not stand for the truth of Scripture, has been confronted and refuses to repent, or has committed an act of immorality and shows no remorse or repentance, these may be valid reasons to consider finding another fellowship of believers (although these things existed at the tabernacle and still Elkanah continued to come and worship!). My point is that many leave churches for much more trivial reasons. We are often quick to be offended and slow to work out our problems with brothers and sisters in the faith.

[13] Robert Polzin, *Samuel and the Deuteronomist* (Bloomington: Indiana University Press, 1989), p. 22, makes this observation. He writes, "These are words of consolation certainly...but listen again, and you will hear an aggrieved tone, a bitterness more plaintive than Hannah's but a bitterness nonetheless."

you mean more to me than ten sons?' rather than 'Don't I mean more to you?', Hannah might have been a little more convinced. Elkanah seems to have been incapable of seeing Hannah's position from anything other than his own perspective.[14]

Elkanah's words certainly seem to demonstrate the need to walk in another person's shoes before judging them. When someone is struggling with a difficult problem (like depression) year after year, it is not only hard on the person but on those around them. Sometimes the passing of time can harden us to the trial that they are experiencing. It is too easy to dismiss their suffering and expect them to "snap out of it!" Elkanah could only see how Hannah's struggle was affecting him. Paul's words are appropriate here, "Love...does not seek its own, is not provoked...bears all things" (1 Cor. 13:4–7). But the picture painted here in 1 Samuel is all too real, for it is not always easy to respond in a loving way. Prayer and a constant supply of God's grace are necessary for any trial, especially one that seems that it will never end. Indeed, prayer and God's gracious hand are the ingredients that eventually bring a resolution to Hannah's desperate situation.

Having indicted Elkanah, there is another possible interpretation of his words that might vindicate him somewhat. Bruce J. Malina points out that in ancient Mediterranean society (meaning the society of Jesus's day) the wife's most important relationship in the family was with her son.[15] If it can be supposed that Elkanah's social context was similar (and there is a thousand-year difference), then his words would be quite appropriate and loving. He would be assuring Hannah that he had tried to fill the void of relationship in her life that a son would normally occupy. His love for her was so great, in fact, that his relationship with her was better than if she had had ten sons. This would certainly put Elkanah in a better light, but the problem is that his words do not live up to his actions. Peninnah's presence and bitter comments overshadow any kind words that Elkanah might speak.

Elkanah's Principles (1 Sam. 1:21–23)

Elkanah's first words expose a number of his failings; his last words remind us that he is also a man of faith, commitment, and principle. After the birth of Samuel we are told that Elkanah makes preparations for his yearly trip to Shiloh. One of his purposes is to honor "his vow" (1:21). We are aware of Hannah's vow (1:11) but the story mentions nothing about a vow by

---

[14] Evans, *The Message of Samuel*, pp. 25, 26.
[15] Bruce J. Malina, *The New Testament World: Insights from Cultural Anthropology* (Louisville & London: John Knox Press, 3rd edition, 2001), p. 144.

Elkanah. Most believe Elkanah's words refer to the law explained in Numbers 30:6–8. This law states that a husband has the right to overrule his wife's vow but, if he does not, then she is expected to honor her vow. In this sense the wife's vow also becomes the husband's responsibility and this may be the meaning here in 1 Samuel.

Elkanah fully expects Hannah to accompany him as usual. Perhaps he is hopeful that this will finally be the joyous family trip he has desired all these long years! But Hannah responds that she will not accompany the family until the child is weaned (1:22). If the statement from 2 Maccabees 7:27 can be taken as normative, this would be a period of three years.[16] Elkanah's words are flexible and firm at the same time: "Do what seems best to you; wait until you have weaned him. Only let the LORD establish His word" (1:23).

Elkanah's statement, "Only let the LORD establish His word," is a little puzzling as we have not been informed of any specific word from the Lord. Among the Dead Sea Scrolls are copies of the books of Samuel which have a slightly different reading, supported also by the Septuagint (the Greek translation of the Hebrew Scriptures). It reads, "May the LORD indeed establish that which goes forth from your mouth."[17] This reading has the advantage of making sense within the immediate context. Elkanah is simply saying to Hannah, "OK, just be sure you do what you've promised to do."

On the other hand, while the reading in the traditional Hebrew text is more difficult, it is not without support in the rest of 1 Samuel. Throughout 1 Samuel there is a concern that the Lord's word be established. The conversation between Samuel and Saul in 1 Samuel 15 is a good example. God says to Samuel in 15:11, "I repent that I have made Saul to rule as king because he has turned back from following Me and *My word he has not established*" (my translation). Samuel subsequently goes to meet Saul and upon seeing him says, "Blessed are you of the LORD, *I have established the word of the LORD*" (15:13, my translation). But Saul has not "established the word of the LORD" and Samuel proceeds to tell him, "Because you have rejected the word of the LORD, He also has rejected you from being king" (15:23).

It is therefore difficult to choose which way to understand Elkanah's words to Hannah in 1:23. Whichever interpretation is chosen, Elkanah is clearly making sure that Hannah remains committed to her vow.[18] This points

---

[16] "My son have pity on me. I carried you nine months in my womb, and *nursed you for three years…*"

[17] McCarter, *I Samuel*, p. 56. Also, Robert Alter, *The David Story* (New York & London: W.W. Norton & Company, 1999), p. 7.

[18] Birch, *The First and Second Books of Samuel*, p. 976, makes a keen observation when he writes, "Elkanah…makes a statement that sounds an important theme for the opening of 1 Samuel…(He) alludes to the larger purpose for which the boy Samuel is to be dedicated." Birch continues, "We become aware in Elkanah's statement that we

to Elkanah's integrity and shows him not only to be a man of his word, but also a man who seeks to ensure that members of his family keep their promises. The same principle is found in the New Testament as Jesus teaches we are to let our "yes" be "yes" and our "no" be "no" (Matt. 5:37; James 5:12). Our witness to an unbelieving world depends upon our integrity, but even more importantly, if we have made a promise to God we need to be faithful to keep it (Eccl. 5:4–6).

Conclusion: Elkanah's Portrait

Elkanah is a picture of many of us. He was not perfect and made his share of mistakes, but he was honest, sincere, and committed to God. He may not always have said or done the right thing, but he was a godly man who sought to lead his family in the ways of the Lord. It is encouraging to know that God works with imperfect people who seek to follow Him. His grace fills in the gaps of our imperfections. If "God redeems" is an appropriate translation of Elkanah's name, then it seems well suited to the story and acts as a perfect balance to Hannah's name which means "grace." Both names remind us that God *redeems* us by his *grace* and, in spite of our imperfections, uses us to accomplish great things for his name and kingdom. In light of this, the portraits of Elkanah and Hannah provide a fitting introduction to the books of Samuel.

---

are not simply beginning the story of Samuel, but the story of God's Word working through Samuel in Israel."

Chapter 2

Peninnah: The Other Woman (Samuel's Stepmother)

And her rival also provoked her severely, to make her miserable (1 Sam. 1:6)

How Would You Want to Be Remembered?

Peninnah only appears in four verses in 1 Samuel chapter 1. It is hardly enough to gain a true portrait of the woman herself, but is enough to give us a negative impression of her. The writer of 1 and 2 Samuel cannot possibly develop fully the story of every person he mentions, but the question comes to mind, "If you were going to be remembered for only one thing, what would you want that to be?" Unfortunately for Peninnah, our only memory of her is that of a bitter and spiteful person. She is described as Hannah's "rival" (1 Sam. 1:6). Birch notes that this is "a term seldom used in describing family relationships and often translated as 'enemy' or 'adversary' in describing relationships between peoples or nations."[1] In a book where family rivalries will sometimes turn into deadly national conflicts, perhaps this word intentionally suggests a "preview of coming attractions." We have already noted that Hannah's prayer is cast in the mold of national as well as family conflict (1 Sam. 2:4–5). If it had been possible to take a photograph of Peninnah, like any good rival, she would have had a frown on her face and a scowl on her lips.

"Facing" the Facts (1 Sam. 1:2)

The meaning of Peninnah's name is obscure. It may be related to the word "ruby" or "pearl." Fokkelman writes it "is a name which suggests a beautiful exterior,"[2] which in the present context would be ironic (that is, beautiful on the outside but jealous and spiteful on the inside). It has also been suggested that her name means "prolific" which would correspond to her role as the childbearing wife in this story.[3] However, I would suggest the significance of Peninnah's name lies more in its sound than in its meaning. Several of the names mentioned in chapters 1 and 2 have the letters "p^eni" (or, "ph^eni") in them.[4] In addition to Peni*nnah*, these letters are also found in

---

[1] Birch, *The First and Second Books of Samuel*, p. 975.

[2] Fokkelman, *Vow and Desire*, p. 17.

[3] Ralph W. Klein, in *1 Samuel*, WBC (Waco: Word Books, 1983), p. 6, quoting a study by Lipinski.

[4] It is the consonants, not the vowels that are particularly relevant since ancient Hebrew was written without vowels.

the names Ho*phni* and *Phine*has. While this easily goes unnoticed in English, it is more obvious in the original language.[5] The word *p^eni* (or, *ph^eni*—the same consonant can be pronounced as a hard or soft "p") in Hebrew means "face," or "before"; and is used frequently throughout the first and second chapters (1:12, 15, 18, 19, 22; 2:11, 17, 18, 21).

This puts a spotlight on the word "face," or "before." There are two significant occurrences of "face" that we will look at later regarding Hannah, but first it is important to note that this word is always connected with the Lord in this story. Perhaps the story is highlighting the importance of seeking the Lord's "face" (or "presence"), or perhaps we are being reminded that all we do is done "before" the "face" of the Lord.

Seeking the Lord's face is certainly important in understanding the change in Hannah's countenance (1:12, 15, and 18). But the sin of Hophni and Phinehas is also done "before the LORD" (2:17), and so we may be justified in saying that this story is reminding us that all we do, whether good or evil, is done "before the LORD." We have all experienced that the presence of certain people can be an encouragement to do what is right. This is one of the important aspects of Christian fellowship. If we are constantly aware of God's presence in our life, setting our minds on heavenly things (Col. 3:2), and having fellowship with him (1 John 1:3), then we will act and think in a Christ-like way. An awareness that we are always "before the face" of the Lord is a great deterrent to sin.

Family Worship or "War"ship? (1 Sam. 1:4–7)

Would Peninnah's actions have been different if she had been conscious of the fact that all she did was "before the LORD"? The only thing we know about Peninnah, besides the fact that she had several sons and daughters, is that she continually rubbed Hannah's nose in this fact. Peninnah's timing makes her actions even more reprehensible. She chooses the time of the yearly pilgrimage to Shiloh to hound Hannah about being barren. What should be a joyous time of celebrating and worshipping the Lord becomes a miserable family fiasco.

It is interesting how everything can be alright until it is time to go to church. All of a sudden, husbands and wives have a fight, or the kids start fighting with one another, or mom and dad are yelling at the kids to behave. In the car, on the way to church, an otherwise godly family can become screaming lunatics!

Each year the pilgrimage to Shiloh for Elkanah's family was the holiday from hell. Once again, our admiration for Elkanah grows. The easy thing

---

[5] This is a well-known device in the Hebrew Scripture known as *paronomasia*. See Bar-Efrat, *Narrative Art*, p. 202. Also see Wenham, *Story as Torah*, p. 21.

to do would be to cancel the trip and save everyone the pain and misery. But Elkanah, this "God-bought" man, knows the importance of worshipping the Lord together as a family.

When one considers the family obstacle, along with going to a sanctuary presided over by a corrupt priesthood, Elkanah's commitment is quite extraordinary. Satan still uses the same methods of discouragement today. He whispers, "If it is this much hassle for your family, you are better off not going to church." Or he says, "Look at the mess your family is in. Who do you think you are, to be going to church!" If he can't persuade us this way, he will turn our eyes to the leaders or other members of the church and say, "You are better off staying at home, look at those hypocrites. Do you really want to worship with them!" Elkanah's response needs to be our response as well.

This painful scene portrays an important truth. Verse 7 states, "So it was, year by year, *when she went up to the house of the LORD, that she provoked her.*" Peninnah fails to make the connection between worshipping the Lord and her treatment of others. It is while she is on her way to worship that she treats Hannah so spitefully! How is it that we can sit in a worship service and praise the Lord, yet immediately think or speak so cruelly of others made in God's image? Speaking of the tongue, James writes,

> With it we bless our God and Father, and with it we curse men, who have been made in the similitude of God. Out of the same mouth proceed blessing and cursing. My brethren, these things ought not to be so (James 3:9–10).

Or as John writes,

> If someone says, 'I love God,' and hates his brother, he is a liar; for he who does not love his brother whom he has seen, how can he love God whom he has not seen? (1 John 4:20).

Conclusion: Should We Pity Peninnah?

It is tempting to feel sorry for Peninnah. After all, she is Elkanah's second choice and she knows it. The reason for her bitterness and spite is because she is not loved with the same measure as Hannah, if at all (1 Sam. 1:5). Elkanah was doubtless guilty of open favoritism, which in a family can be devastating—just ask Isaac, Rebekah, and Jacob, who were guilty of the same thing (Gen. 27 and 37).

There are two lessons here. First, Elkanah is ultimately responsible for the pain he and his family experienced. If he had trusted God in the first place, he would never have married Peninnah and thus they all would have been spared the grief caused by this less-than-ideal situation. Despite the mistake of bigamy, if he had treated his wives more equitably there would have been less room for jealousy.

Second, Peninnah also bears responsibility for her actions. She was clearly seeking her security in the love of her husband rather than in the Lord she was supposedly worshipping. This is not to ignore her very real pain of being loved less; it is only to say that she still had a responsibility for the way she responded.

We will not always be loved by others the way we would like to be. Sometimes the circumstances are of our own making, but sometimes they are not. Circumstances may influence attitudes, but they are not the only determining factor. God has given us an ability to choose. We choose to grow bitter or we choose to grow in grace. Circumstances may help or hinder, but the choice is still ours. Today's society is quick to absolve people of responsibility. "It is my parents' fault" or "my spouse's fault" that I am the way I am. This kind of reasoning is foreign to the Bible. It is right to have empathy for people who are in difficult situations with much pain and suffering, but it is wrong for the person in that situation to allow those circumstances to mold their character in a negative way.

God is the Potter and he can take *any* circumstance and use it for good, but we must yield our lives to his gracious, omnipotent hands. This is the lesson that Hannah learned and proclaimed, and so we will look at her story next.

Chapter 3

Hannah: The Nobody Who Became a Somebody
(Samuel's Mother)

"I am a woman of sorrowful spirit"/ "My heart rejoices in the LORD*"—Hannah*
(1 Sam. 1:15; 2:1)

Hannah: Number One, or No One? (1 Sam. 1:2, 5–8)

The story of Hannah is summed up in the two verses above and points to the God who brought about the transformation. Though she was wife number one she must have felt relegated to secondary status when Elkanah married Peninnah. No matter how much love Elkanah might profess (1:5) or what words of flattery he might use (1:8), the fact is that actions speak louder than words. Peninnah was a constant reminder to Hannah that she was not enough for Elkanah. She had failed in the one area most important for a woman in the ancient world: she could not have a child (1:2).

Hannah and women in her situation bore greater shame in the society of that day than we can imagine in our modern world. Since children were considered a blessing from God (or the gods), an infertile woman would be looked upon with suspicion.[1] "If children are a blessing, then why has God cursed you by not allowing you to have any?" People may have thought, "What have you done to bring such displeasure on yourself?"

The narrator's words, that "the LORD had closed her womb" (1:5, 6), may reflect the inner thoughts of Elkanah and Peninnah,[2] and probably others as well. Except for the kindness which Elkanah continued to bestow on Hannah, she might have found herself isolated and the object of gossip and ridicule.

The initial picture we are given of Hannah is that of a depressed and desperate woman. Perhaps the best way to describe her is *empty*. Hannah has an empty womb, which is reflected in her empty stomach (1:8—"therefore she wept and did not eat"). She empties her eyes of tears as she weeps in anguish (1:10). This emptiness comes from years of heartbreak and pain.

At times like this it is tempting to give up and believe that things will never change. For Hannah, just as for Elkanah, every trip to the sanctuary was the same as the one before. The only change may have been the depth of

---

[1] See for example, Roland de Vaux, *Ancient Israel, Volume 1: Social Institutions* (New York, Toronto: McGraw-Hill Book Company, 1965), p. 41.

[2] Polzin, *Samuel and the Deuteronomist*, pp. 20-21. Birch, *The First and Second Books of Samuel*, p. 975, writes, "Both lover (Elkanah) and provoker (Peninnah) treat Hannah as God-forsaken."

pain with each passing year. It is clear from 1:22 that Hannah had the ability to refuse to accompany the family on this yearly pilgrimage, but to her credit she persevered.

The first lesson therefore that we gain from Hannah's life is similar to that of Elkanah's: perseverance in the midst of difficult circumstances. This is one of the keys to a life of faith. Abraham believed in God—"who gives life to the dead and calls those things which do not exist as though they did"—and "contrary to hope, in hope" believed (Rom. 4:17–18). Year after year Hannah continued to suffer, but she also continued to worship. Like her forefather Jacob (Hos. 11:4), and her future Savior (Heb. 5:7), she sought God through her tears and found him.

The text tells us that God ordained this painful path: "the LORD had closed her womb." 1 and 2 Samuel portray a God who is in total control. "The LORD kills and makes alive; He brings down to the grave and brings up," as Hannah says (2:6). There are no apologies or excuses for the way this all-powerful God acts.

The Way of the Wilderness (1 Sam. 1:10–11)

Hannah's experience has many parallels to that of Israel in the wilderness. Moses says to Israel, "And you shall remember all the way which the LORD your God has caused you to walk these forty years in the wilderness in order to humble you, to test you, and to know what was in your heart, whether you would keep his commandments or not" (Deut. 8:2—my translation). Notice several things here. First, Moses refers to the way "God has *caused* you to walk." The wilderness was no accident. It was ordained by God that Israel would have to go through the wilderness to get to the Promised Land. Second, God's purpose in this was threefold: 1. *to humble them;* 2. *to test them;* and, 3. *to know what was in their heart.* The situation which Hannah faced, and difficult circumstances we may experience, are for these same three purposes.

The first purpose of the wilderness is to bring humility. Moses proceeds to tell Israel that the reason God humbles us is to teach us total dependence on him. The wilderness is to "make you know that man shall not live by bread alone; but man lives by every word that proceeds from the mouth of the LORD" (Deut. 8:3). It took Israel 40 years to learn this lesson. Perhaps this is one of the reasons that Hannah's ordeal lasted so long. As we will see momentarily, when she reached the point of total surrender to God, she was able to move on and leave the wilderness behind. It seems that we first have to exhaust our strength and every option that our society offers, before we are willing to let go and surrender to God. The wilderness teaches us that we do not have the resources to cope with life on our own. It brings us to the end of ourselves, and yet somehow we survive—because we have a God whose grace preserves us even in the midst of our own stubbornness. It is only when we have exhausted all of our reserves that we can truly see the power of God at work in our lives. For some, the wilderness experience may be longer than for others. God's original desire was to bring Israel through the wilderness in a short amount of time; Israel's lack of trust lengthened the experience to 40 years.[3]

The second reason for the wilderness is to test our faith. Will we believe God in the face of overwhelming odds or circumstances? Will we continue to hope when, humanly speaking, there is no hope? As the writer of Hebrews says, "Now faith is the substance of things *hoped* for, the evidence of things not seen" (Heb. 11:1). The first generation of Israelites who came out of Egypt failed the test. They saw the inhabitants of Canaan and their walled cities and said, "There is no way we can conquer that land" (Num. 13). Returning to the example of Abraham, Paul states, "He did not waver at the promise of God through unbelief, but was *strengthened in faith*, giving glory to God" (Rom. 4:20). And the writer of Hebrews says, "By *faith* Abraham when he was *tested*, offered up Isaac" (Heb. 11:17). The purpose of the wilderness is to test our faith that we might grow strong and give glory to God.

One might object that this all seems very unfair of God, but this is to misunderstand God and his purpose. Moses says the purpose of God's humbling and testing is "to do you good in the end" (Deut. 8:16). The wilderness is necessary because otherwise, as human beings, we will always opt to do things in our own strength and utilize our own resources. This is a fruitless endeavor, and only the wilderness teaches us otherwise. The end result for those who cling to God through the wilderness experience is "good." The lives of Abraham, Job, Hannah, and countless others, testify to this truth.

The third purpose of the wilderness is for God "to know what was in your heart." The wilderness either reveals a heart of pride and rebellion, or a pliable heart that bends to the Master's will. To use an old cliché, the wilderness makes us bitter or it makes us better. The choice lies with us and our response to our Creator. It would seem that Peninnah's wilderness experience made her bitter,[4] but Hannah's made her better. Why? Because she was a bet-

---

[3] I am speaking of the wilderness experiences that God ordains for us in order to teach us to rely on him. Some wilderness experiences are of our own making due to sin. We should not seek to blame God when we go our own willful way and "wander into the wilderness" because we are rejecting his guidance and the way he has directed us to walk in. Nevertheless, God will even use these wilderness experiences to teach us and bless us if we are willing to turn to him. Hannah's wilderness experience was not self-inflicted. She had no control over God closing her womb or over Elkanah's decision to take a second wife, but she did have a choice as to how she responded to these situations.

[4] I am suggesting that because Peninnah was the second wife and perhaps loved less, that this was a wilderness experience for her.

ter person? No, but because, as the succeeding verses show, she humbled herself, clung to God in hope, and was strengthened in faith.

Bitterness, anguish, and affliction are the three words used to describe Hannah's condition as she leaves a full plate at the dinner table and rushes to seek the presence of the Lord (1:10–11). When we are experiencing this kind of turmoil and all of our negative emotions rise to the surface, we often think it is inappropriate to approach God. At such times Satan comes and whispers to us, "If you were really a Christian you would not feel this way!" "Do you really think God is going to hear and answer your prayer when you are experiencing these kinds of thoughts and emotions?" Whether it was desperation or faith, and sometimes faith is evoked through desperation, Hannah knows that God is the only one she can turn to, and so she prays.

The first words of Hannah's prayer are reminiscent of the wilderness experience we have been talking about. Hannah pleads, *"remember me"* and do *"not forget your maidservant"* (1:11). These are the same words Moses uses repeatedly in Deuteronomy 8 in his exhortation to Israel (vv. 2, 11, 14, 18, 19). While Moses charges Israel to *"remember and not forget"* the Lord, here Hannah asks the Lord to *"remember and not forget"* her. The language reflects a prayer for deliverance. Hannah is not asking God to remember her in the sense that we as humans forget until something jogs our memory. *"Remember"* is used in connection with God to speak of his gracious saving acts that bring deliverance. For example, the turning point of the Flood story is when, "God *remembered* Noah" (Gen. 8:1). From this point on, the waters begin to recede and creation experiences a rebirth. When God sends destruction on Sodom and Gomorrah, we are informed that "God *remembered* Abraham and sent Lot out of the midst of the overthrow" (Gen. 19:29). Therefore, when Hannah says, *"remember me,"* she is seeking a similar intervention from God to deliver her from her situation. In all of the aforementioned cases, it is clear that any deliverance must come from the mighty hand of God; the situation is beyond human control.

Why Now and Not Before? (1 Sam. 1:11–16)

The question arises, "In all the years of going up to Shiloh, is this the first time that Hannah prayed and asked God for a son?" Although the text is silent on this point, we can hardly suppose that this is the first time. So we are provoked to ask, "What made this year different?" and "Why did God respond to Hannah's prayer this time?" I believe there are hints in the story that provide an answer.

First, notice that Hannah's prayer is not self-centered, as our prayers often tend to be. Without question she wants a son, but she goes on to promise the Lord that if he gives her a son, she will give him back to God all the days of his life. I have found that when I am going through a trial I often develop tunnel vision. My problem seems so large that it's all I can see. I lose perspective of the bigger picture. I am so consumed by my pain and seeking a remedy, any remedy, that I cannot get beyond looking continually at my problem.

I believe this may have been Hannah's perspective until this time. But this particular year something changes. Hannah has a breakthrough and she realizes that there is more to the picture than her personal pain. God can work in the midst of her affliction for a greater good. Remember, God's purpose for the wilderness is to *"do you good in the end"* (Deut. 8:16). Hannah realizes that there is something more important than her trial; it is the glory of God. "How can God be glorified in this situation?" she wonders. She says, "Lord, if you will give me a son, I will give him back to you all the days of his life." Hannah now sees that the son she has longed for is intended for more than covering her shame. If she gives him back to God, then God can be glorified and God's people can be blessed. If there is some doubt that this is the reason behind God's answer to Hannah's prayer, confirmation is available in the naming of her son (1:20—see below).

A second reason for the change in Hannah's circumstances is found in her utter dependence on God. We have already noted the three words which characterize Hannah as she begins to pray (bitterness, anguish, and affliction). These words are expressed through her body language as she prays. It appears that her praying was so animated that Eli, the high priest, was convinced she was drunk (1:14). Imagine Hannah as she speaks no words, but moves her lips (1:12–13), accompanied perhaps by other bodily movements expressive of pain and anguish. She may have attracted the attention of others besides Eli! "Her need is so pressing that it overwhelms public concerns."[5] Certainly, Eli thought that her behavior was inappropriate.[6] But when he confronts Hannah she puts words behind her actions. She tells him, "I have drunk neither wine nor intoxicating drink, *but have poured out my soul before the* LORD" (1:15).

How ironic that this "empty" woman would express herself in terms of "pouring out" her soul! With reckless abandon Hannah sought the throne of God. Her words and her actions show that she had come to the end of herself. She didn't care what she looked like or who was watching. The wilderness had done its work of *"humbling,"* and now, reaching out in faith, she only wants the Lord to glorify himself through her life. This is a picture of total surrender. This woman with the empty stomach has learned that "man (and woman) shall not live by bread alone" (Deut. 8:3).

---

[5] Francesca Aran Murphy, *1 Samuel*, BTCB (Grand Rapids: Brazos Press, 2010), p. 11.
[6] Hannah's spiritual desperation is not something that the self-satisfied Eli can fully comprehend. See my comments in chap. 4, p. 55, n. 7.

This leads us to the third reason for the change which Hannah experienced: her honesty. As Hannah continues her response to Eli's charge she says, "Do not consider your maidservant a wicked woman (literally, *daughter of Belial*—more on this later), for out of the *abundance of my complaint and grief* I have spoken until now" (1:16). We learn here that there are some things this "empty" woman has in "abundance," namely, "complaint and grief"!

It may seem that a person cannot be "empty" and "full" at the same time, yet our experience teaches us differently. People who are full of bitterness usually feel empty inside. Hannah is empty because she has an *"abundance of complaint and grief."* To experience the fullness of God Hannah must *"pour out"* this bitterness. Ironically, Hannah learns that in order to have true fullness, she must pour out the things which led to her emptiness.

Hannah's story demonstrates the true meaning of emptiness and fullness. There is a counterfeit fullness that leads to emptiness and there is a true emptiness that leads to fullness. The world offers a counterfeit fullness which, in reality, leads to emptiness. Some believe by holding on to the things of this world they can experience fullness. This kind of fullness may manifest itself in different ways. Acquiring possessions is one way, but another way is holding on to negative emotions. Hurt is usually perceived as loss. Hannah, for example, feels the loss of a son she never had. Divorce leads to the loss of a spouse, and physical abuse often causes the victim to experience a loss of self-respect. When we have lost something, it is tempting to allow our anger to fill the void. Holding on to our anger may actually make us feel we still have some control over what we have lost. It is hard to let go of our anger because it means giving up hope of retrieving our loss. But as we fill ourselves with bitterness we begin to experience an emptiness that can never be satisfied. The only escape from this living hell is a true emptying of ourselves: a pouring out of our soul, like Hannah. Experiencing authentic emptiness, by laying our anger at the throne of God, banishes the counterfeit fullness—the fullness offered by the world that left us empty. By letting go we are finally free to allow God to fill us up.

Some people allow their anger to prevent them from seeking God. Perhaps they reason that God will not hear them if they voice their anger and frustrations. Or, they may believe they are unworthy to approach God with such "ungodly" emotions. The fact is that God wants us to come to him just as we are. We don't like it when people put up false fronts and pretend to be something they are not. We appreciate honesty and sincerity, and so does God. The Scriptures are full of "tough" prayers—saints of God voicing their complaints to God. Jeremiah complains, "O LORD, You induced me, and I was persuaded; You are stronger than I, and have prevailed" (Jer. 20:7). These are very strong words. Jeremiah uses the language of rape here in addressing God.

My point is not that we should make a practice of using offensive language when talking to God, but that God is already aware of our thoughts and feelings. When we build a wall between ourselves and God, there is little that can be done. Even an all-powerful God respects those walls. God is looking for vulnerability. Relationships only grow where vulnerability exists. Walls are not conducive to healthy relationships. God is not afraid of our brokenness and he is capable of handling our hurt and anger, even if it is directed against him. As I am typing these words, the lyrics of a Chris Rice song are playing in the background. The chorus goes like this:

> *God if You're there I wish You'd show me.*
> *And God if You care then I need You to know me.*
> *I hope You don't mind me asking the questions*
> *But I figure You're big enough.*
> *I figure You're big enough.*[7]

Yes, God is indeed "big enough." By faith, Hannah knows this and so she "pours out her soul" before the Lord, which consists of complaint and grief.

God works best with people like Hannah—people who let go, and experience true emptiness. If we are full of ourselves, full of bitterness, or full of complaint and grief, there is little room for God to work. Like Hannah, it takes a step of faith. Are you ready to be set free from the vicious cycle of this world and experience true fullness?

Hannah Gets a "Face Lift" (1 Sam. 1:5, 18–19)

Notice that all of this is done "before the LORD" (1:12, and 15). It does little good to pour out our souls anywhere except "before the LORD," as he is the only one who has the remedy for our problem. It is particularly noteworthy that in a polytheistic society, Hannah turns only to the Lord. Baal and Asherah were the popular fertility deities of Canaan and many Israelites had succumbed to worshipping them (e.g., Judg. 2:13). "Where the dominance of families is at stake, one worships the deities of child production, the deities believed to enlarge the tribe."[8] Instead, Hannah seeks the Lord and is transparent before him. She lets him know just what she is feeling and thinking, what her hopes and fears are, and this is what brings about the dramatic change in her. We are told in 1:18, "So the woman went her way and ate, and her face was no longer sad."

---

[7] Chris Rice, *Big Enough*, from the CD, *Past the Edges* (Franklin: Clumsy Fly Music, 1998).

[8] Murphy, *1 Samuel*, p. 8.

Hannah is no longer empty. She is now able to eat, having spewed out the poison that had tortured her for so long. More than that, we are told, "her *face* was no longer sad." This is the first time in our English translations that the word "*face*" appears in 1 Samuel, and yet the Hebrew text suggests the significance of this word in the story through the expression "before the LORD" (vv. 12, 15, 19, 22) and through sound-play on the names of the characters of the story (see pp. 30-31).

To appreciate the significance of the statement in 1:18, we must back up to 1:5. There we were told that when Elkanah made an offering he would give portions to Peninnah and her children (1:4), "but to Hannah he would give a double portion" (1:5). The words translated "a double portion" in the NKJV are literally, "a portion for the face" or "nose." This is a strange expression in English and in Hebrew and has perplexed many Bible commentators. But when one sees how the theme of "face" fits into the story, the expression makes more sense.[9]

It is clear that Elkanah hopes by his generous gift to "lift the face" of Hannah, or at least to calm her down. That is, he hopes his generosity will bring a smile to her face, or, at least, take away the anger she is experiencing. However, the story shows us that no physical gift (or bribe?) can change Hannah's attitude. Her wound goes much deeper and it cannot be healed by putting a bandage on it.

Elkanah's action highlights man's vain attempts to deal with spiritual problems in superficial ways. The cure for Hannah's hurt will only be found in the hands of the "Great Physician." This explains the significance of the statement in 1:18. Now that Hannah has fully surrendered to the Lord and laid her burden "before" him (that is, before his face), she can leave with a face that is no longer sad. Thus Peninnah (whose name sounds similar to *face*) provokes Hannah and makes her *face* sad. Elkanah tries to change Hannah's *face* by his gift, but it is only when Hannah seeks the *face* of the Lord and pours out her heart, that her *face* is no longer sad!

It should not go unnoticed that we are told that Hannah's facial expression changed *before* she had any knowledge that the Lord would bless her with a son. Hannah's new countenance was based on her faith and her new, deeper relationship with the Lord. It was not the promise of a son, but her

---

[9] The word used for "face" in 1:5 is *'appāyim*, a different word from *p^{e}ni*. It literally refers to the nose, i.e., the center of the face. Malina, *The New Testament World*, p. 39, points out that challenges in the ancient world were an attempt to dishonor or shame. "In an affront challenged persons are obliged to witness the challenge to *their face*. In return, the recognition of the challenge takes place *on the face*. In Semitic culture, this focus of recognition is the *center of the face, the nose*; a Hebrew word for anger refers metaphorically to flared nostrils, and a reference to flared nostrils is most often translated 'wrath' " (emphasis mine). Therefore, Elkanah's "portion for the nose" is his way of trying to calm Hannah down and assuage her wrath.

relationship with the Lord that put a smile on her face. Total surrender means accepting by faith whatever the Lord chooses to do with our life. God does indeed answer Hannah's prayer and give her a son, but this should not be interpreted to mean that we can follow this formula and force God to answer our prayers the way we want. This is why the text tells us about the change in Hannah before she becomes pregnant. Hannah's faith and deeper relationship with God gave her peace about the future, a peace she had not known in previous years; a peace reminiscent of Paul's words when he writes,

> Be anxious for nothing, but in everything by prayer and supplication, with thanksgiving, let your requests be made known to God; and the peace of God which surpasses all understanding, will guard your hearts and minds through Christ Jesus (Phil 4:6–7).

The next verse (1:19) has two important expressions. First, we are told that the family rose early and worshiped "before the LORD" and, second, we are told, "The LORD remembered her." This is not the last time that Hannah and Elkanah will respond with thankful worship to the Lord (see 1:28). The second statement, "the LORD remembered her" is an exact echo of Hannah's request in 1:11, "remember me." God, the Giver of life, acts to deliver Hannah from her difficult situation as he responds by blessing her with a son.

Ask and It Shall Be Given to You (1 Sam. 1:17–28)

Like Hannah, our story has been in travail, earnestly looking to the announcement of Samuel's birth. The birth of Samuel is the highlight of the story and Hannah's naming of him is significant. Verse 20 states, "Hannah conceived and bore a son, and called his name Samuel, saying, 'Because I have *asked* for him from the LORD.' " The name, Samuel, means, "His name is God," referring to the one Samuel worships,[10] or it may mean "bearing the name of God."[11] However, it is not the literal meaning of Samuel's name which is significant to the story, but, like Peninnah, the significance lies in words that sound similar.[12]

The first word which sounds similar to Samuel's name, and plays an important part throughout his story, is the word *sh^ema'*. The word *sh^ema'* means, "*to listen*," "*hear*," or "*obey*." Hannah makes no reference to this word in 1:20, but it is noteworthy that when she prayed, "her voice was not *heard*"

---

[10] McCarter, *I Samuel*, p. 62.
[11] John T. Willis, *First and Second Samuel*, LWC (Austin: Sweet Publishing Company, 1982), p. 37.
[12] This is another example of paronomasia.

(1:13). Among the first words uttered by Samuel is the reply, "Speak, for Your servant *hears*" (1 Sam. 3:10). Hearing and obeying are also important in Samuel's confrontation of Saul (1 Sam. 15:1, 14, 19, 20, 22, 24).

The word Hannah calls attention to is *sha'al*, which is the Hebrew word for "*ask*." We are told Hannah named her son Samuel because she had *"asked"* for him from the Lord. Jesus said, "Ask and it will be given to you" (Matt. 7:7). Asking is a sign of dependence and it involves humility. We have already noted that these are qualities that God desires to put within us through the wilderness experience. James says, "You do not have, because you do not ask" (James 4:2). God does not want to be taken for granted any more than we do. If we have a godly desire, we are encouraged to come to our Heavenly Father and ask him. God hears even the whispers of our hearts. Remember, God heard Hannah even though her voice was not heard; only her lips moved (1:13).

But the significance of "asking" in the present context goes deeper. The word "ask" is from the same Hebrew root as the name "Saul." To catch the pun we might translate verse 20 this way: "Hannah called his name Samuel saying, ' Because I *sauled* him from the LORD.' " This word occurs seven times in the birth story of Samuel. It is found twice in verse 17, when Eli tells Hannah, "Go in peace, and the God of Israel grant your *petition* which you have *asked* of him (1:17)." The words "petition" and "ask," in verse 27, are also from the same Hebrew word. Finally, *sha'al* occurs twice in verse 28, translated by the NKJV as "lent." It is difficult to show the wordplay in English because the Hebrew word has much greater flexibility in meaning. Most surprising is the seventh and final occurrence of the word in the story (a significant biblical number, often implying completion). The seventh time it appears, it is written in the Hebrew text exactly as the name Saul is spelled. So Hannah's words in 1:28 could actually be translated, "as long as he lives he is *Saul* (shall be lent) to the LORD."[13] So the intriguing question is, "What is the name Saul doing seven times in the birth story of Samuel?"[14]

Robert Polzin points out that the story of Samuel and Eli anticipates the coming kingship.[15] When the people demand a king in 1 Samuel 8 we are told that they "asked" Samuel for a king (8:10). Samuel uses this same language in his speech in 1 Samuel 12 when he says, "your wickedness is great, which you have done in the sight of the LORD, in *asking* a king for yourselves" (12:17). Since the word "ask" is from the same root as "Saul," Samuel is literally saying the people "sauled" for a king. Ironically, they got what they

---

[13] Victor P. Hamilton, *Handbook on the Historical Books* (Grand Rapids: Baker Academic, 2001, hereafter cited as *Handbook*), p. 216, writes, "There are two 'asked-for' ones in this era in the Old Testament. There is the *sha'ul*, who is the son of Hannah, and later there is the *sha'ul*, who is the son of Kish."

[14] It also occurs two more times in 1 Sam. 2:20.

[15] Polzin, *Samuel and the Deuteronomist*, p. 26.

"sauled" for! The prevalence of this "saul" language in chapter 1 cannot be accidental. The writer is clearly inviting us to compare Hannah's "asking" for a son with that of the people's "asking" for a king. In chapter 8 we are told that the people's motivation in asking for a king is so that they might be "like all the nations" (8:5, 20). In contrast, Moses had told the children of Israel,

> The LORD has proclaimed you to be *His special people*, just as He promised you, that you should keep all His commandments, and that He will set you *high above all nations* which He has made, in praise, in name, and in honor, and that you may be a holy people to the LORD your God, just as He has spoken (Deut. 26:18–19).

God's purpose was not for Israel to be "like all the nations," but to set them above the nations as a holy people, and as a light to the nations. Israel's desire to have a king so that they might be like all the nations is a direct contradiction of God's desire and purpose for them. This is why Samuel says in 12:17, "your wickedness is great…in asking for a king for yourselves." Samuel's words, *"for yourselves"* show that Israel is selfishly motivated.

Israel's attitude contrasts greatly with Hannah's. We have already noted how Hannah's focus moves from her own concerns to the greater concerns of the Lord (p. 38). This contrast between Hannah and Israel is further evidence for the unselfish basis of Hannah's request.[16]

Thus what we have in these two chapters is a meditation on "asking." What is the proper motivation for "asking" the Lord for something? If Jesus said, "Ask and you shall receive," is this always a *carte blanche* promise? These two chapters show us that proper "asking" involves considering the bigger picture. It is not simply a matter of having our selfish desires met but a question of what will bring glory to God. The book of James affirms this. After he writes, "You do not have because you do not ask," he continues, "You ask and do not receive because you ask amiss, that you may spend it on your pleasures" (James 4:2–3). Godly "asking" is not all about *me*; it is about what is best for me in light of the glory and purpose of God.

We have already noticed Hannah's refusal to go up to Shiloh on the yearly pilgrimage with the family until she had weaned Samuel, and Elkanah's charge to be sure she kept her vow (1:22–23, see p. 28). Hannah is indeed faithful to her vow. As difficult as it must have been for her to leave her young son in the care of Eli, she seems to approach the task with great enthusiasm. It is easy to hear the excitement in her voice when she says to Eli,

---

[16] My view is different from Polzin's on this point. He believes that the writer is comparing the attitude of Hannah with the attitude of the people in chapter 8, rather than providing a contrast to it.

O my lord! As your soul lives, my lord, I am the woman who stood by you here, praying to the LORD. For this child I prayed, and the LORD has granted my petition which I asked of Him (1:26–27).

Hannah's last line is actually a word-for-word repetition of what Eli said to her years earlier: "the God of Israel *grant your petition which you have asked of Him*" (1:17). With these words Hannah cheerfully fulfills her vow by "lending" (the word "saul" again) Samuel to the Lord (1:28). This payment of her vow is followed by worshipping the Lord.

Conclusion: Strength Displayed in Weakness

It is important to see the change of mood in this story from the beginning to the end of the chapter. The story begins with a family in conflict, caught in a vicious cycle from which there seems no escape. But the chapter ends on a note of praise and joy.

So how does a family move from conflict to joy? For those who enjoy alliteration we may trace four steps Hannah follows which lead her out of the wilderness of pain to a life of fulfillment and joy. First she **prays** to the Lord (1:11–12), second, she **places** her burden on the Lord (v. 18), third, she **pays** her vow to the Lord (vv. 24–28), and fourth, she **praises** the Lord (v. 28).

This is a surprising way to begin a book that deals with power. An ordinary family from the mountains of Ephraim who have no strong political connections or religious authority is its focus. More than that, the heroine of the story is a social outcast—a woman who is considered a failure, who brings nothing to the table but her emptiness—and her complaint and grief! Yet it is this empty, depressed woman, caught up in a family cycle which involves the dysfunctional qualities of bigamy, favoritism, and animosity, who God chooses to use.

We are faced here with a kind of power that is not of this world. It is the kind of power that finds strength in weakness, wisdom in foolishness, and life in death. It is incredible to think that God uses this "nobody" of a woman (in the eyes of her peers) to transform the entire history of Israel!

It is because of Hannah's prayer of faith, and her ability to rise above her personal pain and see the bigger picture of God's glory, that Samuel is born. Samuel will bring reform to the priesthood, revive the prophetic word in Israel, and begin to deliver Israel from its arch enemy, the Philistines. It is also Samuel who will inaugurate a new era in Israel by anointing Saul king, and eventually, and most importantly, David. And it is to David that God promises an "enduring house" which, in turn, will lead to the future messianic expectation (2 Sam. 7:12–16). Yet this chain of events is set in motion by a weak, empty woman, who chose to find her strength in an all-powerful God "who raises the poor from the dust, and lifts the beggar from the ash heap, to set them among princes and make them inherit a throne of glory" (1 Sam. 2:8).

Hannah's story continues in 1 Samuel 2:1–10 with her song of praise. This song is her act of worship referred to at the end of chapter 1. As mentioned in the Introduction (see pp. 1-3), Hannah's song not only applies to her personal situation, it looks beyond and encompasses the entire story of 1 and 2 Samuel.[17] Hannah's song is prophetic and we will return to it a number of times to see how its truth is reflected throughout the books of Samuel; therefore we will not deal with it in detail here. It is a prophetic word that holds sway over all the events recorded in these books—now that's real power!

---

[17] Raymond B. Dillard and Tremper Longman III, *An Introduction to the Old Testament*, p. 141, states, "Hannah's magnificat becomes a proleptic summary of the themes that fill the book as a whole." Also see the comments by Howard, *An Introduction to the Old Testament Historical Books*, pp. 161-162.

Section 2

The Family of Eli

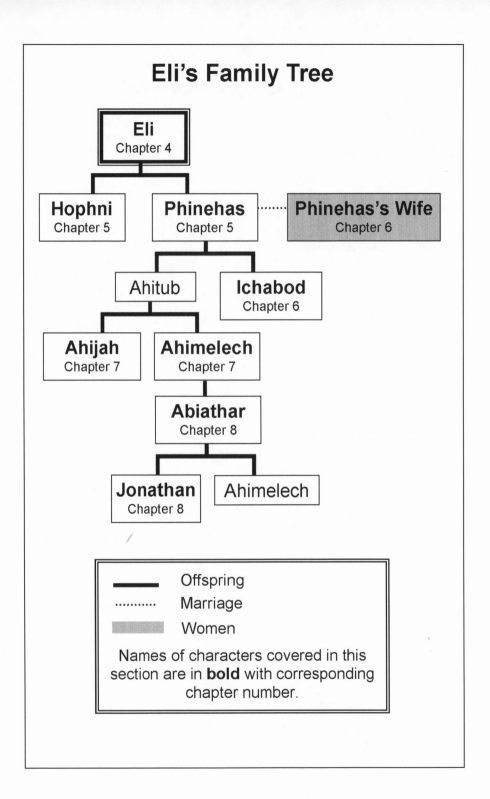

Eli's Family Tree

Eli
Chapter 4

Hophni
Chapter 5

Phinehas
Chapter 5

Phinehas's Wife
Chapter 6

Ahitub

Ichabod
Chapter 6

Ahijah
Chapter 7

Ahimelech
Chapter 7

Abiathar
Chapter 8

Jonathan
Chapter 8

Ahimelech

————— Offspring

············ Marriage

▨▨▨▨ Women

Names of characters covered in this section are in **bold** with corresponding chapter number.

Introduction to Eli's Family

And therefore I have sworn to the house of Eli that the iniquity of Eli's house shall not be atoned for by sacrifice or offering forever (1 Sam. 3:14)

The words of 1 Samuel 3:14 are the climax of what might be termed an avalanche of words of judgment against Eli and his house found in chapters 2 through 3. The story of Eli's house is a troubled one. It begins with his weakness and the wickedness of his sons, followed by their deaths on the same day in fulfillment of prophecy (1 Sam. 2:34; 4:11, 17–18). It culminates in the slaughter of his entire family by Saul. Only Abiathar escapes (1 Sam. 22).

Eli's house is without question a doomed house (1 Sam. 2:31–34), and, as a result, has many parallels with the house of Saul. We will examine some of the similarities between the two later. But the doom that hangs over Eli's house is not the result of a capricious, angry God who is "out to get" people. The man of God who comes in 1 Samuel chapter 2 with a word of judgment reveals that God had given great and precious promises to the house of Eli (2:27–28, 30); the future fate of Eli's house is fully his responsibility and that of his sons. The loss of God's blessing and the resulting judgment is wholly in line with the words of the prophet Jeremiah, who may himself have been a descendant of Eli.[1] In Jeremiah 18:7–11 God declares,

> The instant I speak concerning a nation and concerning a kingdom, to pluck up, to pull down, and to destroy it, if that nation against whom I have spoken turns from its evil, I will relent of the disaster that I thought to bring upon it. And the instant I speak concerning a nation and concerning a kingdom, to build and to plant it, if it does evil in My sight so that it does not obey My voice, then I will relent concerning the good with which I said I would benefit it.

Presumably these words can apply to individuals and families as well as nations and kingdoms (King Ahab is an example of this same principle—1 Kings 21:28–29). Notice the words leave room for repentance and a change in God's plan, not only for evil but for good. Eli and his sons were indeed responsible for the judgment which they brought on their house, but clearly, once they had sinned, repentance could have averted the disaster.

While the story of Eli's house is not the happiest of stories, it has many important lessons for all who desire to live godly lives pleasing to the

---

[1] Note that Solomon banishes Abiathar to his hometown in Anathoth (1 Kings 2:26) which is the same as Jeremiah's hometown, he also being from a priestly family, perhaps Eli's (Jer. 1:1).

Father. One important lesson concerns the holiness of God and the honor and glory due his name. It has been said that the church of today is more afraid of holiness than it is of sin.[2] Our lack of formality and our stress on a personal relationship with our Creator has certainly provided a much-needed emphasis that was lacking in past generations. However, we must be careful not to tip the balance to the other extreme; and it seems in some ways we have. There is a lack in many modern churches of messages that deal with sin, judgment, God's holiness, and our need to appropriate that holiness to our lives. Some may fear being labeled "legalistic" for teaching on obedience, to be sure, a misunderstanding of the biblical concept of obedience (e.g., Rom. 6:15–18). The danger of being too familiar with God is that we take his majesty and holiness for granted and fail to recognize that "our God is a consuming fire" (Heb. 12:29). When the church strays too far in one direction or the other in its overall message, heresy and false doctrine lie at the door. The message of Eli's house is an important one for us, as it deals with the honor due God's name (1 Sam. 2:30). It has been said that "familiarity breeds contempt." If our familiarity with God leads us no longer to give him the honor and glory due to him, then, like Eli and his sons, we have certainly gone too far.

---

[2] Sermon by Leonard Ravenhill

Chapter 4

Eli: The Heavy High Priest[1]

For the man was old and heavy (1 Sam. 4:18)

Is Something Missing?

Eli's name is a shortened form of "Yahweh is exalted." It is interesting that Eli's full name is never given, thus "Eli" simply means "exalted."[2] In light of what we will learn below about Eli this shortened form of his name seems particularly appropriate. Could it be that the writer intentionally avoids using Eli's full name in order to emphasize the point that Eli exalts himself rather than God? Making alterations in biblical names is not uncommon in the Hebrew Scriptures and we will have opportunity to observe other examples of this practice.

Eli the "Kingly" Priest: First Impressions (1 Sam. 1:9, 12–17)

Our first introduction to Eli is somewhat provocative and leaves the reader wondering what to expect.[3] We are told, "Now Eli the priest was sitting on *the seat* by the *doorpost* of the *tabernacle* of the LORD" (1 Sam. 1:9). These words, which look innocent in our English translations, are loaded with double meaning in Hebrew.[4] The word "seat" is the usual word in Hebrew for "throne." To "sit on a throne" is, of course, to be a king (1 Kings 16:11; 1 Chron. 28:5; etc.). If this language is not suggestive enough the writer also chooses the word *hēykal*, translated as "tabernacle" in the NKJV but literally meaning "temple" or "palace."[5] Normally a different word would be used for tabernacle.

---

[1] While Eli is never called "high" priest, several verses indicate this was his position (1 Sam. 2:27–28, 35). 1 Sam. 2:35 is said to be fulfilled in 1 Kings 2:35 where Abiathar, the descendant of Eli, is replaced by Zadok as High Priest.

[2] R.W. Corney, "Eli," *IDB,* vol. 2 (Nashville: Abingdon, 1962), p. 85.

[3] Eli is first mentioned in 1 Sam. 1:3, but he is not properly introduced until verse 9.

[4] Polzin, *Samuel and the Deuteronomist,* p. 23, also makes this observation.

[5] Some scholars believe that this word is evidence that there was an actual temple in Shiloh (thus a temple prior to Solomon's temple). See Joyce Baldwin, *1&2 Samuel,* TOTC (Downers Grove: Inter-Varsity Press, 1988), pp. 65-68. Two passages are cited to support this contention: 1) it is suggested that Jeremiah 7:12 (cf. Jer. 26:6) supports this idea because Jeremiah compares the "house" of the Lord in Jerusalem with the "place" in Shiloh. But Jeremiah does not use the word *hēykal* (temple) or *bet* (house) in reference to the sanctuary at Shiloh. 2) 1 Sam. 1:7, 24 does use the word *bet* (house) in reference to the place of worship in Shiloh but, as Tsumura points out,

51

The writer of Samuel purposely chooses these words as he introduces Eli and the story that follows. This verse could be translated, "Now *Exalted* (Eli) the priest was sitting on the *throne* by the doorpost of the *palace* of the LORD." The royal imagery is important. It is also not the last time we will see Eli "sitting on a throne," for the final picture we are given of Eli is falling backward "off the throne" (cf. 1 Sam. 4:13, 18).

Another important word found in this opening description of Eli is the word "doorpost"(*mᵉzûzāh*). A *mezuzah* in modern Hebrew is a little receptacle, attached to a doorpost, containing the words of Deuteronomy 6:4ff. The commandment in Deuteronomy 6:9 which says, "You shall write them [i.e., God's commandments] on the *doorposts* of your house" is still taken quite literally by many Jews. To say that Eli is sitting by the "doorpost" of the temple (palace) of the Lord, ruling as a priest/king, suggests that he is the guardian or enforcer of God's Law. This is a lofty introduction for anyone and it remains to be seen if Eli can live up to first impressions.

In fact, Eli is removed from his pedestal rather quickly, as his first action in the story involves rebuking poor empty, desperate Hannah, the heroine of the story (1 Sam. 1:12–14). We are told that "Eli watched her mouth" and, because her voice was not heard, he was convinced that she was drunk. Eli, the enforcer of the Law, is quick to rebuke this woman only to find that he has completely misjudged her actions. His rebuke may have included the words "daughter of Belial" since Hannah pleads with him not to consider her as such (1:16). The word "Belial" carries the idea of being without worth, thus, "worthless" (NKJV).[6] It is a strong word used of a wicked individual who is at crossed purposes with the Lord and thus stands condemned. It occurs frequently in 1 and 2 Samuel, and ironically is used accurately to describe the sons of Eli in the next chapter (1 Sam. 2:12). Eli's strong rebuke of innocent Hannah stands in stark contrast to his rebuke later of his own sons (1 Sam. 2:23—25), who are in fact "sons of Belial": in the first rebuke he is quite wrong, and in the second he is ineffective—so much for being a strong enforcer and guardian of the Law!

---

context must be the determining factor. The use of "house" does not necessarily refer to the material the structure is made of (Tsumura, *The First Book of Samuel*, p. 114). It would be a major blunder for the author (or editor) of Samuel to have the Lord say, "For I have not dwelt in a house since the time that I brought the children of Israel up from Egypt, even to this day, but have moved about in a tent and in a tabernacle" (2 Sam. 7:6), if he intended the reader to take 1 Sam. 1:7, 24 as a literal building. We have already noted that the word "house" has different shades of meaning in the books of Samuel (see p. 5, n. 8). Baldwin points out that despite various excavations, no material remains of a temple have been found at Shiloh. Perhaps the new excavations recently begun at Tel Shiloh (2010, continuing to the time of this writing) will finally lead to the identification of the site of the ancient tabernacle.
[6] Willis, *First and Second Samuel*, p. 35.

While we could perhaps excuse Eli for jumping to a rash conclusion about Hannah, the evidence of 1 Samuel chapters 2 and 3 convince us that our "knight in shining armor" (this kingly priest and guardian of the Law), is not all he's made out to be. This is not the only time that the books of Samuel will teach us that first impressions can be deceiving. When Samuel later goes to the house of Jesse to anoint a new king, he sees Eliab, Jesse's firstborn, and exclaims, "Surely the LORD's anointed is before Him" (1 Sam. 16:6). But the Lord says to Samuel,

> Do not look at his appearance or at his physical stature, because I have refused him. For the LORD does not see as man sees; for man looks at the outward appearance, but the LORD looks at the heart (1 Sam. 16:7).

The above verse is certainly a key passage in these books. Over and over again the writer will emphasize to the reader not to trust in what he or she sees (e.g., Saul, Goliath, and Absalom). No matter how often we hear the warning, as human beings we are prone to judge by what we see. We often forget that it is the motives and intent of the heart that truly matter. One of the main messages of Scripture is that God desires that we learn to live a different way: we are to "walk by faith, not by sight" (2 Cor. 5:7); and we are "not to look at the things which are seen, but at the things which are not seen. For the things which are seen are temporary, but the things which are not seen are eternal" (2 Cor. 4:18). In 2 Corinthians 5:16 Paul says, "Therefore, from now on, we regard no one according to the flesh." Christians are to "see" differently than others.

Eli is not as perceptive as we would expect a kingly priest and guardian of God's Word to be. There is a challenge here to all of God's leaders to be people of discernment and not to jump to hasty conclusions. Godly leadership should be undergirded by prayer and the wisdom that comes from God. After all, only God can truly "see" the hearts of people. This message of seeing (or not seeing) will be important to Eli's story as we continue. But, for now, the writer has pulled the literary rug out from under our feet with his impressive introduction of Eli in 1:9 which only proves that "appearances can be deceiving."

1 Samuel 1:17 momentarily presents Eli in a better light. At least Eli is honest enough to admit he has made a mistake. After his harsh words to Hannah, he responds with a priestly blessing. Eli's words can be taken as a prayer, "*May* the God of Israel grant your petition," or as a prophetic statement, "The God of Israel *will* grant your petition." Either way, his words bring encouragement to Hannah and are burned into her memory. When she returns later to present Samuel to the Lord, she repeats these very words to him (1:27).

Words are important and it is especially true that those in leadership must be careful how they use them. We are all human and say things we regret. The example set before us here is to be humble enough to admit our mistakes and to seek to encourage and bless the one we have injured with our rash words. After the initial misunderstanding, Hannah and Eli would become warm acquaintances. 1 Samuel 2:20 tells us, "And Eli would bless Elkanah and his wife, and say, 'The LORD give you descendants from this woman for the loan that was given to the LORD.' " If Peninnah's harsh words could cause Hannah's "face to fall," Eli's kind words, along with Hannah's faith in the Lord, could make that same face "no longer sad" (1:18).

Old, Blind, Heavy Eli: A Closer Look (1 Sam. 2:22–3:18; 4:15–18)

The next scene that specifically concerns Eli is found in 2:22–25. This passage relates Eli's weak rebuke of his sons but it begins in a most curious way. Before telling us about the rebuke, the writer begins with the words, "Now Eli was very old." We might wonder why the author bothers to mention this seemingly insignificant detail, but as we examine the story of Eli we find that he is, in fact, preoccupied with a number of physical features of Eli. The writer tells us three times that Eli is old (2:22; 4:15, 18), twice that he has eyesight problems (3:2; 4:15), and twice that he has a weight problem (2:29; 4:18). For someone who is concerned that his readers not judge by outward appearance, why does the writer pay such attention to these physical features of Eli? The answer lies in how the physical defects of Eli are paralleled to his spiritual condition. It is true that sin often manifests itself in a physical way. A superficial look at Eli may cause one to think he is a royal priest, while closer inspection reveals serious character flaws. Let's look at each one of these physical disorders, starting with the last one.

Weight Watchers Anyone? Eli's Weight Problem (2:22–29)

Eli's weight problem is almost certainly related to his, and his sons', sin of taking the sacrificial meat that did not belong to them and consuming it (God accuses them of making themselves *"fat* with the best of all the offerings of Israel"—2:29). The laws in Leviticus make clear that the "fat" of the sacrifice is not to be eaten. For example, Leviticus 7:23–25 states,

> Speak to the children of Israel, saying: *"You shall not eat any fat,* of ox or sheep or goat. And the fat of an animal that dies naturally, and the fat of what is torn by wild beasts, may be used in any other way; *but you shall by no means eat it.* For *whoever eats the fat* of the animal of which men offer an offering made by fire to the LORD, *the person who eats it shall be cut off from his people."*

The reason for the prohibition against eating the fat is that "*all the fat is the LORD's*" (Lev. 3:16). But Eli and his sons flagrantly disregard this command in Leviticus. Worshippers coming to Shiloh prove this in their protest against the taking of their sacrifices: "*They should really burn the fat first*, then you may take as much as your heart desires" (1 Sam. 2:16). Thus the "fatness" of Eli and his sons is a result of their taking and eating the forbidden "fat" of the sacrifices.[7]

The greediness of the priests is vividly described in 2:12–17 and we will look at this in more detail later in connection with Eli's sons. The point to note here is that, in spite of Eli's rebuke of his sons' sin in 2:22–25, he apparently participated in the benefits of some of their sins. Perhaps he would not actually lie with the women who assembled at the door of the tabernacle as his sons did (2:22—maybe because he was too old!), but he was happy to consume the forbidden portions of meat. Such duplicity may help explain why his sons had little respect for him (2:25). We are vividly reminded of this sin of Eli's in connection with his death, when we are told that he broke his neck because he was "old and *heavy*" (4:18).

There is none so blind as he who will not see: Eli's Sight Problem (3:2, 13; 4:15)

We are also informed that Eli had eyesight problems. 1 Samuel 3:2 states that "his eyes had begun to grow so dim that he could not see." We have already noticed that Eli is capable of having perception problems (Hannah). In this passage his eyesight problem is directly connected with his inability to control his sons. In God's words of judgment in 3:13 he says, "[Eli's] sons made themselves vile, and he did not *restrain* them." The word translated "restrain" in the NKJV is the same word translated "dim" in 3:2. In other words, 3:2 could be translated as "his eyes were *restrained* so that he could not see." Eli's physical eyesight problem is directly tied to his inability to control his sons by the use of the same word. His physical blindness is a symptom of a much bigger problem: his spiritual blindness. The inference is that if Eli had been spiritually perceptive, he would have been able to better guide his sons. The fact that Eli rebukes his sons and then participates in their sins shows his lack of spiritual perception. Parents must be careful of not falling into the trap of "Do as I say, not as I do." Children will always imitate behavior over words. Words must be backed up with godly action; God's Word is to become incarnate in our lives. If it is not lived out in the flesh, then it will have no power to affect those we love.

---

[7] Eli's heaviness stands in contrast to Hannah's emptiness. His consumption of the part of the offerings which he is not entitled to also contrasts with Hannah's unwillingness to eat the portion of the sacrifice that she is entitled to (1:8–9).

You're as old as you feel: Eli's Age Problem (3:1–18)

By now it should be obvious that the writer's frequent mention of Eli's age is also symptomatic of a spiritual problem. This is best exemplified in chapter 3 when a young Samuel hears the voice of God for the first time. To understand the significance of Eli's age we need to look at the first part of this story in some detail.

Chapter 3 begins with a notice that the youthful Samuel ("boy" NKJV) "ministered to the LORD before Eli." Throughout the chapter there is an emphasis on Samuel's eagerness to serve. By way of contrast, Eli is first introduced to us as "lying down in his place" (3:2) and he remains in his bed until at least verse 16, although even this verse does not say that Eli arises from his bed; only that then he "called to Samuel." One might assume that Eli is up and about since it is morning (3:15), but this is by no means clear. In other words, with the absence of any indication otherwise, it can be inferred that Eli never leaves his bed throughout the entire episode in chapter 3!

One thing we can be assured of is that Eli is preoccupied with lying down. This phrase occurs 8 times in the chapter (3:2, 3, 5[2x], 6, 9[2x], and 15). Twice it refers to Samuel lying down (3:3 and 15). The other 6 occurrences involve Eli lying down (3:2), Eli commanding Samuel to lie down (3:5, 6, and 9) or Samuel obediently lying down at Eli's command (3:5, and 9).

At one point, after Eli's sleep has been interrupted for the second time, a measure of exasperation can be sensed in the old man as he commands Samuel to go back and lie down. In verse 6, Eli adds the words "my son" to his exhortation to Samuel to lie down. "I did not call, *my son*; lie down again." His innocent-looking words betray Eli's frustration with this youthful lad who doesn't seem to understand that nighttime is for sleeping! Eli's "my son" is similar to our use of a term of endearment in an exasperating situation. For example, if our spouse or teenager says "you did such and such," we might respond, "No I didn't *dear*." Or, "It wasn't me, *honey*." Our use of such terms of endearment is meant to communicate our dissatisfaction with what has been said. Eli's use of "my son" may be a way of reminding himself that Samuel is young and so he wishes to not be overly harsh with him. The boy is just showing the impetuousness of youth. Or, Eli's "my son" may have been said in a more firm way, making it clear that, "It's time for bed, my son!" Either way, the expression "my son" clearly indicates that Eli is getting fed up with interruptions and wants to get on with a good night's sleep![8]

---

[8] This interpretation of Eli's words is supported by the fact that the first time Samuel disturbs his sleep he does not use the term "my son" (cf. v. 5), and Eli's continued insistence that Samuel "lay down." Eli's use of "my son" in v. 16 is certainly a more tender use of this phrase. Perhaps he uses it apologetically to offset the exasperated use of it from the night before.

In contrast to Eli's preoccupation with sleep is Samuel's youthful enthusiasm to serve. When Samuel first hears a voice speaking to him, he naturally assumes it is Eli, and verse 5 says that "*he ran to Eli.*" Usually if I am awakened at night I am not too excited about having to get out of bed. I will usually respond with an irritated, "What do you want?" I certainly wouldn't "run" unless I knew it was an emergency. In contrast to my typical reaction we are not only told that Samuel "ran," but also that he responds with the words of a servant: "*Here I am*" (3:4). In fact, this is Samuel's constant refrain throughout the story. Five times in chapter 3 Samuel responds to Eli with the words, "Here I am" (3:4, 5, 6, 8, and 16). "Here I am" is a statement of availability. It is a response communicating, "I am at your service, what do you need? I'm here to take care of it for you."

Our story purposely contrasts the youthful enthusiasm and servant's attitude of Samuel with old Eli's desire to "lie down." The point, however, is not to say that all young people are servants and all old people are preoccupied with sleep. Age in our story is a relative term. A person could be young physically but old spiritually, because youth is connected with a desire to serve. An older person with the heart of a servant would be young in a spiritual sense. It is not physical age that matters but the unseen attitude of the heart.[9]

The condition of Eli's heart is revealed by two additional observations. First is the apparently innocuous comment of verse 3: "before the lamp of God went out in the tabernacle of the LORD."[10] In Exodus 27:20–21 the Lord instructs,

> And you shall command the children of Israel that they bring pure oil of pressed olives for the light, to cause the lamp to burn continually. In the tabernacle of meeting, outside the veil which is before the Testimony, Aaron and his sons shall tend it from evening until morning before the LORD. It shall be a statute forever to their generations on behalf of the children of Israel.

Notice that the priests are to tend the lamp "from evening until morning" and that it is to "burn continually." Clearly this could be a tedious task resulting in sleep deprivation. It appears that young Samuel had been given this task which makes his enthusiasm at being awakened all the more remarkable.

---

[9] I am not suggesting that every reference to old age is an indication of spiritual lethargy. Context must be the determining factor. There is an interesting parallel between Eli and the Samuel of 1 Sam. 8:1–3. There, Samuel is said to be "old" and to have two rebellious sons. These similarities recall the story of Eli, but despite the parallels one cannot characterize the old age of Samuel as a spiritual laziness.

[10] The word "tabernacle" here is once again the word for "temple" or "palace."

This further heightens the contrast between Samuel and Eli. Eli's focus on sleep suggests that he had become weary in the work of the Lord. It is possible that his familiarity with the things of the Lord had caused him to become complacent. To use a modern analogy, just as the lamp was in danger of experiencing "burnout" (unless attended), Eli himself was "burned out." When we attempt to do things for the Lord in our own strength, sooner or later we too will experience burnout. To avoid this we need the holy fire of God's Spirit to burn in us and provide the strength we need to serve. Paul's words in Galatians 6:8–9 are appropriate here: "For he who sows to his flesh will of his flesh reap corruption, but he who sows to the Spirit will of the Spirit reap everlasting life. And let us not grow weary while doing good, for in due season we shall reap if we do not lose heart."

The second observation about the state of Eli's heart concerns his reaction once he realizes that God is speaking to Samuel. Verse 8 reports, "Then Eli perceived that the LORD had called the boy." Mention is made here of Eli's "perception," but he is slow on the draw. It is not until Samuel comes to him the third time that blind old Eli begins to realize that there is something significant going on. But it is Eli's response which is most remarkable. He gives the young Samuel great advice. He alerts him to the fact that God may be trying to speak to him, and he even gives him proper words to use in response: "Speak, LORD, for Your servant hears" (3:9). However, having given Samuel good advice, Eli rolls over and goes back to sleep!

Now imagine that you just discovered that God is speaking in the room next to you. Would you say to your friend, "Tell me all about it in the morning," and then roll over and go back to sleep? Not a chance! Hopefully you would be right there in that room waiting to hear the voice of God and what he might have to say. Eli's reaction once again betrays his spiritual age. He is too tired to hear from God. He would rather get a good night's sleep and hear about it in the morning! This is why chapter 3:1 begins with the statement, "And the word of the LORD was rare in those days; there was no widespread revelation." The reason was the lack of godly leadership in Israel interested in hearing what God had to say. Eli's sons were too rebellious and Eli was too tired to hear from God.

Eli is an example of a leader who knows the right thing to say, but has drifted so far from the Lord that he doesn't have the heart to follow his own advice. "Speak, LORD, for Your servant hears," is not something Eli could say himself because he has lost his heart for service. Eli has become too tired to serve the Lord; as a result he has closed his eyes and his ears to the word of the Lord.

This story suggests that, along with the problems of blindness and old age, Eli also has a hearing problem. Notice that, although God is speaking in the very next room, Eli cannot hear the voice that is calling out to Samuel. We will see that Eli's sons also have a hearing problem. But God tells Samuel that when his judgment is poured out on the house of Eli, Israel will clearly hear about it: "Behold, I will do something in Israel at which both *ears* of everyone who *hears* it will tingle" (3:11).

A Word About Mercy (1 Sam. 3:1–3, 10, 15)

Before moving on with other observations about Eli, it is important to digress and point out how 1 Samuel chapter 3 testifies not only to God's judgment on the house of Eli, but also to God's mercy toward Israel. Notice again the statement, "before the lamp of God went out" (3:3).

The story of chapter 3 begins in darkness. It is nighttime—Eli and Samuel are lying down (3:2–3), and there is no mention of morning until verse 15. Eli is blind, which means that he lives in a world of darkness. There was no "widespread revelation"—the word for prophetic visions (3:1)—and "the word of the LORD was rare in those days," more evidence of a spiritual darkness. The only light at the beginning of the story is the light that is coming from "the lamp of God." The fact that the lamp of God had not yet gone out not only hints that the physical dawn was nearing (Lev. 24:2–3), but more importantly that a new spiritual dawn was imminent.

In other words, in a world sunk in darkness, the light of God was shining, however tentatively, and that light would not go out until a new day had dawned. These are words of mercy and hope. Despite the fact that Israel's leadership was rebellious (Hophni and Phinehas) and weary (Eli), and had let God's people drift into a night of spiritual darkness, God had not given up on his people.[11] As long as there is a God such as this, there is always hope. In the midst of the blackest darkness, the light of God still shines (John 1:5).

Light plays an important part in the end of the story. As previously noted, verse 15 announces the coming of the dawn: "Samuel lay down until morning, and opened the doors of the house of the LORD." While this may have been a normal part of Samuel's routine, the writer calls attention to his actions. In a story where the physical world parallels the spiritual world so closely (in fact, is an explicit comment on it) it is significant that night begins turning into day *after* God is given a listening ear by his servant Samuel. The opening of the doors of the Lord's house, letting in the morning light, is a way of saying that a new day has dawned in Israel. Now there is a man who will listen to the word of the Lord and obey. God's light once again streams into his house. Paul's words would have been appropriate to this situation as he exhorted the Christians in Rome saying,

---

[11] It is also significant that Samuel is probably lying down in this part of the sanctuary. Unlike Eli who lays in the dark, Samuel lays in the light of God—a sign of his future destiny and calling.

And do this, knowing the time, that now it is high time to awake out of sleep; for now our salvation is nearer than when we first believed. The night is far spent, the day is at hand. Therefore let us cast off the works of darkness, and let us put on the armor of light. (Rom. 13:11–12)

A second point regarding God's mercy, concerns the references to his "calling" of Samuel. The word "called" is used 12 times in the story (once again, a significant biblical number). In most cases it refers to God calling Samuel (6 out of 12) or Samuel saying "you called" and Eli responding, "I did not call" (5 times). All of this confusion about "calling" and "not calling" highlights further that God is trying to speak, but neither Samuel nor Eli is aware of it. While "the word of the LORD was rare in those days," it becomes clear that it was not primarily because of God's silence, but because of people's inability to hear him.

The words describing the final time God calls to Samuel before he answers, speak volumes about God's mercy. Verse 10 says, "Now the LORD came and stood and *called as at other times.*" These words emphasize God's persistence in trying to get his Word through to his people. God did not call once and give up. God kept calling until Samuel finally responded.

Chapter 1 asks the question, "Does God hear when we speak?" (Hannah's plea for a son) The answer is, "Samuel"—a play upon the words, "God hears," or to use Hannah's words, *"Because I have asked him from the LORD"* (1:20). Chapter 3 asks the question in reverse, "Does anyone hear when God speaks?" Our answer needs to be the same as Samuel's, *"Speak, LORD, for Your servant hears"* (3:9–10). If we are experiencing a spiritual night and it seems like the word of the Lord is "rare," this story assures us that God, in his mercy, is trying to speak. What we need are "ears to hear" and a servant's heart that is willing to respond. This story asserts that God can only be heard by a "servant," because only servants hear and obey.

Those Who Honor Me, I Will Honor (1 Sam. 2:30)

If the main theme of Eli's life was to be summed up in one sentence, I believe it would be found in the statement made by the unnamed man of God sent to proclaim judgment against Eli and his house. In 1 Samuel 2:30 the man of God declares, "But now the LORD says, 'Far be it from Me; for *those who honor Me I will honor, and those who despise Me shall be lightly esteemed.*' " This statement contains three key words, important not only for Eli's story, but also important in understanding the overall message of the books of Samuel. Those words are "honor," "despise," and "lightly esteem." We will look at these words in reverse order, saving the one that is most important to Eli (honor) for last. But first, to understand the impact of these words, it is important to examine the significance of the concept of honor and shame within the cultural context of the ancient Mediterranean world.

Honor and Shame in the Ancient World

Bruce J. Malina has asserted that, "In the Mediterranean world of the past and present, honor is a core value."[12] "Honor is a claim to worth along with the social acknowledgement of worth."[13] Not only do people of equal social status operate interpersonally on the basis of honor and shame, their relationship with superiors (including God) is expected to conform to this important norm. To live in a state of dishonor is intolerable. It means isolation and the contempt of others. There is no meaningful existence without honor in such a culture.

Malina also points out that the physical body plays an important symbolic role in the expression of honor.

> The head and front of the head (face) play prominent roles. To be seated at the head of the table, to be at the head of the line, to head an organization, are replications of crowning the head, of others taking off their hats to you, of others bowing their heads in your presence.[14]

I have noted these observations by Malina about honor for two important reasons. First, 1 Samuel 2 continues the theme of "before the face" which we noted in connection with Hannah and Peninnah (see pp. 30-31, 40-41). It now becomes easy to recognize that the contest between Hannah and Peninnah involved honor. Hannah was ashamed that she could not have a son. Peninnah's action of "getting in Hannah's face" year after year was a way of dishonoring her among the family. When we put ourselves in the cultural

---

[12] Bruce J. Malina, *Windows on the World of Jesus* (Louisville: Westminster/John Knox Press, 1993), p. 1. Also see Malina, *The New Testament World*, pp. 27-57. Another previously cited work that investigates the significance of honor in the ancient world is David A. deSilva, *Honor, Patronage, Kinship, & Purity*. Both of these works focus on the world of the 1st century and the NT, but both cite OT examples. Articles that address the values of honor and shame from an Old Testament perspective include: Gary Stansell, "Honor and Shame in the David Narratives," *Semeia* 68, 1994, pp. 55-79; and Saul M. Olyan, "Honor, Shame, and Covenant Relations in Ancient Israel and Its Environment," *JBL* 115/2, 1996, pp. 201-218. Olyan, p. 203, states, "These concepts are not at all alien to the worldview of ancient Israelites or their neighbors. On the contrary, they are common almost to the point of banality, occurring in discourses concerning many aspects of social relations: war, international diplomacy, marriage, the family, the penal system, and death and the afterlife."

[13] Malina, *The New Testament World*, p. 52.

[14] Ibid., pp. 38-39.

context of ancient Israel we can understand why not bearing a son is such a grievous situation for Hannah. No son means no honor, and no honor is a living death, or worse than death itself. Were it not for the kindness and love of Elkanah, Hannah might have been socially isolated—as good as dead. Continuing this theme, chapter 2:17, 18, 21, 28, and 30 all speak about Samuel or Eli's family doing something "before the LORD."[15] The point of this expression in chapter 2 is that Samuel's ministry "before the LORD" is a way of showing honor to God, while the actions of Hophni and Phinehas "before the LORD" bring dishonor. God says to Eli, "I said indeed that your house and the house of your father would walk *before Me* forever" (2:30).[16] However, since Eli's actions have shown contempt for the Lord's face, thus bringing dishonor, God will no longer honor him.

Second, as Malina points out, honor is both a claim and acknowledgement of worth. The word "worship" means to ascribe worth to someone, especially to deity. Worship should be an expression of the honor and high esteem we hold God in. Notice that God's words of judgment to Eli occur in the context of worship—or rather, a lack of worship. God says, "Why do you kick at My sacrifice and My offering?" (2:29). Because he had taken the part of the sacrifices that belonged to God (the fat), Eli had dishonored God. The word rendered "best" in 2:29 (*"the best* of all the offerings of Israel My people"*) comes from the Hebrew word for "head." Recalling Malina's observation about the head representing honor, God is accusing Eli of taking "the head" of all the offerings. Eli is taking the honor that belongs to God. Furthermore, because Eli put the concern of his sons before God, he showed that he really honored them more than God ("and honor your sons more than Me"—2:29). Therefore, Eli's (and his sons') punishment fits their crime. Because Eli has acted in a way that dishonored God, God will no longer honor him and his house. This provides some cultural context for understanding the significance of Eli's sin. We will return to the concept of honor below and notice its importance for the rest of the story of Eli.

Those Who Despise Me Shall Be Lightly Esteemed

The words "despise" and "lightly esteem" are at the other end of the honor spectrum. They are words of shame and disgrace. The word "despise" is used 7 times in 1 and 2 Samuel.[17] Each time it refers to one who either despises the Lord, or who despises someone or something that belongs to the

---

[15] This expression is also found in 2:35 where it refers to serving "before" the Lord's anointed. 2:11 and 3:1 also speak of Samuel ministering to the Lord "before Eli."

[16] 2:28 also shows that God had honored Eli's father (i.e., ancestor) by choosing him as priest "to wear an ephod *before Me*."

[17] The passages are: 1 Sam. 2:30; 10:27; 15:9; 17:42; 2 Sam. 6:16; and 12:9, 10.

Lord. The result is usually death.[18] Eli's despising of the Lord leads to his and his sons' death on the same day (2:34; 4:11, 18).

The word "lightly esteem" means to treat with contempt and is therefore an antonym for honor.[19] The Hebrew word occurs 18 times in 1 and 2 Samuel.[20] It is particularly prominent in the story of Shimei's cursing of David. Shimei's "lightly esteeming" (cursing) of David is an act of heaping shame and dishonor on David. Once again, when one "lightly esteems" the Lord, or the Lord's anointed, death is the inevitable result, and Hophni and Phinehas, as well as Shimei, experience the consequences of their "cursing." We will have opportunity to notice the effects of "despising" and "lightly esteeming" on several of the characters found in 1 and 2 Samuel.

Honor and Heaviness

This brings us back to God's statement, "Those who honor Me I will honor." The word "honor" in Hebrew (also translated "glory" as we shall see) is from the same root as the word "heavy." In Hebrew thought, a person who was honorable or glorious had a heaviness of presence.[21] We can all relate to an important person walking into a room and everyone "feeling the presence" of that person. It may be an important politician or a well known celebrity, but there is something about the charisma surrounding certain people that causes a stir in the room, a certain thickness in the air, or "heaviness" when they are present. In the 1960's when we were impressed with something or someone we used to say, "Man, that's heavy!" The idea in Hebrew is similar. God's glory was thought to be so impressive that there was a heaviness when one experienced his presence.

The reader may be aware of where all this is headed. God has accused Eli and his sons of making themselves "fat," and upon Eli's death we are told that he was "old and *heavy*" (4:18). The word used for "heavy" in 4:18 is from the same root as the word used for "honor" in 2:30. Ancient Hebrew used words from the physical sphere of life to express abstract ideas. For ex-

---

[18] 1 Sam. 10:27 is an exception because Saul shows mercy to the men who despise him (cf. 1 Sam. 11:12–13). David is another exception because the Lord forgives him (2 Sam. 12:9–10, 13).

[19] The words "honor" and "heavy" come from the same Hebrew root (see comments which follow above). The words "light" and "heavy" are natural opposites and are sometimes used in this literal sense (e.g., 1 Kings 12:10). In the present context "lightly esteem" works as a wordplay on "honor" which causes one to think of "heaviness."

[20] The passages are: 1 Sam. 2:30; 3:13; 6:5; 17:43; 18:23(2x); 2 Sam. 1:23; 2:18; 6:22; 16:5, 7, 9, 10, 11, 12, 13; and 19:21, 43.

[21] The link between "heaviness" and "honor" may have to do with a wealthy person being described as one "heavy with possessions" (cf. Gen. 13:2). This "heaviness" of wealth brought honor and prestige.

ample, there is no word for "power" (an abstract concept); instead Israelites spoke of the "hand." To be delivered into the "hand" of one's enemy means to be delivered into his "power."[22] The same is true with the words "honor" and "heavy" in our present story. The context suggests a clear connection between the two words.[23] Thus, "heaviness" conjures up images of "honor" and vice versa. Eli literally steals God's "honor" by making himself "heavy" with the meat of the sacrifices that belong to God!

Priests with a Similar Problem—Malachi 1 and 2

The situation described in Malachi chapters 1 and 2 provides an interesting parallel to the story of Eli. Malachi chastises the priests of his day for their corrupt practices. In 1:6 he uses two of the key words found in 1 Samuel 2:30.

> A son *honors* his father and a servant his master. If then I am the Father, where is My *honor*? And if I am a Master, where is My reverence? Says the LORD of hosts to you priests who *despise* My name. Yet you say, "In what way have we *despised* Your name?"

Abuse of the sacrificial system by the priests is the issue here, just as it is in 1 Samuel 2. Malachi records the priests' attitude toward their offerings when he writes, "You also say, 'Oh what a weariness!' And you sneer at it" (1:13). Growing weary in the work of the Lord and taking their holy calling for granted sounds similar to Eli's situation. Malachi 2:2 continues,

> If you will not hear, and if you will not take it to heart, to give *glory* to My name, says the LORD of hosts, I will send a *curse* upon you, and I will *curse* your blessings. Yes, I have *cursed* them already, because you do not take it to heart.

Refusal of the priests to give "glory" (show honor) to the Lord results in a curse that God has sent on them. The word for "curse" is the usual Hebrew word, which is stronger than the word "lightly esteem" used in 1 Samuel 2:30. The similarity of language between these two passages can hardly be acci-

---

[22] I have argued in the introduction that "power" is a key concept in 1 and 2 Samuel. But since power is an abstract concept it is communicated in many different ways throughout these books, including the frequent use of the word "hand." An example of a particularly heavy usage of "hand" (meaning "power") is found in 1 Sam. 23:4, 6, 7, 11, 12, 14, 16, 17, 20; 24:4, 6, 10, 11, 12, 13, 15, 18, and 20.

[23] This does not mean that every occurrence of "honor" should conjure up the idea of heaviness, anymore than every occurrence of "hand" suggests power. Context must be the determining factor.

dental. In both situations we have priests who have corrupted the sacrificial system: they are said not to be giving "honor" (glory) to the Lord. Instead they are "despising" the worship of the Lord and, as a result, God promises to "lightly esteem" or "curse" them. Furthermore, Malachi 2:2 says that the problem is a "heart" problem ("you do not take it to heart"). When God pronounces judgment on the house of Eli he tells him he will raise up a faithful priest, "who shall do according to what is in My *heart* and in My mind" (1 Sam. 2:35). Space does not permit further discussion, but it seems clear that there are allusions to the story of Eli in Malachi 1 and 2.

A Weighty Conclusion

The story of Eli teaches us that it is a serious affront to God for anyone to take the glory that belongs only to him. There is an important lesson here for pastors, worship leaders, or any of God's people who are tempted to take credit for things that only God deserves the praise for. "I am the LORD, that is My name; and My glory I will not give to another" (Isa. 42:8). The glory of God is simply too weighty for any human being to handle.

When Moses said, "Please show me Your glory" (Exod. 33:18), God answered, "You cannot see My face; for no man shall see Me and live" (Exod. 33:20).[24] God's presence is too glorious for fleshly man to stand in his presence. God does grant Moses the opportunity to see his back, but he says, "My face shall not be seen" (Exod. 33:23). Eli makes the fatal mistake of trying to steal the glory (honor) of God and, as a result, the heaviness of God's glory crushes him. In the last scene in which Eli, the kingly priest, appears, we see him falling backwards off his *throne* (the same word as 1:9) and his neck breaking because he was "*old and heavy*"! (4:18).

The portrait of Eli that 1 Samuel leaves us with is not of an overtly wicked man, but rather, a weak man. Eli was a man who grew weary and neglectful and who did not finish the race God had given him to run. Eli's concern for what was right is noted several times throughout chapters 1–4. Although he was incorrect, he rebuked Hannah for what he perceived as drunken actions in the presence of the Lord (1:14). The blessing of Elkanah and Hannah (2:20), the ineffective rebuke of his sons (2:22–25), his good advice to Samuel (3:9), his acquiescence to the will of God (3:18), and finally, his concern for the ark of God (4:13, 18), show him to be a man who had a concern for right and wrong.

Eli simply lacked the power and the integrity to follow through on what he knew was right. His appetite for good meat was stronger than his appetite for spiritual things. He was a carnal man in the most literal sense! Because he walked in the flesh, he grew weary, old, blind, and heavy, and his

---

[24] Notice the connection again between "glory" (honor) and "face."

life—which had such potential for godly influence—instead resulted in a legacy of disappointment. To adapt an expression from the apostle Paul, Eli has "become our example, to the intent that we should not lust after evil things as he also lusted" (1 Cor. 10:6).

Chapter 5

Hophni and Phinehas: Sons of Belial (Eli's sons)

Nevertheless they did not heed the voice of their father, because the LORD desired to kill them. (1 Sam. 2:25)

Double Trouble (1 Sam. 2:12)

Hophni and Phinehas never appear separately in the Samuel narrative. Biblically speaking, they are Siamese twins. When one is mentioned so is the other. As a result we will treat them as 1 Samuel does—together. The names "Hophni" and "Phinehas" are both Egyptian. Hophni means "tadpole" and is a rare name. Phinehas means "the Negro" and is the same name as Aaron's grandson.[1] Unfortunately, Phinehas, the son of Eli, does not live up to his namesake. As mentioned earlier, the significance of Hophni and Phinehas's names is more in the way they sound rather than in what they mean. The pronunciation of both names reminds one of the word "face" in Hebrew and we have previously explored the significance of this (see pp., 30-31, 40-41, and 60-62).

While Hophni and Phinehas are first mentioned in 1:3, their full introduction does not come until 2:12ff.[2] The writer leaves no doubt about the character of these men. These literary twins are said to be alike in two ways: First we are told they were "sons of Belial" ("corrupt"—NKJV). Literally it says, "The *sons of* Eli were *sons of* Belial." The expression "sons of" draws a parallel between these two expressions.[3] In fact, the word "Belial" has the same letters found in Eli's name in a different order (with the exception of the "B"), and so there is a wordplay. We have already encountered a similar expression in Eli's description of Hannah (1:16). This phrase occurs nine times in 1 and 2 Samuel[4] and always refers to someone who is rebellious, wicked, and deserving of death. Therefore, the reader should not be surprised by the statement in 2:25, "the LORD desired to kill them," or the prophecy and fulfillment concerning their deaths on the same day (2:34; 4:11).

---

[1] Klein, *1 Samuel*, p. 7.

[2] We have already noticed that the reason for their introduction in 1:3 is to make a comment on Elkanah's faithfulness. The faithfulness of Elkanah's commitment to worship where Hophni and Phinehas preside as priests is only fully appreciated after reading 2:12–17 (see chap. 1, pp. 24-25).

[3] Robert D. Bergen, *1, 2 Samuel*, NAC (Nashville: Broadman & Holman, 1996), p. 78, makes a similar observation. He writes, "The construction has the effect of equating Eli with Belial."

[4] 1 Sam. 1:16; 2:12; 10:27; 25:17, 25; 30:22; 2 Sam. 16:7; 20:1; and 23:6.

Second, we are told, "they did not *know* the LORD." This is a devastating critique about men who are in the ministry of God. Hosea describes people who have no knowledge of God: "There is no truth or mercy or *knowledge* of God in the land. By swearing and lying, killing and stealing and committing adultery, they break all restraint, with bloodshed upon bloodshed" (Hos. 4:1b–2). Knowledge of God is not a mental exercise, or merely knowledge of certain facts *about* God. As most Bible students are aware, the word "know" is used to express *intimate relationship*—"Now Adam *knew* Eve his wife, and she conceived and bore Cain" (Gen. 4:1). Knowing God means having an intimate relationship with God. This relationship leads a person to live obediently. He or she wants to act and live as God acts and lives. This includes treating others the way God treats them. However, as Hosea states, a lack of the knowledge of God is directly related to a lack of truth and mercy. The result is a society in chaos, a people who do not keep the ten commandments—swearing, lying, killing, stealing, and committing adultery become the norm. Hophni and Phinehas clearly fit into this mold. They steal the sacrifices of the people (2:13–14), they threaten them with violence (2:16), and they sleep with the women who serve at the tabernacle (2:22).[5] They are, in fact, guilty of breaking at least five of the Ten Commandments, as coveting (2:16—"all your heart desires"), and disrespect for parents (2:25—"they did not heed the voice of their father") could be added to this list. Thus the fate that Hosea says will befall the priests of his day is also appropriate for understanding the fate of Hophni and Phinehas in our story: "My people are destroyed for lack of knowledge. Because you have rejected knowledge *I also will reject you from being priest* for Me; Because you have forgotten the law of your God, *I also will forget your children*" (Hos. 4:6).

Vegetarians Not Welcome Here! (1 Sam. 2:13–17)

The portrait of Hophni and Phinehas begins by describing their "custom" with the people regarding sacrifice. The "custom" of the priests regarding sacrifice is clearly outlined in Deuteronomy 18:1–8. Deuteronomy 18:3 uses the same word as 1 Samuel 2:13. Thus the "custom" described in Deuteronomy, which speaks of God's provision for the priests, is contrasted with the "custom" of Hophni and Phinehas, who greedily take what they want. The scene would be somewhat comical were it not so sad. 2:13–14 describes the servant of the priests (probably a portly little fellow himself), greedily running to any vessel he can find (pan, kettle, caldron, or pot) with a

---

[5] Contrasting Phinehas, the grandson of Aaron, with Eli's son, Leithart, *A Son to Me*, p. 50, insightfully notes, "The earlier Phinehas pierced through a man and a woman who were fornicating in the camp (Num. 25:1–9), but at Shiloh an anti-Phinehas fornicated in the tabernacle precincts."

three-pronged fork and taking whatever meat he can carry. Instead of being satisfied with the portion that was rightfully theirs, the priests were stealing what belonged to the worshipper and his family.

Not content with this, verses 15–16 describe how the priests even stole the part of the sacrifice that belonged to God. "Also before they burned the fat, the priest's servant would come and say to the man who sacrificed, 'Give meat for roasting to the priest.' " We have already noticed that the Law specified that the fat was to be offered to the Lord and was forbidden for anyone to eat (Lev. 3:17; 7:23–25; see pp. 54-55). Taking the sacrifice even before it could be offered to the Lord highlights the covetousness of the priests. This is why God accuses Eli and his sons of taking *"the best* of *all* the offerings of Israel My people"* (1 Sam. 2:29).

The priests backed up their covetousness with threats of physical harm—"No but you must give it now; and if not, I will take it by force" (2:16). The greed of Hophni and Phinehas is summed up in the word "take." Verse 14 says, "The priest would *take* for himself all the fleshhook brought up," and in 2:16 the priests' servant says, "I will *take* it by force." The "custom" of the priests is therefore one of "taking" what is not theirs. They are indiscriminate in their "taking," they "take" from the people and from God. They act like petty potentates. They take what they want and back it up with force. Once again the priesthood of Eli and his sons is paralleled to the future kingship. In 1 Samuel 8:11 Samuel tells the people the "custom" ("behavior"—NKJV) of the king who will reign over them. Samuel uses the word "take" 4 times in 8:11–17.

There is a temptation within leadership to think that certain privileges go with the territory. A position of servanthood given by God's grace suddenly becomes a position I think I deserve because of my service, my goodness, my education, or my godly pedigree. Rather than serving I expect to be served. I begin to believe that God's people owe me; after all, I'm their pastor, vicar, or bishop. I should be entitled to a "pastoral discount," live in the best house and drive the best car. If I do not have what I think I deserve, I may begin to use the people of God, or the ministry of God, to get it. Ministry loses its biblical focus and becomes a pursuit of wealth, fame, and "the good life." Rather than leading and feeding the sheep, we fleece the flock. Sadly, there are many examples in contemporary ministry that illustrate this attitude and by rushing to a harsh judgment of Hophni and Phinehas, we may find ourselves condemned (Rom. 2:1). Jesus warned the religious leaders of his day not to choose "the best seats" (Matt. 23:6), and he told his disciples:

> You know that those who are considered rulers over the Gentiles *lord it over* them, and their great ones exercise authority over them. Yet *it shall not be so among you; but whoever desires to become great among you shall be your servant.* And whoever

of you desires to be first shall be slave of all. *For even the Son of Man did not come to be served but to serve,* and to give his life a ransom for many (Mark 10:42–45).

The sin of "taking" is a sin of presumption and ingratitude. One who "takes" puts himself in the place of God and proclaims that God's sufficiency is not enough. God is removed from the throne of our hearts and He is dishonored (1 Sam. 2:29—"*honor* your sons more than Me"; 2:30—"Those who *honor* Me I will *honor*"). It is significant that the first sin of mankind is described in terms of "taking"—"she *took* of its fruit" (Gen. 3:6). This act of taking was based on dissatisfaction with what God had provided and a desire to be like God (Gen. 3:5). A servant who takes is a great oxymoron. Servants serve, they do not take! The people of God are not to be "takers." Rather we are to be content with what God has supplied. Paul writing to the Philippians says, "Not that I speak in regard to need, for I have learned in whatever state I am, to be content: I know how to be abased, and I know how to abound. Everywhere and in all things I have learned both to be full and to be hungry, both to abound and to suffer need" (Phil. 4:11–12).

Jesus is the supreme example of one who refused to take. Paul says although he was in the form of God, he did not consider it "something to be held onto" ("grasped"—KJV) but "made himself of no reputation, taking the form of a bondservant" (Phil. 2:6–7). Again Paul writes, "For you know the grace of our Lord Jesus Christ, that though He was rich, yet for your sakes He became poor, that you through His poverty might become rich" (2 Cor. 8:9). The example of Jesus, and the counterexample of Hophni and Phinehas, clearly teaches the ministry is not to be used as a means to an end for our own glorification. Those who preach a "health and wealth" gospel and who use the ministry to glorify their own reputation should look to the One who "made himself of no reputation." If we are getting "fat" off of the ministry, stealing the offerings of God's people, or seeking to glorify our name, then a swift and uncompromising repentance is in order, lest we experience the same fate as these priests. The self-seeking ministry of Hophni and Phinehas stands as a strong warning against modern ministries that do not model servanthood in leadership and do not give God the glory due his name. The following verses show us what God does with ministries, and ministers of this kind.

Dying to Get Out of the Ministry (1 Sam. 2:25)

After recording Eli's mild rebuke of his sons, the author says, "Nevertheless they did not *heed* the voice of their father" (2:25). Verses 22–25 use some form of the word "hear" (*sh^{e}ma'*) 5 times. We are told 3 times that Eli "heard" (22, 23, 24) the "report" (24—also from *sh^{e}ma'*) about his sons' wickedness. Verse 25 then tells us that Eli's sons had a "hearing" problem because, "they did not *heed* the voice of their father." In Hebrew the word *sh^{e}ma'* not only means "to hear" but also "to obey." In Hebrew thought if someone does not "obey" then they really have not "heard." We use the word "hear" in a similar way. When dad used to say, "Didn't you *hear* what I said?" he really meant "Why didn't you *obey* me?" The flagrant disregard of Hophni and Phinehas for their father's warning stands in contrast to Samuel's words in 3:10, "Speak for Your servant *hears.*" Hophni and Phinehas are self-willed, they do not have the heart of a servant therefore they do not "hear" (obey).

What might surprise the modern reader, however, is the reason given for Hophni and Phinehas's disregard of their father's correction: "because the LORD delighted to kill them" (my translation). The Hebrew Scriptures are not as squeamish about attributing things to the Lord that embarrass modern readers. It is important to recall the words of Hannah's prophetic song: "*The LORD kills* and makes alive; He brings down to the grave and brings up" (2:6). These words assert that God is sovereign; if he makes alive, he also kills. Everything in Creation is under his sway and control. God not only extends mercy, he also judges wickedness. Rather than try and explain away these words because they make us uncomfortable, we are better off to let them stand and have their full impact on us. These words assert that there are limits. There is a day of judgment, a time of reckoning for willful disobedience. If it can be said that God "delights" in delivering (2 Sam. 22:20), it can also be said that he "delights" in destroying the wicked. If God is holy and righteous, if he desires to deliver his people from evil, then it must be this way.

On the other hand, Ezekiel writes, " 'For I do not *delight* in the death of one who dies,' says the Lord GOD. 'So *repent* and live!' " (Ezek. 18:32—my translation) God delights more in repentance, but when that repentance is not forthcoming, he delights in ridding wickedness from among his people.[6] In case one thinks that this is just an "Old Testament" teaching, listen to what Jesus tells the church at Ephesus (a church with a pretty good ministry—certainly nothing like the wicked ministry of Eli's sons): "Remember therefore from where you have fallen; *repent* and do the first works, or else I will come to you quickly and *remove* your lampstand from its place—unless you *repent* " (Rev. 2:5). He also says of the woman known as "Jezebel" at the church in Thyatira, "*I will kill her children with death* and all the churches shall know that I am He who searches the minds and hearts" (Rev. 2:23).

---

[6] I am not suggesting that God enjoys killing people, but the fact that 1 Sam. 2:25 uses the word "delight" is a strong indication of God's seriousness about judging sin. I am in agreement with Bergen, *1, 2 Samuel*, p. 81, who writes, "Although it would be misleading to say that the Lord takes pleasure in killing people (cf. Ezek. 18:32; 33:11; 2 Pet. 3:9), it is certainly true that he delights in bringing justice to the world order."

It is important to note that even in the wicked ministry of Hophni and Phinehas God gave time for repentance. Following the warning by Eli, God sends a Man of God with a word of judgment against Eli and his house (2:27–36). Judgment still doesn't come, however, and God delivers yet another word of warning through Samuel (3:11–14). Still, judgment doesn't fall until the events of chapter 4. God is indeed, "longsuffering...not willing that any should perish but that all should come to repentance" (2 Pet. 3:9). If you are living in sin, if your ministry is corrupt, God is speaking a warning to you just as surely as he did to Hophni and Phinehas and the churches of Revelation. God's desire is for repentance and restoration. He is a longsuffering God; nevertheless, there is an end to his mercy. A person, or ministry, that continues in willful rebellion will reach a point of no return. God promises a day of reckoning and that ministry (dare we also say minister?) will be put to death—"For the wages of sin is death" (Rom. 6:23). Turn now before it is too late. "Repent and live" (Ezek. 18:32).

Here Comes the Judge (1 Sam. 2:27–36; 3:11–14)

Before leaving the subject of judgment it is important to examine the words of 2:27–36 and 3:11–14 in more detail. The oracle delivered by a "Man of God" in 2:27–36 begins by reminding Eli of all God had given to him and his father's house. Just as God contrasts David's "taking" with his own "giving" (2 Sam. 12:7–9), so here God contrasts his blessing upon Eli's house with the greediness of Eli and his sons. God had honored Eli's house by "choosing" his father (meaning ancestor) to be priest. He, and his house after him, had the privileged position of approaching God's altar, wearing the ephod of priesthood, and receiving the offerings of Israel for their sustenance (2:28). The wearing of priestly garments in order to minister before the Lord's altar is explicitly stated to be an "honorable" (or "glorious") position (Exod. 28:2, 40). Yet in spite of God's goodness, Eli and his sons had dishonored God (1 Sam. 2:29–30). As a result, God proclaimed certain consequences which would befall Eli and his family.

It is interesting to note how God's judgments parallel the physical condition of Eli. God proclaims to "old" Eli that, "there shall not be an *old* man in your house forever" (2:32), "all the descendants of your house shall die in the flower of their age" (2:33). Furthermore, God says to "blind" Eli, "But any of your men whom I do not cut off from My altar shall *consume your eyes* and grieve your heart" (2:33).[7] To "heavy" Eli God says, "everyone who

---

[7] William McKane, *I&II Samuel*, TBC (London: SCM Press, Ltd., 1963), p. 40, translates this verse differently: "But there is one man whom I will not cut off from my altar to consume thine eyes (with tears)." He believes this is a reference to Abiathar, the only one to escape the massacre at Nob (cf. 1 Sam. 22:20).

is left in your house will come and bow down to him [God's anointed] for a piece of silver and *a morsel of bread* and say, 'Please, put me in one of the priestly positions, that *I may eat a piece of bread*'" (2:36).

Eli and his sons' self-sufficiency, evidenced by their stealing of sacrifices and weight problem, will be eradicated by God, as Eli's descendants will become beggars looking for their daily bread, totally dependent upon God and his anointed for their next meal. This is a judgment to be sure, but there is also a word of mercy here. It is certainly better to be a beggar and realize one's dependence on God, than to be overweight, self-sufficient and headed for destruction.

This oracle also contains the important prophecy of 2:35, which speaks of a "faithful priest" who will do "what is in My heart and My mind." Of this priest God says, "I will build him a sure house." In a happy coincidence of chapter and verse division, this prophecy in 1 Samuel 2:35 is fulfilled in 1 Kings 2:35 when Zadok is given the high priesthood in place of Abiathar (cf. 1 Kings 2:27). While Zadok is said to be the fulfillment of this prophecy, there also seems to be a more immediate fulfillment of it in Samuel, and a more distant fulfillment of it in Jesus. It is the faithful ministry of Samuel that replaces the wicked service of Eli and his sons in 1 Samuel. In fact, 1 Samuel 2 is a study in contrasts between the faithfulness of Samuel and the wickedness of Hophni and Phinehas.[8] Most importantly these words anticipate Jesus, "the *faithful* High Priest" (Heb. 2:17), who does all that is in his Father's mind and heart (John 6:38). Jesus is, of course, *the* faithful priest, and the only One who has totally done the will of the Father. Furthermore, the promise of an enduring ("sure") house is only completely fulfilled in him (Heb. 7:21).

The prophecy of 2:35 once again links the priesthood with the kingship. God's desire for a priest who is faithful and does all that is in his heart, is the same as his desire for a king who will do the same (1 Sam. 13:14; 15:28). When God places this king (David) on the throne, he promises him a "sure house" (2 Sam. 7:16). Just as Jesus is the ultimate fulfillment of the perfect priest, he is also the perfect fulfillment of this promise (Luke 1:32–33). It should not be overlooked, however, that the emphasis in the immediate context is on God's leader being faithful and having a heart that desires to live God's way.

---

[8] Notice how chapter 2 constantly shifts the focus between Samuel and Eli and his sons (2:11, Samuel; 2:12–17, Hophni and Phinehas; 2:18–21, Samuel and his family; 2:22–25, Eli and his sons; 2:26, Samuel's growth; 2:27–36, judgment on Eli and his house). This shifting of the "camera's focus" between Samuel and Eli's family highlights the rise of Samuel and the fall of Eli, and illustrates the truth of Hannah's prophetic words—"he brings low and lifts up" (2:6–8). See John T. Willis, "An Anti-Elide Narrative Tradition From a Prophetic Circle at the Ramah Sanctuary," *JBL* 90 (1971), pp. 288-308, esp. pp. 289-294.

The second oracle of judgment (3:11–14) continues to emphasize the rebellious nature of Eli and his sons. God says in 3:13 that he will judge the house of Eli "for the iniquity *which he knows*." In other words, despite God's warning in 2:27–36, Eli had not taken any further steps to address his sons' wickedness, but had resigned himself to their disobedience. God says that Hophni and Phinehas had made themselves "vile" (NKJV). This is the same word translated "lightly esteem" in 2:30. In other words, Eli's sons lived in a manner that "lightly esteemed" or, blasphemed God. Their "cursed" way of living brought its own "curse" from God upon their lives.

This curse is laid out in 3:14 and, in spite of what we know about Hophni and Phinehas, seems, at first glance, very harsh. God says, "I have sworn to the house of Eli that the iniquity of Eli's house *shall not be atoned for by sacrifice or offering forever.*" If God will not accept sacrifice and offering on behalf of Eli's house then there is no possibility for atonement—his house is doomed. However, when we recall that the chief sin of Hophni and Phinehas involved defiling God's sacrifices and offerings (2:13–17, 29), this judgment is just. 2:17 states that "men abhorred the offering of the LORD." If God mercifully provides a means of forgiveness but it is despised and not accepted, then what other avenue is there for obtaining forgiveness? Hophni and Phinehas had contemptuously treated the very thing intended to bring them forgiveness! As a result, the punishment fits the crime. Since Eli and his sons treated the sacrificial system with such disregard then the system designed to bring them atonement would be useless to them.

Some people believe that Christianity is too narrow by claiming that Jesus is "the Way, the Truth, and the Life" and that "no one comes to the Father" except through him (John 14:6). What they fail to understand is that it is not our place to define how forgiveness and atonement are received. It is God's prerogative to tell us how forgiveness can be obtained. Such an attitude that questions God's way of forgiveness is arrogant and presumptuous. God does not owe anyone forgiveness. We should simply rejoice that he has made atonement possible, and humbly follow his direction to receive it! That God offers forgiveness at all is an amazing testimony of his grace and forbearance. Who are we to attempt to put our own terms and conditions on God's means of forgiveness? The writer of Hebrews addresses the attitude of one who rejects the sacrifice of Christ when he writes, "Of how much worse punishment, do you suppose, will he be thought worthy who has trampled the Son of God underfoot, counted the blood of the covenant by which he was sanctified a common thing, and insulted the Spirit of grace?" (Heb. 10:29). Hophni and Phinehas's actions were an insult to the Spirit of grace, and so are ours if we reject the sacrifice of God's only Son.

Conclusion: The Axe Finally Falls (1 Sam. 4:1b–22)

The end of Eli and his sons finally comes in the tragic story related in 1 Samuel 4. We are told that the Philistines fought with Israel and killed about 4,000 men (4:2). As a result, Israel made the mistake that people frequently make: they equated the things of God with God himself. After the initial defeat Israel asked, "Why has the LORD defeated us today before the Philistines?" (4:3). Unfortunately, they came up with the wrong answer. They believed it was because they did not bring the ark of the covenant into battle with them: "Let us bring the ark of the covenant of the LORD from Shiloh to us, that when it comes among us *it may save us* from the hand of our enemies." Some believe that the manipulation of religious relics will force God to act on their behalf. Israel made the mistake of thinking they had God in a box so they sent back to Shiloh and had Hophni and Phinehas bring up the ark of God to the battlefield (4:4). Israel expected their "box" approach to yield "instant" results, much like a modern recipe. However, they learned that the God of heaven could not be put in a box and the result was not what they (or apparently the Philistines) expected.

God has given us memorials of himself to remind us of his presence. But the power of these rituals (e.g., communion, baptism, prayer) is not in the things themselves, but in the unseen God who supplies them with power and meaning. God's presence cannot be manipulated by ritual. Ritual has meaning and power when God's people live in his presence, but when that presence is absent, the ark (or any relic or ritual) becomes an empty box. Various churches over the centuries have developed rituals including the lighting of candles, the saying of the rosary, or the genuflecting of the cross, but these can never be used to manipulate the sovereign God of heaven. Israel experienced one of its greatest defeats up to this time. 30,000 men were killed, the ark of God was captured, and Hophni and Phinehas were slain (4:10–11); so much for ritual without God's presence. This event was a devastating defeat permanently burned into Israel's memory (Ps. 78:59–64; Jer. 7:12).

It is interesting how little attention is paid to Hophni and Phinehas in this chapter. They are mentioned in verses 4 and 11, but their names appear at the end of the sentence in the Hebrew text. They are nothing more than an afterthought. When news is brought to Eli about the battle, it is not the death of his sons that is said to trouble Eli, but the capture of the ark of God (4:18). Similarly, Phinehas's wife seems much more concerned about the ark and Eli than about her husband, who is consistently mentioned last (4:19, 21)! The point may well be that these rebellious men are of no consequence in the day of calamity. These men of no spiritual stature are relegated to insignificance because there is no power in their lives. The presence of God had already forsaken them, as it would soon depart from Israel (4:21–22). With no pres-

75

ence and no power the sons of Eli were ill-equipped for the day of crisis. They were of no help to themselves, their family, or their nation.

The deaths of Hophni and Phinehas on the same day (4:11) were a fulfillment of prophecy (2:34). Moreover, they provide another link between the priesthood of Eli and the kingship. It is not coincidental that the house of Saul is rejected in similar words to that of Eli. Saul too is accused of abusing the sacrificial system (1 Sam. 13:11–13; 15:22–23). Like Eli, Saul's house is rejected in favor of one who will be according to the Lord's heart (2:35; 13:14). Eli is said to be "heavy" at his death, and on the day of Saul's death we are told, "And the battle was *heavy* against Saul" (1 Sam. 31:3—my translation). Finally, Eli and his sons die on the same day in a devastating defeat by the Philistines who had gathered at Aphek (ch. 4:1). Likewise, Saul and his sons all die on the same day by the hands of the same enemy (the Philistines), who gathered in the same place (Aphek—1 Sam. 29:1), and won another overwhelming victory (chap. 31)! These intentional parallels further establish the truth of Hannah's prophetic words (2:6–10), and confirm the words of God: "Those who honor Me I will honor, and those who despise Me will be lightly esteemed" (2:30).

These truths are important for leaders (priests and kings), and families. The rebellion of Eli and his sons had devastating consequences for his family and the nation. As noted in the introduction, families and the fate of nations are intimately connected. The fragmenting of families will ultimately lead to the downfall of a nation. While the message here is applicable for everyone, the context has a particularly sobering message for the leaders of God's people. When ministry becomes about us, our selfish desires, and our glory, then not only are our families in trouble, our nation, which is only redeemed by its godly families, is headed for certain destruction. Thankfully the truths of 1 Samuel 2:6–10, and 2:30 are mixed with the mercy and grace of God, or else no one would stand. However, as Birch states, "Those who would serve God place themselves under both God's grace and God's judgment—not just under God's grace"[9] (cf. James 3:1). The judgment on Eli's house is a reminder of this important truth.

---

[9] Birch, *The First and Second Books of Samuel*, p. 989.

Chapter 6

Phinehas's Wife and Ichabod: No Glory
(Eli's grandson and daughter-in-law)

Then she named the child Ichabod, saying, "The glory has departed from Israel!" (1 Sam. 4:21)

Where is the Glory? (1 Sam. 4:19–22)

The wife of Phinehas, whose name is anonymous, and her son, Ichabod, play a small but important part in the climax of the story of the destruction at Shiloh. The writer tells us that Phinehas's wife is pregnant and that the distressing news from the battle causes her to give birth (4:19).

The order in which she receives the news is significant. First she is told that the ark of God has been captured; second that her father-in-law (Eli) is dead; and only last that her husband is dead. One might think that the order was constructed to cushion the blow of hearing of her husband's death, but the text makes it clear that the news is given in the order of most important to least important (4:21–22). We can certainly understand how news of the ark and of Eli might be of more consequence to this woman than the death of a husband who had lain with the women at the door of the tabernacle of meeting (2:22). In fact, the commentary of Psalm 78:64 on this event states, "Their priests fell by the sword, and *their widows made no lamentation.*" Nonetheless, the news does bring about a premature labor and, although the child is delivered, it results in Phinehas's wife's death. And so another member of the family of Eli succumbs to death on this tragic day.

Before she dies, however, the wife of Phinehas is able to name her child. The name is a strange one—Ichabod—but she links the name with the most traumatic event of the day: the taking of the ark of God (4:21). There is some debate as to whether Ichabod's name means "No glory" (i.e., inglorious), or perhaps "Where is the glory?"[1]

This scene is reminiscent of the birth of Benjamin. With her dying breath, Rachel gave her son a strange name, Ben-Oni, which means "son of my sorrow." Jacob, however, changed the name to "Benjamin": "son of my right hand" (Gen. 35:18). It seems ironic that a man from the tribe of Benjamin also delivered the bad news to Eli (4:12–14). The parallel between the two birth stories may lie in the contrast they provide to one another. Ben-Oni does not properly reflect the future of Jacob's family, and so Jacob changes his son's name to Benjamin. However, the name, Ichabod, stands because it is a true reflection of the situation—"the glory has departed" (4:22).

---

[1] See McCarter, *I Samuel*, pp. 115-116 for a discussion of the meaning of the name. McCarter also suggests that it could mean "Alas (for the) Glory!"

The significance of the name "Ichabod" lies in the repetition of a key word in the Eli story. If the "I" is removed (in Hebrew this is a separate word meaning "no" or "where?"), we have the word *chabod* (usually transliterated *kābôd* in English) which is the word for "honor" or "glory." This is the same word used in 2:30 where God says, "Those who *honor* Me I will *honor*." As noted above, this word is from the same root as the word "heavy" which is used to describe Eli in 4:18. The reason Phinehas's wife names her child "Ichabod" is because "the glory (*kābôd*) has departed from Israel" (4:21–22). Therefore, the name "Ichabod" brings the story of Eli to a dramatic conclusion. Because Eli had "honored" his sons more than the Lord (2:29), God said to him, "Those who honor Me I will honor" (2:30). We are told at Eli's death that he was old and "heavy" (4:18). By stealing the sacrifices, Eli had made himself fat. That is, Eli had appropriated for himself the glory belonging to God alone.[2] As a result "the glory departed" from Israel.

English translations obscure the fact that the words translated "honor," "heavy," and "glory" are all from the same root in Hebrew. Therefore, to belabor the point one more time, because Eli had not "glorified" God but had "glorified" himself, God would not "glorify" Eli and his house and thus the "glory" departed from Israel. Reinhartz suggests that the anonymity of Eli's daughter-in-law, "is a symbol of this national misfortune, of her death, and, despite the life to which she gives birth, of the moral barrenness of the house of which she is a part."[3]

Conclusion: The Glory Has Been Exiled

Recent Bible scholars have called attention to the fact that a better translation of "the glory has departed" is "the glory has been exiled."[4] The similarities between the situation described here and those of the Babylonian exile are intriguing. In both cases a king is dethroned (Eli, 1 Sam. 4:18 [see footnote 2 below]; Zedekiah, 2 Kings 25:6); one king is blind (Eli, 1 Sam. 4:15), the other is blinded (Zedekiah, 2 Kings 25:7); descendants of the ruling line must beg at another king's table (1 Sam. 2:36; 2 Kings 25:29); the house

---

[2] Eli's stealing of God's glory is also communicated through the "kingly" language used to describe him (1:9; 4:13, 18—see chap. 4, pp. 51-52). When the people ask for a "king" in 1 Sam. 8, God says to Samuel, "They have not rejected you, but they have rejected Me, that I should not reign over them" (8:7). This statement should cause the reader to reflect on the "kingly" language used of Eli, and is another way of showing that Eli took what belonged to God. The many correspondences between Eli and Saul further confirm this.

[3] Adele Reinhartz, "Anonymity and Character in the Books of Samuel," *Semeia* 63, 1993, p. 127.

[4] For example, McCarter, *I Samuel*, p. 116; also Alter, *The David Story*, pp. 25-26.

of the Lord is destroyed (Ps. 78:60; 2 Kings 25:9); and the glory is exiled (1 Sam. 4:21–22; Ezek. 11:23).

These parallels are a warning to any who treat the Lord and the work of the ministry in a comparable way. The Israel of Jeremiah and Ezekiel's day had not learned the lesson of Shiloh (Jer. 7:12–14), and so they made the same mistakes and history repeated itself. Similarly, if we follow the example of Eli, then our name and ministry will also become "Ichabod" because the glory will depart.

Although the final word to the story of Eli is "Ichabod," there are several signs of hope. First, the birth of Ichabod recalls the birth of the only other child mentioned so far in the story: Samuel. These two births act as bookends around the story of Eli. While Ichabod's birth brings a forecast of doom, the story of Samuel's birth was full of hope. The contrast between the priesthood of Eli and the growth and ministry of Samuel (recorded in 1 Sam. 2–3) contains a word of hope for the future. How gracious of God to proclaim a word of hope (in the person of Samuel) before judgment fell! Although the bleak situation of 1 Samuel 4 ends with gloomy words, Samuel's ministry is on the horizon. The words of 3:19 remind us that the Lord was with Samuel and he "let none of his words fall to the ground." Samuel will reappear in chapter 7 to restore Israel's relationship with God (7:3–4).

Second, although the "glory has been exiled" from Israel it does not mean the glory has disappeared. 1 Samuel 5 and 6 are the story of "the glory" making itself known in enemy territory. The key word "heavy" continues to appear in these chapters, as we are informed that "the hand of the LORD was *heavy*" on the Philistines (5:6, 11). As a result, the priests of the Philistines encourage the leaders to "give *glory* to the God of Israel; perhaps He will *lighten* His hand from you" (6:5).

The point is that even if God's people do not give him the glory he deserves, he *will* get the glory for himself—for he is a mighty and awesome God. In the words of Hannah, "The adversaries of the LORD shall be broken to pieces; from heaven He will thunder against them. The LORD will judge the ends of the earth" (2:10; cf. 1 Sam. 7:10). The true God is sovereign and powerful. He needs no one to give him glory; he can get it for himself. The good news is that God graciously allows us to participate in his ministry and to give him the glory that is due his name. As we do, amazingly, he allows us to participate in that glory, and he glorifies us (John 17:22; 2 Cor. 3:18)!

Chapter 7

Ahijah and Ahimelech: Doomed Priests of a Doomed King (Great-grandsons of Eli)

Two Names for One Person?

Ahijah and Ahimelech are both said to be a "son of Ahitub" (1 Sam. 14:3; 22:9) and both act as priest for Saul. As a result some scholars have suggested that they are one and the same person.[1] It is true that some people in the Bible are referred to by more than one name (e.g., Solomon is also called "Jedidiah," 2 Sam. 12:25), but it is more likely that these are two different people.

First, it is quite common in the books of Samuel to refer to pairs of priests, and on several occasions these pairs are brothers. Hophni and Phinehas (1 Sam. 1:3), and Ahitub and Ichabod (1 Sam. 14:3), are examples of this. Other pairs of priests include Abiathar and Zadok (2 Sam. 15:24), and Jonathan and Ahimaaz (2 Sam. 15:27).

However, the most important reason for seeing these two names as separate individuals is the contextual evidence found in 1 Samuel. The prophecy recorded in 1 Samuel 2:32–33 states, "And there *shall not be an old man* in your house forever...and all the descendants of your house *shall die in the flower of their age.*" The seemingly quick change of priests by Saul between the mention of Ahijah in 1 Samuel 14:3 and Ahimelech in 1 Samuel 21 and 22 is better understood against the background of these words of judgment on Eli's house. The obscurity of Ichabod and Ahitub add to this conclusion.[2] The lack of information about these priests and the swiftness with which they disappear reinforce the prophecy against Eli's house.[3]

---

[1] For example, F.T. Schumacher, "Ahijah," *IDB*, Vol. 1, p. 67; and Hans Wilhelm Hertzberg, *I & II Samuel*, OTL (Philadelphia: Westminster Press, 1964), p. 112. The suggestion is that Ahi-"jah" and Ahi-"melech" are similar ways for saying the same thing. "*Jah*" is a shortened form of "Yahweh" and "*melech*" is the word for king. It is argued that the name "*melech*" would be influenced by the Canaanite culture while "*Jah*" would be the more appropriate Israelite form. In the context of Samuel it could also be argued that "Yahweh" is the true "king" (1 Sam. 8:7), and thus the names do have a relationship to one another.

[2] The fact that the sons of Ahitub are acting as priest suggests that Ahitub and Ichabod are already deceased. Samuel could be roughly the same age as Ahitub, possibly older, and we know for sure that he is older than Ichabod, yet Samuel lives on while these men seemingly come to a premature end.

[3] I am in agreement with Peter D. Miscall, *1 Samuel: A Literary Reading* (Bloomington: Indiana University Press, 1986), p. 21, who writes, "The effect of the judgment on

We will begin by examining the scanty information we have on Ahijah in 1 Samuel 14 and then look at the story concerning Ahimelech in 1 Samuel 21 and 22.

Ahijah: A Priest Without Significance (1 Sam. 14:1–3, 17–20, 36–37)

Ahijah the son of Ahitub, Ichabod's brother... (1 Sam. 14:3)

The extended genealogy introducing Ahijah in 1 Samuel 14:3 is ominous. The first hint of trouble is the mentioning of Ichabod. It is unusual that an uncle would be introduced into a genealogy that is otherwise very direct. The writer could easily have written, "Ahijah the son of Ahitub, the son of Phinehas, the son of Eli." The intentional reference to Ichabod is surely meant to recall the circumstances surrounding his birth (1 Sam. 4:21–22). This is further confirmed by the mention of Shiloh. Thus we are reminded that Ahijah is part of a doomed priesthood. He belongs to the family of priests who have "no glory."

The context in which Ahijah is introduced also conspicuously hints at failure. The story begins with Jonathan's bold step of approaching the Philistine garrison. The verse ends by noting, "But he did not *tell* his father" (14:1). Next we are told that Saul was sitting under a pomegranate tree (14:2). This statement provides two important contrasts. Jonathan is boldly "stepping out" (the Hebrew word here is from "walk") and "crossing over." Saul on the other hand is "sitting." One is a picture of activity and the other of non-activity. Second, it appears that Saul is seeking a divine word, and this explains why he is sitting under the pomegranate tree with Ahijah nearby who is "carrying" an ephod (14:3).[4] Before going into battle, kings often sought a word of knowledge from God (cf. 1 Kings 22). The irony is that Saul, his priest, and the entire army are ignorant of Jonathan's maneuvers. Verse 3 emphasizes this lack of knowledge, first mentioned in verse 1. Therefore Saul and his priest, Ahijah, are among those who sit around and know nothing.

Ichabod, Ahijah, and their families is not stated, but we can assume that their insignificance for the continuing story is a sign that the judgment has befallen them."

[4] It is clear from Scripture that an ephod was a garment worn by the high priest which included a breastplate with pockets in which were carried the Urim and Thummim for divining the will of God (Exod. 28:15–30). There is some debate as to whether an ephod might also describe some other kind of object for divining the will of God. Gideon was said to have made an ephod of gold which became an object of worship to many Israelites (Judg. 8:24–27). At times in 1 Sam. the ephod is said to be "carried" not worn and is used for the purpose of inquiring of God (14:3; 21:9; 23:6, 9; 30:7). For further information see Klein, *1 Samuel*, p. 135, and Willis, *First and Second Samuel*, p. 141.

Ahijah is, in fact, Saul's counterpart—as Jonathan's armor-bearer is his counterpart. The word "bearer" in "armor-bearer" (v. 1) is the same word used to describe Ahijah's "bearing" or "carrying" of the ephod (v. 3; The NKJV obscures the parallel by translating the phrase "wearing an ephod").[5] In other words, just as Jonathan's servant "carries" his armor, and is thus his "armor-bearer," so Ahijah "carries" the ephod. The point of the comparison is to show that: just as Jonathan is "in the know" and stepping out in faith, so is his armor-bearer. Likewise, just as Saul is sitting around in ignorance, so is his "ephod-bearer."

Ahijah is supposed to be a man who hears from God, but this relative of Ichabod does not appear to have a direct line to the Almighty. This observation is confirmed when Ahijah is next mentioned in 14:18. Saul notices the commotion going on in the Philistine camp and suspects that some of his soldiers are up to something. He does not know who, however, until he does a roll call (14:17). It is only at this point that he, and the rest of the army including Ahijah, realizes that Jonathan is missing. In spite of the great victory God is orchestrating, Saul (and Ahijah) does not know what to do. Rather than joining the work of God already in progress, Saul calls for Ahijah to ask God what he should do. Ahijah is apparently oblivious to what God wants, so he begins to inquire. His inability to get a quick message from the Lord finally causes the impatient Saul to tell him to "withdraw" his hand (14:19). Saul then proceeds to do what he should have done long before, which is to summon the people to battle (14:20).

With leadership that does not know when to inquire and when to act or when to sit and when to go, Israel is in trouble.[6] In fact, Jonathan will say regarding yet another unwise action by his father that day, "My father has

---

[5] The similarity of language between this story and 1 Sam. 10:3–7 is illuminating. Both stories frequently use the word "carry" (see 10:3 which uses "carry" 3 times). Both stories also speak about Gibeah which means "hill" (10:5—"hill of God"; 14:2) and the garrison of the Philistines (10:5; 14:1, etc.). My point in mentioning these similarities is that chapter 10 is a story about knowing the will of God. In 1 Sam. 10 Samuel is declaring to Saul what God will do. Saul is "in the know" here and he receives the Spirit of the Lord and prophesies (10:5, 11). Saul's lack of knowledge in discerning the Lord's will in chapter 14 stands in strong contrast to this and is highlighted by the use of these similar words. Ahijah is certainly no Samuel!

[6] It might seem that one should always inquire of God before acting and therefore Saul and Ahijah are doing the right thing. But the Scripture teaches there is also a time to step out in faith and do what God calls one to do. Once again 1 Sam. 10 provides an important comment on chapter 14. In 10:7 Samuel advised Saul, "And let it be, when these signs come to you, that you do as the occasion demands; for God is with you." Saul's inactivity in 14:2 reveals a lack of faith to "do as the occasion demands" and stands in contrast to Jonathan's words, "For nothing restrains the LORD from saving by many or by few" (14:6).

troubled the land" (14:29). Only the faith of Jonathan and the grace of God could bring victory out of such confused and incompetent leadership.

Ahijah is mentioned one more time in this story, where he is simply referred to as "the priest" (14:36). His impotence is once again revealed when he tells Saul and the people, "Let us draw near to God here." Ahijah's suggestion sounds very pious, but in light of the events just described it seems misguided. Saul and the people are ready to continue the battle, but instead Ahijah again suggests inquiring before pursuing. This inquiry receives a deafening silence from the Lord. After Saul's inquiry about whether he should pursue the Philistines, we are told, "But He [God] *did not answer* him that day" (14:37). This botched attempt at inquiry nearly leads to the death of Jonathan, the hero of the day (14:45).

The entire story highlights the ineffective leadership of Saul. At times he is indecisive when the situation calls for action (14:2). At other times he is presumptuous, making oaths where none are needed (14:24–34). And still at other times his reversal of decisions inspires no confidence in those who follow him (14:18–19; 44–45). While the focus of this story is Saul's failure and Jonathan's faith, Ahijah plays a small part. Unfortunately for him, he is on the side of indecision, ignorance, and pious irrelevance.

Saul's relationship with the doomed house of Eli does not help him, nor does Ahijah's relationship with Saul benefit him in any way. One person who is conspicuously absent from this story is the prophet Samuel. Saul's lack of association with Samuel, who has left him due to his disobedience in offering up a sacrifice (13:13–15), seems to have brought about a spiritual paralysis in his life. On the other hand, Saul's association with Ahijah, who does not hear from God (14:19, 37), becomes a case of "the blind leading the blind" (Matt. 15:14): a tragic comedy of errors in which Saul constantly makes the wrong decision.

Sometimes there are relationships that are better off terminated. There are friendships that seem to bring out the worst in each other. Paul says, "Do not be deceived: evil company corrupts good habits" (1 Cor. 15:33). It is hard to say whether the lives of Ahijah and Saul could have been different had they broken off their relationship;[7] after all, there were other contributing factors. But it is certain that their relationship only seemed to reinforce each other's weaknesses and brought neither of them closer to God. To adopt (and adapt) Paul's expression from 1 Corinthians 11:16, they came together "not for the better but for the worse."

---

[7] I am speaking hypothetically as it is unlikely that Ahijah even had such a choice. Saul's future slaughter of Ahimelech and the priests at Nob (1 Sam. 22) vividly illustrates the danger posed to one who might be suspected of not fully supporting the king.

Ahimelech: the Duped Priest (1 Sam. 21:1–9)

"You shall surely die, Ahimelech" (22:16)

We are introduced to Ahimelech in 1 Samuel 21 as David flees from Saul. Ahimelech is the leading priest at Nob, a city of priests (22:19) and apparently the place where the tabernacle had been re-established after the destruction at Shiloh (21:6). It is only in 22:9 that we learn Ahimelech is the son of Ahitub and thus a descendant of Eli. This information is kept from the reader until Saul's murderous intentions take shape in chapter 22.

Ahimelech is initially introduced as one who is "afraid" (21:1), and the reason is revealed in his question to David, "Why are you alone, and no one is with you?" David's "aloneness" is suspicious, but we do not know the precise nature of Ahimelech's suspicion. As Saul's priest, he might have been aware of tension between Saul and David. The fact that Saul's leading commander was alone is not a good sign to him. However, David's deception quickly allays his fear (21:2). Ahimelech appears somewhat gullible. David's unorthodox appearance raises suspicions, but rather than probe further he accepts David's explanation. Like his brother, Ahijah, Ahimelech is not very discerning. He is a pawn caught between the present and future monarchs of Israel.

There are two viable ways to view Ahimelech's response to David's requests. First, it is possible that he is hesitant and uncomfortable, yet he does not wish to stand in the way of a secret mission from the king, so he proceeds to give David everything he asks for. David's first request is for bread (21:3–5). Ahimelech responds that the only bread available is the holy bread—bread usually reserved for the priests. While he is unwilling to refuse David, Ahimelech offers a possible reason why David should not take it ("if the young men have at least kept themselves from women," 21:4).[8] Likewise, David appears without a sword or weapon (another very unusual situation for a military commander on urgent business!), and asks Ahimelech if he has one available (21:8). Ahimelech's verbose reply may again suggest he is uncomfortable. His words, "For there is no other except that one here" (21:9) might be his way of suggesting to David, "It's all we've got; are you sure you really want it?" Once again, however, he acquiesces to the will of David who brusquely replies, "There is none like it; give it to me."

Another possibility, suggested by Fokkelman, is that, after his initial suspicion, Ahimelech becomes an enthusiastic helper of David.[9] Among oth-

---

[8] Of course, Jesus uses this passage as an example that the needs of people are more important than sticking to the letter of the law (Matt. 12:3–4). I am not disputing whether Ahimelech's actions are right or wrong, only that he is compliant with all of David's requests despite the fact that there is plenty of reason for suspicion.

[9] Fokkelman, *Crossing Fates*, pp. 352-361.

er reasons, Fokkelman maintains that Ahimelech's increasing verbosity suggests his ease and comfort in David's presence. This ease leads to "his readiness to help (which) borders on enthusiasm."[10]

Whether Ahimelech's words are interpreted as reluctant or enthusiastic, his gullibility remains. He is duped by David. Ironically, he does not want to interfere with a secret mission of the king, so out of loyalty he gives David everything he asks for. But it is this very loyalty that Saul will question in 22:11–13. The aid Ahimelech gives David will convict him (in Saul's eyes) of treason rather than faithfulness (22:16)!

The first lesson that can be learned from Ahimelech is the importance of discernment, especially in leadership. Ahimelech's gullibility not only results in his own death, but the death of an entire community, save one (22:19–20). If we are uncomfortable with a particular person or situation, Scripture charges us to investigate it further. John says, "Beloved, do not believe every spirit, but test the spirits, whether they are of God; because many false prophets have gone out into the world" (1 John 4:1). 1 Samuel 21 may not be asserting that David was a "false prophet," but there are a number of indications that he was out of the will of God on this occasion.[11] The point is that discernment is important for any child of God, but especially for leaders whose decisions affect an entire community. We are told that Ahimelech had the ephod in his possession, an instrument for discerning the will of God (21:9). Rather than seek God's direction, Ahimelech allowed himself to be pressured into making what were, at least for him and the other priests, unwise decisions.

Ahimelech: the Doomed Priest (1 Sam. 22:9–19)

Ahimelech next appears in the story when he is summoned by Saul to account for his actions regarding David (22:9–11). When Ahimelech first encountered David he was afraid. By way of contrast, as he and the other priests come to Saul there is no mention of fear. This suggests that Ahimelech had acted innocently in regard to aiding David, as he himself argues (22:15). However, he has much to fear; but his demeanor suggests he is still either unaware of Saul's hostility toward David, or believes that his defense of ignorance will acquit him.

---

[10] Fokkelman points out that Ahimelech speaks, first one line, then three, and finally four. Ibid., p. 354.

[11] The first clue is David's deception. He lies about being on important business for the king. Second David's request for a "spear or a sword" (21:8) are in direct contrast to his great statement of faith in 1 Sam. 17:47, "The LORD does not save with sword or spear!" Third, David's flight to Gath (21:10–15) is a clear sign he is not in the will of God. In fact, his life is put in great jeopardy and he must flee again. For a different view see Bergen, *1, 2 Samuel*, pp. 221-223.

Saul's first words to Ahimelech are harsh and disrespectful as he refuses to acknowledge him by name and instead calls him "son of Ahitub" (22:12). Saul's address equates Ahimelech with David, as he refers to David contemptuously as "the son of Jesse" (22:7, 8, and 13): in his eyes, the guilt of one implicates the other. Saul says, "Why have you conspired against me, you and the son of Jesse?" (22:13). In the context of the larger story we know that Saul is totally mistaken. David is not guilty of betraying Saul, and neither is Ahimelech; yet both stand accused in his eyes.

Ahimelech responds with an eloquent five-point defense (22:14–15): 1) Who is a more faithful servant than David?; 2) David is the king's son-in-law, so why wouldn't he support him?; 3) David does the king's "bidding"; 4) David is "honorable" in the king's house; and 5) Ahimelech denies that he inquired of the Lord on David's behalf ("Far be it from me..."—v. 15).[12] In spite of Doeg's accusation (22:10), this denial is consistent with the account in chapter 21 which only mentions the giving of bread and the sword.

Ahimelech's defense is his one shining moment. He uses terms loaded with meaning within the context of 1 Samuel. He calls David "faithful," which recalls God's desire for a man who is "faithful" (2:35—here, specifically a priest). He uses the word "servant," and says David does the king's "bidding" (from the word $sh^ema\,$ meaning "obedient"). The picture of an obedient servant recalls the young Samuel of chapter 3. Finally, he says that David is "honorable," which recalls God's promise, "Those who honor Me I will honor" (1 Sam. 2:30). Ahimelech spends more time defending David than himself!

Ahimelech's defense goes beyond the present story, depicting David in glowing terms that remind us of past events and people. But eloquence is wasted on a man whose mind is already made up. In fact, Ahimelech's brilliant defense of David only serves to convince Saul of Ahimelech's guilt. Saul, who has a penchant for wanting to kill the wrong person (Jonathan, 14:44, and David, 20:31), proceeds to pronounce: "You shall surely die, Ahimelech" (22:16). Yet Saul goes even further. Beginning with 22:11 we read that not only did Ahimelech respond to the king's summons, so also did "all his father's house." In his defense, Ahimelech includes the innocence of "the house of my father" (22:15). Thus in 22:16 Saul not only pronounces a death sentence on Ahimelech, but also on all his father's house. To their credit, Saul's servants refuse to carry out the death penalty against the priests of the Lord (22:17). Therefore, Saul turns to a foreigner, Doeg the Edomite, who carries out the wholesale slaughter of eighty-five priests and their city (22:18–19).

---

[12] Scholars are divided over the meaning of Ahimelech's words and whether he did in fact inquire of God on this occasion. For a good discussion of the various points of view see Fokkelman, *Crossing Fates*, pp. 389-391, 398-400, and 415-416.

Saul's slaughter of the priests of Nob is clearly a fulfillment of the prophecy found in 1 Samuel 2:27–36, especially the Lord's words, "I will cut off your arm and the arm of your father's house, so that there will not be an old man in your house" (2:31). However, his fulfilling of prophecy does not mean the Lord condones his act, as the context makes clear that Saul is in rebellion against the Lord.

Saul's act can be compared with Judas's betrayal of Jesus. Jesus said, "The Son of Man indeed goes just as it is written of him, but woe to that man by whom the Son of Man is betrayed! It would have been good for that man if he had not been born" (Matt. 26:24). In other words, prophetic foreknowledge does not absolve individual responsibility. God had foretold the doom on Eli's house, as well as the betrayal of Jesus, but Saul and Judas are held responsible for their actions.

Conclusion: Leaving a Legacy

The fate of Ahijah, Ahimelech and the house of Eli leads to the consideration of an important biblical principle. The Bible makes clear that one generation does not bear the guilt of another (Ezek. 18:2–3); each one bears its own sin. But, one generation can experience the consequences of another generation's sins, just as one person can experience the consequences of another's sins. For example, Jeremiah denies that the people of his generation are bearing the guilt of the previous generation, even though this is what they argue (Jer. 31:29–30). However, he does say that they are experiencing the consequences of the sin of the previous generation of Manasseh (Jer. 15:4).

As an example, one does not have to be an alcoholic to experience the consequences that come from alcoholism. A drunk driver can kill an innocent person, and an alcoholic parent can be abusive to a child. The innocent are not responsible for the other's sin of alcoholism, but they do experience the consequences.

The Bible is clear that sin is deadly. It not only brings death to a particular individual but can affect those around them, even future generations. Such is the deadly power of sin. This truth was stated clearly when God proclaimed his name to Moses in Exodus 34:7. After speaking of his mercy and forgiveness, God added, *"visiting the iniquity of the fathers upon the children and the children's children to the third and the fourth generation."*

Our modern society makes us aware how a problem like child abuse or alcoholism can become a vicious generational cycle. Even if a future generation is freed from this cycle, family members will experience the consequences of it (for example, struggling with problems of self-worth or depression). The stories of Ahijah and Ahimelech are similar. They might not have sinned to the same degree as Eli and his sons, but the sin of Eli had a rippling effect that impacted their generation severely. In light of Exodus 34:7

it is interesting that Ahijah and Ahimelech represent the fourth generation from Eli.

One of the questions raised by a study of 1 and 2 Samuel is, "What kind of a legacy do we want to leave for future generations?" It is an important family question. This issue will confront us again when we look at the houses of both Saul and David. Our sin or our righteousness not only affects our own lives, or the lives of our contemporaries; it also has an impact on future generations.

Chapter 8

Abiathar and Jonathan: The Remnant
(great–[x2] and great–[x3] grandsons of Eli)

Abiathar: The "Soul" Survivor (1 Sam. 22:20–23)

Now one of the sons of Ahimelech the son of Ahitub, named Abiathar, escaped (1 Sam. 22:20)

Because there is only a small amount of information on Abiathar, and his son, Jonathan, we will treat them together in this chapter. While Abiathar is mentioned in a number of passages throughout 1 and 2 Samuel and the beginning of 1 Kings, very little is said about him.[1] He never speaks, except once indirectly when it is said he told David that Saul had killed the priests of the Lord (1 Sam. 22:21); and his character receives very little development in the ensuing story. We are told that he inquired of God on David's behalf (1 Sam. 23:6, 9; 30:7), carried the ark and was faithful to David during Absalom's revolt (2 Sam. 15:24–36; 1 Kings 2:26), and participated in Adonijah's aborted attempt to usurp the throne, thus losing his position as priest (1 Kings 2:27). Beyond this we know very little about Abiathar. Perhaps this silence on his character is yet one more instance of commenting (without commenting!) on the insignificance of Eli's descendants. Yet there are clues in the text that allow us to examine some important truths that relate to Abiathar's life.

One of the most intriguing things about Abiathar is his name, which has an interesting range of meaning. "*āḇ*" means "father" in Hebrew. The second part of his name comes from the Hebrew word *yāṯār*[2] meaning "remainder," or "what is left over," and is also related to the idea of "abundance." Therefore, his name can mean "the father's (God's) abundance,"[3] or "the father's remnant."[4]

Both of these meanings have an important relationship to what we have learned about Eli's family in 1 Samuel. When *yāṯār* is translated as "abundance," it can be used as "a technical sacrificial term that always occurs in conjunction with the liver" (cf. Exod. 29:13, 22; Lev. 3:4, 10, 15). It refers

---

[1] The passages (too numerous to list in the subtitle) referring to Abiathar are: 1 Sam. 22:20–23; 23:6, 9; 30:7; 2 Sam. 15:24–36; 19:11; 20:25; 1 Kings 1:7, 19, 25, 42; 2:26–27, 35; and 4:4.

[2] In English the "y" in the Hebrew *yāṯār* is transliterated as an "i" in Abiathar.

[3] R.W. Corney, "Abiathar," *IDB*, vol. 1, p. 6.

[4] Alter, *The David Story*, p. 139, gives a similar meaning when he translates it as "my father remains."

to an appendage or *covering of fat* that is to be sacrificed along with the liver" (emphasis mine).[5]

It might be recalled that Eli's family has a notorious history concerning "fat" (1 Sam. 2:16, 29; 4:18).[6] In addition, the word for "liver" is from the word *kābēd* (the word "heavy" in the Eli story).[7] This is not to suggest that Abiathar is guilty of stealing the fat as Eli and his sons did, at least not literally.[8] Rather, his name may be a celebration of the "abundance" that his family had experienced since the destruction at Shiloh. In spite of the fact that people like Ichabod, Ahitub, and Ahijah may have died prematurely, 1 Samuel 22:18 tells us that the house of Eli consisted of 85 men before the destruction at Nob. Therefore, "Abiathar" may be an expression of thanks for God's "abundance," in spite of the prophecy of doom which hung over the family. Whatever the reason, it is interesting to note that the idea of "fat" continues to follow the family of Eli. However, this "fatness" becomes "leanness" when Saul kills all the priests at Nob except Abiathar, which leads to a consideration of the second meaning of Abiathar's name.[9]

Because the word *yātār* carries the meaning "what is left over" it can refer to "excess" (hence "fat"), or to "what remains," which invokes the idea of scarcity. This word is sometimes used interchangeably with another Hebrew word which means "remnant" (*sha'ar*).[10] Therefore, *yātār* can be used in the sense of "few," or even "none." This meaning is, of course, very applicable to the name "Abiathar" after the destruction of the priests at Nob, since he alone escapes (1 Sam. 22:20).

Abiathar's "aloneness" is confirmation of the prophetic word of judgment, but it is also a word of grace. The concept of "remnant" in Scripture is set within the context of grace. The idea is that, in spite of mankind's wickedness, God does not utterly destroy, but always leaves himself a remnant. In the days of Ahab and Jezebel, God tells Elijah that he has reserved for himself a remnant of 7,000 that have not bowed the knee to Baal (1 Kings 19:18). The concept of a godly remnant is also very important to the book of

---

[5] David Latoundji, *ytr* I, 3855, *NIDOTTE*, vol. 2, p. 572.

[6] Various Hebrew words are used to communicate the idea of "fatness" in the Eli story.

[7] This is because the liver was considered the heaviest organ in the body.

[8] However, see the discussion below (pp. 92-94) for a possible connection.

[9] Fokkelman, *Crossing Fates*, p. 409, makes a similar observation: "The semantics of his name Abiathar appears to interlock with the contrast of destruction-and-survival."

[10] Latoundji, *ytr* I, p. 573. For example, Joshua 11:11, 14, employs *yātār* in v. 11 which translates as, "there was *none left*," while v.14 uses *sha'ar*, which is similarly translated, "they *left none* breathing."

Isaiah (e.g., Isa. 7:3).[11] Discussing the biblical principle of the remnant, Paul writes, "Even so at this present time there is a *remnant* according to the election of *grace*" (Rom. 11:5). So while Abiathar's name is a reminder of the judgment that fell on the house of Eli, it is also a reminder of God's grace.[12]

The Ephod: A Direct Line to God (1 Sam. 23:6, 9–12; 30:7–8)

After his escape to David, Abiathar is introduced as coming with an ephod in his hand (1 Sam. 23:6). Almost immediately, David avails himself of Abiathar's presence by asking him to bring the ephod—so he can inquire of the Lord's will (23:9–12). The next scene in which Abiathar is mentioned also concerns him inquiring of the Lord on David's behalf (1 Sam. 30:7–8). On both occasions God responds to David's inquiry and tells him what to do. It seems that Abiathar has more success in hearing from God than his uncle Ahijah had (see pp. 82-83 above)! The reason, of course, is the company he keeps. Since Saul had rejected God's word, God had forsaken him and refused to respond to his inquiries (14:36–37; 16:14). At the end of Saul's life we are told: "And when Saul inquired of the LORD, the LORD did not answer him, either by dreams or by Urim or by the prophets" (1 Sam. 28:6). In contrast to this we are told "the Lord was with" David (18:12, 14) and, therefore, responded to his inquiries (23:9–12; 30:7–8).

Abiathar is a living, breathing example of God's rejection of Saul and acceptance of David. Abiathar is the lone survivor of the priesthood Saul slaughtered—a reminder of Saul's heinous crime. On the other hand, his presence with David seems to ensure a direct line to God. Abiathar's significance lies in his association with David. His relationship with David, the man after God's own heart (13:14), brings blessing to him and his house. Not only does he retain the high priesthood during David's reign (sharing it with Zadok—2 Sam. 20:25); he seems to avoid the judgment on Eli's house by living to a ripe old age (1 Kings 2:26).[13] However, his poor choice later, aligning

---

[11] The word used in the above passages is *sha'ar*, which is the normal word for the concept of remnant. However, my point is that *yātār* can have a similar meaning (see e.g., Exod. 10:15; 2 Kings 4:43–44; Dan. 10:13).

[12] Fokkelman, *Crossing Fates*, p. 411 points out that the seemingly needless repetition of "son of Ahitub" in 22:20 is there, "in order to keep the idea of the genealogy alive."

[13] Russell Dilday, *1, 2 Kings*, MTOT (Dallas: Word Publishing, 1987), p. 61, estimates that Abiathar was about 80 years old at the time that Solomon banished him. Whatever his exact age may have been, Abiathar was somewhere around David's age, and 2 Sam. 5:4 allows us to estimate David's age at his death to be 70-71 years old. If McKane's translation of 1 Sam. 2:33 is correct, then this would explain why Abiathar lives to such an old age. See McKane, *I&II Samuel*, p. 40, and also n. 7 in chap. 5, p. 72 above.

himself with Adonijah instead of Solomon, brings about the final fulfillment of these words (1 Kings 2:27).

It is the responsibility of each of us to seek God, but the examples of Ahijah and Abiathar remind us that the company we keep is also important. While godly people are to be salt and light to the world, and thus must be in the world (1 Cor. 5:9–10), it is important that we have a network of godly influences in our lives. "As iron sharpens iron, so a man sharpens the countenance of his friend" (Prov. 27:17).

A Poor Choice: a Bad Result (1 Kings 1:7, 19, 25, 42; 2:26–27, 35)

As with a few other characters in our study, the final scene in which Abiathar appears takes us beyond the books of Samuel. In his old age Abiathar makes the fateful error of aligning himself with the wrong man for the throne. It appears from 1 Kings 1–2 that Solomon was the choice of (both) David and God for the throne (1:17, 29–30; 2:15, 45).[14] A look at other characters teaches us that, not only does God honor those who honor him (1 Sam. 2:30), but those who go against his anointed experience the consequences. Abiathar is an example of this. His association with God's anointed, David, brought him blessing, but his association with Adonijah and his rejection of Solomon, the Lord's chosen, brought judgment down on his head (1 Kings 2:26–27).

To understand why Abiathar joins Adonijah's attempt to gain the throne from Solomon involves a little reading between the lines.[15] The text does not explicitly state Abiathar's motive, and yet, by examining the passages that speak about him, it is possible to suggest a motive. The other passages which speak of Abiathar show him to be a loyal follower of David, who carries the ark of God (2 Sam. 15:24–36; 19:11). However, these passages reveal that Abiathar is no longer the only high priest in David's service. Zadok is also mentioned as high priest along with Abiathar, and seems to have eclipsed him in importance. Not only does Zadok's name always appear before Abiathar's in these texts, but when David flees from Jerusalem, it is striking that David directly addresses Zadok but never speaks to Abiathar (2 Sam. 15:24–29). It seems that Abiathar went from being David's only high priest (during his fugitive days), to playing second fiddle to Zadok during the kingdom years. It is natural to suppose that, under such circumstances, Abiathar could easily succumb to envy.

Scripture provides meager information regarding this dual high priesthood. Zadok's first appearance in the narrative follows the conquest of

---

[14] For further justification of this view see chap. 25 pp. 387-388.

[15] See "Gaps and Ambiguity" in the "Introduction," pp. 11-14.

Jerusalem, where he is mentioned among David's officials (2 Sam. 8:17).[16] Textual evidence suggests that he joined David when the kingdom was unified following Ish-bosheth's death (1 Chron. 12:23, 28). Zadok may have been appointed high priest to appease the northern tribes and strengthen the fragile unity between north and south.[17] Thus, this unusual situation may have resulted in the anomaly of having two high priests during David's reign. Whether David preferred Zadok for political, religious, or other reasons, we are not told. Since Zadok was a "newcomer" to David's regime, having formerly shown loyalty to "the kingdom of Saul" (1 Chron. 12:23), it is possible that Abiathar resented his growing importance. Abiathar's loyal ties to Judah and Zadok's ties to the northern tribes provide a further plausible explanation for their different allegiances at the time of Solomon's accession.

It seems likely that Abiathar was aware of David's oath to make Solomon king in his place (1 Kings 1:17).[18] Yet it is clear that Solomon's inner circle of power consisted of Nathan, Benaiah and Zadok. For Abiathar this would have meant that he, and his son Jonathan, would continue to be subordinate to Zadok. Perhaps he even feared that Zadok would become sole high priest. As a result, it is easy to see how siding with Adonijah and the "old Judahite regime"—which would recognize him as sole high priest—would be extremely tempting. And it seems he succumbed to this temptation. Tired of the "lean" years and of being second on the food chain behind Zadok, Abi-

---

[16] Some argue that Zadok was the Jebusite priest of Jerusalem when David conquered the city and that David integrated him, and other Jebusite leaders, into the political and religious structure of his kingdom. For further elaboration of this view, see, H.H. Rowley, "Zadok and Nehustan," *JBL* 58, (1939), pp. 113-141; C. E. Hauer, "Who Was Zadok?" *JBL* 82, (1963), pp. 89-94; and Gwilym, H. Jones, *The Nathan Narratives*, JSOT Supp. 80 (Sheffield: Sheffield Academic Press, 1990). I do not find this hypothesis convincing. For an alternative view, see Saul M. Olyan, "Zadok's Origins and the Tribal Politics of David." *JBL* 101, 1982, pp. 177-193. For a summary of both arguments see, D. W. Rooke, "Zadok, Zadokites," *DOTHB*, pp. 1012-1016.

[17] The fact that Zadok presided over the tabernacle at Gibeon (1 Chron. 16:39), reinforces the possibility of his northern affiliation as well as his superior status over Abiathar, who appears to have remained in Jerusalem—perhaps presiding over the tent where the ark was kept (2 Sam. 6:17). However, both men appear carrying the ark from Jerusalem during David's flight from Absalom (2 Sam. 15:24–25).

[18] While this verse indicates this promise was made directly to Bathsheba, it is clear that Nathan was aware of it (1 Kings 1:11–13). The knowledge of this oath to make Solomon king would also explain why Zadok, Benaiah and Nathan were excluded from Adonijah's planned coup. Apparently it was already obvious that these men were in favor of Solomon's accession. For further comments, see, chap. 19, pp. 246-247 and chap. 25, pp. 387-388.

athar decided to seize the "fat"![19] With Joab and David's eldest living son, Adonijah, it must have seemed like a foolproof plan.

From this small exercise of reading between the lines, we learn another important lesson about accepting the role that God has assigned us. Grasping for power and importance is a pitfall for many. It is particularly sad to see power and status pursued within the church, and yet, as fallible human beings, like Abiathar, we sometimes succumb to this temptation. Abiathar's example teaches us the importance of contentment. It is far better to have less power and importance and be in the will and blessing of God, than to strive for what God has not ordained for us. Abiathar's striving took him out of God's will and brought God's judgment down on him. Ironically, in his desire to be the only high priest, he lost his position totally. He and his family were relegated to obscurity as he was forced to retire to his hometown of Anathoth. Like the others involved in the attempted coup, Abiathar was deserving of death. It was only the restraint of Solomon and the mercy of God that kept him from that fate (1 Kings 2:26). God is merciful, and will even show mercy when we step outside his will, but in our selfishness we can lose his best for our lives and must experience the consequences of our choices, like Abiathar.

Jonathan: The "Good News" Man with the "Bad News"[20]

You are a prominent man and bring good news (1 Kings 1:42)

With Jonathan we encounter the saying, "like father, like son." Just as Abiathar plays second fiddle to Zadok, so Jonathan is secondary to Zadok's son, Ahimaaz (2 Sam. 15:27, 36; 17:17–21). And just as Abiathar sides with Adonijah, so too does Jonathan (1 Kings 1:42–43).

Jonathan is first mentioned in the story of Absalom's rebellion, where he and Ahimaaz act as intelligence messengers for David (2 Sam. 15:27, 36). Reference to these young men consistently puts Ahimaaz before Jonathan, except in one instance. They are next mentioned in 2 Samuel 17:17–21 which tells of their daring escape from Absalom's pursuers in order

---

[19] As noted above (pp. 89-90), the second part of Abiathar's name (*yātār*) in sacrificial contexts is connected with the word *kābēd* (liver). The reader might recall that it is precisely within a sacrificial context that the word *kābôd* (honor/heavy) highlights the sin of Eli and his sons. It seems ironic that part of Abiathar's name is connected with the very word which causes so much trouble in the family of Eli. Israelites would have been well aware that it was the priest's duty to offer up the *yôteret* (fatty lobe) of the *kābēd* (liver) and thus, might have been cognizant of this irony.

[20] The passages under consideration, too numerous to include in the subtitle are: 2 Sam. 15:27, 36; 17:17–21; 1 Kings 1:42–48.

to bring news to David. Verse 17 is the one occasion in which Jonathan's name is introduced first, but the usual order is resumed in 17:20.

This story is reminiscent of the two spies hidden by Rahab in Joshua chapter 2. In both accounts, a woman protects spies and deceives those who are looking for them by giving them false information. The parallel between the spies of Joshua 2 and Jonathan and Ahimaaz may suggest that Absalom's defeat is as sure as Jericho's.

This particular tale focuses on a few of the many whom God used to return the kingdom to David. Not everyone is a leader. Leaders need loyal followers who will faithfully carry out the tasks they are appointed to. Just as many people of all different ranks played an important role in the kingdom of David, so too all of us have our place in the kingdom of God. There is no insignificant part in the body of Christ (1 Cor. 12:12–27). We all have our gifts and our calling from God, who is no respecter of persons. God only asks that we are faithful in whatever he calls us to do (Matt. 25:14–30).[21] If Jonathan and Abiathar had been content and served faithfully in their roles, who knows how God may have blessed them?

The final scene in which Jonathan appears is full of irony (1 Kings 1:42–48). While Adonijah and his associates are feasting his apparent success, Jonathan arrives with news from Jerusalem. Jonathan's appearance recalls a comparable situation, in which his (former) partner Ahimaaz delivered a message to David (2 Sam. 18:19–30). Both Jonathan and Ahimaaz deliver reports to a king (David) or potential king (Adonijah). In both cases, the men are said to be good men who bring good news (2 Sam. 18:27; 1 Kings 1:42). Although Ahimaaz's news was good—David's men had been victorious over Absalom—it was actually bad news to David because Absalom was dead.[22] Jonathan, on the other hand, has no good news for Adonijah (1 Kings 1:43). He describes the coronation of Solomon in detail, revealing facts previously unknown to the reader (vv. 47–48). Surprisingly, of the various speeches in 1 Kings 1, his is the longest.

Two related questions come to mind as a result of Jonathan's speech. First, "Why was Jonathan not at the feast with all of Adonijah's other loyal supporters?" Second, "How did he know such intimate details about the coronation, including the actions of David within his own bedchamber?" Jonathan's appearances in the narrative of 2 Samuel provide the answers to both questions. We have previously noted in 2 Samuel 15 and 17 that Jonathan appears in the role of a spy for David's camp. Interestingly, he receives the news about Absalom's plan at En Rogel where he is hiding out (17:17). In our

---

[21] See Evans, *The Message of Samuel*, p. 244, for a similar observation.

[22] Ahimaaz, however, does not deliver the bad news to David; he wisely avoids the question. Although it is unlikely, some argue he was truly unaware of Absalom's death (see Youngblood, *1, 2 Samuel*, p. 1025).

current story, he arrives at En Rogel to deliver news to Adonijah (1 Kings 1:9, 41–42). It seems that he is still in the espionage business, and this explains why he was not at the feast with Adonijah and his friends. It is of note that one possible meaning of the name En Rogel is "Well of the Spy."[23] Jonathan's close connections with people in the court also explain the intimate details he discloses in his speech. Having proven his abilities in the past, he becomes the logical choice to gather intelligence for Adonijah. Therefore, Jonathan's actions in 2 Samuel 17 aid the reader in understanding his role in 1 Kings 1. Furthermore, the parallels between these two passages, as well as the similarities with Ahimaaz's situation, connect Absalom's rebellion to Adonijah's attempted coup.[24]

In one sense, the "prominent man" who "brings good news" (1 Kings 1:42) does, in fact, bring good news. The reader who understands that God has ordained that Solomon should succeed his father, can relish the irony in Adonijah's words and appreciate Jonathan's report. However, for those who are seeking to go their own way and reject the Lord's anointed, there can be no good news. Jonathan's words cause the guests to scatter like frightened sheep (v. 49). His message spells the beginning of the end for Adonijah and his closest associates (1 Kings 1:50–53; 2:13–34).

Jonathan is not mentioned again, but it must be assumed that he shared the same fate as his father and was exiled to Anathoth (1 Kings 2:26). From this vantage point, only a few miles from Jerusalem, he and Abiathar would be able to observe Zadok's priesthood without the privilege of participating. While Jonathan and Abiathar ultimately experience the judgment announced long ago on the house of Eli (1 Sam. 2:27–36), the choice was their own and they had to bear the consequences of it.

Conclusion: A Future and a Hope (Jer. 29:11)

The exile of Abiathar and Jonathan is not the final word on the family of Eli. Scripture testifies that God was not finished with the priests who were from Anathoth. In time to come, God would raise up one of his mightiest prophets from among the priests in Anathoth. And that prophet, Jeremiah, (Jer. 1:1), would: remind his people of the days of Shiloh (Jer. 7:12), tell them that not even the prayers of Samuel could save them (Jer. 15:1), and proclaim their own impending exile (Jer. 28:14; 29:1–10).

---

[23] John Gray, *I&II Kings*, OTL (London: SCM Press, 1964), pp. 81-82.
[24] On the relationship between 2 Sam. 17:17–21; 18:19ff.; and 1 Kings 1:41ff., see Fokkelman's helpful chart and comments in, J.P. Fokkelman, *Narrative Art and Poetry in the Books of Samuel*, vol. I: *King David* (Assen/Maastricht & Dover: Van Gorcum, 1981), pp. 373-374.

But Jeremiah also knew how God could change the destiny of a nation, based on its people's response to him (Jer. 18:1–11). Was it the history of his own family that had brought this truth home to him? Having experienced God's mercy and grace within his own family, he knew that the future was not hopeless (Jer. 29:11). Therefore, he also prophesied of better times to come—when God would establish a new covenant with his people (Jer. 31:31–34). Families may fail and covenants may be broken, but the God of Israel (and of Eli) is able to redeem the most unlikely people and circumstances for the glory of his name.

Section 3

The Family of Saul

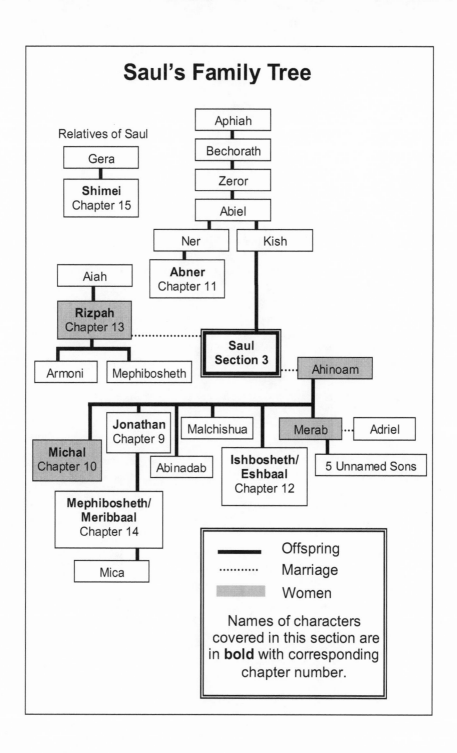

Saul's Family Tree

Relatives of Saul

Gera

Shimei
Chapter 15

Aphiah

Bechorath

Zeror

Abiel

Ner

Kish

Abner
Chapter 11

Aiah

Rizpah
Chapter 13

Armoni

Mephibosheth

Saul
Section 3

Ahinoam

Jonathan
Chapter 9

Malchishua

Merab

Adriel

Michal
Chapter 10

Abinadab

Ishbosheth/
Eshbaal
Chapter 12

5 Unnamed Sons

Mephibosheth/
Meribbaal
Chapter 14

Mica

Offspring

.... Marriage

Women

Names of characters
covered in this section are
in **bold** with corresponding
chapter number.

Introduction to Saul's Family

The house of Saul grew weaker and weaker (2 Sam. 3:1)

Saul's family is introduced in 1 Samuel 9:1 with a four-person genealogy, reminiscent of the introduction of Samuel's family in 1 Samuel 1:1. This similarity, as well as the narrator's glowing introduction of Saul and his family, leads the reader to expect great things. Saul's father, Kish, is described as a "man of valor" ("a mighty man of power"—NKJV), while Saul is twice described in positive terms—"handsome" (literally, "good") and "taller than any of the people" (9:2). If outward appearance can be trusted, then 1 Samuel 9:1–2 holds out great hope. The discerning reader, however, has learned from Eli not to jump to conclusions too quickly.

While there are some storm clouds on the horizon,[25] the story of Saul seems to get off to a good start (1 Sam. 9–11) before things go wrong (1 Sam. 13–31). Saul inspired the fierce loyalty of many, such as the Ziphites (23:19–24) and the inhabitants of Jabesh-Gilead (31:11–13). On the other hand, he could strike out violently against his own people (the priests of Nob—chap. 22), including members of his family (Jonathan, 20:30–32). As a result, even Saul's children are torn between loyalty to their father and the "beloved" David (18:1–4, 20). Both Jonathan and Michal struggle with remaining true to their father while protecting David (19:11–17; 20:31–32). However, it must be said that Jonathan remains with his father even in death (1 Sam. 31:2); and, in spite of everything, David's eulogy is a moving tribute of his loyalty to Saul (2 Sam. 1:19–27). Even those whom Saul pushes away are drawn to him! This tug-of-war, which results in great tensions, is an important theme in the story of Saul. Consequent divisions are not only evident in his family, but also in the nation he ruled. With the death of Saul the nation erupts in civil war (2 Sam. 3:1).

A reader can find him or herself with conflicting emotions about Saul. In spite of his failings, he evokes sympathy. Saul is not so much the sort of character you "love to hate" as the kind you "hate to love." Interestingly, commentators are as divided over Saul as his own nation was. Some see him as a victim of a predetermined fate,[26] while others see him as a man whose disobedience cost him a kingdom.[27] Saul remains a divisive character to this

---

[25] For example, one dark cloud that hangs over Saul's introduction is his hometown of Gibeah (1 Sam. 10:26), last spoken of as the place that caused a civil war in Israel over the rape of a Levite's concubine (Judg. 19–21).

[26] David M. Gunn, *The Fate of King Saul*, JSOT Supp. 14 (Sheffield: University of Sheffield, 1980). Walter Brueggemann, *First and Second Samuel*, IBC (Louisville: John Knox Press, 1990), defends a similar position.

[27] Sternberg, *Poetics*, pp. 482-515, has a brilliant essay on Saul's culpability. Polzin, *Samuel and the Deuteronomist*, also agrees with this viewpoint, as I do.

day! Any treatment of his family must therefore reflect this truth. Saul's ability to polarize not only extends to Jonathan, Michal and David; division follows his family even after his death. Abner and Ish-bosheth become alienated from one another (2 Sam. 3:6–11), as do Mephibosheth and Ziba (2 Sam. 19:24–27). Another descendant of Saul, Shimei, is a vocal supporter of the division caused by Absalom's civil war (2 Sam. 16:5–13).

Jesus said, "every...house divided against itself will not stand" (Matt. 12:25). This truth is part of the reason that the house of Saul deteriorates from strength (1 Sam. 9:1) to weakness (2 Sam. 3:1). The main reason, however, is Saul's failure to honor the Lord.

The many parallels between Saul's house and the house of Eli substantiate this conclusion.[28] Just as Eli's house is rejected from the high priesthood (1 Sam. 2:27–36), so Saul and his house are rejected from being king (1 Sam. 13:13–14; 15:23). Both Eli's and Saul's descendants beg for bread at the king's table (1 Sam. 2:36; 2 Sam. 9:6–7). Hannah had declared, "The LORD makes poor and makes rich; He brings low and lifts up" (1 Sam. 2:7). The same principle that brought about the fall of Eli and the rise of Samuel brings about the fall of Saul and the rise of David. This becomes especially clear in the story of Michal in 2 Samuel 6, which uses the same three key words found in 1 Samuel 2:30 ("honor," "despise," and "lightly esteem").

To some extent, "the more things change, the more they stay the same." Since human nature is similar and the truth of God never changes, each family and generation will exhibit common features. However, this is not to say that we simply have the story of Eli dressed up in the clothes of Saul's family. The portraits of Saul's family will give us glimpses of new personalities confronting new situations.[29] After all, kingship is a new institution in Israel and presents its own set of problems and solutions.

While a number of Saul's family members are mentioned in the text, many receive no development, and so will not be examined. Among these are Saul's father Kish (1 Sam. 9:1), his wife Ahinoam (1 Sam. 14:50), his daughter Merab (1 Sam. 19), his sons Abinadab and Malchishua (1 Sam. 31:2), other sons and grandsons (2 Sam. 21:8), and Saul's great-grandson, Micha (2 Sam. 9:12).

Along with David, Saul and his family dominate the narrative of 1 Samuel chapters 9–31. David and his family are the main focus of 2 Samuel, yet Saul's family continues to play an important role. Although a lot of material is devoted to the reign of Saul, we learn of God's rejection of his kingship and dynasty rather quickly (1 Sam. 13:14; 15:28). This means that a major portion of the story focuses on how Saul and his family deal with this rejection, and how they treat his future replacement. This theme raises an important

---

[28] See chap. 5, p. 76.

[29] As always, some personalities are more developed than others in the text.

question that everyone must confront at sometime. How should we respond when someone is chosen or favored over us, especially when that person ends up in the position we once occupied? In Saul's case it is not simply a matter of David being favored over him, but one in which he disqualified himself through sin. The narrative teaches us that a response of pride, envy, and a refusal to repent, leads to a dead end for Saul—quite literally!

This kind of attitude can lead one to strike out blindly against his own family (1 Sam. 20:33), contributing to its breakdown and destruction. Not only can such a mindset affect an individual, it can permeate a family. Thus all those who follow in Saul's footsteps—Abner, Ish-bosheth, Michal,[30] Shimei, and other descendants of Saul—meet a similar fate. Saul's obsession to destroy David leads to the destruction of many in his family, not to mention the political chaos and destruction that accompanies it. How true it is that the one consumed with hatred ends up destroying him or herself as well as the ones he or she loves.

Hatred and bitterness will destroy a family (and a nation); but just because a family becomes consumed with animosity does not mean that every member must conform. The books of Samuel continually affirm our freedom to choose. No matter what the circumstances in which we find ourselves, our attitude and response are still our choice. While Samuel has godly parents and follows the Lord, and David's sons have a godly father but do not follow the Lord, Jonathan stands alone in these books as a godly son with an ungodly father. Ungodly parents are no excuse for children to continue down the same path. Each must make his or her own choice. Jonathan is an example to all that the cycle of ungodliness can be broken. This beautiful example, followed by his son Mephibosheth, is the silver lining in a family clouded with self-assertion and pride. While it is true that Jonathan's loyalty leads him to die beside his father, his humility and self-lessness point the way to a future for Saul's family. Jonathan's love and de-votion to David turn the family's fortunes from a path of hatred and death to one of life and hope. Jonathan's example points the way for us as well.

---

[30] The author does not tell us of Michal's death, but he does point out her barrenness (2 Sam. 6:23) which, as with Hannah, was as good as a living death. Michal's barren-ness was a consequence of her attitude towards David and his worship of God.

Chapter 9

Jonathan: A Lover and a Giver (Saul's son)

The soul of Jonathan was knit to the soul of David, and Jonathan loved him as his own soul.
(1 Sam. 18:1)

It is More Blessed to Give

Jonathan's name means "The Lord gives," and from the start his actions live up to his name. The first story about Jonathan involves a victory over the Philistines, precipitated by a bold act of faith in which he makes a play on his own name: "*the LORD has given* them into our hand" (1 Sam. 14:10, 12). Jonathan's first encounter with David involves a gesture of covenant love, marked by another act of giving which includes his robe, armor, belt, and weapons (1 Sam. 18:4).

If Saul is suspicious, envious, and selfish, then Jonathan his son is the opposite. Except for an instance of naiveté,[1] a lie to protect David, and problems with his father (Who didn't have problems with Saul?), the reader looks in vain for any shortcomings in the character of Jonathan.[2] This is not to assert that Jonathan was perfect, but only that the author chooses to emphasize Jonathan's noble qualities. There are two reasons for this. First, Jonathan's faith, bravery, loyalty, and love highlight Saul's shortcomings, and thus provide an explanation for his rejection. Jonathan's actions in the same circumstances confirm that other responses are available to Saul. Second, Jonathan is the forerunner to David. In his actions he anticipates the "man after God's own heart" (1 Sam. 13:14).[3]

Steps of Faith (1 Sam. 13:1–14:46)

The first mention of Jonathan shows him to be a man of action. 1 Samuel 13:3 begins, "And Jonathan struck the Philistine governor[4] who was

---

[1] In 1 Sam. 20:2 Jonathan cannot believe that Saul would violate his oath to David.

[2] I disagree with Peter Miscall who asserts, "The text supports a 'good' Jonathan and a 'bad' Jonathan" (Miscall, *1 Samuel,* p. 91). The clear intention of the text is to contrast the bad qualities of Saul with the good qualities of Jonathan.

[3] David Jobling, *The Sense of Biblical Narrative, Jonathan: A Structural Study in 1 Samuel,* JSOT (Sheffield, 1978) writes, "In relationship to David, he (Jonathan) moves between close identification and a self-emptying into David," p. 11.

[4] The Hebrew word can be translated "prefect" (i.e., governor), or "garrison." Many scholars today opt for the translation "prefect," since revolts sometimes began in the ancient world with the assassination of a leader. See V. Philips Long, *The Reign and Rejection of King Saul* (Atlanta: Scholar Press, 1989), pp. 78-79, (Hereafter cited as *Rejec-*

in Geba" (my translation). Saul's subsequent going to Gilgal to wait for Samuel (13:4, 8) suggests that Jonathan does what Saul should have done earlier. In 1 Samuel 10:5–7, Samuel had noted the presence of the Philistine governor (or perhaps here, "garrison") at Geba (v. 5), and told Saul that after the Spirit came upon him he was to "do as the occasion demands"; for God was with him (v. 7). Following this, Samuel instructed Saul to meet him in Gilgal and to wait seven days until he (Samuel) would arrive to offer the sacrifice (v. 8). The fact that these actions are carried out in 13:3–4 suggests that Jonathan did what Saul should have done long before.[5]

While the narrator credits Jonathan with this step of faith and obedience, it is interesting that, "all Israel heard it said that Saul had struck the Philistine governor" (13:4—my translation). It could be argued that the act of a soldier or commander might be credited to the king, but Joab's statement in 2 Samuel 12:27–28 would seem to indicate otherwise. Joab tells David to hurry to the city of Rabbah, as it is about to fall. If David is not present, Joab says that the city will be called by his name.[6] Given Saul's future penchant for making monuments to himself (1 Sam. 15:12), and jealous reaction when others receive more acclaim (1 Sam. 18:7–8), it seems that this is the first in a long line of self-absorbed reactions.[7]

We have already seen what envy can lead to in the example of Abiathar. The difference here, however, is that, unlike Abiathar, Saul is the undisputed leader of the people. But rather than praise and encourage those under his leadership, Saul is so insecure that he must take credit for any success.[8] Sadly, some people perceive others' success as a threat. It is particularly distressing when this dynamic is found in the church. Effective leadership desires to see others use their gifts for the glory of God. Good leaders therefore rejoice in the success of others. It is the act of a petty tyrant who feels threatened by the faith and godly action of one of their own. In seeking the glory for himself, Saul is following in the footsteps of Eli. 1 Samuel 13:16

---

tion). Tsumura, *The First Book of Samuel*, p. 336 argues that the plural form of this word means "garrison" but the singular probably refers to a prefect or governor.

[5] This interpretation of the events is argued very convincingly by Long, *Rejection*, pp. 51-55. Furthermore, 1 Sam. 9:16 states that the king was selected in order to deliver Israel from the hand of the Philistines. Tsumura, *The First Book of Samuel*, pp. 340-345, argues that too much time would have elapsed for the command in 10:8 to refer to this incident. But it seems to me that this is precisely the point. Saul has been slow to act. It can also be argued that the similar wording of these two passages suggests that the author would expect the reader to recall Samuel's command in 10:8.

[6] It is possible, however, that Joab is simply haranguing David. See chap. 20, pp.275-276 for a fuller explanation.

[7] See Long, *Rejection*, pp. 81-82 for a similar view.

[8] A future example of this is when Saul takes credit for the destruction of the Amalekites, but blames the people for sparing the best (1 Sam. 15:15).

informs us for the first time that Jonathan is Saul's son (cf. 13:22 also). Hindsight now shows us that the man Saul upstaged in 13:3–4 was not just the commander of his army, but his own son![9]

Jonathan's next step of faith is mentioned in 14:1, where he proposes to his armor-bearer that they go over to the Philistine army, even though they are outnumbered and "out-gunned." This story further reveals the differences between father and son, as Jonathan once again takes a step of faith while his father "sits" (14:3). Jonathan is bold, but he is not presumptuous. He says to his armor-bearer, "Come, let us go over to the garrison of these uncircumcised; it may be that the Lord will work for us" (14:6). Jonathan makes himself available to God, but does not presume that he can manipulate God by his action.

Boldness without presumption is a good recipe for all of God's people to live by. Boldness gives God the opportunity to use us. On the other hand, Saul and the people with him were paralyzed by fear (13:7). Numbers, or a lack thereof, can often intimidate us. The people were deserting Saul (13:8), and his numbers had dwindled from 3,000 to 600 (14:2). To Saul the greater number of the Philistines must have seemed overwhelming (cf. 13:5, 11). Once again the books of Samuel remind us that looks can be deceiving. While Saul looks at the physical and sees only hopelessness, Jonathan, by faith, looks to the Lord and proclaims, "For nothing restrains the Lord from saving by many or by few" (14:6). Jonathan's words anticipate the words of Elisha, who says to his servant as they are surrounded by the Syrian army, "Do not fear, for those who are with us are more than those who are with them" (2 Kings 6:16).[10]

While Jonathan's faith leads him to bold action, he does not presume that his action can force God to act. Jonathan respects the sovereignty of God and therefore says, "*it may be* that the Lord will work for us" (14:6). Unlike the elders of Israel who attempted to manipulate God by using the ark (1 Sam. 4), and unlike his own father Saul, who will try to use an oath (14:24) to influence the result of the battle, Jonathan leaves the outcome in God's hands. Once again we are reminded that empty ritual without faith is indeed empty. Jonathan's faith leads to a great personal victory (twenty Philistines are killed—v. 14), as well as a great victory for Israel. Devoid of true faith, Saul's oath only leads to "distressing" the army (14:24). Jonathan bluntly says, "My

---

[9] Jobling, *1 Samuel*, p. 94, makes the important observation that Jonathan is not called Saul's son until *after* the possibility of Saul establishing a dynasty is denied: "Jonathan has lost his royal expectations before we knew he had them."

[10] Jonathan's response also recalls the story of Gideon (Judg. 7) who overcame overwhelming odds with only a few men. In fact, Saul has 600 soldiers—twice the number of Gideon (!)—and is afraid to act. The important word "tremble" or "afraid," is another connection between the story of Gideon (Judg. 7:1, 3) and the story in 1 Sam. 14 (cf. v. 15).

father has *troubled* the land" (14:29), recalling the key word in the story of Achan who "troubled" Israel (Josh. 7:25–26).[11] As a result, Israel's victory was not as extensive as it could have been (14:30).

The lesson is easily grasped, but harder to live out. Whenever we step out in faith, we give God an opportunity to work. The problem is that, when a situation seems impossible, we tend to respond more like Saul than like Jonathan. We have a tendency to trust in numbers, rituals, and things we can see. We forget that when the odds are stacked against us we may be staring victory in the face! This is not because God is forced to act, but because he delights in proving himself sufficient when we are weak. Hannah discovered this, and her prayer reminds us that it is the unseen hand of our powerful God that has the final say: "For by strength no man shall prevail" (1 Sam. 2:9).

Love Your Neighbor as Yourself (1 Sam. 18:1–4)

After David's defeat of Goliath, Jonathan was immediately drawn to David. Perhaps he saw in him a kindred spirit. Like Jonathan, David had defied the odds against the Philistines. As Jonathan had trusted in the Lord and said, "For nothing restrains the LORD from saving by many or by few" (1 Sam. 14:6), so David proclaimed, "The LORD does not save by sword or spear; for the battle is the LORD's" (1 Sam. 17:47). Jonathan's act of bravery and faith led Israel to victory, as had David's. Jonathan could have felt threatened by Israel's new hero, but instead, "the soul of Jonathan was knit to the soul of David, and Jonathan loved him as his own soul" (18:1). This says much about Jonathan's character. Jonathan is for God and for God's people, so he is drawn to those with a similar faith and commitment.

Being the crown prince (David's social superior), and the elder of the two,[12] Jonathan takes the initiative in the relationship. Even though age and

---

[11] The word "trouble" and the casting of lots evoke the story of Achan (1 Sam. 14:38–45; cf. Josh. 7:14–18). Furthermore, Saul's willingness to sacrifice his own child following a victorious battle has similarities with Jephthah (Judg. 11:30–31). Jephthah also uses the word "trouble" (Judg. 11:35). The comparison of Saul with Achan and Jephthah, and the contrast with Gideon, does not put him in a positive light.

[12] Warren W. Wiersbe, *The Bible Exposition Commentary: Old Testament History, 1 Samuel* (Colorado Springs: Victor, 2003), pp. 255-256, notes that some Bible chronologists— perhaps Floyd Nolan Jones (The Chronology of the Old Testament), although he does not say who—calculate that Jonathan may have been 25 to 28 years older! This seems high, but is not impossible. A more conservative estimate suggests that Jonathan was between 6 to 15 years older than David. This reckoning comes from comparing various passages. We are told that David was thirty years old when he began to reign in Hebron over Judah (2 Sam. 5:4). During this time, Ish-bosheth reigned over Israel and we are informed that he was forty years old (2 Sam. 2:10) when he began to

social standing might have caused Jonathan to envy David (after all, he was Israel's hero before David came along), his response is one of generosity and kindness. The words of 18:1 recall Israel's second greatest commandment, "You shall *love* your *neighbor* as *yourself*" (Lev. 19:18). Samuel had told Saul, "The LORD has torn the kingdom of Israel from you today, and has given it to a *neighbor* of yours, who is better than you" (1 Sam. 15:28). David is clearly the "neighbor" foretold by Samuel, and Jonathan loves him as he loves himself.[13]

The word "love" in a context such as this carries political overtones. For example, treaties from the ancient Near East often contained the language of "love" between covenant partners. The Book of Deuteronomy, which has similarities with such treaties, is an example of the "love" language between God and his covenant people Israel (e.g., Deut. 6:5; 7:7–8).[14] Therefore, while Jonathan's love for David certainly involves an emotional component, it is important that the modern reader understand the political signifisignificance of this word.

Jonathan not only loves in word, but also in deed (1 John 3:18). 1 Samuel 18:3 tells us that his love motivated him to make a covenant with David, and as tokens of his commitment he gives David his robe, armor, weapons and belt (v. 4). This action is full of significance. Jonathan is not only the initiator of the covenant, but he lives up to his name by being a "giver."

---

reign. Since Ish-bosheth only reigned two years (more on this later), we can presume that he did not gain control of Israel until David had already reigned in Hebron for about five years (David reigned seven and a half years in Hebron, cf. 2 Sam. 5:5), which would make David about thirty-five years old. This means there was at least a five-year difference between David and Ish-bosheth (if David's and Ish-bosheth's ages have been rounded off, the difference could be plus or minus one or two years). Since Jonathan was Saul's oldest son, there must be at least one year between him and Ish-bosheth, assuming that Ish-bosheth was Saul's second born (1 Sam. 14:49 makes this a possibility). But Jonathan had two other brothers, Abinadab and Malchishua (1 Sam. 31:2), who may have been older than Ish-bosheth (1 Chron. 8:33; 9:39). This means Jonathan was at least six years older than David, and most likely, ten years or more. For an alternative view, suggesting that David is roughly the same age, or older than Jonathan, see Jonathan Rowe, "Is Jonathan Really David's 'Wife'? A Response to Yaron Peleg," *JSOT* 34.2, 2009, pp. 183-193 (esp. 186, 192-193).

[13] Markus Zehnder, "Observations on the relationship between David and Jonathan and the debate on homosexuality," *WTJ* 69, 2007, p. 146, states that "conceptually Lev 19:18 and 1 Sam 18:1, 3 are closely connected, to such a degree that 1 Sam 18:1, 3 most probably must be understood as deliberately referring to Lev 19:18."

[14] Dennis J. McCarthy, *Old Testament Covenant: A Survey of Current Opinions*, (Richmond: John Knox Press, 1972), p. 15, states, "…the omnipresent Deuteronomic word love (*'ahab*) is borrowed directly from the treaty tradition and appears in Deuteronomy with a meaning which is exactly that of the 'love' which the vassal owed his overlord."

Throughout the entire passage Jonathan is the active partner: Jonathan loves, Jonathan makes a covenant, Jonathan gives, and so on. No reciprocal action is mentioned on David's part. David only receives! Mary Evans states,

> Jonathan is consistently presented as a great man, the equal of David in faith and in courage and *perhaps his superior in generosity*....It may or may not be significant that all the giving and the loving in the relationship is depicted as coming from Jonathan's side. (emphasis mine)[15]

I believe it *is* significant that Jonathan does all the loving and giving. As Zehnder states, "The reason for the one-directionality can be sought in the social position of the persons involved: as the king's son and designated heir to the throne, Jonathan is socially far above David."[16] It was customary for the socially superior person to be the one to instigate a covenant. Furthermore, as Rowe points out, "imposition of 'gifts' is not meant to be repaid in kind, but in long-term commitment.[17] In other words, by his gift, Jonathan is seeking a response of loyalty from David.

In the larger narrative, Jonathan's actions have theological significance, for he imitates the Lord, who is always the initiator of covenant relationships and who, in turn, seeks a response of loyalty. "We love Him because He first loved us" (1 John 4:19). By acting like God, Jonathan's covenant with David anticipates God's covenant with David (2 Sam. 7); Jonathan's gifts look forward to God's gift of the kingdom to David. Zehnder notes the close connection between words which describe Jonathan's attitude towards David and Yahweh's. For example, regarding the word "delight" (see comments on 1 Sam. 19:1 below) Zehnder states,

> Is Jonathan's delight to be understood as a consequence of YHWH's delight on the human level? Perhaps the connection hinted at here can be described even more specifically: YHWH's delight in David becomes effective in David's political success; Jonathan's delight in David is the means by which YHWH's delight operates. This would mean that Jonathan's delight in David corresponds to the will of YHWH; YHWH would even be its ultimate source. Alternatively, Jonathan's delight could be understood as a correspondence

---

[15] Evans, *The Message of Samuel*, p. 112.
[16] Zehnder, "Observations," p. 156.
[17] Rowe, "Response to Yaron Peleg," p. 186.

to the divine delight: David's way is smoothed by the double support given him both by God and by men.[18]

On a practical level, Jonathan is the friend we would all wish to have and be. Unselfish in his actions and motives, Jonathan gives and initiates relationship. Though he has the most to lose (humanly speaking), he humbly recognizes one on whom the Spirit of God has fallen. So rather than viewing Da-David as a threat to oppose, he welcomes him as a brother and companion. In his eyes, David is not a competitor but a co-laborer, sharing the same faith and values in the common cause of advancing the kingdom. If only all of God's people had such a magnanimous outlook toward their fellow laborers in the kingdom.

From Gladiator to Mediator (1 Sam. 19:1–7)

Jonathan loved David and the people loved David (1 Sam. 18:16), but Saul's envy (18:8), paranoia (18:9), and fear (18:12, 29) turned him against David. As a result, Saul made several clandestine efforts to destroy him (18:17, 21). Failing in these attempts because "the LORD was with David" (18:12, 14, 28), Saul becomes bolder by speaking to Jonathan and "all his servants, that they should kill David" (19:1). At this critical point Jonathan, "who delighted greatly in David," is transformed from war hero to lawyer extraordinaire—from gladiator to mediator.

Though Jonathan plans to intervene on David's behalf, in case that plan fails, he begins by alerting David to the danger (19:2–3). To protect his friend, Jonathan does something unusual—he speaks to his father![19] This might seem a strange observation, but it is one of only a few times that the author points to any communication between father and son. It is not recorded whether Jonathan spoke to Saul before attacking the Philistine governor (13:3), but he clearly did *not* communicate with his father before attacking the Philistines at Michmash ("But he did not tell his father," 14:1). Jonathan's intervention on David's behalf is the only place in 1 Samuel where he initiates a conversation with his father. The only other recorded occasions in which father and son speak involve Saul threatening Jonathan's life or telling him to kill David. Clearly there was a communication problem![20]

---

[18] Zehnder, "Observations," pp. 147-148.
[19] The following comments are based on J.P. Fokkelman's perceptive observations. See *Crossing Fates*, pp. 257-258.
[20] 1 Samuel records four explicit conversations between Saul and Jonathan. The first is Saul's threat to Jonathan's life in 14:43–44. The second is Saul's command to Jonathan to kill David (19:1). The third is Jonathan's intercession for David (19:3–6). The fourth is another angry confrontation over David, at the dinner table (20:27–33). Of the four conversations, only 19:3–6 can be said to be amicable. Three are concerning

This highlights Jonathan's love for David. Apparently, communication between father and son was neither frequent nor pleasant, but for David's sake Jonathan is willing to make the effort. Jonathan's speech is a great lesson on how to approach a hostile person on behalf of another. First, Jonathan's words are respectful. He refers to his father in the proper courtly manner by calling him "the king" (19:4). Second, he speaks boldly and truthfully about the difference between right and wrong: "Let not the king sin." Third, he speaks "good" concerning David and reminds Saul of all that David had done, including risking his life (19:4–5) and fourth, he makes it personal. Rather than simply praise David's acts for Israel (which might arouse Saul's envy), he speaks of how David's killing of Goliath had benefited Saul personally, as well as the nation. Fifth, he reminds Saul that he needs to set an example and not allow personal vindictiveness to override justice: "Why then will you sin against innocent blood, to kill David without a cause?" (v. 5).

Jonathan's speech is also artfully constructed, showing that good communication is often well crafted. It has what literary scholars refer to as a concentric pattern.[21] For example, Jonathan begins and ends his speech by encouraging Saul not to "sin" against David. The full pattern of the speech in 19:4–5, detected by Fokkelman, is reproduced here:[22]

A   "do not sin"
  B   "because his works are very good toward you"
    C   David's contribution—"he took his life in his hands"
      X   result—"killed the Philistine"
    C'   God's contribution—"the LORD brought about a great deliverance"
  B'   "You saw it and rejoiced"
A'   "Why then will you sin…?"

Looking at the speech in this way highlights David's greatest deed: the killing of Goliath—which lies at the center of the dialogue. It is the clearest demonstration of the "good" (B) that David has done for Saul (B'), and it is validated by the fact that David risked his own life (C) and God brought about a great victory (C'). The "package" that Jonathan delivers to Saul is then placed in the "wrapping" of an admonition not to sin (A/A'). Jonathan proves to be a good

---

David—at least he gets father and son talking! In the first and last conversations, Saul threatens Jonathan's life, enveloping their communication in violence.
[21] This terminology comes from the idea of a circle. As one travels into a circle a midpoint is reached; then, moving beyond the midpoint one travels out of the circle on the opposite side, covering similar territory in reverse order. Looking into a mirror and seeing the exact image in reverse conveys a similar idea, known as a chiasm. For a distinction between an envelope structure, a chiastic structure and a concentric structure, see Bar-Efrat, *Narrative Art*, p. 98, n. 2.
[22] Fokkelman, *Crossing Fates*, p. 255.

advocate. He wins his case, as Saul promises by an oath (something Saul is fond of making and breaking!) not to kill David.[23] Jonathan's act of intercession comes to a successful end when he is able to deliver David from the "law court" and personally return him to the king's court (19:7).

Jonathan presents another important dimension of a true friend here, by acting as an intercessor. The very definition of friendship involves peacemaking. A real friend desires wholeness for his or her friend in all relationships. Jonathan did his best to mend David's relationship with Saul. First and foremost, he "spoke well of David." How important it is that we not fall into censure and gossip, especially when it concerns our friends. Inhaling the negative atmosphere of criticism often leads to exhaling insensitive words we later regret. At times we all fall prey to being tactless windbags, but Jonathan's example sets the standard. When faced with the unjustified criticism of a friend, we should respond respectfully and truthfully, defending their good qualities and calling others to a higher standard of conduct.

Parting is Such Sweet Sorrow (1 Sam. 20)

Breaking his oath, Saul makes several more attempts on David's life (1 Sam. 19:9–24). As a result, David once more seeks refuge in Jonathan's friendship. His three short successive questions (only six words total in Hebrew) to Jonathan betray his desperation, and perhaps, a little righteous indignation (20:1). Though guilty of no crime, David has become public enemy number one. Jonathan is taken aback by David's passionate questions, just as the reader is taken aback by Jonathan's ignorance of the problem between Saul and David! With similar passion Jonathan vehemently denies that his father is plotting David's death (20:2). The communication problem between Saul and Jonathan (noted above) finds its most explicit reference here in Jonathan's words, "Indeed, my father will do nothing either great or small without first telling me."

Jonathan seems blissfully unaware of other attempts by Saul to make a dartboard out of David (19:10). He has apparently not communicated with his sister concerning Saul's attempt to kill David in his own bed (19:11–17), and he is unaware of the three squadrons of soldiers that Saul sent (and even led) to apprehend David in Ramah (19:18–24). How is the reader to account for Jonathan's ignorance? The writer chooses not to tell us,[24] which highlights

---

[23] Saul's oath is full of irony. He says, "As the LORD *lives*, he shall not be *killed*" (19:6), juxtaposing God's life with David's death. But Saul will violate his oath by seeking to kill David and, as a result of this and other acts of rebellion, God will put Saul to death (1 Sam. 28:19).

[24] Here is a classic example of a "gap" in the narrative. See the "Introduction," pp. 11-14. My own supposition is that Saul had probably sent Jonathan on some military mission. With Jonathan absent, Saul would be free to pursue his vendetta against

the theme of a lack of communication in Saul's family and kingdom. Ironically, Saul will later complain bitterly about his servant's (and son's) lack of communication with him (1 Sam. 22:8).

There can be a number of reasons for a lack of communication, but the end result is always the same—problems! In the case of Saul and his kingdom, the reason for a lack of communication is clear: there is a lack of trust. And it is this lack of trust between father and son, and father and daughter (19:17), as well as between king and subjects, which contributes to the destruction of Saul's kingdom. Failure to communicate is at the heart of many problems within any kind of human community. Even if lack of trust is not the reason, poor communication will eventually translate into a lack of trust, damaging relationships, destroying loyalties, and ultimately bringing division in a family, a church, or a nation.

David's oath and reason prevails, convincing Jonathan that there is "but a step between me and death" (20:3–4). David proposes a test to reveal Saul's true motives. This test is surely more for Jonathan's benefit than David's, despite the fact that David allows for the possibility of a positive outcome ("If he says thus: 'It is well,' your servant will be safe," v. 7).[25] David is all too aware of Saul's intentions! After explaining his plan to Jonathan, which involves lying,[26] David appeals to the covenant relationship between them,

---

David. Ironically, the biblical writer's silence on this issue causes the reader to experience his or her own ignorance. We are unaware of why Jonathan is unaware, further emphasizing the problem of a lack of communication.

[25] I am in agreement with Polzin, *Samuel and the Deuteronomist*, p. 189, who writes, "It makes little sense for David now to believe that any favorable utterance of Saul about him is credible. When David suggests to Jonathan that any word of approval by the king over David's absence would mean that 'it will be well with your servant' (v. 7), it is difficult to take David seriously."

[26] Bergen, *1, 2 Samuel*, pp. 213-214, excuses the lie David puts in Jonathan's mouth by pointing out that, since the purpose is to preserve innocent life, it does not violate "either the letter or spirit of the Torah." There may be some validity to this observation, as other passages seem to praise characters for similar actions (cf. Josh. 2—the story of Rahab, who lies to protect the Israelite spies—although many would contend it is Rahab's faith that is praised, not the lie itself). A more modern example might be those European Christians who hid Jews from the Nazis during World War II. Would we expect them to tell German soldiers, when asked, that Jews were hiding under their floorboards? This is not to condone lying in general, but simply to assert that people in a sinful world sometimes resort to imperfect means in desperate situations. For an excellent examination of the ethical issues involved in such a situation, and the various interpretations possible, see "Excursus: On Rahab's Lie" in David M. Howard, Jr., *Joshua*, NAC (Nashville: Broadman & Holman Publishers, 1998), pp. 106-112. The writer makes no explicit statement regarding David's deception here. However, he does show that deception becomes a part of David's pattern as he flees

and concludes with a dramatic flair by telling Jonathan to kill him if he is indeed guilty (v. 8). This brings a further protest from Jonathan about his ignorance of his father's plan (v. 9), and leads to David inquiring how Jonathan will get word to him (v. 10).

The next scene takes place in "the field" (v. 11). The words are reminiscent of the story of Cain and Abel, but with a twist. Some scholars believe that the LXX (Septuagint) text of Genesis 4:8 preserves the original reading, and that the Hebrew text may be incomplete.[27] The LXX tells us that Cain said to Abel, "Let us go out to the field," the same words Jonathan speaks to David. Cain's purpose was to get Abel alone in the field, in order to slay him. Jonathan's purpose is to protect David. While Cain should have been "his brother's keeper," Jonathan truly is David's keeper.[28]

Jonathan wants to get David to a safe place where they can continue to discuss their plan. It is also clear from the ensuing verses (14–17) that Jonathan wants privacy in order to confirm his covenant with David—a dangerous deed if David's suspicions about Saul are correct. The conversation that follows, however, takes a surprising turn. While it is David's life that is in danger, Jonathan looks to the future and asks David to protect him and his family (vv. 14–15). Such a conversation could be viewed as selfish on Jonathan's part. (Imagine if your life were being threatened, and your friend, who is presently secure, were to turn the conversation to his own safety!) However, the story makes it clear that Jonathan speaks from faith, motivated by love (v. 17). Jonathan, who is not "in the know" about his father's feelings, clearly is "in the know" about what the future holds. He knows that David will be king, and so he asks David to show him the same "loyalty"[29] that he has shown towards David.

---

from Saul (21:2, 13), and this has severe consequences at least on the family of Ahimelech (22:22).

[27] The Hebrew text literally says, "Then Cain *said* to Abel, his brother," but the Hebrew text does not tell us what Cain said to Abel. The NKJV has tried to smooth out the difficulty by translating it as, "Now Cain talked with Abel his brother" and a marginal note supplies the LXX translation. Some scholars, however, believe the text makes sense as it is. See, for example, Pamela Tamarkin Reis, "What Cain said: A Note on Genesis 4.8," *JSOT* 27.1, 2002, pp. 107-113, and recently, Howard Jacobson, "Genesis iv 8" *VT* 55, 2005, pp. 564-565.

[28] The Hebrew word also means to "guard" or "protect." It is the word Jonathan used in 19:2 when warning David by saying, "be on your guard." Thus Jonathan proves himself to be David's keeper.

[29] The word in the original is *hesed* which is used in covenant contexts and refers to "kindness" and "loyalty." This word occurs three times in this chapter (20:8, 14, 15), and three more times in 2 Sam. 9 which mirrors its fulfillment in the story of Mephibosheth, Jonathan's son.

Robert Bergen observes that 20:11–23 contains Jonathan's longest speeches. There are actually four different quotations, consisting of 162 Hebrew words. What is especially important to note is that Jonathan mentions the Lord (Yahweh) nine times in these verses.[30] This shows that Jonathan is a man of faith. He sees his friendship with David, and their futures as totally dependent on the Lord. Besides these nine occurrences of the Lord's name in these verses, the Lord is mentioned four more times by Jonathan or David in this chapter.[31] As a popular Christian song proclaims, "Friends are friends forever if the Lord's the Lord of them."[32] My wife and I have been privileged to have several lifelong friends due to our mutual relationship with the Lord. The Lord creates a common foundation that friends (and lovers) can spend a lifetime building upon.

Following Jonathan's instructions about how he will inform David (vv. 18–23), David goes off to hide—while Jonathan goes off to find out what David already knows. The first day of the feast is uneventful, except that the author allows us into Saul's thought processes. Although he says nothing, he is clearly anxious about David's absence (v. 26). The next day, however, the time-bomb explodes. Saul, who cannot even speak the name of David civilly,[33] asks derogatorily, "Why has the son of Jesse not come to eat, either yesterday or today?" (v. 27). Jonathan gives the answer provided by David, and dinnertime erupts into a war of words between father and son.

Saul's opening words are especially caustic and intended to publicly shame Jonathan (v. 30). In his tirade he finally says what he has long harbored in his heart: "For as long as the son of Jesse lives on the earth, you shall not be established, nor your kingdom" (v. 31). With these words Saul reveals his rebellion against the Lord, who had said through Samuel, "The LORD has torn the kingdom of Israel from you today, and has given it to a neighbor of yours, who is better than you" (1 Sam. 15:28).

If Jonathan was ignorant of this fact, it is now clearly laid on the dinner table before him—swallow that if you can Jonathan! Indeed Jonathan does swallow it, for he does not care at all about his "right" to the throne. Jonathan's focus is on his friend and the injustice being done to him. "Why should he be killed? What has he done?" Jonathan asks the very questions that David could not ask of Saul (v. 32, cf. v. 1). At this juncture, Jonathan gets the *point* as he sees the tip of Saul's spear heading towards him, as it had headed towards David on three previous occasions.

---

[30] Bergen, *1, 2 Samuel*, p. 214.

[31] God's name is found in the following verses of chap. 20: 3, 8, 12, 13 (2x), 14, 15, 16, 21, 22, 23, and 42 (2x). The Lord's name is notably absent in the scene between Jonathan and Saul.

[32] Deborah D. Smith and Michael W. Smith, "Friends" from the CD, *The First Decade: 1983-1993* (Nashville: Meadowgreen Music Co., 1982).

[33] Saul continually refers to David as "the son of Jesse," rather than speak his name.

Several commentators have noted the remarkable wording of v. 33. Jobling writes, "Saul tries to impale Jonathan…and from this Jonathan deduces that his father seeks *David's* life. The identification of Jonathan and David is total—an act directed at one is an act directed at the other" (Jobling's emphasis).[34]

We have been reminded in this chapter that Jonathan "loved him as he loved his own soul" (v. 17). Now we witness the fruit of that love. In his blind rage to strike out at David, Saul strikes out at the very one he wants to give the kingdom to![35] To see Jonathan is to see David. His hopes, dreams, and ambitions are one with his friend. This is further confirmed in another extraordinary statement in verse 34. Jonathan leaves the table in fierce anger, not just because his father has treated him shamefully, but first and foremost because he is "grieved for David." His refusal to eat is a genuine sign of grief:[36] if David is not welcome at Saul's table, neither is he. It is clear that Jonathan "loves his neighbor as he loves himself " (Lev. 19:18).

Following the confrontation there was nothing left for Jonathan to do except deliver the sad news to his friend. With a pretense of doing some target practice, Jonathan heads for the field where he and David had agreed to meet, perhaps the same field where once Jonathan had been able to persuade his father of David's innocence (19:3). Communication is again at a minimum as the author makes it clear that not even the lad accompanying Jonathan knew what was going on: "Only Jonathan and David knew of the matter" (20:39).

Once the lad is sent on his way, the friends embrace in an emotionally laden scene. The poignancy of this meeting is highlighted in verse 41 by the word "neighbor," which is used not once, but twice.[37] Both men "loved their neighbor as themselves" (Lev. 19:18). Before parting, Jonathan recalls the words of their covenant, emphasizing the God who united them and now sends them in different directions (v. 42 cf. vv. 14–15, 23). The number three has been significant throughout the chapter (three opening questions by David—v. 1; three evenings—v. 5; three days—v. 19; three arrows—v. 20; David bows three times—v. 41; three main characters—David, Jonathan, and Saul). Now, in the final scene, the friends are united (and part) under the oversight of their ever-present God—three in one!

---

[34] Jobling, *Sense*, p. 14.

[35] Stansell, "Honor and Shame in the David Narratives," pp. 60-61, believes that Saul is not intentionally trying to kill Jonathan. In his view, the throwing of the spear is a symbolic action that means death for David.

[36] Fokkelman, *Crossing Fates*, p. 341, says it "shows the interior and gentleness of the prince."

[37] The Hebrew literally says, "And they kissed, each man his neighbor, and they wept, each man and his neighbor."

Jonathan "Lends" David "a Hand" (1 Sam. 23:14–18)

Up to 23:14, David's escape from Saul is described as "fleeing" (19:10, 12, 18; 20:1; 21:10), and his wandering is summarized in the statement of 23:13, "So David and his men, about six hundred, arose and departed from Keilah, *and went wherever they could go*." Although still in the wilderness and being sought by Saul, 23:14 begins to show David as more settled.[38] "And David *dwelt* in the wilderness in the strongholds, and he *dwelt* in the mountain in the wilderness of Ziph" (my translation).[39] This period of settling down coincides with Jonathan's visit—the last time the friends will see one another.

Jonathan came to David and "strengthened his *hand* in God" (v. 16). This statement is connected with the narrator's statement in verse 14, "but God did not give him [David] into his [Saul's] *hand*," and Jonathan's statement in v. 17, "the *hand* of Saul my father shall not find you." Jonathan's encouragement suggests the reason why David becomes more settled. His friend's faith and support have a calming and fortifying result. The narrator's statement in verse 14 has a double-edged effect. On the one hand, it explains why Saul will never catch David: God will not allow it. On the other hand, verse 14 shows how significant Jonathan is in helping David to understand this. The author may be deliberately using a part of Jonathan's name—"but God did not *give* him into his hand." From this point on, the reader is informed that God will not give David into Saul's hand. After Jonathan strengthened David's hand in God, and assured him that the hand of Saul would not find him, David becomes more confident of this same truth. The man whose name means "The Lord gives" gave one final gift to David.

Jonathan strengthened David's hand in God in several ways. First, he calmed his fear—"Do not be afraid" (v. 17). Sometimes we need the reassuring voice of a friend to remind us that things are going to work out, especially when the wilderness seems to have put all of our dreams and plans on hold. Constant upheaval can cause doubt to creep in and rob us of the certainty of God's promises. Jonathan's words are not empty platitudes; he backs up his statement with substance. The second thing he does is to remind David of God's calling and promises—"you will be king." Jonathan becomes part of a chorus of voices in these chapters confirming God's promise to David (see 1 Sam. 21:11; 24:20; 25:28–31). In the midst of trials God is faithful to remind us of his plan for us; and often He uses a friend. Third, Jonathan and David do what has become natural between them: they make a covenant before the Lord (23:18).

---

[38] Once again I am indebted to Fokkelman, *Crossing Fates*, pp. 435-442, for many of the following insights.

[39] The NKJV and NASB use "stayed" followed by "remained," which obscures the fact that the Hebrew uses the same verb.

The reader might wonder why Jonathan does not stay with David; but the author does not tell us. We merely read, "Jonathan went to his own house" (v. 18). Though we might wish Jonathan had stayed with David, his actions are consistent with his speech in these verses. Jonathan twice calls Saul "my father" (v. 17) and the narrator reminds us that Jonathan is "Saul's son" (v. 16).[40] While remaining true to his friend, Jonathan continues to show loyalty to Saul by not defecting to David—which would bring public shame on his father. This is the consistent portrait that we are given of Jonathan: he is a man of integrity.

Eulogy for Jonathan (2 Sam. 1:19–27)

In Jonathan's last appearance, we were reminded that he is Saul's son. By this the narrator may also have been indicating that Jonathan's expectations of being "second" to David (1 Sam. 23:17) would remain unfulfilled. Such a close connection with Saul spells disaster. It is one of several examples in the books of Samuel of how the innocent can fall victim through association with the guilty.[41] Jonathan's loyalty to his father, an admirable quality, results in his death (1 Sam. 31:2). David eulogizes this loyalty when he laments, "Saul and Jonathan were beloved and pleasant in their lives/And in their death they were not divided" (2 Sam. 1:23).

The good die, as well as the wicked. Death does not necessarily mean God's displeasure, for we all must die; it only means that God's purposes in that life have been accomplished. King Josiah, a godly man like Jonathan, dies at a young age (2 Kings 23:28–30). To us this may seem tragic; but Scripture affirms it was part of God's merciful plan:

> Because your heart was tender, and you humbled yourself before the LORD when you heard what I spoke against this place and against its inhabitants, that they would become a desolation and a curse, and you tore your clothes and wept before Me, I also have heard you, says the LORD. Surely, therefore, I will gather you to your fathers, and *you shall be gathered to your*

---

[40] Jonathan's designation as "Saul's son" seems to play a different role from Michal's designation as "Saul's daughter." In chap. 10 we will notice that the reference to Michal as "Saul's daughter" identifies her with Saul's character and attitudes (see pp. 125ff.). Though Jonathan is frequently labeled "Saul's son" it is almost exclusively in contexts which contrast him with the attitude and demeanor of his father (1 Sam. 14:1, 40; 19:1; 23:16). The only exceptions are his initial introduction (1 Sam. 13:16, 22), which seeks to establish his relationship with Saul, and his death (1 Sam. 31:2), where he is mentioned in connection with his other brothers who were killed in the battle on Mount Gilboa.

[41] Uriah is perhaps the best example of this (2 Sam. 11).

grave in peace; and your eyes shall not see all the calamity which I will bring on this place (2 Kings 22:19–20).

Another example is the death of Jeroboam I's son. God proclaims through the prophet Ahijah that his child will die, but the reason is surprising. Ahijah says to Jeroboam's wife:

> Arise therefore, go to your own house. When your feet enter the city, the child shall die. And all Israel shall mourn for him and bury him, for he is the only one of Jeroboam who shall come to the grave, *because in him there is found something good toward the* LORD *God of Israel* in the house of Jeroboam (1 Kings 14:12–13).

It is not our desire to lose any of our loved ones to death, but we should take comfort in the fact that sometimes God seeks to spare them additional pain. For those who believe there is life beyond the grave (John 11:25), Jonathan simply passed from an earthly kingdom to a heavenly one.

David's first mention of Jonathan in this song is a celebration of his courage in battle: "the bow of Jonathan did not turn back" (2 Sam. 1:22). It was Jonathan's bow that was the symbol of his loyalty to David. His bow had announced Saul's hostility toward David and warned David that he must flee (1 Sam. 20:20–22, 35–37); and it was the same bow that Jonathan surrendered to his servant as he went to meet David, showing the trust between them (1 Sam. 20:40–42). Saul might be remembered for his sword (2 Sam. 1:22), or as, in David's case, his spear,[42] but Jonathan was remembered for his bow—the bow that defeated enemies and united friends.

David saves his most personal reflections about Jonathan until the end of his song. Though there is no need to doubt David's love for Jonathan, this is the first expression of it from his own lips,[43] and it is an eloquent expression. Nevertheless, it is Jonathan's love which is highlighted. David's words are a final tribute to the man who always seemed to be giving.

> I am distressed for you my brother Jonathan;
> You have been very pleasant to me;
> Your love to me was wonderful,
> Surpassing the love of women (2 Sam. 1:26).

---

[42] It is not accidental that Saul, a "king like all the nations," would be remembered for his sword and spear. David had once declared, "the LORD does not save with sword or spear" (1 Sam. 17:47).

[43] "And they kissed one another; and they wept together, but David more so" (20:41), is no doubt an expression of David's love; but it could also mean that he is emotional over leaving everything, as well as everyone, he loves.

The intimacy of David's words can be seen in the triple use of "me" and "you" together in these lines.[44] They recall Jonathan's words, "May the LORD be between *you* and *me*, and between *your* descendants and *my* descendants, forever" (1 Sam. 20:42). David also uses the tender expression, "my brother." Although technically they were brothers-in-law, it is unlikely that David is thinking of legal connections.[45] Rather, he is expressing the deep emotions experienced by best friends, which only the language of family can adequately convey.

It is David's final sentence, however, that best communicates how deep the bond between the two really was.

> He selects as a standard that ardour which so many men re-gard as a source of unsurpassed beauty and ecstasy for so much of their lives, "the love of women," and then goes one step further with a comparative, "even more wonderful to me was your love [for me]."[46]

Based on this statement and other factors in the David/Jonathan narratives, some scholars have suggested that their relationship was homosexual, or that Jonathan is described in feminine terms.[47] Other commentators, however, reject this view.[48] There are a number of solid reasons for such a rejection. First, we have noted throughout our study that the Books of Samuel consist-ently uphold the values and teachings of the Torah (the Law of Moses). Levit-icus 18:22 clearly prohibits homosexual relations. Once again it is worth quoting Zehnder at length,

---

[44] Another observation made by Fokkelman, *Crossing Fates*, p. 672. The first line in Hebrew literally says, "Distress is to me because of you."

[45] To sever any family ties, Saul had unlawfully given Michal to another (1 Sam. 25:44).

[46] Fokkelman, *Crossing Fates*, p. 672.

[47] For example, Danna Nolan Fewell and David M. Gunn, *Gender, Power, and Promise: The Subject of the Bible's First Story* (Nashville: Abingdon, 1993), pp. 148-151. See also, Jobling, *1 Samuel*, pp. 161-164. There are also a host of journal articles that deal with this topic. The interested reader can consult the references in Zehnder's article cited earlier in this chapter.

[48] Youngblood, *1, 2 Samuel*, p. 706, states that, "the verb *'aheb* ("love") is not used elsewhere to express homosexual desire or activity, for which the OT employs *yāda'* ("know"), in the sense of "have sex with" (Gen. 19:5; Judg. 19:22). The latter verb is never used of David's relationship with Jonathan. See also Bergen, *1, 2 Samuel*, p. 293 for a similar view.

...for the narrator(s) presents himself as an advocate of the official Yahwism, and there is no clear ground for the assumption that this religion at any point in its history ever took a positive stance on homoeroticism or homosexuality. For the same reason, the underlining of the fact that the relationship between Jonathan and David was connected with the concept of a covenant and with oaths that were witnessed by YHWH has to be taken as incompatible with the assumption of a homoerotic or homosexual nature of that relationship. How can one explain that it is precisely YHWH who takes on the function of guarantor and witness to a covenant if this covenant were connected with a kind of sexual relation for which no affirming evaluation can be found within the official documents of Yahwism, but...only negative evaluations?[49]

Second, Zehnder has conducted a comprehensive study in the Hebrew Bible on the words often used in the Jonathan/David narratives to suggest a homosexual relationship ("love," "knit," "delight," "kiss," and so on) and has found such a suggestion to be highly improbable. In no case does any of the language offer evidence of a homosexual or homoerotic relationship.[50]

Third, the history of interpretation of the Jonathan/David narratives is against a homosexual reading. For over two millennia this story has been read without any hint of a homosexual relationship.[51] Only in recent times has such an interpretation been advocated, suggesting that it is based more on a desire to support current opinions and lifestyles than on an understanding of ancient Israelite society.[52]

Therefore, David's lament over Jonathan is not an expression of a homosexual relationship. Rather, his affection, which could hardly be put in stronger terms, shows the pathos that follows the explosive combination of family and friendship with abusive power-grasping politics. It is not the last example of this deadly combination in the books of Samuel.

---

[49] Zehnder, "Observations," pp. 166-167.

[50] The reader is encouraged to read Zehnder's entire article.

[51] Yaron Peleg, "Love at First Sight? David, Jonathan, and the Biblical Politics of Gender," *JSOT* 30.2, 2005, pp. 171-172 (also see n. 1), suggests that such an interpretation does exist in early Christianity, but I have been unable to substantiate this claim. Even if such were the case, it would be a rare exception.

[52] Robert Alter, *The David Story*, pp. 200-201, writes, "Repeated, unconvincing attempts have been made to read a homoerotic implication into these words....The bond between men in this warrior culture could easily be stronger than the bond between men and women."

Several authors have noted the preparatory role that Jonathan plays in the story.[53] Jonathan is everything that Saul is not, and he causes us to yearn for a better monarch. As Saul's son, Jonathan paves the way for David by his voluntary abdication of the throne (1 Sam. 23:17), and by his close identification with David ("He loved him as his own soul").

As the forerunner of God's anointed king,[54] Jonathan's role anticipates the role of John the Baptist who was the forerunner of The Messiah.[55] Closer examination reveals a number of similarities. First, both begin their "ministry" before their counterpart appears on the scene. Second, as Jonathan is identified with David, so John the Baptist is identified with Jesus (e.g., Mark 6:14). A third similarity is that both confront wicked kings (Jonathan confronts Saul, and John confronts Herod), and die as a result of their contact with that king. The fourth, and most obvious, similarity is that both exemplify true humility by abdicating in favor of their successor. Both Jonathan and John "decrease" so that the coming king (David and Jesus) might "increase" (John 3:30). Jesus said that, among those born of women, there was none greater than John (Luke 7:28). Could the similarities with Jonathan justify a comparable sentiment of him? That would be high praise indeed!

Conclusion: Faith, Bravery, Loyalty, and Love

There is perhaps no better character in 1 and 2 Samuel than Jonathan, unless it be Hannah or Samuel himself. At the outset of this chapter, we noted the qualities of faith, bravery, loyalty, and love that set Jonathan apart from his father Saul. His faith and bravery are evident from the beginning, with the slaying of the Philistine governor (or garrison, 1 Sam. 13:3), and his attack against the enemy with only his armor-bearer's aid (1 Sam. 14:6–14). The same bravery is evident when he confronts Saul on David's behalf (1 Sam. 19:1–7), and later dies with his father on the battlefield (1 Sam. 31:2–4).

---

[53] For example, Jobling, *Sense*, p. 6. While I agree with Jobling on this point, I cannot accept his suggestion (p. 20) that Jonathan may be a literary creation of the author to explain how the kingship passed from Saul to David.

[54] Messiah means "anointed one." An anointing ceremony accompanied the crowning of every king (1 Sam. 10:1; 16:12–13; 1 Kings 1:34, 39; etc.), thus every king was a "messiah." These "messiahs" anticipated the coming of The Messiah—Jesus Christ, the Son of David.

[55] Hertzberg, *I&II Samuel*, p. 193, and Jobling, *Sense*, p. 21, both make reference to the similarity of the two but do not give any detailed comparison. While my focus is on the similarities between Jonathan and John the Baptist, Evans, *The Message of Samuel*, p. 122, notes several similarities between Jonathan and Jesus.

Jonathan is "a man's man."[56] He shows no fear when confronted with danger. He is a hero, but he is also "man enough" to make room for other legitimate heroes, like David. Jonathan exhibits no insecurity, or grasping for power or position, because his eyes are not on himself but on his God.

Bravery and faith make Jonathan an extremely likeable person, but perhaps his greatest characteristics include selflessness and loyalty, which are among the truest expressions of love. Jonathan's loyalty is particularly admirable as he had to negotiate a delicate balancing act between being Saul's son and David's friend. One could argue that Jonathan was not always loyal to his father. After all, he was willing to deceive Saul in order to protect David (1 Sam. 20), and even when he knew of David's whereabouts he did not divulge them to his father (1 Sam. 23:16–18). However, complete loyalty to Saul on such occasions would have meant death for his innocent friend; therefore, one could also argue that Jonathan was protecting his father from shedding innocent blood—a true act of loyalty, whether Saul recognized it or not! As previously noted, Jonathan demonstrated genuine loyalty to Saul by staying with his father while David was in the wilderness, and ultimately by dying with him in battle.

Jonathan's loyalty to David is undeniable. He defends him (1 Sam. 19:1–7), protects him (1 Sam. 20:35–42), keeps his location secret, and willingly takes second-place to David's leadership (1 Sam. 23:16–18). Jonathan's loyalty to David stems from his selflessness. David's life and well-being are as important to him as his own (1 Sam. 18:1, 3). Jonathan willingly faces a spear for his friend, and is grieved when David is misunderstood and mistreated (1 Sam. 20:33–34). Jonathan is not perfect. He can practice deceit if the circumstances call for it; he is capable of communication problems with his father; and he can be trusting to a fault, and at times naive. But in the end, everyone of us longs to have a friend like Jonathan.

---

[56] *Contra*, Yaron Peleg, "Love at First Sight? David, Jonathan, and the Biblical Politics of Gender," pp. 171-189, who asserts that Jonathan is intentionally portrayed by the biblical author with feminine qualities in order to disqualify him from the kingship.

Chapter 10

Michal: Lover and Despiser (Saul's daughter, David's wife)

Michal, Saul's daughter, loved David (1 Sam. 18:20)
Michal, Saul's daughter...saw King David...and she despised him in her heart (2 Sam. 6:16)

When I Fall in Love, Will It Be Forever? (1 Sam. 18:20–30)

We fall in love with the best of intentions. Marriage vows are "for better or for worse," but infatuation does not believe in "worse," only in "better." Passion can blind us to the hardships we may encounter in life. When fiery trials come, the heat of passion can quickly cool. When storms come, what makes the difference between couples who emerge stronger and those who are torn apart? The story of Michal raises such questions.

It has been stated that Michal is the only woman in the Bible said to love a man.[1] While there is, in fact, one other,[2] it is important that Michal's introduction into the narrative is enveloped by statements of her love for David (18:20, 28).[3] However, the highway to happiness faces a major roadblock from the start (a father-in-law's insane jealousy), and the fairytale-like beginning (hero marries princess) quickly degenerates into a nightmare. David's forced departure from the palace leaves little time for this couple to develop a "family photo album" and, when they are at last joined together again, the only picture we are given is one of bitterness resulting in barrenness and isolation (2 Sam. 6:23). How one goes from loving (1 Sam. 18:20) to despising (2 Sam. 6:16) is one of the questions answered by a closer look at Michal's portrait.

The reader is introduced to Michal after the failed match between David and Saul's first daughter, Merab (18:19). She joins a list of those in chapter 18 who are said to "love" David (cf. vv. 1, 3, 16). While the text proclaims Jonathan's love before Saul's initial outburst of jealousy against David (cf. vv. 1–4 with 7–13), Michal's love is noted after (v. 20). This means that Michal's love for David could put her in the precarious position of having to choose between her father and David. This is immediately confirmed by the statement that Saul sees Michal's love as an opportunity to be rid of David. The writer allows us to read Saul's thoughts as he says, "I will give her to him,

---

[1] Alter, *The Art of Biblical Narrative*, p. 118.
[2] See Youngblood, *1, 2 Samuel*, p. 709, who points to the Shulamite woman of the Song of Solomon (1:7; 3:1–4).
[3] Michal is first mentioned in 1 Sam. 14:49 which provides a summary list of Saul's family, but her proper introduction to the story is here in 1 Sam. 18:20.

that she may be a snare to him, and that the hand of the Philistines may be against him" (v. 21).

The early picture of Michal is mixed. Michal's love for David, and her intervention on his behalf—saving his life (19:11–17)—suggests she may be viewed as a female counterpart to Jonathan. However, there are hints of a darker, more ominous side to Michal. One of these is found here in Saul's statement that she might become a "snare." This is Saul's hope and may not be a reflection of the true circumstances; but events in the next chapter (19:13, 16) will recall the associations of this word with idolatry throughout Scripture (e.g., Exod. 23:33; 34:12; Deut. 7:16; Judg. 8:27). Saul may be shrewder than we realize at this point. He clearly hopes that David's betrothal to Michal will lead to him dying in battle against the Philistines (a result of the bride price that he requests—v. 25). But if that fails, perhaps he hopes that Michal's idolatrous ways will alienate the Lord from David. After all, chapter 18 reminds us three times that "the LORD was with David" (vv. 12, 14, 28). Do we give Saul too much credit to think that his plan involved Michal's idolatrous ways weakening David's relationship with the Lord?[4] From what is known of Saul, this motive cannot be easily dismissed.[5]

David is, of course, successful against the Philistines (he is *always* successful against the Philistines, in contrast to Saul!). In fact, he almost seems to flaunt his success in Saul's face by a double payment of the gruesome bride price, and as a result he receives Michal in marriage (18:27). Saul's plan has backfired and David's continued success threatens him even more (vv. 29–30). Jonathan's sane words will calm Saul for the moment (19:1–7), but the demon inside of Saul eventually leads him to a more direct assault (19:9–10). This brings us to Michal's next appearance in the story.

What Light Through Yon' Window Breaks?[6] (1 Sam. 19:11–17)

A number of similarities invite us to compare this scene with the preceding story about Jonathan's intervention (19:1–7). The most obvious is that both stories involve children of Saul saving David. A strong link is made

---

[4] Bergen, *1, 2 Samuel*, p. 204, suggests this as part of Saul's motivation in marrying Michal to David.

[5] Even if it is not a part of Saul's motivation, the larger literary context may suggest the author is making this connection. See the discussion on pp. 125-127 below.

[6] The choice of this subtitle (obviously tongue-in-cheek) is suggested by the importance of the window, and also by Fokkelman's astute observation that the imagery of night and day is reversed in this story (*Crossing Fates*, p. 262). Usually the light of day represents a positive turn, while darkness is a menacing image (cf. chap. 4, pp. 59-60). In this story, however, it is morning that brings danger for David and his flight at night which saves him.

by the use of similar words. Both Jonathan and Michal "warn" David.[7] Both stories speak of Saul's intent to "kill" David, and the words "morning" and "guard/watch" occur in both (19:2, 11). As mentioned above, Michal is clearly Jonathan's counterpart. Yet, as we shall see, she stands in contrast to Jonathan as well.

In 19:11, Michal is introduced as *David's wife*, and this is a statement of where her loyalty now lies. She is not *Saul's daughter* (cf. 18:20, 28).[8] If Saul believed "blood is thicker than water," it appears that Michal—still in the glow of her newly-married state—believed in the triumph of love. She had left father and mother and been joined to her husband (Gen. 2:24). Saul probably thought he could manipulate Michal into delivering David to him; but, he was greatly mistaken.

Somehow Michal gets wind of the plot against David and the next few sentences focus on her response. First, she warns David, "If you do not save your life tonight, tomorrow you will be dead" (19:11). Second, in a scene reminiscent of David's great great grandmother, Rahab,[9] she lets David down through a window (v. 12; cf. Josh. 2:15). It is interesting that David never speaks a word. In fact, we do not know what his feelings toward Michal are, because the text is silent. In relation to David, Michal and Jonathan are givers and lovers—another similarity they share. All we hear from David in this passage is the faint sound of his footsteps as he disappears into the night (v. 12). The next time we see Michal at a window (2 Sam. 6:16), her disposition toward David will be quite different. Perhaps the text's silence about David's feelings for Michal tells us plenty.

While David disappears, Michal must buy him some time. Her subsequent actions recall the words of her father in 18:21 and place her in a less-than-favorable light. To deceive the soldiers, Michal takes a household idol—why does she have one?—and lays it in the bed, covering it with clothes and goat's hair (19:13). The Hebrew word for this image is *teraphim*, and its only other occurrence in 1 Samuel is found in 15:23. There the prophet Samuel speaks of God's view on Saul's disobedience: "And stubbornness is as iniquity and *idolatry*" (i.e., *teraphim*). Michal may be called "David's wife" in this pas-

---

[7] The Hebrew word *nāgid* means, "to declare." The NKJV translates it as *"told."* The NIV translates this verb in vv. 2 & 11 as, *"warned him."*

[8] David J. A. Clines, "X, X Ben Y: Personal Names in Hebrew Narrative Style," *VT* 22, 1972, pp. 266-287, presents a significant study on the use of name-forms attached to individuals in Hebrew narrative. Regarding Michal, Clines writes, "The name-forms used for Michal, daughter of Saul and wife of David, are particularly instructive" (p. 269). Although I became aware of Clines' article after I had written this chapter, I was encouraged to find that his conclusions were similar to mine.

[9] Matt. 1:5 establishes this connection between Rahab and David.

sage, but this word connects her with her father and idolatry.[10] Suspicion about Michal's devotion to the Lord is confirmed in 2 Samuel 6, where she does not partake in the celebration and worship and she scornfully derides David for his uninhibited expression of worship "before the LORD" (vv. 16, 20).

When the soldiers finally come, Michal deceives them by saying David is ill (1 Sam. 19:14). This is comparable to Jonathan's deception (20:28–29), as both lies are designed to protect David. Once the ruse is discovered, however, Michal feels compelled to lie again—putting David in the worst possible light as she depicts him threatening her life. Michal says to Saul, "He said to me, 'Let me go! Why should I kill you?' " (19:17).

Michal's second lie, as well as her religious interests, stand in stark contrast to her brother Jonathan. Jonathan lies to protect David, but not to protect himself. On two occasions he makes it clear to his father that David is innocent (19:4–5; 20:32). Jonathan will deflect Saul's spear from David, if possible, but is willing to face the tip of that same spear when it comes to his own safety. This is the difference between Michal and Jonathan. Though she is willing to protect David, she will not do it at her own expense.[11] Michal has a golden opportunity to protest David's innocence, as Jonathan had; but out of fear of the consequences, she portrays David as the villain Saul thinks he is.[12] Jonathan acts nobly, but as 2 Samuel 6 will show us, Michal has a wrong concept about what true nobility is.

Michal's *teraphim* also stand in contrast to Jonathan's faith in the Lord. Admittedly there is less material devoted to Michal than Jonathan, but not once is the name of the Lord found on her lips. Conversely, Jonathan's mention of Yahweh, and his faith, is constantly put before the reader. If anything can be read into the significance of Michal's name, perhaps it is that her

---

[10] One could also wonder why David permits *teraphim* in his house. There may be a suggestion here that David is not a strong spiritual leader over his family. While this is confirmed elsewhere (2 Sam. 11ff.), the emphasis here remains on Michal. The fact is that the author only connects the word *teraphim* with her and her father.

[11] Clines, "Introduction," *Telling Queen Michal's Story*, Clines and Eskenazi eds. p. 41, seems surprised when he states, "hardly a writer can be found who does not approve of Michal's decision." He continues, "Why is there such unanimity among writers on this issue? We might have expected it to be a point of dissension, since it is a question whether or not to approve of telling lies" (p. 42). It seems to me that many writers have missed the intentional contrast between Michal and Jonathan (see Hugenberger's comments below).

[12] G.P. Hugenberger, "Michal," *Telling Queen Michal's Story*, Clines and Eskenazi eds. p. 205, comes to a similar conclusion: "When Saul confronted her she lied, saying that David had threatened her. This lie sharply contrasts Michal with her brother Jonathan, who defended David against Saul even at the risk of his own life (1 Sam. 20:32f.; cf. 19:4f.)."

name refers to the more nebulous word "God" or "god(s)"[13], whereas, Jonathan's name proclaims the more personal name, Yahweh.

The mention of *teraphim*, the deception with a goat and garments, marriage to a second daughter, and the enmity of a father-in-law have naturally caused many to note the similarities between this story and the story of Jacob, Rachel and Laban (Gen. chaps. 29 and 31; esp. 31:17–42).[14] Although Rachel is one of the matriarchs of Israel, the comparison here is not flattering. It serves to confirm that Michal's religious devotion is misplaced.

From Princess to Pawn (1 Sam. 25:44; 2 Sam. 3:12–16)

Whatever misgiving we may have about Michal, her portrait to this point has led us to expect a strong, resourceful woman full of both passion and cunning wit. With this in mind, the next two scenes which mention her are surprising, for the princess seems to be reduced to a pawn in a game of power-politics. Michal, the main subject of 19:11–17, who speaks and acts decisively and shrewdly, becomes a mere object who is spoken about and acted upon in the verses under consideration. In fact, her mention is so brief in 1 Sam. 25:44 that it could be termed an afterthought. The author reports that Saul has given her to another: Palti, the son of Laish. The description of her being "David's wife" alludes to the illegal activity of Saul, who violates the law in order to sever any legitimate connection David might have to his throne. But, no matter, David has replaced Michal with two others (25:42–43)—one of who, at least, is a much better match for David—Abigail.

The callousness of both Saul and David is evident. We will examine this aspect of David's character in a moment, but first I would like to consider what we may infer from this passage about Michal. Sometimes we can learn by what Scripture does *not* say. For example, Michal's lack of mentioning the Lord's name speaks volumes. Similarly, there is silence about Michal making any attempt to join David after his flight. Is she locked up in the palace tower like the proverbial princess, waiting for her hero to rescue her? Jonathan was able to make his way to David (23:16–18) so may we not infer that Michal must have had an opportunity to join her husband if she so desired? Would not Jonathan have been willing to aid her in this? The real question is, "Why is there no mention of Michal making an attempt to join her

---

[13] Dorothea Harvey, "Michal," *IDB*, vol. 3, p. 373, states that Michal's name seems to be a contraction of the Hebrew phrase, "Who is like God?" Unlike the names of other characters examined in this book, I can find no particular significance between the meaning of Michal's name and her portrayal in the story, unless it is in this contrast. While Michal's name may originally have had a positive meaning, her actions turn the first letter in "God" from a capital "G" to a small "g."

[14] See, for example, Fokkelman, *Crossing Fates*, pp. 274-276, who points out not only the similarities, but also the differences between the two narratives.

beloved husband?"[15] I suggest the answer is found in something we have already learned about her and something we have yet to learn about her.

1 Samuel 19:17 has taught us that Michal is only willing to go so far in identifying with David. Though she loves David, unlike her brother, she does not love David "as herself." Michal seems to choose personal security, and perhaps luxury, over her marriage. Life with David in the palace is one thing. Life with David in the wilderness is another matter. Who knows what will become of David or those who follow him?

Another silence in Michal's life is also notable. Her brother, David's new wife Abigail, and even her own father have confessed that David will one day be king. Michal's silence on this issue suggests she is not as sure. Rather than choosing "to suffer affliction with the people of God," Michal chose "to enjoy the passing pleasures of sin" (Heb. 11:25). In short, she was not a woman of faith. She was indeed her father's daughter. Her attitude is further revealed in 2 Samuel 6:20 by her lecture to David on appropriate kingly behavior. Thus when Palti began to show her attention, we can presume she did not refuse.[16] Being at the king's court where there was power and security, and being with a man who truly loved her (2 Sam. 3:15–16), must have seemed more appealing than a life and future in the wilderness.[17] In retrospect, perhaps Michal was not as passive as we first supposed!

We have, however, characterized Michal as a political pawn, and 2 Samuel 3:12–16 substantiates this claim. Following his feud with Ish-bosheth (3:7–11), Abner sends messengers to David, inviting him to make a covenant in which he promises to bring all of Israel to David (v. 12). David is favorably disposed to Abner's proposal, but he makes one demand: Michal must be returned to him (v. 13). This is clearly a political move on David's part. Michal's return would restore his relationship with a member of Saul's family, giving him a more legitimate claim to the throne in the eyes of Israel. Furthermore, it is a way for Abner to demonstrate good faith, since Michal had been illegally taken away from him. David's words to Ish-bosheth (v. 14), reminding him that he had paid a bride price for Michal (the infamous one hundred foreskins), further confirms the justice of this demand.

---

[15] It is also true, of course, that there is no mention of David trying to retrieve her.

[16] This statement is based on Palti's affection for Michal as noted in 2 Sam. 3:16. It is also just as possible that Saul learned of Palti's interest in Michal and took advantage of the opportunity by giving her to him, regardless of her own personal feelings in the matter.

[17] Some might object that this reads too much into the portrait of Michal and that she had little choice but to comply with Saul's orders. I do not mean to infer that Saul was not an intimidating force in Michal's life; clearly he was. However, I believe the interpretation above is supported by the overall characterization of Michal by the author. The analysis below continues to bear this out.

David's descriptions of Michal are interesting. When speaking to Abner, he calls her "Saul's daughter." No doubt this language is intended to communicate his legitimate connection with Saul's family. When speaking to Ish-bosheth, he calls her "my wife," emphasizing his legal right to her. In the larger context of the story, however, these two designations have other implications. When we first meet Michal, she is of course called "Saul's daughter" (1 Sam. 14:49; 18:20, 28). In 19:11, however, she is called "David's wife." As noted previously, this not only referred to her marriage to David, but was also an announcement of where her loyalty resided. In 1 Sam. 25:44, as in our present passage, Michal is called both Saul's daughter, *and* David's wife. This double designation introduces ambiguity into Michal's character and hints at a split personality. Saul's break with David has made these two expressions oxymoronic. She cannot be both Saul's daughter and David's wife. She must choose.

Therefore, it is fair to ask where her loyalty now lies. As we have seen in our discussion of 1 Samuel 25:44, Michal's loyalty seems to have a definite leaning towards the court of Saul. But the two appellations hint at an inner struggle. Although, on the surface, there are good reasons for David to use both designations here, there is a suggestion that he is aware of her shift in loyalty. After all, he has been king in Hebron for over seven years at this point, and Michal has made no effort to return to him of her own accord. The fact that in her final appearance in 2 Samuel 6 she is only referred to as "the daughter of Saul" (v. 16), shows that Michal's allegiance has come full circle.

There are a few things noticeably absent from 2 Samuel 3:12-16. We would expect in a story that speaks about the reunion of a husband and wife that there would be a word about their feelings, and a scene depicting the actual reunion. Our story, however, is devoid of both. We still have no word that David ever loved this woman. This silence is particularly deafening if we contrast it with the reaction of Michal's current husband: "Then her husband went along with her to Bahurim, weeping behind her" (2 Sam. 3:16). Palti(el) only leaves Michal when he is forced to. When did David ever show an inkling of such emotion towards Michal? Clearly all the problems in this troubled marriage cannot be laid at her feet. For David, despite all of his success, was a tragic failure when it came to family relationships. As observed earlier, Michal has no dialogue in 2 Samuel 3 and we are not given any glimpse into her thoughts or feelings. Treated as an object and forced to leave a man who loved her, what is there to say? The only allusion to love in this scene is the pitiful, brokenhearted Paltiel. When she leaves him behind, she leaves love behind. There will be no warm embraces and no tender reunion between David and Michal.

When Honor Goes Out the Window (2 Sam. 6:16–23)

It used to be popular in wedding ceremonies for the wife to promise to "love, honor, and obey" her husband. For Michal, loving David is clearly a thing of the past. Obedience, albeit begrudging, is not an option; he is the king. But the king cannot control her heart, and just as love has taken flight, so now honor will go out the window—literally!

As David brings the ark of the Lord into Jerusalem, accompanied by great celebration, Michal re-emerges for one last appearance.[18] She is in a window, apart from the joyous festivities; she is distant and aloof (v. 16). As Fokkelman has keenly noted, "Looking down at and on her husband she considers herself to be above him, but at the same time places herself outside what is happening and is isolated from everyone."[19] The last time Michal was at a window she was called David's wife (1 Sam. 19:11–12), but now she is introduced as *"Saul's daughter."* This ascription will be used four times[20] in these verses, matching the total number of times it is used in other narratives,[21] thus identifying her with Saul. She has adopted his outlook and his attitudes.[22]

As she peers through the window, she sees what she considers to be an undignified spectacle, *"King* David leaping and whirling *before the LORD."* As a result, "she *despised* him in her heart." The words make it clear that Michal not only looks down on David, but she looks down on his expression of worship. The addition of the words *"King"* and *"before the LORD"* at the beginning and end of this sentence make all the difference. In her high opinion, David's

---

[18] The Hebrew text (MT) mentions Michal in 2 Sam. 21:8, but a comparison with 1 Sam. 18:19, other Hebrew MSS, and the LXX, demonstrates that the correct reading should be "Merab," Saul's older daughter. Other factors, which strengthen this conclusion, are that Michal was married to Palti son of Laish (1 Sam. 25:44; 2 Sam. 3:15–16), not Adriel the son of Barzillai, and Michal was childless (2 Sam. 6:23). The NKJV of 2 Sam. 21:8 reads "she brought up," suggesting perhaps an adoptive type of relationship between Michal and Adriel's children; but this is the translator's attempt at harmonization. The Hebrew word means "to give birth" and the best explanation is that, in the process of copying, a scribe accidentally wrote Michal's name instead of Merab's. For a similar view see, Robert P. Gordon, *I&II Samuel*, (Exeter: Paternoster Press, 1986), p. 301.

[19] J.P. Fokkelman, *Narrative Art and Poetry in the Books of Samuel: Throne and City*, Vol. III (Assen/Maastricht: Van Gorcum, 1990), p. 196.

[20] The author refers to her as *"Saul's daughter"* 3 times (vv. 16, 20, 23). The fourth occurrence is David's reference to *"your father,"* when speaking to Michal of Saul (v. 21).

[21] I do not count 1 Sam. 14:49, because this is not a proper narrative that involves Michal.

[22] Clines, *X, X Ben Y*, p. 272 writes, "Michal is not behaving as David's wife (contrast 1 Sam. xix) but as his opponent: she is acting like a true daughter of Saul."

complete surrender to the Lord is not very "kingly." This loss of control before the Lord and David's subjects is a shameful display by one who should always be in control. Just as outward appearance mattered to Saul,[23] so it also matters to this daughter of Saul.

The attentive reader is aware of the fact that to "despise" the Lord, or his anointed, puts Michal in the company of Eli (1 Sam. 2:30) and Goliath (1 Sam. 17:42). The parallels with Eli are, in fact, very strong—as all the key words of 1 Samuel 2:30 ("honor," "despise," "lightly esteem") are repeated in this passage.[24] Two other phrases also connect this story with 1 Samuel 2. First, the expression, "before the LORD," which not only occurs in 2 Samuel 6:5, 14 and 16, but also in verse 21 twice, should recall its frequent use in the story of Hannah/Samuel and Eli.[25] Second, David is said to be wearing a linen ephod (v. 14), which evokes the image of young Samuel in 1 Samuel 2:18. All of these similarities cannot be a coincidence, and so have a bearing on the rest of our interpretation of these verses.

Having given us a glimpse of this dark figure in the window, the camera now pans back to David and the celebration in vv. 17–19. After blessing the people (v. 18), the unsuspecting David returns "to bless his household" (v. 20). The impatient Michal, however, cannot wait to spew out her venom, and goes out to meet David full of sarcasm and scorn. There is no blessing on *her* tongue! Her words are intended to cut David down to size as they progress down the social ladder from king, to servants, to "base fellow."[26] She begins sarcastically by referring to the king's "honor," but ends by speaking of his nakedness and shame. She brazenly suggests that his act of worship was nothing more than a façade for lewdly exposing himself before women of lesser status ("maids of his servants"). While she is clearly scandalized by David's "non-king-like" behavior, do we perhaps hear in her threefold use of "uncover"[27] the jealousy of a rejected wife?

---

[23] Since we have not been able to focus on Saul in this volume I will briefly mention two examples of this attitude which occur in 1 Sam. 15. First, we are told that Saul built a monument for himself (v. 12). Second, he pleads for Samuel to honor him before the people even though the Lord has rejected him (v. 30).

[24] Robert Polzin, *David and the Deuteronomist: A Literary Study of the Deuteronomic History, Part Three: 2 Samuel* (Bloomington & Indianapolis: Indiana University Press, 1993), pp. 70-71, overlooks this point. Polzin makes Michal the hero of the passage, which is foreign to the purpose of the author. The equation of Michal with Eli and Saul, not to mention the similarity with Goliath, makes this obvious.

[25] See chap. 2, pp. 30-31, chap. 3, pp. 40-41, and esp. chap. 4, pp. 60-64.

[26] I owe the recognition of this downward spiral in Michal's speech to Fokkelman, *Throne and City*, p. 199.

[27] Michal begins in 2 Sam. 6:20, "How honorable was the king of Israel today, who has *uncovered* himself today..." and ends with "...causing to *uncover*, he *uncovers* himself as one of the worthless fellows" (my translation). The Hebrew obviously translates

Seeking to bless his family after a good day "at church," this can hardly be the welcome David is hoping for! Nonetheless, David is a man "prudent in speech" (1 Sam. 16:18) and can give as well as he gets. David mixes facts with a little venom of his own. His speech silences Michal forever (at least as far as the text is concerned) and, when it is over, so apparently is his marriage.

David's response is twofold. He begins by defending his worship of the Lord against Michal's crude charge. 2 Samuel 6:21 begins and ends with David's phrase, "before the LORD." He is outraged that his sincere worship has been compared with some sleazy burlesque show. In this he is right to be indignant, as the author frequently emphasizes throughout chapter 6 (vv. 5, 14, 16) the sincere nature of David's worship. To use a cliché, at the heart of the difference between David and Michal is a difference of the heart. David's devotion to the Lord is wholehearted. Clearly, Michal would never stoop to the indignity of David's type of worship. Thus she cannot "worship in spirit." The *teraphim* in her house also testify that she does not "worship in truth" (John 4:23–24). David also defends himself by pointing to his election by the Lord. He is God's appointed ruler over the "people of the LORD," which involves setting an example of true worship: "Therefore I will play music before the LORD" (2 Sam. 6:21). But David cannot resist twisting the knife a little, by reminding Michal that his election was at the expense of her father and "all his house" (in other words, "including you, Michal").

David's second response is a brilliant reversal of Michal's downward spiral of words (v. 22). He begins by speaking of his willingness to be "*lightly esteemed*," continues by saying he will be "*humble*" in his own eyes, and ends with a reference to the maidservants who will hold him in "*honor.*" Thus David's speech ends the way Michal's began—with the word "*honor*," while at the same time making a jibe about the maids Michal had mentioned.[28] Touché David! War of words won—but marriage lost.

While there is some spite in David's words, these words also function on another level. Michal's downward spiral of words versus David's upward spiral of words recalls the prayer of Hannah, who said of the Lord, "He brings low and lifts up" (1 Sam. 2:7). David's willingness to humble himself before the Lord versus Michal's proud unbending stature fleshes out the two types of people Hannah describes.[29] In fact, Michal's bitterness and jealousy

---

into clumsy English which explains why English translations do not use the word "uncover" 3 times. For an alternative view, which suggests that Michal is accusing David of acting feminine, see Susan M. Pigott, "Wives, Witches and Wise Women: Prophetic Heralds of Kingship in 1 and 2 Samuel," *Review & Expositor*, 99/2, 2002, p. 170, n. 69.

[28] These insights are once again thanks to Fokkelman, *Throne and City*, pp. 200-203.

[29] Note how the following verses from Hannah's prayer (1 Sam. 2:1–10) can be applied to the lives of Michal and David: "Talk no more so very proudly; Let no arrogance come from your mouth, For the LORD is the God of knowledge; And by Him

are a faint reminder of Hannah's rival, Peninnah. The repetition of the key words of 1 Sam. 2:30 also point in this direction. God said, "Those who *honor* Me, I will *honor*, and those who *despise* Me shall be *lightly esteemed*." Michal "*despises*" David and questions his "*honor*," but David says he will be "*lightly esteemed*"[30] in order that he may receive "*honor*."

Against this background, Michal's childlessness in 2 Samuel 6:23 is a clear judgment from the Lord.[31] Might it be suggested that as Gehazi receives the leprosy of Naaman (2 Kings 5:25–27), so the barrenness of Hannah is transferred to Michal?[32] In any case, it is poignant that Michal's barrenness is juxtaposed to the promise given to David in the next chapter. The Lord says, "I will set up your seed after you, *who will come from your body*, and I will establish his kingdom" (2 Sam. 7:12b). Furthermore, there is a specific reference to the Lord removing his mercy from Saul (2 Sam. 7:15). As Stansell states,

> On one level the passage is about a familial, even a private matter: the estrangement of husband and wife. On another level, particularly in light of its literary context, it is about a political matter: the break is between king and queen, between the House of David and the House of Saul, which will have no political future.[33]

---

actions are weighed" [Michal] (v.3); "The LORD makes poor [Michal] and makes rich [David]; He brings low [Michal] and lifts up [David]. He raises the poor from the dust And lifts the beggar from the ash heap, To set them among princes And make them inherit the throne of glory" [David] (vv. 7–8). "He will guard the feet of His saints [David], But the wicked shall be silent in darkness" [Michal] (v. 9ab). "He will give strength to His king, And exalt the horn of His anointed" [David] (v. 10de).

[30] David's use of "lightly esteem" in 2 Sam. 6:22 is a clever twist of meaning when contrasted with its use in 1 Sam. 2:30.

[31] It has been much debated whether Michal's childlessness is because of David's refusal to be with her again, or whether it is a judgment from the Lord. It may be that David never paid her another conjugal visit, but the parallels noted above, which follow a continual theme in the books of Samuel, indicate that Michal's barrenness is from the Lord. As Peter R. Ackroyd, in *The Second Book of Samuel*, CBC (Cambridge: Cambridge University Press, 1977), p. 71, states: "Michal is barren, a sign of divine displeasure….But the text leaves no doubt that [Michal's barrenness] is to be understood as a divine decision."

[32] Of course 2 Kings 5:27 explicitly states this connection, whereas 2 Sam. 6:23 makes no such claim. I suggest it as food for thought, and because of the similarities in language with 1 Sam. 1-2. It is interesting that R. A. Carlson, *David, the Chosen King: A Traditio-Historical Approach to the Second Book of Samuel*, (Stockholm: Almqvist & Wiksell 1964), pp. 93-94, makes a similar connection between Hannah's fertility and Michal's barrenness. He believes that Michal's barrenness is also "a punishment sent by Yahweh on account of her attitude to the Ark" (p. 93).

[33] Gary Stansell, *Honor and Shame in the David Narratives*, pp. 67-68.

Concluding Reflections: Love and Respect

Two questions arise that nag the reader of this story: "What if David had loved Michal?" and, "What if Michal had respected (honored) David?" Dr. Emerson Eggerichs writes, "scientific research confirms that love and respect are the foundation of a successful marriage."[34] By this he means that a woman's deepest need is to know that her husband loves her, and a man's deepest need is to be respected by his wife. Nearly two thousand years ago the apostle Paul penned these words, "Nevertheless let each one of you in particular so *love his own wife as himself,* and let *the wife see that she respects her husband*" (Eph. 5:33). As we have seen, while the narrative initially affirms Michal's love for David, not once are we told that David loved Michal. It is possible that this circumstance contributed to her love turning to bitterness and spite. When she lashes out at David and dishonors him (probably in front of his courtiers),[35] the door is slammed shut on their relationship.

In his book, Dr. Eggerichs speaks about the "Crazy Cycle."[36] When a woman feels unloved she often communicates to her husband in a way that he interprets as disrespectful. When a husband feels disrespected, he often communicates in a way that his wife interprets as unloving. And so the "Crazy Cycle" begins: no love, no respect, no respect, no love, and so on. The Bible revealed this thousands of years ago. David and Michal are examples of the "Crazy Cycle"; Paul's words are the balm that can heal the wounds.

As important as love and respect are, a home (i.e., a family), like a house, must be built on a proper foundation. We can grow weary in the daily struggle of showing love and respect. Only the Lord, who is the source of unlimited love and power, gives us the strength that we need to persevere, especially if one or both partners are not feeling loved or respected. Scripture provides a clear warning to believers not to be "unequally yoked" (2 Cor. 6:14). Michal and David are an example of the problems that develop in such a relationship. They were clearly mismatched spiritually, and this is the main reason why their problems were irresolvable.

In general, today's world does not have a problem with someone pursuing "spirituality" or speaking about "God," as long as no exact definition is required. Such vague beliefs are safe and non-threatening, but they lead to no substantial change in the lives of those who hold them. It is specifics

---

[34] Emerson Eggerichs, *Love & Respect* (Nashville: Integrity Publishers, 2004), p. 35. On a personal note, this is the best book on marriage that my wife and I have ever read.

[35] The fact that Michal rushes out to meet David, rather than wait for him to enter the private part of the palace, probably means that her disdain was proclaimed in the ears of his courtiers. There is one thing deemed worse by a man than being disrespected by his wife; that is when she shames him in front of others.

[36] Eggerichs, *Love & Respect*, p. 29.

that the world resists. When we specify that we mean the God of the Bible (Yahweh) or we use the name Jesus Christ, difficulties are encountered. Like Michal, many people are content with a vague god, or a god of their own choosing and on their own terms (their own *teraphim*). Scripture refers to such idolatry as "futile" or "empty." Samuel warned the people: "Do not turn aside from following the LORD, but serve the LORD with all your heart. And do not turn aside; for then you would go after *empty things* which cannot profit or deliver, for *they are nothing*" (1 Sam. 12:20b–21; see also Jer. 10:15).

Pursuing emptiness leads to an empty life. This is what happened to Michal; she ended up alone and barren (2 Sam. 6:23). David and Jonathan had their shortcomings, but they served a living God (1 Sam. 17:26). A personal God means a God involved in the world—a God who therefore can make a difference in our lives. A God who is real and who reveals himself means that a relationship is possible. A relationship with the God of the Bible results in fellowship, a sure remedy for loneliness and barrenness.

Fellowship with the living God also causes other relationships to be fruitful. "That which we have seen and heard we declare to you, *that you also may have fellowship with us*; and truly *our fellowship is with the Father and with His Son Jesus Christ*" (1 John 1:3). Fellowship with God gives life and wholeness to other relationships, because we begin to take on his characteristics. His grace makes us more gracious. His peace flows into our relationships, healing wounds, calming tempers, granting forgiveness, and restoring wholeness. His love teaches us how to love others genuinely, and becomes the cornerstone of all our relationships.

Following a vague concept of "a god" which suits our own personal taste, is the same as worshipping ourselves. Instead of the God who has made us in his image (Gen. 1:26), we make a god in our own image. Such a choice dooms us to a life of futility and emptiness as Samuel and Jeremiah declared millennia ago. If you pursue emptiness, don't be surprised when you find it! The divorce rate, broken families, ethnic hatred and violence, and wars to which we are witness, cry out that gods made in our image are no solution. Clinging to man-made gods turns the dream for world harmony into a nightmare. We need an authority whose power and wisdom are much greater than our own. We need a God with a name. We need a relationship with Yahweh, and with his Son Jesus Christ—the loving, personal God of the Bible.

Chapter 11

Abner: Strong Man in a Weak House (Saul's cousin)

And Abner was strengthening his hold on the house of Saul (2 Sam. 3:6)

Anybody Got a Light? (1 Sam. 14:50–51)

Throughout 1 and 2 Samuel Abner is pictured as a military man. He is what we would call a "lifer." The reader never learns whether Abner had a wife or children. The only scene that could even remotely be described as domestic is when Ish-bosheth accuses him of going into Saul's concubine, Rizpah (2 Sam. 3:6–11). This act, if committed by Abner, and the consequences of the dispute, are full of political overtones. Every mention of Abner concerns a battle, a scene at court, or some political action involving the kingdom. So perhaps we should not be surprised that his rank in Saul's army precedes even his name when he is introduced. 1 Samuel 14:50 states, "the name of the commander of [Saul's] army was Abner the son of Ner, Saul's uncle." Abner is first defined by his position, then by his name, and finally by his relationship to Saul.

Abner's name means, "my father is Ner,"[1] and on nine occasions he is called "the son of Ner."[2] The name Ner, however, means "lamp," and thus "Abner" means, "my father is a lamp."[3] As with some other characters we have encountered, no special attention is drawn to Abner's name by the author; however, this does not mean there is no significance to his name within the context of the story.[4] In my opinion, it is interesting that "ner" is found in the name "Ab*ner*," and also that he is called the "son of *Ner*" nine times! This seems excessive by any stretch, and suggests that the author has a deliberate reason for including it so many times. The word "lamp" is used on several occasions in the books of Samuel and Kings to refer to kingship (2 Sam.

---

[1] The first time Abner's name occurs in the Hebrew text (MT) it is spelled "Abiner." *Abi* = "my father."

[2] The passages are: 1 Sam. 14:50; 26:5, 14; 2 Sam. 2:8, 12; 3:23, 25, 28, 37.

[3] The original meaning of Abner's name may have contained a reference to God. "Father" is used of God in the Hebrew Scriptures (e.g., 2 Sam. 7:14; 1 Chron. 29:10), and "lamp" sometimes describes God's ways or his Word (Ps. 18:28; 119:105). Thus, "Abner" means "my father (God) is a lamp."

[4] Our study has revealed a remarkable consistency between a person's name and their character, whether the author draws purposeful attention to it or not. An ancient Israelite would certainly have been aware of the meaning of the names of the various characters and how closely their names parallel the personality traits mentioned in the story.

21:17; 1 Kings 11:36; 15:4; 2 Kings 8:19),[5] and several verses hint at the fact that Saul's family was desirous of the kingship from the beginning (1 Sam. 9:20–21; 10:14–16[6]). Abner is not only a powerful man, but, as we shall see, also a man who likes to wield power. Therefore, it is no accident that this man (whose name means "My father is a *lamp*"—think "king") is introduced as the king's right-hand-man, and later will fancy himself as a king-maker (2 Sam. 2:8; 3:12).[7] The story of Ab*ner* is intimately connected with the story of the "*ner*" (lamp/kingship) of Israel.

Before proceeding, one problem remains. Based on the biblical evidence available, confusion exists over whether Abner is Saul's cousin or uncle. 1 Samuel 14:50–51 indicates that Abner is Saul's cousin by stating that Abner is the son of Ner, and Ner is the son of Abiel. This makes Ner and Kish (Saul's father) brothers, and thus Saul and Abner are cousins. This agrees with 1 Samuel 9:1, which states that Abiel is the grandfather of Saul, and Kish is Abiel's son. 1 Chronicles 9:36 mentions a Kish and Ner in the ancestry of Saul who were brothers. The problem, however, is that 1 Chronicles 9:39 states that the Ner of verse 36 begot another Kish who was the father of Saul. 1 Chronicles 8:29–33 also indicates that Kish was the son of Ner. This would make Abner and Kish brothers, and thus Abner would be Saul's uncle. A firm solution is not yet available. While I remain open to the possibility that Abner is Saul's uncle, I am inclined to follow those commentators who see Abner as Saul's cousin,[8] as this seems to account for the majority of the evidence.

Uninformed (1 Sam. 17:55–58)

Abner's first appearance in the narrative is not a flattering one. He appears as the commander of a terrified army in the service of a condemned king. Saul has already been rejected by the Lord (1 Sam. 15:23) and received an evil spirit to trouble him (1 Sam. 16:14). In chapter 17, Saul's old problems

---

[5] Polzin, *Samuel and the Deuteronomist*, pp. 52-53, also points out the significance of this motif, though his discussion concerns Eli, not Abner.

[6] Note that it is possible that the "uncle" mentioned in these verses may be a reference to Abner.

[7]This is further suggested by the fact that the majority of these occurrences (6) are found in 2 Sam. chaps. 2–3 which concern Abner making Ish-bosheth king and then seeking to transfer the kingship to David.

[8] See for example, McCarter, *I Samuel*, p. 256. Also Gordon, *I&II Samuel*, p. 142, but see his n. 44 which provides a reference for the alternative view. Saul's age is another argument in favor of the cousin relationship. If Jonathan was between 40 and 50 when he died (see pp. 106-107, n. 11, above), then Saul had to be 56–70 years of age at least. If Abner were Saul's uncle, he would presumably be older than Saul by 5–20 years (although in unusual circumstances, an uncle can be younger than his nephew).

of indecisiveness and fear are plaguing him and the army of Israel, as they are bullied by a giant with a big mouth and impressive weaponry (vv. 11, 24). As David goes out to fight Goliath, Saul asks Abner, "whose son is this youth?" Abner replies, "As your soul lives, O king, I do not know" (v. 55).[9]

Abner's first words are thus words of ignorance. Such an introduction is uncomplimentary to any character, but particularly to one who is the commander of the army and should be "in the know." Even though Saul commands Abner to "inquire whose son this young man is," Abner apparently fails to do so, instead bringing David before Saul so that Saul can ask for himself (vv. 57–58). Though a brave soldier with a good reputation (cf. 1 Sam. 26:15), Abner cannot bring himself to face Goliath, nor can he inspire any of his men to do so. When a champion for the kingdom does arise (David), Abner is unaware of where he comes from, suggesting that he is also uninformed about the nature and origin of true kingship. Fokkelman observes, "In this passage Abner must function in his impotence as the general who has no notion of the greatness and destiny of David."[10] It appears that Mr. "my father is a lamp" is in the dark!

Unaware (1 Sam. 26:6–17)

Abner is briefly mentioned in 1 Sam. 20:25 where he is pictured sitting beside Saul. This harmonizes with his next mention in chapter 26, where he is found sleeping beside Saul (v. 7). Saul and his men are encamped on the

---

[9] The fact that Saul and Abner are unaware of David's parentage seems perplexing in the light of David's introduction to court in 16:18–23 where this information is explicitly given. There are about as many explanations for this phenomenon as there are Bible scholars! For example, McCarter, *I Samuel*, pp. 284-309, follows a typical trend by suggesting that the stories of David come from different contradictory accounts. For a summary of views up to 1973 and a different proposal, see John T. Willis, "The Function of Comprehensive Anticipatory Redactional Joints in I Samuel 16–18," *ZAW* 85, (1973), pp. 294-314. As more recent writers have pointed out, the author of 1 and 2 Samuel was far too erudite to overlook such a glaring contradiction. He clearly intended it for a purpose. Tsumura, *The First Book of Samuel*, p. 470, observes that Saul could not be expected to remember the family background of every courtier, and makes the helpful suggestion that, "Saul is asking about David's background—his family and hence his social status, that is, pedigree—so that he may ask his father to let him keep David permanently." Furthermore, if David is to marry the king's daughter and his family is to be exempted from taxes (the reward promised in 17:25), Saul's question is logical. Firth, *1&2 Samuel*, pp. 180-181, makes the suggestion that chapters 16–17 are presented in a non-chronological form. Though I remain unconvinced of any single suggestion, Bergen, *1, 2 Samuel*, pp. 198-199, is typical of those who head in a more constructive direction by trying to understand the author's purpose.

[10] Fokkelman, *Crossing Fates*, p. 191.

hill of Hachilah, once again in pursuit of David (v. 3). Encamped on a hill, surrounded by his army and commander, Saul seems as well protected as is humanly possible. Surely the presence of the "lamp man"[11] (v. 5) will shed light on any potential danger! Yet David and Abishai are able to steal into the camp and confiscate Saul's spear (the weapon frequently used against David), and his water jug. Saul is spared a fatal end when David's cool head prevails over his hot-headed companion (vv. 8–12). In a rare glimpse beyond the natural, the author informs us that, "a deep sleep from the LORD had fallen on them" (v. 12). God's intervention on David's behalf is a sure sign that Abner is associated with the wrong man.

Once a safe distance away, David does not address Saul, but the army—and Abner in particular. "And David called out to the people and to Abner the son of Ner, saying, 'Do you not answer, Abner?'" (v. 14). Once again "the son of Ner" is in the dark, both literally (it is night-time) and figuratively, as he responds, "Who are you, calling out to the king?" Abner's ignorance is highlighted by the fact that although he does not recognize the voice calling out, Saul does (v. 17). This is the second time that Abner has failed to recognize David. Abner's reference to "the king" is also of note. In the context it is quite understandable (a reference to Saul), but read at a deeper level it emphasizes that this "lamp man" is not very bright, as he continues in failing to recognize true royalty.

David's words heap shame upon Abner. To paraphrase, he asks rhetorically, "If you're such a great warrior, why can't you protect your king?" (v. 15). Ironically it is David, not Abner, who has protected the king on this night: "For one of the people came in to destroy your lord the king" (David is referring to Abishai). He proceeds to pronounce a word of judgment on both the army and Abner. "This thing you (singular) have done is not good. As the LORD lives, you (plural) deserve to die, because you (plural) have not guarded your master, the LORD's anointed" (v. 16). David's words turn out to be prophetic. For many of the army perish in Saul's final battle (31:1), while Abner meets a gruesome death at the hands of Joab and Abishai (2 Sam. 3:27, 30).

The King-maker (2 Sam. 2:8–9a)

Following the death of Saul, David is anointed king in Hebron over Judah (2 Sam. 2:1–3). This could have been an opportunity for the entire nation to unite under David's leadership, but instead we are informed that "Abner the son of Ner, commander of Saul's army, took Ishbosheth the son of

---

[11] "Son of…" is a frequent Hebrew idiom. For example, in 1 Sam. 20:31 Saul calls David a "son of death," that is, "a dead man." In a similar manner for purposes of illumination (pun intended), I am translating "son of Ner" as "lamp man."

Saul and brought him over to Mahanaim; and he made him king" (vv. 8–9a). Note the two ways Abner is identified in verse 8. First, Abner is called the "son of Ner"—as if we need reminding! This is the first of six uses of this appellative in 2 Samuel 2–3, its high concentration suggesting its connection with kingship. As "son of Ner" Abner acts as king-maker. Second, Abner is identified as "commander of Saul's army." It is his rank and the loyalty of his troops that give him the ability to make Ish-bosheth king.

Verses 8–9a are significant in several other respects. First, we are told that Abner "took" Ish-bosheth and made him king. The use of this verb suggests that Abner is, in fact, acting like a king himself by crowning Ish-bosheth king! Within the context of the books of Samuel, the verb "take" often signifies the action of a king. When Samuel warned the people about the behavior of the king (1 Sam. 8:10–17), he used this verb four times to foretell the king's oppressive dealings with the people (vv. 11, 13, 14, 16).[12] Furthermore, this verb is often used to describe sin. Most tellingly it is used to describe the sin of *King* David, who "took" Bathsheba (2 Sam. 11:4; 12:9). Abner's act of "taking" Ish-bosheth is a signal of the abusive use of power. He takes because he can. Notice the absence of any mention of God, prophets, or an anointing ceremony (in contrast to 2 Sam. 2:1–4). This is not a God-guided action, but the willful assertion of a man holding the reins of power.[13] The rest of chapters 2 and 3 will reveal the reins slipping through his hands like water.

Second, it is unusual that the writer states no initiative of Ish-bosheth in claiming kingship. Most people desiring royalty instigate a course of action, but all the verbs here describe Abner. He "takes" and "brings" Ish-bosheth over to Mahanaim (v. 8), and "makes him king" (v. 9a). We will note later that passivity is the defining characteristic of Ish-bosheth.[14] What is important here, however, is that the desire for a Saulide king over Israel belongs with Abner rather than with Ish-bosheth and Abner brings it about by the sheer force of his will. In fact, one could speculate that Abner had first tried to rule the kingdom himself. Since Ish-bosheth only ruled for two years (v. 10) and David ruled in Hebron seven and a half years (v. 11), there was a five and a half year gap before Ish-bosheth was made king.[15] Who else but Abner could have been in charge during this time? Perhaps Abner's attempt at ruling was unpopular because Ish-bosheth, as Saul's son, was seen as the legitimate heir. As a result Abner may have installed Ish-bosheth as king while still holding

---

[12] See chap. 5, p. 69, for a further discussion of the significance of this word.

[13] Brueggemann, *First and Second Samuel*, p. 221, writes, "it is Abner who 'made Ish-bosheth king' (v. 9). The kingship of the north is an inside job for which no popular support is reported."

[14] See chap. 12, pp. 153–154.

[15] See J.A. Soggin, "The Reign of Eshba'al, Son of Saul," *Old Testament and Oriental Studies* (Rome: Pontifical Biblical Institute, 1975), pp. 31–49.

on to the reins of power.[16] The fact that Abner continued to strengthen his position in the house of Saul (2 Sam. 3:6) makes this a viable theory, but with no definite word from the author we are left with only speculation.

The third significant aspect of verses 8–9a is the mention of where Abner chooses to establish this kingdom. Mahanaim means "two camps." The division between Judah and Israel, and its deadly consequences, will be the theme of 2 Samuel 2–4. The place name emphasizes this division of God's people.[17] Again the text invites us to look beyond the physical aspects of Abner's actions in order to discern the spiritual consequences. In his willful act of making Ish-bosheth king, without a prophet or a word from God for support, Abner has divided the nation.

Civil War Can Lead to an Upset Stomach (2 Sam. 2:12–32)

It is Abner's march to Gibeon that precipitates hostilities between north and south. Gibeon was not only a city of foreigners, with which Israel had made a treaty during the days of Joshua (Josh. 9:3–27); it was also a Levitical city (Josh. 21:17). Since Saul had previously shown hostility against both the priesthood (1 Sam. 22:6–19) and the Gibeonites (2 Sam. 21:1), perhaps David dispatched his men to prevent possible further bloodshed. Or perhaps enemy troops in Gibeon were just too close for comfort as far as David was concerned. The eventual conflict that erupts may be the result of a territorial dispute. Besides being in the territory of Benjamin (Josh. 18:25), Gibeon may have been close to Saul's family property. Saul was eventually buried in his father's grave in Zela (2 Sam. 21:14), which may have been near Gibeon.[18] Thus Abner may be seeking to claim an area he feels rightly be-

---

[16] Evans, *The Message of Samuel*, p. 175, states, "It may be that Abner waited for some time before making Ish-bosheth king, perhaps because…he had some thought of claiming the throne for himself." It is also possible that it took Abner 5 ½ years to consolidate Saulide rule over Israel. Having accomplished that he set Ish-bosheth up as his puppet king, while retaining the real power himself. Soggin, "The Reign of Eshba'al," pp. 34-40, and Willis, *First and Second Samuel*, p. 291, make the same observations.

[17] Mahanaim is mentioned in three significant stories in Scripture (Gen. 32; 2 Sam. 2; and 2 Sam. 17–19). In each of these stories division and bloodshed are the major concerns. All highlight how family division can lead to national consequences. In Gen. 32 Esau forgives Jacob, so there is no bloodshed. 2 Sam. 17–19 is the story of a son (Absalom) revolting against his father (David) and the bloodshed that ensues. Our current story uses the family language of "brother" to illuminate the significance of the division (2:26–27). This is another example of how a name (in this case a place name) can function to illustrate a particular idea.

[18] Tsumura, *The First Book of Samuel*, p. 263.

longs to Ish-bosheth's kingdom. In any event, as the following verses show, Abner is ready for a fight.

As the armies face each other on opposite sides of the pool at Gibeon, it is Abner who breaks the tension by suggesting a military contest (2 Sam. 2:13–14).[19] Twelve warriors from each side engage in the conflict, resulting in no survivors (vv. 15–16). The addition of twelve plus twelve on the field of contest leads to the subtraction of twenty-four in Israel and Judah which, in turn, leads to a multiplication of the day's death toll (380 in total—vv. 30–31), a result of the division in Israel—all of which amounts to a very bad mathematical equation! The number twelve reflects the number of the tribes of Israel and the resultant death of all the combatants shows that when brothers go to war there is no winner.

The draw results in a fierce battle that turns out badly for Abner's men (vv. 17, 31). In a flashback of the battle, the author's focus narrows to Abner's flight and the man pursuing him. This fleet-footed man is Asahel, a brother of Joab and a nephew of David (v. 18).[20] Although Abner could dispense with this less experienced soldier quite easily (as v. 23 will soon demonstrate), he shows common sense and self-control as he attempts to dissuade Asahel from his objective. Twice he confronts Asahel telling him to "turn aside" (vv. 21–22). Abner's first warning even suggests a valid alternative: "lay hold on one of the young men and take his armor for yourself " (v. 21). Unsuccessful, Abner tries a second time to discourage his pursuer by saying, "Why should I strike you to the ground? How then could I face your brother Joab?" (v. 22). Abner's warnings to Asahel could be considered noble, but they also contain a healthy dose of respect for Joab, a more formidable opponent that Abner does not wish to offend.

With all warnings ignored and the hot breath of the determined Asahel breathing down his back, Abner is forced to defend himself. A scene characterized by words of running and turning suddenly comes to a standstill with the forceful backward thrust of Abner's spear (v. 23). Asahel is not the only one stopped in his tracks; the army also comes to a halt at the gory scene of Abner's spear protruding from Asahel's back. He is not the last person in 2 Samuel who will experience a similar kind of death. Asahel will be followed in short order by Abner himself (3:27).[21] The fact that Abner uses the back end

---

[19] The Hebrew word used by Abner is "play," no doubt the euphemism of a military man who puts the suggested combat in sporting terms. A number of articles have been written on this subject. See for example, F.C. Fensham, "The Battle Between the Men of Joab and Abner as a Possible Ordeal By Battle," *VT* 20 (1970), pp. 356-357.

[20] An examination of Asahel's character can be found in chap. 21, pp. 308-312.

[21] A total of four men "get it in the belly" in 2 Samuel. The other two are Ish-bosheth (4:6) and Amasa (20:10). A.A. Anderson, *2 Samuel*, WBC (Dallas: Word Books, 1989),

of his spear is evidence of self defense and could possibly have been an attempt to injure without killing.[22] However, "the butt end of a spear was sometimes fitted with two prongs so it could be stuck in the ground."[23] If Abner's spear was constructed this way, it would obviously make the back end dangerous as well. Saul may have had such a spear (1 Sam. 26:7).

After a long day of fighting, Abner and his men are able to regroup and gain a tactical advantage by deploying on a hilltop (2 Sam. 2:25). Having lost eighteen men to every one of Joab's (360 to 20), Abner pleads for a cessation in fighting. Perhaps he also has no desire to come face to face with Joab in battle after killing Asahel. His plea includes an emotional appeal using the familial word "brothers." Abner's choice of words highlights one of the themes of these chapters: grasping for power can tear families and nations apart. So now he seeks a truce. A long day of fighting initiated by his words (v. 14) has turned sour. Like Asahel, Abner has no more stomach for fighting.

The story comes to a conclusion when Joab blows the trumpet and both armies return to their capitals (vv. 28–32), but how one interprets Joab's response (v. 27) is important in understanding the portrait of Abner. Most modern versions interpret Joab's words to mean that Abner has convinced Joab to discontinue the fight. This equates Abner's words here with his level-headed advice to Asahel. But this interpretation requires a change in the Hebrew text, or an unnatural reading of it. I prefer Fokkelman's suggestion which leaves the Hebrew unaltered. His translation reads, "If you had not spoken, then truly the soldiery would have left this morning already, each one from following his brother."[24] In other words, Joab says, "If you [Abner] had not proposed a tournament this morning, then as far as I am concerned there would have been no need for a fight."[25] Far from characterizing Abner as the voice of reason, this suggests that Abner is the cause of all the trouble.[26] A review of the chapter seems to agree with this interpretation. It was Abner's initiative that resulted in Ish-bosheth's kingship (v. 8), dividing Israel from Judah. It was Abner's march to Gibeon that prompted a similar response from

---

p. 45, points out that these four passages contain the only occurrence of this particular Hebrew word translated "abdomen."

[22] Bergen, *1, 2 Samuel*, p. 304.

[23] Vannoy, *1–2 Samuel*, Cornerstone Biblical Commentary (Carol Stream: Tyndale House Publishers, Inc.), p. 276, quoting Hoerth.

[24] Fokkelman, *Throne and City*, p. 59. For those interested in a technical discussion of the text and Fokkelman's reason for the above interpretation see n. 61 on p. 59 and Appendix I, p. 369 under 2:27cd. Alter, *The David Story*, p. 207, comes to a similar conclusion, stating that the Hebrew expression, "idiomatically refers to the morning of the day on which one is speaking."

[25] Ibid., p. 60.

[26] Vannoy, *1–2 Samuel*, p. 277, expresses a similar viewpoint: "Joab blamed the entire episode on Abner (2:27) but nevertheless accepted his proposal for a truce."

Joab and David (v. 12), and it was Abner's suggestion that initiated the combat that led to the day of fighting (v. 14). Abner is capable of exercising good judgment, as in the case of Asahel; but it must be admitted that this instance was for his own benefit as much as Asahel's—"How then could I face your brother Joab?" (v. 22). Overall, the author's portrait of Abner is of a man with a strong lust for power which more often than not clouds his judgment. As the end of this story attests (v. 29), the "lamp man" remains in the dark.

Sex and Politics (2 Sam. 3:6–11)

These verses relate a dispute between Abner and Ish-bosheth which leads to a parting of the ways as Abner threatens to turn the kingdom over to David. Insight into Abner's true motivation is found in the author's words, "and Abner was strengthening himself in the house of Saul" (3:6b—my translation). If the reader was under any illusion regarding Abner's act of installing Ish-bosheth as king, the cat is now out of the bag. Bergen's observations are pertinent here:

> Abner's motives for supporting the dynastic claims of this younger member of his clan may have been less than selfless. Perhaps Abner saw in Ish-Bosheth a person who could be manipulated and otherwise controlled, with the result that he himself would be the de facto ruler over Israel. The text's observation that Abner "had been strengthening his own position in the house of Saul" suggests that he was preparing to usurp his nephew's throne.[27]

The author's words in verse 6 are immediately followed by Ish-bosheth's accusation that Abner had laid with Rizpah, Saul's concubine (v. 7). Modern ears can fail to hear the significance of this accusation, but two other examples from Scripture illuminate the problem. In 2 Samuel 16:21–22, Ahithophel advises the usurper Absalom to "go in to" his father's concubines. Likewise, in 1 Kings 2:13–18, Adonijah requests that Abishag, King David's concubine, be given to him as a wife. Solomon's explosive response to Adonijah's request provides the key to understanding all three of these acts. When Bathsheba presents Adonijah's request to Solomon, he answers, "Now why do you ask Abishag the Shunammite for Adonijah? *Ask for him the kingdom also*" (1 Kings

---

[27] Bergen, *1, 2 Samuel*, p. 307. Andersen, *2 Samuel*, p. 55, thinks the Hebrew for "strengthening himself" should be translated as "kept faithful to," stating that Abner is portrayed "as a positive hero." But, as McCarter, *II Samuel*, p. 112, points out, this translation does not reflect the meaning in this context. It also does not reflect the portrait of Abner that we have noted.

2:22). The point is that the one who has the king's wives (or concubines) must be the king! Nathan's words to David confirm this when he states, "I gave you your master's house and *your master's wives* into your keeping" (2 Sam. 12:8a). Ish-bosheth is accusing Abner of more than sexual misconduct; he is accusing him of taking the kingdom.

The writer never states whether Ish-bosheth's accusation is accurate, but it can hardly be otherwise. First, it should be noted that Abner never denies it. He simply responds indignantly that Ish-bosheth would dare question his loyalty to the house of Saul (2 Sam. 3:8). Abner's outburst of anger and lack of denial sound like the guilty boy who got caught with his hand in the cookie jar! Second, Ish-bosheth was surely aware that this accusation would send Abner into a tirade. To falsely accuse the man who had put him on the throne would be utter stupidity, not to mention political suicide. Third, the author's words demonstrate that Abner was acting like a king (2 Sam. 2:8–9a), and had his eyes set on controlling the kingdom (3:6). There can be little doubt that Abner did indeed "go in to" Rizpah.

The intriguing question is, "What prompted this act of defiance?" It is possible that Abner was maneuvering to gain sole control of the throne, and thought the time was now ripe for a coup. Certainly Ish-bosheth must have considered this, or else he would never have dared to confront Abner. The taking of Rizpah was a sure sign to Ish-bosheth that his days were numbered, unless he attempted to do something about it. However, a consideration of other factors presented in the text suggests another tantalizing possibility. 2 Samuel 3:1 states, "Now there was a long war between the house of Saul and the house of David. *But David grew stronger and stronger, and the house of Saul grew weaker and weaker.*" Certainly Abner was too politically astute not to realize the inevitable collapse of the Saulide dynasty.[28] The future clearly lay with David. But how could he keep the loyalty of Israel and gain a position in David's cabinet without looking like a traitor? My suggestion is that Abner used Rizpah as a means to justify his treasonous action. Knowing that in order to retain any semblance of honor the weak Ish-bosheth would be forced to confront him, Abner lay with Rizpah. When confronted, Abner could feign offence and have an excuse to break with Ish-bosheth.[29]

This supposition gains strength by Abner's immediate retort of handing the kingdom over to David (v. 8). It seems a knee-jerk reaction to say, "How dare you accuse me of disloyalty. That does it, I'm delivering the king-

---

[28] Youngblood, *1, 2 Samuel*, p. 832, states, "Ruthless and ambitious, Abner is a canny politician who sees the handwriting on the wall."

[29] Gordon, *I&II Samuel*, p. 216, makes a similar observation. He writes, "Sudden as the conversion of Abner to David's cause may seem, he must have realized for some time that David's progress was irresistible. In that case, the squabble with Ish-bosheth over Saul's concubine was merely the pretext for breaking with this feckless monarch." Wiersbe, *2 Samuel*, pp. 310-311, makes the same suggestion.

dom to David!"[30] Along this line, Walter Brueggemann's words are enlightening:

> We should not misunderstand Abner's move. It was not simply a sexual act. It was a defiant public, political challenge that could not be ignored. *Was it deliberately provocative on Abner's part, so that Abner could justifiably desert the house of Saul?* We do not know.[31] (emphasis mine)

I believe there are enough clues in the text to answer Brueggemann's question, "Yes." If this supposition is correct, Abner would not be the first or last person to use sex for selfish and/or political gain. In fact, this lethal combination is a theme of the books of Samuel (1 Sam. 18:17–30, Saul's attempts to use his daughters to bring harm to David; 2 Sam. 11–12, David and Bathsheba; 2 Sam. 13, Amnon and Tamar; and 2 Sam. 16:21–22, Absalom goes in to David's concubines).

Whether Abner was seeking to take the throne, or seeking an excuse to break with Ish-bosheth so he could hand the northern kingdom over to David, his words in 2 Samuel 3:8 are duplicitous and ironic. "Am I a dog's head that belongs to Judah? Today I show loyalty to the house of Saul your father, to his brothers, and to his friends, and have not delivered you into the hand of David." Abner's question uses clever wordplay. The Hebrew word for "dog" is *keleb*, the same consonants found in the name "Caleb."[32] David was anointed King of Judah in Hebron, the territory given to Caleb (cf. Josh. 15:13). If we interpret the pun we could translate Abner's words as, "Am I the head of Caleb that belongs to Judah?" In other words, "Am I the King of Judah?" The word *keleb* is a very derogatory term and adds spice to Abner's indignant reply.[33] The real irony, however, lies in his use of "loyalty" (*hesed*). Abner is, in fact, being disloyal, but all the while is proclaiming his fidelity!

---

[30] Similarly, Fokkelman, *Throne and City*, p. 72, states, "His rage is more severe than the business in question itself; the decision with its enormous consequences, announced in his long speech, is out of all proportion to the Rizpah affair." Ackroyd, *The Second Book of Samuel*, p. 42, makes a similar statement but fails to follow it through to its logical conclusion. He writes, "Abner's declaration here seems somewhat strange. That he should threaten Ish-bosheth with the risks which would attend his withdrawal of support is natural enough; but one would hardly expect a declaration not only of the total reversal of his policy, but also of his conviction of God's purpose to establish David as king."

[31] Brueggemann, *First and Second Samuel*, p. 226.

[32] The English transliteration sometimes uses a "k" instead of a "c."

[33] The "dog" motif is a favorite theme of the author of 1 and 2 Samuel. The passages are: 1 Sam. 17:43; 24:14; 25:3 (possibly); 2 Sam. 3:8; 9:8; and 16:9.

As he continues his invective, Abner gives away more than perhaps he intends. 2 Samuel 3:9–10 are particularly eye-opening from a reader's standpoint. When Abner swears with an oath to transfer the kingdom to David, he slips up by adding, "as the LORD has sworn to him."[34] These words betray Abner's knowledge that the kingdom rightfully belongs to David and he has known it all along! How could he not know it? Jonathan knew it (1 Sam. 23:17), Saul knew it (1 Sam. 24:20), and based on Abner's words in verse 18, apparently all Israel knew it as well. These statements clearly show Abner to be a man who has been at crossed-purposes with the Lord, but now that it works to his advantage, he can quote the Lord's promises as well as any prophet. Abner's hypocrisy is one more reason to believe that the situation with Rizpah was a setup. Abner was determined to hold on to the reins of power until it became clear that the situation was hopeless. Now he resorts to "plan B." He is a political opportunist who will use sex, religion, and whatever else it takes to maintain his grip on power. Abner is neither loyal to the Lord or to the house of Saul; he is only loyal to himself.[35]

Abner Goes Belly Up (2 Sam. 3:17–39)

In 2 Samuel 3:12, Abner flexes some political muscle by boasting to David, "Whose is the land?...Make your covenant with me, and indeed my hand shall be with you to bring all Israel to you." To prove he can make good on his promise, he fulfills David's request that Michal be returned to him, while snarling at her grief-stricken husband to, "Go, return!" (v. 16). Abner's address to the elders of Israel indicates that he may have been responsible for preventing them from approving David's kingship earlier.[36] This further confirms our interpretation above that he divided the kingdom by making Ish-bosheth king over Israel. In these verses Abner becomes patriot and prophet, beguiling even some Bible commentators who mistake his politically expedient language for altruism.[37]

---

[34] I say "slips up" not because this would be news to Ish-bosheth, but because it is news to the reader, confirming the duplicity of Abner.

[35] Similarly, Wiersbe, *2 Samuel*, p. 308 writes, "Most of what Abner did during those seven and a half years wasn't for the glory of God or the strengthening of Israel, but for his own self-interest. He was taking care of number one."

[36] Note that Abner says to the elders in v. 17, "In time past you were seeking for David to be king over you." Regarding this statement, Fokkelman, *Throne and City*, p. 88, observes, "If that had been absolutely untrue, Abner would have provoked protest and irritation in his audience."

[37] See Andersen's assessment in n. 27 above, and Evans, *The Message of Samuel*, pp., 178-179. Evans, p. 174, writes, "Abner's role...is presented in Samuel in a very positive light." J. Robert Vannoy, *1–2 Samuel*, p. 281 is more accurate when he writes,

Abner saves his best speech for these elders as he says, "For the LORD has spoken of David, saying, 'By the hand of My servant David, I will save My people Israel from the hand of the Philistines and the hand of all their enemies'" (v. 18). Although Polzin's perspective is different from mine, he rightly comments, "Nothing we have learned about Abner so far prepares us to understand why the narrator here uses him as the mouthpiece of the LORD."[38] Abner's statement simply highlights his hypocrisy. Abner is an ancestor of all those who use religion and religious language to accomplish their worldly agenda. In this sense he is a spiritual kinsman to Eli, who used the ministry for his own gain. The difference is that Abner is much more manipulative than Eli. If Abner was truly concerned about prophecy and the Lord's will, he would have acted long before this to bring the kingdom to David, rather than fighting against him. Furthermore, Abner's words to the elders are introduced by the phrase, "And the word of Abner came to the elders of Israel, saying ..." (v. 17a—my translation). Fokkelman concludes that, "Abner imagines that he is equal to God in power,"[39] for this type of construction is usually reserved for the Lord.

Self-seeking or not, Abner's words ring true and have a profound effect on all of Israel. We know from previous passages that David was anointed to lead Israel (1 Sam. 16:12–13), that it was the king's responsibility to save Israel from the Philistines (1 Sam. 9:16), and that David had great success against them (1 Sam. 17:50; 18:27; 19:8). Thus Abner's words (2 Sam. 3:18) may reflect an actual prophecy previously omitted by the author. Abner's reference to such a prophecy certainly suggests that the elders are acquainted with it.

After rallying the support of Benjamin, Saul's own tribe, Abner sets off with a delegation to seal the deal (v. 19). Once again Abner regards himself as a king-maker, as he says, "*I* will arise and *I* will go, and *I* will gather all Israel to my lord the king, that they may make a covenant with *you*, and that *you* may reign over all that *your* heart desires" (my translation—v. 21). Note the triple "*I*" with Abner as subject, balanced by the triple "*you*" referring to David. Abner is proclaiming that he is the one who will make David's dreams of kingship come true.[40] Furthermore, it is probably not accidental that the

---

"...the reader is given further insight into the ambition and duplicity of Abner, the kingmaker in the north."

[38] Polzin, *David and the Deuteronomist*, p. 40. Abner is more of a "full-fledged" character than Polzin's comments allow for.

[39] Fokkelman, *Throne and City*, p. 87.

[40] Abner's words in v. 12 represent a similar boast, again using the comparative language of "*me/you*." "'Whose is the land?' [implied answer—"*mine*"] saying also, 'Make *your* covenant with *me*, and indeed *my* hand shall be with *you* to bring all Israel to *you*.' Note how the "*me*" and "*my*," along with the implied "*mine*," are balanced by three uses of "*you*." This means that Abner's first and last words to David in the chapter

appellative "son of Ner" is found on people's lips four times in this section (v. 23, a soldier; v. 25, Joab; v. 28, David; v. 37, the narrator), reminding us that the "lamp man" is at work once again, attempting to put his own stamp on the kingship of Israel.

The meeting between Abner and David is indeed a positive one. The author not only paints a picture of goodwill between them, but also mentions three times that Abner leaves in *"peace"* (vv. 21, 22, 23). This threefold mention of *"peace"* (*shālôm*) has at least a threefold effect on the narrative. First, it emphasizes David's sincerity and goodwill in the covenant he has just made. Second, it temporarily lulls the reader into thinking a happy reunion is on the horizon. Third, it highlights the heinous nature of the deed soon to be perpetrated by Joab and Abishai (v. 30).

Joab is conspicuously absent during the negotiation between David and Abner—does David do this intentionally? Upon returning from a raid and receiving the news, Joab is quick to (re)act. First, he rebukes the king (not the only time he will do this), and second, he sends for Abner without the king's knowledge (vv. 23–26). For some reason, Abner, the astute politician, has reverted to being the ignorant, unaware Abner to whom we were first introduced. Abner's ignorance of Joab's true intentions may be due to the fact that he had left David "in peace," and also because he was in the confines of Hebron, a city of refuge (Josh. 21:13). Be that as it may, the cunning Joab gets the oblivious Abner alone in the gate, and gives him a taste of the same medicine Asahel had ingested. Rather than a spear, it's a sword—but like Asahel, Abner experiences severe abdominal discomfort. As Abner's blood spills by the gates of Hebron and Joab stands over him, we have the impression that we are looking at two men who have not learned that "the LORD does not save with sword and spear" (1 Sam. 17:47). If Abner had not spoken up on that fateful day and called for a contest (2 Sam. 2:14) resulting in a bloody battle (2:17), perhaps both he and Asahel would have survived the terrible fate of the "sword and spear."

David is, of course, outraged and utters a blistering curse (literally and figuratively) against Joab and "all his father's house" (3:29).[41] He also arranges a state funeral to honor Abner, forcing Joab to march in the procession clothed in mourning attire (v. 31)—a fitting military funeral for a lifelong soldier. David then composes a lament for Abner, as he had for Saul and Jonathan. The lament is intended to honor Abner and to convince the public that David had no part in his death; but it is not as elaborate (perhaps the author

---

are similar, forming an inclusio emphasizing his king-making ability. For an alternative interpretation of Abner's words see Firth, *1&2 Samuel*, p. 348.

[41] We will return to this passage and examine Joab's part in this crime later (see chap. 20, pp. 261-269).

only quotes it partially?) or complimentary as the one for Saul and Jonathan. It reads:

> Should Abner die as a fool dies?
> Your hands were not bound
> Nor your feet put into fetters;
> As a man falls before wicked men,
> so you fell (2 Sam. 3:33b–34).

It is important to note that David's honoring of Abner no more absolves Abner of his shortcomings than it does Saul. David is simply recognizing the wickedness of the deed, demonstrating his innocence in the affair (a political necessity), and trying to preserve the fragile unity that has just been forged. In the wider context of the books of Samuel, the lament is not that complimentary. Abner's death is compared to the death of a *nābāl* (fool), which recalls the story of Nabal in 1 Samuel 25.[42] This suggests that the author invites us to make a comparison between the two characters. Furthermore, no great quality of Abner is extolled—rather, there is only a pathetic sadness over such a senseless way to die. It seems that in this foolish death, which speaks of the quality of ignorance, the character of Abner comes full circle. David's best words for Abner are spoken in a less public setting, when he tells his court ("servants"), "Do you not know that a prince and a great man has fallen this day in Israel?" (3:38).

Conclusion: Lights Out

There is a similarity between the tragic sadness over the death of Abner and the death of Saul. Though willful and worldly, both men elicit a sense of sympathy from the reader. Perhaps it is sadness over an opportunity lost: grief over what might have been. As one reviews the passages that mention Abner, it is telling that the only time the words of the Lord are found on his lips is near the end when it was politically expedient. Abner, like some, had no real use for the Lord; but he could use the Lord when it furthered his cause. A military man from first to last, he lived by the sword and died by the sword (cf. Matt. 26:52). In his desire for power and attempts to attain it through worldly methods, he missed the All-Powerful One, who could have set him on a more productive path. Not having a true knowledge of the Lord, Abner's story begins and ends in ignorance. Throughout, the "son of Ner" always seems to be in the dark, until at last in the corner of the gate in Hebron his lamp is finally extinguished by the avenger's sword (Prov. 13:9).

---

[42] For further comments on Nabal see chap. 18.

Chapter 12

Ish-bosheth: The Puppet King (Saul's son)

And he could not answer Abner another word, because he feared him (2 Sam. 3:11)

Ish-Who?

Ishvi, Ishbaal, Eshbaal and Ish-bosheth are all variant names of Saul's son,[1] who briefly ruled over Israel after the death of his father. Why so many different names? First, it is not unusual for a person in the Bible to have more than one name (Jacob/Israel, Solomon/Jedidiah, etc.). Second, it appears that all of these names are related. The name Ishbaal means "man of Baal"; and "Baal" not only referred to the Canaanite fertility god, but also meant "lord" or "master." In fact, it was used by Israelites to describe Yahweh, as Hosea 2:16 illustrates. It is most likely that this is its meaning in the name "Ishbaal"—"man of the lord/master." Though it is disputed, Ishvi may derive from an original "Ishyo" which means "man of Yahweh."[2] If so, the relationship between the names Ishbaal and Ishvi is obvious. Eshbaal is the name used in 1 Chronicles 8:33 and 9:39, and means "Baal exists" or, "the lord exists." This carries a slightly different meaning, but in Hebrew the names Ishbaal and Eshbaal have the same consonants and thus are indistinguishable.[3]

This brings us to the much-disputed name used throughout 2 Samuel, Ish-bosheth. The Hebrew word *bosheth* comes from a word which means "shame." Thus one meaning of Ish-bosheth is "man of shame." The explanation of many scholars is that since the word "baal" was associated with the Canaanite god by that name, it became a practice in later Israel to substitute "*bosheth*" (shame), since worshipping Baal was a shameful act.[4] Evidence for this is suggested by such passages as Hosea 9:10, Jeremiah 3:24 and 11:13.

This well entrenched scholarly dogma was challenged by M. Tsevat, who showed that a similar root in ancient Babylonian (Akkadian) meant "dignity."[5] This seemed to be refuted by McCarter,[6] but recent evidence present-

---

[1] There is some dispute as to whether Ishvi refers to Ish-bosheth or his brother Abinadab. See McCarter, *1 Samuel*, p. 254.

[2] Ibid. "*Yô*" is the shortened form of Yahweh, seen in other names like "*Yônātān*" (Jonathan). See the comment by Ackroyd, *The Second Book of Samuel*, pp. 32-33.

[3] Vowels were added to the Hebrew text later. Ancient Hebrew, like modern, is written only in consonants.

[4] This is the common explanation in almost every commentary. See for example, Hertzberg, *I&II Samuel*, p. 249.

[5] Matitiahu Tsevat, "Ishbosheth and Congeners: The Names and Their Study," *HUCA* 46, 1975, pp. 71-87. (Hereafter cited as Tsevat, "Ishbosheth").

ed by Gordon Hamilton suggests that Tsevat may have been right.[7] To explain his findings in brief, Hamilton produces evidence of fifteen Canaanite names with this same ending and suggests that it means "protective spirit" (i.e., the deity). If this is correct, Ish-bosheth, like Ishbaal, would be a reference to deity, probably Yahweh. Ish-bosheth would mean "man of (the) protective spirit."[8] This would also mean that Ish-bosheth was a legitimate name of Saul's son, and was not made up by the author of 2 Samuel who replaced "baal" with "*bosheth*." It would also mean that the names Ishvi, Ishbaal and Ish-bosheth mean essentially the same thing[9] and could explain why one man had so many names!

The current state of knowledge and scholarly division over the meaning of *bosheth* in names like Ish-bosheth, makes it impossible to be dogmatic. If indeed, Ish-bosheth means "man of (the) protective spirit," it could still be true that the author of Samuel sees a double meaning in it ("man of shame").[10] For example, when Saul confronts Jonathan about his friendship with David, he uses the word *bosheth* twice—"you have chosen the son of Jesse to *your own shame* and to the *shame* of your mother's nakedness" (1 Sam. 20:30). As readers, we know that Saul's accusation is false; Jonathan is not a "man of shame." But perhaps his brother, Ish-bosheth, is! As we shall see, there is certainly enough evidence in the story of Ish-bosheth to support this meaning.[11] Conversely, if "man of (the) protective spirit" is a correct rendering, 2 Samuel 4 may show an ironic twist on the meaning of this name.

The Making of a King (2 Sam. 2:8–10)

Except for a possible reference in 1 Sam. 14:49, the reader's first introduction to Ish-bosheth is in 2 Sam. 2:8–10. To this point he has been irrelevant to the story; and, even now, every depiction of him will seem to highlight his insignificance. Ish-bosheth is not king by his own power (or by God's); he is king because Abner "took" him, "brought him over" to Mahanaim and "made him king." In this inauspicious introduction, Ish-bosheth says nothing and does nothing. He is a puppet in the hands of the man who

---

[6] McCarter, *II Samuel*, pp. 85-87.

[7] Gordon J. Hamilton, "New Evidence for the Authenticity of *bšt* in Hebrew Personal Names and for Its Use as a Divine Epithet in Biblical Texts," *CBQ* 60, 1998, pp. 228-250. (Hereafter cited as Hamilton, "New Evidence").

[8] Ibid., p. 237.

[9] "Man of God," whether God be called "Yahweh," "Baal," or "Bosheth."

[10] Hamilton, *New Evidence*, p. 244, suggests this may be the case with Hos. 9:10.

[11] The change of Gideon's alternative name Jerubbaal to Jerubbesheth (2 Sam. 11:21) may be an explicit example of the writer substituting "bosheth" for "baal." However, if the author/editor(s) of the books of Samuel was so against the use of "baal" in a name, then it is puzzling why the same name is not altered in 1 Sam. 12:11.

holds the reins of power. A king who does what he's told by his subordinate does not command much respect.

According to verse 9, Ish-bosheth's kingdom includes all of Transjordan and Northern Israel. Since the Philistines controlled the territory as far as Beth-Shan after Saul's defeat (1 Sam. 31:7, 10), it is likely that Abner spent the next five years reconsolidating the kingdom before making Ish-bosheth king.[12]

Verse 10 uses the regnal formula that will become standard for describing the reigns of the kings of Israel and Judah in the Books of Kings (e.g., 1 Kings 11:42). Ish-bosheth was a mature man of forty[13] when he was made king, but the length of his reign is another sign of his ineffectiveness, lasting only two years. Fokkelman makes the point that Ish-bosheth has much territory but little time, while David has little territory but much time.[14]

This short introduction of Ish-bosheth illustrates the problem we face when we attempt to do something that God has not appointed us to do. Often we can feel pressured by friends or church leaders to do things we are not called to do or capable of doing. Permit a little speculation and put yourself in Ish-bosheth's shoes. Who would not want to be king? As Saul's son you have a legitimate claim to the throne. It is your duty; you cannot let the people down. Besides, Uncle Abner is in favor of the move and will be there to help. Whatever Ish-bosheth's real thoughts and motives, failure looms on the horizon. If there is no anointing, then there is no power; and what is a king without power? Perhaps no one is pressuring us to be a "king," but whatever the situation might be, without the call and blessing of God it is doomed to failure—no matter how powerful or influential our friends may be, and no matter how appealing the opportunity may seem.

The Impotent King (2 Sam. 3:6–11, 15)

The only recorded words which Ish-bosheth speaks are his accusation of Abner: "Why have you gone in to my father's concubine?" (2 Sam. 3:7). There are two curious details about this question which bear exploration.[15] First, Ish-bosheth's question is introduced in Hebrew with the vague, "And he said."[16] There is no previous mention of him in the text; his name is

---

[12] See chap. 11, pp. 139-141 (esp. n. 16, p. 141).

[13] It is possible that forty is a round number (give or take a few years), but I cannot agree with Andersen, *2 Samuel*, pp. 34-35, that Ish-bosheth may have been a young boy, "40 years" being a scribal error (there is no evidence of such).

[14] Fokkelman, *Throne and City*, p. 38.

[15] The following observations are based on Fokkelman, *Throne and City*, pp. 47, 63, 70-71.

[16] Many modern English versions (e.g., NKJV) supply the name "Ishbosheth" but it is not in the original.

simply ignored. Only the statement of verse 8, "Then Abner became very angry at the words of Ish-bosheth," informs us of the identity of the inquisitor in verse 7. To say the least, it is unusual in biblical narrative, as in any narrative, for the speaker not to be specified.[17] But this seems to be a characteristic practice of the author concerning Ish-bosheth. For example, in 2 Sam. 2:12–32, the men with Abner are initially identified as "the servants of Ish-bosheth" (vv. 12, 15), just as the men with Joab are identified as "the servants of David" (vv. 13, 15). But throughout the rest of the chapter, while the men of Judah continue to be called "the servants of David" (vv. 17, 30, 31), the men with Abner are called "men of Israel" (v. 17), "children of Benjamin" (v. 25), or "Abner's men" (vv. 29, 31), but never "the servants of Ish-bosheth." The frequent omission of Ish-bosheth's name is a silent commentary on his insignificance.

Second, both the author and Ish-bosheth himself refer to Rizpah as "*Saul's* concubine." This clearly suggests that Ish-bosheth has not appropriated Rizpah into his harem, as would be customary of a new king (cf. 2 Sam. 12:8; 16:21–22). The sexual connotations of Ish-bosheth's accusation of Abner actually turn on himself, suggesting his impotency! This is confirmed by noting that the section preceding this is a list of David's wives and children (3:2–5), a demonstration of his potency in contrast to Ish-bosheth's. Indeed, David is growing stronger and stronger, while the house of Saul is growing weaker and weaker (3:1). Ish-bosheth—whose name is often overlooked—is impotent both sexually and politically. The idea of "man of shame" comes to mind here. His weakness is further emphasized by the fact that he cannot answer one word (v. 11) in response to Abner's threatening barrage of words (vv. 8–10). This feeble, helpless man can only respond by cowering in fear, a characteristic he may have inherited from his father (cf. 1 Sam. 15:24; 17:11).

The other mention of Ish-bosheth in this chapter concerns how he returned Michal to David (vv. 14–15). He almost sounds like a king when the author says, "Ish-bosheth sent and took her" (v. 15a). "Sending" and "taking" suggests dynamic action; but they can be used to describe an abusive use of power (cf. 2 Sam. 11:4). If Ish-bosheth is acting like a tyrant, it is only because of the duress he is under. Abner's lackey dare not refuse David and the deal Abner has brokered with him, even if it leads to his own political demise![18]

---

[17] McCarter, *II Samuel*, p. 106, says that some copies of the LXX wrongly read "Mephibosheth, son of Saul" and that this reading was shared by the MT. Therefore, the MT dropped out the name since it was in error. However, there is no evidence that the MT ever read "Ish-bosheth" here, and if a copyist had accidentally written "Mephibosheth" why delete the entire name rather than simply make the correction?

[18] Ackroyd's comment, *The Book of Second Samuel*, p. 44, is astute regarding Ish-bosheth in this circumstance: "depicted as too weak to resist what can only be a move to supplant him."

Ish-bosheth's story is an example of the perils of a puppet. If God has called us to do something, then we should conduct ourselves according to the authority allotted to us by that call. If, however, we surrender our integrity, submit to the authority of Man, and commit to a course of action that God has not sanctioned, we will find ourselves in Ish-bosheth's position. A puppet often lives and acts within the realm of fear. They allow themselves to be restricted by the constraints of another and cannot be the authentic people that God wants them to be. As a result, they create a legacy of shame for themselves.

The King is Dead (2 Sam. 4:1–12)

Things go from bad to worse for Ish-bosheth. Upon hearing of Abner's death we are told "his hands dropped" (4:1—"he lost heart"—NKJV). A literal translation is important, as we shall see shortly. But first, it should be noted that Ish-bosheth's name has, once again, been suppressed. In 4:1–2 he is only called "Saul's son." Abner is dead and all of Israel is "troubled." So what is a king to do? Ish-bosheth decides that desperate times call for desperate measures: he takes a nap (v. 5)! The picture of him lying on his bed, vulnerable and inactive, speaks volumes about his inability to lead without the guidance and forceful presence of Abner. It could be argued that in the hot Middle East taking an afternoon siesta is a perfectly natural thing to do. But the author purposely juxtaposes Ish-bosheth's hearing of bad news with his lying down.[19] We read of no action taken during this state of emergency. He is not the type to act; he will wait for trouble to come to him, and so it will (vv. 6–7). Given the last scene in which Ish-bosheth appeared, which emphasized his impotence, it is sadly ironic that he finds solace from the bad news in his bed—alone! When I was a young boy and became afraid, I would often hide under the covers. When trouble rears its ugly head, Ish-bosheth seeks the sanctuary of his bedroom, but it will not prove to be a safe haven. Once again, his fear and indecisiveness are reminiscent of his father. No wonder that we are reminded twice that he is "Saul's son."

While Ish-bosheth is lying on his bed—the last thing he will ever do—two of his army officers sneak in and murder him (vv. 6–7). It is this scene that provides the irony for the other possible meaning of his name. Recalling that his name may mean, "man of (the) protective spirit," it is interesting that he dies in such a vulnerable fashion. Apparently there is no "protective spirit" watching over Ish-bosheth during his afternoon siesta.

Ish-bosheth is the third man in as many chapters to be stabbed in the abdomen.[20] The deed is perpetrated by his own officers and also by men of

---

[19] Eli was also preoccupied with lying down (1 Sam. 3:2–9).
[20] Asahel (2 Sam. 2:23) and Abner (2 Sam. 3:27) are the other two.

his own tribe, the tribe of Benjamin (v. 2). Those who might be expected to be most loyal to him are the very ones that turn against him.[21] As noted previously, only four men in Scripture are stabbed in the stomach; and all four of these occurrences are in 2 Samuel. Polzin points out that all four stories share the common word "brother(s)."[22] The first two murders are between members of the house of Saul and the house of David (Abner kills Asahel; then Joab and Abishai kill Abner). The last two murders occur both *within* the house of Saul (Ish-bosheth by fellow Benjamites) and *within* the house of David (Joab kills his cousin Amasa, 2 Sam. 20:10).[23] The presence of the familial term "brother(s)" demonstrates the heinous nature of these deeds, as it emphasizes the murder of one's family member and/or one's fellow Israelite (a national brother). As noted in the Introduction, 1 and 2 Samuel continually emphasize that the pursuit of power together with the absence of godly principles lead to the destruction of families and nations.[24]

Ish-bosheth is dead; but his story continues for a few more verses as the gruesome picture of his severed head leads the way to David. The brothers Baanah and Rechab are hopeful of glory and a reward as they present their horrid trophy before David (v.8). If they only knew what we as readers already know—David's only reward for criminals who lift their hand against Saul and his family is a sure, swift execution (2 Sam. 1:14–16). David's indignant response to the brothers includes his designation of Ish-bosheth as a "righteous person" (v. 11). The modern reader should not confuse this with a moral pronouncement on Ish-bosheth's behavior. David's words apply to the legal sphere and mean "the one who is in the right" versus one who has done wrong.[25]

The execution of the two men involves more body parts being severed, as the hands that committed the deed and the feet that secretly crept into Ish-bosheth's bedroom are cut off (v. 12). Fokkelman has noted the preoccupation with body parts in this chapter, as well as in previous chapters of 1 and 2 Samuel.[26] He points out that the mention of Ish-bosheth's hands (v. 1) and Mephibosheth's feet (v. 4) is nicely balanced by the cutting off of the hands and feet of Baanah and Rechab. On the one hand (no pun intended), the hands of Ish-bosheth and the feet of Mephibosheth " 'embody' the impo-

---

[21] It has been suggested that the brothers committed this murder as an act of revenge for what Saul did to the Gibeonites (see 2 Sam. 21:1–14), since Beeroth was a Gibeonite city (Josh. 9:17). But Youngblood, *1, 2 Samuel*, p. 844, insists that the text emphasizes that these men were members of the tribe of Benjamin and were, thus, loyal to Saul. Their motivation was greed, not revenge.

[22] Polzin, *David and the Deuteronomist*, pp. 49-53.

[23] Ibid., p. 51.

[24] See pp. 2-6.

[25] Hertzberg, *I&II Samuel*, p. 265, and Willis, *First and Second Samuel*, p. 308.

[26] Fokkelman, *Throne and City*, pp. 135-136, 146-147.

tence of the house of Saul," while the "amputated hands and feet of the brothers are an act of revenge in miniature for the crime which had 'cut' such a ghastly opportunistic covenant with calamity."[27] Ish-bosheth had, illegitimately, been made "head" of Israel. The loss of his head, as well as that of his father, Saul, is an indication that the "headship" of Israel has passed to another—the one whose "head" had been divinely anointed—David (1 Sam. 16:13; 2 Sam. 2:4).

While on the subject of "heads" and "headship" it is of note that neither David nor the narrator refer to Ish-bosheth in this chapter as "king" (in spite of my subtitle!). David shows great respect for his adversary by executing his murderers and giving the only body part of Ish-bosheth in his possession a proper burial (v. 12); but in no instance is he called "king." There is irony in the fact that Abner and Ish-bosheth are reunited in death, and in the very city of their rival David. Hebron of Judah is indeed an interesting resting place for the bodies of the two men who sought to divide Israel from Judah.

Conclusion: The Man Who Should Never have been King

The apostle Paul writes that one who has the gift of leadership should lead with diligence (Rom. 12:8). We might add that one who does not have the gift of leadership should not try to exercise it. Ish-bosheth is an example of the problems that can result from unanointed leadership.

The first and most devastating problem is the division resulting from an unqualified leader asserting his or her authority. There is a tendency in our modern society to assume that if one is not leading then he or she is in some sense inferior. Sadly, leadership and authority are often sought for reasons of pride and prestige rather than gifting and calling. An understanding of God-given roles is sorely needed in our families, churches and nation. Jesus magnified the role of servanthood in his ministry and stated it is the basis for true authority (Mark 10:42–45).

Based on the language of 2 Samuel 2:8–9a, it appears that Ish-bosheth was strong-armed into power. There is no indication that he sought for it himself. But whether his motivation was fear of saying "no" to Abner, other peer pressure, pride, a lust for power, or a combination of these, without the gifting and calling of God Ish-bosheth was ill-prepared to lead God's people. Abner and Ish-bosheth made the mistake that some continue to make today: assuming a position of leadership and authority they were not designed to have.

Think of the lives that would have been spared and the difference within the nation of Israel if both Abner and Ish-bosheth had humbly submitted to the will of God. What if, for instance, instead of retiring to his bed-

---

[27] Ibid., p. 135.

room, Ish-bosheth had mounted his horse and humbly submitted to David? David's covenant with Jonathan (1 Sam. 20:14–15), his promise to Saul not to cut off his descendents (1 Sam. 24:21–22), and his history of not taking matters into his own hands, are all indications that David would have spared Ish-bosheth. Better to live in obscurity, than to die by the assassin's sword. But Ish-bosheth's indecisiveness and fear cost him dearly. Not deciding for God meant deciding against him. By not making a decision, it was made for him.

This story again recalls 1 Samuel 2:30, where God says, "Those who honor Me I will honor." Abner and Ish-bosheth achieved the opposite of what they desired: they left a legacy of division and failure. Had they submitted to God, they would have had the seat of honor that they longed for. By submitting to the role that God has designed for us, we are not confessing inferiority or admitting defeat. Instead, we are embracing all that is best for us and God's people and, in the end, we will enjoy the only honor that really matters—the honor that comes from God.

Chapter 13

Rizpah: The Silent One (Saul's concubine)

And David was told what Rizpah the daughter of Aiah, the concubine of Saul had done
(2 Sam. 21:11)

Actions Speak Louder Than Words (2 Sam. 3:7; 21:8–14)

Though Rizpah never utters a word in the two passages in which she appears, her presence in each has a powerful effect on the house of Saul. The first appearance of Rizpah (3:7) coincides with the downfall of Saul's house (3:1). Rizpah's action in her second, and last, appearance (21:8–14), results in a restoration of honor to the house of Saul in the form of a decent burial for him and his deceased family members. Thus Rizpah forms an inclusio[1] around the fate of Saul's family in 2 Samuel.

Rizpah is certainly not responsible for the decline of Saul's house; however, she does become the object of Abner's machinations. Is she compliant because she has no choice? Or may we surmise that Rizpah welcomed this alliance because of the possibility that it might lead to one of her own sons becoming the future king? The question is an intriguing one, but there is too little information in the text to discern Rizpah's thoughts, since the focus is on Abner's motives and action. Abner's act of taking Rizpah as his own precipitates the break between himself and Ish-bosheth.[2] This division, in turn, quickly leads to the assassinations of both Abner (3:27) and Ish-bosheth (4:6), effectively bringing to an end any hope of a Saulide dynasty.

As Fokkelman has demonstrated, Rizpah parallels Michal in 2 Samuel 3.[3] Both are women of the house of Saul who are treated as pawns in the game of power politics. This would be the only enduring image of Rizpah were it not for her reappearance at the end of 2 Samuel. In 2 Samuel 21:1–14 there is another story full of tragedy for the house of Saul, as well as for Rizpah personally, as her two sons are taken from her and executed by the Gibeonites, for the crime Saul committed against the Gibeonites. However, it is also a story of extraordinary heroism and loyalty—not only the loyalty of a mother to her sons, but also loyalty to an entire family. If Rizpah did feel any

---

[1] Chisholm, *Interpreting the Historical Books*, p. 229 defines an "inclusio" as, "A literary technique in which certain words or phrases appear at both the beginning and conclusion of a literary unit to mark it out as a distinct structural unit." Of course, Rizpah's two appearances do not mark out a literary unit as such. Rather, her two appearances coincide with important events in Saul's household and act as "bookends" for the fall and restoration of it.

[2] See chap. 11, pp. 144-147.

[3] Fokkelman, *Throne and City*, pp. 67-70.

guilt for the downfall of Saul's house,[4] might it be suggested that this act of loyalty was not only an act of love, but also a way of seeking atonement for past mistakes? If she felt in any way responsible for bringing shame to the house of Saul, perhaps she hoped to prevent that shame from becoming a permanent stain. Admittedly this is conjecture; the only certain thing is that Rizpah was determined to protect the dead remains of her family. Having lost all political clout (if she ever had any), she could not prevent their execution, nor could she prevent the natural process of decay, so she did the only thing she could: prevent the desecration of the bodies by wild animals and birds of prey (v. 10). Yet in the powerlessness of her lonely vigil she was able to touch the heart of the king and restore a sense of honor to the dead members of her family.[5] With these general observations in mind, we will now take a closer look at this story with particular attention to Rizpah's part in the drama.

She Loves Me Like a Rock (2 Sam. 21:1–14)

The story begins with David's kingdom facing a three-year famine. The seriousness of the famine is emphasized by the expression "year after year" (21:1). When David seeks the face of the Lord, God responds, "It is because of Saul and his bloodthirsty house, because he killed the Gibeonites" (21:1). Though the Gibeonites were originally among the peoples that Israel was to exterminate, Joshua and the elders of Israel allowed themselves to be tricked into making a covenant with them (Josh. 9:3–15). As a result, Israel was bound to protect the Gibeonites, and any violation of this treaty would incur the wrath of the Lord, in whose name they had sworn (Josh. 9:19–20). Saul's violation of this covenant had brought bloodguilt on the land and the result was that the land refused to yield its abundance (cf. Gen. 4:10–12).[6] Though dead, Saul's legacy was still having an adverse impact on Israel, and was about to have a devastating effect on his own progeny!

David sends for the Gibeonites to attempt to resolve the crisis. After some negotiating it is agreed that seven of Saul's descendants will be executed

---

[4] I am suggesting (speculating!) that once Rizpah realized that Abner was using her as a means to an end she may have been remorseful for being a participant in the eventual dissolution of Saul's kingdom.

[5] J. Cheryl Exum, "Rizpah," *Word & World*, vol. XVII Number 3, 1997, p. 261, writes, "As a member of the deposed house of Saul, a woman, and a widow, she has no official power to oppose their execution, yet the dramatic deed she performs afterwards is of such magnitude that it influences a king to give them a proper burial."

[6] The Law taught that bloodshed pollutes the land and "*no atonement can be made for the land*, for the blood that is shed on it, *except by the blood of him who shed it*" (Num. 35:33—emphasis mine). Note that David's question to the Gibeonites is, "And with what shall I make atonement...?" (2 Sam. 21:3).

"before the Lord" (21:6).[7] This is where Rizpah enters the picture, as her two sons, Armoni and Mephibosheth, "whom she bore to Saul" are among those chosen for execution (v. 8).[8] As Fokkelman points out, the execution of Saul's descendants (v. 9) could easily have been the end of the story.[9] But to the reader's surprise, as well as David's, this story does not end with the gruesome deaths of Saul's kin. Every time we think we have seen the last of Rizpah, she reappears. Though the focus of the story is on the bloodguilt of Saul, this lady must have a final say, even if she never says a word![10] Momentarily we will ask why the author has chosen to include this anecdote, but before pursuing that question we must examine the rest of the story.

Rizpah reappears in verse 10 with sackcloth (a traditional garment of mourning) in her hands. She spreads it on a rock, which apparently becomes her home throughout the long ordeal ahead. We are told it is the beginning of harvest (April-May). This is the time of the executions (v. 9). More importantly, harvest time is an ironic reminder of the famine that has robbed the land of its fertility. There has been no fruitfulness for three years—the land mourns. Having lost the fruit of her womb, Rizpah mourns and spreads sackcloth on a rock—a symbol of how hard things are.[11] From harvest time until the late rains, probably October-November,[12] Rizpah has one focus: to keep the birds of prey and wild animals from desecrating the decaying corpses that were once her family.[13] Fokkelman graphically describes her vigil:

---

[7] Bergen, *1, 2 Samuel*, p. 445, points out, "In cases involving the unsanctioned taking of human life, the Torah called for retribution-in-kind (cf. Exod. 21:23; Lev. 24:21; Deut. 19:21), even though the case might involve aliens (cf. Lev. 24:22)." Footnote 6 above (the quote from Num. 35:33), also makes this clear. Bergen also points out, as do others, that the choice of seven probably carried a symbolic value.

[8] The story makes very clear that Mephibosheth, the son of Rizpah, is different from Mephibosheth, the son of Jonathan, whom David spares for the sake of his oath (v. 7). The other five descendants of Saul who are executed are grandsons, born to his eldest daughter Merab (for further information on this see p. 130, n. 18).

[9] Fokkelman, *Throne and City*, p. 285.

[10] Exum, "Rizpah," p. 264, poignantly comments, "In my opinion, impassioned pleas and angry outbursts would lessen the impact of the story and detract our attention from the act itself. Silence gives Rizpah a preternatural [exceptional] magnitude and underscores the gravity of the ritual she performs."

[11] Exum, "Rizpah," p. 285, suggests the rock may have this symbolic function.

[12] Some believe the text refers to an unseasonable early summer rain. See for example, Gordon, *I&II Samuel*, p. 301; but I am in agreement with Fokkelman, *Throne and City*, pp. 287-288, that if this were the case the author could have clearly made this point. Furthermore, the longer Rizpah's vigil lasted the more awe-inspiring it would have been. This is what seems to have impressed David and motivated him to action.

[13] The exposure of bodies to the elements without recourse to a proper burial was considered one of the greatest horrors of the ancient world. It was a sign of being

The stench and the sight of decay can hardly be borne by an outsider let alone a relative—and Rizpah is a mother who, day in and day out, week in and week out, is forced to experience this with her own children! The horror defies description, and the narrator does not describe it either.[14]

Braving the heat of summer which would also exacerbate the sickening odor, and enduring many sleepless nights, she faithfully stands watch.

Rizpah's vigil is brought to the attention of David (v. 11), who responds by gathering not only the bones of those who had been hanged (v. 13), but also the bones of Saul and Jonathan, and burying them in the family tomb of Kish (v. 14).[15] Thus Rizpah's act not only prompts David to honor the seven who were hanged, but also motivates him to pay special tribute to Saul and Jonathan.

It is only after the act of burial that the author provides the concluding statement, "And after that God heeded the prayer for the land" (v. 14). Although the execution of Saul's descendants was necessary to bring atonement to the land (Num. 35:33), the inference is that Rizpah's heroic act motivated David to show proper respect for the dead of Saul's house, which, in turn, moved God to bring the famine to an end.[16] Firth rightly states,

> Although the decision to execute members of Saul's family was judicially acceptable to resolve the bloodguilt, leaving the bodies exposed was not....Justice for genocide could not add excessive punishment. David could respond to Yahweh and resolve the land's need, but he also needed the spur provided by Rizpah in her loyalty to her family.[17]

---

cursed due to divine displeasure (1 Kings 14:10–11; 16:3–4; 2 Kings 9:33–37; Ps. 53:5; Jer. 22:18–19; Ezek. 6:5; etc.).

[14] Fokkelman, *Throne and City*, pp. 285-286.

[15] Even though the text only speaks of the bones of Saul and Jonathan actually being buried, the inference is that David gave all the bones a proper burial, Saul and Jonathan receiving specific mention due to being the most prominent.

[16] As Fokkelman, *Throne and City*, pp. 289-290, states, "It is important to be aware of where this divine forgiveness of, or compassion towards, the nation does *not* occur: not at the end of v. 9, where it would have been a response to the execution, and not at the end of v. 10, where it would have signified a direct response to Rizpah's wake and a reward for her courage...God did not actually decide to end the period of punishment of the famine until there was the added weight of David's creative and conjunctive act as his response to Rizpah's wake" (author's emphasis).

[17] Firth, *1&2 Samuel*, p. 506.

Conclusion: Silence Often Says Much More—Rizpah's Significance

We must now return to the question of why the author included this anecdote about Rizpah. She is a minor character in the overall story, who is given no voice; why include her at all? I believe that the larger context of Samuel helps to provide answers. For example, as previously noted, Rizpah's character acts as a frame around the fate of Saul's house. She is first introduced when the house of Saul is beginning to fall apart (2 Sam. 3). She reappears when the house of Saul seems to be at its lowest point (2 Sam. 21:8). However, what begins as a tragic story concerning Saul's descendants, ends with a measure of honor and peace being restored to his house (21:12–14). God heals the land and David honors Saul's family with a decent burial in the family tomb, but the first link in this chain is the sacrificial act of Rizpah (v. 10). Her appearance in these two stories mirrors the judgment and mercy of God. She is a participant in some of the darkest moments of Saul's family history, yet the final scene is not one of despair but of hope. Through the character of Rizpah, we see that the Lord judges and heals; or to put it in Hannah's words, "The Lord kills and makes alive; He brings down to the grave and brings up" (1 Sam. 2:6).

Speaking of Hannah, the larger context of Samuel also invites a comparison between her and Rizpah. Hannah is the first woman to appear in the books of Samuel, and Rizpah is the last—creating, I suggest, another inclusio. These two women share many common traits. For example, both are involved in marriages including another wife (Hannah and Peninnah/Rizpah and Ahinoam). Both suffer the pain of childlessness. Hannah must endure the ignominy of not being able to conceive, while Rizpah has her sons violently taken from her. Hannah prays in silence (1:13), while Rizpah never speaks. Both women are powerless and social misfits in their society: Hannah because of her barrenness, and Rizpah because she is a concubine of a rejected king. Both women engage in acts that shock their contemporaries, but which lead to a dramatic change when God acts and brings deliverance from shameful circumstances. Hannah's frantic prayer initially causes Eli to rebuke her (1 Sam. 1:12–16), but her desperate action leads to God's blessing of a son (1:19–20). Rizpah's desperate act gains the attention of David, leading to an honorable burial for her family, which, in turn, leads to God healing the land. The similarities are too numerous to be coincidental.

The books of Samuel are framed by powerless women in desperate situations, who step out in extraordinary ways and find hope in an all-powerful God who turns curses to blessing. Thus, power in weakness is a theme that begins and ends the books of Samuel and is surely one reason why Rizpah's story must be told.

Finally, the theme of power in weakness is accentuated by the immediate context. Following Rizpah's last appearance is a sequence of short vignettes, all showing how David and his men overcame intimidating circumstances as they faced their arch-nemesis, the Philistines (21:15–22). The stories each concern a confrontation with the descendants of "Rapha" (men of giant stature, of whom Goliath was one). The first story is particularly interesting, as it highlights the weakness of David, who "grew faint" (v. 15) and was in danger of being killed until Abishai came to his aid (vv. 16–17). These stories speak of men who fight with "swords and spears," but it is clearly the Lord who gives the victory (cf. 1 Sam. 17:47). The stories of men battling one another provide an interesting contrast to a lone woman who battles the elements. In the end, both prevail: not because of their own strength (1 Sam. 2:9c), but because of a sovereign God.

Chapter 14

Mephibosheth and Ziba: The Good and the Bad
(Saul's grandson and servant)

"Your servant is lame and he [Ziba] has slandered your servant to my lord the king"—
Mephibosheth (2 Sam. 19:26c–27a)

Together, Like it or Not!

Given the fact that it is impossible to write about one of these characters without mentioning the other, it is ironic that no conversation between Mephibosheth and Ziba is recorded in 2 Samuel. Furthermore, they never appear together in a single scene, nor do they ever speak the other's name. David is the common denominator for both characters. Yet the same narrative separating them permanently links them together.[1]

It is Ziba who first reveals the existence and whereabouts of Mephibosheth (2 Sam. 9:3–4). Shortly after this, David appoints him to be Mephibosheth's servant (9:9–11), strengthening the tie between them. When David is fleeing from Absalom, Ziba not only brings him provisions; he also brings a bad report about his master, leading the king to turn over all of Mephibosheth's land to Ziba (2 Sam. 16:1–4). At this point it seems as though Ziba has finally gained autonomy. However, after Absalom is defeated, both men appear one final time in the narrative of 2 Samuel.[2] Ziba is the first to arrive and pay his respects to the king (19:17), followed by Mephibosheth who seeks to salvage his reputation from what he claims are the slanderous remarks of his servant (19:24–30). Mephibosheth's pleas result in both men being forced to share the same property (v. 29), and so in the end the two men, previously divided and clearly preferring to remain separate, are permanently brought together. Their story can be summarized in two paradoxical equations: one land equals two men divided, while a land divided equals two men united—like it or not!

---

[1] Since Ziba is probably not a blood relative of Saul, my initial thought was to focus only on Mephibosheth in this chapter. However, it soon became apparent that Ziba was an integral part of any treatment of Mephibosheth, as he affects every part of Mephibosheth's story. Furthermore, as steward over Saul's house (2 Sam. 9:2, 9), Ziba would have been considered an important part of the extended family, and thus can be justifiably included here even though he was not blood related.

[2] Mephibosheth is mentioned one more time in 2 Sam. 21:7.

The Fall (2 Sam. 4:4)

The reader is first introduced to Mephibosheth in the midst of the story of Ish-bosheth's assassination. Though this is not an unusual practice for the author, at first glance it seems quite abrupt. Some have suggested that the point of this intrusion is to emphasize the absence of a fit heir to the throne of the house of Saul.[3] However, it is more likely that the author introduces Mephibosheth here "to dispel the notion that might arise in the reader's mind that Ish-bosheth's death meant the final destruction of the Saulide family."[4] Therefore when David asks in 9:1, "Is there still anyone who is left of the house of Saul, that I may show him kindness for Jonathan's sake?" the reader is well aware of the existence of Mephibosheth. In fact, Ziba's first mention of Mephibosheth in 9:3 recalls the description of him in 4:4 by using identical wording (literally, "stricken of feet").

Perhaps the best reason for this intrusion is the continued emphasis on the decline and weakness of Saul's house (cf. 2 Sam. 3:1).[5] It has already been noted that the "weak hands" of Ish-bosheth (4:1) counterbalance the lame feet of Mephibosheth.[6] There is also a preponderance of language about feet throughout 2 Samuel 2–5, and in each case feet prove to be a weakness. 2 Samuel 2:18 mentions the swift feet of Asahel; while this might normally be considered a great asset, it turns out to be a great liability. David mentions both hands and feet in his lament over Abner in 2 Sam. 3:34, "Your hands were not bound, nor your feet put into fetters." In spite of this fact, Abner's hands and feet were no match for the treachery of Joab and Abishai. Finally, in David's conquest of Jerusalem, the Jebusites taunt him by saying, "You shall not come in here; but the blind and the lame will repel you" (2 Sam. 5:6), yet David responded by taking the city:

> Now David said on that day, "Whoever climbs up by way of
> the water shaft and defeats the Jebusites (the lame and the

---

[3] For example, Alter, *The David Story*, p. 218. This view seems inadequate in light of the future revelation that Saul had other sons and grandsons (2 Sam. 21:8). It is sometimes suggested that the events of 2 Sam. 21:1–14 took place before the events of 2 Sam. 9 and thus before David had any knowledge of Mephibosheth. Since 2 Sam. 21:7 explicitly mentions David's sparing of Jonathan's son, Mephibosheth, it seems most likely that the events of 2 Sam. 21 happen after the events of 2 Sam. 9. Furthermore, Mephibosheth's crippling fall, and Ish-bosheth's assassination certainly take place before the events of 2 Sam. 21:1–14 which makes it unlikely that the author would be asserting in 2 Sam. 4:4 that Mephibosheth is the lone heir to the throne.

[4] Bergen, *1, 2 Samuel*, p. 316; similarly, Polzin, *David and the Deuteronomist*, p. 99.

[5] Fokkelman, *Throne and City*, pp. 127-128 and p. 135.

[6] See chap. 12, pp. 156-157.

blind, who are hated by David's soul), he shall be chief and captain." Therefore they say, "The blind and the lame shall not come into the house." (5:8)

Thus the reference to Mephibosheth's feet and lameness is surrounded by other references, highlighting weakness. So the reference to Mephibosheth is not quite as arbitrary as it may first appear.

The author attributes Mephibosheth's lameness to his nurse dropping him as she tried to flee on the day news was received of Saul and Jonathan's deaths. Here is yet one more result of the rippling effect of sin in Saul's house. Mephibosheth's fall was not only literal, but also a symbol of the fall and crippling of an entire household. Rather than relate this story chronologically (inserting it in 1 Sam. 31), the author chose to withhold it in order to strategically place it here in the account of the final demise of Saul's kingdom. This verse literally communicates that Saul's kingdom does not have a leg to stand on!

2 Samuel 4:4 is bracketed by references to Mephibosheth's lameness (2 different Hebrew words). The reader only learns his name after twice being told of his disability. The facts are placed in the following order: Jonathan, Saul's son, has a son; he is lame; it happened when he was five years old; his nurse dropped him when fleeing; there is another reference to his lameness; and finally, we are told his name was Mephibosheth.

The meaning of "Mephibosheth" presents a similar problem to that of "Ish-bosheth." In 1 Chronicles his name is given as "Merib-Baal" (8:34 [2x], 9:40 first occurrence), or Meribaal (9:40 second occurrence). The basic meaning of the name(s) in 1 Chronicles is, "(The) master (or Baal) contends."[7] Hamilton, following Tsevat, argues that because the first part of the name differs (*mepi*, vs. *meri*), this is evidence that the author has not simply substituted the word for shame (*bôshet*) on the end.[8] Therefore Jonathan's son had two names: Mephibosheth and Meri[b]baal. Hamilton admits that the meaning of "Mephibosheth" is uncertain, but suggests, "What (is the) command (literally 'mouth') of (the) protective spirit?"[9] Tsevat, on the other hand, had previously suggested a meaning of, "From the mouth of (or by the promise of) *Bosheth*."[10] If the definition of "shame" is to be connected to this root, as many maintain, then "Mephibosheth" would mean "from the mouth of shame" or perhaps "he who scatters shame" (depending on the derivation and meaning of *mepi*).[11] All of this uncertainty makes it impossible at the present time to be dogmatic about what meaning, if any, the author might have intended. Below

---

[7] Hamilton, "New Evidence," p. 239.
[8] Ibid., pp. 238-239.
[9] Ibid., pp. 239-240.
[10] Tsevat, "Ishbosheth," pp. 80-81.
[11] E.R. Dalglish, "Mephibosheth" and "Meribbaal," *IDB*, vol. 3 (Nashville: Abingdon, 1962), pp. 350-351, and 354-355.

I will tentatively suggest a couple of possibilities based on the narrative context.

Will the Real Servant Please Take a Bow? (2 Sam. 9)

Keeping a Covenant

In 1 Samuel 20, with David's life hanging in the balance, Jonathan and David had renewed their covenant with each other. While David was concerned about the present (and rightly so), Jonathan looked into the future and bound David to an oath of loyalty (*ḥeseḏ*) to protect his future descendants (20:14–15). It is this oath made years earlier that prompts David to ask in 2 Samuel 9:1, "Is there still anyone who is left from the house of Saul, that I may show him kindness (*ḥeseḏ*) for Jonathan's sake?" No doubt the death of many in Saul's family and the dissolution of his kingdom had caused his remaining relatives to assume a low profile, leaving David to wonder if anyone still existed to whom he might fulfill his promise. Just as Ziba will provide food and provisions for David as he is fleeing from Absalom (2 Sam. 16:1–2), so too on this occasion Ziba is the man who is able to help David with his dilemma (9:2).

As a servant of Saul's house, Ziba is aware of Mephibosheth's existence and whereabouts, of which he informs the king (9:3–4). In language that will mirror David's action with Bathsheba (2 Sam. 11:4), he "sends" and "takes" Mephibosheth from the house of Machir at Lo Debar (9:5). Both Mephibosheth and Bathsheba respond by "coming" to David (9:6; 11:4), and both end up in a horizontal position in his presence: Bathsheba in bed with the king (11:4), Mephibosheth lying on his face before the king out of fear and humility (9:6). These verbal similarities provide a contrast between the good that David will do toward Mephibosheth and the evil he will commit with Bathsheba.

Character Assessment: Appearances can be Deceiving

There is another contrast in the present story—concerning servanthood. The words "servant" or "serve" occur a total of ten times in chapter 9 (v. 2 [2x], 6, 8, 10 [3x], 11 [2x], 12). These words are applied to Ziba and Mephibosheth (although they also include Ziba's servants and sons). Given the future problems that arise, this passage raises the question, "Which, if either, of these two men can truly be called a 'servant' of David?" Although both talk and act like servants of David, we have already learned that one of the sub-themes of the books of Samuel is that appearances can be deceiving. Ziba is not only called the servant of the house of Saul; he also refers to himself as David's servant (vv. 2, 11), and by the end of the chapter he is designated as servant to Mephibosheth (vv. 9–10). However, there is reason to suspect that Ziba is not overly enthusiastic with this appointment, although he is much too wise to say so in front of the king (v. 11).

Early in the narrative, Fokkelman detects a subtle characterization of Ziba and Mephibosheth that will provide a clue to their future actions.[12] When Ziba appears at court there is no mention of an opening gesture of humility (9:2), as there is with Mephibosheth, who "fell on his face and prostrated [the same word used for 'worship'] himself " (9:6). One might argue that perhaps Mephibosheth thinks he has more to fear than Ziba; still, the contrast of this initial approach to the king is a piece of information worth tucking away for later evaluation. There is also a contrast in language. When David first says, "Are you Ziba?" he responds with one word in the Hebrew, "your servant" (9:2). A one-word response is often a sign of abruptness, and one might expect more when responding to a king's question.[13] When David first addresses Mephibosheth, whose face is bowed to the floor, he responds, "Here (is) your servant" (9:6, consisting of two words in Hebrew, the first emphasizing humility and availability). Mephibosheth's short response probably indicates his fear.

As we hear him utter these words we are reminded that this is the second time he is said to "fall." The first fall, through no fault of his own, was caused by the haste of the nurse who dropped him (4:4). But this fall is voluntary and could not have been easy for one who was already lame. This extra (we might add, painful) exertion in the presence of the king may provide an additional contrast to the demeanor of Ziba. Furthermore, Mephibosheth's self-effacing expression of gratitude, "What is your servant, that you should look upon such a dead dog as I" (v. 8), finds no parallel in Ziba.[14] Admittedly, however, Mephibosheth has more reason to express gratitude than Ziba does at this stage.

---

[12] Fokkelman, *King David*, pp. 28-29.

[13] Hertzberg, *I&II Samuel*, p. 300, also makes this point.

[14] Jeremy Schipper, " 'Why do you still speak of your affairs?': Polyphony in Mephibosheth's Exchanges with David in Samuel," *VT* 54, 2004, pp. 344-351. Schipper, pp. 347-348, asserts that the words "dead dog," although often used in the Ancient Near East as an expression of self-abasement, in Scripture carry a more sinister notion referring to one's political enemy. Yet the examples he cites do not fully support his contention. For example, in 1 Sam. 24:14 David calls himself a "dead dog" when speaking to Saul. While it may be true that Saul perceives David as an enemy, the context makes it clear that David is not Saul's enemy and David's use of the term is meant to communicate this. Mephibosheth's use of this expression is meant to communicate humility and gratitude before a sovereign. It is not a double-entendre with a hidden meaning. See for example, George W. Coats, "Self-abasement and Insult Formulas," *JBL* 89, 1970, pp. 14-26 (esp. 14-19), who asserts that when "dead dog" is used in the first person it is a form of self-abasement, but when used in the second or third person it is intended as an insult.

The lameness of Mephibosheth seems to be his defining characteristic and provides another key in distinguishing his character from Ziba's. It is mentioned in every passage in which he appears. We have already noted that it occurs twice as bookends in 4:4 where he is first introduced. It is also mentioned twice here in chapter 9, once at the beginning (v. 3—by Ziba) and once at the end (v. 13). Finally, Mephibosheth himself mentions it in his defense before David (19:26). Ziba's usage in 9:3, however, is of particular interest. When asked if there is someone who still remains from the house of Saul, Ziba responds, "There is still a son of Jonathan who is lame in his feet." Note that Ziba never says his name; what seems to matter most is his handicap. The text leaves us guessing as to what Ziba's motive might be in supplying this information. There are several possibilities. Some have suggested that Ziba's response is probably intended to assure David that Mephibosheth poses no threat to the throne.[15] But given the fact that Ziba does not even acknowledge the name of Mephibosheth, it seems more likely that the reference is meant derogatorily.[16] Ziba probably means that Mephibosheth is not worth a waste of the king's *ḥeseḏ*. As a person who is crippled in both feet, he is a shameful sight and falls under the category of those who are not to be welcomed "into the house" (2 Sam. 5:8).

Besides the possibility of being prejudiced against Mephibosheth due to his handicap, Ziba's current position as steward of Saul's house might have motivated him to discourage David from any expression of *ḥeseḏ* toward a survivor of Saul's family, especially one as unworthy as Mephibosheth. It is clear that Ziba himself is a man of wealth. We are told he has fifteen sons and twenty servants (9:10). It is also likely that he was the caretaker of Saul's land.[17] Ziba's future actions (16:3–4) can easily be interpreted as the actions of a man who resented losing "his" land to an inferior.[18]

---

[15] For example, Hertzberg, *I&II Samuel*, p. 300, and Alter, *The Story of David*, p. 241.

[16] Evans, *The Message of Samuel*, pp. 203-204, makes a similar observation. Brueggemann, *First and Second Samuel*, p., 267, states, "He is a no-name." It might be recalled that Mephibosheth's uncle, Ish-bosheth, encountered a similar problem. See chap. 12, pp. 153-154.

[17] Bergen, *1, 2 Samuel*, p. 354, refers to him as, "Ziba a well-to-do (cf. v. 10) 'servant of Saul's household' (v. 2) who apparently managed the former king's royal estate." Anderson, *2 Samuel*, p. 141, makes a similar suggestion but adds, "it is not made clear to whom the patrimony now belonged. It is likely that it had become crown property." Even if Ziba managed the property for the king, he would have been the overseer and would have benefited greatly from that position.

[18] Along this line, Evans, *The Message of Samuel*, p. 203, presents a third possibility which also impugns Ziba's motives: "Given the later encounter between Mephibosheth and Ziba (16:1–4; 19:24–30) there may be a hint here that Ziba deliberately revealed Mephibosheth's whereabouts in the hope that he would be removed from the picture once for all and with that his right to what Ziba may now have seen as his own farm."

These subtle differences in characterization might be overlooked, were it not for the fact that Ziba's future accusation of Mephibosheth forces us to ask, "Who is telling the truth?" Some believe it is impossible to tell.[19] I am not that pessimistic, nor do I believe that it is the author's intention to leave the reader in the dark. While I have already hinted at Ziba's culpability, I realize that at this stage such a judgment is premature and is only possible because I have read the rest of the story! Part of the art of the biblical author is taking the reader through a surprising journey of twists and turns concerning these two characters. I have indicted Ziba as one whose motives seem to be less than pure, but further evidence is needed in order to convict him.

The Table of Fellowship

Three times in this chapter David states his desire to show "kindness" (*ḥeseḏ*) to one of Saul's descendants. This three-fold mention of *ḥeseḏ* is matched in the former story between David and Jonathan (1 Sam. 20:8, 14, 15). In 2 Sam. 9:7–13 Mephibosheth becomes the recipient of this *ḥeseḏ* which is expressed in two different ways. First David turns over all the land of Saul to Mephibosheth, who is to be the beneficiary of its abundance (vv. 7, 9–10).

Previous to this Mephibosheth had been living in the house of Machir in Lo Debar (v. 4). Lo Debar is located in Transjordan, not far from Mahanaim, Ish-bosheth's previous capital. While this was an exile of sorts, no doubt intended to keep Mephibosheth out of the public eye, there is every indication that he lived quite comfortably. Machir was apparently not only a loyal follower of Saul, but also a wealthy man. Later, during Absalom's revolt, he and two others provide for David and his army's needs (2 Sam. 17:27–29). Machir's generous gesture on this occasion is no doubt a response to David's kindness toward his former ward, Mephibosheth.

---

[19] Peter Cotterell, "Linguistics, Meaning, Semantics, and Discourse Analysis," *NIDOTTE*, vol. 1, p. 142, writes, "Throughout the story we are given no clue at all as to the characters of Ziba or Mephibosheth. The reader today might well be inclined to take the side of the old man [*sic*] Mephibosheth, to see him as a man of integrity, his infirmity exploited by Ziba, and so to assign to Ziba a sneaking, sycophantic, grasping role. But there is no more evidence in support of one view than of the other." While it is true that the biblical author's method of gapping can sometimes create ambiguity, I do not think that is the case in this instance. The issue here is a matter of truth and deceit. Are we to think that the author was so vague in his characterization that he purposely made it impossible for the reader to decide who is in the right? While some subjectivity must be involved in interpreting the text, I believe that the author has left enough evidence for a decision to be made.

Sermons, and some popular works, sometimes depict Mephibosheth as living a destitute existence until he was rescued by David. [20] This picture is derived from an interpretation of "Lo Debar," Mephibosheth's city. One spelling of *lō'* in Hebrew means "no" or "not." "Debar" means "word," "thing," or "matter." It is suggested that Mephibosheth is taken from "nothing" ("nothing") and made to sit at the king's table.[21] The problem is that the "*Lo*" in "Lo Debar" can be spelled two different ways in Hebrew.[22] Another form of *lô* in Hebrew means, "to him." To add to the confusion, "Lo Debar" is spelled both ways in Scripture! In 2 Sam. 17:27 and Amos 6:13 it is spelled *lō'* as in "no." In our present passage, however, it is spelled *lô* as in "to him." While it makes "good preaching" to say that David took Mephibosheth from a destitute place and set him at the king's table, it cannot be substantiated from this passage. If the writer had intended to infer this, he would certainly have used the other spelling (a spelling he is aware of since it is used in 2 Sam. 17:27).[23] Furthermore, as we have noted, Machir is a wealthy man and so Mephibosheth was not living in poverty, although his welfare would have been dependent on the generosity of his host. However, this does not mean that there is no significance to the place name, Lo Debar. Below I will suggest a possible meaning based on David's words to Mephibosheth in 2 Samuel 19:29.

The second way in which David expresses *ḥeseḏ* to Mephibosheth is by inviting him to eat continually from the king's table. This act is so significant that it is mentioned four times in chapter 9 (vv. 7, 10, 11, 13). While Mephibosheth may have been taken care of by Machir, it is still quite a step up to eat at the king's table, "like one of the king's sons" (v. 11). If the author intends any sense of shame to be read into Mephibosheth's name, perhaps it is found in the contrast between his lameness and his eating at the king's table. These two ideas are purposely juxtaposed in the final verse (9:13).

The two ways in which David shows kindness to Mephibosheth are not accidental. They are echoes of what he personally was deprived of under Saul's rule. David was driven from his home (1 Sam. 19:11–12; 20:38–42) and his land (1 Sam. 26:19) and was deprived of his place at the king's table (1

---

[20] For example, Alan Redpath, *The Making of a Man of God: Studies in the Life of David* (Grand Rapids: Fleming H. Revell, 1962), p. 189. Charles R. Swindoll, *A Man of Passion & Destiny: David* (Dallas: Word Publishing, 1997), pp. 172-173.

[21] Swindoll, *A Man of Passion*, pp. 172-173. Swindoll interprets the phrase as "no pastureland" and says, "So this descendant of Jonathan is in a place where there is unimaginable desolation." See also, James S. Ackerman, "Knowing Good and Evil: A Literary Analysis of the Court History in 2 Samuel 9–20 and 1 Kings 1–2," *JBL* 109/1, 1990, p. 43, who makes a similar unsubstantiated interpretation.

[22] For a similar discussion see, Youngblood, *1, 2 Samuel*, p. 917.

[23] I am unaware of anyone who would suggest that 2 Sam. 9:4 and 17:27 are from different authorial hands.

Sam. 20:24–34). Thus 1 Samuel 20 (with its three occurrences of *ḥeseḏ*, being deprived of table fellowship, and being driven from the land) is answered by David's magnanimous gestures in 2 Samuel 9 to Mephibosheth. It is a gracious response, in view of Saul's treatment of him, but above all it is a response of loyalty toward his beloved friend, Jonathan.

Ziba: In the Right Place at the Right Time (2 Sam. 16:1–4)

Chapter 16 provides a very different scenario from that of chapter 9. Instead of David being securely on his throne and in firm control of his kingdom, he is once again a fugitive: this time on the run from his son Absalom, who has patiently and cunningly planned an effective coup. As David flees over the Mount of Olives, he encounters a number of people including Ziba. Ziba's appearance, both timely and helpful, provokes two suspicious questions from David. The first, "What do you mean to do with these?" is in regard to the provisions that Ziba has with him. He explains that they are for the king and his entourage, to aid in their flight from Absalom (16:1–2). Ziba's appearance quite naturally leads David (and the reader) to wonder about the absence of Mephibosheth, which leads to the second question, "Where is your master's son?" Ziba's response is devastating and unexpected to both king and reader: "Indeed he is staying in Jerusalem, for he said, ' Today the house of Israel will restore the kingdom of my father to me' " (v. 3). Such an accusation would place anyone in a bad light, but considering the extraordinary kindness that David had shown Mephibosheth, this serves to villainize him. At this point it appears that both David and the reader have been duped by the self-effacing display of humility in chapter 9.

The author places the reader in the same position as David by not offering any additional information or insight. We know only what David knows. Faced with an obvious gesture of loyalty and support in the tangible form of donkeys and food, David makes an immediate judgment in favor of Ziba (v. 4). The question is, "Should we as readers join David in this hasty decision?" If this was the final word on Mephibosheth, or, more importantly, if there was further corroborating evidence in the text, then perhaps we would be justified in condemning him here. The Law itself states, "One witness shall not rise against a man concerning any iniquity or any sin that he commits; by the mouth of two or three witnesses the matter shall be established" (Deut. 19:15). David is clearly in violation of the Law on this point, and might I suggest that the author is also testing his readers to see if they will follow suit? It should be stressed that, both here and throughout the rest of 2 Samuel, there is only one person who makes an accusation against Mephibosheth, and he is not a disinterested party, but has much to gain by deceiving the king.[24]

Again it must be admitted that knowledge of the events of chapter 19 filters into my understanding of the events here in 16:1–4, but, nonetheless, this text raises its own questions for the discerning reader.[25] First of all it is clear that David's decision is made in haste and under great duress, with only the few facts he has at hand. But when Ziba's accusation is examined carefully, it does not stand up well. As Robert Gordon has observed,

> Only by a monumental miscalculation could Mephibosheth have imagined that events would favour him in the way that Ziba suggested. It was Absalom's rebellion, and it was for Absalom that large numbers of Israelites were declaring themselves. And such was the contrast between the charismatic prince and the crippled pensioner that David should never have fallen for Ziba's preposterous claim. But in an evil day full of uncertain allegiances he was easily deceived.[26]

Thus, Gordon's conclusion is that Ziba "displays the calculated practicality of an opportunist who realizes David's vulnerability to every sympathetic gesture of support."[27]

Second, Ziba's reaction to David's judgment is interesting when contrasted with 9:2. When David tells him that he is giving him "all that belongs to Mephibosheth," Ziba, who made himself conspicuous in chapter 9 by not bowing before David, responds, "I humbly *bow* before you, that I may find favor in your sight, my lord, O king" (16:4). The skeptical reader begins to get the feeling that Ziba only shows humility before the king after he gets what he wants. Ziba's response here not only contrasts with his actions in chapter 9, but also contrasts with Mephibosheth's response in 19:30 (which we will examine below). Nonetheless, in light of Ziba's accusation and David's reaction,

---

[24] Brueggemann, *First and Second Samuel*, p. 306, states, "We must remember, however, that for all the ominous threat of the statement, we have only Ziba's word for it, a word that is not disinterested. Ziba has put the loyalty of Mephibosheth in doubt while simultaneously enhancing his own position."

[25] Hamilton, *Handbook*, p. 349, observes a number of parallels between the encounters in 16:1–14 (which he designates as "A") and 16:15–23 (which he designates as "B"). Hamilton writes, "In both (A) and (B) somebody tricks somebody else. Ziba puts words into Mephibosheth's mouth (v. 3a) that Mephibosheth probably did not say, but Ziba convinces David that he did say it. Hushai fools Absalom into believing that he has shifted his loyalty from David to Absalom (vv. 16–19)." Other parallels between these sections, mentioned by Hamilton, further strengthen this observation.

[26] Gordon, *I&II Samuel*, pp. 276-277.

[27] Ibid., p. 276.

the reader should have doubts about Mephibosheth's character at this point. However, the subtle hints we have already observed, plus an examination of the events of chapter 19 (to which we now turn), will result in a clear conclusion as to who the real servant and real villain are.[28]

Ziba and Bad Company (2 Sam. 19:17)

By chapter 19, David has been victorious over Absalom and is preparing to return to Jerusalem. As a result, any who have slighted the king make it their business to appear before him as soon as possible. The biggest offender is Shimei, and so it is no surprise that he is first to make his way to the king. What is shocking is the person keeping company with this boisterous traitor and hater of David and his throne (see 2 Sam. 16:5–13). It should take the reader by surprise that none other than Ziba, his fifteen sons, and twenty servants, are found in the company of Shimei (v. 17)! Keeping company with a traitor does not bode well for Ziba.[29]

Something else should also surprise the reader. 16:4 left no indication about what had become of Ziba after his meeting with David. Each of David's encounters with individuals, as he is fleeing from Absalom, involves a discussion of going with the king or staying behind in Jerusalem to aid his cause.[30] Ittai insists on going with the king (15:21), while David instructs other loyal servants to return to Jerusalem where they can be of more help to him (15:27–28; 33–37). No such conversation is recorded between Ziba and David. One wonders what possible good Ziba could do for David by returning; therefore, it is not unreasonable to expect that he would accompany the king. In fact, it seems that loyalty to the king would demand accompanying him into exile unless otherwise instructed.[31] But now, for the first time, the reader realizes

---

[28] Willis, *First and Second Samuel*, p. 374, lists 6 reasons why Ziba appears to be lying.

[29] Some might argue that Shimei and Ziba simply make it to the ford of the Jordan at the same time and that they did not come together. Baldwin, *1&2 Samuel*, p. 276, draws this conclusion. However, she still indicates that this scene suggests a problem: "The intense competition between all these groups to prove their loyalty calls in question their sincerity." In my opinion, the language of the Hebrew text links the two together. Either way, Ziba is mentioned in the same breath as Shimei. It should also not go unnoticed that David's meeting with Ziba in chap. 16 is followed by his encounter with Shimei, thus forging a literary link between the two.

[30] Polzin, *David and the Deuteronomist*, p. 163, states, "One final feature of 2 Samuel 16 continues a concern of 2 Samuel 15: a heavy emphasis on who is *with* whom during the constitutional crisis inaugurated by Absalom's revolt." He continues on p. 227, n. 23, "*'et* meaning 'with' occurs proportionately more often in these two chapters (2 Samuel 15–16) taken individually than anywhere else in the book."

[31] One wonders what "legitimate" excuse Ziba might have offered to keep from accompanying the king, but the text is silent on this point. No doubt the reason for this

that Ziba, like Shimei (and Mephibosheth), had stayed behind. Was Ziba over-anxious to get back to the land that the king had given him? If so, what does this suggest about his true motive? Was he attempting to play on both sides by aiding David, yet remaining in the territory under Absalom's control, just in case?[32] The king might well have asked Ziba the same question he later asks Mephibosheth, "Why did you not go with me?" (19:25). If Mephibosheth was expected to go with the king, would not his servant also have been expected to accompany the king?

Ziba's haste in coming to the king could be explained in two ways. First, it is possible he wants to reassert his loyalty to the king, which perhaps could have come into question. Ironically this assertion comes in the company of Shimei and one thousand other Benjamites. As we shall see with Shimei, the accompaniment of a thousand men is a not-so-subtle form of persua-sion![33] To reject the overtures of Shimei and Ziba is to alienate a thousand men who are ready to give their allegiance to David if he will accept their rep-resentatives. It amounts to a friendly form of political blackmail. As chapters 19 and 20 make clear, the path back to the throne is not an easy one, and Da-vid needs all the support he can gather.

Second, knowing that his deception will soon be exposed, Ziba wants to get to the king before Mephibosheth does. If Ziba can secure the king's goodwill (and demonstrate that he has powerful allies in the process!), then he hopes Mephibosheth will not be able to persuade David otherwise. The au-thor is slowly allowing the character of Ziba to unfold before the reader. Zi-ba's affiliation with Shimei and the revelation that he did not accompany David are two powerful strikes against him. Mephibosheth's demeanor and accusation will prove to be strike three.[34]

"authorial" silence is to surprise the reader with Ziba's reappearance (19:17) in the midst of dubious company.

[32] It is true that Ziba takes a risk in helping David, but there is no certainty that Absa-lom would have found out about this aid had he won, or that Absalom would have taken any action against Ziba. Hertzberg, *I&II Samuel*, p. 345, writes, "We may ask whether Ziba's spontaneous action is not the result of certain calculations. If Absa-lom emerges victorious, then nothing much can happen to him, but if David proves the victor—and this seems to Ziba more probable—he will immediately be in favor with the king." Likewise, Firth, *1&2 Samuel*, p. 459, writes, "If things go well, Ziba will be remembered; but if Absalom prospers, Ziba has lost only the provisions."

[33] See chap. 15, pp. 186-187.

[34] Chisholm, *Interpreting the Historical Books*, p. 77, uses these narratives of Ziba and Mephibosheth as an example of the importance of taking the "macroplot" into con-sideration before drawing a conclusion about a character. After examining the evi-dence he concludes, "In retrospect, the explanation given by Ziba for Mephi-bosheth's absence seems unlikely. Apparently Ziba had been lying."

Mephibosheth: A "Lame" Excuse is at Times a Good Excuse (2 Sam. 19:24–30)

A good rule of thumb to follow when interpreting biblical narrative is that when the words of a character conflict with the information provided by the narrator, always believe the narrator. Ziba had accused Mephibosheth of seeking the kingdom for himself (16:3), and now in 19:24–30 we finally hear Mephibosheth's side of the story. But even before the narrator allows him a word in his own defense, he provides a description of his appearance (v. 24). Untrimmed feet and mustache, and clothes that had not been washed since the day the king left, hardly sounds like a man who was planning on taking over the kingdom! As Bergen states,

> Such inattention to details of personal health and hygiene made Mephibosheth look as if he had been profoundly mourning for a considerable period of time—he certainly did not look like a pretender to the throne who had been actively attempting to take back his grandfather's kingdom (cf. 16:3). It also signified that Mephibosheth had deliberately identified himself as ceremonially unclean (cf. Lev. 13:45) during David's absence.[35]

Some, however, have suggested that the narrator is simply stating the facts, and that this gives no indication of Mephibosheth's motives. Perhaps his appearance was all a ruse.[36] But the narrator not only seems to give a sympathetic portrayal of Mephibosheth's appearance; another important detail confirms his innocence. As Fokkelman observes, "The framing alone states exactly what the heart of the matter is for Mephibosheth."[37] What Fokkelman is referring to is the phrase "in peace," which occurs at the beginning of this section (v. 24) and the end (v. 30), forming an inclusio. The sympathetic portrayal of the author is seen in the first of these instances, where he states that Mephibosheth did not attend to his appearance "from the day the king departed until the day he returned *in peace*." This statement is then matched at the end by Mephibosheth's own words stating that his only concern is "my

---

[35] Bergen, *1, 2 Samuel*, p. 430.

[36] Schipper, "Why do you still speak of your affairs?," is one who takes this line of reasoning. Noting Ackroyd's comparison of Mephibosheth's appearance with the Gibeonites (whose appearance was intentionally deceptive), Schipper then points out that Mephibosheth is mentioned later in 2 Sam. 21 in an incident that involves the Gibeonites. He also argues that 2 Sam. 4:4 may suggest another connection between Mephibosheth and the Gibeonites. See his comments on p. 345, especially n. 6, pp. 345-346. See also Ackroyd, *The Second Book of Samuel*, p. 181.

[37] Fokkelman, *King David*, p. 32.

lord the king has come back *in peace* to his own house." This double confirmation (once in the mouth of the narrator and once in the mouth of a character) is characteristic of biblical narrative[38] and serves to assure the reader of Mephibosheth's innocence.

Other factors in Mephibosheth's speech to King David also confirm his sincerity. He claims, "My servant deceived me"[39] (v. 26). It is obvious that Mephibosheth could not saddle his own donkey since he was "lame," so his claim that Ziba left without him is certainly plausible. Mephibosheth's defense is actually quite clever. Not only does he mention his "lameness," but he also accuses Ziba of "slander," which comes from the Hebrew word for "foot" (*rgl*), a constant theme of the Mephibosheth narratives. He falls on the mercy of the king by entrusting his case to David's judgment, as well as reminding David that he has no further right to presume on the kindness of the king, who has already spared him from death and given him a seat at the royal table (vv. 27–28). By these words Mephibosheth infers that he is not guilty of such gross ingratitude. His heart has been true and loyal to David, and he could never forget all that the king has done for him. Once again the language of servanthood is highlighted in Mephibosheth's words, just as they were in chapter 9. He uses the phrase "my lord the king" five times in his speech, and refers to himself as "your servant" four times. When one looks back over Mephibosheth's words to David in chapters 9 and 19 it is impossible to find one word (or thought) of disrespect. He always addresses the king in a polite and humble manner.

Unfortunately, the same cannot be said of David. His response to Mephibosheth is very abrupt. This no doubt comes from a sense of embarrassment and frustration, because he now realizes (and so does everyone else accompanying him) that Ziba has duped him. But Ziba is not there, and in fact, David has just re-pledged his loyalty to him! Mephibosheth has exposed the king's hasty and gullible decision, so because he is present he bears the brunt of David's anger.

The words of the narrator and David combine to form an interesting twist on the place name "Lo Debar." We noted that the word *lô* means "to him." The narrator states, "So the king said *to him*" (v. 29). This is followed by David's statement, "Why do you *speak* anymore of your *matters?*" The words "speak" and "matters" are both from the Hebrew root *dbr* ("Debar"). It appears that the author has included a subtle wordplay here that frames the first

---

[38] To cite another example, Joshua 23:1–2 states, "Now it came to pass, a long time after the Lord had given rest to Israel from all their enemies round about, that *Joshua was old, and advanced in age*. And Joshua called for all Israel, for their elders, for their heads, and for their judges, and for their officers, and said to them, "*I am old, advanced in age*."

[39] Notice how Mephibosheth avoids saying Ziba's name, just as Ziba had avoided saying his name earlier. This hints at the underlying hostility between the two men.

and last meeting between Mephibosheth and David (9:4; 19:29).[40] More significant, however, is David's decision as he proclaims, "I have said 'You and Ziba divide the land.' " It is often suggested that David's motivation for making this decision was recognizing the innocence of Mephibosheth while still wishing to express gratitude to Ziba for his material aid.[41] But David's anger suggests that he feels he has no other recourse. He has just reaffirmed his loyalty to Ziba, who came in the company of one thousand Benjamites, so he dare not go back on his word. Yet he also recognizes that his decision was premature and unjust toward Mephibosheth, so he decrees an uncomfortable compromise—uncomfortable for both Mephibosheth and Ziba, who do not get along (for good reason), and uncomfortable for David, who has put himself in this difficult and embarrassing position because of a rash judgment.

The narrator reserves the final word for Mephibosheth.[42] The fact that his response is so gracious is the final nail in Ziba's coffin, and confirms Mephibosheth's innocence. He diffuses the tension by focusing on the welfare of the king. It is not the land that matters; the fact that the king has returned and is well is what is important. Mephibosheth's gracious words, "Rather let him take it all, inasmuch as my lord the king has come back in peace to his own house" (v. 30), reveal the true nature of his heart, which stands in bold contrast to the words of Ziba in 16:3.[43] As Fokkelman has noted, the immaterial *ḥeseḏ* of Mephibosheth is a sincere response to the *ḥeseḏ* of David, and

---

[40] If the *"mepi"* in Mephibosheth is a reference to "mouth" there may be another (subtle) thought play here. Although the word "mouth" does not occur in this verse, attention is drawn to Mephibosheth's continual speaking. So whether Mephibosheth means "mouth of shame" or "What is the mouth (command) of the protective spirit?," perhaps the writer is suggesting that although this man from "Lo Debar" cannot use his feet, he certainly can make a convincing case with his words (that is, mouth)!

[41] Bergen, *1, 2 Samuel*, p. 431, is an example of this. Others, however, believe David makes this decision because he is unsure of who is telling the truth. Gordon, *I&II Samuel*, p. 291, takes this view.

[42] There is one final mention of Mephibosheth in 2 Samuel 21:7, but he does not speak or play a significant part in the story. He is only mentioned to assure the reader that David faithfully kept his covenant with Jonathan.

[43] *Contra* Charles Conroy, *Absalom Absalom! Narrative and Language in 2 Sam 13–20*, Analecta Biblica 81 (Rome: Biblical Institute, 1978), p. 106, who writes, "The narrator's apparent refusal or inability to come to a clear decision is really a subtle way of showing that both Meribaal and Ziba deserve the reader's contempt. The narrator wants the whole House of Saul to be seen in an unfavorable light." Although Conroy's statement pertains to 2 Sam. 13–20, it is clear that the books of Samuel as a whole do not cast an unfavorable light on the whole House of Saul. Conroy's statement ignores the fact that the story of Mephibosheth in chaps. 16 and 19 must be connected with 2 Sam. 9, which, in turn, clearly alludes to 1 Sam. 20. Jonathan is certainly cast in a favorable light in 1 Sam. 20, as he is elsewhere in 1 Samuel. Similarly, once Ziba's ruse is exposed for what it is, Mephibosheth's character is exonerated.

stands in contrast to the material *ḥeseḏ* of Ziba.[44] Baldwin states, "The one who comes out of the incident unscathed is the crippled Mephibosheth, who rises above financial considerations and takes genuine pleasure in the return of his lord the king in safety."[45]

Mephibosheth: A Picture of the Past, Present, and Future

We have already noted many parallels between the houses of Saul and Eli.[46] Mephibosheth's life and circumstances provide even more connections with the past.[47]

First, both houses have the word "left" in common: "Is there still anyone who is *left* of the house of Saul?" (2 Sam. 9:1); "Everyone who is *left* in your house..." (1 Sam. 2:36). This word emphasizes that judgment will devastate both houses, leaving only a small remnant. Second, Eli's house is told they will "bow down" to the faithful priest God raises up (1 Sam. 2:36). In a similar manner, Mephibosheth "bows down" before David (2 Sam. 9:6), the "faithful" one who has replaced Saul. Third, it is said that Eli's house will be dependent upon another for their bread (1 Sam. 2:36). Mephibosheth becomes dependent upon David as he is assigned a portion at the king's table (2 Sam. 9:7).

In an interesting twist, Mephibosheth's present circumstances also anticipate the future fate of David's house.[48] In 2 Kings 25:30 it is the Davidic king Jehoiachin who now sits and eats at the table of the king of Babylon "continually" (Hebrew *ṭāmîḏ*). This word is also used of Mephibosheth in 2 Sam. 9:7, 10, 13). Just as the house of Saul was devastated by judgment and the oppression of a foreign enemy, so will the house of David be in time to come. Finally, as David shows kindness to Mephibosheth "for the sake of " Jonathan (2 Sam. 9:1, 7), so God shows kindness to the descendants of David "for the sake of " David (e.g., 1 Kings 15:4; 2 Kings 20:6).

Past, present, and future collide in the character of Mephibosheth. Their encounter vividly reveals the certainty of judgment on sin, yet the surety of mercy because of the *ḥeseḏ* of the Lord. Any family (Eli's, Saul's, or David's) that takes God's promises for granted and persistently presumes upon

---

[44] Fokkelman, *King David*, p. 32.

[45] Baldwin, *1&2 Samuel*, p. 277.

[46] See chap. 5, p. 76.

[47] The subsequent observations are based on Polzin, *David and the Deuteronomist*, pp. 102-106, and are neatly summarized by Hamilton, *Handbook*, pp. 323-324.

[48] The similarities between Mephibosheth and the end of Kings is explored in more detail in the following two articles: Anthony R. Ceresko, "The Identity of 'the Blind and the Lame' (*'iwwer upisseaḥ*) in 2 Samuel 5:8b," *CBQ* 63, 2001, pp. 23-30; and Jeremy Schipper, "Reconsidering the Imagery of Disability in 2 Samuel 5:8b," *CBQ* 67, 2005, pp. 422-434.

his goodness will finally face the judgment of God. But against this background amazing grace is unveiled through Mephibosheth. Even in judgment, God is faithful to preserve a remnant.

Mephibosheth: A Type of Us All

While we cannot say that David rescued Mephibosheth from a life of destitution, still David treated him with uncharacteristic graciousness for a monarch of that era. And if we look at what David did for him "through New Testament eyes," there are many valid parallels to the relationship we have with Jesus our King.

David Guzik provides one of the most complete lists of these comparisons. Here are just a few of the many he suggests:[49] 1) We are separated from our King because of our wicked ancestors; 2) We separated ourselves from the King because we did not know him or his love for us; 3) Our King sought us out before we sought him; 4) The King's kindness is extended to us for the sake of another; 5) The King's kindness is based on covenant; 6) The King returns to us more than we lost in hiding from him; 7) We are received as sons (and daughters) at the King's table with access to the King and fellowship with him; and 8) The King's honor does not immediately take away all of our weakness and lameness, but it gives us favor and standing that overcome this sting and transforms the way we view ourselves. We can be thankful that our King does not make rash judgments to our detriment as David later does; David was a fallible foreshadowing of our King Jesus, who is the perfect fulfillment. 2 Samuel 9 therefore contains the gospel in miniature for those who have "ears to hear."

Concluding Reflections: Ziba and Mephibosheth—How's Your Serve?

As the language of these passages suggests, the major theme of the Ziba/Mephibosheth narratives, at least from the perspective of their characters, must be servanthood. The writer demonstrates that we can learn to sound good and look the part of a servant while harboring feelings of envy and greed. Ziba is a reflection of those who take the form of a servant begrudgingly, either because they have no choice, or because it suits their goal of achieving something for themselves. Once again the author has succeeded in reminding us that appearances can be deceiving.

The definition of a servant is one who looks out for the welfare and interests of his or her master. A servant grasping at the first opportunity to improve his or her own standing at the expense of the master does not under-

---

[49] For a complete list see, David Guzik, *Verse by Verse Commentary: 2 Samuel*, EWCS (Redlands: Enduring Word Media, 2004), pp. 70-71.

stand loyalty (*hesed*) or servanthood. Jesus captures the idea in his parable of the servant who works in the field, plowing or tending sheep, and then must come in and prepare supper for his master before he can consider taking care of his own needs (Luke 17:7–8). Jesus concludes by saying,

> Does he thank that servant because he did the things that were commanded him? I think not. So likewise you, when you have done all those things which you are commanded, say, "We are unprofitable servants. We have done what was our duty to do." (Luke 17:9–10)

Looking at the larger picture presented in 1 and 2 Samuel, Mephibosheth becomes a fulfillment of Hannah's words in 1 Samuel 2:8, "He raises the poor from the dust and lifts the beggar from the ash heap, to set them among princes and make them inherit the throne of glory." While he did not live the life of a beggar, Mephibosheth was dependent on the magnanimity of Machir and was certainly "poor" apart from his benefactor, having nothing of his own. The lame man was taken from obscurity and set among princes.

Even more powerful is the exact parallel between Hannah's exhortation in 1 Samuel 2:3 and Mephibosheth's conduct: "Talk no more so very proudly; let no arrogance come from your *mouth*, for the Lord is the God of knowledge; and by Him actions are weighed." It is not just the immediate narrative of Mephibosheth that justifies him, but also this broader context. Mephibosheth presents the picture of a true servant. He unfailingly treats his master with loyalty and respect. Even when he is falsely accused and suffers loss, no arrogance is found in his mouth (Hannah's word is "*mepi*"!). Instead, he accepts it graciously, realizing that all he has is a *gift*. He trusts the judgment of his master and will abide by his decision. After all, it is the safety and well-being of the king that matters most. It is this selfless attitude, expressed so beautifully in Mephibosheth's final words (2 Sam. 19:30), that causes his character to shine more brightly than the majority in 1 and 2 Samuel. In the end, the man crippled in both feet stands tall.

Chapter 15

Shimei: The Ugly (an unspecified relative of Saul)

Shimei went along the hillside opposite him and cursed as he went (2 Sam. 16:13)

Shimei the Mudslinger (2 Sam. 16:5–13)[1]

When I was young and someone called me a name, I used to say the old rhyme, "Sticks and stones may break my bones but names will never hurt me." In Shimei's case there may not have been any sticks but there was plenty of name-calling, stone-throwing, and dirt-flinging (literally and figuratively)! Of course, it is not true that "names will never hurt me." Words are powerful; and the ancients took a curse very seriously. Name-calling is especially hurtful if we detect a note of truthfulness behind the accusation. In David's case, Shimei's mudslinging and stone throwing hit the mark, though not in the way Shimei intended.

We are introduced to Shimei as David is fleeing from Absalom, appearing at the end of a long line of encounters. As the author has slowly tracked David's journey from Jerusalem up and over the Mount of Olives (15:17, 30, 32; 16:1), the reader can note a steady deterioration in these encounters—from loyal followers (Ittai, Zadok & Abiathar, and Hushai), to a dubious follower (Ziba), to the outright hostile encounter with Shimei. While Hushai and Ziba are said "to meet" David and offer him assistance and support, the author says that Shimei "came out" (a more aggressive word—see below), "cursing." It is also no accident that the final two encounters involve people from the house of Saul (16:1, 5), and if there is some doubt about Ziba's sincerity, there is no ambiguity in Shimei's feelings for David.

Ironically, Shimei's assault on David happens at the town of Bahurim, which means, "chosen."[2] In Shimei's view, David is not the "chosen" of the Lord but has been "chosen" to experience Yahweh's wrath (v. 8). The word "curse" occurs seven times in this paragraph (vv. 5, 7, 9, 10, 11, 12, and 13); and based on the wider context, David is certainly experiencing a "curse" from Yahweh.[3] Nathan had told David that because he had "despised" the

---

[1] This paragraph extends to v. 14, but Shimei disappears from the narrative after v. 13. For the outline and chiastic structure of this text see, Walter Brueggemann, "On Coping With Curse: A Study of 2 Sam. 16:5–14," *CBQ* 36, 1974, pp. 177-178, and Youngblood, *1, 2 Samuel*, pp. 1000-1001.

[2] Fokkelman, *King David*, pp. 195-196, points out that this is the first place in the rebellion narrative where the words "king" and "David" are combined, highlighting the irony of this place name.

[3] Carlson, *David, the Chosen King*, entitles a section of his book (pp. 129-193), "David Under the Curse."

word of the Lord, God would raise up evil from his own house (2 Sam. 12:9–11). Once again the theme announced in 1 Sam. 2:30 becomes significant: "Those who honor Me, I will honor, and those who despise Me shall be lightly esteemed," or "cursed."[4]

The words of Shimei's curse give their own portrait of the man. The narrator tells us,

> And thus Shimei said when he cursed, "Get out, get out you man of blood(shed), you man of Belial. The Lord has caused to return on you all the blood of the house of Saul in whose place you reign, and the Lord has given the kingdom into the hand of Absalom your son, and look you [*are caught*] in your own evil because a man of blood(shed) are you!" (vv. 7–8, my translation)

Shimei's words, "Get out, get out..." echo the same word used to describe his coming out to confront David (v. 5). The word means to "come out" or "go forth." It is sometimes used in a military context of an army going forth to battle (e.g., 2 Sam. 18:6; 20:7) and it has a similar aggressive meaning here. Shimei's "coming out" is clearly an act of hostility, as he comes cursing and throwing stones. On the other hand, when he uses this same word against David he clearly means "get out." These words will later return to haunt Shimei and bring about his own demise (1 Kings 2:36, 37, 42).

Shimei follows up his aggressive introduction with two vulgar descriptions of David, that stand parallel to one another—"man of blood," and "man of Belial." It is true that David is a "man of blood," in that he was responsible for the death of innocent Uriah (2 Sam. 11:15–17; 12:9); but this is not what Shimei means. His accusation concerns the "blood of the house of Saul," as he apparently seeks to blame David for the deaths of Abner and Ishbosheth, as well as the deaths of Saul and his other sons.[5] The reader knows that this accusation is unfounded, because the author has repeatedly vindicated David of the deaths of Saul's family (2 Sam. 1:14–16; 3:26–39; 4:8–12).[6]

---

[4] See chap. 4, pp. 60-64.

[5] Many scholars also think that Shimei has in mind the events of 2 Sam. 21:1–14. While this is a possibility, Fokkelman, *King David*, p. 198, states, "Since the adjectival adjunct 'in whose stead you became king' immediately follows this, Shimei is most probably not referring to the bloody affair described in II Sam. 21, but to the Saulide losses at the end of Saul's reign and shortly thereafter."

[6] James Vanderkam, "Davidic Complicity in the Deaths of Abner and Eshbaal: A Historical and Redactional Study," *JBL* 99, 1980, pp. 521-539, contends that later editors of the Samuel material vindicated David of these crimes, but the historical reality is that David was involved in their deaths. However, I am in agreement with Bergen, *1, 2 Samuel*, p. 408, n. 148, who states, "This position runs counter to the bib-

Shimei's curse therefore comes across as the ranting and raving of a bitter man. It is uttered by one who sees through the politically colored glasses of a disenfranchised member of Saul's family. Godly justice is not his objective: it is revenge, not righteous indignation that motivates Shimei. The word "blood," used twice here, will occur two more times in the final denouement of Shimei's story. On his deathbed, speaking of Shimei, David will instruct Solomon, "bring his gray hair down to the grave with *blood*" (1 Kings 2:9). Then, later, Solomon will warn Shimei, "your *blood* shall be on your own head" (1 Kings 2:37)—if he violated his oath and left Jerusalem.

Shimei also uses the loaded expression "man of Belial" in reference to David (2 Sam. 16:7). Previously we have noted that this expression characterizes those who are "worthless," in the sense that they are ungodly people deserving of death.[7] Shimei's characterization of David is just as erroneous as Eli's characterization of Hannah as a "woman of Belial" (1 Sam. 1:16). To incorrectly designate the Lord's anointed as a "man of Belial" puts Shimei in the category of a lawbreaker who violates the commandment, "You shall not revile God, nor curse a ruler of your people" (Exod. 22:28).

Shimei's next contention is harder to deny, "the Lord has given the kingdom into the hand of Absalom your son, and look you [*are caught*] in your own evil." There is some truth to this statement. 2 Samuel 11:27 states, "But the thing that David had done was *evil* in the eyes of the Lord" (my translation). And later Nathan tells David, "Thus says the Lord, 'Look I will raise up *evil* against you from your own house'" (2 Sam. 12:11—my translation). David is truly experiencing the consequences of his evil actions, but not for the reasons Shimei states. Furthermore, it remains to be seen if the Lord has "given the kingdom into the hand of Absalom," as Shimei contends. Events, as well as the explicit statement in 2 Samuel 17:14, will once again prove Shimei wrong.

Shimei's statement yields yet another word that will come back to bite him. In 1 Kings 2:44 Solomon states, "You yourself know all the *evil* which your heart knows, that you did to David my father, but the Lord will cause to return your *evil* on your own head" (my translation). Besides the double occurrence of the word "evil," Solomon also uses the loaded word "return" (or "cause to return"— *hēshîḇ*), the very word Shimei uses at the beginning of 2 Samuel 16:8 when he says, "The Lord has *caused to return* on you all the blood of the house of Saul."[8]

---

lical writer's thematic intentions as expressed in the canonical text and for that reason can be dismissed by those who accept the trustworthiness of the biblical record."

[7] See chap. 4, p. 52 and chap. 5, p. 67. McCarter, *2 Samuel*, p. 373, emphasizes the impact of this word by stating that it refers to "hell." He translates the expression as, "fiend of hell," or "son of hell."

[8] Brueggemann, *On Coping with Curse*, p. 177, has rightly noted the importance of this expression in the present passage. It is not only used here in this verse by Shimei, but

The repetition of the words, "come out," "cause to return," "blood" and "evil," not only make for a nice inclusio, relating Shimei's first appearance to his last, but they lend credibility to his guilt in cursing David. One other indication that Shimei's curse is not to be viewed favorably is that the only other person in the books of Samuel said to curse David is Goliath (1 Sam. 17:43)—not exactly good company to be in![9]

The scene switches to Abishai's and David's reaction to Shimei's curse (vv. 9–12).[10] David's reaction of humility and submission to the will of Yahweh provides a foil to the attitudes of both Abishai and Shimei. As verse 13 shows, there is a gulf between David and Shimei. That gulf is not only the valley that physically separates them, but also the difference in their attitudes and actions. The final picture of Shimei in this text parallels the opening, as he continues cursing and throwing stones at David and his entourage (v. 13). The writer adds an unusual, but colorful, expression to the actions of Shimei which well sum up the entire episode. Shimei is said to be "dirting with dirt"[11] David and his men. Alter observes, "Shimei walking along, angrily persisting in his insults, the dirt flung a material equivalent of the words uttered."[12]

Submission and Confession: Shimei Eats Dirt (2 Samuel 19:16–23)

For all of his faults, Shimei does indeed display boldness. He was not afraid to face down a whole army with nothing but a repertoire of stones and dirt; and after the defeat of Absalom, the king's return to Jerusalem being imminent, he does not waste any time presenting himself before David. However, while it appears that the stone-slinging incident of chapter 16 was a "lone ranger job," this time Shimei does not come alone. While he is quick to respond, he wisely puts himself in the good company of the men of Judah, and, more especially, in the company of a thousand Benjamites, as well as Ziba and his household. If Shimei were a life insurance salesman he could not have put together a more effective threefold package! Being in the company of the king's own tribe is either a stroke of genius or good fortune. Ziba, who is currently in the king's good graces, could perhaps be called on as a media-

---

its correlate is found in David's hopeful words, "Perhaps the Lord will look on my iniquity and the Lord will [cause to] return to me good instead of his cursing this day" (v. 12—my translation).

[9] Hamilton, Handbook, p. 350, makes the interesting observation that, "Shimei's throwing stones at David (v. 6) recalls David slinging a stone at Goliath (1 Sam. 17:49)." In one narrative David slings a stone at the one who curses him (and his God); in the other narrative, the one who curses David throws the stones!

[10] We will examine Abishai's reaction in chap. 21.

[11] Youngblood, 1, 2 Samuel, p. 1003, points out that this is the only occurrence of this expression in the OT. "Dirting with dirt" is his translation.

[12] Alter, The David Story, p. 293.

tor, a character witness of sorts (although, of course, he has his own agenda for being there). Shimei's trump card, however, is the thousand men from Benjamin who come willing to pledge their support to the king if all goes well, or who could withdraw their support if the king responds inappropriately. While he cannot control David's response, he has certainly stacked the deck in his favor.

Shimei further shows his eagerness by plunging into the Jordan River and being the first to present himself before the king (v. 18). This is a case of the last being first. Shimei, who was the last to speed David on his journey with a parade of rocks and curses, is now the first to welcome him back to his kingdom. The contrast between one who had so vehemently cursed the king and one who now lies at his feet begging for mercy is acute. Shimei, who never appears to be at a loss for words (except in his final appearance before Solomon), has prepared a fine confession. He makes no excuses (unlike his long lost relative Saul) but fully accepts the blame for his actions, asking that the king not impute or remember his wrong (v. 19). He confesses that he has sinned and seeks to demonstrate his goodwill by being, "the first to come today of all the house of Joseph[13] to go down to meet my lord the king" (v. 20).

Shimei's choice of words, again, proves interesting. He states that he has come to "meet" the king. We might recall that this was the language used of loyal subjects as David was fleeing Jerusalem (2 Sam. 15:32; 16:1)—language that was not used of Shimei who "came out cursing" (2 Sam. 16:5). Other words that link this story with the previous narrative are the words, "cause to return" (translated "impute" in the NKJV—19:19), "go out" (used here of David's flight from Jerusalem, translated "left" in the NKJV—v. 19), "curse" (v. 21), and the description of Shimei as "Shimei, the son of Gera, the Benjamite who was from Bahurim" (v. 16, cf. 16:5, 11).

The ball is now in David's court, who, unlike some of his courtiers (namely, Abishai—v. 21), has enough political sagacity to know the only proper response to make is a declaration of amnesty. David declares, "Shall any man be put to death today in Israel?"; and then turning to Shimei he swears an oath saying, "You shall not die" (vv. 22–23). David's declaration is reminiscent of Shimei's relative, Saul, who made a similar proclamation after a battle that established him as king (1 Sam. 11:12–15). Ironically, the men that Saul spared are called "sons of Belial" (1 Sam. 10:27), the same name Shimei had called David (2 Sam. 16:7). In the final verse of this scene, David makes an oath not to harm Shimei. However, in Shimei's final scene, Shimei will swear an oath that will lead to his own undoing.

---

[13] Shimei is, of course, from the tribe of Benjamin. The phrase "house of Joseph" is shorthand for the northern tribes, or Israel.

Shimei and David's "Deathbed Vendetta" (1 Kings 2:8–9)

Shimei does not reappear in the narrative until the accession of Solomon to the throne. As David lies on his deathbed he gives some final instructions to the newly-appointed king. Along with instructions about keeping the Word of God, David gives practical advice on how Solomon should deal with certain people (1 Kings 2:1–9). David is especially concerned with how Solomon should treat three people. His speech is arranged chiastically as he recommends death for Joab (vv. 5–6), blessing for the sons of Barzillai (v. 7), and death for Shimei (vv. 8–9).[14] Some think this picture of a dying David is not very becoming. It seems that in two out of three cases he has revenge on his mind.[15] Fretheim states, "The immediate juxtaposition of personal faithfulness and public actions, both merciful and merciless, is striking...the reader cannot but wonder if David hasn't slipped on this one."[16] Others, however, believe there are legitimate reasons for David's actions. Koopmans, for example, writes,

> It is inadequate to view David's charges...as executions of a personal vendetta contrasting sharply with the emphasis on obedience to the law....The beginning of David's reign is characterized by examples of executions which are intended to typify his respect for the office of the anointed rather than a desire for revenge (2 Sam. i 13–16, iv 9–12). His actions won the respect of the people. David now instructs Solomon to act similarly.[17]

Does David die with venom on his lips, revenge in his heart, and as a violator of the law he has just told Solomon to observe? Even though our focus here is on Shimei, this is an important question to address. I am in agreement with those who find David's actions to be legitimate. If we step back and look at the big picture presented by the author(s) of Samuel and Kings, it must be admitted that, despite his shortcomings, David is pictured in a favorable light as a man after God's heart. For example, the author of Kings states,

---

[14] This chiasm (death-blessing-death) is not only thematic but also structural. See W.T. Koopmans, "The Testament of David in 1 Kings 2:1–10," *VT* 41, 1991, pp. 429-449.

[15] For example, House, *1, 2 Kings*, p. 98, writes, "Certainly David does have personal revenge on his mind."

[16] Terence Fretheim, *First and Second Kings*, Westminster Bible Companion (Louisville: Westminster John Knox Press, 1999), p. 25.

[17] Koopmans, "The Testament of David," p. 447.

Nevertheless for David's sake the LORD his God gave him a lamp in Jerusalem, by setting up his son after him and by establishing Jerusalem; because David did what was right in the eyes of the LORD, and had not turned aside from anything that He commanded him all the days of his life, except in the matter of Uriah the Hittite. (1 Kings 15:4–5)[18]

With this kind of portrayal of David, I find it extremely unlikely that the author would be suggesting that David's final words are words of vengeance, or that he is ironically charging Solomon to obey the Law while he himself violates it in his final breath. It is much more likely that those of the 21st century who would indict David do not fully appreciate the cultural setting and beliefs that motivated him. As Richard Nelson has observed,

> The problem of Shimei (vv. 8–9) involves the concepts of the irrevocable curse and the inconvenient oath. In the Old Testament a word is a powerful, objective thing. Even though David had pardoned Shimei for his crime (II Sam. 16:5–11; 19:21–23), his "grievous curse" (literally the "sickening curse") still hung suspended over David's house. Since David's own oath to Shimei was also irrevocable, he was unable to do anything about the problem. Solomon, however, was free to take action and arrange a violent death in order to disarm the curse.[19]

Thus, by modern standards David's actions may appear vindictive, but in point of fact, David has legitimate reasons for his instructions—reasons that the author seems to sanction based on his favorable portrayal of David. Finally, it should be noted that David never violates his oath to Shimei. He is true to his word and does not put him to death.[20] However, he would not be a very good king, or father, if he did not warn Solomon about potential threats to the throne that needed his attention.

In verse 8, David draws Solomon's attention to Shimei and rehearses for him the story covered in 2 Sam. 16:5–13 and 19:16–23. This also acts as a

---

[18] This is only one of many statements in 1 and 2 Kings that pictures David as a faithful servant of the Lord (see also, 1 Kings 9:4–5; 11:4, 6, 32–33, 38; 14:8; 15:11; 2 Kings 18:3; 22:2).

[19] Richard Nelson, *First and Second Kings*, IBC (Atlanta: John Knox Press, 1987), p. 24. See the similar statement by Ackroyd, *The Second Book of Samuel*, p. 152, who writes, "A curse is a terrible thing, because of the power believed to inhere in actual words."

[20] A. Graeme Auld, *Kings*, DSB, (Philadelphia: Westminster Press, 1986), p. 13, states, "Unhappily for Shimei, David's oath was a personal one and a formal one, and was to die with him."

reminder for the reader and provides the setting for David's instructions in 1 Kings 2:9. David tells Solomon "not [to] hold him guiltless."[21] Re-examining the account in 2 Sam. 19:22–23 reveals that David never told Shimei that he would be forgiven for his cursing of the king. He only promised that he would not put him to death. In fact, several passages in the books of Samuel (all spoken by David) declare that one who assaults the Lord's anointed will not be held "guiltless" (1 Sam. 24:6; 26:9; 2 Sam. 1:14–16).[22] Shimei was guilty of violating the Law (Exod. 22:28), and his powerful influence in the tribe of Benjamin, coupled with his clear hostility to the house of David, made him a real threat to the security of Solomon's throne.

David's final words ironically recall Shimei's curse. He says, "bring down his gray hair with blood to Sheol" (my translation). David uses a similar expression with reference to Joab, but instead of using the word "peace," as he does in verse 6, he substitutes the all important word "blood," recalling Shimei's words, "man of blood" (2 Sam. 16:7, 8). The expression is even more ironic in that the word "Sheol" looks exactly like the word "Shaul" (Saul) in Hebrew. Thus this "Saulide" is to descend to "Sheol" in blood! The stage is now set and the reader waits to see how Solomon will exercise his "wisdom" in order to carry out David's instruction.

Shimei's Exit (1 Kings 2:36–46)

Growing up I used to watch a cartoon character called "Snagglepuss." When Snagglepuss was going somewhere he would always say, "Exit stage

---

[21] Hamilton, *Handbook*, p. 226 (in a different context), points out that the word *hēshîḇ* is uniquely used in connection with the guilt, or reparation offering (*'āshām*). Hamilton states, "The implication is that with an *'āshām* offering damage has been done vis-à-vis one of the Lord's 'holy things,' and restitution is mandated." While this word is never used in the context of Shimei and David's relationship, it is interesting that the word *nqh*, meaning "guiltless" is. *'āshām* is a word that denotes the offering itself, *nqh* denotes the state of being free from guilt, that is, "pure or innocent," and so the two concepts are closely related. My point is that use of the word *hēshîḇ* may be yet another possible link to Shimei's guilt, since no restitution has been made for his cursing and no forgiveness has been pronounced. Along this line, Shimei begs David, "Do not let my lord impute (*yaḥashāḇ*) iniquity to me" (2 Sam. 19:19). See footnote 22 below for further discussion on the word *nqh*.

[22] 1 Sam. 26:9 uses the same word found here in 1 Kings 2:9 from the verb *nqh*. This word is usually used in the positive sense of being free or exempt from guilt. However-er, the most frequent occurrence of the adjectival form (*naqî*) connects it with the word "blood" (*dām*), meaning "innocent blood." Because of Shimei's accusation against David concerning the "blood of Saul's house," perhaps David is saying that Shimei is not to be treated as "innocent blood," or guiltless. On this word see, J.P.J. Olivier, "*nqh*," 5927, *NIDOTTE*, vol. 3, pp. 152-154.

right," or "Exit stage left." In this his final scene, Shimei exits the stage of the narrative because of an unwise choice to exit Jerusalem, leading to another exit—down to Sheol in fulfillment of David's words.

For the third time, Shimei is included in a list of encounters between a king and his subjects. For the sake of convenience we will designate these narratives as A (2 Sam. 16:5–13), B (2 Sam. 19:16–23), and C (1 Kings 2:36–46). When compared, these narratives present interesting similarities and differences. In A and C, Shimei is the last in a line of encounters with the king, whereas in B he is first. In A and B, several members of the house of Saul appear in back-to-back scenes. In C, Shimei is the only Saulide. Another similarity between A and B is Abishai's offer to kill Shimei, but David protests and offers him protection. By way of contrast, in C the king (Solomon) puts him to death. A and C involve hostile encounters between Shimei and the king, whereas B concerns reconciliation (of a sort). In A it is Shimei who is hostile, and in C it is the king. In B, David swears an oath and keeps it, and in C Shimei swears an oath and breaks it. Finally, all three narratives share common vocabulary (see pp. 184-186 above, and the immediate discussion below).

David had said to Solomon, "You are a wise man and know what you ought to do" (1 Kings 2:9). Solomon's plan is indeed wise. It should be noted that he does not execute Shimei for cursing his father, but instead puts him under a sort of "house arrest." (Thus neither David, nor Solomon, violate David's oath.)[23] Solomon makes Jerusalem Shimei's city of refuge.[24] As long as he stays within its confines, no harm will come to him. Solomon tells Shimei, "Build yourself a house in Jerusalem and dwell there, and do not go out from there anywhere" (2:36). He continues by warning him that on the day he "goes out" (using the verb that recalls Shimei's initial encounter with David) and crosses the Kidron Valley, he will certainly die. He then adds the words, "your blood shall be on your own head," using the key word "blood" that characterizes the story of Shimei. Shimei agrees (admittedly he doesn't have much choice) and all goes well for three years (v. 38).

The fact that the writer states he dwelt in Jerusalem "many days" and then notes in verse 39 that a period of three years transpired, serves to demonstrate that Solomon kept his side of the agreement and would not have harmed Shimei had he stayed in Jerusalem. However, we are informed that Shimei's slaves ran away. The description of his slaves "running away" is

---

[23] Ackroyd's statement, *The Second Book of Samuel*, p. 180, is worth quoting at length: "David's solemn oath assuring Shimei of his life was carefully observed. Yet the curse remained spoken and at the end of his life David is represented as handing on this legacy to his son Solomon. The latter, by a skilful stratagem, contrived to bring Shimei to a death which was a just judgement upon himself, avoiding any bloodguilt on the royal house."

[24] Peter J. Leithart, *1 & 2 Kings*, BTCB (Grand Rapids: Brazos Press, 2006), p. 30.

probably a wordplay on his hometown. Because Shimei had to stay in Jerusalem, he was not allowed to return to *Bahurim*. But when his slaves "flee" (the Hebrew word is from *bārah* —note the reversal of letters *b*, *h*, *r*), he violates his oath and pursues them to Gath. We are not told what Shimei is thinking, so we are left to guess. Has his concern over lost slaves caused temporary amnesia? Does he think this is a special circumstance? Since he doesn't have to cross the Kidron to go in the direction of Gath, does he think this technically exempts him? Whatever was going on in Shimei's mind, it was a gross miscalculation and provided Solomon with the opportunity to rid his kingdom of this troublemaker.

Upon his return to Jerusalem, Shimei is summoned before Solomon. Despite always having something to say, he doesn't utter a word as he appears before the king. Some impugn Solomon, by saying he does not give Shimei a chance to respond. Furthermore, it is pointed out that the king accuses him of breaking an oath—something not previously mentioned in the text.[25] However, these are not serious objections, and miss the point the narrator is trying to make. First, it is clear that Shimei had given his word not to leave Jerusalem (v. 38). It may be that the writer has withheld the word "oath" until verse 42 for dramatic effect. There seems to be a clear contrast between David keeping his oath to Shimei (2 Sam. 19:23; 1 Kings 2:8) and Shimei breaking his oath to Solomon. Here is yet one more word (like "go out," "blood," "cause to return," and "evil") that is returned "upon the head" of Shimei. Second, the reason Shimei gives no response is because he is clearly guilty—so what can he say? Either Shimei said nothing at all, or the writer has omitted his words as a way of showing that he had no real defense.[26]

In his accusation, Solomon makes a clever play on Shimei's name, which comes from the Hebrew word *sh^{e}ma'*, meaning "to hear" or "obey."[27] In the latter part of verse 42 Solomon, speaking to Shimei, says, "And you said to me, ' The word I have *heard* is good.' " While these words come from Solomon's lips, the narrator may be making a comment on Shimei's overall behavior. Although his name means "obedience," Shimei is not an obedient person. He cannot be expected to live up to his word. Rebellion is in his nature. His cursing of David was the first evidence of this trait, and now his breaking of the oath confirms this truth about him.

---

[25] Hamilton, *Handbook*, p. 387.

[26] Alter, *The David Story*, p. 107, notes a "biblical convention that can be schematized as: And X said to Y; [no response from Y]; and X said to Y, with the intervening silence being dramatically significant." 1 Kings 2:43–44 is a perfect example of this. In other words, Solomon asks Shimei, "Why then have you not kept the oath of the Lord and the commandment I gave you?" Shimei is speechless; he can offer no response, and so we are told that Solomon continues speaking in v. 44.

[27] Fokkelman, *King David*, p. 406, also notes this wordplay.

Solomon has one more stinging rebuke for Shimei, in which he uses the loaded word "evil" twice, and the word "caused to return" once (v. 44). As noted earlier, these words recall Shimei's original curse against David (2 Sam. 16:8). Furthermore, Solomon's words, "the Lord will return your evil on your own head," parallel his words concerning Joab in 1 Kings 2:32 when he says, "So the Lord will return his blood on his head." The only difference is Solomon substitutes "evil" for "blood." As we have seen, either word would be appropriate to Shimei's character, but having already said, "your blood shall be on your own head"[28] (v. 37), Solomon chooses to emphasize his wickedness.

When a guilty person left a city of refuge, he exposed himself to the avenger of blood (Num. 35:26–28). Similarly, Solomon now takes on the role of avenger of blood as he commits Shimei to the executioner's sword (v. 46).[29] The man who first appeared flinging dust at David (2 Sam. 16:13), is now returned to the dust from whence he came (Gen. 3:19).

Conclusion: "I will Curse him who Curses you"

The words that God spoke to Abram in Genesis 12:3 are a fitting summary for the life of Shimei. Because he chose to curse the Lord's anointed, he was cursed in return.[30] One might object that Shimei confessed his sin and sought forgiveness (2 Sam. 19:19–20). But the picture presented of Shimei's confession is not of a truly repentant individual; rather it is a picture of a politically expedient individual. Shimei is caught by his own words, and if he values his life then he has no choice but to apologize. However, the apology is made with the political backing of 1000 men. True repentance does not involve twisting the arm of the one being asked for forgiveness!

Not much good can be said about Shimei based on his portrait in the books of Samuel and Kings, unless, as noted earlier, we laud his boldness. But even his boldness seems to be born more out of his crass nature than any real courage. Shimei is the opposite of his name. He is not "Mr. Obedience." Rather, he is "Mr. Troublemaker," a rebel at heart, looking out for his own causes and family interests. Shimei is a warning to all who would put family loyalty above matters of right and wrong. We *should* be loyal to family, but not at the expense of truth. One who slings mud, unjustly accuses others, kicks God's people when they are down, strong-arms forgiveness out of others when it's politically expedient, and shows no real heartfelt repentance, may, in the end, experience a similar fate to Shimei.

---

[28] It is also significant that David used the same words when he put the Amalekite to death who claimed to have killed the Lord's anointed (2 Sam. 1:16).

[29] Leithart, *1 & 2 Kings*, p. 39.

[30] As noted earlier, this truth clearly follows an important theme in the books of Samuel. One who stretches out his hand against the Lord's anointed will not be guiltless (1 Sam. 24:6; 26:9; 2 Sam. 1:14–16).

Section 4

The Family of David

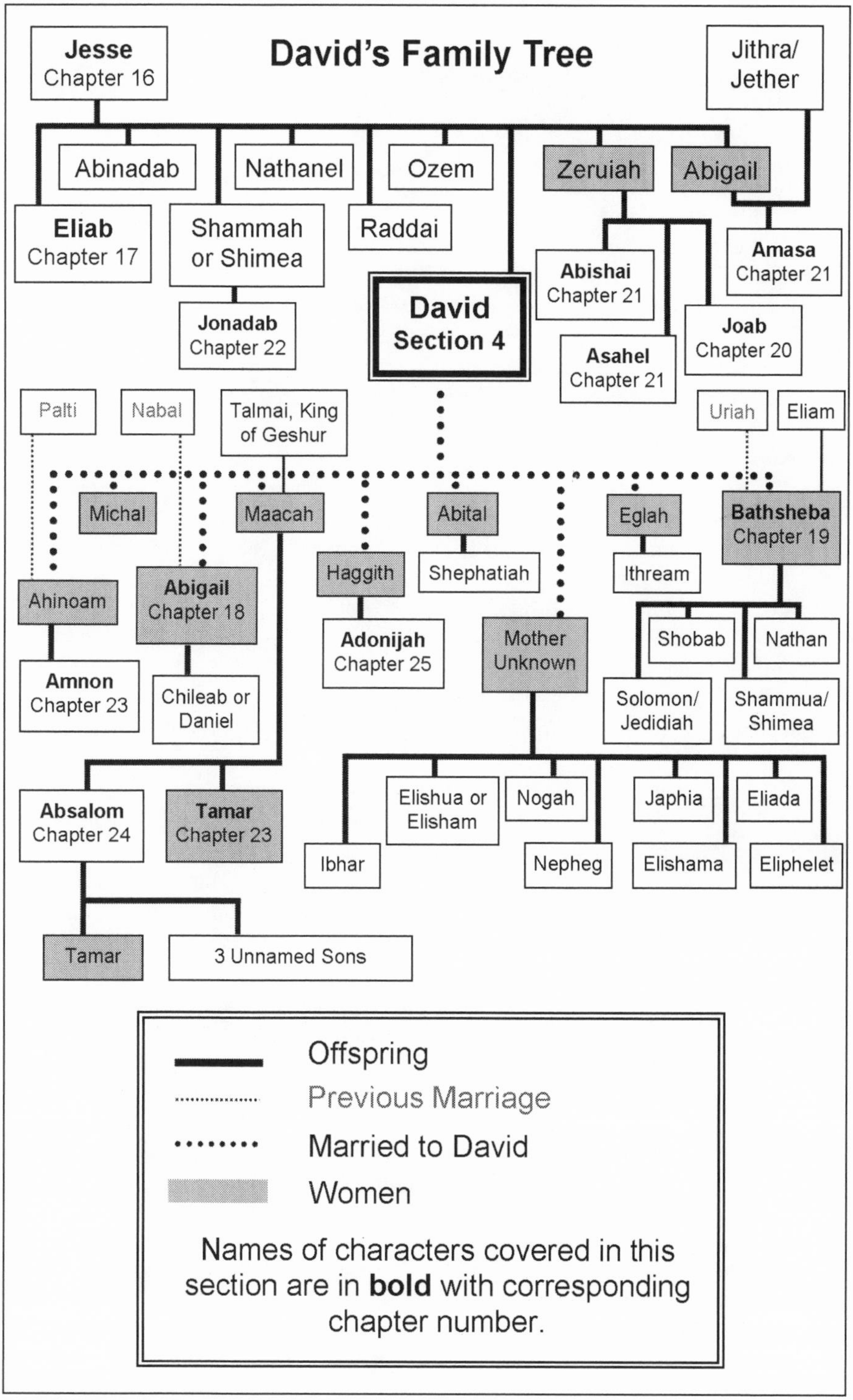
David's Family Tree
Jesse
Chapter 16
Jithra/
Jether
Abinadab
Nathanel
Ozem
Zeruiah
Abigail
Eliab
Chapter 17
Shammah
or Shimea
Raddai
Amasa
Chapter 21
Abishai
Chapter 21
Jonadab
Chapter 22
David
Section 4
Joab
Chapter 20
Asahel
Chapter 21
Palti
Nabal
Talmai, King
of Geshur
Uriah
Eliam
Michal
Maacah
Abital
Eglah
Bathsheba
Chapter 19
Haggith
Shephatiah
Ithream
Ahinoam
Abigail
Chapter 18
Adonijah
Chapter 25
Mother
Unknown
Shobab
Nathan
Amnon
Chapter 23
Chileab or
Daniel
Solomon/
Jedidiah
Shammua/
Shimea
Elishua or
Elisham
Nogah
Japhia
Eliada
Absalom
Chapter 24
Tamar
Chapter 23
Ibhar
Nepheg
Elishama
Eliphelet
Tamar
3 Unnamed Sons
Offspring
Previous Marriage
Married to David
Women
Names of characters covered in this section are in bold with corresponding chapter number.

Introduction to David's Family

"Who am I, O Lord GOD? And what is my house, that You have brought me this far?"
(2 Sam. 7:18)

David is the main character of the books of Samuel so it is not surprising that nearly 40 of his relatives are mentioned within its pages. This is one way in which the author demonstrates that the house of David "grew stronger and stronger" (2 Sam. 3:1). However, the majority of David's relatives are simply names in a genealogy. The author gives us information only on a handful of them. Thus, our character portraits will be limited to those few individuals.

It is obvious that the narrative is primarily about David and his key role in the unfolding purposes of God. Other relatives, whether they are brothers, wives, sons, nephews, etc., are introduced in relation to the author's overall themes, which concern God, his people, and the kingship.

The contours of David's story bear some resemblance to Saul's. There are stories that tell of David's rise to the kingship (1 Sam. 16–2 Sam. 10), his sin (2 Sam. 11–12), and his decline (2 Sam. 13–1 Kings 2). Saul's story followed a similar outline: rise (1 Sam. 9–12), sin (1 Sam. 13–15), and decline (1 Sam. 16–31).[1] This common pattern is not surprising, considering the theme of reversal announced at the outset in Hannah's prayer (1 Sam. 2:1–10), and the words of the man of God to Eli (1 Sam. 2:30). But, unlike Saul, David is the king "after God's own heart" (1 Sam. 13:14). As the story clearly shows, he is not perfect, but his response during his "decline" is different from Saul's. He confesses his sin, without making any excuses (2 Sam. 12:13; 24:10), he continues to seek the Lord in difficult circumstances (e.g., 2 Sam. 15:31–32; 24:14), and he is gracious in the good times and the bad (2 Sam. 9; 16:9–12).

David's faults and faith provide the backdrop for understanding and evaluating his relatives. For example, one of David's biggest problems was his inability to transfer his piety to his children. His affair with Bathsheba and murder of Uriah seemed to paralyze his ability to be an effective father, if he ever possessed that ability (e.g., 2 Sam. 13:21). One of the main themes of 2 Samuel 13–20 and 1 Kings 1–2 is the chaos in David's own family—a direct consequence of his sin (2 Sam. 12:10–11)—and its effects on the kingdom. David's sons imitate his sin and, in fact, push it to another level, without retaining any of his godly characteristics. Likewise, the magnanimity of David contrasts sharply with the ruthlessness of his nephews, Joab and Abishai, while David's fearless courage in facing down Goliath provides a foil to his brothers' (especially Eliab's) lack of faith (1 Sam. 17:13, 28).

---

[1] See the diagram in Hamilton, *Handbook*, p. 299.

On the other hand, the wisdom of Abigail (1 Sam. 25), the purity of Tamar (2 Sam. 13), and the strength of Bathsheba (1 Kings 1), stand in contrast to David's impetuosity, lust, and weakness. In fact, if there are any models of virtuous behavior in David's family, they are to be found among the women. This does not mean that the women are all good and the men are all bad, yet one has to search hard to find positive qualities among David's male relatives. David's father, Jesse, is probably the only exception. For literature that is sometimes accused of being very "patriarchal" in its outlook, this mostly positive portrayal of women and mostly negative portrayal of men is interesting!

Although Solomon was to stray in his later years (1 Kings 11:4), it seems that David's influence on him was positive overall. No doubt, looking back, David would have wished for a positive influence on all of his sons and relatives. Still, the legacy of David was to prove an extremely powerful influence for the good of his family and kingdom (1 Kings 15:4–5). The Davidic kingdom survived for 400 years, with his descendants reigning on the throne of Judah—such was the power of his influence according to biblical testimony.

Moreover, the end of the kingdom of Judah was not the end of the significance of the family of David. In David and his offspring a greater hope was nurtured (2 Sam. 7:12–16)—the hope of a Messiah, a descendant of David who would rule over an eternal kingdom:

> For unto us a Child is born, unto us a Son is given; and the government will be upon His shoulder. And His name will be called Wonderful, Counselor, Mighty God, Everlasting Father, Prince of Peace. Of the increase of His government and peace there will be no end. Upon the throne of David and over His kingdom, to order it and establish it with judgment and justice. From that time forward, even forever. The zeal of the LORD of hosts will perform this. (Isa. 9:6–7)

It is the family of David that carries with it, not only the hope of Israel, but of all mankind. The family of David reaches its climax in the person of Jesus of Nazareth, "the Son of David," the "King of glory," the Savior of the world.

David's family is another testimony to the faithfulness of God. God, in his power, can use even the darkest chapter in our family history for his glory. David's days seem to end in sadness, with a family that is being torn apart, but what some mean for evil, God means for good (Gen. 50:20). Many of the characters we will examine in the following chapters are examples of what *not* to be, yet the unseen hand of an all-powerful, and all-wise God, is present working all things "for good to those who love God, to those who are the called according to his purpose" (Rom. 8:28).

Chapter 16

Jesse: Provider and Supporter (David's father)

Now David was the son of that Ephrathite of Bethlehem Judah, whose name was Jesse, and who had eight sons (1 Sam. 17:12)

Father Doesn't Always Know Best (1 Sam. 16:1–12)

Jesse is first mentioned in the books of Samuel in the narrative of David's initial anointing by Samuel. It is the Book of Ruth that informs us that Jesse was none other than the grandson of Boaz, the illustrious, wealthy and gracious landowner from Bethlehem (Ruth 4:21–22) who married Ruth the Moabitess. *Jesse* was an uncommon name among the Israelites, and its meaning and derivation are uncertain.[1] There are two things, however, that we learn about him in his introduction (16:1). First, we are told he is from Bethlehem, and, second, that God has "seen" a king among his sons. It is possible that he is one of the elders of Bethlehem, although the text is not clear on this (vv. 4b–5).

In some way that the author does not tell us, Jesse becomes aware that Samuel has been sent to anoint one of his sons. Whether Jesse and his sons know that this anointing is for kingship is debatable.[2] However, there are three good reasons for assuming that Jesse and his sons are aware of the meaning of the anointing in spite of the ambiguity: First, Samuel uses the words "chosen" and "the Lord" as he looks over each son. Three times we hear the refrain, "The Lord has not chosen this one" (or "these"), (vv. 8, 9, 10). Since the king was "The Lord's chosen," kingship would be the most obvious meaning to Jesse and his sons. What else would the Lord be "choos-

---

[1] Tsumura, *The First Book of Samuel*, p. 415.

[2] Ibid., p. 423, states, "This verse [i.e., v. 13] is careful not to say David is anointed 'king over Israel' (v. 1). To Jesse and other attendees there, the purpose of this anointing may not have been totally clear." See also, Gordon, *I&II Samuel*, p. 151. Therefore, while the Lord had revealed His divine mission to Samuel, some would argue that it is not clear whether Samuel made this obvious to Jesse or his sons. Scholars who take this position believe the sentence, "He looked at Eliab and *said*, 'Surely the LORD's anointed is before Him'" (v. 6b), refers to Samuel's inner thoughts rather than words spoken audibly. Sternberg, *Poetics*, p. 97, writes, "Considering the ambiguity of the biblical 'said' between thought and speech, he may well have announced his verdict, only to retract it the next moment." One does wonder what Jesse and his sons could possibly have thought if Samuel had not revealed the purpose of his visit to them. "Anointed for what role?" would be the obvious question. Are we to believe that Samuel anointed David and never said a word to the family about what the anointing was for? Such a circumstance would be odd indeed.

ing" one of them for? Second, the anointing by Samuel would automatically point to kingship.[3] Third, Samuel came to preside over a feast in which Jesse and his sons were the special guests. This feast recalls a similar scene involving Saul's appointment by Samuel, when he was guest of honor (1 Sam. 9:22–24; 10:1).

Jesse presents each son to Samuel in order of their birth, beginning with Eliab, the eldest. No doubt Jesse is as surprised as Samuel when Eliab is rejected (1 Sam. 16:6–7). But this surprise must turn to consternation by the time Samuel finishes rejecting each of Jesse's seven sons (v. 10).[4] Like most people of his day, Jesse assumes that special significance is attached to the eldest son; and if not the eldest, then certainly the next, or…the next. This explains why he does not see any need to have David, the youngest, present at this anointing ceremony. Surely Samuel will find the one whom he is looking for among the older sons. Having seven present probably already seems like overkill to Jesse, and so there is no reason to take number eight away from looking after the sheep. That is, until the perplexed Samuel asks, "Are all the young men here?" (v. 11a).

Jesse's response, his first spoken words, which are also the first words that describe David, are pregnant with meaning. He states, "There *remains* yet the *youngest*, and there he is, *keeping the sheep*" (v. 11b). The word "remains" is the same word that is frequently used in the OT to refer to a "remnant" (e.g., 1 Kings 19:18; Isa. 7:3—from the word *sha'ar*). What "remains" may seem insignificant to us—"the leftovers," or the "nobodies." But this word is infused with God's grace throughout the OT and speaks of his power to use what "remains" for his glory.[5] It is parallel to the next significant word Jesse uses, which means "youngest" or "smallest." Because David was the youngest, his absence seemed excusable. After all, if some great political appointment was about to take place, what relevance could that have to a

---

[3] It is true that people could be anointed for other purposes. For example, the priesthood, but this was obviously not the purpose here since only Levites descended from Aaron could qualify. A prophet could be anointed for ministry, but it is not clear that most prophets were anointed, since the OT only cites two examples (1 Kings 19:16; Isa. 61:1). Kingship remains the most obvious reason for the anointing.

[4] There is some debate as to whether Jesse had eight or seven sons. 1 Sam. 17:12 explicitly states that Jesse had eight sons, and this is also implied in 1 Sam. 16:10. However, 1 Chron. 2:13–15 lists only seven sons of Jesse, David being the last. The Chronicler is known to leave out names in other genealogies (a common practice in the ancient world—cf. Matt. 1:8). In my opinion, the Chronicler has omitted one of Jesse's sons in order to make David the seventh son, due to the significance of this number in Hebrew thought. For further discussion, see Steven L. McKenzie, "David's Family," *DOTHB*, eds. Bill T. Arnold and H.G.M. Williamson (Downers Grove: IVP Academic, 2005), p. 212.

[5] For further discussion see chap. 8, p. 90.

youth? He would only be in the way, and he could be much better utilized looking after the family property. On such a "big" occasion, there is no need for the "smallest." This is the usual reasoning of men, and Jesse is no exception.[6] But as God had done many times in the past, choosing the younger over the older (e.g., Isaac/Ishmael, Jacob/Esau, Ephraim/Manasseh), so here he would teach both Jesse and Samuel not to "judge a book by its cover" (v. 7). This is one scenario in which "father knows best" does not apply, unless by "Father" we mean God and not Jesse.

Jesse's final words, "he is keeping the sheep," are perhaps the most significant. It is well known that throughout the ancient Near East a favorite symbol of kingship was that of a shepherd. So it is not accidental that David is introduced as a shepherd here (16:11), as well as three more times in the succeeding narratives (16:19; 17:15, 34–35). Later, David will be anointed king over (all) Israel with the words, "You shall *shepherd* My people Israel, and be ruler over Israel" (2 Sam. 5:2). Nathan will convict David of sin by a parable that involves a "*ewe lamb*" (2 Sam. 12:1–4) and, in the final narrative of the book, David will show himself to be a compassionate protector of the flock with the words, "Surely I have sinned, and I have done wickedly; but these *sheep*, what have they done? Let Your hand, I pray, be against me and against my father's house" (2 Sam. 24:17b).

Jesse is a lesson to us all not to underestimate what God can do with the most "unlikely" members of our family. When we live with people it is easy to take them for granted. We can be all too aware of our loved ones' weaknesses and shortcomings, which can cause us to underestimate how God could use them. The Bible regularly affirms that God uses "small" people to do his "biggest" jobs.

Jesse—The Provider (1 Sam. 16:18–23; 17:12–18)

Jesse was taken by surprise when Samuel anointed his youngest son, but he excelled when it came to providing for his family, showing fatherly concern, and supporting the kingdom. At least this is the portrait that has been left for us in the present passages under consideration.

When Saul learns that there is a "son of Jesse" who can help him with the distressing spirit that God has sent upon him (16:14–18), he sends to Jesse and has David brought to court (v. 19). Jesse not only sends his son to the king, but he also sends a gift along with David (v. 20). The gift recalls an

---

[6] Jobling, *1 Samuel*, p. 114, sees "a lot of distance between this father and son from the outset." However, I do not detect any mistreatment of David as Jobling's words suggest ("Shades of Cinderella"). The "distance" between Jesse and David in this passage is related more to the lack of any political expectation for the youngest son— a common presupposition in ancient cultures.

earlier incident concerning Samuel's instructions to the newly-anointed Saul (1 Sam. 10:3). Samuel had told Saul that he would meet men carrying goats, bread and wine. Likewise, Jesse has David take these same three items to Saul. One could argue that these are normal daily provisions, but the fact that the author draws attention to this detail suggests that the newly-anointed David is beginning to walk the same road as the man that he is now coming to serve, and will eventually replace! Furthermore, it is interesting that Jesse, the man from Beth*lehem* (house of *bread*), sends bread (*lehem*) with David.[7] Jesse's provision of bread and other items may symbolize God's greater provision of David, who will prove to be a blessing to Saul (16:23)—David is true bread for Saul!

Chapter 17 moves us on to the battlefield where Israel is confronted by Goliath, the intimidating champion of the Philistines (vv. 1–11). Verses 12–18 inform us that the impending battle has separated Jesse and three of his sons. While Jesse remains at home due to his old age (v. 12), his three oldest sons have followed Saul to the battle (v. 13). The gulf between them is bridged by David, the youngest, who goes back and forth between Saul and the family home at Bethlehem, where he continues to "feed his father's sheep" (vv. 14–15). When concerned for his sons' welfare (literally, "peace"—*shālôm*), Jesse sends David to check on them. And once again, David does not go empty handed. Jesse sends provisions to them. As he did earlier for Saul (16:20), the man from Bethlehem sends "ten loaves" (*lehem*) to his sons (17:17), as well as dried grain. Besides providing for them, he also shows support for the war effort by sending their captain "ten cheeses" (v. 18).

Jesse charges young David with four tasks, three of which pertain to his brothers. He is to: 1) take food to his brothers; 2) take food to the captain; 3) see about the welfare of his brothers; and 4) bring back a tangible sign that they are well. For this fourth charge, the NKJV reads, "bring back news of them" (v. 18). However, this does not convey the strength of Jesse's request. He wants David to bring back a token that his brothers are indeed alright.[8] This is reminiscent of Jacob sending his young son Joseph to check on the welfare of his brothers (Gen. 37:13–14), the differences being that Jacob's sons were not on the battlefield, and there seems to be no animosity between Jesse and his sons.[9] Thus, Jesse's actions portray a concerned father who is actively involved with his sons. He cares about their welfare and seeks confirmation of it, as well as doing what he can to provide for them.

---

[7] Fokkelman, *Crossing Fates*, pp. 155-156, makes this observation.

[8] Tsumura, *The First Book of Samuel*, p. 450.

[9] There is, however, some animosity between David and his brothers (at least Eliab), though this is not life threatening to David. This is another similarity between him and Joseph.

David Protects His Parents (1 Sam. 22:3–4)

By chapter 22 David has become *persona non-grata* with Saul, which means that David's family is automatically in jeopardy. Attempting to put his parents out of harm's way, David takes them to Moab and petitions the king for asylum on their behalf. The reader might find this a curious move, were it not for the fact that the Book of Ruth reveals Jesse's (and David's) Moabite roots.[10] Furthermore, 1 Samuel 14:47 declares that Saul fought against the Moabites during his reign. Thus, the king of Moab, like King Achish of Gath later (1 Sam. 27), may have provided support to David in order to contribute to the political instability of Saul's kingdom. Whatever the king of Moab's motives were, the text indicates that David was successful in gaining a place of sanctuary for his parents, at least temporarily ("they dwelt with him all the time that David was in the stronghold"—v. 4).

Considering the event that follows—the slaughter of Ahimelech and the priests at Nob (22:9–23)—David's actions seem wise. Saul is out for blood. Ahimelech and his priestly family become the sacrificial substitute for David and his family. Saul connects the two households when he says, "Why have you conspired against me, *you and the son of Jesse?*" (v. 13a) "You shall surely die, Ahimelech, *you and all your father's house!*" (v. 16). Saul's ambition was to kill David and "all his father's house." Having failed, he chose to vent his anger on the family of Ahimelech. On this occasion it was David who provided a way of escape for Jesse who was used to providing for all his sons.

Conclusion: A Family Man

Jesse is not even mentioned by name in the final narrative in which he appears. Instead, the author has David refer to him and his wife as "my father and my mother" (1 Sam. 22:4). David "honors his father and his mother" (Exod. 20:12) by protecting them. As he flees for his own life, David does not forget his family and the perils that they face. This is an example of a son who has been raised well.[11] David had witnessed, and experienced, his father's concern and support for him and his brothers. Based on the few verses allotted to him in 1 Samuel, we can only conclude that Jesse was a family man. As he makes his sons pass before Samuel (1 Sam. 16:8–10), we can sense his

---

[10] Ancient readers were probably well aware of the Moabite origins of David's great-grandmother.

[11] A more cynical interpretation might be that "misery loves company," but there is surely more to it than that. David's effort to leave his aging parents with the king of Moab speaks well of him. He goes "the extra mile," quite literally, to secure their safety. Furthermore, the parallels with Joseph suggest that any previous animosity that existed between David and his brothers is forgiven and forgotten.

pride in them (even if a little misguided). His support for David and the rest of his sons, as well as his loyalty to Saul and the army, speak well of him. The author's brief sketch of Jesse portrays him as a patriot and a caring, faithful man who was involved in the lives of his children. No wonder that Israel's greatest king is not only remembered as "David," but also as "the son of Jesse."

Chapter 17

Eliab: The Rejected One (David's oldest brother)

But the LORD said to Samuel, "Do not look at his appearance or at his physical stature, because I have refused him." (1 Sam. 16:6–7a)

Sibling Rivalry

A Psalm attributed to David begins, "Behold, how good and how pleasant it is for brethren to dwell together in unity" (Ps. 133:1). One would hope that this obvious truth does not need stating. Yet, human experience and Scripture are both keenly aware that brothers do not always get along. Cain and Abel, Jacob and Esau, and Joseph and his brothers, are all examples of this sad fact.

We can also add David and Eliab to this list. The rivalry, only implicit in 1 Samuel 16:1–13, comes to the fore in 1 Samuel 17:28. The question arises: Does this rivalry result from Eliab's jealousy, as most commentators believe,[12] or is Eliab trying to warn his ambitious younger brother of potential danger, as Keith Bodner has suggested?[13] While Bodner is willing to accept either conclusion,[14] the answer to this question is germane to our character study of Eliab. Therefore, can we determine whether Eliab's words in 1 Samuel 17:28 are intended graciously or maliciously? I believe there is enough evidence in the text to suggest a firm conclusion. The good news regarding this rivalry is that—as with Joseph and his brothers—circumstances eventually brought David and his brother(s) together (1 Sam. 22:1).

It's All About the Heart (1 Sam. 16:1–7)

When Samuel comes to Bethlehem in 1 Samuel 16, it is with the intent of anointing a new king. At God's command, and against his better judg-

---

[12] For example, Walter Brueggemann, in *David's Truth in Israel's Imagination & Memory* (Philadelphia: Fortress Press, 1985), p. 32, writes regarding Eliab's reaction, "his anger is not against the passive Israelites as it might have been, or against the intimidating Philistines as it could have been. No, he is angry with little David. Well, of course, little brothers bother bigger brothers, especially if big brothers are pretending to be mighty men of valor—who are immobilized in fear and cannot fight. David's presence immediately exposes Eliab as a coward."

[13] Keith Bodner, "Eliab and the Deuteronomist," *JSOT* 28, 2003, pp. 55-71.

[14] While Bodner proposes that Eliab's words may have "David's best interests in mind," he contends that whether Eliab is seen as jealous or benevolent does not affect his thesis that Eliab's words have a deeper meaning in the overall context of 1 and 2 Samuel. See ibid., pp. 66-67. We will discuss Bodner's proposal in more detail later in this chapter.

ment ("If Saul hears it, he will kill me"—v. 2), Samuel arrives with the divine instruction, "You shall anoint for Me the one I name to you" (v. 3). However, Samuel's judgment fails him again when he rushes to the conclusion that Jesse's firstborn, Eliab, must be the Lord's anointed (v. 6). God had told Samuel, "I have *seen* among his sons a king for Myself " (v. 1—my translation). The Hebrew word "seen" could be translated "provide" in this context (cf. NKJV, NRSV); however, I opt for the literal translation because the word "see" is integral to the story. Rather than waiting for God to reveal the son that he has "seen," Samuel "sees" Eliab (v. 6) and is immediately convinced by his appearance that he must be the Lord's chosen. The inability of Samuel the "seer" (1 Sam. 9:18–19) to "see" correctly leads to God's rebuke in verse 7, which includes the Hebrew word "see" four more times in some form.

The fact that Eliab appears to be something that the Lord says he is not, automatically casts a shadow over his character. We are reminded of Eli, who also resembled royalty (1 Sam. 1:9), but in reality was old, heavy, and blind. I have already noted that the theme "looks can be deceiving" is prominent in the books of Samuel.[15] The story concerning Goliath will continue this theme in the next chapter (1 Sam. 17).

This puts Eliab in bad company (Eli and Goliath), but the wording of verse 7 associates him with Saul, which clinches the case. The reference to Eliab's stature making him look like a king is a clear reference to Saul (1 Sam.10:23–24), as is the word "rejected" (used frequently of Saul in the immediate context—16:1, as well as in 1 Sam. 15:23 and 26). The reference to Eliab's stature is particularly poignant as we recall Hannah's words, "Talk no more so very proudly" (1 Sam. 2:3), or as Robert Polzin translates it, "Do not multiply your words, 'Tall! Tall!' "[16] Polzin's translation points out that the same word used to describe Eliab here (as well as Saul and Goliath) is the word used by Hannah. The fact that the "looks can be deceiving" theme is prominent in three consecutive chapters (1 Sam. 15–17)[17] further suggests that Eliab is being put in a bad light.

It is true that at this point (1 Sam. 16:7) the text has given no hint of Eliab's thoughts or feelings,[18] but the attentive reader has been put on guard about his character. The Lord's statement to Samuel strongly suggests that God has looked into the heart of Eliab, as well as the other brothers, and

---

[15] See, for example, the character study of Eli in chap. 4.

[16] Polzin, *Samuel and the Deuteronomist*, p. 34.

[17] Samuel's statement to Saul in 1 Sam. 15:22, "Behold, to obey is better than sacrifice," affirms that Saul tried to "appear" obedient by using sacrifice. Thus Saul attempts to look good even though he knows he has disobeyed the Lord's command (cf. v. 24). Saul continues to be concerned about outward appearance when he says to Samuel, "I have sinned; yet honor me now, please, before the elders of my people and before Israel" (v. 30).

[18] A point made by Bodner, *Eliab and the Deuteronomist*, p. 60.

found something lacking. Earlier, when Samuel told Saul that his kingdom would not continue, he stated, "The Lord has sought for himself a man after His own heart" (13:14b). So the Lord's statement, "I have seen among his [Jesse's] sons a king for Myself " (16:1), indicates that God has found the person he was looking for. 1 Samuel 16:12 confirms that it is David.

This contrast between David's heart and his brothers' is similar to the contrast made between Eli and the faithful priest that God promises to raise up. This priest "shall do according to what is in My heart and in My mind" (1 Sam. 2:35). The contrast between Eliab and David is further heightened (excuse the pun) by the reference to David as the "smallest"[19] of the brothers (16:11). While Eliab is taller in stature, David is larger in heart.

Clearly the immediate, and wider, context of 1 Samuel creates a negative impression of Eliab. When all of the evidence is gathered, including allusions to Eli, Saul and Goliath, as well as the intentional contrast between David and his brothers, it must be said that Eliab creates a bad first impression. It remains now to be seen if this impression will be sustained or altered by his appearance in the next episode.

We're in the Army Now (1 Sam. 17:13–28)

Eliab's next appearance in the story transports us from the home front to the battle front. In fact, 17:13 tells us that, "The three oldest sons of Jesse had gone to follow Saul to the battle." Just as in 1 Samuel 16:6–9, we are once again given their names—Eliab, Abinadab, and Shammah. A superficial reading of the story might suggest that it is admirable that these brothers are demonstrating their loyalty to Israel by going to the battle. After all, perilous times call for patriotism. However, at another level the language used of these three brothers is troubling. We are told twice that they "followed after Saul" (17:13, 14), and this expression is a proclamation of loyalty or discipleship. It is used of believers who "follow after" God, but more ominously, it is also used of those who "follow after" false gods (e.g., Deut. 6:14; 8:19). Based on the (immediate) context, "following after" Saul is not a good thing. We are told that God has sent a distressing spirit on Saul to trouble him (16:14), and 17:11 informs us that Saul's state of mind is one of dismay and fear. Therefore, to "follow after Saul" is, at the very least, ambiguous. It may imply loyalty to Israel, but it suggests that the brothers are captives of the same fear and dismay that control Saul. In fact, it must be so because Goliath challenges the army for forty days (17:16), and neither Eliab nor the other two brothers have the courage to face him. Thus, while "tall Saul" and "tall Eliab" cower before "tall Goliath," it is "small" David who will stand tall by confronting the giant. For a second time Eliab is linked with Saul. In neither

---

[19] The word, usually translated "youngest," also means "small."

case has the comparison been a flattering one. Eliab's character portrayal remains consistent so far.

As the brothers wait on the battlefield, Jesse sends David to bring provisions and inquire about their welfare (17:17–18). While there, he hears Goliath's challenge and begins to ask about what would be done for the man who kills this Philistine (vv. 23–27). Some scholar's characterize David's first words as ambitious.[20] Alter states that David's inquiry is about personal profit, and then suggests that the accompanying theological language ("For who is this uncircumcised Philistine that he should defy the armies of the living God?"—v. 26) might be a cover-up to disguise his true motive.[21] Against this background, Bodner suggests that Eliab's words may be those of a concerned wiser brother, who knows the ambition of his younger brother all too well.[22]

While I agree that David's initial words sound ambitious, they are balanced with his concern for Yahweh's honor—a major theme in the books of Samuel, as we have seen.[23] Furthermore, ambition, in and of itself, is not a terrible crime; other criteria must determine whether ambition is to be admired or disdained. David's anointing in the previous chapter, his concern for God's honor,[24] and his heroic action against Goliath, suggest that his ambition is not out of place—and, in fact, may be divinely motivated.[25]

We are told that Eliab overheard David's inquiry, and that his "anger burned against David" (v. 28—my translation). Next, Eliab issues a strong rebuke to David. The question is: "Are these the words of a concerned older brother, or do they reinforce the portrait of Eliab that the author has painted to this point?" I am immediately struck by the fact that Eliab's rebuke is full of sarcasm and scorn—not unlike many older brothers! His question, "With whom have you left those few sheep in the wilderness?" is derogatory and belittling. Is "small" David getting too big for his britches, or is "tall" Eliab embarrassed that his younger brother displays courage and faith that he lacks?

Eliab's statement is wrong on at least two counts. First, he is accusing David of being irresponsible, claiming that he cannot take care of even a simple job. But the reader knows otherwise. The author establishes that David is careful at each stage of his journey. David has left the sheep with a "keeper" (v. 20). Thus Eliab's charge is in error; David has not been irrespon-

---

[20] Polzin, *David and the Deuteronomist*, p. 91, "From the moment David enters the picture, he…is as much self-serving as God-fearing."

[21] Alter, *The David Story*, p. 105.

[22] Bodner, "Eliab and the Deuteronomist," pp. 63-66.

[23] See the discussion in chap. 4, pp. 60-64.

[24] Birch, *The First and Second Books of Samuel*, p. 1110 states, "David understands the lack of Israelite response as shameful."

[25] Ibid., p. 1111, "David becomes the first to describe the confrontation in theological terms. It is not Saul, the king anointed to bring God's deliverance, who invokes the power of God. It is this newly arrived shepherd boy."

sible with the sheep. Furthermore, as if to emphasize David's attention to detail, the author notes that upon arriving in camp, he leaves the supplies he has brought "in the hand of the supply keeper" (v. 22—"keeper" being the same word as in v. 20). Thus both the sheep and supplies are in proper hands while David searches for his brothers in the camp. He is not simply a youth caught up in the excitement of the moment and throwing caution to the wind—rather, David is portrayed as thoughtful and responsible in his actions.

Second, Eliab's response is wrong because of its tone. If he is seeking to give wise counsel to David, as Bodner suggests, then we must conclude that Eliab is indeed unwise. What person seeking to give good advice would couch it in sarcasm? A wise person would know that advice delivered in this way would not be accepted. Eliab does not come across as the concerned older brother; his words are intended to belittle and discourage David. In the context of the story, Eliab is an impediment to the great deed God will accomplish through David; he is a temporary roadblock on the path to victory. In fact, Eliab's sarcastic reply suggests a parallel with the enemy Goliath, who also speaks disdainfully of David (17:42–43). Ironically, small David will overcome all three tall men in this chapter![26]

There are further problems with Eliab's response. Eliab's first question is, "Why did you come down here?," which he presumes to answer himself by saying, "you have come down to see the battle" (v. 28). Once again the text proves him wrong. David might have been interested in the battle—what young man wouldn't be? But, the reason he had "come down" was because Jesse had sent him with supplies and to inquire about the welfare of his brothers (vv. 17–18). Eliab also presumes to know that David's true motives are based on his pride and his "evil heart." However, just as Eliab's first presumption is wrong, so is this one. How can his judgment of David's heart be taken seriously, when we already know that Eliab's heart does not meet with God's approval (1 Sam. 16:6–7)? The author has made clear that the heart of David *is* acceptable to God. In fact, as the reader already knows, David is the man after God's own heart (1 Sam. 13:14).

Eliab and the Author of Samuel

Before leaving Eliab, it is important to address the question of whether his words have meaning beyond the present context. I have frequently noted in this book that the words of a character may convey meaning

---

[26] Saul, the other "tall" person in this story also seeks to discourage David with his words (17:33). My continued use of "small" does not suggest that David was short in stature. Rather, it is to highlight the contrast being made in the text between "small" and "tall"—symbolic of impressive versus unimpressive, powerful versus insignificant in the world's eyes.

that goes beyond the immediate context of a given story in which they appear (most notably, Hannah's prayer). Bodner's contention is that, no matter what we think of Eliab (wise or jealous big brother), his words about David are "a voice of warning." Bodner believes that, "Through the voice of Eliab, the reader receives a signal that the characterization of David will not be entirely straightforward, and that his personality will be subjected to rigorous scrutiny."[27] Specifically, Eliab's description of David as having an "evil heart" anticipates his future adultery with Bathsheba and murder of Uriah.[28]

Given the author's penchant for stating the themes of the book through his characters, this is a provocative suggestion. Certainly the author will go on to show that David is a complicated figure. David is capable of great good, but for a "man after God's heart" we must admit that he is capable of the most despicable crimes. This fact makes Bodner's thesis attractive, but I detect two problems. First, if the author wanted to make this assertion about David, it seems that using Eliab is a poor choice. It is true that Eliab might be expected to have insights into his brother's character.[29] However, given the portrayal of Eliab, what reader would take his sarcastic words seriously?

Second, and this is the most important problem with Bodner's thesis, while the author admits that David is capable of evil, he never suggests that David's *heart* is evil. 2 Samuel 12:27 says, "But the thing that David *had done* was *evil* in the Lord's sight" (my translation), and Nathan asks, "Why have you despised the commandment of the Lord, *to do evil* in His sight?" (2 Sam. 12:9) It is one thing to *do evil*, but it is an altogether different matter to have an *evil heart*. The difference is between a person who desires to follow God, but through weakness gets caught up in sin, and one who deliberately, and defiantly, seeks his own way apart from God. No one would ever deny that David gets caught up in sin, even sin of the worst kind, but he is consistently portrayed as a man who seeks after God. David is never said to have an "evil heart"; furthermore, the writer of Kings consistently portrays him as having a heart of integrity (e.g., 1 Kings 9:4; 11:4).[30] Based on these observations, it is very unlikely that we are to take Eliab's words about David's heart seriously.

Conclusion: Are You are Roadblock or a Signpost?

When picking sides for a ball game we usually choose the biggest players to be on our team. After all, they "look" like a winner. When I was young, I was tall for my age, and so I was frequently chosen to play the posi-

---

[27] Bodner, *Eliab and the Deuteronomist*, p. 67.

[28] Ibid., pp. 70-71.

[29] Gros Louis, *King David of Israel*, p. 209.

[30] For further discussion of this point, see chap. 15, pp. 188-189.

tion of Center on a basketball team. The problem was, I was terrible at basketball! No matter how many times we learn the lesson that "things aren't always what they seem," we still make the mistake all over again of trusting our eyes. When Samuel first laid eyes on Eliab, he looked like a signpost for the future; but, in fact, he proved to be a roadblock (albeit a small one) to victory. Sometimes we wonder why God doesn't choose us, and instead of supporting God's choice, we become a roadblock. We may think, "It's not fair, God. I'm more qualified than they are!" Perhaps from a human perspective we are, but the story of Eliab reminds us that God's standards are different to ours. In fact, such a reaction tells us more about our own heart than we may want to know. When pride rises up it usually seeks to tear down another. Eliab may have been "tall," but his desire to "tear down" David demonstrated what God already knew—he was not fit to lead his people.

Our world emphasizes the exterior. We spend a lot of time and money trying to look beautiful and appear successful. There's nothing wrong with good looks—David was good looking (1 Sam. 16:12); but it was not his looks that enabled him to defeat Goliath. In writing to Timothy, Paul contrasted the outward and the inward this way: "For bodily exercise profits a little, but godliness is profitable for all things, having promise of the life that now is and of that which is to come" (1 Tim. 4:8). Eliab reminds us of the importance of paying more attention to what is inside than what is outside.

It's sad but sometimes true that nothing brings people together as much as a common foe. This may well have been the case with David and his brothers. We read nothing further of Eliab, or any of David's brothers, until the author tells us, "David therefore departed from there (Gath—cf. 1 Sam. 21:10) and escaped to the cave of Adullam. So when his brothers and all his father's house heard it, they went down there to him" (1 Sam. 22:1). It seems that adversity finally brought David and his brothers together. Certainly, Saul's desire to kill David extended to the entire family, and so they had no choice but to join him. We might hope that the result was a happy reunion, or at least a deeper bond. Of David's brothers, only Shammah (or Shimea, as he is later designated) is referred to again, and that simply to introduce his son, Jonadab (2 Sam. 13:3). But the mention of several nephews in the remaining narrative (Joab, Abishai, Asahel, Jonadab and Amasa) is a strong indication that David's brothers and sisters reconciled themselves to his leadership of the kingdom.

Chapter 18

Abigail: The Peacemaker (David's wife)

A woman of good understanding and beautiful appearance (1 Sam. 25:3)

Introduction: Good and Evil (1 Sam. 25:3)

Abigail is introduced in 1 Samuel 25 in a story that proves to be pivotal in David's rise to the kingship. Surrounded by stories of Saul's pursuit (1 Sam. 24, and 26), the encounter with Abigail teaches David a valuable lesson about God's providence and not taking vengeance into his own hands. The harsh words of the rich but boorish Nabal (Abigail's husband) to David's men (25:10–11) portend doom for Nabal and all the males of his house (25:21–22), but the gracious words and humble spirit of Abigail prove to be an emollient for the wounded honor of David (25:32–35). The wise words of Abigail not only restrain David from bloodguilt; they also provide a glimpse into his future when she states, "For the LORD will certainly make for my lord an enduring house" (25:28b). When the Lord strikes Nabal, David is vindicated (25:38–39) and proposes marriage to the intelligent and beautiful Abigail (25:39–42).

Although Abigail is mentioned a few more times in 1 and 2 Samuel,[1] only 1 Samuel 25 provides insight into her character. Unlike other people, the author provides an evaluation of Abigail (as well as her husband Nabal) immediately upon her introduction. At the very outset of the story (1 Samuel 25:3) she is contrasted with her husband, and the contrast is written chiastically (ABBA), with Nabal's name first and then Abigail's. This is followed by a description of Abigail and then of Nabal. The contrast could not be more stark; it is a contrast between good and evil. While Abigail is of "*good* understanding," Nabal is "harsh and *evil* in his doings." The words "good" and "evil" are important throughout the story, occurring seven times each.[2] Gunn summarizes their significance for the story:

> At face value this is a tale about good and evil—about good and evil people, and good and evil actions. Abigail is good, Nabal evil. Nabal does an evil action; David, a good person, is about to do an evil action in return but is stopped in time by Abigail's good action.[3]

---

[1] The other passages are: 1 Sam. 27:3; 30:5, 18; 2 Sam. 2:2; and, 3:3.

[2] David M. Gunn, *The Fate of King Saul*, p. 96.

[3] Ibid., p. 101. Although I agree with this summary, I do not agree with Gunn's conclusion.

Abigail and Nabal's words and actions in the narrative will confirm the initial impression given by the author. Although our intention is to focus on Abigail, it is important to view the story as a whole and to understand its function within 1 and 2 Samuel. In addition, the Book of Genesis will provide valuable insights for our character sketch. It is only within this broader context that Abigail's character can be fully appreciated and understood.

Peace and War (1 Sam. 25:4–13)

This subtitle is an intentional turn of phrase of Tolstoy's monumental work. It well describes the opening and final verses of this section. Our story is not one of "War and Peace" but of peace followed by the threat of war. As David sends ten of his young men off to request a favor from Nabal, he instructs them to seek after Nabal's welfare. "And when you come to Nabal then you shall inquire of him in my name *for peace*" (v. 5—my translation). This of course is a typical Israelite greeting, but it emphasizes David's goodwill. This statement is followed by David telling the young men to say: "To you *peace*, and to your house *peace*, and to all that is yours *peace*" (my translation). Although awkward in English, I have translated the Hebrew literally to show that not only does David wish Nabal peace, but he ends each of the three phrases with the word "peace." Thus peace is emphasized by its repetition and also its position in the sentence.[4] David's warm greeting is to be followed by a request for provisions in the humblest manner possible (*"favor* in your eyes...*please*...*whatever* comes to your hand to your *servants* and to *your son* David"—v. 8). David could hardly be more deferential.

David has been accused of running a protection racket[5]—expecting payment for a job he was never asked to do. Such an accusation, however, reveals contemporary ideas and prejudices, and does not take the ancient cultural situation seriously enough.[6] Not only were ancient Israelites to provide for the sojourner and those less fortunate, but the threat from marauding bands and wild animals was a real one. Bergen states, "The value of David's protection is suggested by a previous narrative account, which noted that after the Philistines attacked nearby Keilah, they were in possession of livestock

---

[4] Alter, *The David Story*, p. 153, misses the mark when he affirms that David's greeting of peace "contains a veiled threat—let us hope that you continue to fare well a year from now." The clear intention of David's language, and the author's purpose in reporting it, is to show that David approaches Nabal in a humble and well-intentioned manner. It is Nabal's rude and insulting response that creates the tense situation that follows.

[5] For example, Gunn, *The Fate of King Saul*, p. 96.

[6] Birch, *The First and Second Books of Samuel*, p. 1166, aptly writes, "This view seems more influenced by old gangster movies than by the biblical narrative."

(23:5).'[7] For David and his men to protect Nabal's flocks and servants, while not taking anything for themselves, would have been considered a great kindness—which any honorable man would have desired to repay. "David conceives the good deportment of his men as a gift to the big man [Nabal], and it is a rule of archaic cultures that a gift requires a return."[8] David affirms that he has acted with integrity (vv. 7–8), and his assertion is later confirmed by one of Nabal's servants (vv. 15–16).

Nabal, however, is not an honorable man. He lives up to his name: "Excellent speech is not becoming to a *fool*" (the word is *nābāl*—Prov. 17:7a).[9] He insults David's name, refers to him as a rebellious slave, and refuses to offer any assistance to such a group of nobodies (vv. 10–11). When David's men inform him of Nabal's hostile answer, David's response is immediate: "Every man gird on his sword" (v. 13). In fact the word "sword" occurs three times in verse 13, matching David's original threefold salutation of "peace." Indeed, "Death and life are in the power of the tongue" (Prov. 18:21a). The words of James 3:5–6 offer a stern warning concerning dangerous use of the tongue:

> Even so the tongue is a little member and boasts great things. See how great a forest a little fire kindles! And the tongue is a fire, a world of iniquity. The tongue is so set among our members that it defiles the whole body, and sets on fire the course of nature; and it is set on fire by hell.

The section began with David's greeting of peace, but Nabal's rude response precipitates warlike actions. To assume that it is only Nabal's refusal to give provisions that provokes David's hostile response would be a mistake. The situation described goes much deeper. The cultural dynamics of honor and shame provide the basis for understanding David's violent reaction.[10] Nabal has not simply refused provisions to David; he has insulted him in every way. David is honor-bound to respond, less he lose the respect of his men (and everyone else). This is not to justify David. The text clearly shows that his response is wrong. It is simply to observe that David is a man of his time and culture, and reacts accordingly.

---

[7] Bergen, *1, 2 Samuel,* p. 246.

[8] Murphy, *1 Samuel,* p. 239.

[9] Jon D. Levenson, "I Samuel 25 as Literature and as History," *Literary Interpretations of Biblical Narratives,* vol. II, ed. Kenneth R. R. Gros Louis (Nashville: Abingdon, 1982), p. 221, states, "The Hebrew word *nābāl,* often translated as 'fool,' designates not a harmless simpleton, but rather a vicious, materialistic, and egocentric misfit."

[10] Although I came to this conclusion independently, Stansell, *Honor and Shame in the David Narratives,* pp. 61-65, demonstrates that the values of honor and shame play an important role in the story.

A Soft Answer Turns Away Wrath (1 Sam. 25:14–31)

The opening verses of Proverbs chapter 15 sum up the contrast between Nabal's response and Abigail's intervention:

> A soft answer turns away wrath,
> But a harsh word stirs up anger.
> The tongue of the wise uses knowledge rightly,
> But the mouth of fools pours forth foolishness (Prov. 15:1–2).

Knowing that it will do no good to reason with his master, one of Nabal's servants makes his way to Abigail to relate the recent event and sound a warning of approaching danger (vv. 14–17). Not only is he confident that she will listen, but also that she will act. Abigail does not disappoint; she begins with "haste" to prepare a generous gift of food for David and his men (v. 18). Unlike others we have discussed, she does not wait for danger to come to her.[11] Her quick action shows her to be a resourceful person, and her neglect of informing Nabal demonstrates her prudence (v. 19). These two characteristics remind us of Jonathan, who also was willing to act in a dangerous situation, but wise enough not to tell his father (1 Sam. 14).[12] Furthermore, David's approach with four hundred men (v. 13), and Abigail's command for her servants to go before her while she would follow after, remind us of Jacob when Esau approached him (Gen. 32:6, 13–16).[13] The allusions to these biblical characters, plus others we will note later, portray Abigail in a favorable light, adding depth to the resumé presented in 1 Samuel 25:3.

Abigail has entered the story at its most dangerous moment, and as she rides down under the cover of a hill she is about to come face to face with a very angry and offended David. To highlight the suspense, the author gives us a glimpse into his thoughts (vv. 20–22). David is seething over the wrong done to him as he meditates on the important words "good" and "evil": "He has repaid me evil for good." Unfortunately a thousand years separates David from Paul's godly advice: "Do not be overcome by evil, but

---

[11] Saul and Ish-bosheth are two such examples.

[12] The refusal of a family member to confide in them as head of the family is one of many similarities between Saul and Nabal. All recent commentators are agreed that Nabal is a surrogate in this story for Saul. Nabal's insulting language resembles Saul's remarks and attitude towards David. For other similarities see Polzin, *Samuel and the Deuteronomist*, pp. 211-212.

[13] See Mark E. Biddle, "Ancestral Motifs in 1 Samuel 25: Intertextuality and Characterization," *JBL* 21, 2002, pp. 617-638, for a more in-depth comparison.

overcome evil with good" (Rom. 12:21). David is intent on revenge, swearing an oath to destroy all the male[14] inhabitants that belong to Nabal by morning.

The only thing that stands between David and his intention to exterminate Nabal's house is Abigail. She is enough. As David was a wall of protection for Nabal's flocks (v. 16), so this wise and beautiful woman will prove to be a wall of protection around his household. "Abigail's ability to act halts the negative progress of the story."[15]

Haste and Humility (25:23–25)

When Abigail sees David she again acts in haste by dismounting from her donkey. Her descent doesn't stop there, however, as she falls on her face before David and bows down to the ground. In these three quick actions she assumes a posture of humility before David, or more literally, before "David's nose" (v. 23). We noted a similar expression before, when Elkanah gave Hannah a "portion for the nose" (1 Sam. 1:5).[16] David's honor has been challenged and his nose is burning—that is, he is angry. Abigail's great humility in falling on her "face," and thus burying her nose in the ground, is the first step in restoring David's honor. Now fallen at David's feet (v. 24a), she begins to speak.

Bergen has noted that Abigail's speech consists of 153 words, and is the longest quote from a woman in the United Monarchy accounts (1 Sam. 8–1 Kings 11).[17] Her words not only have great significance for the story at hand, but also play an important role in the message and themes of 1 and 2 Samuel as a whole. Like Hannah, her words have an impact on the future kingship. Once again in the books of Samuel, a woman bears an important message.

Abigail's first words are well chosen at this critical moment: "On me my lord, on me let this iniquity be!" These words foreshadow the words of the wise woman from Tekoa, who also addresses David about a violent situation (2 Sam. 14:9). David is ready to spill the blood of every male in Nabal's household, but he is apparently not prepared to pour out his wrath on one

---

[14] The literal rendering of this oath is a crude expression in both Hebrew and its English equivalent: "every one who pisses against a wall." This phrase serves to highlight David's agitated state. Youngblood, *1, 2 Samuel*, p. 765, points out that this expression also occurs in 1 Kings 14:10; 16:11; 21:21; and 2 Kings 9:8, always in the context of exterminating an entire family or household.

[15] Alice Bach, "The Pleasure of Her Text," *USQR* 43, 1989, p. 43.

[16] See chap. 3, p. 41.

[17] Robert D. Bergen, "Authorial Intent and the Spoken Word: A Discourse-critical Analysis of Speech Acts in Accounts of Israel's United Monarchy (1 Sam. 1–1 Kings 11)," in *Giving the Sense: Understanding and Using Old Testament Historical Texts*, David M. Howard Jr. and Michael A. Grisanti eds. (Grand Rapids and Leicester: Kregel Publications and Apollos, 2003).

lone beautiful woman.[18] Abigail's first words defuse the situation by accepting responsibility for the offense. She is a true intercessor.

Hoftijzer illuminates the significance of this statement, noting, "By confessing guilt one acknowledges one's own inferiority and throws oneself at the mercy of the other party."[19] Her words are disarming and they create a space for her to continue her plea. Abigail continues with the language of an inferior: "Please let your maidservant speak in your ears, and hear the words of your maidservant" (v. 24). It is not only her posture that indicates humility; she chooses her words carefully, voicing the honor that was absent from her husband's reply. In this speech, Abigail refers to herself 6 times as David's "servant" (two different Hebrew words), while calling David "lord" 14 times.[20] Gunn succinctly notes the contrast in attitude between Nabal and Abigail: "For Nabal, David is 'servant'; for Abigail, he is 'master.' "[21]

Her next few sentences address with candor and wit the man and the act that precipitated the present crisis. "Please, let not my lord regard this scoundrel Nabal. For as his name is, so is he: Nabal is his name, and folly is with him!" (v. 25). Alice Bach questions whether Abigail can be viewed as a model wife, since her words insult her husband and her actions place her on the enemy's side.[22] We should first admit (as if it needs acknowledging!) that the Bible is not here suggesting that every wife should forsake and insult her husband when a crisis arises due to his error. However, an important consideration validates her behavior. Abigail is acknowledging that her husband has committed a great injustice. This is a necessary step in the restoration of David's honor. Nabal has publicly shamed David and it is necessary to publicly renounce his behavior in the strongest language. It is not David who deserves to be shamed, but Nabal for his disgraceful behavior. For justice to be restored the reproach must be removed from the innocent party and placed on the perpetrator. As we might say, Abigail must "call a spade a spade." This is an act of wisdom, not disloyalty. Any attempt to sugar-coat or lessen the se-

---

[18] Of course Abigail was not totally alone. She had sent her servants on ahead with the gift of food, but apparently that would have been insufficient to halt David's advance. This is another clue that more was at stake than the refusal of provisions. David's honor still needed restoring.

[19] Jacob Hoftijzer, "David and the Tekoite Woman," *VT* 20/ 4, 1970, p. 426. He further explains, "But uttering the formula in question both women [Abigail and the Tekoite woman] throw themselves on the mercy of David: they hope by doing so to further the chance that their request will be granted.

[20] Miscall, *1 Samuel*, p. 152.

[21] Gunn, *The Fate of King Saul*, p. 99.

[22] Bach, "The Pleasure of Her Text," p. 49.

verity of the insult would be counterproductive.[23] Abigail only speaks the truth—a truth well known to her servants (v. 17).

The first expression she uses to describe her husband is "man of Belial," a label already pinned on Nabal by one of his own servants (v. 17). This phrase is familiar to the readers of 1 and 2 Samuel, and within that larger context puts Nabal in the company of Eli's sons (1 Sam. 2:12), and a future rebel named Sheba (2 Sam. 20:1),[24] not to mention others. Abigail follows this statement with a clever wordplay on the meaning of Nabal's name. As noted earlier, Nabal means "fool" in Hebrew.[25] It is unlikely that this is the original meaning, as the letters can also mean "wineskin."[26] Abigail, however, sees a connection between the man and his actions. He is a "fool" and therefore he commits "folly" (fool/folly = *nābāl/nebālah*).

We have all been in tense situations where a witty saying or a bit of humor has helped bring some relief. One wonders if David couldn't help a wry smile, or one of his men a little snicker, at Abigail's turn of phrase. This is not to suggest that Abigail has turned comedian at this serious moment, but only that she may recognize that injecting a bit of wit may relieve some of the anxiety of the situation.[27] Any wise sage would recognize the power of well-timed humor. Certainly, the original Israelite audience would have gotten a chuckle out of it. Though encapsulated in a clever statement, the word "folly" itself is no laughing matter. It is a word only used to describe the most despicable crimes in Scripture (Gen. 34:7; Judg. 19:23–24; etc.).[28] Abigail could hardly have chosen a stronger word to describe her husband's guilt.

---

[23] Although I am convinced that the cultural dynamics of honor and shame provide the best explanation for Abigail's behavior, Tikva Frymer-Kensky suggests that Abigail's language is intentionally insulting toward her husband in order to convince David she is not acting as Nabal's emissary. She notes that the same technique was used by the Hebrew midwives in Exodus 1:19, who call Hebrew women "animals" in order to protect them. See Tikva Frymer-Kensky, *Reading the Women of the Bible* (New York: Schocken Books, 2002), p. 319. However, given the values of honor and shame reflected in this story, it is much more likely that Abigail takes on the role of a mediator between two disputing parties. See Stansell, *Honor and Shame in the David Narratives,* p. 64.

[24] Besides also being called a "son of Belial," Sheba's disparaging language toward David is similar to Nabal's.

[25] See p. 213, n. 9.

[26] For other possible meanings, and the possibility that Nabal's real name has been deliberately altered from its original form, see Levenson, "I Samuel 25 as Literature and as History," pp. 222-223.

[27] The cleverness of Abigail's statement is further enhanced by recognizing that the words "his name" and "with him" rhyme in Hebrew, both ending in a long ō sound.

[28] For a helpful list of all the passages, see Hamilton, *Handbook*, p. 280.

Some commentators misunderstand the final sentence in verse 25 as Abigail attempting to distance herself from her husband's crime.[29] Bergen is on target, however, when he states, "Abigail implied to David that since she knew these facts about her husband, she should have been more watchful to protect her husband from himself. Unfortunately, in the present instance she 'did not see the men' David sent and thus became blameworthy."[30] Abigail is merely explaining why she hadn't responded sooner.

Looking to the Lord (25:26–31)

The wisest thing that Abigail does is to turn David's eyes from himself to the Lord. "Abigail's language in this section of her speech makes constant reference to the Lord (Yahweh) and to what the Lord is doing in these events."[31] She "counters David's vow with a vow of her own"[32]—based on the "life" of the Lord and David's own "life" (v. 26). "Life" is a recurring word in this story, where the threat of death hangs so heavy (25:6, 26 [2x], 29, 34). Abigail swears by "the life of the Lord" and by "David's life," reminding him that with a living God there is no need for him to take matters into his own hands.

Abigail suggests that her presence is God's way of preventing David from bloodshed, and she ends her vow with the powerful imprecation, "let your enemies and those who seek harm for my lord be as Nabal." Some have interpreted this as referring to Nabal's death,[33] as well as Saul's.[34] However, in the present context Abigail need only mean that all David's enemies would prove to be as foolish as Nabal. It is true, however, that the ultimate end of a fool is death (Prov. 8:36; 14:12) and, given the prophetic context, Abigail may foresee Nabal's doom.[35] In fact, if Abigail's action is the Lord's doing, as she implies (v. 26) and as David later confirms (v. 32), then her words are also the Lord's words. Furthermore, her statement not only concerns Nabal, but all of David's enemies, including Saul who is the one that is "seeking" harm against David.

Abigail now requests that David accept the gift (*berākāh* = blessing) she has brought (v. 27). The word recalls the Jacob and Esau story. Jacob had stolen his brother's blessing (Gen. 27:35–36), but upon returning to Canaan he sought to make amends by giving gifts to Esau, which he calls a "blessing"

---

[29] For example, Alter, *The David Story*, p. 156.

[30] Bergen, *1, 2 Samuel*, p. 250.

[31] Birch, *The First and Second Books of Samuel*, p. 1168.

[32] Ibid.

[33] McCarter, *I Samuel*, p. 394.

[34] Birch, *The First and Second Books of Samuel*, p. 1168.

[35] I am in agreement with Tsumura, *The First Book of Samuel*, pp. 588-589, who writes, "The reference to Nabal can be taken either as a prophecy of his death or as just a curse of folly upon David's enemies."

in Genesis 33:11. David had originally approached Nabal with words of blessing, but had been rebuffed. Abigail acts like her forefather Jacob by presenting to David a tangible demonstration of goodwill. Nabal had referred to David as one of many slaves breaking away from their master (v. 10), but Abigail's gift (we might call it tribute) and language of maidservant/lord reverses the insult by treating David like a royal figure. Indeed, she will acknowledge his royal status in the forthcoming verses (vv. 28, 30). Whenever someone has been injured by thoughtless words, it is not only important that we say the right things in order to repair the relationship, but, like Abigail, we should also be willing to demonstrate it in a concrete way.

Abigail's supplication continues with a plea for forgiveness of her transgression (v. 28). By this she may mean that she had not seen the men David sent (v. 25), but as a representative of Nabal's household she has accepted responsibility for his deed (v. 24). To this point she has laid the groundwork of reconciliation by a posture of humility, words of reason, a curse on Nabal and all of David's enemies, and a tangible gift. Now she comes to her most persuasive point. Abigail pleads with David to forgive the past by looking to the future, so that a tragic mistake is not made in the present. She assumes a prophetic role (she is, after all, God's emissary to David) as she speaks of the "sure house" that God will establish for David.[36] As Bach has noted:

> Her prescience is a clear indication that Abigail is God's chosen prophet-intermediary. Abigail's assurance to David that he is YHWH's intended ruler and must remain innocent to do God's will is the link between the anointing prophecy of Samuel and the dynastic prophecy of Nathan.[37]

In fact, Abigail's words in verses 28–31 anticipate three promises made in the oracle given to Nathan in 2 Samuel 7. First, David receives the title "prince" (7:8); second, the Lord will deal with his enemies (7:9); and third, the Lord will give him an enduring house (7:16).[38] Thus the most compelling reason for David to restrain himself in the present is the glorious future that God has in

---

[36] Abigail's prophecy is the climax to a chorus of voices in the preceding chapters that recognize David as king (the Philistines, 1 Sam. 21:11; Jonathan, 23:17; and Saul, 24:20).

[37] Bach, "The Pleasure of Her Text," p. 45. Similarly, Susan M. Pigott, in "Wives, Witches and Wise Women," p. 152, writes, "It is interesting that Abigail is introduced immediately following the announcement of the prophet Samuel's death (1 Sam 25:1). Significantly, the prophetic voice is not silenced with the death of Samuel; instead it finds its expression through the mouth of a bold woman who portrays herself as a humble handmaid."

[38] Frymer-Kensky, *Reading the Women of the Bible*, p. 322.

store for him. Moreover, he is one who "fights the battles of the LORD." This is a clear allusion to his public victory over Goliath (1 Sam. 17:47), the inference being that taking revenge on Nabal certainly does not fall into that category. As one who fights the Lord's battles "evil is not to be found" in him.[39]

Abigail now directly addresses Saul's pursuit of David, but assures him in vivid metaphoric language that the Lord will protect him. "The life of my lord shall be bound in the bundle of the living with the LORD your God; and the lives of your enemies He shall sling out, as from the pocket of a sling" (v. 29). The first metaphor may refer to a shepherd's bag, where pebbles were put to keep count of the sheep.[40] Alternatively, it may be translated "the document of the living" and be a reference to the book of life mentioned elsewhere in Scripture (Ps. 69:28; Phil. 4:3).[41] If it is a shepherd's metaphor, then it would fit well with Abigail's next statement about David's enemies being slung from the pocket of a sling. This is another clear reference to David's victory over Goliath. When facing down the giant, David had said, "The LORD does not save with sword and spear for the battle is the LORD's" (17:47). Abigail would remind David that, if the Lord wins battles and they are not won by the sword, then David should not take up his sword on this occasion to avenge himself.[42] Her words will prove to be true when Nabal becomes hardened like a "stone" and the Lord strikes him (vv. 37–38).

Abigail presses the point home in verses 30–31 by reassuring David of the "good" that the Lord will do for him by appointing him as "prince." She also reminds him that past actions do affect the future. Therefore, David should do nothing that would be a "grief" or "offense of heart to my lord." The word "heart" is another key word in the story and provides a contrast between David and Nabal.[43]

The written text of 25:3 describing Nabal literally says, "He is like his heart."[44] If Nabal's character is described as evil in verse 3, then his heart is

---

[39] Sadly, once he is king, David will take matters into his own hands and shed innocent blood. This act will tarnish his throne and be "evil" in the Lord's eyes (2 Sam. 11:27). What Abigail warns him of now will come to pass. This will be explored further in chap. 19.

[40] Willis, *First and Second Samuel*, p. 246.

[41] Tsumura, *The First Book of Samuel*, p. 590.

[42] Vannoy, *1–2 Samuel*, p. 226, writes, "David's confrontation with Nabal was not a 'battle of the LORD.' It was a personal affront that provoked David to take personal revenge."

[43] Based on the Hebrew text, the word "heart" occurs in the following verses: 3, 25, 31, 36, and 37.

[44] Most English translations follow what is called the Qere (that which is read). Although the written text is, "He is like his heart," what is read is, "He was a Calebite"—the words "like his heart" looking similar to the word "Calebite" in Hebrew. For a more detailed discussion see Levenson, *I Samuel 25 as Literature*, p. 223.

evil too. Two other statements about Nabal's heart occur in this chapter: 1) his heart is said to be "merry within him," due to an over-consumption of wine (v. 36); and 2) his heart "dies within him" when he becomes a "stone" (v. 37). Abigail is concerned that David not take Nabal's insult to heart (v. 25), and that he not experience an "offense of heart" due to a rash act of taking matters into his own hands (v. 31). The previous chapter informed the reader that David was so sensitive about taking vengeance that even cutting Saul's robe had troubled his heart (24:5). We have previously established that David, while capable of great evil, does not have an evil heart like Nabal, in spite of Eliab's charge.[45]

When all this information is processed, the following picture emerges: Abigail understands the nature of a *nābāl* (fool), being married to one, and that Nabal is "like his heart" (v. 3). She knows that David is not a *nābāl* and therefore believes he can be reasoned with (v. 24), unlike her husband (v. 17, 19). David must not take vengeance into his own hand, for this would be to commit *nebālah* (folly), which only a *nābāl* would do. Abigail knows that David is too principled to do this without experiencing "grief" and "offense of heart" (v. 31).

Abigail ends her entreaty with a supplication for future favor: "But when the LORD has dealt well with my lord, then remember your maidservant." It is doubtful that Abigail's request refers to marriage, as supposed by some.[46] The word "remember" implies "act favorably in behalf of,"[47] and is used by an inferior seeking the favor of a superior. It provides yet another parallel with Hannah, who asked the Lord to "remember" her (1 Sam. 1:11), and further confirmation that Abigail believes what she says about David's future.

Blessed are the Peacemakers[48] (1 Sam. 25:32–35)

David now speaks for the first time since commanding every man to "gird on his sword" (v. 13) and threatening to destroy every male of Nabal's house (vv. 21–22). His words could not be more opposite as he begins with "Blessed be the LORD" (v. 32). In fact, David's blessing is threefold, countering the earlier threefold mention of the sword. First he blesses the Lord for sending Abigail to meet him, recognizing that their encounter was providential. Second, he blesses her discernment, validating the author's earlier comment about Abigail's intelligence (v. 3). Third, he blesses Abigail herself for

---

[45] See chap. 17, p. 209.

[46] For example, Gunn, *The Fate of King Saul*, pp. 100-101.

[47] Bergen, *1, 2 Samuel*, p. 251.

[48] Matt. 5:9

preventing him from taking matters into his own hand and shedding innocent blood—incidentally, also the third time this phrase is used (26, 31, 33).[49]

Next David repeats his violent intention using the same crude words spoken earlier (v. 34)—words that Abigail had not previously heard. Literarily, these repeated words act as an inclusio around Abigail's speech and David's response (v. 22, 34), bringing the threat of violence to an end. These harsh words must have rolled from David's lungs like thunder when first uttered, but now there is a hollow ring to them.[50] Vengeance melts away, replaced by words of acceptance and peace (v. 35). *The hand* that had been restrained from shedding innocent blood now receives the gift from *the hand* of the peacemaker; and David's declaration of "peace" with which the story began (vv. 5–6) now becomes the possession of Abigail (v. 35).

By this point it should not surprise the reader that David makes *three* pronouncements to Abigail. First, he tells her to go up in peace to her house. Second, he says, "I have heard your voice," in response to Abigail's request, "please let your maidservant speak in your ears, and hear the words of your maidservant" (v. 24). This also confirms that David is not a *nābāl*; and in the broader context of 1 and 2 Samuel it sets him apart from Nabal (v. 17), as well as Saul. Third, David says, "I have lifted up your face" (my translation). Abigail has restored David's honor and now he honors her in return. The language of uplifted "face" reminds us yet again of Hannah, not just because of the actual word "face" in her story, but because of her words that the Lord lifts up the humble (2:7–8). Abigail's downward movement which preceded her speech (vv. 23–24) is now reversed, as she "goes up" to her house with her "face lifted up."[51]

If we review the story, noting key words and phrases that occur in groups of three or more, we have the following pattern: the greeting of **peace**; the taking up of the **sword**; the guidance of **providence**; the thirst for **vengeance** quenched; the pronouncement of **blessing**; and the restoration of **peace**. The story comes full circle.

---

[49] Vannoy, *1–2 Samuel*, p. 226.

[50] Fokkelman, *Crossing Fates*, pp. 515-517, notes that there are three oaths in the story that play off against each other. David's initial oath in v. 22 is "an assurance of murder." Abigail's oath (v. 26) is introduced with the counter-proposal of life—"by the *life* of the LORD and by your *life*." David's repetition of his oath to Abigail (v. 34) now picks up on Abigail's expression, "As the LORD the God of Israel *lives*." Even though David repeats his oath, the threat of death is clearly gone and the insertion of "lives" into the oath shows that Abigail's intervention has been successful in transforming the situation from death to life.

[51] I owe this insight to Fokkelman, ibid., p. 519.

A Heart of Stone (1 Sam. 25:36–38)

Abigail returns home to find her husband "feasting like a *king*" (words full of irony), with his heart "merry" with wine (v. 36). She decides it is best to wait until morning light to speak with him, for it is difficult enough to speak to a fool, let alone a drunken fool. Since the consonants in "Nabal" can also mean "wineskin," verse 37 begins on a humorous note, stating, "When the wine had gone out of Nabal," thus equating the man with his bladder![52] In a story that has twice mentioned wiping out those who "*urinate* against a wall by *morning*" (vv. 22, 34), this pun is surely intentional. It seems fitting that this is the last action we read of Nabal undertaking. Following this, Abigail informs him of the preceding day's events. David had intended that Nabal and all his men would be dead by morning, and the next statement tells us that Nabal's "heart *died* within him and he became a stone" (my translation). Many have interpreted this statement as Nabal suffering a heart attack or stroke upon hearing Abigail's words,[53] but this seems unlikely. It is more probable that "stone" is a metaphor for a hard heart.[54] This is its meaning elsewhere in Scripture (Exod. 15:16; Ezek. 36:26), and it corresponds to Abigail's metaphor of the sling in verse 29. Along this line, Deuteronomy 15:7–8 is particularly illuminating:

> If there is among you a poor man of your brethren, within any of the gates in your land which the LORD your God is giving you, you shall not *harden your heart* nor shut your hand from your poor brother, but you shall open your hand wide to him and willingly lend him sufficient for his need, whatever he needs (emphasis mine).

Nabal's hardness of heart after hearing Abigail's words corresponds with her servant's statement, "For he is such a scoundrel that one cannot speak to him."[55] The mercy of God waits "ten days," then when no change occurs God slings Nabal and his stony heart into the grave (v. 38) just as Abigail had foreseen would happen to all of David's enemies (v. 29). Nabal experiences

---

[52] Levenson, *I Samuel 25 as Literature*, p. 227.
[53] For example, Ackroyd, *The First Book of Samuel*, p. 199 (stroke), and Alter, *The David Story*, p. 160 (heart attack or stroke).
[54] Marjorie O'Rourke Boyle, "The Law of the Heart: The Death of a Fool (1 Samuel 25)," *JBL* 120, 2001, pp. 401-427, has examined the cultural, medical, and Scriptural evidence behind this expression and convincingly argued for the metaphorical usage. My comments are indebted to her insights.
[55] Fokkelman, *Crossing Fates*, p. 522, points out that the Hebrew root for "speak" (v. 17) and "words" (v. 37) is the same (*dbr*), making the correspondence between these two verses even stronger.

the truth of Proverbs 28:27: "He who gives to the poor will not lack, but he who hides his eyes will have many curses." In the end, Nabal is cursed, but Abigail remains blessed.

Wedding Bells (1 Sam. 25:39–43)

When David hears of Nabal's death, he once again blesses the Lord, "who has pleaded the cause of my reproach from the hand of Nabal" (v. 39). "Reproach" is another word that is part of the honor/shame vocabulary of this chapter, and may recall the story of Goliath where it occurs frequently (1 Sam. 17:10, 25, 26, 45).[56] David experiences the truth of Abigail's counsel (vv. 26, 29) and rejoices that the Lord has "kept His servant from *evil*" (cf. v. 28), while returning "Nabal's *evil* on his own head." "Yahweh, not David, must resolve such issues. David cannot wrongly bring about a just cause."[57]

David then sends a proposal of marriage to this wealthy widow, whose beauty and intelligence (v. 3) seem to be a match for his own good looks and wisdom (1 Sam. 16:12; 18:5, 30). Baldwin comments, "Eastern wedding customs do not seem to have changed through the ages. David sent his *servants*, 'friends of the bridegroom,' to fetch his bride who took her *five maidens* and went to the marriage feast" (author's emphasis).[58] Abigail responds with the same courtesy and humility that she had shown previously. She prostrates herself "nose to the ground" and says, "Here is your maidservant, a servant to wash the feet of the servants of my lord" (v. 41). Though humble in word, Abigail rides on a donkey attended by five maidens (a sign of wealth), having apparently become the heiress of Nabal's estate (v. 42).[59] David's marriage to her, as well as to Ahinoam of Jezreel (v. 43), builds a strong power base for him among the clans in southern Judah, which will later help to pave his way to being anointed in Hebron (2 Sam. 2:2–4).

The Widow of Nabal (1 Sam. 27:3; 30:5; 2 Sam. 2:2; 3:3)

Although Abigail shares in David's adventures in Philistia (1 Sam. 27:3), is even kidnapped by the Amalekites (1 Sam. 30:5), is present at his anointing over Judah (2 Sam. 2:2), and eventually bears him a son (2 Sam. 3:3), she never plays a major role after 1 Samuel 25. It is a curious fact that every time her name is mentioned she is called "the wife (widow) of Nabal the Carmelite;" and she always appears in the company of Ahinoam of Jezreel, consistently being mentioned after her. It has been suggested that the tag

---

[56] Miscall, *1 Samuel*, p. 154.
[57] Firth, *1&2 Samuel*, p. 272.
[58] Baldwin, *1&2 Samuel*, p. 152.
[59] There is no indication that Nabal and Abigail had any children.

after her name may be a reminder of David's link to the region of Hebron.[60] While this could potentially explain its use in 2 Samuel 2:2, it does not provide a satisfactory explanation for its use elsewhere. Perhaps the author desires to remind us that this is the Abigail who interceded for her former husband Nabal, prophesying of a "sure house" for David, of which she has subsequently become a part.

Because the only other Abigail mentioned in Scripture is David's half sister (2 Sam. 17:25; 1 Chron. 2:15–16), it has been suggested that David's wife and half-sister are one and the same person.[61] This equation is used as a possible explanation for David's close ties to Nahash king of Ammon (2 Sam. 10:1–2). There are a number of reasons, however, that could explain David's relationship with Nahash, not the least being that Nahash was an enemy of Saul (1 Sam. 11). Furthermore, the text of 2 Samuel 17:25 is difficult; and even if the Abigail mentioned there is the progeny of Nahash, this does not prove she is the same Abigail found in 1 Samuel 25. Just because there are only two Abigails mentioned in Scripture, it doesn't mean they are one and the same person. Surely many other women bore this name at the time of David. Finally, the Abigail of 1 Samuel 25 is only called David's wife and/or Nabal's wife; she is never called David's sister.

The Many Faces of Abigail (Scriptural "Look-alikes")

We have noticed similarities Abigail shares with Jacob, Hannah, Jonathan, and the wise woman of Tekoa. In this section we will explore these parallels in more depth, as well as note other biblical characters not previously mentioned. The term "look-alikes" is only intended to mean that Abigail shares certain characteristics and/or vocabulary with other biblical figures; it does not suggest an exact similarity. This is common in biblical typology. Noting these connections will add depth to our character portrait of Abigail.

Jacob

Many of the similarities between Abigail's encounter with David and Jacob's encounter with Esau have already been noted. To briefly summarize:[62] David approaches with four hundred men (1 Sam. 25:13), as does Esau (Gen. 32:6). Abigail sends servants on ahead[63] carrying provisions, while she follows behind (1 Sam. 25:19); Jacob does the same (Gen. 32:16). Both stories use the same Hebrew word for "encounter" (Gen. 32:18; 33:8; 1 Sam. 25:20).

---

[60] Firth, *1 & 2 Samuel*, p. 331.

[61] Jon D. Levenson and Baruch Halpern, "The Political Import of David's Marriages," *JBL* 99, 1980, pp. 507-518; supported also by Youngblood, *1, 2 Samuel*, p. 754.

[62] I am indebted to Biddle, "Ancestral Motifs in 1 Samuel 25," pp. 630-632, for many of the following insights.

[63] Abigail gives the same command to her servants ("pass over") that Jacob gives.

Abigail uses the deferential language of servant/lord (1 Sam. 25:23–31, 41) constantly, just as Jacob also does (Gen. 32:1–21; 33:1–17), and both bow before their opposition (Gen. 33:11; 1 Sam. 25:27). Like Jacob, Abigail refers to the gift she brings as a "blessing" (Gen. 33:3; 1 Sam. 25:23). Finally, the word "face," which is prominent in the Genesis story (32:20, 30; 33:10), also occurs in 1 Samuel 25:23 and 35. Vengeance, God's providence, and forgiveness are themes in both stories. What are we to make of these similarities? It appears that Abigail is being compared with the best qualities of her forefather Jacob. Admittedly Jacob began as an unsavory character, but Genesis 32–33 demonstrates a transformation from the old deceitful Jacob to a new humble Jacob who trusts in God. It is these qualities of humility and trust that are highlighted in Abigail's character, making her a "chip off of the old block."

Rebekah

Before leaving the Book of Genesis, we should note that Abigail also shares certain characteristics with Jacob's mother Rebekah. Both are said to be beautiful, although different words are used to describe them (Gen. 24:16; 26:7; 1 Sam. 25:3). They are both industrious, which is communicated through the word "hastened" (Gen. 24:18, 20, 46; 1 Sam. 25:18, 23, 34, 42). And both demonstrate great energy and resourcefulness. Finally there are similarities between their encounters with their future husbands. "The verbal similarities between the texts that narrate the departures of Rebekah and Abigail (Gen. 24:61//1 Sam. 25:42) as they set out for new husbands are unmistakable."[64] These similarities put Abigail in a favorable light, likening her to one of the great matriarchs of Israel, especially in regard to industriousness.

Hannah

One of the greatest connections, as far as the books of Samuel are concerned, is between Abigail and Hannah. Again I will summarize similarities already noted, while adding a few not previously mentioned. First, both Hannah and Abigail find themselves in desperate situations. Although these situations are different, the future of a household is at stake in each case. Second, both women make supplication to a superior, using the term "maidservant" to describe themselves (1 Sam. 1:11; 25:24ff.).[65] Third, in making their supplications both ask to be "remembered" (1 Sam. 1:11; 25:31). Fourth, Hannah makes a vow (1 Sam. 1:11), while Abigail swears an oath (1 Sam. 25:26). Fifth,

---

[64] Biddle, "Ancestral Motifs in 1 Samuel 25," p. 630. All of the similarities with Rebekah that I mention are based on this article.

[65] It could be argued that this is the typical language of supplication. Certainly if it were the only similarity it would not be convincing. But it is one of several correspondences between the two characters.

the Lord causes Hannah's *face* to be sad no longer (1 Sam. 1:18), while David lifts up Abigail's *face* (1 Sam. 25:35). Sixth, both share the theme of "strength through weakness" because of their dependence on the Lord. Seventh, words from Hannah's prayer are reflected in the story of Abigail and Nabal. Abigail assumes a lowly position and is lifted up (1 Sam. 2:7; 25:23–24, 35), while arrogance proceeds from Nabal's mouth (1 Sam. 2:3; 25:10–11) resulting in the Lord striking him (1 Sam. 2:6; 25:38). Eighth, and perhaps most important, both adopt a prophetic role that has significance for the future kingship (1 Sam. 2:1–10; 25:26, 28–31). It was Hannah who first proclaimed, "He will give strength to His king and exalt the horn of His anointed" (2:10); and it was Abigail who first announced the "sure house" that the Lord would give to David. The books of Samuel testify that these women were the first to foresee and utter these great truths, which would change the course of Israel's history. The stories of Hannah and Abigail thus highlight the important role that women played in inaugurating the monarchy. Although Israel, like the nations around it, was a patriarchal society, clearly Israel's God "shows no partiality" (Acts 11:34).

Jonathan

The correspondences with Jonathan continue to accentuate Abigail's good qualities. We have already noted that Nabal is a Saul in miniature,[66] so it is not surprising to find there are similarities between Jonathan and Abigail. The most obvious resemblance is her refusal to tell Nabal what she is doing (1 Sam. 25:19), as Jonathan refused to tell Saul about his dangerous venture (1 Sam. 14:1). Nabal's inability to recognize the serious nature of his offense, and the impossibility of effectively communicating with him makes this a wise choice on Abigail's part. As Proverbs 23:9 warns: "Do not speak in the hearing of a fool, for he will despise the wisdom of your words." Jonathan's willingness to step out in faith and put himself in danger for the good of others is another trait that he and Abigail share. Jonathan's foreknowledge of David's kingship and of God's punishment of David's enemies (1 Sam. 20:14–15) finds a parallel in Abigail's words (1 Sam. 25:28–31). Finally, Jonathan's focus on the Lord (e.g., 1 Sam. 20) makes Abigail, who continually refers to the Lord, his female counterpart in this regard.

Future Characters: Bathsheba, Tamar, and the Woman of Tekoa

Abigail's story also anticipates other women who will appear in the narrative of 1 and 2 Samuel. Similarities of wording and contrasting situations provide insights into the stories of Bathsheba and Tamar. These characters will be examined in later chapters.[67] The other future connection, previously

---

[66] See footnote 12 p. 214.
[67] See chap. 19 for Bathsheba and chap. 23 for Amnon and Tamar.

noted, concerns the wise woman of Tekoa. Gunn affirms that "both scenes involve a woman interceding with the king for herself and her family, and both are concerned with themes of bloodshed and revenge."[68] He also points to four similarities in wording that are striking. In both stories, the women fall with their faces to the ground and bow down (1 Sam. 25:23–24; 2 Sam. 14:4). They both ask David to lay the blame on them (1 Sam. 25:24; 2 Sam. 14:9). Both word their petitions to David similarly, "Please let you servant speak a word(s)..." (1 Sam. 25:24; 2 Sam. 14:12). Lastly, David tells each woman to go to her home (1 Sam. 25:35; 2 Sam. 14:8). While the order and circumstances differ, there are enough similarities to indicate that both ladies are "wise." The difference between them is that Abigail is more forthright while the woman of Tekoa is more deceptive.

When one evaluates her similarities with various biblical characters, Abigail stands head and shoulders above most of them. While she possesses all of their good qualities, their negative traits are absent. One might object that the way she spoke about her husband is a negative quality, but we have demonstrated that her language was not disloyal, but rather an act of wisdom on her part. This is not to say, of course, that Abigail was perfect—only that the writer chose to accentuate her positive attributes. In this too she resembles Jonathan.

Conclusion: A Woman of Humility

A host of adjectives could be strung together to describe Abigail: wise, prudent in speech, industrious, beautiful, prophetic, honorable...; but perhaps her greatest quality is humility. We will focus on this because it is the foundation for all the other attributes.

It is somewhat surprising to find humility in the wife of a wealthy man: a member of the aristocracy in Judah. Abigail is not caught up in her wealth, her position, or her own self-importance. She is a striking contrast to her husband, who is enamored with these things. Where does Abigail's humility come from? She is certainly a wise woman, and is described as such from the outset of the story (1 Sam. 25:3). Is it Abigail's wisdom then that makes her humble? Proverbs 11:2 would suggest otherwise: "When pride comes, then comes shame; but with the humble is wisdom." This proverb contends that wisdom comes from humility, not the other way around.

Again we ask, "Where does her humility come from?" Proverbs 22:4 links humility with the fear of the Lord: "By humility and the fear of the LORD are riches and honor and life." The answer is that Abigail fears the Lord; this is evidenced throughout her speech in 1 Samuel 25:24–31. The

---

[68] David M. Gunn, "Traditional Composition in the 'Succession Narrative,' " *VT* 26, 1976, p. 221.

name of the Lord is frequently on her lips. It is this fear that translates into humility.

It is not social status, hard work, or physical beauty, but a recognition of who God is, that gives one the proper perspective on life. We all need to learn this from Abigail, because we often overvalue things that don't matter and undervalue things that do. Abigail's wisdom comes from a humility that gives her the proper perspective, and therefore she understands what is truly important. When our possessions and social standing are of supreme importance to us, we act like Nabal. When wounded pride is paramount, we act like David. Abigail teaches us to ask, "Why do I act the way I do?" Our answer reveals a lot about what we think is important and what we are basing our lives upon.

All of the qualities mentioned above (except outward beauty) flow from humility. Indeed, it could be argued that humility enhances even physical beauty. One might rightly assert that prudent speech is an aspect of wisdom, but we have already seen that wisdom flows from humility. The humble know the importance of carefully-chosen words. Abigail is industrious because she is humble. She is not above doing hard work or "getting her hands dirty." Pride often blinds one to the truth; humility provides insight. Thus, Abigail's prophetic insight relates directly to her humility and her relationship with God. Honor is the icing on the cake for a humble person. "The fear of the LORD is the instruction of wisdom, and before honor is humility" (Prov. 15:33).

Abigail treats David differently than Nabal because her eyes are not blinded by pride. She sees clearly that David is the future king. By humbly acknowledging David, she honors the Lord because David is the Lord's anointed. The story of Abigail and Nabal again highlights the truth of 1 Samuel 2:30: "Those who honor Me I will honor, and those who despise Me shall be lightly esteemed." We have noted the honor and shame language occurring throughout this chapter. Nabal insults the Lord's anointed and is therefore despised and lightly esteemed. Abigail honors David and thus is honored by the Lord. Honor issues from humility.

In summary, whether we talk about controlling the tongue and choosing our words carefully (Nabal), controlling our reactions and leaving vengeance to the Lord (David), or the positive quality of being a peacemaker (Abigail), the bottom line is that we need a heavy dose of humility. How many family quarrels could be ended and how many wars avoided, if disagreements were approached with humility? Humility heals many wounds; in fact, it prevents many from occurring in the first place. We began this chapter by speaking of "good" and "evil," as key words in this story. Paul writes, "Abhor what is evil. Cling to what is good" (Rom. 12:9). One of the ways he defines what is "good" is, "Do not set your mind on high things, but associate with the humble. Do not be wise in your own opinion" (v. 16). Paul concludes with a reminder that, " 'Vengeance is Mine, I will repay,' says the Lord" (v. 19). As Abigail could testify, that is *good* advice. We are less likely to be offended if we follow Paul's exhortation: "Let nothing be done through selfish ambition or conceit, but in lowliness of mind let each esteem others better than himself" (Phil. 2:3). Our society is high on self and low on humility. We need to remember the Scripture: "God resists the proud, but gives grace to the humble" (James 4:6). Abigail is a shining example of this truth.

Chapter 19

Bathsheba: The Ambiguous One (David's wife)

"Is this not Bathsheba, the daughter of Eliam, the wife of Uriah the Hittite?" (2 Sam. 11:3)

Ambiguity with a Capital "A"

Of all the characters examined in this volume, Bathsheba is without question the most difficult to assess. From beginning to end her appearance in the narratives of 2 Samuel (chaps. 11–12) and 1 Kings (chaps. 1–2) is full of ambiguity. She is first introduced in the famous story of 2 Samuel 11 where David commits adultery with her. The narrator "presents external occurrences alone, deeds and words, leaving his agents' inner lives opaque."[1] The opening verses of 2 Samuel 11 evoke a host of questions without offering any definitive answers. For example, why does David remain in Jerusalem? Did Bathsheba position herself in a place where she knew David would be able to see her or does his vantage point on the roof of the palace allow him viewing access into the privacy of her home or courtyard? Is Bathsheba's bath in verse 2 connected to the statement of her purifying herself in verse 4? Does the statement, "she was cleansed from her impurity" (v. 4) refer to the end of her menstrual cycle, or to bathing after having intercourse with David? Is Bathsheba a foreigner or an Israelite? Why does David send for her knowing that she is a trusted soldier's wife? Why does Bathsheba come? Does David take her by force, or does she come willingly? These are only a few of the questions raised in reading the first four verses of 2 Samuel 11.[2]

How one answers these questions clearly determines how one perceives Bathsheba's character. Is she a calculating and clever woman who seeks to entrap the king?[3] Is she a victim,[4] or merely a passive participant?[5] Is she a naive,[6] and perhaps foolish woman,[7] or does she start out naive only to

---

[1] Sternberg, *Poetics*, p. 190.

[2] For a summary of the various types of questions raised see: Gale A. Yee "Fraught with Background: Literary Ambiguity in II Samuel 11," *Int.* 42, 1988, pp. 240-253. Also see, Birch, *The First and Second Books of Samuel*, p. 1284.

[3] George G. Nicol, "The Alleged Rape of Bathsheba: Some Observations on Ambiguity in Biblical Narrative," *JSOT* 73, 1997, pp. 43-54.

[4] J. Cheryl Exum, "Bathsheba, Plotted, Shot, and Painted," *Semeia* 74, 1996, pp. 47-73, not only accuses David but also the biblical narrator and other interpreters of the story of victimizing Bathsheba!

[5] Joel Rosenberg, "The Institutional Matrix of Treachery in Second Samuel 11," *Semeia* 46, 1989, pp. 103-116 (hereafter cited as "Institutional Matrix").

[6] Moshe Garsiel, "The Story of David and Bathsheba: A Different Approach," *CBQ* 55, 1993, pp. 244-262.

mature into a "mistress of language—shrewd, energetic, politically astute"?[8] These varying views of Bathsheba demonstrate the challenge of evaluating her character and suggest that the conclusions that are drawn here leave room for further discussion and debate.

Before attempting an assessment of Bathsheba's character, it is important to note with Birch that, "Perhaps the most common distortion of this story through the ages is the effort to portray Bathsheba as a seductress or co-conspirator, thereby transforming David to some degree from perpetrator to victim."[9] Examples of this are the interpretations of ancient rabbis seeking to excuse David by stating that Bathsheba was divorced at this time (because every soldier divorced his wife before going into battle), or Uriah deserved to die because he disobeyed David's order to go down to his house, thus committing treason.[10] Hollywood has also done an injustice by romanticizing David's act with Bathsheba, and even picturing Uriah as a harsh unloving wife abuser![11] Again, Birch poignantly states, "Romances do not begin with 'taking' and end with murder, and we romanticize this tale at our own peril."[12] Whatever conclusions may or may not be drawn about Bathsheba it is important to realize that David is fully responsible for his actions. In fact, it is the narrator's main purpose in this story to focus on his culpability (2 Sam. 11:27).

Beauty and the Beast (2 Sam. 11:2–5)

It is ironic that, although Bathsheba is a minor character in this story, there would be no story without her, making her extremely significant. The author suggests no sinister motive in Bathsheba's bath and therefore we should not read into it that she is purposely exposing herself to the king. There are good reasons to believe that this is a chance sighting by David. The narrative states that David is "walking about"[13] on his roof when he happens to see a woman bathing. There is no suggestion that he is purposely being voyeuristic. While this is a possible motive, it reads something into the text.[14] Whatever his motive, David's vantage point makes it possible to view some-

---

[7] Rost, *The Succession to the Throne of David*, p. 69.

[8] Alter, *The David Story*, p. 366. Rosenberg, "Institutional Matrix," p. 109.

[9] Birch, *The First and Second Books of Samuel*, p. 1288.

[10] McCarter, *II Samuel*, p. 288.

[11] Exum, "Bathsheba, Plotted, Shot, and Painted," pp. 48-51.

[12] Birch, *The First and Second Books of Samuel*, p. 1289.

[13] This is the meaning of the Hebrew tense. See for example, the NIV.

[14] It could also be argued that David is simply taking pride in surveying his city, or enjoying a stroll in the cool evening air. The many possible explanations demonstrate the problem of superimposing a motive when none is explicitly stated.

one else in the privacy of their own home without them realizing it.[15] As for Bathsheba, her evening bath some distance from the palace (how near or far we cannot tell) does not look like a purposeful display of immodesty. Furthermore, "Her marital status is another obstacle, for she cannot assume that David will indeed endanger himself by an affair with a married woman and plot to remove her husband."[16]

It asks too much of the text to assume that Bathsheba has cleverly planned a seductive rendezvous with the king. How does she know he will send for her? How can she be certain that she will become pregnant? How can she be sure that David will dispense with her husband and marry her? After all, David's first action upon hearing of her pregnancy is to try and cover it up by sending Uriah home for a visit (2 Sam. 11:8–11). Had his plan succeeded, Bathsheba would never have become his wife. The most that can be said is that Bathsheba is either naive or unaware that she is bathing in a place that exposes her to the view of someone on the palace roof.

It is Bathsheba's beauty that causes the beast in David to begin to stir. He "sends and inquires about the woman" (v. 3). How this happens is not exactly clear in the text. The question (or statement) "Is this not Bathsheba, the daughter of Eliam, the wife of Uriah the Hittite?" is a definitive way in Hebrew of confirming the identity of the woman. It could be translated, "Why that's Bathsheba…!"[17] The question is, "Who makes this statement?" The Hebrew text reads, "And he said." Most translators and commentators assume that the "he" is an anonymous messenger or person who confirms Bathsheba's identity. However, the only subject in the sentence is David and it is possible that he is the one speaking.

If David is the subject, then he already knows that the woman he has seen is Bathsheba. So what is he inquiring about? Birch believes he is seeking confirmation but receives no reply.[18] If this is correct then the lack of a reply could infer apprehension on behalf of the palace staff concerning David's inquiry. If David is inquiring about something other than her identity, then

---

[15] Anyone who has had the opportunity to visit the ancient site in Jerusalem known as "The City of David" realizes that standing at the top of the city (where David's palace probably was located) gives one a commanding view of the entire city. For the intriguing possibility that David's palace has recently been discovered see: Eilat Mazar, "Did I Find King David's Palace?" *BAR* 32:01, 2006, pp. 16-27, 70.

[16] Garsiel, "The Story of David and Bathsheba," p. 254.

[17] Rosenberg, "Institutional Matrix," p. 108. Vannoy, *1–2 Samuel*, p. 329 notes, "a surprising communication is introduced in this way in order to show it to be absolutely true." See Gesenius, F. W., *Gesenius' Hebrew grammar*, E. Kautzsch & S. A. E. Cowley, ed. 2d English ed.; (Oxford: Clarendon Press, 1976), § 150e, p. 474.

[18] Birch, *The First and Second Book of Samuel*, p. 1284.

the text leaves us guessing as to what that could be.[19] Of course, the traditional interpretation that David has asked about the woman's identity and received a response from someone else is also a possibility. The exact meaning is just one more ambiguity among others! The important point, however, is that David knows full well who this woman is *before* he sends for her.

When it comes to Bathsheba's identity, David knows more than the modern reader. Are Uriah and Bathsheba both foreigners, or is Bathsheba an Israelite who is married to a foreigner? Is Bathsheba's father the Eliam who is mentioned among David's mighty men in 2 Samuel 23:34? If so, this would make her the granddaughter of David's infamous counselor, Ahithophel (2 Sam. 15:31). It is difficult to answer these questions with any certainty. The fact that Bathsheba is not only identified by her husband's name but also by her father's suggests that there is some significance to her father.[20] The best explanation is that her father is indeed the Eliam mentioned in 2 Samuel 23:34. David's treatment of Bathsheba would then provide a plausible explanation for Ahithophel's animosity toward him.[21]

Whether Bathsheba is an Israelite or a foreigner is an intriguing question. Does David think he can take advantage of her because she is not an Israelite? Or is she an Israelite but David thinks he can take advantage of her because her husband is a foreigner?[22] This could possibly explain why David has no qualms about violating the wife of one of his mighty men (2 Sam. 23:39).[23] Such speculations are interesting but they take us beyond the words of the text. Outside of knowing the names of Bathsheba's father and that her husband was one of David's mighty men, her identity must remain something of a mystery.

---

[19] For example, is he inquiring about her availability? Perhaps making sure that there are no potential obstacles that could prevent him from sending for her?

[20] McCarter, *II Samuel*, p. 285. Also see Anderson, *2 Samuel*, p. 153. Although both men note the significance of Bathsheba's father being mentioned, both are skeptical that he is the Eliam of 2 Sam. 23:34.

[21] J. W. Wesselius, "Joab's Death and the Central Theme of the Succession Narrative (2 Samuel IX–1 Kings II)," *VT* 40/3 (1990), p. 347, argues, "It is hardly accidental that Bathsheba's grandfather Ahithophel was the person who advised Absalom to have sexual intercourse with his father's concubines (2 Sam. xvi 20–2)....This is, of course, another piece of evidence for the supposition that the narrator expected the reader or hearer to be aware of Ahithophel's family relationship with Bathsheba, whether through 2 Sam. xxiii 34 or because it would be generally known."

[22] Uriah (Yong-Hwan) Kim, "Uriah the Hittite: A (Con)Text of Struggle for Identity," *Semeia* 90-91, 2002, pp. 69-85, argues that it is Uriah's foreign status that makes him a vulnerable target.

[23] It must be admitted, however, that David shows no evidence of prejudice against friendly foreigners. Note for example his interaction with Ittai which suggests that David commanded great loyalty from the foreign mercenaries in his army (2 Sam. 15:18–22).

As verse 4 begins, the (metaphorical) beast within David rises to the surface as he "sends, takes, and lays." No psychological insight is provided and there is no reference to emotion. It is an act of unrestrained power and lust, and is reminiscent of Samuel's warning about the king who will "take" people and things for himself (1 Sam. 8:10–18). All three of these verbs will reappear in the narrative describing David's conviction and judgment.[24] David's act is reprehensible, but it is softened somewhat by the insertion of three actions that refer to Bathsheba. We are told that "she came," "was purifying herself from her uncleanness,"[25] and "returned to her house" (v. 4). These verbs interrupt the harsh succession of verbs that describe David's sin. We have already asserted that David is fully responsible for his actions. Indeed, the event would never have taken place had he not initiated it and followed through with it. However, the fact that Bathsheba "came" at least suggests compliance on her part if nothing else.[26] It could be argued that she came out

---

[24] "Send" occurs in 12:1 where it is the Lord who "sends" Nathan to convict David and pronounce sentence. "Take" occurs in 12:4, 9, and 10. "Lay" occurs in 12:3, and 11.

[25] This phrase is almost universally acknowledged to refer to the week following the end of Bathsheba's menstrual cycle. It is argued that this is the writer's way of asserting that Bathsheba was not pregnant at the time that David had intercourse with her, and, therefore, the child she carries cannot be Uriah's. Two recent studies, however, suggest that this expression, as well as Bathsheba's bath (v. 2), should not be connected with the menstruation law in Leviticus 15:19–24. Tikva Frymer Kensky, *Reading the Women of the Bible*, p. 147, believes the phrase in v. 4 refers to the cleansing bath that was taken while Bathsheba was still in the palace following her sexual encounter with David. J. D'ror Chankin-Gould, Derek Hutchinson, David Hilton Jackson, Tyler D. Mayfield, Leah Rediger Schulte, Tammie J. Schneider, E. Winkelman, "The Sanctified 'Adulteress' and her Circumstantial Clause: Bathsheba's Bath and Self-Consecration in 2 Samuel 11," *JSOT* 32, 2008, pp. 339-352, perform a comprehensive study of the words contained in this phrase and find no evidence that it refers to the menstruation law in Leviticus. Rather, they believe it refers to "an innocent bath" (p. 339). While I do not agree with all of the conclusions of this article, the authors, as well as Frymer Kensky, have raised significant objections about the traditional interpretation of this phrase.

[26] I am in agreement here with Nicol, "The Alleged Rape of Bathsheba," p. 49 who writes, "If David 'takes' Bathsheba, it should not be ignored that the following phrase states that she 'comes' to him, suggesting that their encounter is one in which each plays a part." Even as severe a critic as Exum, "Bathsheba, Plotted, Shot, and Painted," p. 49, admits, "Although 'sent' and 'took' indicate aggression on David's part, 'came' and 'returned,' the two verbs of which Bathsheba is the subject, are not what one would expect if resistance were involved." Alter, *The David Story*, p. 251, goes so far as to wonder whether the author may be toying with the double meaning of the phrase "came into," which can be used of a man's first sexual encounter with a woman. See for example, Gen. 38:16, and 18. Thus, Bathsheba's "coming into" David would be an ironic use of this expression.

of fear, or she came because the king summoned her and she didn't know what the summons was about, but once again we would be in the realm of speculation. The fact is, the narrator chose to balance David's three actions with Bathsheba's three actions, although admittedly the scale of guilt still tips in favor of David. However, it is notable that Bathsheba is not "sent" home, which would be yet another coercive deed on David's part giving him four actions to her two, rather, she "returns" home of her own accord. Later we will look at other evidence that suggests Bathsheba is not totally innocent,[27] although the majority of blame must rest on David's shoulders.

Verse 5 begins, "And the woman conceived." The word *'iššāh* (pronounced *ish-shah*) in Hebrew is the word "woman" or "wife." This word is skillfully used by the narrator to note an ironic progression in the story. When David first sees Bathsheba she is "a woman bathing," in fact, she is a "very beautiful woman" (v. 2). At this point she appears to be an eligible candidate for David. Next, however, David realizes, or finds out through inquiry, that she is the "wife" of Uriah the Hittite (v. 3). This recognition should have made her off limits to David, but continuing his pursuit he commits adultery with her which leads to the opening statement of verse 5—the "woman" is about to become a mother![28] Thus, through the use of one Hebrew word there is a progression in four verses from woman, to wife, to expectant mother. Of course, under other circumstances it would be joyous news for a wife to become a mother, but not when it is another man's child!

In yet another ironic twist, it is Bathsheba who does the "sending" this time. From an historical point of view we can only guess why she "sends" a message to David instead of going to the palace personally. Perhaps she fears there would be more talk if she appeared in person, we do not know. What we do know is that David's sending resulted in the planting of a seed which was now growing in the womb of Bathsheba. Bathsheba's sending teaches us that David now reaps what he has sown. He receives the devastating message, "I'm pregnant," the only two words Bathsheba speaks in the entire story. With these two simple words the king loses control of the situation. The king who "sent" and "took" and did as he pleased now finds him-

---

[27] Fokkelman's statement, *King David*, p. 53, that "the text is…not at all interested in her possibly having shared the responsibility," is over zealous in my opinion. Certainly the focus is on David, and the narrator is mainly interested in his actions. However, even though Bathsheba did not initiate the action and is therefore innocent in that sense, nonetheless she did commit adultery. Whatever her motive was (fear, attraction, etc.), she would still be considered guilty under the Law of Moses. I believe the three actions describing her in 11:4 substantiate this conclusion as well as evidence we will examine below.

[28] Yee, "Fraught with Background," p. 245, notes the significance of this word in the story although she does not mention its connection with the idea of motherhood.

self in a dilemma of his own making. This is always the consequence of ignoring God's way and choosing our own.

If Bathsheba were a cunning manipulative woman, the words "I'm pregnant" would be words of strength—blackmail even. This would be a dangerous game to play with the king, however, and as we have already seen, it is an extremely unlikely scenario. Rather, Bathsheba's words are words of weakness. They are a cry for help.[29] While the affair is surely known to the messengers and perhaps others at court, it will soon become common knowledge to all unless something is done. If Bathsheba is somewhat naive and passive as I am inclined to believe, then she may not know what to do. Whether naive or not, she is powerless to do anything about the situation so she turns to the only one who can. The plan to "send" for Uriah is David's (v. 6). Indeed, only David has the power to send for him. When Bathsheba sends her distressing message we do not know what she hopes the king will do. We do not know if she has any plan at all. We are only told that she sends to David. As the plot thickens, having informed the king of the shameful predicament they are in, she disappears from the narrative; we do not see her again until her husband is dead and she becomes David's wife (vv. 26–27).

From Widow to Queen (2 Sam. 11:26–27)

Verse 26 begins with "a sentence that…implicitly condemns David's adultery by stressing three times the husband-wife relationship between Uriah and Bathsheba."[30] There is one reference to Bathsheba as "Uriah's wife" and two to Uriah as "her husband." She is never called by name in these verses, the emphasis being on her relationship with Uriah. Upon hearing of her husband's death, Bathsheba mourns. It appears that the customary period for mourning was seven days (1 Sam. 31:13). If the character sketch we are painting is correct, then there is no reason to assume that her mourning is anything but genuine.[31] The narrator does not give us a "wink" when he says she mourned for her husband. There is no detectable irony; therefore the statement should be taken at face value. In fact, one would imagine Bathsheba's mourning to be a mixture of guilt and true grief: Not guilt in the sense that

---

[29] *Contra*, C.Y.S. Ho, "The Stories of the Family Troubles of Judah and David: A Study of Their Literary Links," *VT* 49, 1999, p. 518, who states that Bathsheba's words are more a "cry of triumph than an S.O.S. signal."

[30] Youngblood, *1, 2 Samuel*, p. 932.

[31] McKane, *I&II Samuel*, p. 232, notes that her affection could be genuine but it may also be no more than a formality. If one accepts that Bathsheba is a master manipulator then the obvious conclusion would be that her grief was not genuine.

she is aware of how her husband has been dispatched (although that is possible), but because of the affair with David.[32]

Time is of the essence and David wastes none, "gathering" her "into his house" (v. 27a). In other words, he incorporates her into his already large harem. This fact will be exploited in Nathan's parable about the rich man (David) who has "exceedingly many flocks and herds" (2 Sam. 12:2), in contrast to the poor man (Uriah) who only has "one little ewe lamb" (2 Sam. 12:3). The word 'iššāh (woman/wife) occurs yet again, but this time with reference to David. Uriah's wife (v. 26) has become David's wife (v. 27), but the threefold mention of Bathsheba's identity in verse 26 outweighs the single reference in verse 27. In case there is any doubt about the matter, for the first time the narrator lets us in on God's thoughts: "And the thing that David had done was evil in the eyes of the LORD" (my translation).

The Miracle of Forgiveness: From Object to Person (2 Sam. 12:24–25)

By the time Bathsheba appears in the narrative again the Lord has sent Nathan to convict David of his sin and to pronounce judgment on him (12:1–12). David has also confessed, repented, and been forgiven (12:13), but the first of several severe consequences has been experienced as the child born to David and Bathsheba dies (12:14–23). For the first time since 2 Samuel 11:3 Bathsheba is referred to by name. It is also the first time that David treats her like a person instead of like an object to be used. Following the death of their child we are told that, "David comforted Bathsheba his wife" (v. 24a). There was no mention of comfort at the loss of her husband (11:26–27), only the cold efficiency of David gathering her into his harem. Although the narrative has focused on David's sin and its consequences, this statement reveals that Bathsheba has experienced some very real pain of her own. In a short time she has lost both a husband and a child. How quickly one sin can change the direction of many lives! However, what is done is done; Uriah is dead, and the beloved child cannot be brought back (12:23). Repentance and forgiveness may not bring back the dead or remove all of the consequences of past actions, but it does resurrect the compassion that is destroyed by sin and allows people once again to be treated as human beings instead of objects.

There are four ways in which the Lord's grace and forgiveness is communicated in these two verses. First, Bathsheba's name is restored and she is now called David's wife without any qualifications. In connection with this, the word 'iššāh now occurs in a positive context. Second, two of the

---

[32] The text never addresses the issue of when Bathsheba found out about David's part in her husband's death. Certainly she knew after Nathan's confrontation with David (2 Sam. 12), if not before.

verbs which described David's sin and punishment "send" and "lay," now occur in a context of the Lord's acceptance.[33] David "lays" with Bathsheba and she gives birth to another child, replacing the one who had died (v. 24). This is followed by the Lord "sending" Nathan and giving the child another name (v. 25). Third, it is explicitly stated that the Lord "loved" this child (Solomon) and gave him a special name, Jedidiah, "beloved of the Lord." Fourth, the birth of Solomon, as with any child in Scripture, is a joyous occasion and represents a new beginning. Indeed, God's favor on Solomon anticipates his future kingship (1 Kings 1–2).

Bathsheba Through the Eyes of Abigail (1 Sam. 25; 2 Sam. 11)

Many scholars have noted the connection between the stories of Abigail and Bathsheba. In some ways Abigail's account is a mirror image of Bathsheba's story with a few interesting twists.[34] Both are married when David meets them and both become his wife after the death of their respective husbands. Abigail's husband is an evil man, Bathsheba's a good one. Abigail's words that the one who fights the Lord's battles should not be guilty of "evil" (1 Sam. 25:28–31), anticipate David's actions in 2 Samuel 11 (see esp. v. 27). At the nadir of his power, a woman saves him; at the height of his power, he is imperiled by a woman.[35] Nabal commits a foolish act potentially leading to his death at the hands of David, but Abigail intercedes and saves him thus saving David from shedding innocent blood. Uriah is innocent, yet Bathsheba commits (or is coerced into committing) a foolish act which leads to his death. David becomes guilty of shedding innocent blood and she does nothing (perhaps can do nothing) to prevent it. When a crisis strikes, Abigail knows what to do, Bathsheba does not. Nabal refuses to take from his abundant flocks and so does David. Both Abigail and Bathsheba are said to be beautiful women (different Hebrew words). One important difference is that sex plays no part in the story of Abigail but acts as the catalyst in Bathsheba's.

A survey of these stories also demonstrates that they share a host of similar vocabulary. The following list is a sample of these similarities with Scripture references to Abigail's story occurring first (1 Sam. 25), followed by those in the Bathsheba story (2 Sam. 11–12):

---

[33] It could be argued that the third word "take" is also used in a positive context in the next episode which describes David "taking" the crown of the king of Ammon—a sign of God's blessing in victory.

[34] Adele Berlin, "Characterization in Biblical Narrative: David's wives," *JSOT* 23, 1982, pp. 69-85, hereafter cited as "David's Wives." The words "mirror image" are Berlin's and many of the following comments are based on her observations.

[35] Rosenberg, *King and Kin*, p. 152.

David sends and inquires (25:5; 11:4, 6–7)
David sends messengers (25:14, 42; 11:4)
David takes (25:40; 11:4)
Nabal is evil in his doings; David does evil (25:3; 11:27)
evil should not be found in David; David commits evil (25:28; 11:27)
threefold use of "peace" (25:6; 11:7)
sword (25:13; 11:25; 12:9, 10)
dead or died (25:37, 38, 39; 11:15, 17, 21, 24, 26)
wash the feet (25:41; 11:8)
descend (25:23; 11:8–13)
morning (25:22, 34, 37; 11:14)
drinking and being drunk (25:36; 11:11, 13)
swearing an oath, "As the Lord lives…" (25:26, 34; 11:11)
wall (25:16; 11:20, 21, 24)
"hasten" and "tomorrow"—same letters in Hebrew (25:18, 23; 11:12)

Although words are often used in different ways between the two stories, and some occurrences may be coincidental, the similarities are striking. In particular, David's sending messengers, the threefold use of the word "peace," the words "sword" and "dead," the description of Nabal and David doing "evil," and the phrase "wash the feet" (which only occurs in these two passages in the books of Samuel), strongly suggest correspondences between these two accounts. The correlation of theme and vocabulary indicates that a comparison between Abigail and Bathsheba would be fruitful and might unveil some of the ambiguity present in Bathsheba's character in 2 Samuel 11.

Carole Fontaine has noted "the clustering of typical wisdom motifs in vocabulary and theme" found in 2 Samuel 11–12.[36] In the previous chapter we observed that the story of Abigail also contains vocabulary and motifs consistent with the themes of wisdom and folly. This recognition creates yet another link between the stories of Abigail and Bathsheba. The most ironic contrast between the two is that Abigail's action saves her "good-for-nothing" husband Nabal from death, while Bathsheba's action sends her good husband Uriah to his death. This contrast highlights the wisdom motif of the woman who brings death. Fontaine notes the similarity of language in

---

[36] Carole Fontaine, "The Bearing of Wisdom on the Shape of 2 Samuel 11–12 and 1 Kings 3," *JSOT* 34, 1986, pp. 61-77. The partial quote above is from p. 62. For the classic treatment of the influence of wisdom on the narrative of 2 Sam. 9–20 and 1 Kings 1–2, see R. N. Whybray, *The Succession Narrative: A Study of II Sam. 9–20 and 1 Kings 1 and 2* (London: SCM Press, Ltd., 1968).

Proverbs 6:22 with the opening of the story in 2 Samuel 11.[37] Speaking of the commandments and teachings of one's parents (which ultimately derive from the Lord), Proverbs 6:22 states, "When you *walk* they will lead you; when you *lie down* they will watch over you" (ESV). I have highlighted the words "walk" and "lie down" because they are precisely the words that characterize David's action in 2 Samuel 11:2, 4.[38] The proverb goes on to warn that the commandment will "preserve you from the evil woman, from the smooth tongue of the adulteress. Do not desire her beauty in your heart" (Prov. 6:24–25a). The proverb continues,

> Can a man carry fire next to his chest and his clothes not be burned?
> Or can one walk on hot coals and his feet not be scorched?
> So is he who goes into his neighbor's wife;
> None who touches her will go unpunished. (Prov. 6:27–29, ESV)

The correspondences, though not exact, cannot help but make one think of the David and Bathsheba affair. While Bathsheba may not have intentionally seduced David she is, nonetheless, the woman who brings death, not to her fellow adulterer in this case, but to her husband. The counterpart of the adulteress in Proverbs 6 is "Woman Wisdom" in Proverbs 9. Similarly, Bathsheba's act foolishly puts her husband in harm's way while Abigail acts wisely in saving her husband. When one adds up Bathsheba's naiveté and passivity the sum total is foolishness.

It is not just these similarities, however, that associate Bathsheba with the woman who brings death; a reference within the story of chapter 11 also suggests this equation.[39] When Joab sends a messenger back to David with the news of Uriah's death, he refers to the story of Abimelech in Judges 9 (2 Sam. 11:21). Uriah has just died because the Israelite army got too close to the city wall. Similarly, Abimelech, the petty tyrant king of Shechem, died when he got too close to the city wall and a woman cast a millstone on his head (Judg. 9:50–54). This may have become a proverbial story in Israel about the dangers of getting too close to an enemy's wall and may explain why Joab anticipates David citing it. Within the context of the story, however, it takes on a deeper meaning, for it was Bathsheba's act of lying with David that directly resulted in Uriah's death at the foot of the wall in Rabbah. Like the

---

[37] Fontaine, "The Bearing of Wisdom," p. 65.

[38] This is not to infer that the story in 2 Samuel 11–12 is dependent on Proverbs 6, or any other passage of the Wisdom Literature. My point in this comparison is similar to that of Song-Mi Suzie Park, "The Frustration of Wisdom: Wisdom, Counsel, and Divine Will in 2 Samuel 17:1–23," *JBL* 128/3, 2009, p. 457, who states that "wisdom-like themes and language were part of the larger cultural milieu."

[39] Park, "The Frustration of Wisdom," p. 457.

other correspondences, this one is not exact. It is simply one more nail in the coffin that convicts Bathsheba of a foolish action.

Bathsheba Through the Eyes of Tamar (2 Sam. 11 and 13)

The story of Amnon and Tamar in 2 Samuel 13 is the sequel to the story of David and Bathsheba. It is the beginning of the fulfillment of the Lord's word of judgment in 2 Samuel 12:11: "Behold I will raise up evil against you from your own house" (my translation). Just as David has illicit sex in his house, so too does his son Amnon. Verbs once again draw a parallel between the actions of father and son. Just as David "sent" for Bathsheba, so he innocently "sends" his daughter Tamar to Amnon's house (13:7). Ironically Amnon "lies down" on his "bed" (13:5), the posture David was in at the beginning of 2 Samuel 11:2. The word "lie" also describes Amnon's sin (13:11, 14), as it does David's (11:4). Wisdom motifs and vocabulary are once again prevalent in 2 Samuel 13, indicating a further link with chapters 11–12.[40] These parallels once again suggest that we may profit from a comparison between Bathsheba and Tamar in order to gain a clearer understanding of her character.

Like Bathsheba, Tamar is said to be beautiful (13:1, although a different Hebrew word is used). Tamar is sent by David to Amnon's house in order to make him some food so that he might recover from his "illness" (13:6–8). She remains unsuspecting of any ulterior motive, even when Amnon orders everyone else out of the house and tells her to come into his bedroom (13:9–10). Our portrait of Bathsheba in 2 Samuel 11 proposed that she was naive; may we suggest that the parallel with Tamar adds weight to that proposal? We also inferred the possibility that Bathsheba may not have known why she was sent for. The same is true of Tamar. She believes she was sent to minister to her sick brother; the true purpose of her visit has been concealed from her. Here, however, the similarities end. When Amnon forcefully expresses his intentions,[41] Tamar protests (13:12–13). Her language invokes the words "fool" and "folly" as she tries to dissuade her brother from his predetermined course of action. We note an important difference here between Tamar and Bathsheba.[42] The words describing Bathsheba's actions in 11:4–5 gave no hint of resistance, and certainly the text records no words of protest. Tamar protests the foolish act being forced upon her; Bathsheba acquiesces.

---

[40] There are also many parallels in vocabulary with the story of Abigail, including wisdom vocabulary. These parallels will be explored in more depth in chap. 23 which examines the story of Amnon and Tamar.

[41] The word "take" which describes David's sin (11:4) is replaced by the word "seize" (13:11, 14), showing Amnon's act to be more aggressive than his father's.

[42] *Contra* Fokkelman, *King David*, p. 53, n. 7, who does not think the two can be compared.

Once again a comparison of stories yields a verdict of foolishness in regard to Bathsheba.

Scripture affirms the importance of more than one witness in determining a conviction (Deut. 17:6; 19:15). Although Bathsheba's portrait in 2 Samuel 11 is ambiguous, there is enough circumstantial evidence to suggest a certain understanding of her character. The witness of Abigail and Tamar seems to solidify our suggestion that Bathsheba is a naive and passive woman who does not have the wisdom or strength to extricate herself from a dangerous situation. If we were to hold court on Bathsheba's character, based on the evidence of 2 Samuel 11 and our two witnesses, we would have to conclude she is not a cunning, manipulative, or malicious person. She is simply foolish. It remains to be determined if the future will alter our verdict, but for the moment court stands adjourned.

David's Wives: A Picture of Ethical Deterioration

Having examined in detail the three wives of David highlighted in the narratives of Samuel (Michal, Abigail, and Bathsheba), a closer look at his acquisition of them is instructive. It is noteworthy that each of these three women had another husband who was displaced by David.[43] The manner in which David obtained these women reveals a progressive ethical deterioration on his part. Although Abigail was originally the wife of Nabal, God's judgment on him freed her to marry David. The marriage was legal and ethical and provides a satisfying closure to the story.

While David had previously, and legitimately, married Michal (1 Sam. 18:25–27), the reader is informed at the end of the Abigail story that Saul had taken her and given her to another man named Palti (1 Sam. 25:44). This unlawful move by Saul clearly left David within his rights to take Michal back, but the manner in which he does so reflects poorly on him. David uses Michal as a political pawn in a game of power politics with Abner and Ishbosheth. In contrast, Palti, an adoring husband, (also called, "Paltiel") shows great emotion at the loss of Michal who is forcibly taken from him (2 Sam. 3:13–16). Though Michal is rightfully David's wife, this incident lacks the warmth and charm of his encounter and marriage to Abigail. The securing of Abigail's hand resulted from David listening to her wise counsel and ultimately trusting in the Lord. Conversely, Michal had no voice in being returned to David. Rather than trusting in the Lord, David's own ingenuity orchestrated a power play that forced Michal to return and become a member of his growing harem.

---

[43] John Kessler, "Sexuality and politics: the motif of the displaced husband in the Books of Samuel," *CBQ* 62, 2000, pp. 409-423. I am indebted to Kessler for the following insights.

Taking Bathsheba is the final step in David's ethical deterioration. This time he does not wait for the husband to die (Abigail), nor does he take one who was previously his (Michal). Bathsheba should have been off limits to David, and yet he took her knowing she was married to Uriah, one of his mighty men. When she turned up pregnant he dispensed with her husband and married her himself. Comparing David's acquisition of these wives thus becomes an important way of observing his spiritual descent. We are reminded of Samuel's warning about the king who "takes" (1 Sam. 8:10–18), and perhaps more importantly of the Torah's instruction that a king must not "multiply wives for himself" (Deut. 17:17).[44] Fortunately, David's treatment of Bathsheba is not the end of the story; as we have seen, the nature of a gracious God who confronts and forgives sin (when repented of) provides a new starting point for the king and his wife.

The Impotent King and His Ewe Lamb (1 Kings 1:1–4)

The Book of Kings opens with the portrait of a feeble David confined to his bed and unable to keep himself warm. A young virgin named Abishag is brought to care for him and to "lie" in his "bosom" (1 Kings 1:1–4). This language recalls the imagery of Nathan's parable who described the ewe lamb (Bathsheba) as lying in the bosom of the poor man (Uriah—2 Sam. 12:3). Abishag has become David's ewe lamb! This imagery is reinforced by the comment that David did not "know" her (1 Kings 1:4), thus like the ewe lamb of 2 Samuel 12:3 Abishag's relationship with David is more like a "daughter" who serves and cares for him, than a concubine. The description of her as a "young woman" may further enhance this connection. Lastly, she is described as "very beautiful." Is she even prettier than Bathsheba? Bathsheba is described as "very good in appearance" (2 Sam. 11:2), whereas Abishag is described by the Hebrew word "beautiful." Both women are given the adverb "very" to heighten the description of their appearance.

Like other allusions we have encountered, the similarities between Bathsheba and Abishag are not intended to be an exact parallel. The author's purpose is to recall the former story and thereby plant a suggestion in the reader's mind that there may be a connection between the two women. The reader awaits the unfolding of the drama to see if any parallel or contrast will become clearer.

In the introductory verses of 1 Kings, the author skillfully weaves together the portraits of two people who will play a part in the ensuing drama. The first portrait is that of a once virile and powerful king who has grown impotent with age; the second, of a young beautiful virgin who serves the king. Their relationship is reminiscent of David and Bathsheba's with a twist:

---

[44] Ibid., p. 421.

there is no sexual intimacy between them. David's impotence sets the stage for the political crisis which is about to take place with Adonijah's seizure of the throne. If he can do nothing with a young beautiful woman, can he do anything about the kingdom? Will the old king lie passively while the kingdom is taken by force, or does he have enough strength left to determine the future of the kingship? Just as Bathsheba's personal relationship with the king once had an effect on kingdom politics (unintentionally on her part), so now Abishag, who is a younger reflection of her, will also impact future affairs of state (also unintentionally).[45]

Kingship in Crisis (1 Kings 1:11–31)

Nathan's Plan (1:11–14)

Adonijah's attempt to seize the throne (1 Kings 1:5–10) creates a political crisis that elicits a quick response from Nathan the prophet.[46] 1 Kings 1:10 informs the reader that Nathan, as well as Solomon, were among those excluded from Adonijah's attempted coup. Nathan's first act is to go to Bathsheba, the mother of Solomon, and formulate a plan that will motivate the supine king to action (v. 11). Although Bathsheba's return to the narrative has been anticipated in the description of the young Abishag, this is her first appearance since 2 Samuel 12:24–25. Obviously many years have passed: what Bathsheba will we as readers encounter? Have the intervening years as David's wife and the time spent at court brought a maturity, a sagacity that was lacking to the younger woman we last encountered?

The initial answer seems to be, "No." Nathan begins with the question, "Have you not heard that Adonijah the son of Haggith has become king, and David our lord does not know it?" The construction of this question is similar to the question asked in 2 Samuel 11:3. In other words, it could be translated as a declaration: "Surely you have heard...!" The implication is that Bathsheba knows what Adonijah has done, but she has not yet considered what, if anything, she should do about it. Nathan's words are intended to stir "Bathsheba's maternal instincts by referring to Adonijah as 'son of Haggith.' "[47] Nathan continues to make the mother-son connection by stating, "Come, please, let me now give you advice, that you may save your own life and the life of your son Solomon" (v. 12). Once again we encounter a crisis situation in which Bathsheba does not seem to know what to do. It takes the counsel of the wise Nathan to formulate a plan and motivate her to action. It

---

[45] Fokkelman, *King David*, p. 382, also notes that only Abishag and Bathsheba are said to "stand before the king" in this chapter (1:4, 28), thus drawing another parallel between the two.

[46] For further information on Adonijah and his attempted coup see chap. 25, pp. 386-390.

[47] Dilday, *1, 2 Kings*, p. 39.

seems she has not grasped the ramifications of the day's events. Adonijah has proclaimed himself king, and this now threatens the very lives of Bathsheba and her son. That this implication appears to have escaped Bathsheba seems incredible and, once again, confirms that she is either very naive, helpless, or unintelligent.

Before looking at Nathan's advice it is important to pause and note that Nathan and Bathsheba are on the same team. The significance of this recognition lends support to our caricature of Bathsheba as a naive and passive individual. If Bathsheba had cunningly manipulated her way into David's court one has to wonder if she could have secured the friendship and support of Nathan so easily. Furthermore, this support is not of recent making due to the present political crisis, but goes all the way back to 2 Samuel 12:25. Garsiel makes a similar point from Bathsheba's view when he writes,

> If she had been so anxious to become David's wife, would she not have harbored deep resentment against the prophet who exposed the affair and brought about her child's death? Exactly the opposite happens: Nathan does not condemn her, her next child is "loved by the Lord," and it is Nathan who gives him the appropriate name of Jedidiah. She puts complete faith in Nathan when together they counter Adonijah's manipulations. This relationship of trust would be incomprehensible if she were the cunning or opportunistic woman [others conjecture her to be].[48]

Nathan's advice begins by telling Bathsheba to remind David of the "oath" he had sworn to place Solomon on the throne (1 Kings 1:13). The use of "oath" is a clever wordplay on Bathsheba's own name which can mean "daughter of an oath." Thus, Bathsheba's very presence can invoke the idea of an oath! The oath becomes the focal point of Bathsheba's and Nathan's plea. It is their leverage to convince David to act in favor of Solomon. Since there is no previous mention of an oath to put Solomon on the throne, many scholars believe that this is a fabrication by Nathan and Bathsheba.[49] There are, however, several good reasons to accept the oath as factual. Perhaps the most significant is Adonijah's actions. If Adonijah believed that he would be the next king there would have been no need to take matters into his own hands prematurely as he does here. Furthermore, the fact that he invites "all

---

[48] Garsiel, "The Story of David and Bathsheba," p. 254.

[49] For example, David M. Gunn, "David and the Gift of the Kingdom," *Semeia* 3, 1975, p. 31. It is somewhat startling to me how many scholars convict Nathan of deceit, or suggest that it cannot be known whether such an oath was ever given. Although not previously stated in the text, there are several good reasons to assume the oath is legitimate. See the argument above.

of his brothers, the king's sons" (v. 9), except Solomon and those close to him, strongly indicates that he knows Solomon is in line to succeed David.[50]

Another compelling reason is David's affirmation that he had sworn such an oath to Bathsheba (1 Kings 1:30). Some call David's mental prowess into question and suggest he has been duped by Bathsheba and Nathan into thinking that he had made such an oath.[51] This goes beyond the text, however, which only comments on his physical disability, never a lack of mental capabilities. In fact, David's subsequent actions in having Solomon anointed (1 Kings 1:32–35), and his instructions to Solomon (1 Kings 2:1–9), suggest that he is in full control of his mental faculties. David's repetition of the oath quoted by Bathsheba is additional corroboration to the reader that neither she nor Nathan have fabricated the oath. Such confirmation is typical of biblical narrative.[52] Furthermore, Bathsheba affirms that David had "sworn by the LORD your God" (v. 17), a fact that David confirms in repeating the oath. If this assertion were not true, Bathsheba would be guilty of blasphemy and so would Nathan who had counseled Bathsheba to remind David of his oath (v. 13). This would discredit both characters and such is clearly not the case. Bathsheba may be naive but she is no blasphemer, nor is Nathan who has guided David in the way of the Lord throughout his reign.[53]

For those who respect the veracity of Scripture, 1 Chronicles 28:1–6 removes all doubt that David did indeed make such an oath concerning Solomon. Note especially verse 5: "And of all my sons (for the LORD has given me many sons) he has chosen my son Solomon to sit on the throne of the kingdom of the LORD over Israel." The most obvious answer for the lack of such a pronouncement in 2 Samuel (or 1 Kings) is simply the narrative art of the biblical author. Information is frequently withheld by the author in order to create suspense or surprise the reader later.[54]

---

[50] D.A. Carson, *1 and 2 Kings*, NBC (Leicester; Downers Grove: Inter-Varsity Press, 1994), states, "...the fact that Adonijah did not invite Solomon to his celebrations suggests that he recognized him as having some claim to the throne...."

[51] For example, Alter, *The Art of Biblical Narrative*, p. 99.

[52] For example, 1 Sam. 25:7–8, 15–16. A similar example may be found in Joshua 14:9 where Caleb states that "Moses swore" that he would receive an inheritance in Canaan. Although a promise can be found in Num. 14:24 and Deut. 1:36, as M. H. Woudstra, *The Book of Joshua*, NICOT (Grand Rapids: Wm. B. Eerdmans, 1981), p. 228, points out, there is no previous mention of an oath.

[53] Fokkelman states, "We simply do not know if Nathan's words, repeated by Bathsheba, recall an actual event," but then goes on to note, "The idea that the oath is pure invention on the part of the faction (i.e., Nathan) is hard to reconcile with the portrait and allure of Nathan presented in II Sam." See Fokkelman, *King David*, p. 354, especially n. 12.

[54] For example, the author withholds Israel's idolatry as a reason for their defeat by the Philistines (1 Sam. 7:3–4), and the fact that Jonathan had a son (2 Sam. 4:4), and

Nathan concludes his advice to Bathsheba by telling her to inform the king of Adonijah's proclaimed kingship and assures her he will support her by coming in while she is still speaking to confirm her words (v. 14). It is (the better part of) wisdom to plan how best to persuade the king at this critical moment. There will be no time for David to check the facts, or to discuss the situation. He must be made aware of the situation so that he can act quickly and decisively. Once again, the biblical principle of "by the mouth of two or three witnesses" (Deut. 17:6), is being followed.

Bathsheba's Plea (1:15–21)

Bathsheba's speech before David is clearly her best moment in the narratives in which she appears. It is this speech which has convinced some that she is indeed a clever and resourceful woman.[55] It is true that she not only takes Nathan's directives to heart, she improves on them in dramatic fashion. This could be resourcefulness, or it could simply be the actions of a desperate woman as Nelson states, "Characters reveal themselves through their speech: Bathsheba as the frantic mother...and...the fearful co-conspirator."[56]

Before we hear her plea, the narrator notes "So Bathsheba went into the chamber to the king" (v. 15). The chamber is the king's bedroom where he lies cold and shivering on his bed; the repetition that the king was old (see v. 1) reminds the reader of his impotency. The scene is truly ironic as we recall Bathsheba's presence here on another, more intimate, occasion. The irony continues with the notice of Abishag attending to the king (is she lying in his bosom?). Bathsheba, once the attractive woman who used to share this room with David has been replaced by a younger model, although Abishag's function is different. Do any of these thoughts cross Bathsheba's mind as she enters the king's bedchamber? We do not know for sure: our old friend ambiguity has returned. However, what other need is there to remind the reader of the king's old age or that Abishag is attending him? These are things we have already been told. It is only with the entrance of Bathsheba into the room that we are reminded of these facts. Therefore it seems logical that their repetition here is because they are the things Bathsheba notices.[57] Is there a twinge of jealousy on Bathsheba's part?[58] We cannot tell, but it is not the last

---

that Saul had additional descendants (2 Sam. 21:1ff.). Other possible examples include 1 Sam. 22:10; 24:4 and 2 Sam. 3:18.

[55] For example, Alter, *The David Story*, p. 366, and Nicol, "The Alleged Rape of Bathsheba," p. 43.

[56] Richard Nelson in, *First and Second Kings*, p. 19. Even Alter, *The Art of Biblical Narrative*, p. 99 states, "Bathsheba's presentation reveals the distressed mother and suppliant wife emphasizing the injustice done to her son."

[57] I owe these insights to Adele Berlin, *David's Wives*, p. 74.

[58] Ibid.

time in the story that Abishag's name will appear in conjunction with Bathsheba (1 Kings 2:13–22).

Bathsheba approaches the king showing the proper respect by first kneeling and then bowing before him (v. 16). The king replies by asking, "What is your wish?" The king's question consists of two words that, when put together, are identical to the Hebrew word for "king" or "reign" minus one consonant. So his question puns on the issue at hand.[59] Bathsheba begins with a direct appeal to David's oath, quoting it in full and noting that "you swore by the LORD your God" (v. 17). This is a positive embellishment of Nathan's original instruction. In fact, Bathsheba's speech is three times longer than Nathan's original directives.[60] Hamilton provides a helpful summary of all the changes and additions:

1. She changes Nathan's "swear" into "swore by the Lord your God," thus making her husband's…earlier promise even more binding.
2. She changes Nathan's rhetorical question, "Did you not swear?" into fact, "My lord, you swore."
3. She changes Nathan's question to David, "Why then is Adonijah king?" into a fact, "Adonijah has become king," and adds the words "although you do not know it."
4. On her own, she draws attention to Adonijah's banquet (v. 19).
5. She mentions on the excluded list from Adonijah's festivities only Solomon (cf. v. 19c with v. 8).
6. She adds, hyperbolically, that all Israel is waiting with bated breath for his announcement of a successor (v. 20), and that should Adonijah succeed, her life and Solomon's are in great danger (v. 21).[61]

Bathsheba's appeal is direct and full of emotion. In fact, desperation may be a better explanation than wisdom for the changes she makes. Nathan's counsel pointed her in the right direction and her survival instinct took it from there. For the first time in the narrative Bathsheba takes a stand. Her final sentence demonstrates that she fully appreciates the desperate straits that she and her son are in: "Otherwise it will happen, when my lord the king rests with his fathers, that I and my son Solomon will be counted as offenders" (v. 21). She had lost a husband through passivity; she is determined not to lose a

---

[59] Fokkelman, *King David*, p. 355.
[60] Ibid.
[61] Hamilton, *Handbook*, pp. 383-384.

son and her own life in the same way. At this point Nathan, true to his word, seeks an audience with the king and in his own skillful way reinforces Bathsheba's words (vv. 22–27).

With Nathan's final question ringing in his ears, David, who is now called "King David," emphasizing his authority, summons Bathsheba back into the room (v. 28). In her hearing he repeats the oath, solemnly swearing in the Lord's name that Solomon will sit upon the throne "this day" (vv. 29–30). Bathsheba and Nathan have been successful in alerting David to the critical situation and motivating him to act. Before the king swings into action, Bathsheba pays one last act of homage as she bows "nose to the ground" and proclaims, "Let my lord King David live forever!" (v. 31). In the next scene in which she appears, also her last, Solomon will be king and she will be queen mother.

Stupid Is as Stupid Does (1 Kings 2:13–22)

Following Adonijah's aborted coup attempt, he approaches Bathsheba with a request. We are reminded that Adonijah is the "*son* of Haggith" and Bathsheba is the "*mother* of Solomon." These labels recall that the son of Haggith would have destroyed Solomon and his mother had his usurpation of the throne been successful (1 Kings 1:11–12, 21). This naturally leads to Bathsheba's first question: "Do you come peaceably?" (2:13). Adonijah responds with one word, "Peaceably" (*shālôm*). The reader of the books of Samuel, however, is aware that situations that seem "peaceable" often end up with deadly consequences (1 Sam. 25:6; 2 Sam. 3:21–30; 2 Sam. 11:7); this occasion will prove to be no exception. It is Adonijah's turn again and he says, "I have a word for you" (my translation), to which Bathsheba responds, "Speak" (2:14). Adonijah and Bathsheba have now both responded to each other with a one word response using the same word the other had previously used:[62]

(A) Bathsheba: Is it *peace?*
(B) Adonijah: *Peace.*
(B') Adonijah: "I have a *word* for you."
(A') Bathsheba: "*Speak.*[63]

The exchange is terse by both parties, suggesting the tension that exists between them. Before coming to his request, however, Adonijah feels it necessary to justify why he deserves something from this situation. His words show that he is still brooding over his lost kingdom: "Then he said, "You know that the kingdom was mine, and all Israel had set their expectations on me,

---

[62] See Fokkelman, *King David*, pp. 390-391 for a more in-depth analysis.
[63] In Hebrew "word" and "speak" are from the same three letter root "*dbr*."

250

that I should reign" (v. 15a). This seems an unwise opening statement as it would surely put Bathsheba on the defensive, but apparently Adonijah hopes playing the "guilt card" (or is it the "pity card"?) will help him achieve his purpose. He quickly softens his statement by saying, "However, the kingdom has been turned over, and has become my brother's; for it was his from the LORD" (v. 15b). Having now established how much he has lost (thanks to the Lord), he asks one request of Bathsheba and pleads, "do not deny me" (literally, "do not turn my face"—v. 16). Bathsheba has another one word response, the same as before, "Speak." In other words, no progress has been made in the narrative by Adonijah's little "pity party." Bathsheba, and the reader, still await the purpose of his visit (although Bathsheba's forthcoming intercession on his behalf might indicate it had an effect on her). Adonijah finally comes to his request; he has approached Bathsheba because he wants Abishag, the young Bathsheba look-a-like, for himself! (v. 17).

Why does Adonijah come to Bathsheba with this request instead of going directly to Solomon? There are at least two reasons that can be suggested. First, it is clear that Adonijah realizes that approaching Solomon directly would, at the very least, result in a rejection of his request, and at most could be dangerous. Therefore, Adonijah must believe that Bathsheba is a soft touch. Is she a soft touch because her naiveté is well known, or because he believes he can appeal to her motherly instincts?[64] Clearly he thinks that if he can persuade her, then her motherly influence on Solomon will prevail.

At a deeper level of the text, the correspondence between Bathsheba and Abishag suggests a second possibility. As David had once taken Bathsheba from her former husband, now Adonijah seeks to take David's former concubine by none other than Bathsheba! One would think that, of all people, Bathsheba would realize that wife-swapping always has serious consequences, but, incredibly she agrees to help Adonijah with his request (v. 18).

Before asking why Bathsheba would agree to help Adonijah we must meditate a little longer on what his approach to Bathsheba suggests about her character. If he believes her to be a soft touch, this suggests that he does not believe her to be very insightful. Of course, Adonijah could be totally mistaken in his assessment, but it is consistent with the woman who must be counseled by Nathan to know what to do (1 Kings 1:11), and with the portrait of her in 2 Samuel 11 that we have suggested.

The inherent danger of Adonijah's request seems to be the idea that possessing the king's concubine makes one the king (2 Sam. 3:6–7; 12:8; 16:21–22). This is certainly how Solomon will interpret it (1 Kings 2:22–24). So why does Bathsheba agree to bring Adonijah's request before Solomon? Is it because she is in fact insightful, and sees this as a way to be rid of her son's

---

[64] Fokkelman, *King David*, p. 393.

chief rival?[65] In the short time from Nathan's counsel until now, has she developed a keen political savvy? As much as some may want the mother of the wise Solomon to be pictured as a shrewd and crafty woman, she is not. Nothing in the text suggests that her motive is to plot the demise of Adonijah. She simply appears to be one of those people who cannot say "no." She does not say "no" to David in a more obvious situation of danger, and she does not turn down Adonijah, apparently oblivious to any danger.[66] I suggest her motive, other than an apparent desire to please others no matter what the circumstance, is found in the introductory exchange with Adonijah. When Adonijah approaches her she asks, "Do you come peaceably?" and he responds, "Peaceably." I believe it is this desire to maintain or promote peace that motivates Bathsheba. The outcome then is extremely ironic. In her desire to promote peace, her request results in Adonijah's death. Her inability to say "no" always seems to get someone killed!

Bathsheba's entrance before Solomon is described in painstaking detail. It is the king who rises and bows to his mother and who has a throne prepared for her at his right hand (v. 20). The honor and courtesy that Solomon accords his mother prepares the reader for a positive response to Adonijah's request. Bathsheba's opening words to the king are almost identical to Adonijah's, but instead of saying, "I have one request to request of you, do not refuse me" (my translation), she says, "I have one *small* request to request of you, do not refuse me" (my translation). Her addition of the word "small" shows that she comes as Adonijah's advocate. She hopes the word *small* will *enlarge* his chance of a positive response from Solomon. We often do the same thing when seeking a favor from someone. We know we are presuming on their good graces and, therefore, want them to know that we will not inconvenience them any more than necessary. After all, it's not a *big* favor; it's just a *small* favor that we seek.

Solomon's reply causes the reader to continue to expect a positive response: "Ask it, my mother, for I will not refuse you." With this positive encouragement, she drops the bomb on Solomon: "Let Abishag the Shunammite be given to Adonijah your brother as wife" (v. 21). Bathsheba tries to soften the request even further by using a passive tense. She does not say, "Please give" as Adonijah does, but rather, "Let Abishag…be given," as if Solomon doesn't even have to bother about personally doing the favor. He can have someone else give her to Adonijah!

---

[65] Robert I. Vasholz, "The Wisdom of Bathsheba in 1 Kings 2:13–25," *Presbyterion* 33, 2007, p. 49.

[66] P. R. House, in *1 & 2 Kings*, p. 100 states, "As for not realizing the significance of Adonijah's plea, who would understand harem politics more than the queen of the harem?" But this is precisely the point. She *should* realize the significance but she is either so naive, or so desirous of pleasing others, that she never takes the consequences into consideration.

At these words Solomon's respectful demeanor towards his mother morphs into a sarcastic retort, followed by an oath to do away with his brother. There will be peace in the kingdom, not because Abishag will be given to Adonijah but because Adonijah will forfeit his life (vv. 22–25). Solomon's explosive response in contrast to his previous pleasant demeanor is another indication that Bathsheba's request is sincere. Had he detected any irony, or a wink of the eye, his response would surely have been more like: "I hear you mother, we'll give Adonijah exactly what he deserves." The contrast, however, is too sudden and too sharp to be ironical or to be staged. Bathsheba's request on behalf of Adonijah is genuine and so is Solomon's response.[67] Based on these facts it seems hard to improve on R. N. Whybray's assessment of Bathsheba when he writes, "We thus have a consistent and thoroughly credible picture of Bathsheba as a good-natured, rather stupid woman who was a natural prey both to more passionate and to cleverer men." [68]

Before concluding our study of these verses, we must ask if there might also be another motive behind Bathsheba's action. We have noted the correspondence between Abishag and Bathsheba, and how the text draws attention to Abishag when Bathsheba first comes into the king's bedchamber (1 Kings 1:15). Regarding Bathsheba's entrance Berlin writes, "One can feel a twinge of jealousy pass through Bathsheba as she silently notes the presence of a younger, fresher woman."[69] Speaking of Abishag in the present episode Berlin states, "Perhaps Bathsheba is really jealous of her and does not want Solomon to have her."[70] Given the correspondences between Bathsheba and Abishag, and the deliberate mention of David's young concubine as Bathsheba enters the room, one cannot totally rule out that jealousy could have played a role in Bathsheba's motivation. However, this must be inferred from 1 Kings 1:15 and the characterization of Abishag in 1 Kings 1:1–4 as David's "ewe lamb." The conversation between Bathsheba and Adonijah only suggests a naiveté on her part with a desire to please her petitioner and encourage peaceful relations. This seems to be consistent with Bathsheba's portrait throughout her appearances in 2 Samuel and 1 Kings.

---

[67] Similarly, Fokkelman, in *King David*, p. 395 states, "She really does her best and nothing in the text justifies speculations concerning her having secret intentions or even counting on a bad outcome."

[68] Whybray, *The Succession Narrative*, p. 40.

[69] Berlin, "David's Wives," p. 74.

[70] Ibid., p. 75. Dilday, *1, 2 Kings*, p. 58, also suggests a possible motive of jealousy.

A Four-pointed Triangle Never Works

Although geometry was never a favorite subject of mine, it provides an interesting way of examining the relationships of the four characters in these two scenes, particularly in the form of triangles.[71]

The triangle of Bathsheba-Adonijah-Abishag is uncomfortable yet manageable; it is also potentially dangerous.

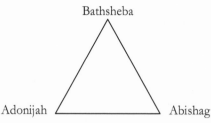

If Adonijah were at the top (as king), the triangle would not be manageable because Bathsheba and Solomon would probably be dead, while Adonijah would make a straight line for Abishag. Arranged in the above order, however, it is tolerable. The tension evidenced in Adonijah's meeting with Bathsheba is tolerable so long as "peace" is the goal (1 Kings 2:13). If Bathsheba is indeed jealous of Abishag this would create tension, but it does not seem to be unbearable or dangerous to either lady. Adonijah, of course, desires a relationship with Abishag, and Bathsheba is in agreement with the arrangement. Thus the agreement that Adonijah should have Abishag brings stability to the triangle. The inclusion of Solomon, however, explodes the stability of this triangle: in fact, geometrically speaking, it destroys the triangle. It is doubtful that Solomon would be happy with any kind of relationship between his mother and Adonijah, and he certainly is opposed to one between Adonijah and Abishag. The foolishness of both Bathsheba and Adonijah is exposed by them imagining they can include Solomon within their triangle!

---

[71] Hans J.L, Jensen, "Desire, Rivalry, and Collective Violence in the Succession Narrative," *JSOT* 55, 1992, p. 44, also notes that many of David's familial relationships occur in the form of triangles. We could add others from the books of Samuel such as Elkanah, Hannah, and Peninnah; Saul, Jonathan and David; Michal, Saul, and David; Jonathan, David and the Lord; Nabal, David and Abigail; etc.

The triangle of Solomon-Bathsheba-Abishag is workable.

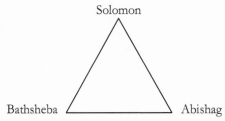

The relationship between mother and son is solid. Abishag has apparently become a part of Solomon's harem and, as long as she remains there, there is harmony between them. There may be some discomfort between Bathsheba and Abishag but, if it does exist, it is nothing they cannot live with. It is only the inclusion of Adonijah that can disrupt the stability of this triangle. Once again, a triangle by definition can only have three points and three sides. Adonijah simply doesn't fit in.

The triangle of Solomon-Bathsheba-Adonijah is dysfunctional at best.

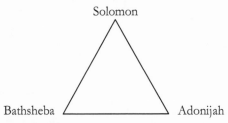

The relationship between two brothers who both desire the kingship is potentially dangerous. Fear and suspicion are not the best building blocks for a healthy relationship, yet Solomon is willing to take the risk unless Adonijah proves himself unworthy (1 Kings 1:50–52). We have already seen that Bathsheba is willing to coexist with Adonijah as long as he seeks peace. But it is doubtful that Solomon would tolerate any kind of association between his mother and Adonijah.

The triangle of Solomon-Abishag-Adonijah is deadly.

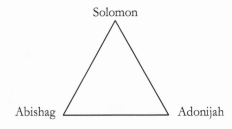

This is the one triangle that is absolutely intolerable. It is a major miscalculation on the part of both Adonijah and Bathsheba to think that Solomon will accept David's former concubine Abishag, becoming Adonijah's wife. Even the love and respect that Solomon has for his mother cannot keep this triangle from blowing apart. Bathsheba's attempt to glue this triangle together by "one *small* favor" is the very ammunition that causes it to explode.

Finally, a comparison of Bathsheba's two conversations in 1 Kings 2 is instructive. Her conversation with Adonijah begins with suspicion but ends in harmony (vv. 13–18), while her conversation with Solomon begins with extreme deference on the king's part only to end in violence (vv. 19–24). This contrast suggests that Bathsheba has been drawn in by Adonijah's machinations and has succumbed to his manipulation. Solomon, on the other hand, is too insightful to be manipulated by Adonijah, or by Adonijah's use of his mother.[72] There is no change in Bathsheba's character. She is neither wise nor cunning. Except for her speech before David where her desperation causes her to shine for one brief moment, I find it difficult to improve on Leonard Rost's (unpopular!) assessment who years ago wrote, "In the end Bathsheba is…a not especially distinguished lady; she lends an all-too-ready ear to commissions, apparently quite happily, because she herself does not possess the requisite acumen and insight."[73]

Conclusion: Just Say "No"

Although Bathsheba was a very attractive woman, one wonders if she suffered from a lack of self-esteem. There is not a text that can prove such a supposition, but pleasing others at all costs suggests such a possibility. Generally speaking, most of us desire to please others and, within certain boundaries, this can be a positive trait. However, when pleasing others becomes more important than moral boundaries or obeying God's word, serious consequences will always result. Saul's mistake of listening to the voice of the people and desiring their esteem above God's word cost him a kingdom (1 Sam. 15:24–30). Peter and John model the correct perspective when they tell the Sanhedrin, "Whether it is right in the sight of God to listen to you more than to God, you judge. For we cannot but speak the things which we have seen and heard" (Acts 4:19–20).

---

[72] Some interpret this story differently, asserting that Solomon used this occasion as a pretext to kill his brother. We will examine this more carefully when we discuss Adonijah's character in chap. 25, pp. 392-394.

[73] Rost, *The Succession to the Throne of David*, p. 69. Sean E. McEvenue, "The Basis of Empire, A Study of the Succession Narrative," *Ex auditu* 2, 1986, p. 40, goes as far as to classify Bathsheba as a stereo-typical "dumb blond."

Sometimes it is important just to say "No." Some would argue that Bathsheba had no choice. Summoned by King David, what could she do? We always have a choice however; Tamar is an example of that (2 Sam. 13). While Tamar could not prevent the horrible crime perpetrated against her, she still resisted, and that is to her everlasting credit. It may have been dangerous for Bathsheba to resist, but it was also dangerous for Abigail to put herself between an angry David with four hundred men and her husband. Sometimes saying "No" exposes us to potential harm, but not saying it can lead to more devastating consequences. Passivity can be dangerous, just ask Ish-bosheth (2 Sam. 3–4).

One cannot always be blamed for naiveté; in fact, there is a certain innocence about it. In the beginning, Bathsheba may have been totally unconscious of David's gaze, and so she is not to be blamed. As life progresses, however, it is important to shed the naiveté of youth and to grow and mature. Bathsheba never seems to make this transition. From her bath in 2 Samuel 11:2, to the kingship crisis in 1 Kings 1, to being manipulated by Adonijah in 1 Kings 2, she never appears to grasp (on her own) the significance of the issues at hand. Bathsheba gave birth to a very wise son, but her naiveté was responsible for some serious blunders that cost two men their lives.

Some wisdom can be gained through experience, but above all, wisdom comes from God. James writes, "If any of you lacks wisdom, let him ask of God, who gives to all liberally and without reproach, and it will be given to him" (James 1:5). James may have been referring to a young man named Solomon, Bathsheba's son, who asked God for this gift and was granted wisdom that exceeded anyone of his time (1 Kings 3:7–12). In the end, Bathsheba was not an evil woman; she was, however, a weak woman because she allowed people and events to control her thoughts and actions, rather than allowing God and his word to direct her life.

Chapter 20

Joab: The Hard Man (David's nephew)

"These men, the sons of Zeruiah, are too harsh for me"—David (2 Sam. 3:39)

Joab, the "Mama's Boy"?

However one evaluates Joab, there can be no doubt that 2 Samuel characterizes him as one of the toughest men in David's court. Given this "tough-guy" image, it might seem surprising to describe Joab as a "mama's boy"; yet the author frequently refers to him and his brothers as the "son(s) of Zeruiah." Of course, the modern expression "mama's boy" and Joab's actual demeanor are worlds apart: Joab is no "sissy"! Still, the author's repeated use of this label (fifteen times in 1 and 2 Samuel) deserves consideration.[1]

1 Chronicles 2:16 reveals that Zeruiah is a sister of David, thus making Joab and her other sons David's nephews. If "son(s) of Zeruiah" was used by the author to establish a family connection with David, surely once, or at most a few times, would have been sufficient. Like the designation "son of Ner" that frequently accompanies Abner,[2] one wonders whether the phrase "son(s) of Zeruiah" has another function in the narrative. While Joab's father might have died prematurely (2 Sam. 2:32), or perhaps "the ancient custom of tracing descent by the female line [has] been preserved in this case,"[3] it does not explain the frequency of this description.

David's use of this expression suggests a deeper meaning. For example, he uses it several times in a derogatory manner (2 Sam. 3:39; 16:10; 19:22). Presumably, David is not reminding himself of a family connection in all these contexts. His disparaging remarks suggest there is more to this designation than meets the eye.

---

[1] There is one occurrence in 1 Samuel (26:6). The other occurrences are all in 2 Samuel, and are as follows: 2:13, 18; 3:39; 8:16; 14:1; 16:9, 10; 17:25 (here Zeruiah is described as the mother of Joab); 18:2; 19:21, 22; 21:17; 23:18, and 37.

[2] See chap. 11, pp. 136-137.

[3] D. Harvey, "Zeruiah," *IDB*, vol. 4, p. 956. F. H. Cryer, "David's Rise to Power and the Death of Abner: and Analysis of 1 Samuel 26:14–16 and Its Redaction-Critical Implications," *VT* 35, (1985), pp. 388-389, n. 9, supposes the probable death of Zeruiah's husband and states, "It is thus likely that Zeruiah then returned to live in her father's house (cf. Gen. xxxviii 11), and her children will then have assumed her name in acknowledgement of their special status. It may further be pointed out, with R. R. Wilson, *Genealogy and History in the Biblical World* (New Haven, Conn., 1977), that Semitic genealogies have a habit of shifting in order to align their members towards the centres of political power, so it is possible that the 'Zeruiah connexion' was an effort in this direction."

The meaning of "Zeruiah" has not received much attention from scholars; thus, I am treading on virgin territory here. Part of the difficulty is that there are several possible Hebrew roots from which the name could be derived. It is thought that the basic meaning is "balm."[4] If this is accurate, then "Zeruiah" would refer to a balm often used for medicinal purposes (cf. Jer. 8:22). This would associate her name with the positive qualities of healing. David's use of the name could be considered ironic, since he uses it in contexts where the "sons of Zeruiah" have either murdered, or desire to kill, someone. These men want no "balm" for healing others; their spirit is quite the opposite!

Another feature of Hebrew names is that they often play off the meaning of other words with similar sounds. We have noted this already with such names as Peninnah, Hophni, Phinehas, and Samuel.[5] The consonants in the name Zeruiah are similar to two words that can mean: "showing hostility," "distress," "adversary," "foe," "hard," and "rock."[6] These meanings are *apropos* to the actions and demeanor of Joab and his brothers. In fact, several contexts in 2 Samuel link words with these meanings to the expression "sons of Zeruiah."

In 2 Samuel 2:14, as the armies of Israel and Judah meet, Abner proposes to Joab a combat involving twelve men from each side. After all are killed in the combat, the field is named "Field of Flints." The word "flint" comes from a word that means "rock" or "hard." It is sometimes used to describe a knife or sword (Exod. 4:25; Josh. 5:2, 3). The reference to the "Field of Flints" is surrounded by references to the "son(s) of Zeruiah" (vv. 13, 18). The words "flint" and "Zeruiah" sound similar, and this would catch the ear of someone reading in Hebrew. Furthermore, there is a conceptual link between these words, as the sons of Zeruiah are well known for their use of the sword.

Another passage which associates the sons of Zeruiah with "hardness" is 2 Samuel 3:39. Following the murder of Abner, David declares, "and these men, the sons of Zeruiah, are harder than me" (my translation). A different Hebrew word is used here to describe the "hardness" of Joab and Abishai. We will look at this verse in greater detail later; the important point here is that David connects the expression "sons of Zeruiah" with the quality of hardness.

Finally, in 2 Samuel 19:22 David rebukes Abishai by referring to him as an "adversary/accuser" (*śāṭān*).[7] In this context, *śāṭān* is parallel to the expression "sons of Zeruiah." Although 2 Samuel 3:39 and 19:22 express Da-

---

[4] Harvey, "Zeruiah," and *BDB*, p. 863.

[5] See chap. 2, pp. 30-31 and chap. 3, pp. 40-41.

[6] The words are *ṣur* and *ṣrr*. See *BDB*, pp. 849 and pp. 864-866, respectively.

[7] For further discussion on the meaning of this word see chap. 21, pp. 304-305.

vid's point of view, this phrase suggests a certain "hardness" or "adversarial" role that characterizes Joab and his brother, in contrast to David. As we examine Joab's role in the story, it will be important to determine whether this hardness is a negative or positive quality, or perhaps a mixture.

In summary, the description "sons of Zeruiah" may originally have had a connotation of "healing," but its relationship to similar-sounding words, as well as the actions and demeanor of the brothers themselves, suggests the meaning of "hard" or "adversary" in some contexts.

Joab and Abner: Body Double (2 Sam. 2:12–18; 24–32)

After a brief mention in 1 Samuel 26:6, Joab finally takes the stage in 2 Samuel, where he becomes a pivotal character in the plot.[8] In this initial story he is pictured as Abner's counterpart. As Abner leads the "servants of Ish-bosheth" (v. 11), so Joab leads "the servants of David" (v. 12). Like Abner, Joab is pictured as a military man and an influential leader in the king's court. There is never any specific mention of a wife or children.[9] His brothers and fellow-warriors seem to be his true family. He leads, he fights, he plots, he manipulates; but he is never said to love. The omission of these "softer" qualities—qualities which David possesses in abundance—influence his character portrait.

Joab's initial word mimics his counterpart. Abner says, "Let the young men arise," to which Joab responds curtly (one word in Hebrew), "Let them arise" (v. 14). This first word suggests that Joab is not one to back down from a fight. When the contest results in a draw, a full-scale battle develops in which David's men are victorious (v. 17). Since this account frequently draws similarities between Abner and Joab, it is somewhat surprising that, while Abner is twice credited with defeat, Joab is never credited with victory. Verse 17 states that, "Abner and the men of Israel were beaten before the servants of David." One would expect Joab's name to appear before "the servants of David" to balance the line, but it is conspicuously absent.

At the end of the chapter, Joab is associated with nineteen dead plus Asahel (v. 30), while it is said that "the servants of David had struck down, of Benjamin and Abner's men, three-hundred and sixty men who died" (v. 31). Once again Joab appears as a counterpart to Abner, as both men's names are associated with loss of life, but only the "servants of David" are mentioned in

---

[8] Rosenberg, *King and Kin*, p. 165, notes that Joab is "second only to David and Absalom in frequency of reference, and surpassing Absalom in *range* of textual space occupied." Filip Čapek, "David's ambiguous testament in 1 Kings 2:1–12 and the role of Joab in the Succession Narrative," *Communio Viatorum*, 52/1 2010, p. 16, notes that Joab is mentioned 74 times in 2 Samuel and 11 times in 1 Kings: a total of 85 times.

[9] There is, however, a mention of "Joab's house" (2 Sam. 3:29), and Joab's descendants (1 Kings 2:33).

connection with the victory. Do these omissions suggest that it was not Joab but the Lord who gave David victory—with, or perhaps in spite of, Joab's leadership?

The battle is called off when Abner manages to take higher ground with his troops. His words, and Joab's response, have been previously examined.[10] Based on our understanding of Joab's response, he is not *compliant* with Abner's plea; he is *defiant*. Joab's response should not be misconstrued. He is not saying, "I am sure glad you spoke up, Abner! That is great advice, and if you had not given it we would have pursued you until the morning." Rather, Joab's response is caustic: "This is all your fault to begin with, Abner! If you had not spoken up this morning, none of this would have happened." With these parting words of spite, and recognizing that Abner and his men have gained a superior fighting position, Joab blows the trumpet to end the pursuit (v. 28).

Joab's willingness to give up the pursuit at this point highlights his wisdom, in comparison with his brother Asahel. Even though Asahel was at a distinct disadvantage in pursuing the more experienced Abner, he would not give up his pursuit despite several warnings (2:19–23). No matter how badly Joab may wish to avenge the loss of his brother, he is astute enough to realize that Abner has the tactical advantage, and so he is willing to wait for a more opportune time to exact his revenge. It is not the last time that Joab will take the advice of someone he is opposing in battle (2 Sam. 20:16–22). Like his brothers, Joab can show great impetuosity, but, if the circumstances dictate, he is pragmatic enough to show restraint. As this story suggests—and future stories will confirm—Joab's actions are based on what is most advantageous for him. "He is David's hard man, but one who has his own agenda."[11]

Joab Gets a "Belly-full" of Abner (2 Sam. 3:22–39)

By the time Joab reappears in the text, David has concluded a treaty with Abner to bring all Israel under his domain (v. 21). The late arrival of Joab, suggests that David either attached no importance to him being present, or purposely concluded the treaty in his absence. The latter seems more likely. Either way, it suggests a lack of respect for Joab. This is the first of many signs of the troubled relationship that existed between David and his commander. Read in light of the events in chapter 2, David probably considered that Joab's presence would be an impediment to good relations with Abner. It is hard to believe that Joab would have, or could have, kept his seething desire to avenge his brother's blood from David. Whatever David's reason

---

[10] See chap. 11, pp. 143.
[11] Firth, *1&2 Samuel*, p. 337.

for proceeding without Joab, forthcoming events would soon demonstrate the volatile effect of Joab's presence.

Apparently there were some among David's court (or troops) who were unhappy about recent events—because, upon his return, Joab is informed that Abner had been with David and "had gone in peace" (v. 23). Upon hearing this news, Joab immediately goes to the king and issues a harsh rebuke (v. 24). This is the first scene in which Joab and David appear together, and it is a particularly shocking one. The commander acts like a king rebuking a subordinate! All of the words in this scene belong to Joab; David does not speak. It is reminiscent of an earlier scene when another commander (Abner) rebukes his king (Ish-bosheth), who also says nothing in return (3:8–11).

Joab's first words, "What have you done?," are words frequently used to convict someone of wrong-doing or sin (e.g., Gen. 3:13; 4:10; 1 Sam. 13:11; 20:1, 32; etc.). He quickly follows his first question with a second, detailing the wrong he is accusing David of: "Look, Abner came to you; why is it that you have sent him away, and he has already gone?" Joab continues, charging Abner with deception and espionage (v. 25). Having barraged David with accusatory questions and insinuations ("Abner is a spy and you are too dull-witted to realize it"), Joab storms out, not waiting for a reply.[12] His abrupt exit from the king's presence demonstrates that he is only interested in venting his frustration; Joab could not care less what David's response is. Furthermore, he is in a hurry to put his scheme into action before Abner gets too far away.

Joab's first three speeches (2:14, 27; 3:24–25) can be characterized as aggressive or confrontational. If each of them is examined one after the other, they display an escalation of hostile speech from the mouth of Joab. In fact, Joab's harshest words are not reserved for his enemy (Abner), but for his own king!

This initial encounter between Joab and David leaves us wondering, "Is this any way for a commander to treat his king?" Joab acts like the one in charge. He does not formulate an appeal to the king, as an underling should; nor does he use polite address (e.g., "your servant," "my lord the king"). He does not wait for the king's response, nor does he seek any orders about what should be done next. His language is insulting and belittling and, after he has voiced his irritation, he angrily leaves the king's presence to implement his own plan.

---

[12] Baldwin, *1 & 2 Samuel*, p. 190, believes that David's lack of a response may suggest he was having second thoughts; but Bergen, *1, 2 Samuel*, p. 312, is surely closer to the truth when he asserts, "Without waiting for orders from David, Joab left the king's presence."

As mentioned previously, the scene is reminiscent of Abner's rebuke of Ish-bosheth.[13] Joab continues to mirror Abner! In fact, when Joab leaves the king's presence, he does exactly what Abner had previously done: he *sends messengers* in order to bring his plan to fruition (cf. 3:12 and 26). Joab's messengers are dispatched to go "after" Abner and "return him." Abner is being pursued again—a theme enunciated by the key word "after" (*'aḥarē*), which is so prevalent in the account of the sons of Zeruiah's pursuit of him in 2 Samuel 2:19–28.[14]

Even though we could have been led to believe that Joab is another Abner, the event that transpires next in the midst of the gate at Hebron (3:27) changes the reader's perception of Joab's character.

In certain ironic ways, Joab's actions continue to mimic Abner's. As he "turns him aside" in the gate and stabs him "in the belly" (v. 27), we are again reminded of similar words used to describe Abner's encounter with Asahel. In that previous story, Abner had pleaded with Asahel to "turn aside" (2:21) and when Asahel could not be dissuaded, Abner struck him "in the belly" (2:23). Thus the death of Asahel, and Abner's reconciliation with David, was enough to give Joab a "belly-full" of Abner. Joab seeks to return the favor with one skillful thrust—giving Abner a "belly-full" of his sword.

No doubt Joab would see this as a sort of "poetic justice"—"you reap what you sow"—but the similarities serve to highlight the many differences. First, Abner's confrontation with Asahel took place during wartime. Joab's killing of Abner takes place during a truce between Abner/Israel and David/Judah. The author is clear (repeating three times in vv. 21, 22, 23) that "peace" existed between Abner and David upon his departure.

Second, Abner did not wish the confrontation with Asahel, and tried to discourage his pursuer twice (2:21–22).[15] Joab, on the other hand, deceives

---

[13] Hertzberg, *I&II Samuel*, pp. 260-261, states, "The reader can only be amazed at the general way in which the commanders talk to their kings."

[14] See chap. 21, pp. 310-311.

[15] *Contra* Eschelbach, in *Has Joab Foiled David* (pp. 23-25, 67-68) who, in my opinion, misinterprets the text and justifies Joab's killing of Abner, while maintaining that Abner "murdered" Asahel (p. 25)! I am in agreement with Gregory T. K. Wong, "Ehud and Joab: Separated at Birth?" *VT* 56/3 2006, p. 409, who states, "From the way this chain of unfortunate events is described, one gets the impression that the author of the account clearly desired to absolve Abner from bloodguilt in the death of Asahel. For not only did the death of Asahel take place in a battle where loss of life is almost inevitable, Abner had also given his pursuer two chances to disengage before finally acting in self-defence. In this way, the responsibility for Asahel's death was presented as resting squarely on his own stubbornness rather than on Abner. What this means is that Joab actually had no legitimate grounds to seek revenge of Abner over the death of his brother."

Abner and catches him off guard.[16] Third, the murder takes place "in the midst of the gate" of Hebron. The gate was a place where justice was meted out. It is where the king, or the elders of a city, often adjudicated cases brought to them (Deut. 16:18; 21:19; 22:15; Ruth 4:1–6; Jer. 39:3). Since Abner killed Asahel in battle, there is no evidence that he was guilty of an offense, but if there was any question, his case would have been decided in the gate. The fact that Joab dispenses punishment without a trial, in a part of the city known as a place of justice, is clearly ironic: it is a commentary on the injustice of his deed.[17] Fourth, that this killing takes place in the gate at Hebron, a city of refuge (cf. Josh. 21:13), compounds the heinous nature of the crime.

The revelation of Joab's motive in killing Abner is another confirmation of his guilt. Joab had upbraided David for his naiveté, saying, "Surely you realize that Abner the son of Ner came to deceive you, to know your going out and your coming in, and to know all that you are doing" (v. 25). However, after Joab kills Abner we are informed that the reason was "for the blood of Asahel his brother" (v. 27). So that we do not miss the point, it is reiterated in verse 30: "So Joab and Abishai his brother killed Abner, because he had killed their brother Asahel at Gibeon in the battle." In other words, when Joab rebuked David, it was not because he was concerned about the security of the kingdom; the frustration revealed in his rebuke of the king now comes to be understood in the light of his desire for vengeance. Joab is unmasked by this statement. This revelation shows that his words to David were an attempt to manipulate him. He accused Abner of being deceitful, but in reality Joab was the duplicitous one. In the end he deceived both David and Abner. Wong rightly concludes, "By portraying the assassination as an act of revenge, the author was thus subtly indicating his disapproval of Joab's action."[18]

Two other features of verse 30 confirm Wong's statement. First, two different verbs are used to describe the deaths of Abner and Asahel. If the author had sought to parallel the deaths of the two men, the same verb would no doubt have been chosen. The word used to describe Abner's death is a verb associated with homicide in the Hebrew Scriptures, while the other verb used of Asahel is the more common word for describing someone's death.[19]

---

[16] Alter, *The David Story*, p. 213, suggests that the word translated "privately" (NKJV) may be from a Hebrew root that means "to delude." Thus Alter translates the phrase as, "Joab drew him aside into the gate to speak with him deceptively." Whichever translation is correct, Joab's attack on Abner was based on deception.

[17] *Contra*, Caleb Henry, "Joab: A Biblical Critique of Machiavellian Tactics," *WTJ* 69, 2007, p. 332, who suggests that Joab avoided committing a sacrilege against the Mosaic Law by killing Abner in the middle of the gate.

[18] Wong, "Ehud and Joab," p. 409.

[19] The verb describing Abner's death is *hrg*. Although *hrg* does not always refer to homicide or murder (see NIDOTTE, vol. 1, pp. 1055-1057), I am in agreement with

Second, when speaking of Asahel's death, the narrator attaches the phrase "at Gibeon in the battle," reminding the reader that the circumstances of his death were much different, occurring during a time of war.[20]

In between the two statements of Joab's intent, David's initial reaction to the murder is recorded. The reader has previously been informed that David was unaware of Joab's plan (v. 26), so it is not surprising that, upon hearing of the murder, David immediately proclaims himself and his kingdom free of bloodguilt (v. 28). He follows up this declaration by pronouncing a severe curse on Joab and his family (v. 29). Earlier, the king had not been given an opportunity to respond. Having been rebuked and deceived by Joab, David now explodes. His curse more than offsets Joab's rebuke, and for the remainder of the chapter David will be the only speaker, while Joab will lose his voice. David's curse upon Joab and his family encompasses the three main types of disaster common to Old Testament and Ancient Near-Eastern curses—pestilence, famine, and sword (e.g., Jer. 15:2–3; Ezek. 5:12).[21]

Next, David stages an elaborate state funeral for Abner, forcing Joab and his fellow soldiers to assume the traditional signs of grieving by tearing their clothes, wearing sackcloth and mourning for Abner (v. 31).[22] There may

---

Fokkelman, *Throne and City*, p. 115, n. 64, that the difference in the two verbs seems to be noteworthy and suggests the connotation of murder.

[20] Gordon, *I&II Samuel*, p. 221, similarly notes, "The words *in the battle*, which come at the end of the sentence in MT, make the point that the law of revenge should not have operated on this occasion (cf. 1 Ki. 2:5)" (author's emphasis).

[21] Steven W. Holloway, "Distaff, Crutch or Chain Gang: The Curse of the House of Joab in 2 Samuel III 29," *VT* 38/3, 1987, p. 370.

[22] It is commonplace among many scholars today to look at David's actions in this chapter with suspicion. Some are suspicious of David's actions, claiming that he works too hard to demonstrate his innocence. Others are suspicious of the author, or some editor, putting his own apologetic spin on the story. The claim is that David is somehow involved in Abner's death, and the elaborate means that he (and the author/editor) goes to in order to demonstrate his innocence is evidence of his guilt. Among those who advocate this view are: Vanderkam, "Davidic Complicity in the Deaths of Abner and Eshbaal," and Eschelbach, *Has Joab Foiled David?* In my opinion, the problem with this approach is that it begins with a negative assessment of the author or editor, and a negative assessment of the biblical hero. One is given the impression that the author or David is trying to cover something up and make the reader believe something that is untrue. Only careful scholarly detective work reveals the true facts! Those who advocate this "hermeneutic of suspicion" begin by presupposing David's guilt. If the author shows that David is guilty, then David is guilty. If, on the other hand, the author insists on David's innocence, then David is still guilty! I find myself in agreement with Hans J. L. Jensen, "Desire, Rivalry, and Collective Violence in the Succession Narrative," pp. 53-54, who states, "almost all scholars are extremely critical of the non-violent, non-combative David whom we see in these chapters [his reference is to the Absalom story, but it is also applicable to 2 Sam. 3].

be a hint of irony, as the word for "girding" on sackcloth contains similar consonants (in a reversed order) to the word "murder."[23] Thus, Joab has *murdered* Abner; now he must *gird* on sackcloth and pretend to mourn Abner's death! For the first time in the story Joab does not have his way, but must bend to the demands of the king.[24] "David is in charge and Joab is humiliated. David honors Abner and rebukes Joab."[25]

During the funeral, both brothers (Joab and Abishai) find themselves indicted in David's lament as he chants, "As a man falls before wicked men, so you fell" (v. 34). The word "wicked" has the basic meaning "iniquity" and is often translated this way in other passages (e.g., Ps. 125:3; Ezek. 28:15; Hos. 10:9, 13). Isaiah 59:3 is relevant, as it connects this word with those who have blood on their hands. Thus, the brothers are pictured in David's lament as sinners, or, iniquitous men with blood on their hands.

Considering that the narrator has clearly revealed Joab's guilt in the death of Abner, David's words should be taken at face value—they are the narrator's words as well. This same sentiment concerning the sons of Zeruiah is echoed at the end of the chapter: "The LORD shall repay the evildoer according to his evil" (v. 39—my translation). "Evil" and its synonym "iniquity" are therefore said to characterize the brothers. The words of Psalm 141:4, which are attributed (or dedicated) to David, seem particularly appropriate to his words and actions here:

> Do not incline my heart to any evil thing,
> To practice wicked works
> With men who work iniquity;
> And do not let me eat of their delicacies.[26]

We have certainly learned to master the hermeneutic of suspicion; today, it is child's play to suspect dark motives behind a seemingly pious person, and there is rarely a more comforting position than to be able to demonstrate one's lack of naive credulity towards the Biblical text...by repeating what everybody else says." Vanderkam himself admits that if the story is taken at face value, no one can question David's innocence (p. 521).

[23] "To gird" (*hgr*) as compared with "to kill/murder" (*hrg*)—there is, however, a slight difference in the first Hebrew consonant of each word. The same wordplay occurs in 1 Kings 2:5.

[24] Many commentators note that this is the first place where David is explicitly called "King David." See, for example, Brueggemann, *First and Second Samuel*, p. 230.

[25] Ibid.

[26] Not only does this verse include the words "evil" and "iniquity," but David's refusal to eat the "delicacies" of the wicked reflects his action in the narrative where he refuses to partake of the usual funerary meal, choosing instead to fast until sundown (2 Sam. 3:35).

Verse 39 also contains David's famous contrast between himself and his nephews. He says, "I am gentle though anointed king, but these men, the sons of Zeruiah, are harder than me" (my translation). Having established that the words of David are the same as the narrator, in this context, we can be confident that this is an accurate description of the sons of Zeruiah. Therefore, by looking at the contrast made here, we gain a better understanding of the character portrait of these men.

The word that David chooses to describe himself can also mean "weak," but "gentle" or "tender" fits the context better. Auld points to the later actions of Josiah as a way of understanding David's description of himself. In 2 Kings 22:19 Josiah is said to be "*tender* of heart" (the same word). Furthermore, he tears his clothes and weeps at the reading of the Law. Similarly, our passage speaks of David tearing his clothes (v. 31), weeping (v. 32) and being tender (v. 39).[27] This parallel is strengthened by the fact that Josiah is said to have "walked in all the ways of his father David" (2 Kings 22:2). Thus, Josiah is a latter David.

McCarter states, "David's passive attitude toward this part of his destiny is consistent with his behavior as presented elsewhere in the larger story."[28] For example, David's "gentleness" is evident in his earlier treatment of Saul, when he refused to take matters into his own hands concerning the kingship. In contrast, Abishai, one of the sons of Zeruiah, had to be restrained by David from killing Saul when he had the opportunity (1 Sam. 26:8). Later in his career, when driven from his throne by his own son, David exhibits the same tenderness, as he tells his soldiers, "Deal gently for my sake with the young man Absalom" (2 Sam. 18:5). The Absalom narrative also contrasts the harsh response of the sons of Zeruiah, as Abishai must be restrained twice from killing Shimei (2 Sam. 16:9–10; 19:21–23), while Joab defies David's orders by killing Absalom (2 Sam. 18:14, 15).

In contrast to his own "gentleness," David describes the sons of Zeruiah as "hard" or "harsh." Elsewhere in the books of Samuel, this word is used to describe the troubled spirit of Hannah (1 Sam. 1:15) and the fierceness of the battle between Abner and the servants of David (2 Sam. 2:17). Perhaps most tellingly, it is used to describe Nabal's character (1 Sam. 25:3).[29] The parallel made with Nabal is far from complimentary; coupled with the descriptions of them as "men of iniquity" and "evil doers," we are left with a very negative impression of the sons of Zeruiah.

---

[27] Auld, *I&II Samuel*, p. 384.

[28] McCarter, *II Samuel*, p. 121.

[29] The parallel between Nabal and the sons of Zeruiah is strengthened by the number of verbal similarities between 1 Sam. 24–26 and 2 Sam. 3. See the impressive list compiled by Auld, *I&II Samuel*, pp. 384-385.

As noted above, the name "Zeruiah" may well have a double function here. On the one hand, if "Zeruiah" means "balm," it would provide an ironic contrast to the deed just perpetrated by Joab and Abishai. On the other hand, if "Zeruiah" recalls similar-sounding words like "rock" or "adversary," then the hardness of the brothers' character receives a stronger emphasis. Thus, the expression "sons of Zeruiah" is a brilliant sarcastic turn of phrase by David. Not only does it carry a deeper meaning; it is also a contemptuous way of referring to these brothers, by not acknowledging their personal names.[30]

David continues his invective by saying, "The LORD shall repay the evildoer according to his evil." Having already discussed the word "evil," a comment on the word "repay" is also in order. "Repay" (*shallēm*) is frequently used in the context of bloodguilt. David's initial exclamation upon hearing of the murder of Abner was to absolve himself and his throne of any bloodguilt (3:28).[31] Now he calls on the Lord to "repay" those who are guilty of shedding innocent blood. In the larger context, a wordplay is created that emphasizes the magnitude of Joab's crime. The author informs the reader three times that Abner had left "in peace" (*shālôm*—vv. 21, 22, 23). Consequently, the murder of Abner threatened the fragile union that was being formed between Israel and Judah. Thus, Joab disrupted *shālôm*, and therefore deserves *shallēm* from God.

David's complaint and harsh words about the sons of Zeruiah leave one wondering what the exact nature of their relationship was. Why, for instance, does David not have them executed for murder? His execution of the Amalekite who claimed to have killed Saul (2 Sam. 1:14–16), and his execution of the sons of Rimmon who murder Ish-bosheth (2 Sam. 4), demonstrate his usual response to those who kill members of the Saulide clan.

The execution of the sons of Rimmon is particularly interesting, in that it immediately follows the present story. The fact that two brothers murder a member of Saul's family in both stories, and that each are referred to with the formulaic expression "sons of X," makes the different outcomes of the murderers more surprising. Joab and Abishai are cursed, but Rechab and Baanah are executed (2 Sam. 4:9–12). David's reasons for tolerating the sons of Zeruiah are never given, unless we are to read into his words here a be-

---

[30] This is similar to Saul's refusal to acknowledge either David or Ahimelech by calling them "son of Jesse" and "son of Ahitub" (1 Sam. 22:12–13). However, "son of X" is not always a derogatory term; context must be the determining factor. For a further discussion of this usage see Clines, "X, X Ben Y," pp. 282ff.

[31] Some disparage David for this initial response. For example, Eschelbach, *Has Joab Foiled David?*, p. 24. But note Brueggemann's discussion about the serious nature of bloodguilt, *First and Second Samuel*, p. 229, as well as Youngblood, *1, 2 Samuel*, p. 839.

grudging acknowledgement of his dependence upon them.[32] Although a curse was a very grievous utterance, David's inability to take sterner measures suggests his impotence regarding the sons of Zeruiah.[33] One thing that is clear is the ongoing feud between David and his nephews, that is evident from the first episode in which Abishai appears (1 Sam. 26:6–11), right through until David's deathbed scene, where he tells Solomon to execute Joab (1 Kings 2:5–6).

Victorious Commander (2 Sam. 8:16; 10:7–14)

Except for the brief notice of being "over the army" (2 Sam. 8:16), Joab does not reappear in the narrative until chapter 10. Surprisingly, his presence in the capture of Jerusalem (2 Sam. 5:6–9) is glossed over by the books of Samuel, in contrast to 1 Chronicles 11:6–8.[34] However, the mostly-positive portrayal of Joab in 10:7–14 makes one wonder if a character transformation has taken place, during his prolonged absence from the narrative. While Joab is always pictured as fearless and victorious in battle, his speech of encouragement, and especially his devout words (vv. 11–12), leave the reader with a more positive impression of him.

Joab's victory occurs during the initial engagement between Israel and the combined forces of Syria and Ammon (vv. 6–8). The war is precipitated by the suspicions of Hanun's advisers, who believe that David has come to spy out the city and overthrow it rather than show "kindness" to the new monarch (10:1–5). It is this war with the Ammonites that provides the context for the infamous story of David and Bathsheba (2 Sam. 10–12). Joab's pious words and faithfulness to the war effort provide a stunning contrast to David's act of remaining in Jerusalem (11:1), and subsequent adultery and murder. While Joab's true colors will resurface (11:14–21), the current story

---

[32] Willis, *First and Second Samuel*, p. 305, suggests family connections as well as popular opinion as reasons for David's inability to further punish Joab and Abishai, while Firth, *1 & 2 Samuel*, p. 352, states, "David knows that although kings rule, they do so only with their generals' support."

[33] Rosenberg, *King and Kin*, p. 166, notes that, "David's carping at 'the sons of Zeruiah' has a peculiar ring of powerlessness about it, and hints of complicated infighting between David and his chief allies, the exact nature of which remains unknown." Similarly, Fokkelman, *Throne and City*, p. 119, states, "In a political reading we establish the fact that David is either not able, or not prepared, to correct Joab effectively."

[34] Henry, "Joab: A Biblical Critique of Machiavellian Tactics," p. 332, suggests that David is already seeking to replace Joab by giving leadership to whoever would capture the city.

demonstrates that difficult circumstances can bring the best out of even the worst kind of people.[35]

Upon arriving at Rabbath-Ammon, Joab initially finds himself in a difficult position as he is surrounded by the enemy (v. 9). It is argued by some that this was a tactical blunder on Joab's part, and that his reason for returning to Jerusalem following the battle (v. 14) was because this mistake "weakened him to the point that he could not follow up with a siege of the capital."[36] While this would dampen Joab's victory somewhat, it is difficult to determine if this is part of the author's purpose. It seems more likely that the author seeks to show how Joab's resourcefulness, courage, and faith enable Israel to overcome the enemy in a desperate situation. Blunder or not, there is more positive than negative in this circumstance.[37]

For the first time in the narrative, Joab speaks to instruct, encourage, and exhort. His bravery is evident in choosing the most difficult part of the fight for himself. He "chooses" the "choice ones" of Israel (i.e., "the best") to face the Syrians (v. 9). The reason for this is twofold: 1) the Syrians appear to be the most numerous (v. 6); and 2) being hired mercenaries, the Syrians would no doubt be the most seasoned and battle-hardened soldiers. Joab puts the rest of the troops under the command of Abishai to face the Ammonites (v. 10). Auld's comment on Joab's words in verse 11 is instructive:

> Though seemingly unremarkable at first, they are in fact unusual in several respects. The plan itself that they describe is straightforward: only after engaging the enemy will Joab know whether the division of troops between the brothers was the right one—if not, and one comes under enemy pressure, the other can help.[38]

---

[35] I disagree with Eschelbach's depiction of Joab as a "flat" character (a word he is also somewhat uncomfortable with). Eschelbach contends that Joab is always portrayed consistently in the narrative (a hero in his understanding). I am in agreement with Whybray, *The Succession Narrative*, p. 40, who states, "He [Joab] is depicted in a variety of situations which enable his complex character to take on flesh and blood." For examples of Eschelbach's view, see *Has Joab Foiled David?* pp. 60-61, 76, and n. 18, p. 106.

[36] McCarter, *II Samuel*, p. 274. However, McCarter's argument is derived from Yigael Yadin whose theory has, in my view, been successfully challenged by Michael M. Homan, in "Booths or Succoth? A Response to Yigael Yadin," *JBL* 118/4, 1999, pp. 691-697.

[37] Anderson, *2 Samuel*, p. 147, states, "Joab may have committed a tactical error by allowing his troops to be caught between two enemy forces. Equally well one could argue that he showed a great tactical skill being able to deal with a military emergency."

[38] Auld, *I&II Samuel*, p. 446.

Joab then gives some words of encouragement: "Be of good courage, and let us be strong for our people and for the cities of our God" (v. 12a). Literally, he says, "Be strong, let us be strong!" Joab's double exhortation to be "strong" counters his two-fold description of the enemy as "strong" (v. 11). The context seems to indicate he is still speaking with Abishai; but it is possible that his words are said in the hearing of all the soldiers. His exhortation is followed by remarkable words of acquiescence to the divine will: "And may the LORD do what is good in His sight" (v. 12b).

Of the sixteen, or so, times that Joab speaks in the narrative,[39] this is the first time he uses the name "Yahweh." In fact, 2 Samuel records Joab using the words "God" and "Yahweh" only three times each.[40] In every case the words are used in an oath or common idiomatic expression.[41] While we must give Joab (whose name means "Yahweh is father") credit for his "God language" in this moment of crisis, his infrequent usage of it, coupled with the fact that he only uses these words in stereotypical ways, suggests a man who is more acquainted with "God language" than he is with God Himself.[42] Nevertheless, Joab's words of encouragement, combined with a victorious outcome (vv. 13–14), prove to be one of the high points in his portrayal.

Willis identifies four principles Joab follows, which should be imitated by all God's people who are engaged in a spiritual battle. (Eph. 6:10–18).

> First, he places his strongest and most capable soldiers against the best of the enemy, and pits the weaker and less experienced against the enemy's inferior warriors. Second, he charges his two forces to help each other if either side seems to be losing. Third, he urges his soldiers to be courageous in view of the fact that they are fighting to save God's people and God's cities. Finally, he leaves the victory to God.[43]

---

[39] The number depends on how one counts the various conversations of Joab.

[40] Joab speaks 379 words in 2 Sam.–1 Kings 2. This means that his use of "God" or "Yahweh" only amounts to 1.58% of his speech.

[41] The passages are: 2 Sam. 2:27 ("God" is used in an oath formula); 10:11–12 ("God" and "Yahweh" are used once each in common idiomatic expressions); 19:7 [Heb. 19:8] ("Yahweh" is used in an oath formula); and, 24:3 ("Now may Yahweh your God add..."—a common expression used to wish someone blessing or prosperity). Joab only speaks eight words in 1 Kings 1–2, and "God" or "Yahweh" are not among them.

[42] Given these facts, Baldwin, *1&2 Samuel*, p. 230, may be a bit too optimistic when she writes, "It comes as something of a surprise to find the tough Joab exhibiting faith in this way; now we know him a little better, and see him as a worthy general of David's army."

[43] Willis, *First and Second Samuel*, p. 344.

Murder, He Wrote (2 Sam. 11:14–25)

After David's crushing defeat of the Syrian troops (10:15–19), Joab and the army are dispatched by the king to punish the Ammonites (11:1). While Joab fights (11:11), David commits adultery and plots murder. The contrast between loyal troops battling the enemy (including Uriah and Joab) and David's actions is shocking, and serves to highlight his descent into sin.[44] However, when Uriah returns to the frontline with his own death warrant in hand (vv.14–15), the reader quickly learns that Joab is a willing accomplice to murder. Although the author never explicitly reveals the reason for Joab's complicity, the murder is expedient for Joab because it puts David in his debt, and Joab is a man who likes to be in control.[45]

That Joab has another motive and is not simply "following orders" is clear from the narrative, which has already established that, Joab is not afraid to say when he disagrees with the king (3:24–25). Furthermore, he is known to defy the king's orders on other occasions (e.g., 2 Sam. 18:11–15). Here, however, there is no indication that he questions Uriah's death sentence.[46] Instead, he sets about to "improve" on David's plan, which means he gives some thought as to how this execution should be carried out. The fact that Joab does not deliberate on "why," but only on "how," suggests something sinister in his character.

The alteration Joab makes to David's plan is also revealing.[47] That David would order Joab to, "set Uriah in the forefront of the hottest battle, and retreat from him, that he may be struck down and die" (v. 15), shows David's ineptitude in plotting a murder. Such an action would reveal that Uriah was intentionally being targeted, creating morale problems for the other soldiers and engendering distrust with those in charge. Joab, on the other hand, knows how to kill. "A born pragmatist as well as an experienced soldier, he realized that the saving in casualties, however desirable in itself, is

---

[44] It is not the first or last time that Joab and the army would confront an enemy without David (2 Sam. 2:12ff.; 10:7–14; 18:2–4; 21:16–17), but this episode emphasizes David's absence (11:1, 11).

[45] Evans, *The Message of Samuel*, p. 211, writes, "A further consequence, almost certainly perceived by Joab with his understanding of David's character, was that Joab now had a permanent hold over David. This was not so much that Joab could reveal David's sin, but that David would no longer be able to take the high ground. He was not by nature a hypocrite and having been complicit in Joab's excesses on this one occasion would find it hard to restrain or rebuke him on other occasions."

[46] Fokkelman, *King David*, p. 66, notes that Uriah could have been executed in Jerusalem, "which therefore presents some doubts as to Uriah's guilt."

[47] Keith Bodner, "Is Joab a Reader-Response Critic?," *JSOT* 21A, 2002, p. 34, states, "Joab's interpretation of the king's letter betokens a calm and calculating demeanor, in contrast to David's lack of clear thinking and insipid orders."

also the weak spot in the king's plan. It is better for many to fall, he decides, than for the conspiracy to stand revealed."[48]

Although Joab may welcome the opportunity to have David in his debt, it is also possible that he resents being put in a position that will cost the "necessary" loss of good soldiers and, in turn, make him look like a poor field general. Such poor battle tactics could cost him the respect of his soldiers. It is notable that, on other occasions, Joab seeks to minimize casualties (2:28; 18:16; 20:20–22). His correspondence with David throughout the duration of the Ammonite war will reveal his disdain for the king.

Following the death of Uriah, Joab sends a messenger to tell David "all the things concerning the war" (v. 18). Since Joab withholds the information about Uriah, Fokkelman says, "it follows, therefore, that 'all the matters of the war' are not really *all* the matters of the war" (author's emphasis).[49] Joab's initial communication seems designed to frustrate the king. He anticipates the king exploding in rage, and mockingly imitates his response (vv. 20-21). According to Joab's instructions, it is only *after* the king has vented his frustration that the messenger is to respond, "Your servant Uriah the Hittite is dead also."

Joab knows that David will be anxious to hear the news concerning Uriah; thus, there appears to be no reason to withhold this information, except to play a sadistic joke on his king. Why give David all the information up front, when he can make him squirm a little? Why let him off the hook so easily, when this "necessary" defeat has made Joab look bad and has cost him the lives of some good men?

If Joab had really respected his king, he would have delivered the news about Uriah in the context of the other "matters of the war." However, by withholding this piece of information and playing his trump card at just the right moment, Joab is able to defend his actions and deliver a backhanded reply to David—that the loss of quality soldiers is really his fault. He hopes to make David look foolish by stirring up his anger, and then by supplying one well-timed response that will cause a reversal in David's attitude. Surely the messenger (unless he is in on the joke, which is unlikely), and those in David's court, will be mystified by the king's dramatic change in outlook.

How the next scene plays out depends upon whether one follows the Hebrew or Greek text of 11:21–24. In the Hebrew text, David does not respond as Joab anticipates, because the messenger "spills the beans" by mentioning the death of Uriah in the context of the defeat. This version suggests that the messenger loses his nerve and, rather than take the risk of angering the king, gives him all the information up front. As Sternberg states,

---

[48] Sternberg, *Poetics*, p. 214.

[49] Fokkelman, *King David*, p. 65.

The messenger must have considered Joab's logic to be twisted and strange. It is surely difficult for the messenger to understand how the king, tearing his hair about all these needless casualties, can be soothed by means of a follow-up about an additional casualty: such an addition would seem most likely to prove the last straw. Therefore, the messenger tries to forestall this danger and save himself from the king's wrath. And how can danger and wrath be averted except by deviating from Joab's text?[50]

I am persuaded, however, that the Greek text (Septuagint) is the more original reading.[51] "In the longer Greek text, the audience with the king proceeds just as Joab has expected, and just as he has briefed his messenger; and the messenger is almost word perfect in what he says to David."[52] Thus, according to this version, David responds as Joab predicts, and the joke succeeds in embarrassing the king. Whether one accepts the Hebrew or Greek text, however, does not affect Joab's intent and, therefore, our characterization of him here. In one version, he is successful, while in the other he is not; but his objective to embarrass David can be detected in both.[53]

A comment should also be made on Joab's inclusion of the incident of Abimelech's death (v. 21), which, at first glance, seems a bit odd. Judges 9 relates the story of Abimelech, the self-made king of Shechem, who attacks the city of Thebez and is killed by a woman when he gets too close to the city wall. The fact that Joab (and apparently David, if the Greek text is accepted here) refers to this incident, might suggest that it had become a notorious example in Israel's history of what not to do during a siege.[54] However, its inclusion here is more profound than a simple observation of siege tactics. Both stories detail a king's abuse of power. "Both kings, David and

---

[50] Sternberg, *Poetics*, p. 216. The other possibility is that the messenger respected the king too much to play such a sadistic joke on him.

[51] For arguments as to why the Greek text is more original, see: S. R. Driver, *Notes on the Hebrew Text and the Topography of the Books of Samuel*, 2nd ed. (Oxford: Clarendon Press, 1913), p. 290; McCarter, *II Samuel*, pp. 282-283 (who thinks that even the Greek text has some issues); and Gordon, *I&II Samuel*, pp. 57ff. (esp. p. 59), and p. 255.

[52] Auld, *I&II Samuel*, p. 459. For a translation of these verses which includes both the Hebrew and Greek text, see Auld, pp. 449-450.

[53] Fokkelman, *King David*, pp. 67-68, suggests that Joab's guilt over the loss of many men causes him to fear an angry response from the king, and thus he tells the messenger to inform David of Uriah's death. But if this were the case, Joab would deliver the information about Uriah sooner, rather than wait until after the king's angry response.

[54] Alter, *The David Story*, p. 254, makes this suggestion.

Abimelech, fall because of a woman,"[55] and both seek to cover up a secret that becomes known to all.

How much of this correspondence Joab intends is debatable. As previously mentioned, he may simply be alluding to an analogy from Israel's history regarding siege warfare, anticipating that David will cite this common example. On the other hand, it is possible that Joab sees some of the parallels between Abimelech's and David's situations. For example, both kings sought to cover up a deed they did not want others to know about. It is also obvious that both kings used their power in an abusive manner. I find it doubtful (but not impossible) that Joab would already be aware of David's liaison with Bathsheba, and so the female connection in both stories is less likely to have occurred to him. Whatever Joab's thoughts and motives may have been, David never hears him utter these words. Therefore it is unlikely that he intends any kind of subtle rebuke by this reference. The irony in these similarities is there for the reader to ponder; it is only in the larger context of the story that they take on a greater significance.

Joab's Jibe: "Take It, or I Will" (2 Sam. 12:26–28)

With the siege at Rabbah nearing a successful conclusion by Joab's capture of the city's water supply (v. 26), Joab summons David to the battlefield. While some scholars see Joab's action as a sign of loyalty and respect for David,[56] his language suggests otherwise. Joab says:

(a)   I have fought against Rabbah.
(a)   Yes, I have captured the city's water (supply).
(b)   So now, gather the remainder of the people
(b)   And camp against the city
(b)   And capture it.
(a)   Otherwise, I, I will capture the city
(a)   And my name will be called over it. (vv. 27–28, my translation)

This layout suggests that Joab has prepared a well-made sandwich, which David would certainly have found hard to swallow. The outer layers marked "a" are the bread and consist of four "I"s and one "my" statement. Thus Joab's short speech begins and ends with statements about his own ac-

---

[55] Sternberg, *Poetics*, p. 221.

[56] Hertzberg, *I&II Samuel*, p. 319, states, "Joab's request to David…is framed in such a way that he seems concerned for the prestige of the king." Birch, *1&2 Samuel*, p. 1300, writes, "But out of loyalty to David, he sends word that he believes it more appropriate that David's name be associated with the fall of the city rather than his own (v. 28). It is a worthy and perhaps prudent gesture on the part of a loyal commander."

complishments, or possible accomplishments. In short, he views himself as the true conqueror of the city. The middle sections, marked "b," are the meat, and consist of three imperatives for his king. David is commanded by Joab to "gather," "camp against," and "capture" the city. No doubt Joab's "Ego sandwich" left a bad taste in David's mouth, but at this point David was powerless to do anything but comply.

It is just as important to look at the language that Joab does not use. Once again there is no language of deference toward the king. Joab does not use the typical Hebrew form of polite address,[57] nor does he use words like, "your servant" or "my lord." He speaks only of the great things he has done and is capable of doing, while barking orders to his superior.

Alter believes that the first two lines of Joab's message are in the form of a victory poem, "in which it is he who figures unambiguously as conqueror." Alter continues, "This coy and dangerous game Joab plays with David about who has the real power will persist in the story."[58] I suggest this power game is what irks David about the sons of Zeruiah, and yet, as we will see in the next episode (2 Sam. 14), David willingly plays the game. Joab knows that, for the sake of kingdom stability, it is important for David to remain the "front-man." Many mistake this shrewd acknowledgement as loyalty. As Joab's actions regularly betray, and as this speech clearly proclaims, Joab is a man of self-interest and self-confidence.

One Good Trick Deserves Another (2 Sam. 14:1–3, 19–24)

After Absalom's murder of his brother Amnon and subsequent flight to Geshur (2 Sam. 13:23–38), the narrative turns to the events that conspire to restore him to the king's court (2 Sam. 14). Joab is a key figure in this turn of events (14:20). The context suggests that David is in no mood for reconciliation with his wayward son.[59] However, through the machinations of Joab, and the skillful implementation of his scheme by a "wise woman" from Tekoa (v. 2), Absalom is allowed to return (v. 21).

Many have speculated about Joab's motive in seeking the return of the prince, but the text is silent.[60] Any conjecture (and it can be only that) should be based on what the reader has learned or will learn about Joab. Con-

---

[57] The word *nā'* is typically used in polite forms of address, just as English uses the word "please."

[58] Alter, *The David Story*, p. 263. More recently, several scholars have noted the negative tone of Joab's words. For example, Bodner, "Is Joab a Reader-Response Critic?" p. 34, and Hamilton, *Handbook*, p. 336.

[59] For a clear and concise argument demonstrating that David continues to be angry with Absalom, see, Davis, *2 Samuel*, pp. 175-176. My reasons for supporting this interpretation are presented in chap. 24, pp. 358-359.

[60] For a list of possible motives, see Evans, *The Message of Samuel*, pp. 225-226.

sidering his abiding self-interest, I surmise that he must have seen some personal benefit in Absalom's return. Perhaps Joab believes that he will be able to manipulate a grateful Absalom and use him to his advantage; or, Joab might see the potential of a young protégé and admire the similar characteristics of deception, ruthlessness, and self-interest that are a part of his own makeup. After all, Absalom's murder of Amnon was very "Joab-esque." Whatever his expectations, Joab will soon learn that Absalom walks to the beat of his own drum (14:30–32). Given the ongoing feud between David and Joab, the one speculation I cannot accept is that he acts out of loyalty to his king.[61]

The fact that relations between David and Joab are strained explains the reason why Joab selects a go-between. Knowing that David is a sucker for a good story (see 2 Sam. 12:1–6!),[62] Joab employs a wise woman and tells her to pose as a widow "who has been mourning a long time for the dead" (14:2). The use of deception not only suggests that David would oppose a direct request for Absalom's return, but it also provides Joab with another opportunity to use an intermediary to embarrass the king in front of his court (see 2 Sam. 11:18–21).

Since the text tells us that "Joab put the words in her mouth" (14:3), in one sense this is his longest speech in the entire narrative of 2 Samuel.[63] However, although the plan and substance of the words are Joab's, the woman must have had the flexibility to improvise, in order to steer David's declarations toward the desired outcome. This is why she is described as a "wise woman."[64]

Despite the freedom she may have possessed in guiding the conversation, much of her words and actions mirror those of Joab. For example, as

---

[61] Brueggemann, *First and Second Samuel*, p. 291, is among those who make this supposition.

[62] There are, of course, a number of similarities between these two incidents. In both, the king is told a fictitious story, only to be trapped into pronouncing judgment on himself. One significant difference, however, is that "Nathan's parable was designed to rouse the king's conscience as against his feelings; the woman of Tekoah's, as prompted by Joab, to rouse his feelings as against his conscience"—Davis, *2 Samuel*, p. 179, quoting W. G. Blaikie.

[63] Regarding the expression, "putting words in someone's mouth," see Exod. 4:15; Num. 22:38; and Ezra 8:17. For an informative discussion on the various ways the Hebrew Scriptures make use of this technique, see Hamilton, *Handbook*, pp. 342-343.

[64] Susan M. Pigott, "Wives, Witches and Wise Women," pp. 159-160, notes thematic and linguistic similarities with the Abigail story (1 Sam. 25), but observes the important contrast that "unlike Abigail, the wise woman's words result in violence rather than peace, in bloodletting rather than avoidance of bloodshed. As a result, she is tied much more closely to Jonadab in 1 [*sic*] Samuel 13 (also described as wise) whose advice results in violence culminating in the death of the first successor to the throne."

she approaches the king she is said to "fall" and "bow" before him (v. 4). Surprisingly, and for the first time in 2 Samuel, Joab does the same (v. 22). The woman frequently refers to herself as "your maidservant" (vv. 6, 7, 12, etc.) and respectfully addresses David as "my lord, the king" (vv. 9, 12, 15, etc.). Again, Joab surprises the reader with similar language (v. 22). In spite of all the courtly language used by the wise woman, however, she can also be very direct and accusing ("For the king speaks this thing as one who is guilty," v. 13c), which is much more customary of Joab's speech.

Once the woman manipulates David into pronouncing an oath (v. 11), she reveals the real purpose in her coming (vv. 12–14). Whether Joab has approached David about this subject in the past, or whether David simply begins to recognize his handiwork, he asks the woman: "Is the hand of Joab with you in all this?" (v. 19). In the midst of a copious amount of flattery, she concedes: "Your servant Joab commanded me, and he put all these words in the mouth of your maidservant." Perhaps she says too much when she adds, "In order to turn the face of the matter, your servant Joab has done this thing" (v. 20, my translation). These words will come back to slap Joab. For the moment, however, David agrees to the petition and shows no animosity about being duped and manipulated. Perhaps Joab expected an angry retort; he was used to such from David. However, David's response is polite and magnanimous: "Look, please, I will do this thing. Now go, bring back the young man Absalom" (v. 21, my translation).

The fact that David grants the request, but also responds politely, seems to move Joab. As noted above, for the first time in the narrative Joab responds by showing great respect to the king in both word and action. It is possible that Joab is playing the part of the grateful courtier, all the while relishing his victory over the king. His words could all be for show, and there could be a hidden barb in his statement, "the king has done the word of his servant" (v. 22, my translation). In other words, "Gotcha David! Don't you know I always get my way?" David's response in verse 24 could justify reading Joab's words this way.

On the other hand, Joab might believe that David is reaching out an olive branch and so Joab is responding with true gratitude. Without hearing the tone of voice, it is difficult to know which interpretation is correct. The difference is important. One interpretation suggests that Joab is acting like the same old Joab. The other suggests that part of the feud between Joab and David results from his desire to receive some acknowledgement from his uncle and king. If Joab is fatherless, he may have looked to David for approbation. In spite of Joab's manipulative tactics, David responds positively, which softens Joab in return. Perhaps an ancient audience would be more in tune with the author's true intention, but since the context does not obviously lend itself to sarcasm, I am inclined to accept the option that Joab is showing genuine gratitude to David.

Whether gratitude or sarcasm, the game is not over between these two men. David's polite response proves to be ingenuous. When Joab returns with Absalom, the king responds employing two key words used earlier by the wise woman (v. 20a): "Let him *turn* to his house, for my *face* he will not see" (v. 24, my translation). The woman had said that Joab sought to "*turn* the *face* of the matter." Now David responds by *turning* Absalom away from his *face*. In other words, Joab had tried to change the situation, but David throws the words back in his face and says in effect, "You thought you could manipulate me and get your way, but nothing has changed." As Fokkelman states, "David surprises us, and undoubtedly Joab, by announcing a sort of quarantine for the prince....All the way up to his return in Jerusalem Joab has had the illusion of being totally successful in his design. Only afterwards does David disclose his step backwards."[65] Although Joab seemed to have won the verbal sparring, David delivers a "left hook" and "turns the face" of Joab and Absalom! Who knows whether things might have turned out differently had David shown a kinder response to both men. Instead, Absalom grows more bitter, eventually fomenting a rebellion against his father, while Joab grows ever harder and more callous towards his king.

Joab Gets Burned (2 Sam. 14:28–33)

After waiting two full years to be received back into his father's good graces, Absalom grows impatient and sends for Joab, hoping he can help break the stalemate (vv. 28–29). Joab has already been burned trying to help Absalom, so he ignores his request—not once, but twice. Little does he know that spurning Absalom's requests will lead to a burning of a more serious nature. Absalom, not one to be refused, promptly has his servants set Joab's barley field on fire (v. 30). The economic loss propels Joab into action, as he first confronts Absalom, and then does his bidding by interceding on his behalf before the king (vv. 32–33).

This incident is revealing. First, while anyone would be upset at the wanton destruction of his property, it further confirms that Joab only acts/reacts to those things which are of personal interest to him. Second, and most importantly, it demonstrates the folly of Joab's plan in returning Absalom. It is clear from this incident that Absalom feels no particular loyalty to Joab for his past efforts. Joab is someone Absalom uses to get what he desires. This suggests that Joab's plot involving the "wise woman" may not have been so "wise" after all. Future events will provide further confirmation. Joab has misjudged the situation. He has let the devil loose in his own backyard. But Absalom will do much more damage than burning a field: he will set the nation itself ablaze with civil war. If some were inclined to think that

---

[65] Fokkelman, *King David*, p. 147.

the return of Absalom might be a good thing, hindsight proves otherwise. In the burning of his field, we might say that Joab "reaps what he sows." The destroyed harvest not only anticipates the devastation to come; it also reveals the fruitlessness of Joab's plan. McCarter's insightful words sum up the situation well:

> In its disregard for larger moral questions and consequences in the interest of the attainment of an immediate goal, the woman's masquerade exhibits what has become familiar to us as the Machiavellian spirit of the sons of Zeruiah....Behind the scenes lurks the sinister figure of Joab, manipulating the king and his authority to purposes that he, Joab, thinks good.[66]

Joab Reveals No "Hang-ups" About Killing Absalom (2 Sam. 18:1–5, 10–16, 19–23)

Joab's prevalence throughout 2 Samuel leads Rosenberg to note that, during Absalom's rebellion, "We are perhaps surprised to find him conspicuously *absent* from the scene of David's flight from Jerusalem" (author's emphasis).[67] It is peculiar that such a key figure in David's army should go unmentioned. Indeed, the first reference to Joab in this part of the narrative is in connection with Absalom, not David! 2 Samuel 17:25 informs the reader that Absalom "made Amasa captain of the army instead of Joab."

What are we to make of this statement? Does it mean that, had Absalom chosen Joab, Joab would have joined the rebellion? Furthermore, why does David demote Joab on this occasion? Could it be that suspicions of Joab's loyalty are the basis for why he is given charge over only a third of the army (2 Samuel 18:2) rather than full command?

These suspicions seem to be allayed by 1 Kings 2:28, which states, "Then news came to Joab, for Joab had defected to Adonijah, *though he had not defected to Absalom.*" However, Joab's reason for defecting to Adonijah is related to maintaining a prominent position in the kingdom (1 Kings 1:7, 19)—something Absalom denies him. Does all of this suggest that Joab aligns himself with the one he thinks will benefit him the most, or does the comment in 2 Samuel 17:25 simply help to explain Joab's animosity toward both Absalom and Amasa, two men he later kills?

No definitive answer can be given to these suspicions, for Joab does remain with David during Absalom's revolt. However, his absence (i.e., lack of mention) during the crucial withdrawal from Jerusalem is curious, particu-

---

[66] McCarter, *II Samuel*, p. 352.
[67] Rosenberg, *King and Kin*, p. 165.

larly in light of the emphasis on the loyalty of David's Philistine captain, Ittai (2 Sam. 15:18–22). The mention of many of David's loyal followers as he flees Jerusalem provides a sharp contrast to the narrator's silence on Joab.[68]

This observation is important, because much is often made about Joab's loyalty to David by other scholars.[69] The narrator, however, does not seem to share this view, as references to Joab seem to highlight his disdain for David and David's commands. Joab's actions during Absalom's rebellion can be explained on the basis of loyalty to himself and what *he* thinks best. This is also the way one of Joab's own soldiers characterizes him (2 Sam. 18:12–13).

David's command to Joab, Abishai, and Ittai to "deal gently for my sake with the young man Absalom" (18:5), sets the stage for Joab's subsequent actions. David's order is highlighted by four successive words (five, if the narrator's introductory word is included) beginning with the letter "l" in Hebrew. The alliteration makes the command more memorable. David's appeal to his commanders to show his son mercy is not based on Absalom's merit, but on their loyalty to their king—literally, "deal gently for me." Whatever one may think about Joab's supposed prudence in dispatching Absalom, his disobedience to David's command demonstrates *dis*loyalty, not loyalty. "Joab is left no excuse by the narrator: *all* the people heard what David commanded *all* the officers—nothing else in this paragraph is so total until the flight of 'all Israel' at its end" (author's emphasis).[70]

Joab's disloyalty is underlined through his conversation with an anonymous soldier, who happens upon Absalom while he is hanging in a tree (v. 10). Joab's response, when the soldier says he had seen Absalom, is probably sarcastic—as he throws the soldier's words back in his face ("Look, you saw…"—v. 11).[71] He then asserts that he would have enriched and honored the man by presenting him with ten pieces of silver and a belt, if he had struck Absalom to the ground.

The soldier's response reveals how Joab is perceived by one of his troops. Indeed, there is no reason for the narrator to include this conversa-

---

[68] The lack of reference to Joab is all the more startling when it is noted that the narrative goes to great lengths to highlight key people who show their loyalty to David during this time. Besides the mention of Ittai, reference is made of Hushai (2 Sam. 15:32–37), as well as Zadok, Abiathar, and their sons (2 Sam. 15:24–29). The inclusion of Abiathar, who will later join Joab in Adonijah's attempted coup (1 Kings 1:7), makes the absence of any mention of Joab even more noticeable.

[69] For example, E. J. Bridge, "Joab the Commander," *Lexham Bible Dictionary*, (Bellingham, WA: Logos Bible Software, 2012) states, "He had an independent policy from his king; yet he remained loyal to David."

[70] Auld, *I&II Samuel*, p. 542.

[71] Some scholars would translate this more mildly, but however one looks at Joab's initial words, it is clear that he is upset that the soldier did not kill Absalom immediately. For further discussion see, Youngblood, *1, 2 Samuel*, pp. 1019-1020.

tion except to illuminate Joab's character and convict him of disregarding David's command.[72] The soldier shows his fidelity to the king by multiplying the reward a hundred times and saying he would still refuse it (v. 12). His refusal is based on three assertions: 1) the king had commanded that Absalom was not to be harmed (v. 12); 2) nothing remains hidden from the king (v. 13); and 3) when the news reached the king, Joab would have set himself against him (v. 13). "Unfortunately for Joab, his tendency to put expedience above morals appears to have been well known, at least among the soldiers."[73] The fact that Joab's only response is, "I cannot linger with you" (v. 14), is evidence that the soldier has spoken accurately. Brueggemann rightly states, "As we might expect, Joab does not bother to refute the man's analysis. Most likely Joab can make no defense."[74]

As Joab marches off to kill Absalom, he has many "good" reasons for disregarding the king's order. First, the advice that Ahithophel had earlier offered Absalom, "kill the king and the people will flee" (2 Sam. 17:2) is sound strategy. Of course, Joab had not heard Ahithophel's counsel, but he is enough of a pragmatist to see the logic in this course of action. The narrative intends the reader to see the irony: Absalom, who had previously rejected Ahithophel's advice to strike quickly and kill David, is struck down, thus bringing the war to an end as Ahithophel had suggested.

Second, and perhaps most importantly, Joab has a number of personal reasons for slaying Absalom. The last two encounters between them involved loss and humiliation on Joab's part. Absalom had burned his field (14:30–32) and spurned him as commander over the army (17:25). Joab was not the kind of man to forget these slights, especially considering the huge favor he had performed on Absalom's behalf in restoring him to the kingdom and, eventually, to his father. Wartime provided the perfect excuse for repaying such ingratitude.

Certainly the killing of Absalom provided another personal pleasure for Joab. In striking the heart of Absalom (18:14), not only would he avenge himself against the upstart rebel, but he would strike the heart of David as well. In the ongoing power struggle between these men, evidenced in a continual game of "tit-for-tat," Joab would achieve an overwhelming triumph against his uncle. No curse and no insult that David could dispense would equal Joab's feat on this occasion. What could hurt David more, and what could he possibly do about it? Joab had killed a dangerous rebel in a legiti-

---

[72] The soldier's comments about Joab are very damaging to Eschelbach's portrayal of Joab as a hero in, *Has Joab Foiled David?* Eschelbach offers no comment on this incident. Anderson, *2 Samuel*, p. 225, is correct when he states, "These verses give a negative picture of Joab: he is dealing perfidiously with David, and he would, most likely, leave his obedient servant in a tight spot had he killed Absalom."

[73] Henry, "Joab: A Biblical Critique of Machiavellian Tactics," p. 334.

[74] Brueggemann, *First and Second Samuel*, p. 320.

mate battle. He had saved the kingdom, spared a considerable amount of bloodshed, and exacted revenge on Absalom and David all at the same time!

The exact nature of Absalom's death is unclear. Joab's act of taking "three staffs" and "thrusting" them into Absalom's "heart" is capable of various interpretations. For example, are the "three staffs" three spears? Does "heart" mean "chest" in this context? If Joab thrust three spears into Absalom's actual heart, he would surely have been dead before his ten armorbearers could finish him off (v. 15). Could it, therefore, mean that Joab used the staffs to dislodge him from the tree and then his armor-bearers killed him?[75]

While we may not be able to ascertain the exact circumstances of Absalom's death, a closer look at these words demonstrates that they have significance beyond their literal meaning. The word "staffs" (translated "spears" in NKJV) can, in other contexts, mean "tribes." At the beginning of Absalom's rebellion he intercepted people at the gate who would say, "Your servant is from such and such a *tribe* in Israel" (2 Sam. 15:2). Furthermore, we are told, "Then Absalom sent spies throughout all the *tribes* of Israel" (2 Sam. 15:10). The use of this word in describing Absalom's death thus ironically recalls the original nature of his crime.[76] The significance of the words "heart" and "thrust" are explored in the chapter on Absalom.[77]

One final word that stands out in this context is the word "surrounded." As Joab's ten armor-bearers move in for the kill, we are told that they "surrounded Absalom" (18:15). This is the same word used of Joab who sought to "*turn* the face of the matter" by bringing Absalom home from exile (2 Sam. 14:20). It is also the same word used by David when he said, "Let him *turn* to his house" (2 Sam. 14:24). Once again, a word used to describe Absalom's death reminds us of an event that precipitated the rebellion.

With Absalom dead, Joab now turns to the task of informing the king about the outcome. Ahimaaz, the son of Zadok, is eager to deliver the report of victory (18:19), but Joab refuses, noting that the death of the king's

---

[75] Charles Conroy, *Absalom, Absalom!*, p. 44, n. 5 states, "Joab's personal involvement in the death of Absalom…took the form of a symbolic act of violence. With three stout sticks he prodded Absalom in the chest (*lb*) to dislodge him from the tree (see NEB); this was the signal for the ten attendants to move in and finish off the helpless Absalom." Another interpretation suggests that Joab merely attempted to stun or wound Absalom and then allowed his armor-bearers to finish the job. See, for example, Alter, *The David Story*, p. 306.

[76] Auld, *I&II Samuel*, pp. 542-543. Auld notes the connection of this word with foolishness and a rebellious child in the Book of Proverbs (Prov. 10:13; 26:3; 13:24; 22:15; 29:15). He also states, "Proverbs 13:24 is the only other passage in the Bible to link key words of [2 Sam. 18] vv. 14, 16 in this narrative: 'Who holds back the staff hates his son.' "

[77] See chap. 24, p. 378.

son will not make this a welcome day for news (v. 20).[78] The contrast between Ahimaaz's outlook and Joab's reveals an important difference between them. Ahimaaz is youthful and enthusiastic about delivering the good news of victory. Joab, however, is much more realistic, knowing that news of Absalom's death will not be welcomed by David.

Are we to discern some sensitivity in Joab by preventing Ahimaaz from delivering the news? He knows that David will be upset by the news of Absalom's death. Does he fear that David may react harshly towards the messenger (cf. 2 Sam. 1:15; 4:12)? Or, does he put himself in David's shoes and project how he might react to a messenger who brought such devastating news? It is hard to be certain, but as Ahimaaz asks a second time to "run," Joab's words do seem to show the concern of an older, more experienced, man as he says, "Why will you run *my son*?" (v. 22). Such concern on the part of Joab is surprising, but it reflects the complex nature of his character. It reveals that even the hardest of men can have a soft side.

Joab's words to Ahimaaz also contrast with his words to the Cushite, whom he addresses with imperatives, the way a commander would to a subordinate (v. 22). The identity of the Cushite is ambiguous. Is he Nubian or Ethiopian, as most scholars suggest, or is he perhaps from Mesopotamia?[79] Is he a foreigner or an Israelite of mixed blood?[80] Is he a lowly servant, or an important personal attendant to the king himself?[81] While certainty is impossible, it seems most likely from the task he is assigned, and the way Joab addresses him, that he is a foreigner of low rank in the army. This would also explain why Joab prefers to send him, as opposed to Ahimaaz. Better to risk the fate of a foreigner, than an Israelite of priestly descent! Such an attitude lines up with what we have come to expect of Joab.

After the departure of the Cushite, Ahimaaz refuses to be denied and presses Joab once again. Whether it is resignation or frustration, Joab finally capitulates with one word, "Run!" (v. 23). It is possible that, since the Cushite left first, Joab believes that he will arrive with the news before Ahimaaz. In

---

[78] I accept these words as the words of Joab to Ahimaaz, but McCarter, *II Samuel*, p. 406, thinks they are the narrator's parenthetical comments and that Ahimaaz is unaware of Absalom's death. The fact that the Cushite, who left before Ahimaaz, knows of Absalom's death, makes it unlikely that Ahimaaz was unaware of it.

[79] Youngblood, *1, 2 Samuel*, p. 1025, notes that either is a possibility.

[80] McCarter, *II Samuel*, p. 408, defends the possibility that he is a Benjamite. Most scholars, however, believe he is a foreigner.

[81] R. L. Omanson, & J. Ellington, *A handbook on the Second Book of Samuel*, UBS Handbook Series (New York: United Bible Societies, 2001), p. 1016, identify the Cushite as an important personal servant to David based on 2 Sam. 18:29. Furthermore, they note 2 Kings 22:12 uses the expression "servant of the king" as a designation of a royal official. While this expression may denote a royal official, this is not always the case and does not seem warranted in the present context.

fact, Ahimaaz arrives first, but does not deliver the crushing news of Absalom's death to David; that is left to the Cushite who speaks in a triumphant but diplomatic tone (vv. 27–32). Joab himself will follow shortly, armed with words that are anything but diplomatic!

Hard Words From a Hard Man (2 Sam. 19:1–7)[82]

Joab's softer tone with Ahimaaz, as well as the courtly language and manner of both messengers as they deliver the news of victory to David (18:28–29, 31), contrast sharply with Joab's severe rebuke of the king. Joab's invective, consisting of seventy-five words, is his longest recorded speech. In fact, his first sentence is a barrage of twenty-four words. "It is the longest sentence of the spoken word in I/II Sam! Thus he machine-guns the king with words."[83] It is reminiscent of his first rebuke of the king (2 Sam. 3:24–25). Once again, Joab unceremoniously invades the king's presence and unloads on him and, once again, the king makes no verbal response.[84] This incident brings us full circle and suggests that the relationship between David and Joab continues to steadily deteriorate.[85]

Joab's reprimand can be broken into two sections. In the first section (vv. 5–6), Joab attributes three offenses to David: 1) He has shamed his army who fought to save his life and the life of his family; 2) by staging a private "pity-party," and showing no concern for his commanders or servants, David demonstrates that he "loves" his enemies and "hates" his friends, and; 3) David would be happier if Absalom had lived and all of his faithful followers were dead. The emotional and accusatory nature of Joab's harangue is evident in the contrasts he makes (shame/honor, love/hate, and life/death), as well as his use of the second person plural ("your"—16 times!).[86] The second part of the speech consists of three imperatives—"Arise, go out, and speak to the heart of your servants" (v. 7, my translation). Thus, in Joab's eyes, his three commands provide the remedy for David's three offenses.[87]

The important question for us is, "What do Joab's words tell us about Joab?" Is he correct in rebuking David? Does he, in fact, behave as a

---

[82] By way of reminder, the verses of the English text are being followed for the convenience of the English-speaking reader.

[83] Fokkelman, *King David*, p. 271.

[84] Joab's speech has been brilliantly dissected by Conroy, *Absalom, Absalom!*, pp. 77-80, and Fokkelman, *King David*, pp. 271-275. Therefore, my comments will focus mainly on how his words contribute to his character portrait.

[85] This is one of several similarities between the two civil wars recorded in 2 Samuel. For further parallels see chap. 24, p. 377.

[86] Conroy, *Absalom, Absalom!*, pp. 78-79.

[87] Fokkelman, *King David*, p. 273.

statesman and save the kingdom, as many contend?[88] Is it fair to characterize Joab as "suitably brutal in order to shake David into acknowledging the situation?"[89]

To answer these questions, it is important to keep the whole flow of the narrative in mind. Before the battle, the narrator tells us that David gave an explicit order, in the hearing of the commanders and "all the people," that they were to "deal gently for [his] sake with the young man Absalom" (18:5). The importance of this command is stressed in the conversation between the unknown soldier and Joab (18:10–13). As previously noted, this conversation casts Joab in a negative light. The narrator shows Joab purposely acting against the command of the king.

Furthermore, if Joab's concern had merely been for the State, Absalom could have been dispatched in a much more humane way. Whatever the exact meaning is of the three rods thrust into Absalom's heart while the ten armor-bearers administered the *coup de grace* (18:14–15), it is clear that Absalom's death was not an easy one. The tense narrative about the messengers which follows (18:19–32) demonstrates Joab's knowledge that David will be extremely agitated when he learns of Absalom's death (18:20, 22). Therefore, when Joab arrives at Mahanaim and is told, "Behold the king is weeping and mourning for Absalom" (19:1), this would not come as a shock to him. In fact, I suggest that David reacts precisely as Joab expects him to. It is ironic that the one responsible for causing David this grief is now the one who administers these harsh words. David has fallen into Joab's trap. By striking Absalom he has struck David, and now he will deliver the knock-out punch with a blistering rebuke.

There are several other factors that contribute to the above interpretation. First, if Joab was genuinely concerned about David, why did he not approach him in a more compassionate way? "How is it that Joab defines and shapes his meeting with David as a conflict instead of extending understanding to the father and leading the king forth with gentle insistence?"[90] As in his previous rebuke of David, there is no courtly language or polite speech; only accusations and commands. Is such language "suitable" and necessary? Again we ask, is this the way a subordinate should address his king? The contrast between Joab's "fatherly" treatment of Ahimaaz in the previous episode and his "let me kick you while you are down" treatment of David should not go unnoticed.

---

[88] Whybray, *The Succession Narrative*, pp. 41-42, asserts that Joab's main concern is with the State and that he is willing to forfeit even his own life in the service of it. Others echo these sentiments, referring to Joab as a statesman. See, for example, Brueggemann, *First and Second Samuel*, p. 324, who writes, "It is loyal, unmoved Joab who watches over the public trust."

[89] Baldwin, *1&2 Samuel*, p. 273.

[90] Fokkelman, *King David*, p. 277.

Second, a major theme of 1 and 2 Samuel involves honoring God (1 Sam. 2:30) and those whom God has chosen. Even when fleeing from Saul, David still addressed him with the respect due his office (1 Sam. 26:17–18,"my *lord* O *king*"/"why does my *lord* thus pursue his *servant?*"), and consistently refused to harm him. Joab speaks of David's actions shaming the people (19:5), but by his words and actions he dishonors his king. Joab's reproach of David puts him in the same camp as Goliath, or any other person in 1 and 2 Samuel, who dishonors the Lord's anointed.

Third, it is often claimed that if it were not for Joab's hard words, the people would have deserted David. What is often overlooked is that only Joab claims that the people will desert David. Joab's previous rebuke of David proved that he could twist the truth to his own advantage (3:24–25). Since most of Joab's reproof in 2 Samuel 19 consists of half-truths,[91] it casts doubt on this statement as well. In fact, his statement may be a veiled threat that he himself will lead the people away from David.[92] It is most likely a threat aimed to motivate David to action.

Although it is possible to see the narrator's description of the people's attitude in 19:2–3 as a confirmation of Joab's words,[93] it is also possible to interpret it differently. Alter suggests that the people "hear of his [David's] grief and are smitten with shame and apprehension—either out of empathy for their beloved leader, or guilt over the complicity some of their number share in Absalom's death, or fear of potential violence between David and Joab."[94] The text lends support to this interpretation. The expression "the people heard" (19:2) is also found in 18:5, where David gave the original command regarding Absalom. Thus, the expression "the people heard" connects David's former command with David's present grief. Recalling David's previous command, the people now share in his grief.

Finally, as Vannoy suggests, fatherly affection "is not the only way to evaluate David's desire to spare Absalom, nor to assess his grief when he learned of his death."[95] He states, "David's desire to spare Absalom was not the expression of parental sentimentality but rather was the expression of a forgiving spirit rooted in David's own experience of having been forgiven by

---

[91] Bar-Efrat, *Narrative Art*, pp. 60-61, and Fokkelman, *King David*, p. 271, who states that the beginning of Joab's first accusation is true "but, from 7a onwards [6a English], there follow reproaches which show an increasing disregard for the truth."

[92] Ackroyd, *The Second Book of Samuel*, p. 173, as well as others, makes this observation.

[93] Olyan, "Honor, Shame, and Covenant Relations," pp. 208-211, provides a solid argument for the potential truth of Joab's words in light of the cultural context of honor and shame.

[94] Alter, *The David Story*, p. 311.

[95] Vannoy, *1–2 Samuel*, p. 381.

God."[96] This is certainly consistent with David's attitude throughout 1 and 2 Samuel. David's forgiveness of Saul and Abner are exhibits "A" and "B" of his "gentle" attitude toward former adversaries. How much more so his own son, particularly in light of the forgiveness that God had extended to him? Whether this interpretation is correct or not (and I am inclined toward it), it serves to highlight a glaring flaw in Joab's character. Joab is never said to forgive anyone. Joab's *modus operandi* is first, and always, revenge!

The point is not to absolve David of all guilt. The text shows that David had his faults and was responsible in large part for the trouble that came upon him and his kingdom. However, David's faults in this part of 2 Samuel are often used by scholars to justify Joab's words and actions. Although Joab's faults are noted, he is frequently lauded as a statesman and a loyal supporter of David. David's weaknesses and faults, however, should not be used to legitimize Joab's words and actions.

Amasa and the Kiss of Death (2 Sam. 19:13; 20:2–13)

Since a closer examination of these texts is found in the next chapter, only a few observations are made here. Following the battle, David attempts to heal the rift between himself and those who followed Absalom by appointing Amasa, his nephew and Absalom's former general, as commander in place of Joab (19:13). David may have thought this a shrewd move, a way of "killing two birds with one stone." Amasa's appointment not only holds out an olive branch to the former rebel army, but it allows David to strike back at Joab. It is to be understood as David's response to Joab's blistering rebuke. It is also possible that David has learned of Joab's involvement in Absalom's death by this time. Thus, the game between David and Joab continues. It is, however, a costly game for the kingdom, and a deadly game for Amasa—who is caught in the middle of the power struggle between David and Joab.

When Amasa fails to respond quickly enough to the rebellion precipitated by Sheba son of Bichri (2 Sam. 20:1–5), David, still intent on overlooking Joab, puts Abishai in command of the troops (v. 6). As Abishai leaves with the troops, however, the reader is informed, "So *Joab's* men…went out after him" (v. 7). "The fact that they are called 'Joab's men' suggests where the real power is, and where Joab's brother Abishai assumes it must be."[97]

David's demotion has (had) little effect on Joab's command of the troops! The only thing preventing Joab from assuming full control at this point is Amasa, but that is only a minor problem which will be addressed immediately upon Amasa's arrival. As the murder of Amasa demonstrates,

---

[96] Ibid., p. 382. Vannoy cites M. R. Van den Berg as his inspiration for this interpretation.

[97] Alter, *The David Story,* p. 323.

Joab's authority is not inspired by hard-won respect, but by fear and intimidation. "Joab's creed [is] simple: When someone stands in your way, kill him."[98] This brutal act secures his character portrait as a cold-blooded, ruthless killer, who will do whatever it takes to hold on to the reins of power. From the murder of Abner, to the death of Uriah, and the slaying of Absalom, Joab consistently marches to the mantra, "The end justifies the means!"

As Joab approaches Amasa to deliver the fatal blow, his words, which speak of "peace" and familial affection ("my brother"), coupled with his gesture of a welcoming kiss (v. 9), belie his true feelings and motive. They also highlight the vicious nature of his crime. Once again he uses deception in order to disarm his victim and administer the deadly strike (cf. 2 Sam. 3:27).[99] In fact, Joab never faces his victims "man to man." He gains an unfair advantage in each of the three killings he is involved in. Absalom is helplessly hanging in a tree when Joab strikes him, while Abner and Amasa are purposely caught off-guard. Joab does not bravely face his rivals; he finds cowardly ways to dispose of them.

Immediately following the kill, while Amasa "wallows in his blood," Joab's bullying tactics are imitated by an unnamed underling who stands over Amasa and cries out, "Whoever favors Joab and whoever is for David—follow Joab" (v. 11)! This statement is very revealing. First, the bold assumption that being loyal to David means following Joab is a convenient and intimidating misconstrual of the facts! "What in David's view would not be in the least self-evident, is presented as being quite ordinary by skilful propaganda."[100]

Second, it should not go unnoticed that Joab's name precedes David's. David's men are even called "Joab's men" twice in this episode (vv. 7, 11). So who is really in charge, Joab or David? Third, the occurrence of Joab's name holds a two-to-one advantage over David's name in this statement. Is it proper that the battle-cry of a soldier should use the name of a deposed general twice as much as the name of the king? Finally, the fact that Joab's name surrounds David's acknowledges Joab's superiority. David is trapped; he is engulfed by Joab. As Leithart notes, Sheba is not the real threat in this episode—Joab is.[101]

---

[98] Leithart, *A Son to Me*, p. 289.

[99] Wong, "Ehud and Joab," pp. 401-405, notes a number of similarities between Ehud's murder of Eglon in Judges 3 and Joab's murder of Amasa. He believes that Ehud is an unsavory character and that "the author of Samuel was seeking to portray Joab as a 'latter-day Ehud' " (p. 405). I believe the similarities between Ehud and Joab are to draw a *contrast* between the two. While Ehud leads the underdog Israelites in victory over an oppressive foe, Joab uses similar tactics to kill his own countryman and cousin.

[100] Fokkelman, *King David*, p. 330.

[101] Leithart, *A Son to Me*, p. 290.

Joab Gets "A Head" (2 Sam. 20:15–22, 23)

Joab's pursuit of Sheba leads him to the city of Abel of Beth-maachah (20:15) in the northern territory of Israel, where he encounters a "wise woman" (v. 16). It should be recalled that Absalom's rebellion, and the ensuing revolt by Sheba, was precipitated by Joab and a wise woman from the southern town of Tekoa (2 Sam. 14) who deceived and manipulated David into returning Absalom. McCarter notes that there are several verbal links between chapters 14 and 20, and that "in both cases the fate of a man who causes trouble for Israel is decided."[102] Therefore, 2 Samuel 13 and 14 act as a private prologue to these events, while 2 Samuel 20 becomes a public epilogue.[103]

McCarter's contrast between "private" and "public" is significant. What begins as a private family matter (Amnon's rape of Tamar/Absalom's murder of Amnon), later explodes to engulf all of Israel in the fallout. Acting as a parenthesis around this entire series of events is the interaction of Joab with certain "wise women." This recognition is important, for as McCarter states, "If the verbal echoes of chap. 14 in chap. 20 carry a message, it is that *Abishalom* [Absalom] *should not have gone unpunished, that he certainly should not have been permitted to return to court,* a parlous flaw in the fabric of Israelite society" (emphasis mine).[104] In other words, Joab's interaction with the wise woman of Abel lends further confirmation to the fact that his original plan of returning Absalom, implemented by the wise woman of Tekoa, was sheer folly. The events following Absalom's return amply demonstrate this foolishness, and the rebuke by the wise woman of Abel in the current story adds an exclamation point.

When Joab and the army arrive at Abel the city is put under siege. A siege mound is raised against it and they begin to batter the wall (20:15). At this point, the reader's focus is the same as Joab's and the army—the capture of Sheba. However, the focus shifts to the wise woman and the inhabitants of the city in verses 16–19. "With the change of perspective, we suddenly realize that the city under attack is Israelite, part of the people David ruled and wants to rule again."[105] Suddenly, Joab's act of aggression against a city in Israel comes under scrutiny by both the woman and the reader. Abel is characterized as a noble city, with an ancient reputation for settling disputes (v. 18). The wise woman, who is clearly a leader within the city (perhaps its judge),[106]

---

[102] McCarter, *II Samuel*, p. 351. See also, Claudia Camp, "The Wise Women of 2 Samuel: A Role Model for Women in Early Israel?," *CBQ*, 43/1, 1981, pp. 14-29.

[103] McCarter, p. 351.

[104] Ibid.

[105] Marcia L. Geyer, "Stopping the Juggernaut: A Close Reading of 2 Samuel 20:13–22," *USQR* 41, 1986, p. 36.

[106] Ibid., p. 38.

identifies herself as one who is "peaceable and faithful in Israel" (v. 19). The woman indicts Joab by stating, "You seek to destroy a city and a mother in Israel. Why would you swallow up the inheritance of the LORD?"[107]

> "The inheritance of Yahweh" asserts claims against Joab on a number of levels. Most fundamentally, Abel is Israelite, and Joab's siege on it is an outrage. At the level of metaphor, the woman caps her charge of matricide with a charge that Joab wars against God. Finally, Israelite law comes from Yahweh, not from the king. Joab has broken Yahweh's law on several counts. First, as the monarchy's representative, he had no right to make war on an Israelite city. Second, he gave the city no opportunity to submit voluntarily before opening siege against it. Third, Joab's target is the seat of the institutional conservator of Yahweh's law and of social stability in its region. Fourth, Joab's siege threatens to precipitate another civil war, this time along regional lines which could destroy the unity of "the inheritance of Yahweh." The charge that Joab is destroying the inheritance of Yahweh has a substantial foundation in law as well as in metaphor.[108]

The charge is, indeed, a serious one. Joab's actions are revealed as rash and cruel. He did not consult the Lord or the inhabitants of Abel before laying siege to it. He gave no consideration to a diplomatic solution. He assumed the worst and would have destroyed the city and those in it, were it not for the intervention of this wise woman. The woman's words, "I am peaceable/you seek to destroy," are surely intended as a characterization of Joab that goes beyond the present scene. In fact, in the previous scene, Joab had greeted his cousin Amasa with the word "peace," only to destroy him. Joab's actions prove to be consistent: if you are in the way of him achieving his goal, prepare for destruction!

This stark indictment forces Joab into a strong denial, which sounds ironic considering his past actions: "Far be it, far be it from me, that I should swallow up or destroy" (v. 20)! What? Joab destroy? Never! ("Yeah right," winks the narrator.) Joab's denial leads to his reason for the attack which, in turn, leads to negotiations (where the process should have begun in the first place). Joab demands that Sheba be handed over; then he will depart from the city. The woman goes one better: "Watch, his head will be thrown to you

---

[107] "Inheritance of God/Yahweh" is one of the verbal parallels between the two wise women of 2 Sam. 14 and 20. Cf. 2 Sam. 14:16 with 2 Sam. 20:19.
[108] Ibid., pp. 38-39.

over the wall" (v. 21). Thanks to the wise woman's intervention, Joab gets "a head" (v. 22).

True to the agreement, Joab blows the trumpet and the men return to their tents, a verbal echo of the way Sheba's revolt began (v. 1), and a reminder of the end of similar conflicts in the past (2 Sam. 2:28; 18:16). The scene concludes by saying, "So Joab returned to the king at Jerusalem." One can only imagine what kind of reception greeted Joab upon his return! It is possible, however, that David responded with his customary silence, and perhaps this is why the story ends as it does. Whatever happened, verse 23 informs us that Joab remained in his usual position "over all the army of Israel."[109] In the ongoing sparring match between David and Joab, this round goes to Joab; but it is David who will have the final word.

David's Census "Plagues" Joab (2 Sam. 24:1–9)

2 Samuel 24 is not only the concluding chapter of the book, it is also the counterpart of 2 Samuel 21, resulting in a chiastic arrangement to the final chapters of 2 Samuel.[110] In chapters 21 and 24 there is a crisis precipitated by a king, that involves the punishment of people in the kingdom, ultimately resulting in a display of God's mercy. In chapter 24, the crisis is motivated by God's anger against Israel which results in God "inciting" David to number the people (v. 1). Although this story provokes many interesting theological questions, our concern is Joab and the small part he plays in the narrative.[111]

In verse 2 Joab, is called "commander" of the army for the first and only time in the book,[112] and is told to go and number the people throughout

---

[109] Leithart, *A Son to Me*, p. 291, states that Joab's "name stands in the text where we expect to find David's name (v. 23)." Therefore, he concludes that, "Textually, Joab has replaced David." On the other hand, Firth, *1&2 Samuel*, p. 498, thinks that David's name is omitted because his kingship has been stressed in the previous chapters.
[110] A Crisis in David's kingdom due to Saul's sin (21:1–14)
   B David's heroes and their exploits (21:15–22)
      C David's psalm (22:1–51)
      C' David's psalm (23:1–7)
   B' David's heroes and their exploits (23:8–39)
A' Crisis in David's kingdom due to Israel's sin (24:1–25)
[111] In pursuing the larger questions and issues raised by this narrative, the reader is referred to the commentaries listed in the Bibliography.
[112] Joab is said elsewhere to be "over" the army (2 Sam. 8:16; 20:23), and we are informed that Absalom made Amasa "over the army" instead of Joab (2 Sam. 17:25); but he is never called "commander" in 2 Samuel except here. However, even here the reference to "commander" is ambiguous, as the Greek text reads, "to Joab and *to the commanders of the armies that were with him.*" The Hebrew text makes a similar distinction in v. 4 (twice), suggesting the Greek text may be the more original reading. If this is

the kingdom. It is not surprising that Joab offers resistance to David's command (he has done so before), but on this occasion his resistance is made politely and with a pious motive in mind. Joab responds, "Now may the LORD your God add to the people a hundred times more than there are, and may the eyes of my lord the king see it. But why does my lord the king desire this thing?" (v. 3). It is only the second time in the entire narrative that Joab uses polite language when addressing David (see 2 Sam. 14:22). Furthermore, he voices the devout wish that God would multiply the people and that David would live to see it. He is also backed up by the other commanders who, apparently, also have misgivings about this order (v. 4).

Joab's polite address is very "un-Joab-like." His pious-sounding words give the reader pause for thought. Not only are they unusual, but they seem contradictory to the Joab we have come to know and love/hate. They recall the Joab who encouraged his men to be strong, while leaving their fate in the hands of the Lord (2 Samuel 10:12).

On the one hand, Joab's objection reminds us that he is a complex character. He has moments of courage (2 Sam. 10:9–14); he is capable of soft words and perhaps even fatherly concern (2 Sam. 18:20, 22); and now even he can be reluctant to commit an irreverent act. On the other hand, it seems that the purpose of Joab's objection serves more to highlight the gravity of David's sin, than to emphasize the piety of Joab. His reaction acts as a foil to David's command in this story. The point is, if even Joab hesitates to number the people, and we all know how unscrupulous he can be, then David's command must involve a serious infraction!

There is yet another way to view Joab's reaction that has been overlooked. While Joab's words sound devout, they are actually opposed to God's purposes. The narrator specifically says that God "incited David" (v. 1). Therefore, David's command to number the people is, in effect, in line with God's purpose to bring judgment on Israel. Joab's resistance to David is, therefore, resistance against God, in spite of his religious vocabulary. This view treads on very controversial ground,[113] but follows the logic of the text. Of course, Joab and the other leaders acquiesce to David's order, and thus God's purposes are ultimately fulfilled. Perhaps it is the invisible hand and purposes of God that explain why "the king's word prevailed against Joab" (v. 4a).

A superficial reading of this story makes it possible to add a little light to the dark character sketch of Joab. It is indeed surprising to see Joab

---

the case, then the author of 2 Samuel consistently avoids calling Joab "commander." However, Joab is called "commander" unambiguously in 1 Kings 1:19.

[113] Controversial questions include such things as: God's sovereignty vs. human free will; does God incite someone in a direction that leads to sin, etc.? Again, I refer the reader to the various commentaries in the Bibliography, as such questions take us far beyond a character sketch of Joab.

dispensing spiritual advice to David! It must also be admitted that Joab's language toward David is polite and respectful. This makes Joab's character more interesting and even a little less predictable.

At a deeper level, Joab's objection serves to highlight David's sinful motivation and says more about David than Joab. If Joab does have scruples, then they seem easily overcome by David's insistence. On the other hand, I have also suggested a more controversial reading of the story (on the previous page) that paints Joab as one who initially resists the will of God, but who eventually capitulates under the pressure exerted by his king. It is difficult to choose between these options but, either way, a mixed portrait of Joab is presented in which one can observe both positive and negative qualities.

Joab Joins the Coup but "Flies the Coop" (1 Kings 1:7, 19, 25, 41, 49)

Although Joab had been a part of David's political inner circle for a long time, he had never been a part of David's personal inner circle. As the old king nears the end of his life, political factions vying for control of the kingdom begin to emerge. Solomon, the heir apparent,[114] has a loyal following that includes Zadok the priest, Benaiah captain of the guard, and Nathan the prophet (1 Kings 1:8). Joab joins forces with Adonijah and Abiathar (v. 7), hoping to maintain his power base. Adonijah invites all of his supporters to En Rogel, just outside the city of Jerusalem, where he participates in a coronation feast and is proclaimed king (vv. 19, 25). The coup is short-lived, however, when his guests hear commotion coming from the city. When a horn is sounded (the same instrument used frequently by Joab—2 Sam. 2:28; 18:16; 20:22), the seasoned veteran, Joab, is the first to voice his concern: "Why is the city in such a noisy uproar" (v. 41)? Bewilderment turns to fear, causing all of Adonijah's guests to flee (v. 49), as it becomes apparent through Jonathan's (the son of Abiathar the priest) report that there is another king in town. It is Joab's association with Adonijah that eventually presents Solomon with legitimate grounds to have him eliminated (1 Kings 2:28–34), fulfilling the death-bed counsel of his father (1 Kings 2:5–6).

Slaying Joab: The "Horns" of a Dilemma (1 Kings 2:5–6; 28–34)

Having charged Solomon with keeping the word of God (1 Kings 2:1–4), David dispenses some final political advice to Solomon. Instruction for the gracious treatment of Barzillai's sons is surrounded by grim counsel

---

[114] Some dispute this and claim that Adonijah, being the eldest living son, was the true heir to the throne. For a defense of Solomon as the true heir see chap. 19, pp. 246-247, and chap. 25, pp. 387-388.

on how to deal with two troublemakers in the kingdom (2:5–9).[115] At the top of the list is Joab (vv. 5–6). Our portrait of Joab has shown him to be far from the loyal commander that many suppose him to be, and thus, David is not unjust in telling Solomon to see that he is punished.[116] David cites the murders of Abner and Amasa as justification for Joab's death.[117] As Bar-Efrat has noted, this statement by David is another indication of his genuine grief at the death of Abner and further confirmation of his words and actions in 2 Samuel 3:28–39.[118]

Furthermore, David's concern over bloodguilt should be taken seriously. Bloodguilt is a major theme in the narratives of 1 and 2 Samuel,[119] not to mention a serious concern of the Law (Num. 35:30–34; Deut. 19:1–13; 21:1–9). While Saul was guilty of shedding innocent blood, the author consistently disassociates David from bloodguilt, except in the case of Uriah. David equates Joab's murder of Abner and Amasa with "what he did to me" (2:5), suggesting that, as king, David was liable for the innocent blood shed by his subordinate Joab. Solomon will later proclaim, "Their blood shall therefore return upon the head of Joab and upon the head of his descendants forever. But upon David and his descendants, upon his house and his throne, there shall be peace forever from the LORD" (1 Kings 2:33). These are not merely politically expedient words, covering an aggressive act with religious jargon, as some suppose.[120] Nelson captures the ancient mindset on shedding innocent blood:

> The issue of bloodguilt is raised by verse 5…to indicate that Joab's bloody deed led to a persistent, objective guilt borne by David, who as king was responsible for his subordinate's actions….Bloodguilt, viewed as something objectively real,

---

[115] We have previously discussed the nature of David's advice to Solomon. I am not in agreement with those who see it as a "death-bed vendetta." For my views, see chap. 15, pp. 188-190.

[116] *Contra* Provan, *1 and 2 Kings*, NIBC (Peabody: Hendrickson Publishers, Inc., 1995), p. 33, who refers to him as "loyal Joab."

[117] Wong, "Ehud and Joab," p. 400, n. 2, is correct in asserting that David and Solomon could legitimately have other reasons for eliminating Joab, but it does not mean that the stated reason must be false.

[118] Bar-Efrat, *Narrative Art*, p. 183.

[119] Passages include: 1 Sam. 22:17–19; 24:10; 25:30–32; 26:9, 11; 2 Sam. 1:14–16; 3:29, 37, 39; 4:9–12; 12:9; 16:7–8; 21:1–9.

[120] For example, Iain Provan, "Why Barzillai of Gilead (1 Kings 2:7)? Narrative Art and the Hermeneutics of Suspicion in 1 Kings 1–2," p. 110.

had to be neutralized lest the Davidic house be put in mortal danger.[121]

Because Joab had "shed the blood of war *in peace*(time)," David tells his son Solomon not to "let his [Joab's] gray hair go down to Sheol [the grave] *in peace*" (2:6—my translations). Thus, Joab is to reap what he has sowed. Although David was fully justified in seeking to punish Joab and clear his kingdom of bloodguilt, he was certainly wrong in passing on the responsibility to Solomon.[122]

Adonijah's blunder in asking for the hand of Abishag (1 Kings 2:13–25) creates the opportunity for Solomon to put David's words into action. Anderson notes, "Joab ironically found himself in a position similar to Abner and Amasa. He was now the man who had supported the rival of Israel's king, and his loyalty to Israel's king would now be held in suspicion."[123] Upon hearing of Adonijah's execution and Abiathar's banishment, Joab takes a page out of Adonijah's book and flees to the altar of the Lord (2:28). Originally, Solomon spared Adonijah when he had fled and taken hold of the horns of the altar (1 Kings 1:50–53); no doubt Joab hopes for similar treatment.

This action appears to be based on Exodus 21:12–14. However, the law in Exodus only protects the man who did not murder with premeditation.[124] Joab's murders of Abner and Amasa clearly do not qualify him for clemency. Grabbing the horns of the altar is the act of a desperate man, and perhaps Joab thought that Solomon did not have the stomach for slaying someone who refused to leave the sanctuary.[125] It is ironic that this man who only used the Lord's name in religious clichés, in the end, runs to find sanctuary at the Lord's altar. Like many, Joab seeks to use the Lord and the things of the Lord when it comes to self-preservation, but he exhibits no repentance

---

[121] Nelson, *First and Second Kings*, p. 24. Similarly, Alter, *The David Story*, p. 375, states, "The concentration on blood reflects a general belief that blood shed in murder lingers over not only the murderer but also over those associated with the victim like a contaminating miasma until it is 'redeemed' or 'taken away' by vengeance."

[122] Donald J. Wiseman, *1 and 2 Kings*, TOTC (Leicester: IVP, 1993), p. 77.

[123] Joel Edmund Anderson, "A Narrative Reading of Solomon's Execution of Joab in 1 Kings 1–2: Letting Story Interpret Story," *JESOT* 1.1, 2012, p. 56.

[124] For a further discussion of this passage, see chap. 25, p. 391.

[125] Jonathan Burnside, "Flight of the Fugitives: Rethinking the Relationship Between Biblical Law (Exodus 21:12–14) and the Davidic Succession Narrative (1 Kings 1–2)," *JBL* 12/3, 2010, p. 430, states, "Joab might have been counting on the fact that, since no action had been taken against him in David's lifetime, Solomon might not see him as being close to the paradigm of the recent, premeditated killer. There was a chance that his distance from the paradigm would mean that he would not be treated the same as an illegitimate asylum seeker. If so, it was a political miscalculation."

or remorse. He is obstinate to the end, refusing Benaiah's command to come out (v. 30).

It is of note that Joab does not face his death bravely, as we might expect a battle-hardened warrior to do, but instead he tries one last time to manipulate circumstances toward a favorable outcome for himself. Benaiah's hesitation at killing Joab by the altar (v. 30), demonstrates what a strong ploy this was on Joab's part. However, "not even presence at YHWH'S altar is sufficient to protect the premeditating killer. This being so, Solomon's actions may be seen as consistent with Exod. 21:14, rather than a violation of the law."[126] Thus in Solomon, Joab meets his match. He encounters a king who acts with wisdom (1 Kings 2:6) and cannot be manipulated by words or circumstances.

As in the story of Shimei's execution, the words "innocent" (translated "guiltless" in 1 Kings 2:9) and "blood" are significant.[127] Joab has shed innocent blood and therefore, it is imperative that his own blood be required in payment. Allowing the murderer to go free would bring blood upon the house of David (vv. 31–32). Thus when Joab tells Benaiah, "No, but I will die here" (v. 30), Solomon shows no hesitation in having Benaiah carry out the execution.

While Joab's association with Adonijah provides Solomon with a political motive to remove him, Solomon's stated reason for Joab's execution echoes the words of David (cf. vv. 5 and 32). Two times in 1 Kings 2 we are told by two kings (David and Solomon) that Joab was deserving of death for the murders of Abner and Amasa. This is surely not accidental. Through the words of David and Solomon the narrator makes the point that God's justice is not thwarted. We are reminded again of Hannah's words, "By strength no man shall prevail" (1 Sam. 2:9), and, "He will give strength to His king, and exalt the horn of His anointed" (1 Sam. 2:10).

Scholars who view 1 Kings 2 as "pro-Solomonic propaganda," or who use a "hermeneutic of suspicion" to interpret these events, overlook the connection between 1 Samuel 2:10, 2 Samuel 22:51, and 1 Kings 2:12, 33, and 45–46. Furthermore, Joab is put to death because "The LORD kills and makes alive; he brings down to the grave and brings up" (1 Sam. 2:6). He dies because he trusts in his own might and wits rather than the strength and wisdom of the Lord. He dies because he has not learned the lesson that, "The Lord does not save with sword and spear" (1 Sam. 17:47).

From a New Testament perspective, Joab dies because, "all who take the sword will perish by the sword" (Matt. 26:52). Finally, he dies in fulfillment of David's words who said, "The LORD shall repay the evildoer according to his wickedness" following the murder of Abner (2 Sam. 3:39). If

---

126 Ibid., p. 430, n. 43.
127 See the discussion in chap. 15, pp. 184-186.

Solomon's kingdom is to be established in righteousness and justice, people like Joab must be removed.

The fact that Joab is given a proper burial in his own house (v. 34) is evidence that all is done properly and in accordance with the Law (Deut. 21:23). By murdering Abner and Amasa, Joab had maintained his standing as commander of the army. It is only fitting then that, following Joab's execution, Benaiah is awarded that same position (v. 35). Once again, the story shows "what goes around comes around."

Joab's Bloody Legacy (1 Kings 11:14–16)

One final incident recorded in 1 Kings 11:15–16 puts an exclamation point on the brutal nature of Joab's leadership. It is the lead story within the context of people who became adversaries to Solomon's kingdom (1 Kings 11:14–40). At least one of Joab's actions continued to have a negative effect on Israel, long after his death. This story details an incident not recorded in the defeat of Edom in 2 Samuel 8:13–14. Joab is dispatched on a burial detail which, surprisingly, turns into a six-month campaign to annihilate every male (of military age?) in Edom. Thus, "it was the needless barbarism of one of David's officers on a burial detail which was now rebounding in resentment against David's son."[128] As with any pogrom, this military action left a deep scar on the inhabitants of Edom. Consequently, Joab's ruthless exploit against Edom results in hostile repercussions for Solomon and the kingdom of Israel. The reader of 2 Samuel may recall a similar incident in which violence on the part of Saul caused problems for David and Israel (2 Sam. 21:1–14). Whereas David's actions result in future blessing for his descendants (e.g., 1 Kings 11:32; 15:4–5), Joab's legacy, like Saul's before him, brings harm to God's people.

Conclusion: Joab and Machiavelli

Caleb Henry is correct when he asserts, "To a surprising degree, the OT historical narrative of Joab reads like a practical manual of Machiavellian tactics."[129] For Joab, "might makes right," and "the end justifies the means." What is frequently (mis)construed by some as loyalty for David has, on further examination, proven to be what Joab thought was best for himself.[130] Many are motivated by self-interest, but what sets Joab apart was his ruthless pursuit of that goal. It can be confidently asserted that the characteristics of

---

[128] Auld, *Kings*, p. 81.

[129] Henry, "Joab: A Biblical Critique of Machiavellian Tactics," p. 330.

[130] It is also possible that Joab deceived himself into thinking his way was also best for Israel. Self-centered people often delude themselves.

"love, joy, peace, longsuffering, kindness, goodness, faithfulness, gentleness, and self-control" (Gal. 5:22–23) were not a normal part of his repertoire: nor, we might add, was forgiveness. On the other hand, "hatred, contentions, jealousies, outbursts of wrath, and selfish ambitions" (Gal. 5:20), not to mention "envy" and "murders" (Gal. 5:21), describe his character more accurately.

Joab's few "good" moments are evidence that no human being is utterly evil. That distinction is reserved for the "Prince of Demons." The good moments in Joab's story are an illustration of the Bible's realistic portrayal of its characters. However, when Joab's character is measured against the lists in Galatians his portrait becomes clear. He is unequivocally a man of the flesh (Gal. 5:19, "Now the works of the flesh are evident...").

In terms of the theology of 1 and 2 Samuel, Joab was a man who grasped for power and control—he was a taker. He was a master of manipulation and intimidation. He was no stranger to lies and half-truths, when these suited his purpose. Although he paid lip-service to God's sovereignty (2 Sam. 10:12, "may the LORD do what is good in His sight), he lived by a different ethic. In this sense he was the ancestor of all those today who can quote a religious slogan, but do not apply it to their life and actions.

One of the most telling facts regarding the author's evaluation of Joab is his absence from the list of David's mighty men, as Henry insightfully observes:

> Although the OT describes his martial spirit, he is specifically not called a great warrior; among the two OT lists of David's mighty men, Joab is nowhere to be found despite the inclusion of Joab's two brothers and Joab's armor bearer (2 Sam 23:8–39; 1 Chr 11:10–47). What are the authors of Samuel and Chronicles implying by calling everyone around Joab, but not Joab, mighty warriors?[131]

This impression is reinforced by the narratives that describe his killing of Abner, Absalom, and Amasa. As noted above, Joab never faced his adversaries "man to man." In each case, whether through deception or physical circumstances, he saw to it that he had a decided advantage. When Joab finally faced his own death, his reaction is unimpressive. Rather than facing it bravely, he fled and begged for his life by attempting to take advantage of a law that did not apply to him. It is ironic that he died at one of the most sacred sites in Israel. On the one hand, his blood stained an altar he had no right to touch. On the other hand, he died before the Lord in just retribution for his crimes.

Joab's obstinacy to the end and his unwillingness to even show any remorse are a warning to all who live their lives with a similar ruthless aban-

---

[131] Ibid., pp. 330-331.

don. He seemed to escape justice for many years, but his end teaches us that there is a "day of reckoning," when evil will be repaid. It is ironic that willful people like Joab think that they are in control of their own, as well as others', destinies. Ultimately, as the books of Samuel and Kings teach, God's will is accomplished either with or without our co-operation. No power-hungry human being can thwart the plans and purposes of an almighty God—who breaks the bows of mighty men but girds with strength those who stumble (1 Sam. 2:4). Joab would have done well to have heeded these words of Hannah. As Henry states:

> The OT is full of individuals who attempted to fool providence. "And it happened" that their actions were the means God used to fulfill his word. This was also true for Joab. Joab attempted to manipulate David's divinely ordained rule for his own purposes, but God used Joab's ambition to ensure David's rule. Who was using whom? Machiavelli should have better appreciated the OT stories he appropriated. David's actions were successful and celebrated because David was concerned with divine ends. Joab has been largely forgotten because Joab was only concerned with necessity and personal ambition.[132]

---

[132] Ibid., p. 332.

Chapter 21

Abishai, Asahel, and Amasa: Warriors (David's nephews)

The three men examined in this chapter have three things in common: they are David's nephews (by his two sisters), they are warriors, and their appearances in the narrative of 1 and 2 Samuel are limited, making them less than full-fledged characters.[1] Two of the three share other similarities. For example, Abishai and Asahel are brothers, while Amasa is their cousin. Abishai and Asahel are loyal to David, but Amasa vacillates in his devotion. On the other hand, Asahel and Amasa share the unenviable characteristic of being ineffective soldiers, while Abishai is very effective. There is no account of Abishai's death, but the deaths of Asahel and Amasa are graphically recorded sharing similar words and details. Finally, while Asahel may have been captain over a division of the army,[2] he never exercised the authority that Abishai and Amasa did.

Abishai: Eager for the Kill (1 Sam. 26:6–11)

"What have I to do with you, you sons of Zeruiah?"—David (2 Sam. 16:9)

Abishai's initial appearance in the story portrays him as brave, impetuous, and ready to kill. For good and for ill, these qualities characterize him throughout the narratives of 1 and 2 Samuel. He is introduced in two ways. First, as the "son of Zeruiah"—an unusual description, as noted in the previous chapter. Second, he is introduced as the "brother of Joab" (v. 6). Presumably the author expects his readers to know who Zeruiah and Joab are, although this is the first mention of either. As noted before, the phrase "son(s) of Zeruiah" can be a loaded expression. It may contrast the ruthless deeds of these men with the original meaning of their mother's name "balm," or it may be a play on similar-sounding words which mean "hard," "adversary," etc.[3] Although Abishai is the first to appear in the story, he will later be eclipsed by his brother Joab.

The first quality evident in Abishai is his eagerness to perform a daring deed. David approaches him and another soldier, Ahimelech the Hittite, and asks who will go down with him to Saul's camp. Although Ahimelech is

---

[1] Such characters are often labelled "flat" characters. See the "Introduction," p. 10.

[2] 1 Chron. 27:7 indicates that in the fourth month he was captain over a division of David's army. Some believe this honor was accorded Asahel posthumously since this verse reflects David's reign over all Israel, and Asahel was killed while David reigned only over Judah.

[3] See chap. 20, pp. 259-260.

mentioned first, it is Abishai who responds. Ahimelech's silence highlights Abishai's enthusiasm for the dangerous task.[4]

1 Samuel 26 is the third part of a triptych (chaps. 24–26) centering on the theme of bloodguilt and vengeance. Like his future descendant Jesus, David is tempted three times in these chapters to take matters into his own hands (see Matt. 4; Luke 4). This theme has already been noted in the Abigail story where David nearly succumbed to the temptation of killing Nabal (chap. 25).[5] Now, however, as David sneaks into Saul's camp, it is not with the intention of taking vengeance, but proving a point.

David's first encounter with Saul in the cave at En Gedi (chap. 24), and the wise advice he received from Abigail (chap. 25) had taught him the valuable lesson of leaving outcomes to God. Abishai had not learned the same lesson. Now as they reach the middle of the camp where Saul is lying down, his spear at his head, Abishai is the first to speak: "God has delivered your enemy into your hand this day. Now therefore, please, let me strike him at once with the spear, right to the earth; and I will not have to strike him a second time!" (26:8).

Abishai's opening words, "God has delivered your enemy into your hand" are reminiscent of David's men's words in 24:4. On that occasion David arose and cut off the edge of Saul's robe. Perhaps that situation had taught Abishai that David would not strike Saul (24:6–7),[6] or perhaps Abishai was hoping for the glory of the kill. Either way, he offers to efficiently put an end to Saul's life. The desire to *pin* (literal translation) Saul to the earth, while not having to strike *twice*, ironically recalls the *two* occasions Saul tried to *pin* David to the wall with the very same spear (1 Sam. 18:11).[7] Abishai's words also anticipate the actions of his brother Joab, who murders Amasa with one blow (2 Sam. 20:10), highlighting the fact that the sons of Zeruiah are masters of the craft of killing.

David is quick to prevent Abishai from taking any deadly action. He "refuses to accept an argument that associates providence with the right to initiate violence."[8] David has learned from his experience with Abigail and Nabal that the Lord will handle Saul in his own way. He suggests three ways in which Saul might meet his fate: "the LORD shall strike him, or his day shall come to die, or he shall go out to battle and perish" (26:10). The first of these alternatives happened to Nabal (25:38), while the third will eventually happen to Saul (1 Sam. 31:1–6). David uses the Lord's name five times in 26:9–11, but it is clear that Abishai does not possess the same sensitivity towards the

[4] Klein, *1 Samuel*, p. 257.
[5] See chap. 18, "Abigail: The Peacemaker."
[6] Firth, *1&2 Samuel*, p. 277.
[7] Fokkelman, *Crossing Fates*, "Abishai now wishes to avenge and surpass that attack on his master by dispatching Saul in one blow with the same weapon," p. 535.
[8] Firth, *1&2 Samuel*, p. 277.

Lord's will that David does. In his first appearance, Abishai seems to be a man who prefers to act hastily with the sword (or spear), rather than consider the larger picture or the consequences associated with such actions.

Off with His Head (2 Sam. 16:9–11)

Although Abishai appears in other passages between 1 Samuel 26 and 2 Samuel 16, he plays only a minor role as co-conspirator or co-commander with his more dominant brother Joab (2 Sam. 2:18, 24; 3:30; 10:10, 14).[9] It is as David is fleeing from Absalom and being pelted by rocks and dirt from Shimei, that Abishai once again steps to the foreground (16:9–11). The picture is consistent with the Abishai first met in 1 Samuel 26. Abishai sees no reason to tolerate Shimei's cursing, and asks David for permission to go over and take his head off (v. 9). Is it coincidental that it is once again another Saulide that Abishai is ready to do in?[10]

His reference to Shimei as "this dead dog" is extremely derogatory. When this expression is used of oneself, as when David (1 Sam. 24:14) or Mephibosheth (2 Sam. 9:8) use it, it is an expression of humility.[11] When used of another, however, it is equivalent to "trash or riffraff."[12] Abishai's contrast of "this dead dog" with "my lord the king" could not be starker,[13] yet David once again refuses to accede to Abishai's violent request. As in 1 Samuel 26, David's answer is threefold: 1) perhaps the Lord has told him to curse; 2) if my own son is against me, then it is not surprising that this Benjamite is; and 3) perhaps the Lord will look on Shimei's cursing and be gracious (vv. 10–12). Once again Abishai has failed to take into account the religious and political consequences of his proposed rash act. As Brueggemann states,

> David's response to Abishai (vv. 10–12) again shows David's
> capacity to hold together political realism and genuine piety.
> The realism is that the sons of Zeruiah must not commit a
> provocative act. The piety is that David must take his chan-
> ces with the curse of Shimei, believing that even the curse is
> subject to the rule of Yahweh.[14]

---

[9] The same is true in 2 Sam. 18:2, 5, and 12.

[10] The sons of Zeruiah seem to have a vendetta against Saul and his family. Perhaps it is because of Saul's persecution of David, and in particular the fact that *all* of David's family were forced to flee their homes and live with him in the wilderness (1 Sam. 22:1–2).

[11] See the discussion on p. 169, n. 14.

[12] McCarter, *II Samuel*, p. 373.

[13] Alter, *The David Story*, p. 292.

[14] Brueggemann, *First and Second Samuel*, p. 308.

David's willingness to accept the Lord's punishment, and trust the Lord's grace, stands in contrast to Abishai's hot-tempered response. His question, "What to me and to you, O sons of Zeruiah?" (literal translation) has been variously translated,[15] but its meaning draws a clear distinction between David's way and that of Abishai and Joab. Although Abishai is a "stalwart follower of David," his violent reaction equates him with Shimei.[16]

The Accuser (2 Sam. 19:21–23)

As David prepares to return to Jerusalem after Absalom's defeat, Abishai seizes one final opportunity to condemn Shimei. Acting as an uninvited prosecuting attorney, Abishai follows up Shimei's confession of guilt and plea for mercy with a recitation of his crime and pronouncement of the death sentence (v. 21). In fact, Abishai asks for the death penalty before citing Shimei's crime! Abishai's rashness is again obvious, as he interrupts the proceedings with his statement before David even has a chance to respond to Shimei. Abishai does show a bit more prudence on this occasion as he appeals to the law about cursing the king (see Exod. 22:28). Ironically he appears to be using David's own reasoning about the sacrosanct nature of the Lord's anointed (1 Sam. 24:6; 26:8). The question inferred is, "Does not pelting you with stones constitute stretching out one's hand against the Lord's anointed?" Had not David himself said that such a one would be guilty?

Abishai appears to have a strong argument, but once again he has not taken the full set of circumstances into account; or, has he? Why does Abishai feel compelled to interrupt the proceedings and make this accusation? Is David not aware of Shimei's actions? Is David also not aware of his own previous words about the Lord's anointed? The natural expectation is that David will condemn Shimei, but Abishai seems to know that David will not. His response seems to be geared to force David to make the "right" decision. After all, why speak up if he is convinced that David will condemn Shimei?

Two factors suggest why Abishai felt compelled to speak. First, Abishai was all too aware of David's gracious side; he had seen it on many

---

[15] McCarter, *II Samuel*, p. 374, translates it as, "What do you sons of Zeruiah have against me, that you continuously cause me trouble?" He is in disagreement with R. E. Brown, who suggests that the idiom here can mean, "This is not our concern." Peggy L. Day, "Abishai the *śāṭān* in 2 Samuel 19:17–24," *CBQ* 49, 1987, p. 544, n. 6, admits to various shades of meaning for this phrase, but opts for the translation, "How does it concern you, you sons of Zeruiah?" I am inclined to accept the NIV's rendering, "What do you and I have in common, you sons of Zeruiah?" This rebuke recalls David's words in 2 Sam. 3:39, where he states in strong terms the difference between himself and the sons of Zeruiah. For further comments on the meaning of 2 Sam. 3:39 see, chap. 20, pp. 267–268.

[16] Fokkelman, *King David*, p. 198.

occasions (1 Sam. 24:4–7; 26:8–12; 2 Sam. 3:20–39; 16:9–11). Second, Shimei is accompanied by one thousand Benjamites, a not-so-subtle political ploy on Shimei's part to make David deal favorably with him. It appears that Abishai does not want David to "soften" (2 Sam. 3:39), either due to his gracious nature or the political pressure that now confronts him. Like any "tough guy," Abishai wants to make it clear that David and his men are not going to be bullied into making a lenient decision; Shimei deserves to die, period.

This interpretation suggests that Abishai is aware of the political pressure placed upon David at this moment, and he does not want him to give in to it. This implies a certain machismo about Abishai, which is very consistent with his character portrayal. However, the problem with machismo is that it dictates a response based on the need to appear tough, rather than on true wisdom. While Abishai, to his thinking, has taken all the circumstances into account, in reality he has not. His response is wrong on two counts: 1) He seeks to use the law to achieve his own selfish goal of killing Shimei. In this he is not so different from Abner who used the Lord's name when it suited his purpose (2 Sam. 3:9–10, 17); and 2) His machismo underestimates the damage that could be done to the fragile unity of David's kingdom. "The sons of Zeruiah have no political sensitivity. They impress one as military men who are unknowing and uncaring about diplomacy."[17] Later, Sheba's action demonstrates the animosity that some in Benjamin still had for the king and how delicate the political situation was (2 Sam. 20:1–2).

David is not as short-sighted as Abishai, and responds with the same expression used in 2 Samuel 16:10: "What do you and I have in common, you sons of Zeruiah?" (19:22). Once again, David is disassociating himself from Abishai's intentions, and his use of the tag "son(s) of Zeruiah" is derisive. It is possible that it was a title they wore proudly, but in David's mouth it becomes a label voicing contempt for these brothers.

"This day you have become my adversaries" is best rendered, "that you are becoming today an accuser on my behalf?"[18] The word *śāṭān* can mean either "adversary" or "accuser."[19] Shimei does not wish to wait for the formalities of a court hearing; his confession of guilt and plea for mercy to David, who is acting as judge, has established a trial right on the banks of the Jordan. Abishai has taken it upon himself to step forward as prosecutor. The forensic context suggests that David is rebuking Abishai for interfering and acting like a prosecuting attorney. He assures him that he is perfectly capable, as king, of making his own decision in this case, without any interference from the sons of Zeruiah. Shimei's life is spared in spite of Abishai's argu-

---

[17] Brueggemann, *First and Second Samuel*, p. 327.
[18] Day, "Abishai the *śāṭān* in 2 Samuel 19:17–24," pp. 544-545.
[19] By New Testament times the word *śāṭān* had come to describe the prince of demons, but in ancient times it referred to an adversary or accuser.

ment. For a third time, the vengeful impulse of this son of Zeruiah has been thwarted by David.

Celebrated Warrior and Commander (2 Sam. 21:15–17; 23:18–19)

The final two passages in which Abishai appears are found in the "B" sections of an elaborate chiasm stretching from 2 Samuel 21–24.[20] These "B" sections (2 Sam. 21:15–22; 23:8–39) contain anecdotes about the military exploits of some of Israel's most outstanding heroes during the reign of David. Both sections describe Abishai in glowing terms.

Abishai resurfaces in 2 Samuel 21:15–17, which is the first of four vignettes describing victories over "the Rapha" (21:15–22). The Rapha may be related to the gigantic people mentioned in Deuteronomy (2:11, 20; 3:11).[21] Hence the word is sometimes translated "giant." The mention of Goliath in this section (2 Sam. 21:19) adds weight to this translation. Whatever the exact meaning is,[22] the Rapha were definitely fierce warriors, and these verses celebrate the brave men who confronted and killed them.

The first story opens with David accompanying his men into battle and becoming exhausted. Whether David was older at this point (as most commentators suppose), or whether the Philistines made a concerted effort to kill him, thus tiring him,[23] is not clear. The important point is that one of the Philistine champions, Ishbi-Benob, noticed David's exhaustion and boasted he would kill him (v. 15–16). The danger to David is highlighted by a description of Ishbi-Benob's weaponry. He had a spearhead that weighed three hundred shekels (7.5 lbs.) and possessed some type of "new" weapon, perhaps a sword.[24] However, the Rapha's deadly purpose was cut short by the appearance of Abishai who, like the cavalry in an old Western movie, arrived just in time to save David and kill his opponent.

Verses 15–17 contain words of a percussive nature suggesting the sounds of battle.[25] In fact, it is tempting to hear the clash between the two

---

[20] For a more detailed analysis of this structure see Vannoy, *1–2 Samuel,* pp. 14-18, and 393-396. Also see chap. 20, p. 292, n. 111.

[21] The word used in these verses is "Rephaites" or "Rephaim." Verses mentioning this people group include: Gen. 14:5; 15:20; Deut. 3:13; Josh. 12:4; 13:12; 17:15.

[22] McCarter, *II Samuel,* pp. 449-450, lists several possible meanings.

[23] Bergen, *1, 2 Samuel,* p. 448.

[24] The MT simply says "new." Most modern translations assume that it refers to a sword. For a further explanation see Youngblood, *1, 2 Samuel,* p. 1058.

[25] The "sh" sound is particularly prominent in vv. 15–17, occurring a total of 14 times. The "b" sound occurs 6 times, as does the "k" sound found in the Hebrew letters *kaph* and *qoph*. A hard "p" sound also occurs 3 times. The alternation of these various sounds in the ear of the hearer of the story may mimic the kind of sounds heard in battle. In a similar vein, Moshe Greenberg notes the recurring "p" sound

men in the very sound of their names, for "Abishai" and "Ishbi" share several consonants. Even in English, the "i," "sh," and "b" sounds are prominently heard, suggesting the swi*sh*ing of swords, the whoo*sh*ing of spears and the *b*anging together of weapons and armor. Whether such an intention can be attributed to the author or not, it is an interesting effect when reading the Hebrew text. In the end, Abishai stands atop his defeated foe, David is rescued, and the "lamp of Israel" is not quenched (v. 17).

Abishai's last appearance occurs in the list of David's mighty men in 23:8–39. A description of Abishai (vv. 18–19) follows an account of David's top three men (vv. 8–17). There is some discrepancy as to whether Abishai is head over a second group of Three,[26] falls between the Three and the Thirty,[27] or is commander over the Thirty.[28] Furthermore, some interpret the Hebrew to mean he is less honored than the Three,[29] while others believe he was "held in greater honor than the Three."[30] These discrepancies demonstrate the confusion that exists in understanding this text. I have no firm opinion on the subject and will leave the interpretive issues to those more qualified to debate it. Suffice it to say, Abishai is reckoned among the greats of David's army and was held in high esteem. The fact that "he lifted his spear against three hundred" compares him with Jashobeam (v. 8), the greatest of David's men, the only difference being the number killed.

These final two passages in which Abishai appears change the tenor of his overall characterization. If we only had the incidents with Saul and Shimei to judge him by, the critique would be much harsher. Though there is much to criticize about him, it must be tempered by his heroic deeds and the honor accorded him at the end of 2 Samuel.

Conclusion: Hero and Villain

Abishai's desire for vengeance against Saul and Shimei is harsh, but understandable; after all, they were the enemy. Is it fair then to paint Abishai as a villain? Would not any loyal soldier have responded in the same way? There is a part of Abishai in all of us. His loyalty to David is admirable and his vengeful approach is very human. It is natural to want to strike back

---

that "dominates [Job] 16:9–14, a passage in which Job pictures himself as a battered and shattered object of God's pitiless assaults." See Moshe Greenberg, "Job," *The Literary Guide to the Bible*, eds. Robert Alter & Frank Kermode (Cambridge: Harvard University Press, 1987), p. 302. However, I must also note Bar-Efrat's caution on attributing meaning to certain sounds, *Narrative Art*, p. 201.

[26] For example, Youngblood, *1, 2 Samuel*, p. 1090.

[27] Firth, *1 & 2 Samuel*, p. 535.

[28] For example, Birch, *The First and Second Books of Samuel*, p. 1376.

[29] Anderson, *2 Samuel*, p. 273, note on v. 18d.

[30] Bergen, *1, 2 Samuel*, p. 470.

against those who have tried to harm us. While we might sympathize with Abishai, it would be wrong to condone his vengeful nature.[31] Scripture calls us to a higher ideal (Deut. 32:35; Rom. 12:19).

David is the perfect foil for Abishai in the episodes concerning Saul and Shimei. He shows us that there is an alternative response. His gracious actions and love for his enemies foreshadow the words and actions of Jesus (Matt. 5:43–44; Luke 23:34). David's willingness to entrust himself and his enemies to God's hands sets a nobler standard when contrasted with Abishai's attitude. It is Abishai's seeming inability to do this that marks him as a secular man. He does not understand that "the LORD does not save by sword or spear; for the battle is the LORD's" (1 Sam. 17:47). He is the picture of all those who trust in the flesh (Jer. 17:5; Rom. 13:14). This characteristic, along with his complicity in the murder of Abner (2 Sam. 3:30), is what places him in the villain camp.

Given this negative image of Abishai, it is surprising that his appearances at the end of 2 Samuel only highlight his good qualities. When compared with the final narratives about his brother Joab, who is pictured as a murderer and traitor to the state (1 Kings 1–2), this fact is even more significant. Abishai shares similar characteristics with his brother but, in the end, he is no Joab. David seems to recognize this difference when he puts Abishai in charge of pursuing Sheba, while refusing to acknowledge Joab's leadership (2 Sam. 20:6). No one can dispute Abishai's bravery, loyalty, or ability to command and lead David's men, facts also noted in earlier narratives that include him (2 Sam. 10:9–14; 18:1–5). In fact, if Abishai had not intervened against Ishbi-Benob to save David's life, Israel's history would have been very different. Abishai, then, is an example of the best and the worst of us. His insensitivity toward the Lord tips the scales in favor of a villain portrait, but we would do well to show the same loyalty and commitment to others that he demonstrated toward David.

Asahel: Running into Trouble (2 Sam. 2:18–23, 30–32)

And Asahel was as fleet of foot as a wild gazelle (2 Sam. 2:18)

"Brave, impetuous, and ready to kill," are the words we used to describe Abishai's introduction in 1 Samuel. These same words are perhaps even truer of Asahel, proving him to be Abishai's brother and a genuine son of Zeruiah. Together with Joab, all three brothers appear in 2 Samuel 2:18 in the midst of a conflict between Israel and Judah. The conflict was precipitat-

---

[31] Although stated in terms a bit too Freudian for my taste, Fokkelman, *King David*, p. 198, makes the excellent point that Abishai's desire for vengeance enslaves him and takes away his ability to choose as a free man.

ed by Abner, who had marched his troops to Gibeon where he was met by Joab and "the servants of David" (2:12–13). When an initial competition, also proposed by Abner, failed to produce a victor, the confrontation erupted into a full-scale battle, with Abner's troops experiencing a sound defeat at the hands of David's men (2:14–17).

The victory, however, was not without great cost to the men of Judah. In a flashback of the battle, the author follows Asahel as he pursues Abner. The outcome of this altercation not only results in the death of Asahel one of Judah's valiant warriors, it also sets the stage for a blood feud between Abner and the two remaining brothers (Joab and Abishai), culminating in the murder of Abner (2 Sam. 3:27, 30).

Asahel is described as one who is "as fleet of foot as a wild gazelle" (v. 18). It is Asahel's running ability that provides the setting for the chase scene described in verses 19–23. However, Asahel's greatest asset will prove to be his greatest liability—a liability perhaps hinted at in his description as a "gazelle." While gazelles are fast and nimble, they are not known for their strength or predatory nature. Gazelles are not usually "pursuers" (v. 19): they use their speed to flee from danger, not to run towards it! What chance does a gazelle have if it pursues a battle-hardened warrior like Abner?

Furthermore, the word "gazelle" sounds a note of familiarity with a statement found in the previous chapter: "The beauty (gazelle) of Israel is slain on your high places! How the mighty have fallen!" (2 Sam. 1:19). The gazelle that David laments is probably Jonathan (cf. 1:25) but could also include Saul. While Asahel's equation with Jonathan may seem complimentary, it has an ominous ring to it. The previous gazelle (Jonathan) had been slain and had fallen in battle; likewise, Asahel the gazelle will soon be slain and "fall" in battle (2:23).[32]

The chase begins in earnest in verse 19. Two expressions characterize the dogged determination of Asahel. The first expression, "he did not turn to the right hand or to the left (vv. 19, 21), is language frequently used in Deuteronomy–2 Kings in reference to not deviating from the path of the Lord (Deut. 5:32; 17:11, 20; 28:14; Josh. 1:7; 23:6; 2 Kings 22:2). The second term is *'aḥarē*, occurring seven times in verses 19–23 and variously translated as "after," "behind," or "back."[33] It is also used frequently to express following "after" the Lord, or not following "after" other gods (Deut. 4:3; 6:14; 13:4; 1 Kings 14:8; 18:21; 2 Kings 23:3). Thus, Asahel's pursuit of Abner uses language that articulates the resolve Israel should have in following the Lord.

---

[32] The word "fall," which occurs in 1:19, and 25, occurs twice in 2:23 describing Asahel's death.

[33] This word occurs 12 times in vv. 19–30, and a total of 15 times in 2 Sam. 2. For the specialized use of this word see Polzin, *David and the Deuteronomist*, pp. 29-31 and Youngblood, *1, 2 Samuel*, p. 826.

While pursuing the Lord leads to life (Deut. 5:32–33), Asahel's single-minded pursuit of Abner ironically leads to his death (v. 23). An outline of 2 Samuel 2:19–23 demonstrates Asahel's determination as it alternates between his pursuit and Abner's warnings: Asahel pursues (v. 19); Abner turns and speaks (20–21d); Asahel continues his pursuit (21e); Abner speaks and cautions (22); Asahel continues (23a); Abner finally strikes (23b–d).[34]

Still at some distance, Abner turns "behind him" to see Asahel hot on his trail (v. 20). Wishing to confirm the pursuer's identity Abner calls out, "Are you Asahel?" to which Asahel responds with one breathless word, "I." It is the only word he speaks in the entire narrative, highlighting his resolute focus on pursuing his prey. He is not interested in conversation; he is interested in catching Abner. As his name implies, Asahel is all about "doing" ("God has done," or "made") rather than talking. The doing, however, seems to have little to do with God and more to do with Asahel himself. Hence, Asahel's answer, "I," takes on a deeper significance.[35]

Although the language is reminiscent of one pursuing God, the fact is that Asahel is in pursuit of his own glory. What could bring greater honor to a soldier than to kill the commander of the enemy's army? This quest not only makes Asahel mute, but also deaf to the sound advice Abner tries to dispense. Using language that parallels the narrator's, Abner says, "Turn aside to your right hand or to your left, and lay hold on one of the young men and take his armor for yourself" (v. 21). This is Abner's way of telling Asahel to pick on someone his own size, or, in other words, to take on someone of his own skill level and not to tangle with a more experienced soldier like himself. Asahel is undeterred.

Next, Abner is more direct and makes Asahel aware of the deadly consequences he will face if he does not cease his pursuit: "Why should I strike you to the ground? How then could I face your brother Joab?" (v. 22). Abner interjects an emotional element into his plea ("your brother Joab"), hoping it will slow down the fleet-footed Asahel. The advice, threats, and emotional pleas are all to no avail, however, as the narrator reports, "He refused to turn aside" (v. 23a). It is the last decision he will ever make, and it is a deadly one.

Asahel will not stop himself, so Abner must stop him. So far, Abner's rhetoric has not caused his thick-headed opponent to "get the point." Ironically, he will also not get the point of Abner's weapon. Instead, with a thrust of the *back* end of his spear, Abner brings Asahel's pursuit to an abrupt halt as the spear travels through his abdomen and proceeds out of his *back* (v.

---

[34] Fokkelman, *Throne and City*, p. 55.
[35] Similarly, Fokkelman, ibid., pp. 51-52.

23).[36] It is ironic that with one blow of his spear, Abner did to Abishai's brother what Abishai had wanted to do to Saul (1 Sam. 26:8). Asahel's pursuit of glory causes him to "wind up on the wrong end of the stick." Abner's military prowess is so superior that it is not even necessary for him to assume the normal fighting posture of facing his adversary. This accords Asahel no respect. His death appears foolish and needless. Indeed, David's lament over Abner in the next chapter (3:33) could well have been sung over Asahel: "Should [Asahel] die as a fool dies?"

Asahel is the first of four characters to be stabbed in the abdomen in 2 Samuel. The first and the last (Amasa) to experience this fate are of the house of David, while the middle two (Abner and Ish-bosheth) are of the house of Saul, forming a deadly chiasm within 2 Samuel.[37] Later in this chapter we will notice that the wording of Amasa's death evokes images of Asahel's, adding irony to the gruesome inclusio formed by their demise.

The conclusion of the battle underscores an important difference between Asahel and his brother Joab.[38] After Abner pleads with Joab to, "return from following *after* his brothers" (v. 26—my translation), verse 30 informs the reader, "Then Joab returned from following *after* Abner." The use of "after" reminds us of Asahel's pursuit of Abner, and highlights Joab's wisdom. Joab knows when to stop pursuing; he will wait for a more convenient opportunity. The contrast between the two brothers is stark. The body count for Judah says it all: nineteen men *plus Asahel*—the man who did not know when to quit. Asahel's pursuit leads to a tomb in Bethlehem, while the wiser Joab lives to fight another day (v. 32).

Conclusion: Stop and Listen

The honor paid to Asahel by listing him first among David's Thirty mighty men (2 Sam. 23:24) does not diminish the unnecessary tragedy of his death. Asahel proves himself to be much like his brothers: impetuous, hard, stubborn, and preferring violence to diplomacy. The one valuable quality of his brothers that he desperately lacks is discernment. McCarter rightly ob-

---

[36] In a clever wordplay, 'aḥarē which has been used in the pursuit of Abner meaning "after" or "behind," now appears in reference to the *back* end of the spear as well as Asahel's *back*.

[37] (A) Asahel, (B) Abner, (B') Ish-bosheth, (A') Amasa. For more information on the interrelationship of these four deaths, see the comments in chap. 12, pp. 155-156 and pp. 317-318 below.

[38] Fokkelman, *Throne and City*, pp. 60-61, states, "At this stage we are able to compare the two sons of Zeruiah. Asahel cannot let go, but Joab can. Asahel does not let go even though it is necessary and it is pointed out to him. Joab does let go, for as long as it is necessary at any rate" (p. 61).

serves of Asahel that, "[He] appears in the present story as one so headstrong that he will not listen to reason even to save his own life."[39]

The Hebrew Scriptures frequently associate the act of listening with following the Lord. They are full of exhortations to listen, hear, heed, etc.; and the Scriptures record the consequences of those who do not (e.g., Exod. 15:26; Lev. 26:14–39; Judg. 2:17; 1 Sam. 15:22). Although Asahel's story is not directly about listening to the Lord, the formulaic language used in the story recalls the frequent exhortation in Scripture to follow the Lord. Asahel's wrong-headed pursuit took him down the enemy's path and far from the safety of his comrades. Likewise, our pursuit of our own selfish goals can take us down the wrong path and lead us far from the safety of God's people.

In one sense Asahel's real-life tragedy becomes an analogy and warning to the nation of Israel, who often stubbornly chose to follow their own way (2 Kings 17:13–14) and closed their ears to God's word and the way of wisdom (Isa. 6:10; Jer. 5:21). The same attitude is vividly portrayed in the New Testament, when members of the Sanhedrin refused to listen any longer to Stephen's words. Luke reports: "Then they cried out with a loud voice, *stopped their ears*, and ran at him with one accord" (Acts 7:57).

Of course the story of Asahel is not just a warning to Israel, but to anyone who stubbornly pursues their own agenda while ignoring the wisdom of God and others. The grisly account of his death demonstrates how vain the all-out pursuit of glory is. If Asahel had stopped to consider Abner's warnings, then he would not have been stopped by Abner's spear. The message is clear: a stubborn refusal to stop and listen to good advice may have deadly consequences.

Amasa and the "Relative" Clause (2 Sam. 17:25; 19:13)

But Amasa wallowed in his blood in the middle of the highway (2 Sam. 20:12)

In contrast to his cousins Abishai and Asahel, Amasa's military exploits are never mentioned. Although Absalom appoints him as his commander, he is never referred to in the battle that takes place between David's and Absalom's forces. Perhaps due to his treasonous defection, he is not listed among David's mighty men; or he may not have done anything worthy of note. The textual silence presents him as a warrior with no exploits. His introduction in 17:25 provides no resumé or flattering description of his abilities. He seems to get the job because of his family connections.[40] The au-

---

[39] McCarter, *II Samuel*, p. 99.

[40] Anderson, *2 Samuel*, p. 236, following Payne suggests that, "Amasa must have been a man of considerable influence, perhaps even a potential candidate for the kingship." His assertion is based on the fact that Amasa's name is the first word in the sentence.

thor's concern is to demonstrate his relationship to David (and Absalom), and most importantly, to Joab. Of the seven names mentioned in 17:25, only the names of Amasa and Joab occur twice, highlighting the important connection between these two men. Amasa's fate is closely connected to Joab. Joab's "displacement" by Amasa is a "preview of coming attractions" (19:13), which will ultimately result in deadly consequences for Amasa when the two meet one final time (20:8–10).[41]

While the focus of 17:25 is on Amasa's family ties, the relationships are somewhat obscured by textual difficulties. The Hebrew text states that the father of Amasa is "Jithra the Israelite." 1 Chronicles 2:17, however, states that his father is "Jether the Ishmaelite."[42] While the names Jithra and Jether are similar, the main problem is whether this man was an Israelite or an Ishmaelite. Most scholars believe that "Ishmaelite" is the correct identification for two reasons: 1) If he were an Israelite, there would be no need for him to be identified as such; and 2) the word "Israel" occurs in 17:24 and 26 and therefore might have been copied into verse 25 by accident.[43]

Jithra is not said to be Abigail's husband, but rather to have "gone in to Abigail." This could mean that Amasa was the product of rape, or, as some have proposed, the offspring of a special type of marriage (still known in the Arab world) where the wife remains a part of her father's family.[44] Thus, if Abigail was married to Jithra the Ishmaelite, she may still have resided in her father's house.

The identity of Abigail's father is the third difficulty in this verse. If Abigail is the sister of Zeruiah, then she is also the sister of David. One would assume then, that she was the daughter of Jesse. This verse, however, states that she was "the daughter of Nahash." Two explanations are possible: 1) Another copyist error has occurred in this verse and the name "Nahash," which occurs in verse 27, was accidentally written in place of Jesse;[45] or, 2)

This is slim evidence for such a claim. If Amasa was an important man, the author gives no hint of it; his portrait of Amasa is less flattering.

[41] Amasa's brief introduction is similar to that of other characters in Samuel whom the author mentions because of their significance later in the narrative (e.g., Hophni & Phinehas, 1 Sam. 1:3; Mephibosheth, 2 Sam. 4:4).

[42] LXX^A of 2 Sam. 17:25 also reads "Ishmaelite."

[43] See for example, McCarter, *II Samuel*, pp. 392-393. For the possibility that the text should read "Jezreelite," see, Youngblood, *1, 2 Samuel*, pp. 1015-1016.

[44] Hertzberg, *I&II Samuel*, p. 357, among others, makes this suggestion. This type of marriage is known as a *ṣadîqa* marriage. It may be the type of marriage that Samson had with the woman of Timnah (Judg. 15:1), although this is not certain.

[45] Alter, *The David Story*, p. 302. While McCarter, *II Samuel*, p. 392, asserts a similar position, he states that Nahash "is an apparent error, but there is no reliable textual witness to contradict it." 1 Chron. 2:13–17 seems to indicate that Zeruiah and Abigail

Jesse married the mother of Abigail after Nahash, her first husband, died.[46] This would mean that Abigail was Jesse's step-daughter and, therefore, a step-sister of David. In spite of the ambiguity, it is clear that Amasa is related to David as a nephew, and to Joab as a cousin. In light of this verse, the civil war takes on even more tragic proportions, as it pits son against father, nephew against uncle, and cousin against cousin.[47] As noted in the "Introduction," one of the themes of 1 and 2 Samuel is the abusive use of, and desire for, power that tears apart nations and families.[48]

Nations and families that are torn apart do not heal easily. This is illustrated in the tense post-war negotiations between David and the men of Israel and Judah in 2 Samuel 19. David, using familial and covenant language,[49] appeals to the men of Judah as "my brethren" and "my flesh and bone" (19:12). Following Absalom's defeat, David's choice of Amasa as his new commander-in-chief plays an integral part in the reconciliation of the two sides (19:13). David's reference to Amasa as "my bone and my flesh" is an open-armed approach to heal the division within his own family, while at the same time healing the division within the nation. True unity must begin at the most basic level. By welcoming Amasa as his own "flesh and bone," he welcomes back the estranged nation.

This union, however, is tenuous because all is not completely well within David's family or the nation. By choosing Amasa to be commander of the army, Joab is displaced by him for the second time in the narrative.[50] Once again, the fate of Amasa becomes tied to Joab. Furthermore, as Amasa's name begins verse 13, so Joab's ends it. In hindsight, this is an ominous sign. We are not informed of Joab's reaction to his demotion, but we will learn soon enough. The attentive reader knows that while David is attempting to heal one breach in his family, another one is being exacerbated: Sheba's rebellion demonstrates that the same dynamic is at work within the nation (20:1–2). David's move might be a politically astute one, to repair the rift within the nation, but it is also a disciplinary act to punish Joab for the murder of Absalom, and for the severe rebuke he had administered to David (2 Sam. 18:14–15; 19:5–7). This mixture of political motives and use of family members to counter one another will blow up in David's face in the next chapter (20:8–13). Nonetheless, it will establish "equilibrium" within the family as Amasa and Joab experience one final, and fatal, brotherly embrace. Joab's cold-blooded murder of Amasa, coupled with the death of Sheba will

---

were Jesse's daughters, but this does not preclude the possibility that one or both were from a previous marriage.

[46] See for example, Vannoy, *1–2 Samuel*, p. 372.

[47] Wiersbe, *2 Samuel*, p. 358.

[48] See "Introduction," pp. 2-6.

[49] Walter Brueggemann, *Of the Same Flesh and Bone*, pp. 532-542.

[50] The wording of Amasa replacing Joab in 17:25 and 19:13 is similar.

complete the balancing act, restoring the status-quo within the family and the nation, at least for the time being.

Amasa and Joab: Kissing Cousins (2 Sam. 20:4–13)

Amasa's appointment as commander results in an immediate assignment to quell the new crisis involving Sheba ben Bichri (20:4). Amasa is given three days by the king to assemble Judah's militia. Fearing that the rebellion might be extensive, it appears that David wanted every able-bodied man he could assemble to pursue Sheba. It has been suggested that, given the circumstances, David's command to summon the troops within three days was an impossible task for Amasa.[51] The troops may not have been so eager to support David after their recent defeat, or, on the other hand, may not have been enthusiastic about following Amasa, the man who had lost the last war. From David's vantage point, time was of the essence, no matter how daunting the task might have been. Whatever the reasons for Amasa's delay,[52] he failed in his first commission as commander. This failure adds to the overall impression presented by the narrative that Amasa was not a competent leader. When contrasted with Joab's and Abishai's leadership, this deficit is even more pronounced.

It is possible that Amasa's delay caused David to doubt his loyalty. Whatever his thoughts on Amasa, he voiced his concern to Abishai that, "Sheba the son of Bichri will do us more harm than Absalom" (v. 6). It is instructive that David still refused to acknowledge Joab's leadership, putting Abishai in charge of the mission. Ironically, however, verse 7 begins, "So Joab's men...went out after him," and from this point on, Joab again assumed command.

Any doubts about Amasa's loyalty are dispelled by the fact that he catches up with Joab's men at Gibeon (v. 8).[53] The author now slows the pace of the story, zooming in on Joab's appearance and actions. Joab's battle attire is described with particular focus on the belt around his hips, where a sword

---

[51] Fokkelman, *King David*, p. 324.

[52] For a list of possible reasons for Amasa's delay see Birch, *The First and Second Books of Samuel*, p. 1351, and Willis, *First and Second Samuel*, p. 393.

[53] *Contra* Gunn, *David and the Gift of the Kingdom*, p. 28, who states, "What little is said about Amasa both here and elsewhere in the story suggests that the elements of disloyalty, treachery and incompetence belong to the configuration of this cameo." Firth, *1 & 2 Samuel*, p. 496, notes that Gibeon, which is 6 miles north of Jerusalem, is a strange meeting place. If Amasa was travelling with a larger army, it would seem difficult for him to be able to catch up to Joab and his men. Therefore, Firth suggests he may have been unsuccessful in recruiting any men. Verse 11 does seem to suggest, however, that Amasa did recruit some men.

(or dagger) is sheathed.[54] The focus on the sword, as well as the verb describing Joab's movement, portends danger. Joab is said to "go out," the same word used to describe the army's pursuit in verse 7, and Shimei's assault on David with stones and dirt (2 Sam. 16:5).

The mechanics of what happens next are not totally clear. In some way Joab contrives for his sword to fall out. Whether it falls to the ground and is picked up, as many suppose,[55] or falls into a fold in his garment,[56] is hard to determine. What is clear is that Joab's sleight of hand catches Amasa off guard. Joab's callous deception is emphasized in both language and action. As he approaches Amasa, he calls him "brother" and speaks of "peace": "Is it *peace* with you (are you well), my *brother*?" (v. 9—my translation). Once again in the books of Samuel, words of peace are followed by the use of a sword.[57] As he speaks these words, Joab reaches out with his right hand and grasps Amasa by the beard to kiss him. The kiss is a kiss of death, as Joab plunges the sword into Amasa's belly with his other hand (v. 10). The fact that Joab does not use his fighting hand (right hand) to deliver the fatal blow, coupled with his deceptively friendly words and actions, catches Amasa unaware. Amasa's death is described in gruesome detail, as his intestines spill onto the ground. Joab's cold efficiency is noted in the expression, "he did not strike him again," words almost identical to those used by his brother Abishai (1 Sam. 26:8).[58] Then, as if nothing significant had happened, Joab and Abishai continued their pursuit of Sheba.

In spite of one of Joab's men encouraging loyalty to David and Joab (v. 11), the army is not as quick to respond. Seeing their commander wallowing in his blood in the middle of the road causes them to stand motionless,[59] perhaps at the horror of what has just been done, and perhaps because no one wishes to tread on the blood of their fallen comrade.[60] It is only when

---

[54] The Hebrew words present some challenges in translation, but the overall intent is clear enough. For further discussion see, Edward A. Neiderhiser, "2 Samuel 20:8–10: A Note For a Commentary," *JETS* 24/3, 1981, pp. 209-210.

[55] Ibid. See also McCarter's comments, *II Samuel*, p. 427, who notes that this suggestion originally comes from Josephus (*Ant.* 7.284).

[56] Hertzberg, *I&II Samuel*, p. 372, and Anderson, *2 Samuel*, p. 240.

[57] The ironic contrast between "peace" and "sword" is a continual theme in the books of Samuel. See for example, 1 Sam. 25:6, 13; 2 Sam. 3:21–27; 11:7; 12:9.

[58] Anderson, *2 Samuel*, p. 241, might be right in stating, "Joab may have wished to prolong his suffering, and therefore he did not administer the *coup de grace*."

[59] The word "stand" occurs twice in v. 12, emphasizing the revulsion of the troops (probably the troops Amasa had gathered) at this sacrilege. There is also a contrast with v. 11 where Joab's man "stands" triumphantly over Amasa and calls out, "Whoever favors Joab and whoever is for David—follow Joab!"

[60] Alter, *The David Story*, p. 324.

Amasa is unceremoniously removed from the road, thrown into a field, and his body covered by a garment, that the soldiers take up the pursuit of Sheba (v. 13). Gunn sums up the scene by stating, "There is something almost cruelly comic about the portrait; Amasa was the man whose loss of a battle gained him a command, who failed to keep an appointment, and who could not spot the sword in his rival's hand."[61]

While the story portrays the ruthless brutality of Joab, it leaves the reader with an unimpressive view of Amasa. Davis comments, "Amasa is still an obstacle. [He] has been all chapter long. First, Amasa's delay was an obstacle to David's urgency in crushing Sheba (vv. 4–6). Then Amasa's leadership was an obstacle to Joab's designs (vv. 8–10). Now Amasa's corpse is an obstacle to rousing the troops after Joab."[62] Thus the career of Amasa comes to an ignominious conclusion, with not even the mention of a proper burial. He is not only forgotten by the soldiers: he is forgotten by the narrator.

Conclusion: Amasa and His "Blood Brothers"

One cannot read the account of Amasa's death without recalling the violent deaths of other men in 2 Samuel. As Polzin notes, "2 Samuel makes it clear that Joab's smiting of Amasa in the belly looks backward to the murders of Ishbosheth in 4:6, Abner in 3:27, and Asahel in 2:23. Moreover, these instances of 'smiting in the belly' occur only here in 2 Samuel, and always in the context of an explicit reference to 'brother.' "[63] These similarities invite the reader to compare and contrast the four different stories.

Parallels between the deaths of Abner and Amasa are especially noteworthy. They both share the same murderer: Joab. In both cases Joab deceived the men he murdered by catching them off guard and striking them in the stomach (3:27; 20:10). Both were commanders over their respective armies, who fought and lost a civil war against David (2 Sam. 2:12–17; 17:25). Joab perceived the reconciliation of both men to David as a threat, and both were killed in an atmosphere of "peace" (3:21–23; 20:9). Joab's murder of these men threatened to disrupt the tenuous unity recently forged in both situations. Finally, David himself drew a parallel between these two murders, advising Solomon to deal with Joab accordingly (1 Kings 2:5–6).

These similarities provide the backdrop for the contrast between the two deaths. Although the narrative makes it clear that Joab was wrong in murdering Abner, at least the author provided him with some motivation: Abner's killing of Joab's brother Asahel (3:30). No such explanation is provided for the murder of Amasa; indeed, none can be. The silence of the text

---

[61] Gunn, *The Story of King David*, p. 140, n. 21.

[62] Davis, *2 Samuel*, p. 255.

[63] Polzin, *David and the Deuteronomist*, p. 198.

convicts Joab.[64] Perhaps the text's silence also suggests that Joab had reached such a hard-hearted state in his killing of others that he no longer felt the need to justify his actions.

A final contrast that highlights the heinous nature of Amasa's murder is that he was a blood relative of Joab from the house of David, whereas Abner belonged to the rival house of Saul. The murder of Amasa sounds a climactic note in 2 Samuel on the consequences of the abuse of power. Joab's unrestrained lust for power begins with killing his fellow-countryman (Abner) and ends with killing his own kinsman (Amasa).

Besides the act of "smiting in the belly," a number of other similarities also connect Amasa's death with Asahel's.[65] Both stories center on Gibeon (2:12; 20:8). Each story speaks of "pursuing" an enemy, and in each case the battle ends by Joab blowing the trumpet (2:28; 20:23). The root *'aḥar* ("after") occurs frequently (11 times) in the account of Amasa's death, as it does in the story of Asahel. Furthermore, in both accounts the author vividly relates the gruesome nature of the death and comments that those who came upon the scene "stood still" (2:23; 20:12).

The difference between Asahel's death and Amasa's highlights again the brutality of Joab's action. Since Asahel and Abner are on opposite sides in the battle, it is not surprising that one would kill the other. Amasa and Joab, however, are on the same side. Abner warns Asahel twice (2:21–22) before delivering the deadly blow, whereas Joab lulls Amasa into a false sense of security, and then kills him without warning (20:9–10).

The similarities of Amasa with Abner and Asahel also suggest certain character traits that they share. Both Abner and Amasa are caught unaware and "die as a fool" (3:33). Asahel's inexperience contrasts with Amasa's experience, but both prove to be naive in their own way.

Sadly, there is not much of a positive nature that can be said of Amasa. He was the nephew that betrayed his uncle the king. He was the general who lost a war, and the ineffective commander of David's troops who could not fulfill his commission. In the end he dies the death of a fool, his body disgraced by being dumped in a field, ultimately forgotten by his men, and by the narrator as the story continues without him. Amasa, as commander of the army (both David's and Absalom's), has all the outward trappings of success, but his life is a dismal failure. His cruel death evokes sympathy, but his betrayal of the Lord's anointed appears to reap consequences that go beyond the civil war. His under-achieving seems to be related to his lack of true perception (he did not recognize the Lord's anointed or the sword in Joab's

---

[64] Geyer, "Stopping the Juggernaut," p. 41, states, "The text itself accents Joab's ruthless brutality and does not justify the murder."

[65] The similarities that follow are based on Polzin's observations. See Polzin, *David and the Deuteronomist*, p. 199.

hand). As such, he becomes a warning to all who might "dress for success" and look the part, but inwardly lack the real quality of greatness: a quality that comes only by aligning oneself with the Lord and His purposes.

Chapter 22

Jonadab: The Wise Guy (David's nephew)

Now Jonadab was a very wise man (2 Sam. 13:3b)

Jonadab's "Friendly" Advice (2 Sam. 13:3–5)

Considering the Scripture's celebration of Solomon's wisdom (1 Kings 10:24), it comes as a surprise that Jonadab is the only person in the Bible described as "very wise."[1] When Jonadab's cousin Amnon came down with a case of lovesickness for his half-sister Tamar, it was Jonadab who proposed a plan that gave Amnon access to her. To modern ears, the description of Jonadab as "very wise" is disconcerting since his advice seems devoid of ethical and moral content.

English translations have attempted to explain the meaning by using words such as "crafty" (NKJV, ESV) or "shrewd" (NIV). While the English adjective usually has a more positive connotation, in Biblical Hebrew wisdom has "a purely intellectual and morally neutral quality."[2] "It was used for attaining goals, whether admirable or not."[3] There is, after all, not only godly wisdom, but a "wisdom of this age" (1 Cor. 2:6) or "fleshly wisdom" (2 Cor. 1:12). Perhaps a better description of Jonadab in modern terms is that he was a man who understood human nature and knew how to get things done.[4]

As a blood relative of David (the son of Shimeah,[5] David's brother), Jonadab had close connections at court. He was the "friend" of David's firstborn son Amnon (v. 3). While some have interpreted this description as an official court position,[6] or as a technical term for one who connects a man to a woman,[7] it most likely has the basic meaning of an intimate acquaintance.[8] It does appear, however, that Jonadab also functioned in the capacity of a court adviser or counselor (2 Sam. 13:32–35).

---

[1] Bergen, *1, 2 Samuel*, p. 380.

[2] Whybray, *The Succession Narrative*, p. 58.

[3] Ibid. Bar-Efrat, *Narrative Art*, p. 248, states, "The Rabbis and many [others] have solved this problem by saying that Jonadab was clever in evil-doing. Thus, even though wisdom in itself is positive, Jonadab uses it for ignoble purposes."

[4] R.B.Y. Scott, *The Way of Wisdom in the Old Testament* (New York & London: MacMillan Publishers, 1971), p. 7, writes, "The term is applied also to other particular skills in [the] general sense of knowing what to do and how to do it."

[5] He is called "Shammah" in 1 Sam. 16:9; and 17:13.

[6] Firth, *1&2 Samuel*, pp. 436-437.

[7] The word "friend" might have this meaning in Gen. 38:20 and Judg. 14:20. See McCarter, *II Samuel*, p. 321.

[8] Anderson, *2 Samuel*, p. 174.

In spite of the sometimes neutral meaning of the word "wise," Jonadab's description as a *very wise friend* brings certain expectations to the table. While we would hope any friend would give us sound advice, this would be especially true of a *very wise friend*. What the reader expects and what Jonadab delivers are worlds apart. Instead of being helpful, his advice proves to be fatal for Amnon and destructive to the house of David.

Jonadab's appearances in the text act as an inclusio around the story of Amnon's rape of Tamar and Absalom's murder of Amnon. The introduction of Jonadab in 13:3–5 consists of sixty-two words and is balanced by his appearance at the end of the story which consists of sixty-one words (13:32–33, 35). Of these one hundred and twenty-three words, Jonadab speaks eighty-five, and another fifteen describe him beginning to speak.[9] This means that the initial description of Jonadab in 13:3 should also be evaluated by the content of what he says, as well as the results of his advice. The narrative's focus on Jonadab's verbal skills supports the proposal that he was a counselor in David's court.

Jonadab's first words (v. 4) demonstrate that he has the ability to get to the heart of a problem by asking provocative questions. He asks, "How is it that the king's son (who supposedly can have anything he wants) looks so haggard day after day?" The question highlights the incongruity of the situation.[10] While Amnon has made himself sick over his inability to get near his sister, after hearing the problem, Jonadab appears to have an immediate answer (v. 5). The nature of Jonadab's question and his quick solution validate the author's description of him as "very wise." But the advice he dispenses makes the reader aware that his counsel is not based on *godly* wisdom. It is, however, pragmatic. He suggests that Amnon turn his liability into an asset: "If you are sick, then use it to your advantage!" Employing the same verb that the author had used to describe Amnon's love*sickness* (v. 2), Jonadab proposes that Amnon *pretend to be sick* (v. 5).[11]

He tells him to "lie down" on his "bed"—words which recall the previous story of David and Bathsheba (11:2, 4), and anticipate the deed that Amnon will perform (13:11, 14). Although these words foreshadow the sin of Amnon, there is no indication that Jonadab's advice included the raping of Tamar. His strategy is simply designed to secure a private meeting between the two.[12] Amnon's conduct shows that he takes the advice of Jonadab and

---

[9] Thus 81% of the vocabulary in these verses consists of Jonadab's dialogue or describes him beginning to speak.

[10] Phyllis Trible, *Texts of Terror: Literary-Feminist Readings of Biblical Narratives* (Philadelphia: Fortress Press, 1984), p. 40.

[11] Fokkelman, *King David*, p. 104 states, "Jonadab very adeptly converts a negative circumstance into an effective instrument, powerlessness into power."

[12] Note especially Bar-Efrat, *Narrative Art*, p. 249, who states, "We as readers, draw conclusions about Jonadab's intentions from what actually happens afterwards, and

twists a word here and an action there, to suit his own desire.[13] This acknowledgement, however, does not release Jonadab from culpability in the crime. As many have noted, Amnon's desire may have ended in frustration if not for the counsel of Jonadab.[14]

Any advice to carry out deception cannot be considered "sound wisdom" (Prov. 2:6–9; 8:12–14). Jonadab's counsel "concerns itself only with methods and fails to calculate the consequences."[15] Ultimately, Jonadab's "wise" advice demonstrates how foolish the wisdom of the world is (1 Cor. 1:20, 25). In light of coming events, "very wise" Jonadab comes off looking very foolish. Perhaps the wisdom contained in Proverbs 27:12 indicts both Jonadab and Amnon when it states, "A prudent man foresees evil and hides himself; the simple pass on and are punished."

Blessed Assurance? (2 Sam. 13:30–36)

After Absalom's murder of Amnon, a rumor quickly spreads that all of the king's sons have been killed (v. 30). Believing the worst, grief seizes David and his servants as it appears that all the royal seed has been wiped out in one blow (v. 31). In the midst of all the confusion, the cool head of Jonadab prevails as he reappears in the narrative to assure the king that the disaster is not as great as the rumor portends (vv. 32–33). When the king's sons appear on the roadside coming towards the city (v. 34), Jonadab affirms the truth of his assertion to David (v. 35). The king is reunited with his sons and they all raise their voices, weeping over the tragedy that has befallen the royal family (v. 36).

Jonadab's reappearance at the end of the story raises many questions. If he was Amnon's friend, why did he not attend the feast? If he suspected foul play as his words suggest (v. 32), did he try to warn Amnon? Did he regret his former association with Amnon? Was he repentant for having played a part in this disaster? How did he know that Absalom had determined to kill Amnon? Had he disassociated himself from Amnon and become Absalom's friend, or had he been part of a conspiracy with Absalom from the begin-

---

suppose that what took place between Amnon and Tamar is in accordance with Jonadab's plan. But this assumption could well be mistaken." See also Fokkelman *King David*, p. 109, echoed by Baldwin, *1&2 Samuel*, p. 251.

[13] Amnon's words and actions will be examined in more detail in chap. 23.

[14] See for example, Gordon, *I&II Samuel*, p. 262. Rosenberg, *King and Kin*, p. 140, notes the potential double meaning of the word *wayyippālē'* (wonderful/marvelous, or hard/difficult) and states, "After Jonadab's intervention, the thought becomes, as if automatically, a *permitted* rather than a forbidden thing" (author's emphasis).

[15] Whybray, *The Succession Narrative*, p. 59.

ning?[16] If he had not been part of a conspiracy, did he fear retaliation from Absalom for his part in Amnon's crime? Did Absalom even know about the advice he had given Amnon? Did David know? When he saw how his advice was utilized, did he perhaps distance himself from both men, despising Amnon and fearing Absalom?

All of these questions convey the ambiguity that surrounds Jonadab's character at the end of chapter 13. Some of these questions are difficult to answer, given the sparse information we have about Jonadab and his motivations. An attempt to answer them is important, however, if we are to sketch a character portrait of him. For example, if Jonadab was involved in a conspiracy with Absalom to entrap Amnon, then he is a monstrous villain. If, on the other hand, he regretted his advice to Amnon and sought to truly comfort David, then he may be a fallible person who has learned from his mistake. It is probable that the real truth lies somewhere between these two extremes.

Hill suggests that Jonadab conspired with Absalom in order to secure his political future.[17] He believes that Jonadab, as a wise man of the court, would have had knowledge of Egyptian love poetry. One such poem bears a striking resemblance to the advice that he gives Amnon (feigning illness in order to be alone with the woman he desires). Therefore, Hill believes that Jonadab's counsel was intended to lead Amnon to commit rape, which would then give Absalom a justifiable cause to kill him.[18] He maintains that Jonadab's foreknowledge of the murder (v. 32) is proof of this conspiracy.[19]

While Hill's theory is interesting, and certainly makes for good storytelling, I believe it reads too much into the text. Other explanations are more plausible. For example, we never read that Jonadab is Absalom's "friend." The text says that he is Amnon's "friend," and although there is a certain irony in the "friendly" advice he gives, there is no indication that it is insincere. Jonadab is concerned with helping his friend achieve his goal.

The irony of Jonadab's wisdom is that he is wise enough to know how to help his friend get his way, but his wise advice opens the door for his friend to play the fool and commit an act of despicable folly (vv. 12–13). At this point, Jonadab's wisdom is exposed as shortsighted (which godly wisdom never is). Friendship, and perhaps a desire to impress with his own cleverness, blinds him to the possible consequences.

There are two reasons for believing that Amnon's deed shocks Jonadab back to his senses. First, Jonadab describes Amnon's act as "forcing" or "humbling" Tamar, the same word used by the narrator (13:14, 32). He does

---

[16] Andrew E. Hill, "A Jonadab Connection in the Absalom Conspiracy?" *JETS* 30/4, 1987, pp. 387-390.

[17] Ibid., p. 390.

[18] Ibid., p. 389.

[19] Ibid., p. 390.

not try to soften or overlook the violence done to her. This suggests a distance between him and Amnon for he sees the act for what it was, while Amnon does not.[20]

Second, rather than suggest a possible conspiracy with Absalom, Jonadab's foreknowledge of the murder reminds the reader that he is a "very wise" man. Jonadab understands human nature. Once Amnon had violated Tamar, Jonadab foresaw what his pride, or friendship had blinded him from seeing: Absalom would avenge the dishonor perpetrated against his sister (and thus against himself). Moreover, Jonadab's insight into Absalom's motives provides a foil for David's obtuseness in the story.[21] Jonadab then is a wise man, meaning he knows human nature and how to get things done, but his friendship and ego caused his advice to Amnon to focus on immediate results instead of long term effects.

This understanding of Jonadab provides a basis for examining the questions asked above. First, why did Jonadab not attend Absalom's feast? All scholars are agreed that, following the rape of Tamar, Jonadab distanced himself from Amnon. There are several possible reasons for this. Viewed positively, perhaps Jonadab's conscience was troubled, even repulsed, by the outcome of his counsel to Amnon. Viewed negatively, perhaps he was concerned for his own reputation and position at court, or feared being in Amnon's company, lest he get caught up in the violence that awaited Amnon. It is also possible that a combination of reasons factored into his absence from Absalom's party.[22] Therefore, further evidence is necessary to determine which of these options should be chosen.

"If Jonadab suspected foul play, did he try to warn Amnon? The most likely answer to this next question is, "No." The distance that the rape created between him and Amnon probably precluded Jonadab from warning Amnon of potential danger. If this were the case, it suggests that Jonadab was not much of a friend. Jonadab seems to have been a friend "in the good times," but when danger loomed he was nowhere to be found. Of course, there is the possibility that Jonadab attempted to warn Amnon and, being the fool he was, Amnon refused to listen (see 13:14, 16). However, the distance between them, and Jonadab's cool reference to Amnon in 13:32, suggests that he did not warn him.

The next two questions can be answered together. Did Jonadab regret his former association with Amnon, and was he repentant for having played a part in the disaster? It seems clear that Jonadab did regret his asso-

---

[20] Fokkelman, *King David*, p. 109 states, "the Jonadab of 13:32e two years later speaks notably coolly and objectively of Amnon."

[21] David is first duped by Amnon (13:6–7) and then by Absalom (13:24–27).

[22] Of course a third explanation is that he simply was not invited, but if he were still a close friend of Amnon it seems likely he would have accompanied him.

ciation with Amnon. The fact that Jonadab does not seem to be closely associated with him in 13:32–35 suggests that the former friends have parted company. It should also be noted that while everyone else in the palace is rending their garments and lamenting, there is no evidence that Jonadab sheds a tear for Amnon.[23]

Jonadab's desire to comfort David repeatedly with the assurance that only Amnon is dead (vv. 32–33), and his quickness to confirm the obvious after all of David's other sons have returned (v. 35), suggests a guilty conscience or a contrite one. But which is it? The fact that he wants David to be reassured that the catastrophe is not as great as originally reported, and is quick to take the credit for being right, suggests some insecurity on his part. Insecurity leans in the direction of guilt. A repentant person who has been forgiven does not need to press his case as strongly as Jonadab does.

The answer to a related question helps to clarify whether Jonadab's actions are motivated from guilt or penitence. Did David know about Jonadab's advice to Amnon? Based on inferences in the text, the answer is "No." First, Amnon was never rebuked by David (13:21), so there would have been no need for him to implicate Jonadab by saying, "Well it was Jonadab's idea." Second, David is in the dark throughout the entire chapter, never knowing his sons' true motives, so why would he know about Jonadab's input? Third, the fact that Jonadab remains a counselor in David's court suggests that David does not know. Finally, Jonadab does not seem to be the sort of person who would confess to David, "It's all my fault for giving Amnon that bad advice." Thus, the reason for Jonadab's response is more likely a guilty conscience than a repentant and contrite heart.

If David did not know about Jonadab's advice, we can be certain that Absalom did not know about it. If Jonadab and Absalom did not conspire together, then there would be no reason for Absalom to find out about Jonadab's counsel to Amnon. The author tells us that Absalom did not speak to Amnon about anything significant over the next two years (13:22). Therefore, Amnon would not have told him about Jonadab's advice. Jonadab does not seem to have a close relationship with Absalom, and he would certainly not volunteer such dangerous information and jeopardize his own safety. One might also expect that if Absalom had somehow gotten wind of Jonadab's part in the rape of his sister, he might have invited him to the party as well in order to "kill two birds with one stone." Therefore, when looked at as a

---

[23] Speaking of Jonadab's references to Amnon's death in 13:32, 33, Bar-Efrat, *Narrative Art*, p. 249, makes the following observation: "This gives the impression that Amnon's death is not a particularly serious matter, and it is even more surprising that this dismissive tone is adopted by the friend of the murdered man, especially since he uses the phrase, 'for Amnon alone is dead' twice (vv. 32, 33), as if he considers Amnon's death to be a matter of trifling importance."

whole, the evidence suggests that Jonadab concealed his secret for a long time, and had a guilty conscience as well.

Wise Men and Friends

As we have seen, Jonadab is introduced as a friend and a wise man (13:3). These two descriptions invite a comparison with other friends and wise men in 1 and 2 Samuel. How does Jonadab's description as a "very wise man" compare with other wise men in Samuel and what can we learn about Jonadab through this comparison? Similarly, if Jonadab was a "friend" of Amnon, how does his friendship compare with other friends mentioned in the books of Samuel? So as not to overextend this section, we will confine our comparisons to a few examples.

Since 2 Samuel 11–20 is heavily influenced by the wisdom tradition,[24] we do not need to look far for a comparison with other wise men and counselors. The most obvious is Ahithophel. At one time Ahithophel was a trusted counselor of David's court, but during Absalom's rebellion Ahithophel betrayed David and sided with Absalom (2 Sam. 15:31). His wisdom was so renowned that 2 Samuel 16:23 states, "Now the advice of Ahithophel, which he gave in those days, was as if one had inquired at the oracle of God. So was all the advice of Ahithophel both with David and with Absalom."

Several parallels stand out between Jonadab and Ahithophel. First, each man's wisdom is described in an unusual way. Jonadab is called a "very wise man" while Ahithophel's advice is said to be "as if one inquired at the oracle of God." Second, both men's counsel is based on worldly wisdom which proves to be foolish (2 Sam. 13:12–13; 15:31; 17:14). Third, both men turn their backs on previous friendships. Fourth, both give advice that leads one of David's sons to commit sexual sin. While Jonadab's advice opens the door for Amnon's rape of Tamar (2 Sam. 13:4–14), Ahithophel explicitly advises Absalom to go in to his father's concubines (2 Sam. 16:20–22). Finally, two of David's sons die as a result of following the advice of these two men. Amnon, who followed Jonadab's counsel is slain (2 Sam. 13:28–29), as is Absalom, who followed Ahithophel's advice (2 Sam. 18:14–15).

The similarities with Ahithophel do not put Jonadab in a very positive light, but in spite of the similarities, it must also be said that Jonadab was no Ahithophel. The differences between the two men also help in sketching a character portrait of Jonadab. While Jonadab's advice led Amnon to commit sexual sin, he did not explicitly recommend it as Ahithophel did. Jonadab turned his back on Amnon and showed no remorse at his death, while Ahithophel plotted the death of David and requested to execute him personally (2 Sam. 17:1–2). The similarities between the two men definitely put Jonadab in

---

[24] Whybray, *The Succession Narrative*.

the villain camp, but the differences suggest he was not a villain to the same degree that Ahithophel was.

Jonadab may also profitably be compared with Hushai, another wise counselor of David's. In fact, Hushai was not only a counselor; he was also called David's "friend" (2 Sam. 15:37). In this instance, the term "friend" designates a royal official.[25] However, the King's Friend would also have to be a trusted individual who had a close relationship with the king. When David asked Hushai to remain in Jerusalem during Absalom's attempted coup, Absalom made a play on the word "friend," saying to Hushai, "Is this your loyalty to your friend? Why did you not go with your friend?" (2 Sam. 16:17). Hushai was not only David's political ally; he showed the true meaning of friendship by putting his life on the line and confounding the counsel of Ahithophel in order to protect David (2 Sam. 17:5–16). Jonadab shed no tears at the death of a friend, nor as far as we know did he do anything to save his friend from death. Hushai, on the other hand, risked his own life to help save his friend. Jonadab used his wisdom in a way that got his friend into trouble, while Hushai used wise words in order to protect his friend. The contrast between these two men presents a damning portrait of Jonadab.

Finally, if we are going to talk about friendship in the books of Samuel, we must refer to David and Jonathan. The mere mention of this friendship alongside the friendship of Jonadab and Amnon is commentary enough. David and Jonathan's friendship was defined by covenant loyalty (1 Sam. 18:1–4; 20:12–17; 23:18). Jonathan "loved David as his own soul" (1 Sam. 18:1; 20:17) and proved it on many occasions by risking his life for David (1 Sam. 20:33; 23:16–18). The two of them were known to have shed many tears for each other (1 Sam. 20:41; 2 Sam. 1:17, 26). We probably do not need to be reminded again that Jonadab shed no tears at the death of Amnon, nor did he ever risk his life for him. The words of covenant that Jonathan and David shared were words of life. The words shared between Jonadab and Amnon led to death. "A genuine **friend** does not necessarily do what his friend desires, but what is best for him" (author's emphasis).[26]

This brief survey helps to clarify some of the ambiguity in Jonadab's character and presents a dark portrait of him. While Jonadab is not as malevolent a villain as Ahithophel, the contrast with Hushai and with the friendship of David and Jonathan clearly align him with the less savory characters of the books of Samuel.

---

[25] McCarter, *II Samuel*, p. 372. Although this term is from the same root as the word "friend" in 2 Sam. 13:3, it is spelled slightly different and is less common. McCarter, following de Vaux, argues that this less common word is based on an Egyptian designation which evolved into a title for a royal official.

[26] Willis, *First and Second Samuel*, p. 358.

Conclusion: With a Friend Like Jonadab, Who Needs Enemies?

When one reflects on the narrative of 2 Samuel 13, it is interesting to note that every character in the story experiences severe trauma; every character that is except one: Jonadab. David is duped by two of his sons and experiences the rape of a daughter, the murder of one son, and the banishment of another. Absalom endures the rape of his beloved sister and must flee the kingdom as a result of Amnon's murder. Amnon pays the highest price of all with his life. By the end of the story, however, Jonadab seems no worse for the wear. Although it is his counsel that sets the chain of events in motion, Jonadab experiences nothing more serious than perhaps a guilty conscience. Even the loss of his friendship with Amnon does not seem to faze him. After all, a "wise man" like Jonadab is certainly better off without a "fool" like Amnon for a friend. With the house of David crumbling all around him, Jonadab comes off as the wise counselor who comforts poor king David in all of his troubles by saying, "There, there David, it is not as bad as it seems. Ah look! Here come your other sons now! See, I told you everything would work out."

It is also possible to make a comparison between Jonadab and another unsavory character—Joab. Although there are significant differences between Jonadab's actions in 2 Samuel 13:3–5 and those of Joab in 2 Samuel 11:14–21, at least two parallels exist. First, the tragedies of both chapters are facilitated by family members of David. Jonadab and Joab are cousins, sons of David's siblings. Second, the reader is left to wonder in both stories what the exact motivation of these men is. Why does Joab help David murder Uriah, and why does Jonadab help Amnon gain access to Tamar?[27] These similarities are a further indictment of Jonadab's character.

It would certainly be an understatement to say that Jonadab was not a nice man. His biggest problem was that his wisdom was not informed by a godly morality. In the beginning he had no qualms about giving Amnon advice on how he could deceive his father and gain access to the vulnerable princess, and in the end he stood by, seeking to give comfort for a situation he helped to create, without taking any responsibility for it. Jonadab may not have sought to kill intentionally like Ahithophel, but his ego, hypocrisy, and reckless wisdom were just as deadly.

The words of James 3:13–17 provide a fitting conclusion for understanding the deficiencies in Jonadab's character:

> Who is wise and understanding among you? Let him
> show by good conduct that his works are done in the meek-

---

[27] I owe this insight to Rosenberg, *King and Kin*, pp. 142-143. Rosenberg would add another similarity, stating, "Jonadab's name evokes echoes of the name 'Joab.' "

ness of wisdom. But if you have bitter envy and self-seeking in your hearts, do not boast and lie against the truth. This wisdom does not descend from above, but is earthly, sensual, demonic. For where envy and self-seeking exist, confusion and every evil thing are there. But the wisdom that is from above is first pure, then peaceable, gentle, willing to yield, full of mercy and good fruits, without partiality and without hypocrisy.

Chapter 23

Amnon & Tamar: Desire and Innocence
(David's son and daughter)

"And I, where could I take my shame? And as for you, you would be like one of the fools in Israel."—Tamar (2 Sam. 13:13)

Family Matters

There are thirty-nine references to family relationships in 2 Samuel 13.[1] Therefore, we can confidently say that this is a chapter *about* family matters, and a chapter in which family *matters*.[2] This chapter is also a prime example of the interrelationship between family and nation[3] for, as Polzin states, "This immediate emphasis on family also involves deeper associations of tribe and nation."[4] Amnon's crime sets in motion a chain of events that eventually culminates in Absalom's rebellion. Sin in the *house*(hold) of David, affects the *house* (dynasty and nation) of David.

Amnon's rape of his sister Tamar is the beginning of the fulfillment of Nathan's oracle to David: "Behold, I will raise up adversity against you from your own house" (2 Sam. 12:11). Likewise, Absalom's subsequent murder of Amnon begins to fulfill the statement, "The sword will never depart from your house" (2 Sam. 12:10). The sins of the father are reflected in the sons, albeit in a darker and more sinister way. David's destruction of Uriah's *house* bears fruit in the calamity that strikes his own *house* (meaning both family and nation).

Since the character portraits of Amnon and Tamar are intertwined within the story of 2 Samuel 13, they will be treated together. "Togetherness" is, in fact, an important theme of the story. At first, Amnon believes that it is impossible for him and Tamar to be together (v. 2). The heart of the story focuses on the destructive nature of their togetherness. Once Amnon has forced this "togetherness" on Tamar (vv. 11–14), she insists that they must stay together (v. 16), but Amnon rejects her plea by having her thrust outside

---

[1] There are 16 references to "son" or "sons" (vv. 1[2x], 3, 4, 23, 25, 27, 29, 30, 32[2x], 33, 35, 36, 37[2x]—I do not count the expression "sons of valor" in v. 28 as this is not a reference to family but a Hebrew idiom); 12 references to "brother" (vv. 3, 4, 7, 8, 10, 12, 20[4x], 26, 32); 9 references to "sister" (vv. 1, 2, 4, 5, 6, 11, 20, 22, 32); one use of "father" (v. 5); and one use of "daughters" (v. 18).

[2] Polzin, *David and the Deuteronomist*, p. 133, points out that "chapter 13 refers to children and siblings more often than any other chapter in the book."

[3] See the "Introduction," pp. 2-6.

[4] Polzin, *David and the Deuteronomist*, p. 133.

and bolting the door behind her to prevent any further opportunity for to-getherness (v. 17). As a result, Tamar ends up "desolate" in the house of her brother Absalom (v. 20), which provokes him to hate Amnon (v. 22). Thus Amnon's illicit desire for togetherness ends up fracturing a family, and eventually, a nation.[5]

Love and Sickness (2 Sam. 13:1–5)

The first verse introduces the three main characters of the story—Absalom, Tamar, and Amnon, in that order. The order is important, as well as suggestive of coming events. Tamar is surrounded by her brothers.[6] Initially, her situation between two brothers may seem like a safe place for a sister to be. However, we are immediately informed that only one brother views Tamar as a sister, while the other views her as a love interest.

Considering the outcome of the story, the order of introduction may also suggest that Absalom is in front of his sister because he is her protector.[7] Amnon, on the other hand, follows Tamar from behind where she is vulnerable. Similarly, he will seek to deceive her and catch her off guard in the story. Being introduced last seems unusual, considering Amnon is the older brother (2 Sam. 3:2–3), but this position of "weakness" gains him literary access to Tamar. In the same way, the story shows how Amnon learns to use weakness in order to overpower his victim. Absalom may appear to be a formidable obstacle, but the order in which the three siblings are introduced may hint that there are ways of "getting around" him.

The significance of these literary observations is confirmed near the conclusion of this episode. In verse 20, references to Tamar ("my sister") are surrounded by references to Amnon ("your brother"), but Amnon himself is

---

[5] There are a plethora of recent studies which provide valuable insights into the literary quality and events of 2 Sam. 13. I cannot hope in my treatment of Amnon and Tamar to repeat all the insights I have gained through the work of others, but for those who would like to read further on this subject, I would especially recommend the following studies: Conroy, *Absalom Absalom!*, pp. 17-42; J. P. Fokkelman, *King David*, pp. 99-125; Phyllis Trible, *Texts of Terror*, pp. 36-63; and Shimon Bar-Efrat, *Narrative Art*, pp. 239-282. For other works, see the footnotes which follow.

[6] Absalom is Tamar's full-blood brother, having the same father and mother. Amnon, however, has a different mother (2 Sam. 3:2) and is thus the half brother of Tamar and Absalom.

[7] This is not to ignore the frequent assertion by some scholars that Absalom is introduced first because the subsequent narrative will focus on the events that lead to his rebellion; it is only to say that the word order also plays a suggestive role in the present narrative.

surrounded by references to Absalom.[8] Mention of Absalom not only leads the way in verse 20; it also ends the verse, bringing Absalom in behind Amnon, and thus surrounding him. The literary structure suggests that Absalom will not leave his sister unprotected a second time! It anticipates the trap that Absalom will set for Amnon a few verses later (vv. 26–29). In the end, Amnon is no match for Absalom. The one who sought to deceive will be deceived himself.

We are told that Amnon's "love" for Tamar causes him such distress that he becomes sick (v. 2). Amnon is *obsessed* with his sister, leading to him being *distressed* because she is a virgin and because it seems "impossible" for him to "do anything to her." A review of these first two verses raises a number of red flags about Amnon's character.[9] First, is it proper for a brother to love a half sister to the point of obsession? Second, is it not a brother's duty to protect the virginity of his unmarried sister, rather than be distressed over it (see e.g., Gen. 34:7)?[10] Third, should a brother want to "do anything" to a sister, other than protect her?

Much ink has been used in recent years over the question of whether Amnon's crime was one of rape or incest.[11] Tamar tells Amnon, "Please speak to the king; for he will not withhold me from you" (v. 13). Propp observes, "The author describes Tamar as *assuming* she will be allowed to wed her half brother, and, after the rape, she claims marriage as her due. For Tamar, then, half sibling marriage is evidently conscionable"[12] (author's emphasis). Furthermore, Phoenician and Egyptian kings (some of Israel's closest neighbors) were known to marry their full or half sisters.[13] Therefore, this line of reasoning suggests that Amnon's crime was rape and not incest.

---

[8] Bar-Efrat, *Narrative Art*, p. 272, provides a helpful diagram of the literary structure of v. 20:

her brother	your brother	my sister	your brother	her brother
(Absalom)	(Amnon)	(Tamar)	(Amnon)	(Absalom)

[9] I disagree with Bar-Efrat, who believes that the reader would be positively disposed towards Amnon at this point. See ibid., pp. 242-243.

[10] The story in Gen. 34 has many connections with the story here in 2 Sam. 13. We will look at some of these connections and note how they act as a commentary on the story of Amnon and Tamar.

[11] Besides the various commentaries and special studies already mentioned, see also, Gordon J. Wenham, "*B^E TÛLAH* 'A GIRL OF MARRIAGEABLE AGE,' " *VT* 22, 1972, pp. 326-348; William H. Propp, "Kinship in 2 Samuel 13," *CBQ* 55, 1993, pp. 39-53; Mark Gray, "Amnon: A Chip Off the Old Block? Rhetorical Strategy in 2 Samuel 13:7–15: The Rape of Tamar and the Humiliation of the Poor," *JSOT* 77, 1998, pp. 39-54.

[12] Propp, "Kinship in 2 Sam. 13," p. 45.

[13] Ibid., p. 44.

On the other hand, if marriage would have been an acceptable option, then why does Amnon consider it "impossible" to do anything to Tamar? This suggests that there might have been some legal barrier, such as the laws against incest.[14] There are also other reasons to see Amnon's crime as an incestuous rape. Even if we allow that David and Tamar may have been agreeable to this union, this does not mean it was sanctioned by the author of Samuel. Biblical authors sometimes show characters following socially acceptable customs that are not in accordance with God's Word (e.g., Gen. 16:1–4; 1 Sam. 1:2–8). Furthermore, the writer of Samuel consistently upholds the values of the Torah, which suggests that he would view the crime as incest (Lev. 18:9–11; 20:17; Deut. 27:22).[15]

The story of Genesis 34 (the rape of Dinah) provides a negative commentary on Amnon's actions. There the brothers of Dinah are outraged at the rape of their sister, and seek to avenge the crime against her (Gen. 34:7, 31). Guarding the virginity of a sister was the natural duty of a brother in the ancient world, because it protected the family's honor.[16] Amnon does not seek to protect his sister, but to exploit her.

Verses 1 and 2 also echo another important passage which provides a contrast to Amnon's desire. David's lament over his beloved friend Jonathan (2 Sam. 1:26) contains four words also found in 2 Samuel 13:1–2. The words are "brother," "love," "distress," and "wonderful" (translated "impossible" by the NIV and "improper" by the NKJV in 2 Sam. 13:2). When compared with David's "wonderful love" for his "brother" Jonathan, and his "distress" over his death, the "love" of "brother" Amnon who is "distressed" over the "impossibility/wonderfulness" to do anything to his sister appears as something cheap and dirty. David's lament over Jonathan's death and the "wonderful love" they shared as fellow warriors and brothers, makes Amnon— who can find nothing better to do with his plush life at court than desire his half sister— look "sick" indeed!

---

[14] Wenham, $B^E TÚLAH$ etc. (full title in n. 11), p. 342. Although Stansell allows for the possibility of other interpretations, he states, "The 'sacrilege' Tamar so emphatically speaks of (vv. 12–13) suggests that this case is more than rape." See Stansell, *Honor and Shame in the David Narratives*, p. 72.

[15] Wenham, ibid., makes a similar point. Bergen's commentary is especially adept at showing the correspondence between the books of Samuel and the Torah. For example, he states, "Evidences of 1, 2 Samuel's interconnections with the Torah are wide-ranging and abundant. They include explicit references and inferences to historical details found in the Torah, awareness of Torah legal materials, theology, prophecies, and even literary techniques," Bergen, *1, 2 Samuel*, p. 46. See especially his charts on pp. 47-50 which provide ample evidence for this contention.

[16] See for example the discussion by Bruce J. Malina in *The New Testament World*, pp. 46-51.

"Sick" is one word, among several, that seems to carry a double entendre in the narrative.[17] Amnon's "love" for his sister makes him "sick." But is he not "sick" to "love" his sister in this way? The narrative will bear out just how "sick" Amnon really is, and it will show that Amnon's "love" is nothing more than illicit desire (another double entendre).[18]

Jonadab enters the story at this point (vv. 3–5), and we have commented on his character and advice in the previous chapter.[19] Trible sums up the situation before Jonadab's appearance: "Full of lust, the prince is impotent; full of sight, he lacks insight."[20] Jonadab's advice provides the power and vision for Amnon to fulfill his desire. Amnon now understands how he can use his weakness to his advantage. By becoming weak, he can become strong; by exploiting his sickness he can appeal to the power of the king and thereby gain access to what once seemed inaccessible—the princess of his desire.

House of Horrors (2 Sam. 13:6–18)

In verse 6, Amnon begins to put Jonadab's plan into action, with a few twists of his own.[21] It is ironic that when David comes to see his son, Amnon is "lying down" (v. 6). This word occurs in both its verbal and noun form (meaning "bed" in v. 5) in the story, and recalls a similar usage in the narrative of David's sin with Bathsheba (11:2–4). Its use in verse 6 infers deception, since lying down is part of the ruse of pretending to be ill. Speaking to his own generation, the prophet Micah warns, "Woe to those who devise iniquity, and work out evil on their beds! At morning light they practice it, because it is in the power of their hand" (Mic. 2:1).

David is referred to here as "the king" (2x), because Amnon is in need of royal permission to gain access to Tamar. While David was unsuccessful in duping Uriah into going down to his house (11:6–13), Amnon is successful in duping his father into believing that he is sick. How ironic that

---

[17] Another is the word "wonderful/impossible." On the significance of this see, Rosenberg, *King and Kin,* p. 140.

[18] Trible, *Texts of Terror,* pp. 38, and 58 n. 6, translates the Hebrew word for "love" here as "desire." She argues that this translation is ambiguous and allows the plot to draw out its precise meaning. I would argue that the translation "love" does this better, as the story shows that what is originally called "love" is anything but that. The true irony of the story is revealed as the reader discovers that Amnon's feeling for Tamar is far from any true definition of "love." Similarly, Jonadab's description as "very wise" is another example of double meaning. See chap. 22, p. 320.

[19] See chap. 22.

[20] Trible, *Texts of Terror,* p. 38.

[21] For a complete breakdown of the differences between Jonadab's words in v. 5 and Amnon's in v. 6, see Trible, *Texts of Terror,* pp. 58-59, n. 16.

the son whose name means "true" or "faithful" would be so effective at deceiving his father.

Amnon's first words to his father repeat Jonadab's verbatim ("Please let Tamar my sister come"), but his choice of the word "cakes" rather than Jonadab's word "food" is important. In the expression, "make a couple of cakes," the Hebrew uses both a verb and a noun that comes from the word for "heart." Therefore, this expression is sometimes translated "heart-cakes."[22] Once again, we encounter words with a double meaning. On the one hand, Amnon probably wants his father to think that he wishes Tamar to come and make him some health food: that is, food that will strengthen him ("hearty" food as we might say today). The reader knows, however, that these words betray his true intentions.[23]

Convinced by Amnon's duplicitous words, David "sends" Tamar from "the house" to Amnon's "house" (v. 7). There is more irony here, as the "sending" of David will lead to an illicit relationship which will fragment yet another "house" (his own!). Although David does the "sending," as he did so often in the Bathsheba and Uriah episode (e.g., 11:3, 4, 6, etc.), he is not a perpetrator of any crime here, but one of its victims. Amnon, who had no power to access Tamar, uses the sending power of the king to gain that access. By manipulating the king's authority, Amnon is no longer impotent; and he will use his new-found power in a show of brute force to get what he wants (v. 14). In fact, this meeting between father and son seems to create a role reversal in the story. Amnon's previous impotence appears to be transferred to David the king, who, upon hearing of Amnon's deed, can do nothing but be angry (v. 21). Another irony of verse 7 is David's command for Tamar to "go" to her brother's house. It is the same command that Amnon will use to send her away (v. 15), and thus acts as a parenthesis around this tragic incident.[24]

Obeying the king's request, Tamar goes dutifully to her brother Amnon's house (v.8). The focus on her preparation of the cakes has a two-fold effect. First, it demonstrates Tamar's diligence in seeking to help her brother and betrays her innocence regarding what is about to befall her. Second, it allows the reader to see what Amnon sees.[25] Amnon's voyeuristic stare (note the emphasis on seeing in vv. 5 and 6—literally, "before my eyes") while he is "lying down," contrasts with the hard work of Tamar.

The food also provides a metaphor that plays an important part in contrasting this brother and sister. While Tamar's focus is on the food that she hopes will restore her brother to health, Amnon is not concerned one bit

---

[22] Youngblood, *1, 2 Samuel*, p. 959.

[23] McCarter, *II Samuel*, p. 322.

[24] Conroy, *Absalom Absalom!*, p. 33.

[25] Trible, *Texts of Terror*, p. 43.

with the food Tamar is preparing, or the hard work she is putting in; his taste leans toward other delicacies,[26] and so he lies on his bed contemplating another scenario that will remove Tamar from the kitchen and bring her into the inner sanctum of his bedroom. This objective is accomplished when he orders everyone out of the house (v. 9) and tells Tamar to bring the food into his bedroom, where he may eat it from her own hand (v. 10).

With everyone out of the house and Tamar within reach, Amnon dispenses with the charade of weakness and seizes his prey (v. 11). The sister's hands that reached out to give nourishing food are forcefully grabbed and Amnon makes known an appetite of another kind. "Breakfast in bed" takes on a different and ominous meaning for Tamar.

Three key words of the story employ new and ironic meanings as Amnon says, "Come, lie with me my sister." Amnon's previous request of the king to let Tamar "come" (v. 6) takes on a more intimate meaning within the chamber of his bedroom. Deception and obsession now become invitation as the word "lie" also draws on a new shade of meaning. "Sister," a word which clearly refers to sibling relationships in this story, is perverted by Amnon and filled with an erotic meaning often used by lovers in the ancient world (e.g., Song of Sol. 4:9–10; 5:1–2).

To this point, Tamar has been the beautiful object of adoration, as well as the obedient and dutiful sibling in the story. Confronted with Amnon's indecent proposal, she finds her voice and proves herself wise as well as beautiful. Showing complete revulsion toward his intentions, four negative statements roll from her tongue. "*No*, my brother, do *not* force me, for *no* such thing should be done in Israel. Do *not* do this disgraceful thing" (v. 12). Tamar's use of "brother," in the familial sense, counters Amnon's erotic use of "sister" and contrasts with the heinous nature of his proposal.

Her protest is full of significant language, that recalls horrific incidents of Israel's past. There are, once again, a number of similarities with the rape of Dinah in Genesis 34. Dinah is described as being *violated* by Shechem (34:2), the same word used by Tamar who says, "Do not *force* me." This word can refer to a stronger person afflicting a weaker person with the express intent of humiliating (e.g., Gen. 16:6; Exod. 1:12; Judg. 16:19). It can also refer to illicit sex or sexual abuse (Deut. 22:24; Judg. 19:24).[27] Since a woman's

---

[26] Mark Gray, *Amnon: A Chip Off the Old Block*, p. 45, notes that there are "only three occasions in the Hebrew Bible where…[dough] and…[knead] are used in conjunction, one in particular (Hos. 7.4) explicitly links the activity of dough kneading to sexual impropriety, while the other two bespeak, respectively, a situation of social dislocation and wrongdoing (Jer. 7.18), and one of spiritual transgression (1 Sam. 28.24). For some reason, reference to the kneading of dough is always found in texts dealing with something amiss!"

[27] David Noel Freedman, "Dinah and Shechem Tamar and Amnon," *Austin Seminary Bulletin* 105, 1990, p. 54.

honor was bound up in her sexual purity, any illicit or sexually abusive act would humiliate her. This is why one of Tamar's pleas to Amnon is, "And I, where could I take my shame?" (v. 13).

Tamar's words, "For no such thing should be done in Israel. Do not do this disgraceful thing," are also found in Genesis 34:7. Like Shechem, Amnon is a spoiled prince. However, the similar incident in Genesis 34 not only highlights the despicable nature of Amnon's deed, it amplifies it in several ways. First, Shechem does not have sexual relations with a family member as Amnon does. Second, after "humbling her," the text tells us that Shechem loved Dinah, spoke tenderly to her and sought to marry her (Gen. 34:3–12). By contrast, following his rape of Tamar, Amnon is said to hate her and to throw her out of his house (13:15–18). All in all, the Gentile prince comes off looking much better than the son of David, and the similarities in the two stories draw our attention to the different outcomes.[28]

A close link also exists between Tamar's words and the story related in Judges 19–20 (the rape of the Levite's concubine). All three of the above words/phrases are found there as well (Judg. 19:24, 30; 20:6). Here I will particularly focus on Tamar's third expression, "Do not do this *disgraceful* thing." This word is found in Judges 20:6 where the NKJV translates it as "outrage." It is the word, *nebālah* (folly), the same word used by Abigail to describe her husband Nabal (1 Sam. 25:25). The ancient Mesopotamian (Akkadian) root for this word means a "breaking away" (like a stone) or "tearing away."[29] Its connection in Hebrew with sexually illicit situations (see its use also in Jer. 29:23) suggests the same idea of a breaking away or rupturing of the norm.[30] Just as the breaking away of stone from a wall will weaken the wall, so a person who commits *nebālah* threatens the structure of society. "Folly, therefore, consists in failing to observe life's essential rules. The fool is unable to see the order in things....It is this idea of lack of order, unruliness, which lies behind the use of *nebalah*."[31] Tamar's protest seeks to persuade her brother that such an outrageous act will not be countenanced in Israel. Princes are subject to the same law that governs society as a whole.

Moving from society at large to personal consequences, Tamar attempts to point out the devastating effect this will have in her life and Amnon's: "And I, where could I take my shame? And as for you, you would be like one of the fools in Israel" (v. 13). Attempting to reason with him by appealing to his conscience, Tamar asks the self-centered Amnon to consider

---

[28] Bergen, *1, 2 Samuel*, p. 380, states, "Amnon is portrayed as one who chose the way of the Canaanite; thus, readers are prepared to accept the fact that he will suffer the fate of the Canaanite."

[29] Schwartz, "Adultery in the House of David," p. 48.

[30] Ibid.

[31] Anthony Phillips, "NEBALAH—a term for serious disorderly and unruly conduct," *VT* 25, 1975, pp. 237-238.

for one moment how this act will alter her life. Since selfish people rarely consider or care how their actions will affect others, she also pleads with him to consider the consequences for his own life. Amnon, she argues, will be deemed "one of the fools in Israel." The word for "fools" is the plural form of *nābāl*. Like Abigail, Tamar makes a play on the words "folly" (*nebālah*) and "fool" (*nābāl*),[32] hoping to accentuate the ruinous outcome of this deed.

Tamar's final argument to Amnon involves going through the proper channels to obtain her, so that neither one will be disgraced: "Now therefore, please speak to the king; for he will not withhold me from you" (v. 13). As noted earlier, there is much debate over the significance of these words. The following scenarios are possible: 1) In spite of the Law's clear prohibition, Amnon, David, and Tamar are influenced by prevailing social customs and would therefore be agreeable to a brother/sister marriage;[33] 2) Tamar knows how her father indulges his sons and believes that he would override the clear teaching of the Law in favor of his son's desire; 3) Since Amnon has experienced the overindulgence of his father in the past, Tamar believes this argument will make sense to him, even though her father might not be favorable to such an arrangement; or, 4) Since Amnon is about to have sexual relations anyway, Tamar desperately pleads that it be done "legally" to avoid disgrace. In this she may believe what she says, or she may simply be trying to extricate herself from the situation.[34] In the end, since Amnon ignores Tamar's plea, there is no way to establish which of these scenarios reflects the real situation. Although Tamar's pleas fall on deaf ears, her words project a sense of propriety and wisdom for one so young.

One of the characteristics of fools is that they do not listen to wise advice (1 Sam. 25:17, 19), and so we are told, "he would not heed her voice" (v. 14). The brutality of Amnon's deed is emphasized by the repetition in

---

[32] 1 Sam. 25:25.

[33] As noted above, the books of Samuel uphold the teachings of the Torah and so it does no good to argue, as some scholars do, that the laws of the Torah were written later than the time of David. The author would then be inconsistent in holding up the Law as a mirror by which to judge people's actions, when, in fact, they were ignorant of its contents. If David (and Amnon and Tamar) were willing to accept such an arrangement, it must be because they were influenced by prevailing cultural norms. This would be their view, however, not the view of the author. Furthermore, appealing to the case of Abraham and Sarah (Gen. 20:12), as is sometimes done to condone the acceptability of brother/sister marriages, is also illegitimate since this reflects the practice of the patriarchs *before* the giving of the Law. This is clearly noted by David Daube, "Absalom and the Ideal King," *VT* 48/3, 1998, p. 315.

[34] McCarter, *II Samuel*, p. 324, gives a similar, though not identical list, of four alternatives. Defining his fourth alternative, he writes, "The laws were in full effect. In this case Tamar's words, unless she is simply temporizing, imply that David would have been willing to permit the marriage despite its illegality, and Aminon [McCarter's spelling] is guilty of both rape and incest."

verse 14 of three verbs used previously in the story. First, "being stronger than she" is from the same word in verse 11 translated "he took hold of," or "seized her." This verb demonstrates "that Tamar not only argued verbally but also resisted bodily."[35] Amnon's act is one of "seizure" and is thus more violent than the act of his father who "took" Bathsheba (2 Sam. 11:4).

Second, in contrast to his sister's plea, "Do not force/humble me" (v. 12), we are told "he forced/humbled her." Finally, the act is consummated in the expression, "he laid her." The vulgarity of the deed is expressed by eliminating the preposition "with," the customary way of speaking about sexual intercourse (2 Sam. 11:4).[36] Once again, the son eclipses his father in the crude manner of his deed, and the oft' repeated word "lay" notes the progression in the story from deception (v. 6), to obsession (v. 7), to invitation (v. 11), to coercion (v. 14).

The turning point of the story is marked in verse 15 as Amnon's hatred of Tamar overpowers his previous feelings of "love" for her. The vocabulary itself demonstrates this overwhelming change, as the word "hate" occurs four times attached to adjectives like "exceedingly" and "great," whereas "love" occurs only twice, unadorned by superlatives. "Love" is unmasked as unbridled lust, as the dish Amnon once hungered for now tastes rotten to the core. Such is the nature of sin, which seems alluring and desirable until ingested (Gen. 3:6–8).[37] Amnon's words are curt and callous as he says, "Arise, be gone" (two words in Hebrew). With two words he had beckoned her ("come," "lie," v. 11), and with two words he dismisses her.

Tamar's response to this command parallels her earlier response as she once again replies, "No" (v. 16). If Amnon's hatred is now *greater* than his love, Tamar says that his cruel command to leave is a "*greater* evil" than what he had already done to her. The Hebrew is less eloquent than her previous response and may imply the unnerving effect that Amnon's crime has had on her.[38] However, just as Tamar's response parallels her previous response, so too does Amnon's: "But he would not listen to her" (v. 16).

It is suggested that Tamar's insistence on staying with Amnon confirms her belief that the relationship was not incestuous.[39] The situation has drastically changed, however. Whether she was sincere or not in her plea for Amnon to ask the king for her, she now sees no other alternative. She must either stay and become Amnon's wife or give up hope of ever being a wife

---

[35] Bar-Efrat, *Narrative Art*, p. 265.

[36] All commentators are agreed on the crudeness of this expression. See for example, Firth, *1&2 Samuel*, p. 433.

[37] Rosenberg, *King and Kin*, p. 145, insightfully notes that the key words "eat, see, and lie with" which relate to Gen. 3 and 2 Sam. 11 picture Amnon as "a yielder to temptation and a sinner."

[38] Frymer-Kensky, *Women of the Bible*, pp. 163-164.

[39] Propp, *Kingship in 2 Samuel 13*, p. 45.

and mother. Tamar is apparently referring to the commands in such passages as Exodus 22:16 and Deuteronomy 22:28–29. The passage in Deuteronomy is especially pertinent, as it uses many of the key words found in our story. In the following quote I have italicized the key words which occur in 2 Samuel 13:

> If a man finds a young woman who is a *virgin*, who is not betrothed, and he seizes her and *lies* with her, and they are found out, then the man who *lay* with her shall give to the young woman's father fifty shekels of silver, and she shall be his wife because he has *humbled* her; he shall not be permitted to *divorce* her all his days.

The words "virgin," "lies/lay," and "humbled" are obvious even in an English translation. The word translated "divorce" is the word "send,"[40] which is what Amnon tells his servant to do with Tamar in verse 17: "Please send this away" (my translation). The word "seizes" is a different Hebrew verb than the one found in 2 Samuel 13:11, 14, therefore I have not italicized it, but it is a synonym. The question, of course, is whether this law would apply to an incestuous relationship. Either way, Tamar knows no other option and her outlook may, or may not, represent the ideals of the narrator.

Since Tamar will not leave voluntarily, Amnon wants her thrown out (v. 17). Amnon recalls one of his servants (whom he had previously ordered to leave the house, v. 9) and politely asks him to remove Tamar from the premises.[41] The language reveals Amnon's contempt for Tamar. There is a strong contrast in his polite words to his servant, "Please send...," and his refusal even to acknowledge Tamar's name. He refers to her only as "this." The terrible deed has erased all trace of familial language. The words "brother" and "sister" no longer fall from the lips of either Amnon or Tamar. From the beginning, he has treated her as an object. At first she was an object to be gazed upon, then an object on which to consume his lust. Having shamed Tamar and made a fool of himself (as she had warned), Amnon now notices a severe stench in his house and dehumanizes her by comparing her to rubbish that needs to be taken outside. Although Tamar is forcefully removed from Amnon's house, the reader knows that the stench remains. The bolted door, which prevents a togetherness that Tamar sought for only after Amnon's crime against her, serves also to lock Amnon away in his own prison of sin

---

[40] This word which was so important to the David and Bathsheba narrative now comes home to roost.

[41] Trible, *Texts of Terror*, p. 48, perceptively states, "At the start, Amnon wanted the servants out and Tamar in (13:9de); at the close, he wants the servant in and Tamar out."

(Rom. 6:16). The locked door not only seals the fate of Tamar (v. 20); it seals the fate of Amnon as well (vv. 22, 28).[42]

Between the command to "Send away" and the actual implementation of it, we are reminded of better days. We are told that Tamar wears a garment (like Joseph's, Gen. 37:3) that celebrates her status as one of the virgin daughters of the king (v. 18). This, however, only serves to contrast the ignominy with which she is treated as she is thrust out.[43] Should a princess be raped and then thrown out like rubbish by an errand boy? Is this the way royalty should treat royalty, let alone a family member and fellow human being? This is no fairytale, but if it were it would be a fairytale gone wrong, as the beautiful princess, who had nobly responded to a brother in need, is despoiled and cast out by the prince's servant.

Home Alone (2 Sam. 13:19–22)

"Tamar, the good girl who stayed at home until her father sent for her, is now 'outside' in the most devastating of circumstances."[44] Having been thrown out, Tamar assumes the traditional posture and look of one who has been humiliated and suffered loss (v. 19). She places ashes upon her royal head (did she find them in the rubbish outside Amnon's house?) with face bowed, no longer able to look anyone in the eye because of her shame. Her royal garment has been torn, a symbol of grief at the loss of what once was. The hand that had reached out to feed a brother (v. 10) is now placed upon her head, assuming the posture of a lowly captive (Jer. 2:37). As she "goes," she "cries out." The word describing her departure, "went away" (NKJV) is the same word David used to send her when he commanded, "Now *go* to your brother Amnon's house" (v. 7). The repetition of this word creates a purposeful contrast between Tamar's condition before she went to Amnon's house and her condition as she leaves. It also reminds us of her plea to Amnon, "And I, where could I *go* with my reproach?" (v. 13, my translation).[45]

While the word "cry out" may refer to Tamar's literal pain, it is also a word used in judicial contexts, as well as contexts of deliverance (Deut. 26:7; 1 Sam. 7:8; 2 Sam. 19:28; 2 Kings 8:3; etc.).[46] Tamar seeks justice for the

---

[42] Conroy, *Absalom Absalom!*, p. 33, states, "On the surface, it is Tamar who is shut out, but upon Amnon too a door has closed. His fate is sealed from this moment."

[43] Bar-Efrat, *Narrative Art*, p. 270, notes, "In order to stress the depths of her humiliation through contrast—the daughter of the king, wearing a long robe (the symbol of her status), is thrown out by a boy servant—the details about Tamar's apparel are situated at this particular point, between Amnon's command and its implementation by the servant."

[44] Frymer-Kensky, *Women of the Bible*, p. 164.

[45] I am indebted to Trible, *Texts of Terror*, p. 50, for this insight.

[46] Bar-Efrat, *Narrative Art*, p. 271.

wrong done to her, and deliverance from her pitiful situation. When the actions of this verse are viewed as a whole, "she acts as those who see a ruin" (Ezek. 27:30).[47]

When Absalom witnesses her condition, he asks, "Has Amnon your brother been with you?" (v. 20). Either Absalom knew of Tamar's trip to Amnon's house, or was suspicious of Amnon's intentions toward his sister. We cannot be sure, but if Tamar was living in Absalom's house, then he would have known of her visit to Amnon.[48]

Absalom's words are at first surprising and disconcerting. It seems as though he would have Tamar hush up the whole ugly incident and forget about it. Ironically, the word "heart" reappears in the narrative. When Absalom says, "Do not take this thing to heart," we are reminded of the "heart-cakes" (vv. 6, 8) that led to Tamar's current distress. Absalom's advice may have a two-fold purpose. On the one hand, if word gets out about Amnon's actions, shame will be brought on the house of David. More specifically, I believe Absalom is concerned about his own honor. As the older brother he failed to protect his sister's virginity. Later chapters reveal Absalom's vanity (14:25–26; 15:1), so his desire to silence Tamar, at least for the moment, may anticipate this weakness.

On the other hand, verse 22 makes clear that Absalom is not content to let the matter rest. But does Absalom plot revenge against Amnon for the sake of his sister, or for the sake of his own wounded honor? Perhaps it is a little of both. Absalom may have tender feelings for his sister, as implied in the naming of his only daughter, Tamar (14:27). However, from what we will learn of Absalom's ego, his revenge is also based on a desire for personal vindication.[49]

Another look at the beginning of the story suggests an interesting parallel between Absalom and Jonadab. Absalom is to Tamar what Jonadab is to Amnon. "In urging Amnon to 'act ill,' Jonadab counseled pretense for a specific time and purpose....With their own nuances, Absalom's advice to Tamar may also conceal a plan for revenge."[50]

It is of note that sibling language returns in verse 20 with a vengeance (pun intended). As previously noted, Tamar is surrounded by her brothers, as she was in verse 1, but here references to Amnon surround Tamar (suggesting the consequences of the trap he laid for her), while references to Absalom surround Amnon (suggesting the trap he will lay for him). The lan-

---

[47] Frymer-Kensky, *Women of the Bible*, p. 165.
[48] As McCarter, *II Samuel*, p. 236, notes, we cannot be certain where Tamar lived before the rape. If, however, the "house" mentioned in verse 7 is the palace, Absalom may still have known about her visit to Amnon's house.
[49] See chap. 24.
[50] Trible, *Texts of Terror*, p. 51. The parallel is not exact, as Jonadab only provides advice, whereas Absalom advises Tamar but also carries out the deception.

guage of "brother/sister" not only speaks of the shocking nature of the crime committed by Amnon; it also highlights the division within the family and anticipates the fratricide to come.

Though Tamar remains in her brother Absalom's house, in another sense she is "home alone." With no hope of a husband, children, or a home of her own, her devastated life is summed up in the word "desolate," a word that conjures up the destruction of an enemy (Lam. 1:16), or a lion tearing its prey to pieces (Lam. 3:11).[51] The "date palm" (the meaning of Tamar's name) has been deflowered and will never bear fruit.

Will there be any justice for this woman? When we read of *King* David hearing of the incident and being angry (v. 21), we are momentarily hopeful. However, David's anger only reveals his impotence. Is it because of his over-indulgence of Amnon (as the additional phrase in the Septuagint suggests),[52] or does David's past sin paralyze him? Whatever the reason, David's inactivity fuels the hatred in Absalom's heart. We are told that "Absalom spoke to his brother Amnon neither good nor bad. For Absalom hated Amnon, because he had forced his sister Tamar" (v. 22). Some have interpreted this to mean that Absalom did not say a word to his brother over the next two years.[53] This seems unlikely, however, because it would betray the animosity Absalom had for Amnon. Furthermore, this same expression occurs in Genesis 31:24, when Laban tells Jacob that God had appeared to him in a dream and said, "Be careful that you speak to Jacob neither good nor bad." Laban clearly had a conversation with Jacob, a somewhat heated one at that, but was not allowed to act in a harmful way toward him. Thus, Absalom kept up the ruse of pretending all was well in order to plot his revenge against his brother.[54]

The first episode of this chapter closes with the notice that "Absalom hated Amnon" (v. 22). While the story opened speaking of the "love" Amnon had for Tamar (v. 1), the curtain comes down with Absalom hating Amnon because of what he had done to her. The transformation from "love" to "hate" first takes place in the heart of Amnon, with Tamar as object (v. 15). That hatred now passes to Absalom with Amnon as object. The episode ends on a "cliff-hanger," leaving the reader eagerly waiting for the next installment.

---

[51] Ibid., p. 52.

[52] Anderson, *2 Samuel*, p. 176, translates it as, "But he did not curb the excesses (lit., 'spirit') of his son Amnon; he favored him because he was his firstborn." The scroll from the Dead Sea, 4QSam^a reads similarly.

[53] Brueggemann, *First and Second Samuel*, p. 289, among others.

[54] Fokkelman, *King David*, p. 112, translates as, "He did not treat him in a hostile way."

Dead Man Walking (2 Sam. 13:23–29)

After Amnon's death, Jonadab will tell David, "For by the command of Absalom this has been determined from the day he violated his sister Tamar" (v. 32). The focus in these verses (23–29) is on the words and deeds of Absalom.[55] Amnon is given no further voice in the narrative; he is only an object that is manipulated and acted upon. His final tyrannical act of sending Tamar out and bolting the door has left him powerless. He is an insect caught in the web of Absalom's machinations. The prince has become a pawn on the chessboard of love and hate that he has created; he is out-thought and out-maneuvered by Absalom. At least Tamar could struggle and protest, but Absalom's plot is so masterful that Amnon is dead before he can offer the slightest resistance (vv. 28–29). Only David's inquiry, "Why should he go with you?" (v. 26) offers any potential threat to the plan. However, it is overcome easily by Absalom's insistence (v. 27).

The structure of these verses offers interesting parallels with the first part of the chapter. Davis has a very helpful chart which is reproduced here:

Absalom's sister, v. 1
  Amnon, Jonadab, and David: getting Tamar accessible, vv. 2–7
    Amnon's rape of Tamar, vv. 8–17
      Reaction: grief, tearing garment, vv. 18–19
        Solace from Absalom, v. 20
          Reactions of David and Absalom, vv. 21–22

Absalom's sheep-shearing, v. 23
  Absalom and David: getting Amnon accessible, vv. 24–27
    Absalom's murder of Amnon, vv. 28–29
      Reaction: grief, tearing garments, vv. 30–31
        Solace from Jonadab, vv. 32–33, 34–35
          Reactions of David & Absalom & others, vv. 36–39[56]

These parallels suggest the theme of "reaping what you sow." Absalom's hatred, deceit, and murder are a direct result of Amnon's deceit, rape, and hatred. Furthermore, Amnon is struck down when he is most vulnerable and least suspecting: "Watch now, when Amnon's heart is merry with wine, and when I say to you, 'Strike Amnon!' then kill him" (v. 28). Similarly,

---

[55] Absalom's part in these verses will be considered in more detail in chap. 24.

[56] Davis, *2 Samuel*, p. 171. Also see, Polzin, *David and the Deuteronomist*, pp. 134-135, who notes some of the verbal and thematic similarities. Fokkelman, *King David*, p. 121, suggests these verses are arranged chiastically, while Youngblood, *1, 2 Samuel*, p. 968, suggests a double chiasm for these verses. Each suggestion has its own merit and provides different insights into the meaning of these verses.

Tamar is unsuspecting, and when she is most vulnerable Amnon makes his move (vv. 9–10). This theme also encompasses David as he experiences being deceived by two of his sons (as he had deceived Uriah), while having a daughter raped (an intensification of his sin with Bathsheba), and a son murdered (as he had murdered Uriah).

Amnon and Tamar: Looking in the Mirror of Scripture

Stories from Genesis

We have already noted similarities between the story of Amnon and Tamar, and that of Dinah and Shechem (Gen. 34). When these two stories are contrasted, Amnon, the prince of Judah, appears more wicked than Shechem, the Gentile prince, while Tamar looks more virtuous than her counterpart Dinah. Tamar only leaves home when asked by her father (2 Sam. 13:7), whereas Dinah goes out to "see the daughters of the land" (Gen. 34:1),[57] an unwise move particularly in view of what transpires. Tamar, then, is not only more virtuous, but also wiser than Dinah.

Words and motifs from the Joseph story also highlight some of the qualities of Amnon and Tamar.[58] The most obvious similarity is that Tamar and Joseph are the only two in Scripture said to wear the same kind of garment (Gen. 37:3; 2 Sam. 13:18). The words "love" and "hate" play an important part in the Joseph story, as they do in 2 Samuel 13. Joseph is hated by his brothers, and Tamar is hated by Amnon (Gen. 37:4, 8; 2 Sam. 13:15). Tamar attempts to resist an illicit sexual relationship, as does Joseph (Gen. 39:7–13; 2 Sam. 13:11–14); and both suffer consequences in spite of their innocence. Amnon and Potiphar's wife invite their victims by saying, "lie with me" (Gen. 39:7, 12; 2 Sam. 13:11), while Joseph and Tamar give several reasons why they should not do so (Gen. 39:8–9; 2 Sam. 13:12–13).

These similarities with Joseph place Tamar in a very positive light, whereas Amnon is once again compared with a Gentile—this time a woman, who like Amnon, is used to getting what she wants. Spoiled and self-indulgent become apt descriptions of Amnon as we note the similarities with Shechem and Potiphar's wife. Tamar's virtue and wisdom, already noted by the contrast with Dinah, is further heightened by the comparison with Joseph.

One final similarity in the two stories are the words, "Have everyone go out from me" (Gen. 45:1; 2 Sam. 13:9), spoken by Joseph and Amnon.

---

[57] Malina, *New Testament World*, pp. 47-48, points out that the proper sphere of a woman in the ancient world was the home. Any woman who strayed too far away without a legitimate reason was considered a "loose" woman. A woman on her own might have her virtue compromised, as was the case with Dinah in Gen. 34.

[58] See especially Robert Alter, *The World of Biblical Literature* (London: SPCK, 1992), pp. 114-116.

Although they speak the same words, this similarity intensifies the disparity between these two men. "The momentary irony is clear and pointed: the same words that were a preface to a great moment of fraternal reconciliation are now a prologue to a sexual violation of the fraternal bond."[59]

Finally, many have noted similarities between 2 Samuel 13 and the story of Judah and Tamar in Genesis 38.[60] While I am not convinced by all the "parallels" that are adduced, the following are persuasive: 1) both women are named Tamar; 2) both are involved in an illicit sexual relationship with a family member; 3) this family member (Judah in Gen. 38/Amnon in 2 Sam. 13) never engages in sexual activity again with the respective Tamar; 4) both Judah and Amnon are deceived at a sheep-shearing festival (Gen. 38:12–13; 2 Sam. 13:24); and 5) the plots of each story develop in opposite directions (Gen. 38, two sons die, then an illicit sexual encounter; 2 Sam. 11–13, illicit sexual encounter followed by the death of two sons).[61] Other potential links include the mention of clothing in connection to sexual acts (Gen. 38:14, 19; 2 Sam. 13:18); and the fact that both Tamars end up in different houses (Gen. 38:11; 2 Sam. 13:20—if in fact, Tamar did not already live with her brother Absalom).

These similarities are enough to suggest that a parallel and/or contrast is being made between the two Tamars, and Judah and Amnon. In Genesis 38, Judah is a despicable character who has a change of heart by the end of the episode. By contrast, Amnon remains despicable throughout 2 Samuel 13. Judah's confession regarding Tamar, "She has been more righteous than I," demonstrates that he is a man who learns from his mistakes. The same cannot be said of Amnon; he is an unrepentant sinner.

While the Tamar of Genesis 38 engages in sinful activity (deception and incest), she is held up in certain ways as a heroine, because she persists in her rightful quest to raise an heir to her dead husband. When her first two husbands die, she finds herself in a difficult circumstance, through no fault of her own. To her credit, she finds a way to rise above her difficulty and become a productive member of the family. Similarly, the Tamar of 2 Samuel 13

---

[59] Ibid., p. 114.

[60] G.A. Rendsburg, "David and His Circle in Genesis xxxviii," *VT* 36, 1986, pp. 438-446; C.Y.S. Ho, "The Stories of the Family Troubles of Judah and David: A Study of Their Literary Links," *VT* 49, 1999, pp. 514-531 (hereafter cited as *Family Troubles*). While some of the parallels noted by these studies are illuminating, I am not inclined to agree with the conclusion advocated by both: namely, that the story of Judah and Tamar was composed as a commentary on life at David's court. I believe that the dependence goes in the opposite direction. Once again I would cite the fact that the author(s) of Samuel are very familiar with the Torah and constantly allude to it. For other studies that relate similarities between these two passages, see the bibliographies in the two articles mentioned in this note.

[61] Ho, *Family Troubles*, p. 516.

finds herself in a difficult family situation, through no fault of her own. In contrast to the Tamar of Genesis 38, she is more virtuous. The difference is that she is unable to extricate herself from the circumstance and so becomes a non-productive member of the family. The contrast between the two Tamars underscores the disaster that befalls the Tamar of 2 Samuel 13. Genesis 38 has a "happy ending," whereas 2 Samuel 13 ends tragically.

The Levite and His Concubine (Judges 19–21)

The parallels between Judges 19–21 and 2 Samuel 13 are instructive. Polzin has listed eight similarities:[62] 1) familial language—*brothers*, *sons* ; 2) sexual abuse of a woman leads to fratricidal conflict, with similar words being used: "Arise, let's go" (Levite to his concubine, Judg. 19:28), "Arise, go" (Amnon to Tamar, 2 Sam. 13:15); 3 and 4) we have already pointed out that the word *nebālah* (folly), the word "to humble/force," and the expression of something that is "not to be done in Israel" occur in both passages; 5) "the rape of a virgin is suggested in Judges 19 and accomplished in 2 Samuel 13"[63] (see Judg. 19:24); 6) the language of protesting the impending rape is similar in both stories (Judg. 19:23; 2 Sam. 13:12); 7) a double expression of "familial unwillingness" (the son-in-law is unwilling to stay longer, Judg. 19:10; David is unwilling to attend Absalom's feast, 2 Sam. 13:25; the rapists of Gibeah are unwilling to listen, Judg. 19:25; Amnon is unwilling to listen, 2 Sam. 13:14, 16—the same Hebrew word is used in each instance); and 8) similar plot structure. Polzin also notes that the frame of the story in Judges states that there was "no king in Israel" (19:1; 21:25), whereas the narrative in 2 Samuel 13 takes place while there is a king in Israel; in fact, it takes place within the king's family![64]

The correspondences between these two stories are indeed impressive. The similarities suggest the brutality of Amnon's rape, and the ungodliness of his character. While the concubine's experience must be considered even more horrendous than Tamar's, both emphasize the helplessness of the victim as they are overpowered by their attacker(s). The fact that one story is set within the context of national struggle, while the other occurs within a familial struggle, continues to underline the powerful connection between public and private events. Although modern politics would try to insist that the two can be separated, these stories are a commentary on the fact that such a dichotomy is false. The link between public and private actions is not only made by comparing these two stories; it is a significant ingredient in understanding the unfolding story of David's house. As in the days of the Judg-

---

[62] Polzin, *David and the Deuteronomist*, pp. 136-138.

[63] Ibid., p. 137.

[64] Ibid., p. 136.

es, so also here—the rape of a woman will (eventually) lead to civil war in Israel.

Stories from 1 and 2 Samuel

Tamar's wordplay of *nebālah* (folly) and *nābāl* (fool) in 2 Samuel 13:12–13 recalls the similar wordplay by Abigail in 1 Samuel 25:25. This wordplay associates Amnon with Nabal. Indeed, Amnon proves himself to be as self-centered and boorish as Nabal. Closer inspection of these two narratives reveals other significant associations. Nabal is a wealthy man (1 Sam. 25:2) who feasts "like a king"[65] (25:36), while Amnon enjoys the luxuries of court life.

Food plays an important role in both stories. Nabal's refusal to share his food with David, along with his degrading comments (1 Sam. 25:10–11), ignites a crisis (25:13) that is only averted by Abigail's offering of food, and humble words (25:18–31). Food has a somewhat different function in 2 Samuel 13. Food becomes the ruse by which Amnon is able to get Tamar alone with him in his bedroom (vv. 6–10). In both stories food is involved in precipitating the crisis; it is also a symbol of greed and self-centeredness. Nabal's food is something he refuses to share, even though he has an abundance of it. For Amnon, food is a symbol of his sexual appetite, and he will let no one or nothing stand in the way of satisfying his hunger.

Amnon's food, described as "heart-cakes" (2 Sam. 13:6, 8), provides another link with Nabal's story where the word "heart" occurs frequently (1 Sam. 25:3, 25, 31, 36, 37). Just as Nabal's heart is merry within him because he is drunk (v. 36), so Absalom advises his servants to strike Amnon when his "heart is merry with wine" (2 Sam. 13:28).[66]

Not only are both men unwilling to listen to wise counsel (1 Sam. 25:17, 19; 2 Sam. 13:14, 16), David's actions in 1 Samuel 25 provide a foil for Amnon's in 2 Samuel 13. In 1 Samuel 25:24, Abigail pleads with David, "Please let your maidservant speak in your ears." Responding to her advice, David says, "See, I have heeded your voice" (v. 35). In contrast, we are told on two occasions that Amnon "was not willing to listen to her [Tamar]" (2 Sam. 13:14, 16). With so many similarities, it is surely not a coincidence that both Nabal and Amnon are said to die during a sheep-shearing festival (1 Sam. 25:4; 2 Sam. 13:24).

If Amnon shares many similarities with Nabal, then it is not surprising that there are also correspondences between Abigail and Tamar. Besides

---

[65]The LXX of 2 Sam. 13:27 includes the words, "So Absalom prepared a feast fit for a king." If these words were accidentally omitted from the Hebrew text, this would be yet one more correspondence between the stories of 1 Sam. 25 and 2 Sam. 13. For further discussion see Vannoy, *1–2 Samuel*, p. 346.

[66] Absalom also makes the comment to Tamar, "Do not take this thing to *heart*" (v. 20).

making a similar play on the words fool/folly, both are said to be "beautiful" (1 Sam. 25:3; 2 Sam. 13:1, same Hebrew word). Abigail and Tamar both seek to prevent a crisis that would ruin a family. They both prepare food (1 Sam. 25:18; 2 Sam. 13:8–9), and they both offer wise advice (1 Sam. 25:25–31; 2 Sam. 13:12–13).

The preceding similarities serve to illuminate the very different outcomes of both stories. Whereas Abigail is able to save her house from the *sword* (1 Sam. 25:13), Tamar's tragedy contributes to the fulfillment of Nathan's words to David, "the *sword* will never depart from your house" (2 Sam. 12:10). The responses of wisdom (David listening to Abigail's words) and folly (Amnon's refusal to listen to Tamar) are thus defined and contrasted by these two narratives.

David's sin with Bathsheba and murder of Uriah provide the immediate background for understanding the narrative of Amnon and Tamar.[67] As noted above, it is the first step in the fulfillment of Nathan's prophecy which not only includes the judgment, "the sword will not depart from your house," but also, "I will raise up adversity from your own house" (2 Sam. 12:10–11). The word translated "adversity" (NKJV) is the word "evil." 2 Samuel 11:27 states, "But the thing which David did was *evil* in the eyes of the Lord" (my translation). Because David had done "evil," the Lord said he would raise up "evil" from his own house. When Amnon attempts to throw Tamar out of his house, she replies, "No indeed! This *evil* of sending me away is worse than the other you did to me" (2 Sam. 13:16).

The connection between Amnon's evil and David's evil is made more explicit by employing the same three key verbs that described David's sin, with a few twists. We have previously noted how the verbs "send," "take," and "lay" occur throughout the David and Bathsheba narrative, appearing particularly at the beginning, middle, and end of the story.[68] Earlier in this chapter we examined how these words are used in the narrative of 2 Samuel 13. Here we bring all the words together for a summary look, and to compare and contrast them with the narrative of 2 Samuel 11–12.

First, the word "send" is used to bracket Amnon's crime, as David unwittingly, and ironically, "sends" Tamar to Amnon's house (2 Sam. 13:7), while Amnon heartlessly "sends" her away (v. 17). Furthermore, as David uses other intermediaries to send for Bathsheba, so he acts as the intermediary in sending Tamar.[69] Second, instead of describing Amnon's sin as "taking," as in the case of David (2 Sam. 11:4), the more forceful word "seize" is

---

[67] Concerning the initial words of 2 Sam. 13:1, Firth, *1 & 2 Samuel*, p. 436, states, "'Afterwards' provides a clear link to preceding events, indicating that we are to read in the light of what has gone before."

[68] See chap. 19, p. 235, esp. n. 24, and p. 239, including n. 33.

[69] Firth, *1 & 2 Samuel*, p. 435.

used (2 Sam. 13:11, 14), amplifying the violence of the son in contrast to his father. Third, the word "lay" which described David's sin with Bathsheba (2 Sam. 11:4) is used to describe Amnon's sin with Tamar, but in a cruder way (2 Sam. 13:14), so the text does not say that Amnon "lay with her" but that he "laid her."

Noting the verbal similarities communicates that the father's sin continues in the son, but the differences emphasize the more brazen nature of Amnon's crime.[70] Amnon's callous disregard is most evident when he casts Tamar "outside" (vv. 17–18). David had desperately tried to conceal his sin ("you did it secretly," 2 Sam. 12:12), but Amnon does not seem to care who finds out. David brings Bathsheba into his house (2 Sam. 11:27); Amnon throws Tamar out.

Whereas David comes off looking better than his son, a comparison of Tamar and Bathsheba favors Tamar. Tamar speaks wise words and offers resistance, while Bathsheba appears to go along compliantly.[71] Spiritually speaking, Tamar also looks superior to David. The most obvious contrast between the two is that David is the instigator of sin in 2 Samuel 11, while Tamar is the innocent victim of sin in 2 Samuel 13. A more subtle contrast occurs in chapter 13, where David's protest to Absalom, "No, my son, let us not all go now" (v. 25), "is curiously reminiscent in syntax to Tamar's pleas to her brother" Amnon, "No, my brother, do not force me" (v. 12).[72] In both cases, the one protested against has his way. Tamar is forceful and resolute in her response, but lacks the physical strength to overcome her brother. David, on the other hand, proves himself weak by allowing Absalom to manipulate and flatter him into allowing Amnon to go along to the feast. This parallel in weakness emphasizes the strength of character in Tamar as opposed to her father. If it were up to her, she would not give an inch to Amnon's offensive invitation. David, however, has all the power of "king" at his disposal but is worn down by the importunity of his whiny son. Rosenberg calls it a "failure of will—rooted in habit, impasse, and shame."[73]

Finally, David's murder of Uriah and Absalom's murder of Amnon suggest a parallel. As David deceived Uriah (2 Sam. 11:6–15), so Absalom deceived David (2 Sam. 13:24–27). Just as David used others to murder Uriah (2 Sam. 11:16), so Absalom commands his servants to murder Amnon (2 Sam. 13:28–29). Once again, the sins of the father are visited upon the sons,

---

[70] Mark Gray, *Amnon: A Chip Off the Old Block*, p. 47, also notes the contrast between David's refusal to eat (2 Sam. 12:17) and Amnon's refusal to eat. He states that David's refusal to eat "is a serious matter, carrying a positive connotation. But Amnon refuses to eat as part of a ruse of perversion, something which pleases no-one. That there is a patent difference between these two men is strongly accentuated."

[71] See chap. 19, pp. 235-236, and 242.

[72] Rosenberg, *King and Kin*, p. 147.

[73] Ibid.

only in a more sinister way. Whereas David kills a faithful soldier, Absalom kills a brother. Like his adultery with Bathsheba, David tries to cover up the murder of Uriah by having him look like a casualty of war. Absalom, like his brother Amnon, is unconcerned with any kind of cover up. The words of Jeremiah 6:15 seem particularly appropriate to David's wayward sons: "Were they ashamed when they had committed abomination? No! They were not at all ashamed; nor did they know how to blush." The misdeeds of David's sons demonstrate that sinners become bolder and more blatant in the next generation.

Conclusion: Safe at Home

Yairah Amit states, "Spatially, this is a story of houses."[74] Tamar leaves her house, a place of safety and refuge, to go to her brother's house, presumably a place of safety, where the unthinkable happens. The result is desolation in the house of Absalom, which ultimately results in division and damage to the house of David.

The concept of "house" intrinsically conveys the ideas of separation and boundaries. Practically speaking, that which separates one house from another is a property line or boundary. Furthermore, houses have doors and walls that create structure and either provide or deny access. This makes a house inhabitable and, in turn, provides security. Within a household, or family, there are also lines of definition that mark one out as a father or mother, a son or daughter, a brother or sister, or some other relative. When any of these lines is blurred, the safety and security of a household is threatened. If there is no respect for property lines, if walls are randomly demolished, or if family members do not observe appropriate behavior in relation to one another, the roof ultimately caves in. Houses, whether we are speaking of the physical building or the familial unit, need structure; without it, they fall apart. The crime of the fool (*nābāl*) is that he ignores or deliberately assaults proper God-given boundaries by committing "folly" (*nebālah*). This is what happens in the story of Amnon and Tamar.

Sadly, the story of Amnon and Tamar continues today. It is reenacted every time a woman or child is sexually abused and every time a cry for justice is silenced.[75] Whether we speak of the Western male who forces himself on an unsuspecting relative behind closed doors, threatening and shaming her into silence, or gang rape by soldiers in the Congo, or the advice of local

---

[74] Yairah Amit, *Reading Biblical Narratives: Literary Criticism and the Hebrew Bible* (Minneapolis: Fortress Press, 2001), p. 132.

[75] For a contemporary application of the story of Amnon and Tamar, see Pamela Cooper-White, *The Cry of Tamar: Violence Against Women and the Church's Response* (Minneapolis: Fortress Press, 1995).

African witchdoctors to rape a virgin in order to cure the HIV virus, Amnon is alive and his "sickness" continues to plague our world. The personal tragedy of many reminds us that we are no longer "safe at home."

The story of Amnon and Tamar is about more than sexual abuse, however. The books of Samuel consistently connect sexual conquest with political power. As Regina Schwartz has stated, "politics and sexuality are so deeply and complexly integrated as to be one."[76] Whether we are talking illicit sex (1 Sam. 2:22; 2 Sam. 3:7; 11:4; 13:14; 16:22) or controlling a woman's sexual choices (1 Sam. 18:19, 21; 25:44; 2 Sam. 3:13–16), every instance in the books of Samuel highlights the abuse of power. By men controlling the sexual boundaries of their women (e.g., Michal and Rizpah) or breaking down the proper boundaries that should be maintained (e.g., Bathsheba and Tamar), we witness a groping for power that wreaks havoc and destruction on the "houses" of Saul and David.

This observation discloses two important truths. First, satisfying our own appetite (be it power, sex, fame, etc.) does not achieve the intended goal. The "fruit" of our selfish endeavors is bitter to the taste, and not only unsatisfying, but destructive in the end. As Hannah might remind us, "The wicked shall be silent in darkness, for by strength no man shall prevail" (1 Sam. 2:9). Second, God-given boundaries, which may seem prohibitive and restrictive, are for our good. Life without boundaries leads to chaos and anarchy. No quality of life can exist apart from order and structure; this is one of the lessons of the Creation story in Genesis 1, where God, through his Word, creates order out of chaos. As in the beginning, so this principle remains.

Regrettably, modern society is very keen on blurring lines and on ignoring, or destroying, important traditional boundaries. In an attempt to make all truth relative, healthy distinctions delineated in Scripture are often labeled as narrow-minded, fundamentalist, or bigoted. If we seek to be "politically correct" in all our pronouncements and attitudes, we ignore important differences to our own peril. In our sophistication, we have chosen to disregard the words of the apostle Paul who wrote, "Although they knew God, they did not glorify Him as God, nor were thankful, but became futile in their thoughts, and their *foolish* hearts were darkened. Professing to be wise, they became *fools*" (Rom. 1:21–22). We have committed *nebālah*. By dismissing God and biblical boundaries from our lives, we have created a society where schools and neighborhood streets are often dangerous places to be. As in previous times, "the nations rage" (Ps. 2:1) and seek to "break [God's] bonds" (Ps. 2:3); as a result, we are no longer safe at home. However, a day of judgment is coming when God "shall break them with a rod of iron" (Ps. 2:9), but "Blessed are all those who [will] put their trust in Him" (Ps. 2:12).

---

[76] Schwartz, "Adultery in the House of David," p. 46. See a fuller version of this quote in the "Introduction" p. 6, n. 12.

Chapter 24

Absalom: The Rebel (David's son)

"See how my son who came from my own body seeks my life"—David (2 Sam. 16:11)

Absalom's Rebellion in the Context of 1 and 2 Samuel (2 Sam. 13–20)

In 2 Samuel chapters 13–20 the "strong" house of David (2 Sam. 3:1–5) un-ravels in fulfillment of the prophetic word announced in 2 Samuel 12:10–11. There the prophet Nathan, who formerly had announced to David an endur-ing house (2 Sam. 7:11–16), proclaims that the sword will never depart from his house, and that God will also raise up "evil" from his own house.

Within this framework, the sinful actions of Absalom and others (Amnon, Ahithophel, etc.) recounted in these chapters become viewed as the repercussions of David's own sin with Bathsheba and Uriah (2 Sam. 11).[1] Viewed from this perspective, the events are a divine judgment. David recog-nizes this in his flight from Absalom, when he rebukes Abishai over Shimei's cursing and says, "Let him alone, and let him curse; for so the LORD has or-dered him" (2 Sam. 16:11b). One writer has even entitled these chapters: "David under the curse."[2]

Although David suffers greatly in these chapters, he is ultimately vin-dicated. While one might be hard-pressed to describe this as a "happy end-ing" as Frolov does, nonetheless it is a positive ending for David.[3] Paradox-ically then, David's road becomes one of blessing and curse in these chapters. How is this to be explained? Furthermore, does David's sin provide an ex-cuse for Absalom? Can Absalom say in defense, "It's not my fault; daddy made me do it"? Can he blame his rebellion on divine determinism which had decreed problems in David's house? The story will clearly show that Absalom is responsible for his own decisions and bears the weight of his own guilt, but

---

[1] Whybray, in *The Succession Narrative*, p. 37, writes, "The author never states baldly that the tragedies of Amnon, Absalom, and Adonijah were due to David's own weaknesses, but he suggests it quite unmistakably in two ways: by portraying the sons as having inherited the weaknesses of their father and by describing in detail, quite objectively, the relations between David and *Absalom*" (author's emphasis). I would also add that Nathan's statements make this connection.

[2] Carlson, in *David the Chosen King*. However, we will see this designation is only par-tially correct.

[3] Serge Frolov, "Succession Narrative: A 'Document' or a Phantom?," *JBL* 121/1, 2002, p. 101, states, "2 Sam 1–1 Kgs 2 moves from negative to positive, steering its main character, David, toward a happy ending."

how does the text perceive this interlocking of divine sovereignty and free will?[4]

I suggest the answer to all of the questions above is found in the introductory chapters of 1 Samuel. In a key statement made to Eli in 1 Samuel 2:30 God declares, "Those who honor Me I will honor, and those who despise Me shall be lightly esteemed" (cursed). In Nathan's rebuke of David he asks, "Why have you *despised* the commandment of the LORD, to do evil in His sight?" (2 Sam. 12:9). We have already noted that David accepts Shimei's "cursing" because he believes it comes from the Lord (2 Sam. 16:11). The word used for "curse" in this passage is the same word translated "lightly esteem" in 1 Samuel 2:30. Thus, following the logic of 1 Samuel 2:30, the reason for David's divine punishment (curse) in these chapters is because he has *despised* the Lord. Likewise, the sin of Absalom (and of Amnon and others) dishonors both David (the Lord's anointed) and the Lord Himself, as we shall see. As a result, Absalom experiences divine punishment too (2 Sam. 17:14b).

Judgment, however, is only part of the story. As we have noted, David also receives blessing from the Lord. This is explained by David's humble submission to the Lord throughout the ordeal of Absalom's revolt (e.g., 2 Sam. 15:30–31; 16:11). In fact, 2 Samuel chapters 15–18 alternate between David and Absalom, contrasting their actions and words just as 1 Samuel 2:11–36 shifts the focus between Samuel and Eli and his sons, comparing them.[5] This contrast highlights David's humility which results in his vindication, and Absalom's ungodliness which results in his defeat.

In conjunction with 1 Samuel 2:30, Hannah's prayer (1 Sam. 2:1–10) also provides the proper background for understanding Absalom's revolt and its outcome. 2 Samuel 17:14b: "For the LORD had purposed to defeat the good advice of Ahithophel, to the intent that the LORD might bring disaster on Absalom," is a direct reflection of Hannah's words, "The LORD kills and makes alive; he brings down to the grave and brings up" (1 Sam. 2:6).[6] Absalom's self-exaltation resulted in the Lord bringing him down. Similarly, David's low point was the result of his sin, but his final vindication was based on his humble response to the Lord's discipline which, in turn, resulted in the Lord lifting him up (1 Sam. 2:7). Putting these two passages together from 1

---

[4] Whybray, *The Succession Narrative*, p. 63 states, "He [the author] believed that a man's evil deeds lead, by a natural process, to their own evil consequences; but he also believed in the working of a divine providence which is beyond man's understanding." Whybray seeks an answer to this theological dilemma by appealing to the point of view expressed in wisdom circles and evidenced in biblical books like Proverbs. While I do not disagree with this possibility, I am convinced there is a more immediate answer within the books of Samuel.

[5] This is a frequent technique in the books of Samuel. A similar contrast is made between Jonathan and Saul in 1 Sam. 14, and David and Saul in 1 Sam. 27–2 Sam. 1.

[6] The connection between 2 Sam. 17:14b and 1 Sam. 2:25b should also be noted.

Samuel 2 (vv. 1–10 and v. 30) helps us to understand the themes of divine sovereignty and free will and how these two seemingly contradictory principles work together. It also explains how David walks the road of cursing and blessing in these chapters. God is sovereign. It is he who "brings low and lifts up" but God's actions are not arbitrary. They are based on the decisions of people who either choose to honor or despise him.[7] In the analysis that follows, we will see more clearly how Absalom's character measures up against these principles.

Anything You Can Do, I Can Do Better (2 Sam. 13:23–38)

Absalom is no Amnon

Although Absalom is one of the central characters of 2 Sam. 13:1–19:8, he does not emerge as a full-fledged character until Tamar arrives at his house following her encounter with Amnon (13:20). Indeed, Amnon's crime is the driving force that propels Absalom to center stage (13:22). Nevertheless, it is Absalom's name that opens scene one (13:1) and it is the revelation of his thoughts of hatred toward Amnon that bring the curtain down at the end of it (13:22). From this point on, the narrative will alternate between the *actions* of Absalom and the *reactions* of David. [8]

We have previously noted that Absalom's murder of Amnon contains many echoes of Amnon's crime in the first part of 2 Samuel 13.[9] A comparison of each incident also reveals Absalom's superiority over Amnon. First, unlike Amnon, his plan is conceived without the counsel of a friend, suggesting that he is smart enough to figure things out for himself. Second, he is patient in implementing it (two full years—v. 23). Amnon's delay in acting upon his desire for Tamar was his inability to know what to do (vv. 2–4). In contrast, Absalom's delay is based on his shrewdness, waiting for the perfect time and place. Third, as previously noted, Absalom is an active character in these verses, while Amnon is passive; he is an object who is acted upon.[10] Finally, unlike Amnon, he has given thought to the consequences of his ac-

---

[7] This is an important aspect of biblical truth, but it is only *one* aspect. We dare not make the mistake of Job's friends and assert that every act of suffering must be due to sin while every good person will experience nothing but blessing. The biblical wisdom literature (esp. Job), as well as some of the Psalms (e.g., 73), provide a corrective balance to the principle expressed here. Having said that, it is interesting how wisdom themes and motifs abound in the chapters under consideration here. As previously noted (see footnote 4 above), Whybray believes the wisdom theme of "you reap what you sow" explains the divine retribution found here.

[8] I have chosen to begin my focus on Absalom here with 13:23–38 because his appearance in 13:1–22 has already been commented on in chap. 23.

[9] See chap. 23, pp. 344-345.

[10] Ibid.

tion and, therefore, has planned a way of escape (vv. 37–38). These contrasts, as well as the parallels with his father (planning a murder and using servants, etc.), suggest that Absalom has more of David's qualities than Amnon's.[11] This makes Absalom more appealing than Amnon. The fact that the murder seems somewhat justified, and that Absalom potentially forfeits his future by protecting the family honor (Tamar's and his own honor), creates some sympathy for him.[12] True, his deed is more sinister than his father's and this gives the reader pause in forming a positive critique of Absalom. The reader, therefore, awaits further revelations of Absalom's character in forming an opinion about him.

David is Tamar!

Absalom sees the opportunity to implement his plan of vengeance at his annual sheep-shearing festival (v. 23). The fact that such an event took place yearly suggests Absalom's patience in carrying out his plot. Acting too quickly would create suspicion and Absalom seems aware of this and thus waits "two full years."[13] His invitation to "the king and his servants" (v. 24) is also well thought out. It seems likely that Absalom realized that David would refuse his invitation because of the excessive burden the king's entire entourage would create. As Fokkelman notes, "He deliberately asks for too much at first."[14] David's wish to not be a "burden" to Absalom (v. 25) is ironical to the reader, who later realizes that, if he *had* come, he would truly have been a burden as Absalom would not have been able to carry out his plan![15] David's refusal to accept Absalom's invitation puts him in an awkward position and Absalom knows it. This allows him to make a second request which includes a special plea for his "brother Amnon" to attend (v. 26). Even after two years

---

[11] This observation will prove important in understanding the unfolding events of 2 Sam. 15–18.

[12] In my opinion, Absalom's motivation at this point is to avenge the shameful treatment of his sister and his family. I am not in agreement with the proposal made famous by Leonhard Rost, in *The Succession to the Throne of David* (and followed by many others), that Absalom's chief purpose was to eliminate Amnon as his main rival to the throne. As Frolov, "Succession Narrative: A 'Document' or a Phantom?," p. 85, states, "The account of Tamar's rape, Amnon's assassination, and Absalom's exile does not foreshadow the latter's subsequent revolt against David." Gunn, in *The Story of King David*, as well as a host of recent articles and commentaries, has demonstrated that succession to the throne is only one of several themes that permeate these chapters, and that succession is not the main theme.

[13] Does he also wait hoping that his father will finally do something?

[14] Fokkelman, *King David*, p. 115.

[15] Conroy, *Absalom, Absalom!*, p. 113. The word translated "be a burden" is from the verb "to make heavy," which comes from the same root as "to honor" (see chap. 4, pp. 63-64). In other words, David does not wish to shame Absalom by bringing the entire court, because he knows Absalom would be unable to provide for them all.

of showing no animosity (v. 22), David is still suspicious of Absalom's request: "Why should he go with you?" (v. 26). However, no matter how fishy the situation may smell, Absalom knows that David will take the bait because he will not wish to shame his son by refusing him twice. Absalom's plea for Amnon to "go" and the king's debate about him "going" recalls David's use of this word when he told Tamar to "go" to Amnon's house (v. 7). Furthermore, just as David "sent" Tamar (v. 7), he now "sends" Amnon (v. 27). David is once again being duped by another son in a similar manner![16]

Closer inspection of the language and motifs surrounding David in this episode reveals strong parallels with Tamar in the previous episode. Both David and Tamar reject invitations from one of David's sons using similar language (cf. vv. 12 and 25).[17] In both instances initial resistance is overcome and the one making the request eventually gets his way (vv. 14 and 27). Both Tamar and David rend their garments (vv. 19 and 31) and weep (vv. 19 and 36). Both are consoled by someone using the words, "do not take this/the thing to heart" (vv. 20 and 33).[18] These parallels reveal that, in his own way, David ends up experiencing Tamar's plight.

Attention to these similarities reveals that Absalom's plan accomplishes two goals. First, the rapist is dealt with and a sense of honor is restored to Absalom and Tamar. Second, and perhaps just as important, Absalom creates a circumstance that allows David to be put in Tamar's situation. The king who once sat idly by and did nothing to help Tamar or punish her offender (v. 21), now experiences her pain in two ways: 1) just as Tamar's virtue could not be retrieved, neither could Amnon be brought back from the dead; and 2) just as Amnon escaped any consequences pertaining to his crime, so Absalom escapes by fleeing to his grandfather in Geshur (vv. 37–38). By the end of the chapter David, like Tamar, is found desolate in his own house (vv. 20 and 36).

By proving his superiority to his brother Amnon, and by making his father experience Tamar's pain, Absalom has bested both of his opponents. His carefully laid plan to murder Amnon is also superior to his father's clumsier attempt to murder Uriah. One wonders if another ambition of Absalom's in concocting this scheme against brother and father was to demonstrate, "Anything you can do, I can do better!"

---

[16] The verbal parallels continue as Absalom tells his servants to "be strong" using the same verb that describes Amnon's action of "seizing" Tamar (vv. 11, 14, 28).

[17] See chap. 23, p. 350 for a fuller explanation.

[18] For a helpful chart that explores some of these same similarities, see Hamilton, *Handbook*, p. 337.

"Feelings, Nothing More Than Feelings" (2 Sam. 13:39–14:1)

Chapter 13:39–14:1 is pivotal in understanding David's attitude toward Absalom following the murder of Amnon. Furthermore, one's interpretation of 13:39 guides the interpretation of 14:1. There is a difficulty, however, in translating these verses. The problem is that several of the Hebrew words are capable of different meanings, and there appears to be a word that has accidentally dropped out of the Hebrew text of 13:39.[19] Since it is not my desire to become overly technical in this book, the interested reader is referred to other commentaries and studies that explore this issue in more depth.[20] Most English readers are not even aware that there is a question about translation here, unless they check a commentary, because almost invariably the English translations read the same. The translation found in most Bible versions portrays the idea that David has been comforted over Amnon's death, longs to reach out to Absalom, and Joab makes this possible.

This understanding of the text has several problems, however. Fokkelman identifies three important issues: 1) the length of Absalom's exile noted in 13:38 (which suggests David's hostility toward Absalom); 2) David's refusal to see Absalom upon his return (14:24, 28); and 3) the fact that Joab does not feel he can directly approach the king but must resort to trickery.[21] Furthermore, the verb translated "long" ("And King David longed to go…" v. 39) has a stronger meaning of to "be spent."[22] Also, the word translated "to go" can mean "to go out" in the sense of marching to war or attacking someone.[23] When we recall that Absalom's deed was not only intended to harm Amnon, but also David, it is easier to comprehend why David's feelings might be hostile toward him. Based on these considerations, I believe that Anderson's translation best captures the author's meaning:

---

[19] The word "spirit" found in the LXX and apparently a part of the text of 4QSam[a] (one of the Dead Sea Scrolls) seems to have fallen out of the Hebrew text. For a more detailed discussion see, McCarter, *II Samuel*, pp. 338, 344. An interpretation which illustrates the ambiguity of these verses can be found in James S. Ackerman, "Knowing Good and Evil: A Literary Analysis of the Court History in 2 Samuel 9–20 and 1 Kings 1–2," *JBL* 109/1, 1990, pp. 46-47.

[20] Besides the two sources mentioned in the previous footnote, one can check the various commentaries listed in the bibliography in the back of this book, as well as the special studies of Polzin, *David and the Deuteronomist*, p. 133, and Fokkelman, *King David*, pp. 126-127. The reader will note that scholarly opinion is divided on how to best translate these verses.

[21] Ibid., p. 126.

[22] McCarter, *II Samuel*, p. 344, followed by Davis, *2 Samuel*, p. 175, although Vannoy, *1–2 Samuel*, p. 346, cannot decide between the two meanings.

[23] A few examples of this meaning in the books of Samuel include, 1 Sam. 8:20; 29:6; 2 Sam. 16:5, 7; 18:2–3, 6; 20:7, 8. See my comments on Shimei in chap. 15 p. 184, regarding the use of this same verb.

By the time Absalom, having fled to Geshur, had been there three years, the king's anger ceased to be actively directed against Absalom for he had become reconciled to the fact that Amnon was dead. When Joab, son of Zeruiah, perceived that the king's heart was still set against Absalom... (2 Sam. 13:38–14:1).[24]

If this interpretation is correct, it means that the majority of English translations (unintentionally) mislead the reader regarding the author's true intent. The fact is, we want David to "feel good" about his estranged son, but the real intent of the author is best expressed by McCarter when he states, "The meaning is rather that David is no longer openly hostile to Abishalom [Absalom] and, therefore, ready to be prodded step by step towards a reconciliation."[25]

The importance of discerning David's attitude properly is that it helps us to better appreciate Absalom's hostility toward his father. Absalom's rebellion is best understood as the result of a steady progression of years of frustration over his father's actions, or inaction. Only in this section of the books of Samuel does the author constantly draw attention to the span of years being covered. These years are all in relation to Absalom.[26] The author is at great pains to constantly remind the reader how much time has passed: two years between Amnon's rape of Tamar and Absalom's murder of Amnon (13:23); three years in exile (13:38);[27] another two years before he is allowed an audience with the king (14:28); and finally, four years before the start of

---

[24] Anderson, *2 Samuel*, p. 182.

[25] McCarter, *II Samuel*, p. 344. "Abishalom" is an older form of the name and is McCarter's spelling. It is possible to interpret these verses in an even stronger fashion. Fokkelman, *King David*, pp. 126-127, following his colleague, J. Jongeling, translates 13:39–14:1 as, "David longed intensely to march out against Absalom, for he was grieved about Amnon, that he was dead. Joab now, the son of Zeruiah, discerned that the king was ill-disposed toward Absalom." I am not unsympathetic toward this translation, but I believe McCarter's and Anderson's interpretation is closer to the author's intent.

[26] Conroy, *Absalom, Absalom!*, p. 92, refers to it as "Absalom-time."

[27] Ibid., p. 97 states, "The corrosive change in Absalom's character begins, very probably, during his exile in Geshur and is given impetus by David's mishandling of Absalom when at length he returns to Jerusalem." I would modify this statement in two ways: 1) I believe the effects on Absalom's character are already beginning to be evidenced in the first two year period as he plots the demise of Amnon and revenge on his father; 2) Rather than call it "corrosive change" (although this is a vivid description of the effects of time), I would prefer the word "revelation." While events may contribute to a "change" of character, more often they "reveal" it. I think this is one of the important lessons of the books of Samuel.

the revolt (15:7).[28] As the years go by, Absalom's frustration and anger with his father grow, and consequently his heart becomes hardened.

David Rolls Out the "Unwelcome" Mat (2 Sam. 14:2–24)

Just as God had sent Nathan with a parable paralleling David's actions (2 Sam. 12:1–12), so Joab sends a "wise woman" from Tekoa with a concocted story designed to get David to change his mind about Absalom.[29] The woman's appearance is similar to David's own state. "[She] is to act like she has been mourning 'many days' 'over the dead.' Just as David was said to mourn 'all the days' 'over the dead.' "[30] The story she relates is also similar to David's, without being identical so as not to raise suspicion. The woman states that she had two sons and that one was killed by the other (v. 6). Pretending to be a widow, she pleads with David to protect her living son, because the family desires to put him to death; but he is all she has left to carry on her husband's name (v. 7).

The circumstances are sufficiently different not to arouse David's suspicion. David is not a widower and has many sons to carry on his name. However, the mistranslation of 13:39–14:1 has caused some scholars to miss the connection of the death threat that hangs over the widow's son with Absalom.[31] Ironically, David not only shares parallels with the widow; he is also the aggrieved family in the story who wants to put the son to death! As Anderson states, "It is possible that in the past few years the king had acted somewhat like the avenger of blood (v. 11) in respect of Absalom, while the people of God or Israel in general had been seeking Absalom's restoration."[32] This is further confirmed by the woman's accusation that David is guilty of a similar crime (v. 13). According to our understanding of 13:39, David's origi-

---

[28] The Hebrew text of 15:7 reads "forty" instead of "four" years. We will address this issue in our discussion of 2 Sam. 15.

[29] Many have noted the parallels between 2 Sam. 11–12 and 13–14. E.g., Firth, *1&2 Samuel*, p. 443.

[30] Fokkelman, *King David*, p. 128.

[31] George W. Coats, "Parable, Fable, and Anecdote: Storytelling in the Succession Narrative," *Int.* 35/4, 1981, p. 380, suggests there is a "loose relationship" between the woman's story and Absalom's situation. He argues that her story is based on blood revenge, whereas, her plea to David is that he return his banished one. He does not make the connection, however, that the blood revenge in the woman's story matches David's attitude in 13:39.

[32] Anderson, *2 Samuel*, p. 188. Propp's failure to realize that David is both the woman *and* the clan in her story causes him to come to the wrong conclusion that the clan probably represents "either David's clan or the entire nation of Israel." Propp, "Kinship in 2 Samuel 13," p. 50. The woman's words in v. 13, as well as the narrator's words in v. 25, indicate that Absalom was a favorite of the people.

nal desire was to "march out against Absalom." Apparently there was a time when David would have put Absalom to death for the murder of Amnon, and although this feeling may have subsided (or exhausted itself), David was not yet willing to forgive his son or welcome him home from exile. Once again, his situation is different enough not to raise suspicion because the woman speaks of two parties' attitudes toward her son (herself and her family), while David embodies both (grief for the dead son, and desire for revenge against the perpetrator).

Once the woman is able to elicit a positive verdict from David regarding her fictitious son's protection—a verdict which includes a solemn oath (v. 11)—she moves on to her main objective:

> Why then have you schemed such a thing against the people of God? For the king speaks this thing as one who is guilty, in that the king does not bring his banished one home again. For we will surely die and become like water spilled on the ground, which cannot be gathered up again. Yet God does not take away a life; but he devises means, so that His banished ones are not expelled from Him (vv. 12–13).

The woman argues that David has convicted himself. David can demonstrate mercy to other families but he is blind to his own situation. In fact, the woman argues that the injustice being perpetrated by the king on his son is adversely affecting all of God's people. Furthermore, she claims that God would not act as David has, because God "does not take away a life,"[33] but even finds ways to return "His banished ones." This line of argument also reminds us of Nathan's confrontation with David. In chapter 12, David is convicted of having "no pity" (vv. 4, 6). He is not like God because God "gives" instead of "takes" (vv. 7–9). Here David has no room for pitying his own son and he seeks to take away a life, while God seeks to restore it. Did these parallels suggest themselves to David, and, if so, did they open old wounds and weaken his resolve regarding Absalom's banishment? Or was it the oath he uttered in the Lord's name that compelled him to acquiesce?

Whatever the cause of David's compliance, the trap set by Joab was successful. While David does relent and agree to allow Absalom to return, it has been argued that future events bring into question the "wisdom" of Joab and this woman.[34] Although Absalom is responsible for his own actions, in one sense, both Joab and David shoulder some of the blame for future

---

[33] This is an admittedly difficult phrase in Hebrew and its translation is much disputed. For a different view see Hoftijzer, "David and the Tekoite Woman," pp. 437-438.
[34] See chap. 20, p. 290. See also, Sean E. McEvenue, "The Basis of Empire," p. 37, as well as the discussion by Davis, *2 Samuel*, pp. 177-180.

events. Joab's "wisdom" proves to be similar to Jonadab's; it accomplishes an immediate purpose, but the long term effects are disastrous. Likewise, David's lack of response to Tamar's situation, Absalom's three year exile (although deserved), and David's treatment of Absalom upon his return, serve to embitter Absalom against his father. In fact, as previously noted,[35] David plays a game of his own to get back at both Joab (for his manipulation) and Absalom (for his murder of Amnon). Having granted Joab's request that Absalom may return (v. 21), David waits to issue the order that Absalom must return to his own house and not see the king's face until *after* both men return to Jerusalem (vv. 23–24).[36] This "change in the rules" is all the more poignant because David had used the phrase "young man" when speaking to Joab about Absalom, suggesting a softening of his attitude toward him (v. 21). Rather than a dramatic turnabout in his feelings between verses 21–24, I suggest that David was setting Joab and Absalom up for a severe disappointment upon their return. Ironically, he will use this same expression later to communicate his affection for his son while pleading with Joab and the other troops to "deal gently" with him (18:5, 12, 29).[37]

That David does not send for Absalom because of a change of heart seems clear from his command, "Do not let him see my face." This conviction is so firm in David's mind that the narrator allows us to hear it three times (14:24 [2x], 28). "David has not executed the spirit of the oath, merely its letter. In this we see how great his resentment was."[38] Like many people, David seems to have a difficult time balancing his parental responsibilities. He is either too lax in his discipline, or too harsh. Comparing this incident with the story of the prodigal son, Hamilton rightly notes, "If Absalom had said, 'I will get up and go to my father' (Luke 15:18), he would have discovered that David had hung out the 'Not Welcome' sign."[39] Oddly enough, the wise woman's words (v. 13) will, in one sense, prove to be true. David's continued rejection of Absalom will result in harming the people of God.[40]

---

[35] See chap. 20, pp. 278-279.

[36] I owe this insight to Fokkelman, *King David*, p. 147.

[37] Does Joab perhaps recall this event when he deals harshly with this "young man" in 2 Sam. 18? See my comments about Joab's motives and actions in chap. 20 pp. 282-283.

[38] Fokkelman, *King David*, p. 147.

[39] Hamilton, *Handbook*, p. 344.

[40] Besides the points enumerated above, there is a recurrent phrase throughout the story that might further suggest David's and Joab's culpability. It is the expression "this thing." We have encountered these words before. They were used to describe David's sin and subsequent judgment (2 Sam. 11:11, 25, 27; 12:6, 12), as well as Amnon's sin (13:20). These words are found four times in the current story. In 14:13, they refer to David's treatment of Absalom, and this is probably their meaning in verse 15 as well, although the woman relates it to her fictitious situation. The woman,

If we step back to look at the overall picture created in 2 Samuel 13–15, (and even beyond these chapters), it is evident that they are filled with examples of manipulation and deception:[41] Amnon, with the help of Jonadab, deceives and manipulates David and Tamar (13:6–11); Absalom deceives and manipulates David and Amnon (13:22–29); Joab and the wise woman of Tekoa deceive and manipulate David (14:1–20); David deceives Joab and Absalom (14:21–24); Absalom deceives David (14:32–33); Absalom deceives and manipulates all of Israel (15:2–6); and Absalom deceives David and manipulates two hundred men (15:7–11). Regarding this prevalent theme Evans observes, "The interest continues in the way in which people exercise power over others and the reader is certainly being invited to reflect on the process of manipulation, its morality—or otherwise—and its consequences."[42]

Man in the Mirror (2 Sam. 14:25–27)

These verses provide a short interlude, dividing "Absalom's return to Jerusalem from his return to the palace."[43] They allow the reader to experience the passing of time; the reader must wait as Absalom waits. Suspense is created as the reader wonders, along with Absalom, how long he must live in this state of limbo. Will he ever be accepted back into the king's good graces? Meanwhile, this interlude gives a personal glimpse of the man himself. He certainly makes for a pretty picture. In fact, among all the various descriptions of beauty mentioned in the books of Samuel, none excels the description of Absalom who is *beautiful*[44] "from the sole of his foot to the crown of his head." Indeed, there is "no blemish in him" (v. 25).

The focus becomes more particular as the narrator zooms in on his luxuriant head of hair (v. 26). As frequently noted, one is reminded of the king's statement when he promised the woman of Tekoa, "As the LORD lives, not one *hair* of your son shall fall to the ground" (14:11). In the context, the

---

and David himself, also use this phrase once each in reference to Joab's plan to return Absalom (vv. 20, 21). In the first two instances the expression may refer to David's mishandling of Absalom, while in the last two occurrences it may take on an ominous warning about the future and refer to Joab's error in seeking to return Absalom. My point is that there is no one in this story without fault. Absalom, David, and Joab, are all guilty in one way or another of mishandling the situation.

[41] Sean E. McEvenue, "The Basis of Empire," pp. 38-39, extends this insight to the entire narrative spanning 2 Sam. 9–20 and 1 Kings 1–2. See also, Hans J.L, Jensen, "Desire, Rivalry, and Collective Violence in the 'Succession Narrative,' " pp. 39-59.

[42] Evans, *The Message of Samuel*, p. 227.

[43] Firth, *1 & 2 Samuel*, p. 447.

[44] Absalom seems to be surrounded by beauty. The same word is used to describe his father David (1 Sam. 16:12; 17:42), his sister Tamar (2 Sam. 13:1), and his daughter of the same name (2 Sam. 14:27).

(fictitious) son is obviously Absalom. So why all the fuss over hair? Of all the things the narrator could tell us, why focus on Absalom's hair and why the interest in his cutting it and its weight?[45] In a recent study, Susan Niditch writes about the significance of hair in ancient Israel. Her insights on Absalom are worth quoting at length:

> It seems clear that Absalom is portrayed as trying to project a certain image with his hair. The long-haired man is special. It is no coincidence that this description is followed by the mention of his offspring…the long hair is clearly associated with fertility and manly fecundity. The author may be suggesting that long hair is evocative enough in ancient Israelite culture that the man whose hair is luxuriantly thick and long is regarded as set apart like a Nazir [Nazirite]. He looks as if he is meant to lead and as if God's blessing is on his head. He will be an excellent warrior. The richness of the story, however, lies in the fact that these expectations prove to be wrong. The long hair becomes Absalom's undoing. The author is able to play on this irony, however, only because of cultural associations with hair….He [Absalom] is adept at projecting an image of power, an image to which the hair contributes.[46]

We have already noticed that the books of Samuel frequently connect political power with sexual prowess and physical fertility (e.g., 2 Sam. 3:2–7). Niditch's insight that luxuriant hair is connected with fertility not only explains the notice of Absalom's children in this context (14:27), it suggests a solution to a dilemma that has puzzled scholars for years. Upon Absalom's death, the narrator informs the reader that Absalom had a monument built for himself because he said, "I have no son to keep my name in remembrance" (2 Sam. 18:18). This statement appears to be a glaring contradiction to what we read here in 14:27. A number of scholars suggest that Absalom's three sons may have died in infancy, which would explain the

---

[45] Estimates of the weight range between 4-5½ pounds! Some believe the description is hyperbolic. For example, Firth, *1&2 Samuel*, p. 447.

[46] Susan Niditch, *'My Brother Esau is a Hairy Man': Hair and Identity in Ancient Israel* (Oxford: Oxford University Press, 2008), pp. 79-80. Michael Avioz, "The Motif of Beauty in the Books of Samuel and Kings," *VT* 59 (2009), p. 352, makes a similar linkage between long hair and kingship, only he connects it with the concept of beauty rather than power: "Growing hair is intended to signal Absalom's intentions for kingship to the People, since long hair was related to beauty and was characteristic of kings. In Mesopotamia, only people of the high class were permitted to grow their hair, whereas slaves were obligated to cut their hair."

contradiction.[47] Be that as it may, this explanation doesn't account for why there are two notices about Absalom's children (or lack thereof).[48] Given that hair and children suggest virility, we can now see that the author's purpose in bracketing Absalom's revolt with these two statements is to suggest that before the revolt, Absalom gave the appearance of strength and virility, but his defeat, and ignominious death, demonstrated the reality that Absalom was not powerful at all; in fact, he was impotent![49]

Bergen provides further insight concerning Absalom's annual haircuts. He states,

> The Torah provided two primary reasons for a man to cut his hair: one was to give the hair to God following the successful completion of a Nazirite vow (cf. Num 6:18), and the other was to enter into a state of ceremonial cleanness before the Lord (cf. Lev 14:8–9; Num 8:7). Absalom's stated motive for getting a haircut was totally devoid of any connection with service to Yahweh; it was secular and self-serving. This detachment of Absalom's act from any religious motivation underscores the profane nature of the man's life.[50]

Absalom's hair then projects an image of power, but also suggests carnality. The reader of 1 and 2 Samuel is well aware that power in the hands of a carnal man is a dangerous thing. Furthermore, the reader knows that appearances can be deceiving (e.g., Eli, Saul, Goliath, and Eliab). In fact, the focus on appearance is very suggestive of a shallow individual. We will note later that Absalom's story is also filled with vocabulary about the "heart" (e.g., 13:20; 14:1; 15:6, 13, to name only a few instances). The books of Samuel clearly

---

[47] See the discussion by McCarter, *II Samuel*, pp. 407-408.

[48] Many scholars attribute one of these passages to the hand of a redactor reasoning that the author would not include both statements since they are contradictory. Alter's statement is typical along these lines: "The two reports can be harmonized only with considerable strain, and it is best to view them as contradictory traditions incorporated in the final text." Alter, *The David Story*, p. 281. See also the comments in Anderson, *2 Samuel*, pp. 190, 225-226. Anderson rightly notes, "There must have been some reason for the divergent statement," p. 190, but neither he nor anyone I am aware of has been able to provide an explanation. The above explanation demonstrates that it is possible for both passages to come from the same authorial hand, and that they are deliberately placed in their respective contexts to communicate an important truth about Absalom.

[49] For further comments on the significance of these two verses see the remarks below on 2 Sam. 18:18.

[50] Bergen, *1, 2 Samuel*, pp. 393-394.

teach that the Lord's concern is with the heart of a person (1 Sam. 2:35; 13:14; 16:7). Although David was "beautiful" like Absalom, it was his heart that commended him to God. In this description of Absalom, one searches in vain for a comment on any internal quality. Absalom is defined by externals: his good looks; his hair; his children. When viewed within the context of the book, the description of Absalom that seems to be so flattering is not flattering at all.[51] Despite a lot of "heart" language in Absalom's story overall, it is conspicuously absent in these verses. If Nabal was defined by his possessions (1 Sam. 25:2), Absalom is defined by his physical attributes, and the reader has learned by now, "by strength no man shall prevail" (1 Sam. 2:9). This, however, will not stop people from praising (2 Sam. 14:25) or flocking to Absalom (15:6). It seems that it is part of the human condition to be beguiled by good looks and charm. People continue to look on the outward appearance, even though God looks on the heart (1 Sam. 16:7). Ultimately, the author's statement, "There was no blemish in him," will prove to be ironic. Though it may remain true physically, Absalom's character is spotted with many blemishes.[52]

Father and Child Reunion: So Close and Yet So Far (2 Sam. 14:28–33)

When the narrative resumes, we learn that nothing has changed except the passage of time. It has been two long years since Absalom's return and still he has not seen "the king's face" (v. 28). His beauty and popularity have made no inroads with the king. This continues to suggest that David's "heart was against Absalom" (see my comments on 14:1). If David had simply been trying to make a point ("Don't think you can come waltzing back into my kingdom and expect everything to be alright young man") he may have waited six months or a year before allowing Absalom back into his presence. "Two full years" however is an indication that David's mind has not changed and, if Absalom had not grown impatient, we can only assume that this situation would have continued indefinitely. In other words, it is not the soft parental heart of David that finally breaks the stalemate between the two; it is Absalom's impatience and frustration. "Tension is created between the physical proximity to the king and the emotional distance from him. This situa-

---

[51] Stuart Macwilliam, "Ideologies of Male Beauty and the Hebrew Bible," *BibInt.* 17, 2009, p. 280, states, "We could interpret 14:25–26, then, as a deliberate ploy by the narrator, who, taking the theme of male beauty as signifying hero, deliberately undercuts the reader's expectations by gradually revealing Absalom as villain."

[52] Similarly, Avioz, "The Motif of Beauty in the Books of Samuel and Kings," p. 352, states, "If a king must be beautiful or even perfect, then Absalom meets this criterion. However, the continuation demonstrates that this beauty is exploited for manipulations by Absalom in order to achieve the throne. This beauty is empty, he is not a wise or kindhearted man."

tion...involves serious humiliation for the proud-spirited Absalom."[53] This episode makes it clear that Absalom has had enough. He wants the situation settled once and for all, even if it means experiencing dire consequences (v. 32). However, it is doubtful that Absalom really thinks the king would take his life. After all, if this had been David's intent, he would have had plenty of opportunity over the past two years to effect Absalom's execution. It's more likely that Absalom's words are melodramatic and continue to express his frustration. Ironically, he parrots the same words that his father had used years before in a conversation with Jonathan ("if there is iniquity in me, let him kill me," [my translation] compare with 1 Sam. 20:8); it is not the last time we will see Absalom imitating David.[54]

Absalom's frustration is most notable in the burning of Joab's field when the latter twice refuses to respond to his message (14:29–32). This encounter has similarities with 13:23–29, where Absalom also experienced two refusals only to persevere and have his servants commit a violent act.[55] Absalom is not one to take "No" for an answer! The comparison of these two episodes reveals that Absalom is a spoiled child of royalty who is used to getting his own way, and when he does not he is more than willing to use any bullying tactics at his disposal. As Fokkelman notes, "In this way we develop a negative appreciation for the prince's powerful assertiveness."[56] This negative character evaluation is reinforced with the narrative similarities to Samson, another man with long hair who burns fields to get his own way (Judg. 15:4–5). Furthermore, Samson's demanding nature regarding his parents (Judg. 14:2–3) reinforces the spoiled disposition of Absalom.[57]

Absalom's nature is perhaps best revealed if we ask the question, "Why does he seek reconciliation with his father?" The natural response would seem to be that every son wants the approval and love of his father. Perhaps at one stage this may have been true,[58] but, at this point, Absalom's

---

[53] Bar-Efrat, *Narrative Art*, p. 156.

[54] The fact is that Absalom truly is guilty while David's words reflect his innocence. This is one of many contrasts that will be made between David and Absalom in the coming story.

[55] Fokkelman, *King David*, p. 155.

[56] Ibid., p. 151.

[57] Alter, *The David Story*, p. 280, also suggests that, "Perhaps the parallel with Samson is meant to foreshadow Absalom's fate as a powerful leader whose imprudence brings him to an early death."

[58] It is possible to argue, as I have earlier, that years of rejection by his father caused Absalom to become bitter, which, in turn, led to the revolt. The continued emphasis in the text on the amount of years involved makes this a plausible supposition. However, it could also be argued that Absalom's revolt was precipitated by his own ambition. This is usually the perspective of those who view these chapters as part of a succession narrative.

motives for reconciliation are more sinister. Very simply, he seeks the advantages and connections that come with being a part of the king's court. The events of chapter 15 bear this out. Absalom is not seeking any warm fuzzy feelings between him and his father; his actions are pragmatic. The description of the reconciliation in 14:33 reveals that neither father nor son is inclined toward an affectionate relationship at this point.

The long-awaited reconciliation is deeply disappointing, at least from a reader's standpoint. True, the son is once again allowed to be in his father's presence, but that is as far as it goes. The reader might recall that a former family reconciliation between Michal and David ended abruptly without so much as a reunion scene (2 Sam. 3:13–16).[59] At least this time we do see father and son come together but, once again, all the things that one expects in such encounters are missing. There are no tears, no hugs, no words of love exchanged. David does not seem to be very good at family reconciliations! His tears, emotion and expression of love will come too late (2 Sam. 18:33, 19:4). It is true there is a kiss, but this is not the kiss of a father, it is the kiss of a king. The fourfold mention of "king" in this verse eclipses any sense of fatherly expression. As Whybray insightfully states, "The scene is enacted in total silence....Absalom had forced his father's hand, the interests of the State required a formal reconciliation, and David bowed to those interests; but the reconciliation was no more than formal. The author has told us plainly by his silence how cold and formal was that kiss."[60]

As for Absalom, there is no admission of guilt, no request for forgiveness. He bows because he has to, but there is no respect for the king as 15:2–4 will make plain. How different are the actions of father and son in Jesus's parable of the Prodigal. David does not run to meet Absalom, nor does he fall on his neck and kiss him (Luke 15:20). He does not adorn his son with the best attire (v. 22), nor call for the killing of a fatted calf (v. 23). There is no celebration and he does not say anything remotely like, "for this my son was dead and is alive again; he was lost and is found" (v. 24). Absalom makes no statement of humility, nor does he express that he would be grateful just to be one of his father's hired servants (v. 19). In fact, in the very next verse (2 Sam. 15:1) Absalom is seen promoting an image of royalty and power, not one of humility.

Lest it be considered unfair to compare this New Testament reconciliation of father and son with David and Absalom, we will consider two other reconciliation scenes from Genesis. When Jacob greets his estranged brother Esau for the first time in twenty years, he bows seven times, speaks very humbly, and both parties shed plenty of tears. In fact, like the father of the prodigal, Esau runs to meet Jacob, falls on his neck and kisses him (Gen.

---

[59] See the discussion in chap. 10 p. 129.
[60] Whybray, *The Succession Narrative*, p. 28.

33:3–4). Interestingly, this reconciliation occurs at Mahanaim (Gen. 32:2), the very place David will flee to during Absalom's rebellion (2 Sam. 17:24)! Moreover, if we look at the reconciliation between Joseph and his brothers, we also read of tears, kissing, intense emotion and much conversation (Gen. 45:14–15). These scenes present a stark contrast to 2 Samuel 14:33. Summarizing the difference, Fokkelman states, "In II Sam. 14, David is not as far as Joseph, and Absalom is not so far as Jacob."[61]

It is only upon reading the next episode (15:1–6) that we come to understand the sinister suggestion of the matter-of-fact vocabulary used in 14:33. Four words describe Absalom's transformation from humble prince to royal pretender. First, just as Absalom is "called" before the king, so he "calls" to individuals coming to present a lawsuit (15:2). Second, as Absalom "comes" to David for a judgment, so he wishes out loud that all could "come" to him for judgment (15:4). Third, as Absalom "bows" before David, so the people come to "bow" before Absalom (15:5). However, before the person can finish bowing, Absalom takes them by the hand and "kisses" them (15:5), just as the king had "kissed" him.[62] Now that Absalom has been accepted by the king, he begins to act more and more *like* the king.

Absalom "Stirs the Pot" (2 Sam. 15:1–12)

2 Samuel 15:1–12 combines two episodes that describe the beginning of Absalom's revolt. While 15:7–12 builds on the events of 15:1–6, both episodes share a similar dynamic. In each, Absalom deceives people by his words and actions, resulting in a popularity increase. Both scenes also end with a value judgment by the author. Scene one concludes with the statement, "So Absalom stole the hearts of the men of Israel" (v. 6), while scene two concludes with a statement about Absalom's "conspiracy" (v. 12).[63]

Recipe for Rebellion (15:1–6)

15:1 opens with an audacious display of royal power as Absalom gathers horses and chariots and fifty men to run before him. This provides a (not-so-subtle) contrast to his behavior in 14:33 when he pressed his nose to the ground in front of the king. There is only one reason for such a gaudy spectacle: Absalom is on parade! It is ironic that Absalom's self-promotion campaign begins with fifty men who "run." Following his death, the story will focus on two men who "run" to take news to David about Absalom's defeat and death (2 Sam. 18:19–32). Ahimaaz pleads with Joab that he might "run"

---

[61] Fokkelman, *King David*, p. 154.

[62] I owe these insights to Bar-Efrat, *Narrative Art*, pp. 156-157.

[63] Fokkelman, *King David*, 169.

and carry news to the king, but Joab responds by telling him that it is not the right occasion "because the king's son is dead" (18:19–20).

15:2–5 summarizes Absalom's daily routine. He is diligent about his deception as he rises early every morning to stand by the gate (v. 2). There he intercepts all who are going to the king with a lawsuit. The author rehearses a typical exchange between Absalom and these people, and includes formulaic responses by Absalom including, "your case is good and right; but there is no deputy of the king to hear you" (v. 3). Absalom would then add, "Oh, that I were made judge…then I would give him justice" (v. 4).

Is it really possible that *everyone's* case was *right?*[64] By this stereo-typical conversation the author demonstrates that Absalom appeals to everyone but cares about no one; the people are nameless and faceless, what matters to him is his own popularity. Polzin notes that, "This aspect of Absalom's preparations for revolt succeeds in surrounding his *character zone* with a negative evaluation from the very beginning" (Polzin's emphasis).[65] Furthermore, Absalom's antics undermine David's authority by implying no one within the present government can give them justice. This contradicts the narrator's comment in 2 Samuel 8:15: "So David reigned over all Israel; and David administered judgment and justice to all his people."

Absalom follows the age-old strategy: "If you want to make it to the top, tear the one in authority down—while building yourself up." (It is important to note that the Lord works in exactly the opposite way according to Hannah in 1 Sam. 2:1–10). Verse 6 informs us that all Israel took the bait. In an uncharacteristic vein, the narrator shares his opinion of Absalom's action, comparing it to robbery: "So Absalom *stole* the hearts of the men of Israel." Absalom's strategy may be perverse, but it is effective. Sadly, people today still fall for the same ploy.

Stewed to Perfection: The Rebellion Begins (15:7–12)

Verse 7 commences with a reference to "forty years," but this is not possible. David only reigned over Israel for forty years (2 Sam. 5:4–5). Most scholars maintain that the reading here should be "four" years, agreeing with the Septuagint and Josephus. This again shows the patience of Absalom in planning his strategy.[66] Absalom's reason for asking for leave is to pay a vow

---

[64] Polzin, *David and the Deuteronomist*, pp. 149-150, has an excellent discussion comparing Absalom's actions here with Deut. 25:1 and 1 Kings 8:32, the only other two passages from Deut.–2 Kings that use the word "righteous" in verbal form. Absalom's actions contradict the law (Deut. 25:1), and contradict his brother Solomon's words (1 Kings 8:32), because judging involves discerning the righteous from the guilty.

[65] Ibid., p. 150.

[66] Bergen, *1, 2 Samuel*, p. 397 n. 136, refers to an article by R. Althann who argues that the text should read "forty days" based on the readings of two other Hebrew manuscripts. I do find this suggestion attractive because it better explains Absalom's ex-

(v. 7). While he was in Geshur, he had made a vow: that if the Lord brought him back to Jerusalem then he would "serve the LORD" (v. 8). This is the first and only time that the Lord's name is found on Absalom's lips. Although it would appear that Absalom was lying, we cannot be certain. Nevertheless, he uses the Lord's name and religious obligation to initiate his revolt. In this he is similar to Abner, who also used the Lord's name only when it was politically expedient (2 Sam. 3:9–10, 18).[67]

The irony in the next verse is nearly unbearable, as David (for the first time since 13:25) speaks graciously to Absalom, saying, "Go in peace" (v. 9). The word "peace," of course, matches the second part of his son's name, Ab*shalom*. The son whose name means, "My Father (i.e., God) is peace," hears his human father wish him *peace* just as he is going off to make *war* against him! The narrative also resounds with other ironic overtones. For example, when Absalom tells David he needs to "pay" the vow (v. 7), the Hebrew word is *'ashallēm*, which is from the same root as "peace" and also sounds like "Absalom." Fokkelman explains, "Instead of fulfilling (*shallēm*) a pious duty towards God, he perpetuates a revolt from Hebron."[68] In yet another play on the word *shālôm*, the reader soon learns that Absalom's ultimate destination is Jeru*salem* (15:14), a city whose name is reminiscent of "peace," especially in its more ancient form "Salem" (=*shalēm*, Gen. 14:18; Ps. 76:2).

Once in Hebron, Absalom dispatched spies to tell everyone, "As soon as you hear the sound of the trumpet, then you shall say, 'Absalom reigns in Hebron!' " (v. 10). The son thus aims to imitate his father by being made king in Hebron, David's original capital (2 Sam. 2:1–4). Following his anointing, he will march north and capture Jerusalem, as his father did (2 Sam. 5:6–9).[69]

---

cuse of going to Hebron to fulfill a vow. If Absalom had been in David's "good graces" for the past four years, it is hard to understand why David would accept this as a viable excuse. In other words, Absalom's story about a vow makes much more sense within the time frame of forty days, as opposed to four years. Unfortunately, I have not been able to obtain access to Althann's article and, therefore, am not in a position to evaluate the evidence he offers. Another possibility is that the four year period encompasses two of the years that Absalom had already spent in Jerusalem, in which case, the time period since his reconciliation with David would only be two years. This is still a long time, however, to fulfill a vow. If a two or four year time period is to be understood, then the story characterizes Absalom as a sinner according to the Torah (Deut. 23:21). Yet another explanation is offered by Leithart, "*A Son to Me*," pp. 263-264, who suggests that "fortieth year" refers to David's reign. Thus Leithart puts the revolt of Absalom in David's final year.

[67] See chap. 11, pp. 147-148.

[68] Fokkelman, *King David*, p. 172.

[69] Jensen, "Desire, Rivalry, and Collective Violence 'In the Succession Narrative,' " p. 46, states, "They are identical because they want the same object and therefore act identically."

Absalom's deception not only extends to David and his loyal supporters, but also to two hundred invited men who, the author informs us, innocently go along with him to Hebron (v. 11). Absalom thus uses various methods to swell his ranks. Is this why he offers sacrifices (v. 12)? By carrying out the pretense of the vow, he gives an appearance of dedication to the Lord. Does he believe that sacrifice will aid his cause like Saul did? If so, then he is unfamiliar with Samuel's words (1 Sam. 15:22–23), and with the truth that lies behind a passage like Proverbs 21:27: "The sacrifice of the wicked is an abomination; how much more when he brings it with wicked intent!"

The scene ends with the ominous news that Ahithophel, David's counselor, has joined the rebellion (v. 12). Ahithophel's allegiance is a coup within Absalom's coup. The reader will soon learn the formidable qualities that make Ahithophel such a valuable asset (2 Sam. 16:23). With this news, the curtain falls on Absalom, and the camera pans back to David (2 Sam. 15:13–16:14). From this point on, father and son will never speak or be together again. The author carefully sketches the difference between the divergent paths they take. Their two diverse journeys illuminate the character differences of David and Absalom,[70] much as a former narrative once illuminated the differences between King Saul and his son (1 Sam. 14).

There's a New King in Town (2 Sam. 16:15–23)

Picking up where 15:12 had left off, 16:15 reminds us that Ahithophel had joined Absalom. However, the focus quickly shifts to another important counselor, Hushai, the "friend"[71] of David (16:16–19). Hushai has the difficult task of convincing Absalom of his changed loyalty (see 2 Sam. 15:34). After hearing that Ahithophel was among the conspirators with Absalom (15:31), David said, "O LORD, I pray, turn the counsel of Ahithophel into foolishness!" In the very next verse, David encountered Hushai at the top of the Mount of Olives as he worshipped God (15:32). David's prayer and worship provide a contrast to the tactics of Absalom (cf. Prov. 15:8). The fact that Hushai appears just after David prays, and is sent back into the city by David to confound the counsel of Ahithophel (15:34), suggests God's unseen hand at work. 2 Samuel 15:37 leaves the reader in suspense concerning Hushai's fate, as the king sends him off to Jerusalem, while the narrative re-

---

[70] James A. Wharton, "A Plausible Tale: Story and Theology in II Samuel 9—20, I Kings 1—2," *Int.* 35/4, 1981, p. 352, eloquently illustrates David's demeanor in these chapters when he writes, "I hear David saying that the key question in all these events is the future God chooses for Jerusalem, the place of God's dwelling, and for the kingdom there established. It may or may not be that David has some special further role to play in the service of that kingdom. With or without David, it is God's purpose for Jerusalem that will prevail and is to be served."

[71] On the significance of this term, see chap. 22, pp. 320, 327.

mains focused on David (16:1–14).[72] However, just as 16:15 picks up the thread from 15:12 about Ahithophel, so 16:16 picks up the thread from 15:37 about Hushai. While Absalom is not immediately convinced of Hushai's loyalty, Hushai's clever response (consisting of carefully chosen words that feign loyalty to Absalom, but actually maintain his loyalty to David) earns him a future hearing (2 Sam. 17:5).[73]

Having heard out Hushai, Absalom then turns to his "main man" Ahithophel and asks for counsel on how to proceed (16:20). Absalom's words are curt and, according to Fokkelman, "somewhat unusual" having "an undertone of impatience and impetuosity."[74] No doubt, he is trying to sound like a king. The reader has previously been made aware that David left ten concubines behind to "keep the house" (15:16).[75] Ahithophel's first piece of advice is for Absalom to "Go into your father's concubines, whom he has left to keep the house" (16:21a). Ahithophel says that this will draw a line in the sand: "All Israel will hear that you are abhorred [the word means literally, 'become odious' or 'stink'] by your father" (v. 20b). It will also, "make strong all the hands that are with you" (my translation, v. 21c). The word "make strong" is the same verb used of Amnon "forcing" Tamar (13:14). It suggests that Absalom will force an unwanted situation on David, as Amnon did on Tamar. In fact, Absalom's act of incest will be ten times greater (in scale) than what Amnon did to Tamar, as he "goes into" each of the concubines (16:22).[76]

A later reference will sadly note that these ten women will share the same fate as Tamar (2 Sam. 20:3). In Absalom's eyes this must be sweet revenge; and it confirms that this former tragedy was the cornerstone of his rebellion and that he has not fully recovered from his or his sister's humiliation.[77] Not only is Absalom's crime ten times greater, it is also more heinous

---

[72] These verses have been examined in previous chapters. On 16:1–4 see chap. 14, pp. 173-175. On 16:5–13 see chap. 15, pp. 183-186. In his *Handbook*, Hamilton pp. 349-350, notes that 2 Sam. 16 is divided into two parts: vv. 1–14, and 15–23, and has a very insightful discussion on the parallels between these two sections.

[73] For a closer examination of Hushai's words here see, Fokkelman, *King David*, pp. 206-209, and Bar-Efrat, *Narrative Art*, pp. 70-72, whose analysis is somewhat different but comes to similar conclusions.

[74] Fokkelman, p. 209.

[75] It is unclear why David would leave these women behind. For a possible explanation see, Andrew E. Hill, "On David's 'Taking' and 'Leaving' Concubines (2 Samuel 5:13; 15:16)," *JBL* 125/1, 2006, pp. 129-139. Hill's proposal is interesting but he admits it rests on conjecture.

[76] The connections between these two incidents lends further weight to the contention that the sin of Amnon was not just rape, but also incest. See the discussion in chap. 23, pp. 332-333.

[77] Daube's comments "Absalom and the Ideal King," pp. 319-320, are on target when he states that Absalom's act is "a public requital for the brutal unexpiated outrage.

than Amnon's. If a person had sexual relations with a sister, the law declared they were to be "cut off in the sight of their people" (Lev. 20:17); but if a man had sexual relations with his father's wife, both were to be put to death (Lev. 20:11).[78] Of course, Absalom's act has another significance: to possess the king's wives is to *be* the king. This bold act will assert to all Israel that Absalom's intentions are serious and there is no turning back. Yet again, Absalom imitates Abner by usurping the kingship and taking the king's concubine(s) (2 Sam. 3:7–11).[79] The reader is also aware that this is a fulfillment of Nathan's statement to David, "I will take your wives before your eyes and give them to your neighbor, and he shall lie with your wives *in the sight* of this sun" (2 Sam. 12:11). The narrator notes that "Absalom went in to his father's concubines *in the sight* of all Israel" (16:22). There is further irony in the fact that Absalom commits this act on the very roof where this series of events began—when David first spied Bathsheba bathing (2 Sam. 11:2).

16:23 helps us understand why the counsel of Ahithophel was considered so valuable: "Now the advice of Ahithophel, which he gave in those days, was as if one had inquired at the oracle of God. So was all the advice of Ahithophel both with David and with Absalom." This statement is to be taken seriously, and it aids the reader's appreciation for David's prayer in 15:31. However, the placement of this acknowledgement right after Ahithophel's advice for Absalom to take his father's wives demonstrates that Ahithophel's counsel might be formidable, but it certainly is not godly.

All the King's Men (2 Sam. 17:1–14)

The conclusion of chapter 16 would seem to give Absalom the tactical advantage over David. After all, every good leader needs wise counselors and, in Ahithophel, Absalom appears to have the cream of the crop. From Absalom's point of view, he has the best of both worlds—Ahithophel, and now, Hushai. This arsenal of wise counselors is only apparent, however, as the reader is aware that Hushai has been dispatched by David to "defeat the counsel of Ahithophel" (15:34). Nonetheless, after the glowing description of Ahithophel in 16:23, one wonders what chance Hushai has.

The usurper's ceremonious contempt for their standing is in manifest retaliation for the pitiless desertion, long ago, of his innocent sister by their master."

[78] Some understand both of these expressions to refer to death but Leviticus 20 seems to make a deliberate distinction in the penalty of various relationships. For a further discussion see, Gordon J. Wenham, "The Book of Leviticus," *NICOT*, (Grand Rapids: Wm. B. Eerdmans, 1979), pp. 278-280, 285-286.

[79] See chap. 11, pp. 144-147.

Some form of the word "counsel" (noun or verb) occurs a total of 18 times in 2 Samuel 15–17,[80] suggesting it is an important theme in these chapters. Furthermore, it is the only part of the books of Samuel where this word occurs. This focus on counselors, however, can ultimately be misleading, for while it may be true that, "in the multitude of counselors there is safety" (Prov. 11:14), one should not lose sight of the greater fact that it is "the counsel of the LORD [that] stands forever" (Ps. 33:11a). This is something that Absalom has either forgotten or ignored. Nowhere in these chapters do we read that Absalom sought the Lord. All of his wisdom and strategy comes from human beings. He relies on "the strength of man" (1 Sam. 2:9). David, on the other hand, is portrayed as praying, worshipping and submitting himself to God (15:31–32; 16:11–12).

Ahithophel continues by advising Absalom to take an army and strike David quickly (17:1–3). The advice is pleasing to Absalom and all the elders (v. 4), but Absalom then makes the mistake of calling in Hushai and asking for his counsel (v. 5). Several interpreters have noted that Hushai's advice, though not as sound, is more persuasive than Ahithophel's for two reasons: 1) it is more verbose and full of figures of speech, giving the appearance of wisdom; and 2) he appeals to Absalom's vanity by using second-person speech ("you") instead of first-person ("I") as Ahithophel did.[81]

It should also be noted that Hushai's appeal suggests that Absalom slow down his pursuit. In the past, taking things slowly had proven to be one of Absalom's strengths. Here, however, this "strength" will prove to be a liability. Ahithophel's advice to strike quickly is more prudent, but Hushai's flashy counsel carries the day. In most cases in the books of Samuel, substance usually triumphs over appearance; but not in this case. There is a solid reason: "For the LORD had purposed to defeat the good advice of Ahithophel, to the intent that the LORD might bring disaster on Absalom" (17:14b). Absalom reaps what he sows. In the past he appeared to be concerned about the welfare of individual Israelites (15:2–6), but he was not. Now he accepts counsel that appears to be wise but it is not.

The three occurrences of the word "counsel" (advice), in 17:14 nullify the three occurrences in 16:23 that made Ahithophel's advice so awe-inspiring. Indeed, who else but God could nullify the counsel of one whose advice was "as if one had inquired at the oracle of God"?[82] Ultimately, "There are many plans in a man's heart. Nevertheless the LORD's counsel—that will

---

[80] The references are: 15:12, 31, 34; 16:20, 23[3x]; 17:4, 7[2x], 11, 14[3x], 15[2x], 21, and 23.

[81] For an in-depth comparison of Ahithophel's and Hushai's speeches see, Bar-Efrat, *Narrative Art*, pp. 223-237; Fokkelman, *King David*, pp. 203-222; and Park, *The Frustration of Wisdom*, pp. 453-467. Once again, Hamilton, *Handbook*, p. 351, has a very helpful chart comparing the two speeches.

[82] Fokkelman, *King David*, p. 205, makes a similar observation.

stand" (Prov. 19:21), for, "There is no wisdom or understanding or counsel against the LORD" (Prov. 21:30).

In a rare glimpse into the workings of God in these chapters, the narrator allows us to know the outcome of the coming confrontation. It is a clear answer to David's prayer in 15:31. It is also a divine response to the actions of both David and Absalom. As David honored God and humbled himself by relinquishing all control to Him (16:11–12), so God will honor David by delivering him from Absalom. Likewise, Absalom despised God by taking His name in vain (15:7–8), never consulting Him, and lifting up his hand against the Lord's anointed (cf. 1 Sam. 26:9). Thus, 17:14b informs us that God will curse him (see 1 Sam. 2:30). In this way, divine sovereignty and human free will combine to give the kingdom back to David. As Proverbs 16:9 affirms: "A man's heart plans his way, but the LORD directs his steps."

The Battle is the Lord's (2 Sam. 17:24–26; 18:6–8)

After an exciting escape by Jonathan and Ahimaaz to inform David of Absalom's plans (17:15–22), there is a matter-of-fact account of Ahithophel's suicide (v. 23). Ahithophel's death forebodes the disaster that will soon befall Absalom, adding further confirmation to the words of 17:14. The story then returns briefly to Absalom, recounting his advance across the Jordan River (v. 24). Following Hushai's advice (v. 11), Absalom leads his army. In contrast, David's men will refuse to allow him to enter the battle (18:3). The difference between the two strategies will prove important.

We are also informed of Amasa's appointment as commander "instead of Joab" (17:25). This anticipates Joab's confrontation with Absalom in the coming battle (18:14–15). Verse 26 forms an inclusio with verse 24 by noting that "Israel and Absalom encamped in the land of Gilead." This time Absalom's name comes after Israel, forming an ABBA pattern with verse 24 (Absalom, Israel, Israel, Absalom). This brief notice of Absalom's journey and preparation for battle contrasts with the much lengthier report of David's journey (15:16–16:14) and preparation (17:27–18:5) and suggests where the narrator's sympathy lies. Ironically, David's focus on Absalom in the coming chapters is greater than the author's, suggesting that perhaps David's view is distorted by his fatherly affection.[83]

The much-anticipated battle is summarized in 18:6–8. The rugged terrain and the experience of David's more seasoned troops nullify the numerical advantage of Absalom's army. The unusual expression, "the woods devoured more people that day than the sword devoured" (v. 8), reminds the reader that the Lord intended to bring disaster on Absalom (17:14b). Just as the Lord had used the waves of the sea in the days of Moses (Exod. 15:1–21),

---

[83] Similarly, Conroy, *Absalom, Absalom!*, p. 49.

the sun and moon in the days of Joshua (Josh. 10:12–14), and the stars and the river Kishon in the days of Deborah and Barak (Judg. 5:20–21), so now He uses the forest to fight against Absalom.

The battle account here can be compared with the one recorded in 2 Samuel 2. In chapter 2, at the end of a long day of battle, Abner calls out to Joab, "Shall the sword devour forever?" (v. 26). The battle of chapter 2 is also between "Israel" and "the servants of David," and in both cases Israel suffers a major defeat (2:31). Other parallels include the similarity of language between 2 Samuel 2:17 and 18:7; the "seizing" of someone's head (2:16; 18:9); Joab's sounding of a trumpet to end hostilities (2:28; 18:16); the use of the verb "crossing over" (2:15; 18:9);[84] the places of origin of both kings (Hebron and Mahanaim—2:1, 8; 15:10; 17:24); and the general summary of the battles followed by a more detailed account of an important confrontation during the battles (2:17, 18–23; 18:7, 9–15). These correspondences suggest that Absalom continues to follow in his father's footsteps except that, whereas his father succeeds, he fails. He is the great counterfeit; an anti-messiah. He looks and acts like his father, but he is in fact very different. Evil often finds its appeal by imitating what is good. In the end, however, it is revealed for what it is.

Just "Hanging Around" Can Get You into Trouble (2 Sam. 18:9, 14–18)

How the "forest devours" is vividly illustrated in 18:9, as Absalom becomes entangled in an oak tree. While riding under the tree, Absalom's head is caught in the branches. Most scholars are agreed that "head" here is a reference to Absalom's luxuriant hair.[85] A number of images are effectively combined in this verse. First, the narrator's use of *head* instead of *hair* enables him to communicate two messages at once. Absalom's head is symbolic of his supposed leadership (cf. 1 Sam. 15:17), as well as his vanity (hair); and it becomes the instrument of his undoing. People who construct their reputation on hypocrisy and pride will eventually discover they have built their lives on an unstable foundation—in the end they will lose their footing. Since Absalom has illegally seized the headship of Israel, his head is seized by the oak.[86]

The mule is a second image and represents the chosen mount of royalty (2 Sam. 13:29; 1 Kings 1:33, 38, 44). It reinforces Absalom's kingly demeanor and aspirations. The loss of his mule represents the loss of his

---

[84] On these similarities see, Polzin, *David and the Deuteronomist*, pp. 183-186. He notes that only 2 Sam. chaps. 2 and 18 share these parallels.

[85] In some passages "head" is a synecdoche referring to the hair of the head (e.g., Num. 6:5, 9; and Ezek. 44:20).

[86] See Polzin, *David and the Deuteronomist*, p. 185. See also chap. 12, p. 158.

kingdom.[87] The kingship is violently pulled out from under him, as Creation itself (the tree and the mule) does not recognize his legitimacy.

The oak tree is the third significant image in this verse. It often has sacred connotations.[88] It is a place where the Lord appears, or where sacred events transpire (e.g., Gen. 12:6–7; 35:4; Josh. 24:26; Judg. 6:11). As such, the oak here may be a way of speaking of the hand of God reaching down and seizing Absalom. As Absalom hangs suspended between heaven and earth, the reader should call to mind that the Torah states, "For he who is hanged is cursed of God"[89] (Deut. 21:23).

When Joab learns of Absalom's predicament, he is quick to take advantage of the situation. Whatever the actual manner of death may be,[90] Absalom is a helpless victim. He is caught in a trap and can do nothing but receive the deadly blows. His inability to say or do anything as he is killed by Joab and his servants has eerie similarities with the death of his brother Amnon. Once again, Absalom has reaped what he has sown.

In reporting Absalom's death, the author chose to use the word "heart" twice in this verse (18:14), much as he had earlier chosen the word "head" for specific purposes. Not only is Joab said to strike Absalom in his "heart," but the author also tells us he did it while Absalom was "still alive in the 'heart' of the oak tree" (my translation).

As noted earlier, "heart" is a key word in the Absalom story. It occurs 18 times from 13:1–19:8.[91] It is used in various ways, but it is never used to describe the internal state of Absalom. No matter how much he may have tried to imitate his father, Absalom was no David. He was not "a man after God's own heart (1 Sam. 13:14). The one who stole "the hearts of the men of Israel" (2 Sam. 15:6) is vanquished by being struck in the heart three times (18:14). With Absalom dead, Joab *blew* the trumpet (18:16), the same word translated *thrust* in 18:14. Thus the act of Joab "thrusting" three spears in Absalom is equated with his "blowing" of the trumpet. In other words, with Absalom's death the "heart" of the rebellion is broken.

The soldiers then dispose of Absalom's body by "casting" it into a large pit in the forest while stones are heaped over it (v. 17)—hardly a proper burial for a king! In fact this verse recalls Joshua's dishonorable treatment of Canaanite kings who were "hanged on a tree," "cast" into a grave, and covered with a "great heap of stones" (Josh. 8:29; 10:26–27). Absalom's "hanging" also recalls the death of Ahithophel. However, Absalom's ignominious

---

[87] Conroy, *Absalom, Absalom!*, p. 60.

[88] Niditch, *My Brother Esau is a Hairy Man*, p. 80.

[89] The word "curse" is from *qālal*, the same word used in 1 Sam. 2:30 ("lightly esteem").

[90] See chap. 20, p. 283.

[91] The passages are: 13:6[2x], 8[2x], 10, 20, 28, 33; 14:1; 15:6, 13; 17:10[2x]; 18:3[2x], 14[2x]; and 19:7.

death and burial contrasts greatly with that of his counselor who "put his household in order" and "was buried in his father's tomb" (17:23).[92]

Verse 18 tells us that Absalom had earlier "*taken* and *set* up a pillar for himself." The verbs here are the same as those just used to describe what was done to Absalom's body ("And they *took* Absalom...and *set* a very large heap of stones over him"—my translation, v. 17). Bar-Efrat writes,

> The item of information concerning the erection of the monument is inserted here and not in its chronological place in order to create a sharp contrast between the imposing monument in the Valley of the King and the ignoble pit in the forest, signifying the contrast between Absalom's aspirations, pride and self-love, on the one hand, and the calamitous results to which these aspirations gave rise, on the other. The antithesis is given additional emphasis by the repetition of the same (Hebrew) roots.[93]

Only one other person in the books of Samuel is said to erect a monument to himself—that is Saul (1 Sam. 15:12). A brief review of Absalom's life shows that he shares other similarities with Israel's first king. Both men were physically impressive: they looked like kings (1 Sam. 9:2; 10:24; 2 Sam. 14:25–26). Both men pursued and tried to destroy David. Saul clung to a throne that was no longer his, while Absalom tried to take a throne that was not his to take. And, as the monuments testify, Saul and Absalom both sought the honor of men, rather than God's honor (1 Sam. 2:30).

We have already observed that the notice of Absalom's lack of a son to carry on his name acts as an inclusio around the story of the rebellion (see pp. 364-365 above). Along with his dishonorable burial, this highlights his impotence. Absalom's strength and leadership ability were only illusions.

Another effect, however, is the confusion created in the mind of the reader who recalls that Absalom was said to have three sons (14:27). This forces a comparison of the two verses. Many have presumed that Absalom's sons must have died in infancy, or that the verses preserve an irreconcilable contradiction. I suggest that the solution is to be found in comparing who is speaking in each passage, and also in noting the timeframe mentioned by the author. In 14:27 it is the narrator who states that Absalom had three sons, while in 18:18 it is Absalom who asserts, "I have no son." Here I fall back on the assumption that, when the narrator's assertion contradicts a character's statement, it is the character's statement that should be questioned. At first glance it might seem absurd to question Absalom's statement. After all, if he

---

[92] Fokkelman, *King David*, p. 249.

[93] Bar-Efrat, *Narrative Art*, pp. 178-179.

said he had no son when in fact he had three, this would be evident to all. I do not question that, at the time Absalom made the statement, he had no son; rather I question *when* the statement was made and what this might reveal about Absalom. Notice that the narrator's timeframe is very vague. He says that Absalom set up the monument "in his lifetime." While it is possible that he set up the monument *after* all of his sons had died, it is also possible that he set it up *before* any of his sons were born. If this is the case, having no son becomes a convenient excuse for Absalom to erect a monument to himself (in the King's Valley no less!). What Absalom really wants is *his* name to be remembered, and having no son provides a plausible explanation to the masses.

By now, the reader has learned enough of Absalom's megalomaniac tendencies to realize that what he says cannot be trusted. Absalom is good at saying one thing while having a completely different agenda. Therefore, I conclude that the author has pulled a statement from Absalom's past that precedes the assertion of 14:27,[94] and this obvious contradiction reveals Absalom's hypocrisy in building a monument for himself. It is possible that the original readers might have been more familiar with the chronology of events in Absalom's life. If so, and if what I have suggested is accurate, they would have relished the narrator's "delicious" irony in this observation. Whatever the correct order of circumstances, the verse maintains an ironical twist, as noted by Sheriffs: "Absalom intended to be remembered positively. He succeeded in memorializing his name, but he is remembered for all the wrong reasons."[95]

"O Absalom My Son!" (2 Sam. 18:19–19:4)

Now that Absalom is dead, the focus shifts to bringing the news to David. Joab dispatches a certain Cushite, while Zadok's son, Ahimaaz, also insists on carrying the news (18:19–23). The drama builds as the narrative switches to David's perspective (vv. 24ff.). Since the reader already knows the news, the drama lies in observing David's anxious waiting and in wondering how he will react. David sits between two gates, in Mahanaim (meaning "two camps"), as he waits for two messengers to bring an account of a nation that has been divided in two. Continuing this theme of duality, the messengers carry two important pieces of information. The first concerns the victory of David's servants over the forces of Absalom. As the story unfolds, it is clear that David cares little about this aspect of the battle; what interests him is the

---

[94] This is a common technique in the books of Samuel. See for example, 2 Sam. 4:4; and 21:1ff.

[95] Deryck Sheriffs, "The Human Need for Continuity, Some ANE and OT Perspectives," *TynB* 55/1, 2004, pp. 4-5.

second piece of information—Absalom's welfare. According to Joab, this preoccupation nearly costs him the loyalty of his troops (19:7). This division over important matters within David's heart has the potential of creating a division between the king and his army.[96]

When Ahimaaz arrives to deliver his news, his first word is "*shālôm*" ("All is well," 18:28). What David wants to know, however, is, "Is it *shālôm* for the young man Ab*shalom*?" (v. 29, my translation). Ahimaaz neatly avoids answering the question. When the Cushite arrives, he too gives the good news about the enemy's defeat (v. 31), but David's true concern is again betrayed by repeating the same question from verse 29, "Is it *shālôm* for the young man Ab*shalom*?" (v. 32a). The Cushite delivers the long-awaited answer clearly, but diplomatically: "May all the enemies of my lord the king, and all who rise against you to do you harm, be like that young man" (v. 32b). The king's agonized response reveals that, for him, there is no *shālôm* without Ab*shalom* (18:33–19:4).

Before examining David's response in more depth, the similarities between this, the last battle report in 2 Samuel, and the first battle report in 1 Samuel 4, merit attention. As David waits at the gate for news of the battle, so also does Eli (1 Sam. 4:18). Eli hears the sound of a "tumult" (4:14), while the reason Ahimaaz gives for not being able to tell David about Absalom's fate is, "I saw a great tumult" (2 Sam. 18:29). Although the following language might seem characteristic of such accounts, both stories speak of someone "watching" as they await news (Eli in 4:13; a "watchman" in 18:24ff.) and someone "running" to tell the news (4:12; 18:19–26). In both stories, Israel is defeated with a "great smiting" (4:10; 18:7), and we are told "every man fled to his tent" (4:10; 18:17). In the first story, the city "cries out" (4:13), and in the second, David "cries out" (19:4). Eli "trembles" (4:13); David "shakes" (18:33). Eli loses two sons (4:17); David loses one. Eli loses his throne (4:18); David is restored to his.

These parallels and contrasts give the reader pause to consider that, in the beginning of the book, Israel is battling its enemy the Philistines, while at the end of the book Israel wreaks the same destruction on itself.[97] Along this line, it seems ironic that God gave Israel a king saying, "that he may save My people from the hand of the Philistines" (1 Sam. 9:16). Kingship does not seem to have provided the solution the people had hoped for. Little did they realize when they demanded of Samuel, "No but we will have a king over us...that our king may...go out before us and fight our battles" (1 Sam. 8:19b–20), that the kings would end up fighting against their own people!

---

[96] We have noted, however, that this is Joab's construal of the situation and that it may not be accurate. See chap. 20, p. 287.

[97] A similar phenomenon can be observed in the beginning and ending of the book of Judges. Compare Judg. 1:1ff. with 20:18ff.

Such is the outcome when human beings grasp for power instead of recognizing that the Lord is their king (1 Sam. 8:7).

Returning to David's response, the word used to describe his reaction to the news ("deeply moved," NKJV) is unusual. It means "to shake," "to tremble," or "to be perturbed."[98] The author gives voice to David's agony in his tortured cry, "O my son Absalom—my son, my son Absalom—if only I had died in your place! O Absalom my son, my son!" (18:33). These words act as an inclusio around David's expression of grief, as they reoccur in 19:4. The narrative is in no hurry at this point (18:33), but dwells on David's sorrow. His tears and desire to trade places with his son are a perfect contrast to Absalom's self-centeredness.[99] "To Absalom, the possession of power, kingship, is all, and the relationship with his father is nothing. To David blood-relationship is everything."[100] It is unfortunate that David did not arrive at this conclusion until it was too late. "David's blocked feelings only become clear to us (and perhaps also to him) at the death of Absalom. He is a divided man no longer; but the division has been set forth in the land, resulting in civil war, fratricide, and secession."[101]

Besides the word *shālôm* in the name of David's son, it is also not without importance that Absalom begins with *'āḇ* = "father." Regarding David's cry, Bar-Efrat insightfully states, "The numerous repetitions of the elements 'son' and '*'āḇ*' echo continually in our minds, thus highlighting the bond between father and son as well as the preceding conflict between the two."[102] It is of note that Absalom is usually referred to by his personal name but in 2 Samuel 18–19 his relationship to David is constantly emphasized. He is called "young man" (18:5, 12, 29, 32), "son of the king" (18:12, 20), and most poignantly, "his/my son" (18:33; 19:2, 4).[103] Once again, national tragedy meets family pain.[104]

Several key words converge in this scene to draw Absalom's story to a conclusion.[105] Three act as inclusions around the story of Absalom's rebel-

---

[98] See Conroy's discussion, *Absalom, Absalom!*, p. 75.

[99] Roy Battenhouse, "The Tragedy of Absalom: A Literary Analysis (II Samuel 13–18)," *Christianity and Literature*, 31/3, 1982, p. 56.

[100] Fokkelman, *King David*, p. 295.

[101] Ackerman, "Knowing Good and Evil," p. 48.

[102] Bar-Efrat, *Narrative Art*, p. 70.

[103] Conroy, *Absalom, Absalom!*, p. 81.

[104] Although David's grief as a father is very real, David's forgiving heart is another reason we have suggested for his sorrow over Absalom's death. See chap. 20, pp. 287-288 above.

[105] As all scholars note, the effects of the rebellion continue all the way through to the conclusion of Sheba's revolt (2 Sam. 20:22), but Absalom's part in the drama comes to an end in 19:8 when David overcomes the grief of his son's death in order to present himself publicly to the people.

lion, while seven others reach back all the way to the first episode of Absalom's story in 2 Samuel 13. First, as noted above, David's weeping takes place at "the gate" (18:33). It is at the gate that Absalom began his intrigues (15:2), and it is at the gate that David spoke with his troops before battle (18:4–5), asking that they "deal gently for my sake with the young man Absalom." It is also at the gate that he waited in hope of good news (18:24). So it is fitting that David now weeps in a chamber "over the gate," and will, after being rebuked by Joab, greet the people "sitting in the gate" (19:8).

Second, the rebellion began when we were informed that Absalom had *stolen* "the hearts of the men of Israel" (15:6). In an interesting reversal, David's victorious army now *steals* "back into the city...as people who are ashamed *steal* away when they flee in battle" (19:3). It seems in both instances that it is the people who are cheated.

Third, the prelude to the rebellion began with fifty men who "ran" before Absalom's chariot (15:1). At the rebellion's end, two men "run" to proclaim the victory of David's men and the death of Absalom (18:19–32).

The seven words that reach back beyond the rebellion and round off the entire story of Absalom are "heart," "cry out," "weep," "mourn," "over/against," "love," and "hate." Joab demands that David "speak to the heart" of his servants, otherwise not one will stay with him through the night (19:7).[106] While Absalom had stolen the hearts of Israel, according to Joab, David had crushed the heart of his men by mourning over Absalom and not celebrating their hard-fought victory. The second word suggests that David once again experiences the pain of Tamar (13:19) as he "cries out" over a loss that cannot be recovered (19:4). David's reluctance to respond to Tamar's tragedy has created a tragedy greater than he could ever have imagined.

In yet another poignant connection, as David had "wept" and "mourned" "over" Amnon (13:36–37), he now "weeps" and "mourns" "over" Absalom (18:33–19:2). There may be further irony in the use of the preposition 'al which clearly means "over" in 19:1 and 2, for it is the same preposition which meant "against" in 14:1. There the heart of David was "against" Absalom. Here he mourns and weeps "over" his son. This contrast reveals the pathos of a king who realized too late that he was also a father.

The final words "love and hate" act as a pair. "Love" was first mentioned as the feeling that Amnon had for his sister Tamar (13:1, 4). That "love" quickly turned to "hate" following his heinous crime against her (13:15), and fostered a hatred of its own in Tamar's brother, Absalom (13:22). Absalom's hatred ignited a chain of events that eventually led to his rebellion. Now, as David weeps for his rebellious son, Joab chides him by saying, "you

---

[106] The use of "heart" occurs one other time in relation to the rebellion, but it is beyond the bounds of our present investigation. Shimei's plea for forgiveness (19:19) includes the familiar expression "take it to heart" found in 13:20, 33.

love your enemies and hate your friends...for today I perceive that if Absalom had lived and all of us had died today, then it would have pleased you well" (19:6). The repetition of key words thus unites the story of Absalom as a whole and provides a fitting conclusion.

Conclusion: A Hypocrite Wears Many Masks

The Greek word "hypocrite" can mean "actor," and thus, "one who wears a mask."[107] This seems a suitable evaluation of Absalom's character. Absalom certainly showed the ability to wear masks. He could wear the mask of affection for his father (2 Sam. 13:24–25), the mask of brotherly love (13:26–27), the mask of humility (14:33), the mask of the just judge (15:2–4), the mask of religiosity (15:7–8), and, most presumptuously, the mask of kingship (15:10). As we have seen, Absalom was a master manipulator and his words and actions could rarely be taken at face value. It was only when he tried to usurp his father's throne that he was *un*masked once and for all.

Absalom's masks are not only seen in his words but in his deeds. Foremost was his imitation of David. We have noted that his action of killing Amnon resembled his father's murder of Uriah. His words of innocence also mimicked those of David (2 Sam. 14:32; 1 Sam. 20:8). His anointing at Hebron, his seizure of Jerusalem, and his confrontation of the enemy at Mahanaim all echo earlier episodes in the life of David. Furthermore, Absalom stole his father's people (2 Sam. 15:6), his father's counselor (15:12), and his father's concubines (16:21–22). He gave a masterful performance, acting like David, but in the end there was no encore. He could never be his father, because he did not have the heart or the humility of his father. He was an imposter and in his shameful death the trappings of his vanity (his hair) conspired to do him in.

Not only was Absalom's true nature unmasked by David's superior qualities: ironically, in other people he imitates we glimpse his real character. Absalom's similarities with Saul, which we have previously noted, do not speak well of him. At least it can be said of Saul that he was chosen by the Lord (1 Sam. 9:17). Absalom, however, is a usurper, plain and simple. Ultimately, Saul was rejected by the Lord from being king of God's people (1 Sam. 15:11, 26), and so was Absalom (2 Sam. 17:14).

His use of the Lord's name for political gain, his taking of the king's concubines, his rebellion against the Lord's anointed, and attempt to take the kingship by force, all have echoes of Abner. Absalom's similarities with Abner, however, also accentuate the differences between the two men. As Saul's relative, Abner tried to protect the house of Saul by making Ish-bosheth king.

---

[107] The transformation of the meaning of this word has a complex history. See *TDNT*, Vol. VIII, pp. 563-571.

In contrast, Absalom gave no thought to the destruction of David's house by making himself king. While Abner may have had political motives, at least he attempted to be reconciled with David in the end; Absalom never did.

Going outside the books of Samuel, Absalom's resemblance to Samson also shapes his character portrait. Once again, he shares the bad qualities of the person he imitates without any of the good. Like Samson, Absalom was spoiled, and could bully others to get his own way. But unlike Samson, whose long hair designated him a Nazirite set apart to the Lord (Judg. 13:5), Absalom's long hair portrayed his trust in his own physical prowess. Samson was a divinely-sanctioned deliverer of God's people who destroyed many of Israel's enemies (Judg. 13:5; 16:30), but Absalom was not divinely called and only brought destruction on his own nation.

Perhaps Absalom's most negative association concerns the characteristics he shares with Cain. Most scholars recognize similarities between Cain and the wise woman of Tekoa's description of her fictitious son (who in reality is Absalom).[108] She tells the king that her sons were in a field when one rose up to kill the other (2 Sam. 14:6), a similar situation to that of Cain and Abel (Gen. 4:8). Just as Absalom was banished, so was Cain (Gen. 4:12); and just as Cain pleaded with God for protection from blood vengeance (Gen. 4:13–15), so also the woman pleads that her son (representing Absalom) would be spared (2 Sam. 14:11, 14). The New Testament makes a final link between Absalom and Cain. 1 John 3:12 speaks of Cain who "murdered his brother" and concludes that "Whoever hates his brother is a murderer" (1 John 3:15). Absalom's hatred of Amnon is what led to his murder of him (2 Sam. 13:22, 32). Absalom is thus an imitator of the first and most infamous murderer in Scripture.

Ultimately, the various disguises of Absalom serve to unmask a very unsavory character. If we were to argue who the greatest villain in the books of Samuel is, Absalom would come in a close second to Joab.

---

[108] For example, Alter, in *The David Story*, p. 276.

Chapter 25

Adonijah: The Pretender (David's son)

Then Adonijah the son of Haggith exalted himself, saying, "I will be king" (1 Kings 1:5)

Absalom Redivivus[1] (1 Kings 1:5–10)

In contrast to the cheerless description of David in 1 Kings 1:1–4, Adonijah is introduced for the first time as a young, ambitious, spoiled, but dashingly handsome son of David (vv. 5–6). The contrast is intentional: David's impotence suggests that he no longer has the ability to rule, therefore, Adonijah says, "I will be king" (v. 5). The narrator's description of Adonijah exalting himself, along with his first words, "I, even I will be king" (the Hebrew pronoun gives emphasis) suggest an opportunistic, self-absorbed young man. This impression is bolstered by the observations that follow. Adonijah's preparation of chariots, horsemen, and fifty men to run before him in Absalom-like style (2 Sam. 15:1), immediately raises a red flag. Furthermore, the author adds his own comment about Adonijah's spoiled nature: "And his father had not rebuked him at any time by saying, 'Why have you done so?' " (v. 6a). He is thus characterized as a young man who had never been constrained or received fatherly correction (Prov. 13:24; 23:13–14).

One may automatically think of another son of David (Amnon) whose undisciplined ways caused great problems (2 Sam. 13:1–22). However, Adonijah's good looks, and the narrator's statement that he was born "after Absalom," link him most closely with this rebellious brother. Furthermore, in verse 6 the author of Kings explains Adonijah's present actions by looking at his past: "his entire life, starting from his childhood and including his position within the family as a son and a brother, sheds light on the action Adonijah is about to take. Thus, the glimpses into the past hint at the causes for the developments in the present."[2]

Another connecting link between Adonijah and Absalom is made in the verb used to describe David's lack of discipline given to his son. Verse 6 literally begins, "And his father never *pained* him" (my translation). Following Absalom's death, the people heard the king was "*pained* over his son" (2 Sam. 19:2, my translation). This verb also reminds us that David was a failure as a

---

[1] The expression is from Hamilton, *Handbook*, p. 382, who states, "Adonijah is Absalom redivivus" (i.e., Absalom come back to life). For an excellent outline of 1 Kings 1 and a defense of its unity see, Burke O. Long, "A Darkness Between Brothers: Solomon and Adonijah," *JSOT* 19, 1981, pp. 79-94.

[2] Bar-Efrat, *Narrative Art*, p. 176.

father.[3] We might say that through the misadventures of David's sons (Amnon, Absalom, and Adonijah), the text has been at *pains* to show us the inadequacy of his relationship with them. His inactivity regarding Amnon's crime (2 Sam. 13:21), his harsh treatment of Absalom (2 Sam. 14:24, 28), and his lack of discipline of Adonijah combine overwhelmingly to present him as a disappointing father. While accolades can be showered upon David for his kingly abilities (cf. 2 Sam. 3:36; 8:15; 1 Kings 15:4–5), the same cannot be said for his parental aptitude. In our own time, when disciplining children has become politically incorrect, David stands as a warning to those who do not correct their children, either because they are preoccupied with other interests, or because they lack the wisdom to do so.[4]

The verb "to pain" also suggests that Adonijah may be headed toward the same end as Absalom.[5] Noting the many similarities between the two, Nelson eloquently states, "Adonijah is skillfully tarred with Absalom's brush....The subtle invocation of Absalom's ghost constrains us to see Adonijah's moves in the worst possible light."[6] Bar-Efrat summarizes the parallels between Adonijah and Absalom well:

> Both Absalom and Adonijah attempt to seize the crown, both prepare themselves adherents and establish a *fait accompli* (their proclamation as king). Both start their rebellion by sacrificing a great number of beasts in the presence of guests, and both bring disaster on themselves in the final event as the result of their lust for power. The narrator draws our attention to the parallel between the two brothers by saying of Adonijah: "He too was a very handsome man; and he was born next after Absalom" (1 Kings 1:6).[7]

In these two verses (vv. 5–6), the narrator has colored the lens through which we are to view Adonijah's actions. As a result, it is somewhat surprising to find a number of commentators who seek to defend Adonijah

---

[3] The dynamic of David as king and father was also an important component of Absalom's story. Fokkelman, *King David*, p. 355, notes, "Here, as in the Absalom affair, an unmistakable friction has arisen between David's sub-personalities as father and king."

[4] My words should in no way be misconstrued to condone verbal and physical abuse of children. I am speaking of the loving correction and discipline that every child needs (Eph. 6:4).

[5] Iain W. Provan, *1 and 2 Kings*, p. 24, states, "In associating Adonijah so clearly with his brother, the authors have already hinted to us that this son, too, is heading for disaster."

[6] Nelson, *First and Second Kings*, p. 19.

[7] Bar-Efrat, *Narrative Art*, p. 88.

and villainize Nathan and Solomon. For example, Jones states, "Adonijah assumed that he was to succeed David....This expected and apparently legitimate progression to the throne was thwarted by an unexpected move on behalf of Solomon, who had a less obvious claim to succeed his father."[8] If Adonijah had "assumed that he was to succeed David," there would have been no need for a covert operation. Jones believes that because he is David's oldest surviving son, he *deserves* the throne, but there are a number of factors that indicate such thinking is wrong.

First, Israel was still a new kingdom, so the right of primogeniture had not yet been established.[9] Yahweh had always been the one to designate Israel's leader, and He had done so with Saul and David (1 Sam. 9:17; 16:1, 12–13). The Torah states, "you shall surely set a king over you whom the LORD your God chooses" (Deut. 17:15). 1 Kings 1 continually emphasizes that Solomon was the Lord's choice. It is first emphasized in the oath David made with Bathsheba. She recalled, "You swore by the LORD your God to your maidservant, saying, 'Assuredly Solomon your son shall reign after me, and he shall sit on my throne' " (1:17). We have previously addressed the issue that there is no reason to doubt the validity of the oath's existence.[10] David confirms that he had spoken it (1:30).[11]

Second, God's sanction of Solomon as David's successor is repeatedly emphasized (1:36–37, 48). Third, Adonijah was well aware that he was not going to inherit the throne. This is why he rallies his supporters to a pre-coronation feast before the death of his father (1:9). The fact that he invites all of the king's sons except Solomon (1:9–10), and excludes those who support Solomon, indicates that he is aware that Solomon stands in line for the throne. Later, Adonijah begrudgingly admits that the kingdom was Solomon's because, "It was his from the LORD" (1 Kings 2:15). This statement is reminiscent of Abner, who after years of struggling against David for the throne, finally admitted that the Lord had sworn to give David the kingdom (2 Sam. 3:9–10).

The contrast between Adonijah's attempt to seize the throne and Solomon's passivity suggests the dynamic of grasping the kingdom versus receiving the kingdom, so evident in the stories of Saul and David, and Absa-

---

[8] Gwilym, H. Jones, *The Nathan Narratives*, p. 48.

[9] Ibid., p. 47, is in agreement with this: "Admittedly, it is difficult to prove that primogeniture was an accepted principle in Israel at this very early period in the history of the monarchy; the dynasty was too young yet to have acquired an established pattern."

[10] See chap. 19, pp. 246-247.

[11] Some argue that the old king was senile. However, David's impaired condition was physical, not mental. 1 Kings 1–2 consistently shows him in charge of his mental faculties (1:28–35, 48; 2:1–9); not once does it suggest otherwise.

lom and David.[12] "Ironically, Adonijah means 'Yah is master.' In spite of his efforts to make himself master, Adonijah's life history demonstrates that Yah is indeed Master."[13]

In his attempt to take the throne, Adonijah has procured some formidable allies: Joab, the commander of David's army, and Abiathar, priest and former loyalist of David (1:7). While having the backing of Joab and Abiathar may seem impressive, this too should influence the reader's view of the attempted coup. Even at his best, Joab remains an unsavory character—infamous for his lack of moral qualities. Although Abiathar has previously appeared in a positive light, we will be reminded that he belongs to a rejected house. Adonijah's attempt to take the throne will ultimately lead to Abiathar's banishment and fulfillment of the Lord's word against the house of Eli (1 Kings 2:26–27). Our studies have revealed that the company a character keeps, as well as comparisons with previous characters in Scripture, are devices the narrator uses to suggest his assessment of that individual's nature. The many similarities with Absalom (and we will note a few more) suggest the villainy of Adonijah; the company of Joab and Abiathar further confirm this negative portrait.

Politically speaking, there appears to be a division between what might be termed the Hebron faction and the Jerusalem faction. Adonijah was born in Hebron (2 Sam. 3:4) and Joab and Abiathar had been with David since his wilderness days and the beginning of his kingship in Hebron (1 Sam. 22:20–23; 2 Sam. 2:13). Also supporting Adonijah were "all the men of Judah, the king's servants" (1 Kings 1:9). In contrast, Solomon was born in Jerusalem (2 Sam. 5:14), while his supporters, Nathan, Zadok, and Benaiah, are not mentioned until after David's move to Jerusalem (2 Sam. 7:2; 8:17–18).[14] Therefore, as Provan suggests, the different parties may represent a "conflict between old, Judah-based comrades of David from the Hebron days, and newer, Jerusalem-based associates."[15] He believes these two distinct parties

---

[12] Whybray's comments are insightful on this point: "It is perhaps significant that no mention is made of him [i.e., Solomon] at all between the notice of his birth and naming (II Sam. 12.24f.) and the story of his enthronement (from I Kings 1:10). He thus remains an unknown, mysterious figure during the period when his brothers are attempting to usurp the throne. This impersonal treatment is perhaps intended to emphasize that he stood aloof from the conflict. Absalom's and Adonijah's plots stand condemned as arrogant attempts to snatch the kingdom by force." Whybray, *The Succession Narrative*, p. 52.

[13] Leithart, *1 & 2 Kings*," p. 30.

[14] 1 Chron. 12:28 mentions Zadok joining David in Hebron, but this is in connection with those who "came to David at Hebron to turn over the kingdom of Saul to him" (1 Chron. 12:23)—a reference to the event spoken of in 2 Sam. 5:1–3.

[15] Iain Provan, "Why Barzillai," *TynB*, 46/1, 1995, p. 114, esp. n. 10. Also see, Iain W. Provan, *1 and 2 Kings*, pp. 24-25. Jones, *The Nathan Narratives*, pp. 40-46 (referenced

should be seen "in the light of the Judah-Israel tensions already evident in Samuel (e.g., 2 Sa. 20), and soon to explode into schism again in 1 Ki. 12 (cf., in particular, 2 Sa. 20:1 and 1 Ki. 12:16)."[16]

Adonijah is said to offer up sacrifices "by the stone of Zoheleth, which is by En Rogel" (1 Kings 1:9). As previously noted, Absalom's revolt began in a similar fashion (2 Sam. 15:12). Such meals were customary at coronation ceremonies (1 Sam. 9:19–10:1; 16:1–13).[17] The meaning of the place names where Adonijah holds his feast seem significant. "Zoheleth" can mean "the Serpent Stone." However, Grey notes that this is its secondary meaning and that the Hebrew verb actually means "to slip" and so might refer to "some rock mass detached from the overhanging cliffs by an earthquake."[18] If Zoheleth means "Slippery Stone" it could suggest that Adonijah's usurpation is not on a firm footing! On the other hand, if it is to be translated "Serpent Stone," serpent frequently carries evil connotations (Gen. 3), so this might be suggestive of Adonijah's attempted coup. The place name "En Rogel" has several possible meanings, of which "Well of the Spy" is one.[19] It is certainly connected with spying in 2 Samuel 17:17–21 (see comment below). Does this place name perhaps point to Adonijah's subversive activity? Whatever the case, it is ironic that Adonijah's feast to proclaim himself king happens at the same location where David's men had left to bring him word of Absalom's plans. Thus, En Rogel provides another connection to Absalom's revolt.

News Arrives: "Adonijah, Your Goose is Cooked!" (1 Kings 1:41–53)

Solomon's coronation becomes the focus of 1:11–40, while Adonijah reappears in 1:41ff.[20] Fat and satisfied from his feast, thinking his mission is accomplished, Adonijah and his guests hear noise coming from the city. Being an experienced soldier, Joab seems especially disconcerted about the uproar. Jonathan arrives to bring the news, and Adonijah's optimistic, "Come

---

by Provan) proposes a similar view, although he maintains that Zadok, Nathan, and probably Bathsheba, are Jebusites who were integrated into the religious and political system when David conquered Jerusalem.

[16] Provan, "Why Barzillai," p. 114, n. 10.

[17] Some question whether Adonijah's feast was, in fact, a coronation ceremony. For example, Jones, *The Nathan Narratives*, p. 48, and Nelson, *First and Second Kings*, p. 20. However, Adonijah's assertion, "I will be king" (v. 5), and Nathan's report that the guests were saying "Long live King Adonijah" (v. 25), put the matter beyond doubt.

[18] Gray, *I&II Kings*, p. 82.

[19] Ibid., pp. 81-82.

[20] For a treatment of the intervening verses as they pertain to Bathsheba see, chap. 19, pp. 245-250.

in, for you are a prominent man, and bring good news" (v. 42), looks foolish in retrospect.

Jonathan rehearses the recent activities in the city, citing that Solomon has been proclaimed king with David's blessing (vv. 43–48). One wonders how Jonathan received all this inside information (e.g., that David bowed himself on his bed, v. 47), and why he was not present at Adonijah's feast. As previously suggested, it appears that Adonijah had left him behind in the city to act as an informant of any events that might transpire there, good or bad.[21] Once again Jonathan seems to be connected with spying activity at En Rogel, lending support to the definition "Well of the Spy" mentioned above.

As Jonathan recounts Solomon's coronation, it becomes the third time in the narrative that it is described (David's instructions—vv. 32–34, the actual event—vv. 38–39, and Jonathan's retelling—vv. 43–48).[22] In fact, Jonathan's retelling of the events is the most detailed account in the chapter. He becomes a "party-pooper," as his bad news strikes terror into Adonijah and his guests (vv. 49–50). There is a balance between the "rising" and "going" of the guests and the "rising" and "going" of Adonijah, while different words are used to describe the panic of each (guests—"trembled," Adonijah—"feared").[23] Moreover, there is a difference in the paths they take. The guests flee to safety (v. 49), while Adonijah flees to take hold of the "horns of the altar" (v. 50). Robert Alter likens the terrified dispersal of Adonijah's guests to that following Absalom's murder of Amnon.[24] In both instances, the king's sons flee (2 Sam. 13:29) as does the perpetrator, taking a different path from that of the guests (2 Sam. 13:34, 37f.). Here is yet one more link between Adonijah and Absalom.

Adonijah's seizure of the horns of the altar might be related to Exodus 21:12–14. In these verses the Lord speaks of a place where people may flee if they have committed an unpremeditated murder (v. 13). If the act was premeditated, however, the Lord instructs, "You shall take him from My altar, that he may die" (v. 14). It was on the horns of the altar that the atoning blood of sacrifice is smeared (Ezek. 43:19–20). Thus, the horns came to represent a place of mercy. "The fugitive from vengeance, having thus made contact with the part of the altar where union with God was effected by the blood of sacrifice, was regarded as…the protected sojourner with God."[25]

Although Adonijah had not yet killed anyone, there is no reason to doubt that Bathsheba's fear (1 Kings 1:21) would have proven true had he become king. His words, "Let King Solomon swear to me today that he will

---

[21] See chap. 8, pp. 95-96.

[22] See comments by Leithart, *1&2 Kings*, p. 33.

[23] Gunn, *The Story of King David*, p. 140, n. 22.

[24] Alter, *The David Story*, p. 372.

[25] Gray, *I&II Kings*, p. 94.

not put his servant to death with the sword" (v. 51), proclaim that he expects the same treatment and, therefore, seeks sanctuary at the altar. Solomon does not swear such an oath, however. He only states, "If he proves himself a worthy man, not one hair of him shall fall to the earth; but if wickedness is found in him, he shall die" (v. 52).[26] This anticipates the wisdom that Solomon will later be lauded for (1 Kings 3:12, 28). To assure Adonijah his life by swearing an oath, with no guarantee of his future loyalty, would be folly indeed.

Solomon's words draw one more ironic parallel between Adonijah and Absalom. His words "not one hair of him shall fall to the earth" are an echo of David's to the Tekoite woman in 2 Samuel 14:11. The picture of Adonijah alone, begging for his life, and ultimately prostrating himself before Solomon (vv.50–53), presents a profound contrast to the self-assured, ambitious young man of 1:5–10.[27] "The man who attempted to 'lift himself up' comes low."[28] Such is the fate of those who seek to take what is not theirs.

One "Small" Request, One Big Problem (1 Kings 2:13–25)

Since these verses have been examined in some detail already,[29] I will deal with them more briefly here. We are not told how much time passed between Solomon's command, "Go to your house" (1:53), and the *son of Haggith's* approach to the *mother of Solomon* (2:13). One thing that is certain is that it takes place after David's death. Thus, Solomon is no longer a co-regent with his father (1:48), but has assumed complete responsibility for the kingdom. It is within the context of David's death (2:10–11) and Solomon's full assumption of the throne (2:12) that Adonijah approaches Bathsheba with his request.

This context suggests that Adonijah's request for Abishag is colored with political overtones. It appears that, since David is dead, Adonijah sees another possible way of obtaining support for the throne through David's still-virgin concubine, Abishag. He realizes that David is no longer an obstacle (as he was in 1 Kings 1) and, if he is going to take the throne, he must act while Solomon's reign is still new. He hopes to use a "loop-hole" to destabilize the new king's reign. Adonijah knows there are still plenty of political enemies afoot for Solomon. Joab and Abiathar are still forces to be reckoned

---

[26] Critics who accuse Solomon of ascending the throne through a political blood-bath overlook the fact that he does not execute Adonijah immediately. Instead he grants him mercy. It is only when Adonijah persists with suspicious activity that he is put to death.

[27] Fokkelman's chart comparing and contrasting the two opposing parties, as well as his concentric layout of 1:5–53, helps the reader to gain the "big picture" of this chapter. See *King David.*, pp. 365, 367, 381.

[28] Leithart, *1&2 Kings*, p. 33.

[29] See chap. 19, pp. 250-253.

with, not to mention a potential trouble-maker like Shimei. Ambitious eyes do not always see clearly. Where the author sees stability (v. 12), Adonijah sees opportunity.

The political overtones of Adonijah's request are reinforced by the similarity with Absalom. Just as Absalom went into his father's concubines to strengthen the hands of those who were with him (2 Sam. 16:21), so Adonijah hopes to gain possession of Abishag. However, the matter must be handled delicately. Adonijah is well aware that he dare not approach Solomon with such a request, so he finds an easier target to prey upon. Through Bathsheba he thinks he has the perfect person to help his cause. Her position as queen mother, her lack of good judgment, and inability to say "no," make her the ideal individual to approach the king.

Adonijah's manipulative ability is evident in the "guilt/pity trip" he places on her (vv. 15–17). His "wheedling tactics: 'Feel sorry for me (v. 15). It is only one thing. He will not turn you down,' "[30] present an unsavory picture. He makes it appear that his desire for Abishag is purely romantic.[31] Solomon (the rich man in the story) has everything else; all he (the poor man) wants is "one little ewe-lamb."[32] Bathsheba becomes convinced that it is only "one small request" (v. 20). Although a risky venture, Adonijah banked on the hope that Bathsheba's persuasive powers would win the day over her son. He may also have been counting on the fact that his younger, less-experienced, brother would be distracted/influenced by the fact that it was his mother making the request. It is evident from the text that Solomon accorded his mother great honor, and sought to please her if possible (vv. 19–20). However, the text also bears witness that Adonijah greatly underestimated his brother's political acumen. Solomon's response is explosive and immediate (vv. 22). Adonijah has "spoken this word against his own life" (v. 23). Solomon's oath seals Adonijah's doom and Benaiah is dispensed to carry out the execution (vv. 24–25).

While some accuse Solomon of heartless political opportunism, the converse is actually the case.[33] The narrator is already demonstrating the wis-

---

[30] Nelson, *First and Second Kings*, p. 26.

[31] There is much debate among scholars as to whether Adonijah's request for Abishag was politically or romantically motivated. Gunn, *The Story of King David*, p. 91, states, "Perhaps Adonijah's inability to suppress his desire (so impolitic) for this woman is the last faint echo of David's former sexual aggression." This sounds like a viable possibility until it is realized that Adonijah's motives are purposely ambiguous. He is a younger version of Absalom, who, it will be remembered, had the ability to make things appear one way, while having an entirely different motive.

[32] On the comparison of Abishag with the ewe-lamb of 2 Sam. 12:1–4, see chap. 19, pp. 244-245.

[33] I quote at length and acknowledge my agreement with R. D. Patterson and H. J. Austel, *1, 2 Kings*, EBC vol. 4 (Grand Rapids: Zondervan, 1988), p. 38: "In the view

dom of Solomon. David has acknowledged it (2:9), and God will crown him with an abundant supply (3:12). With the death of Adonijah, the banishment of Abiathar (2:26–27), and the death of Joab (2:28–34), Solomon took several giant steps forward in securing his throne.

Conclusion: Adonijah, or Should We Say, Absalom Jr.?

In the vein of his older brother Absalom, Adonijah was a master at self-promotion and manipulation. Although he had the support of at least one significant priest (Abiathar), like his brother, the Lord's name was only found on his lips when it was politically expedient (1 Kings 2:15). The similarities between the two brothers are impressive. Do we have a set of identical twins here?

Perhaps the best way to construct a character evaluation of Adonijah is to note differences between him and Absalom. Absalom's rebellion was fueled by hatred as well as ambition. Adonijah seemed to have no ulterior motive other than self-exaltation. Is it worse to hate one's father, or to care so little for him because of self-absorption? Perhaps in the end, self-love that eclipses concern for others is no different than hatred. In such circumstances, love and hate become one, so we must still ask if there are any differences between these brothers.

The fact that Absalom mounted a claim to the throne while his father still had some vitality makes Adonijah's attempted coup of a weak, sickly old man look pathetic. Absalom was able to assemble an impressive fighting force that was willing to do battle for him, while Adonijah's followers scattered at the first sign of trouble. Clearly Adonijah had not planned his coup as carefully as Absalom, nor did he inspire the same loyalty. One could interpret Absalom's silence while dying as a sign of bravado. And although it might have been more talk than substance, Absalom put himself in potential danger by insisting on seeing the king (2 Sam. 14:32). Adonijah, on the other hand, ran to take hold of the horns of the altar and pleaded that Solomon swear an oath not to take his life. Although it is difficult to speak of Absalom as "no-

---

of those who see a Solomonic apologetic in the first two chapters of 1 Kings, Solomon is the usurper rather than Adonijah. The latter is to be pitied, especially in having his romantic aspirations toward Abishag so unjustly and cruelly thwarted. The difficulties and inconsistencies in adopting such a view are considerable and can only be maintained by resorting to unfounded presuppositions and historical reconstructions that compound the uncertainties and problems. On the other hand, there is a clear and consistent testimony in the narrative as it stands to the grace and sovereign purpose of God in choosing David and Solomon, with all their shortcomings and failures, to be kings and forerunners of the Messiah who would be provided by God for his people, Israel, and for the world."

ble," at least in this sense he was willing to pay the price for his ambition, whereas, Adonijah looks more cowardly by comparison.

What conclusions can be drawn from these differences? Perhaps most surprisingly we must conclude that Absalom's character portrait looks better than Adonijah's! After recovering from this initial shock, we realize this is true by noting another difference: the reader has more of an emotional investment in Absalom's death than Adonijah's. Note that there is no father figure to weep with halting sobs, "O my son Adonijah, my son, my son." If Absalom proved to be a poor imitation of David, then Adonijah was a poor imitation of Absalom; and if nothing good could be said of Absalom, even less can be said of Adonijah (if it is possible to say less than nothing!). In the end, both sons suffer a similar fate, but the reader has a different emotional response. Absalom is dead: the reader suffers with the father. Adonijah is dead: the reader is relieved and rejoices with Solomon.

It is noteworthy that Adonijah led a party of people who sought places of importance, without relying on the call of God. Joab continually maintained his position as commander by the mantra, "Might makes right." As we have noted in an earlier chapter, Abiathar and his son Jonathan were not content with their position. They sought to be on "the winning team" and wound up big losers.

Adonijah defines "blind ambition." It is a sad and ironic truth that self-absorbed people have a difficult time achieving their goal. Often they want to be successful so that they will be loved and admired, or at least in control. Unfortunately, the character flaw of self-centeredness that fuels their ambition becomes their undoing. Their success turns sour, and they lose the power and admiration that they so desire. This is why we do not linger over the death of Adonijah. There are many petty tyrants in this world. We are more captivated by those who live to serve others and who fulfill the call of God on their lives. The Adonijahs are quickly forgotten. It is the Davids who are remembered in this world...and the next.

Conclusion: Family Life and the People of 1 and 2 Samuel

"As for me and my house, we will serve the LORD." (Josh. 24:15)

A Guide to Good Housekeeping

From the joyous birth of Samuel (1 Sam. 1) to the anguished cry of David over the death of Absalom (2 Sam. 18:33ff.), 1 and 2 Samuel realistically depict the range of highs and lows of family life. As gripping as the real stories of families and individuals in these books are, they were not written merely for the purpose of historical record or entertainment; they were written for instruction. The inspired author desired his readers to know that the God of Hannah, Eli, Saul, and David is a God of knowledge and power, who weighs the actions of people and who lifts up the lowly and brings down the proud (1 Sam. 2:3–7). He deserves to be honored and when He is not, there are consequences (1 Sam. 2:30). He is not fooled by pretense, ritual, or appearance, but looks at the heart (1 Sam. 16:7). He is a God who willingly fights for His people because His ultimate desire is their salvation (1 Sam. 17:46–47). Above all, He is a God who desires to bless. As all the families of 1 and 2 Samuel could bear witness to, He is:

> The LORD, the LORD God, merciful and gracious, longsuffering, and abounding in goodness and truth, keeping mercy for thousands, forgiving iniquity and transgression and sin, by no means clearing the guilty, visiting the iniquity of the fathers upon the children and the children's children to the third and the fourth generation (Exod. 34:6–7).

To some in our modern world the stories and principles of Scripture seem alien and antiquated. It is true that the Bible records events from the distant past, using a language and depicting a culture that is different from ours in the western world. However, human beings of every age are the same and we ignore the biblical message at our own peril. The stories of Eli or Saul are there to show us what happens when God is not an integral part of our daily lives. Too many have failed to heed the words of Samuel who warned his people not to turn away from God and go "after empty things which cannot profit or deliver, for they are nothing" (1 Sam. 12:21). We see the consequences of rejecting God all around us and yet we remain oblivious to the cure. God has been chased from our governments, our schools, and our families. The result is greater violence in our society, misguided and dishonest politicians, and fragmented families. Too many in our world know the story of Amnon and Tamar (2 Sam. 13), not because they have read it in Scripture, but because they have experienced it personally. In spite of the story of David and Bathsheba, politicians promote the lie that there is no connection between their private and public lives; and "we the people" buy into it. We are reliving the ugly side of the books of Samuel because we have rejected the God of Samuel. Because we no longer honor Him, He does not honor us. Because we despise Him, we have been lightly esteemed (1 Sam. 2:30). If we can relate to the family and national violence recorded in 1 and 2 Samuel it is because our society is following a similar path. The main sin of Eli's sons, Saul, Nabal, and Amnon was their refusal to hear (1 Sam. 2:25; 15:22; 25:17; 2 Sam. 13:14, 16). Many in our world are turning a deaf ear to the God of Israel. Sadly, there are few who have "ears to hear" (Matt. 13:9, 11–15).

In writing about the various characters and families of 1 and 2 Samuel, I have been particularly distressed over the fact that there are many more negative stories than positive. This observation reveals the ugly truth of how infatuated the human race is with sin. Just as at the beginning, with Adam and Eve, the human race would much rather believe the devil's lie than accept the simple truth of what God says. Like Joab we are independent, sometimes hard, and too full of self-interest. As I have read over the manuscript of this book, I have noted how frequently I have referred to Hannah's phrase, "For by strength no man shall prevail" (1 Sam. 2:9). The modern world has as much trouble learning this lesson as the world of Samuel and David. We are not interested in God's strength or God's answers; we would rather provide our own. It is for these reasons that there are many more negative character portraits in 1 and 2 Samuel than positive, and it is for the same reasons that there is more bad news in this world than good. The words of Jesus illustrate the essential issue of David's world and our own when he said: "Enter by the narrow gate; for wide is the gate and broad is the way that leads to destruction, and there are many who go in by it. Because narrow is the gate and difficult is the way which leads to life, and there are few who find it" (Matt. 7:13–14). The problem with our world is that there are too many "broad-minded" people missing the "narrow way."

While the character studies in this book seem to tip in favor of the "broad way," there were those who chose the more "narrow way which leads to life." 1 and 2 Samuel are books about the houses of Samuel, Eli, Saul, and David, but they are also books that provide guidelines for our own households. Although the "heroes" of 1 and 2 Samuel are far from perfect they illuminate the path that leads to life through their humility, repentance, and trust in God. The positive role models of Elkanah, Hannah, Jonathan, and Abigail (to name a few), point us in a more constructive direction—they point us toward God, and in doing so, they point us toward true life. The books of Samuel are consistent with the rest of Scripture in proclaiming a God who desires to give life to His people (e.g., Deut. 30:19–20). Even when those people are hard and unrepentant, God waits patiently. Doom does not come immediately to the houses of Eli or Saul for God "is longsuffering toward us, not willing that any should perish but that all should come to repentance" (2 Pet. 3:9).

David and his house are an example of this mercy, and the promise that God gives to him (2 Sam. 7) becomes the foundation for the messianic hope in Israel. That promise is the establishment of the throne of David forever (2 Sam. 7:13) which is fulfilled in the birth of Jesus (Luke 1:32). The Gospel of Luke couches Jesus's birth story in the language of 1 Samuel 2. Mary's recognition of God's faithfulness to the Davidic promise leads her to utter words of praise reminiscent of Hannah's prayer (Luke 1:46–55), and in the growth of Jesus we are reminded of the young Samuel (Luke 2:52, cf. 1 Sam. 2:26). Thus the birth of Jesus fulfills what is originally anticipated in 1 and 2 Samuel. He is the True and Righteous King (Rev. 15:3). Jesus Christ from the house of David is the hope of all nations and He is the only hope for your house and mine. As Joshua challenged the people long ago, "Choose for yourselves this day whom you will serve...but as for me and my house, we will serve the LORD" (Josh. 24:15).

Bibliography

Ackerman, James, S. "Knowing Good and Evil: A Literary Analysis of the Court History in 2 Samuel 9–20 and 1 Kings 1–2." *JBL* 109/1, 1990, 41-60.

Ackroyd, P. R. "The First Book of Samuel." *CBC*. Cambridge: Cambridge University Press, 1977.

_____. "The Second Book of Samuel." *CBC*. Cambridge: Cambridge University Press, 1977.

Alter, R. *The Art of Biblical Narrative*. New York: Basic Books Inc., 1981.

_____. *The David Story*. New York & London: W.W. Norton & Company, 1999.

_____. *The World of Biblical Literature*. London: SPCK, 1992.

Amit, Yairah. *Reading Biblical Narratives: Literary Criticism and the Hebrew Bible*. Minneapolis: Fortress Press, 2001.

Anderson, A. A. "2 Samuel." *WBC*. Dallas: Word Books, 1989.

Anderson, Joel Edmund. "A Narrative Reading of Solomon's Execution of Joab in 1 Kings 1–2: Letting Story Interpret Story." *JESOT* 1.1, 2012, 43–62.

Arnold, Bill T. & Williamson, H.G.M eds. *DOTHB*. Downers Grove: IVP Academic, 2005.

Auld, A. Graeme. "Kings," *DSB*. Philadelphia: Westminster Press, 1986.

_____. "I&II Samuel." *OTL*. Louisville: Westminster John Knox Press, 2011.

Avioz, Michael. "The Motif of Beauty in the Books of Samuel and Kings." *VT* 59/3, pp. 2009, 341-359.

Bach, Alice. "The Pleasure of Her Text." *USQR* 43, 1989, 41-58.

Baldwin, J. G. "1&2 Samuel." *TOTC*. Downers Grove: Inter-Varsity Press, 1988.

Bar-Efrat, S. *Narrative Art in the Bible*. Sheffield: JSOT Press, 1989.

Battenhouse, Roy. "The Tragedy of Absalom: A Literary Analysis (II Samuel 13–18)." *Christianity and Literature*, 31/3, 1982, 53-57.

Bergen, R. D. "1, 2 Samuel." *NAC*. Nashville: Broadman & Holman, 1996.

_____. "Authorial Intent and the Spoken Word: A Discourse-critical Analysis of Speech Acts in Accounts of Israel's United Monarchy (1 Sam. 1–1 Kings 11)." *Giving the Sense: Understanding and Using Old Testament Historical Texts*, eds. David M. Howard Jr. and Michael A. Grisanti. Grand Rapids and Leicester: Kregel Publications and Apollos, 2003.

Berlin, Adele. "Characterization in Biblical Narrative: David's wives." *JSOT* 23, 1982, 69-85.

_____. *Poetics and Interpretation of Biblical Narrative*. Sheffield: Almond Press, 1983.

Biddle, Mark E. "Ancestral Motifs in 1 Samuel 25: Intertextuality and Characterization." *JBL* 121/4, 2002, 617-638.

Birch, Bruce C. "The First and Second Books of Samuel: Introduction, Commentary, and Reflections." *NIB*, vol. II ed. L.E. Keck et al., pp. 947-1383. Nashville: Abingdon Press, 1998.

Bodner, Keith. "Is Joab a Reader-Response Critic?" *JSOT* 21, 2002, 19-35.

_____. "Eliab and the Deuteronomist." *JSOT* 28, 2003, 55-71.

Bridge, E. J. "Joab the Commander." *Lexham Bible Dictionary*. Bellingham, WA: Logos Bible Software, 2012.

Brueggemann, Walter. *David's Truth in Israel's Imagination & Memory*. Philadelphia: Fortress Press, 1985.

_____. "First and Second Samuel." *IBC*. Louisville: John Knox Press, 1990.

_____. "Of the Same Flesh and Bone." *CBQ* 32/4, 1970, 532-542.

_____. "On Coping With Curse: A Study of 2 Sam. 16:5–14." *CBQ* 36/2, 1974, 175-192.

Burnside, Jonathan. "Flight of the Fugitives: Rethinking the Relationship Between Biblical Law (Exodus 21:12–14) and the Davidic Succession Narrative (1 Kings 1–2)." *JBL* 12/3, 2010, 418-431.

Camp, Claudia V. "The Wise Women of 2 Samuel: A Role Model for Women in Early Israel?" *CBQ*, 43/1, 1981, 14-29.

Čapek, Filip. "David's ambiguous testament in 1 Kings 2:1–12 and the role of Joab in the Succession Narrative." *Communio Viatorum,* 52/1 2010, 4-26.

Carlson, R.A. *David, the Chosen King: A Traditio-Historical Approach to the Second Book of Samuel*. Stockholm: Almqvist & Wiksell, 1964.

Carson, D. A. "1 and 2 Kings." *NBC*. Leicester; Downers Grove: Inter-Varsity Press, 1994.

Ceresko, A. R. "The Identity of 'the Blind and the Lame' *('iwwer upisseah)* in 2 Samuel 5:8b." *CBQ* 63/1, 2001, 23-30.

Chankin-Gould, J. D'ror and Hutchinson, Derek and Jackson, David Hilton and Mayfield, Tyler D. and Schulte, Leah Rediger and Schneider, Tammie J. and Winkelman, E. "The Sanctified 'Adulteress' and her Circumstantial Clause: Bathsheba's Bath and Self-Consecration in 2 Samuel 11." *JSOT* 32, 2008, 339-352.

Chisholm, R. B. Jr. *Interpreting the Historical Books: An Exegetical Handbook*. Grand Rapids: Kregel, 2006.

Clines, D. J. A. and Eskenazi, Tamara C., eds. "Telling Queen Michal's Story: An Experiment in Comparative Interpretation." *JSOT* Supp. 119. Sheffield: Sheffield Academic Press, 1991.

Clines, D. J. A. "X, X Ben Y: Personal Names in Hebrew Narrative Style." *VT* 22/3, 1972, 266-287.

Coats, George W. "Self-abasement and Insult Formulas." *JBL* 89/1, 1970, 14-26.

_____. "Parable, Fable, and Anecdote: Storytelling in the Succession Narrative." *Int.* 35/4, 1981, 368-382.

Conroy, Charles. *Absalom Absalom! Narrative and Language in 2 Sam 13–20.* Analecta Biblica 81. Rome: Biblical Institute, 1978.

Cooper-White, Pamela. *The Cry of Tamar: Violence Against Women and the Church's Response.* Minneapolis: Fortress Press, 1995.

Cotter, David W. *Genesis,* Berit Olam: Studies in Hebrew Narrative & Poetry. Collegeville: The Liturgical Press, 2003.

Cryer, F. H. "David's Rise to Power and the Death of Abner: and Analysis of 1 Samuel 26:14–16 and Its Redaction-Critical Implications." *VT* 35/4, 1985, 385-394.

Daube, David. "Absalom and the Ideal King." *VT,* 48/3, 1998, 315-325.

Davis, Dale Ralph. *1 Samuel: Looking on the Heart.* Ross-shire: Christian Focus, 2000.

_____. *2 Samuel: Out of Every Adversity.* Ross-shire: Christian Focus, 1999.

DeSilva, D. A. *Honor, Patronage, Kinship & Purity.* Downers Grove: IVP Academic, 2000.

de Vaux, R. *Ancient Israel, Volume 1: Social Institutions.* New York, Toronto: McGraw Hill Book Company, 1965.

Dilday, R. "1, 2 Kings." *MTOT.* Dallas: Word Publishing, 1987.

Dillard, R. B. and Longman III., T. *An Introduction to the Old Testament.* Leicester: APOLLOS, 1995.

Driver, S. R. *Notes on the Hebrew Text and the Topography of the Books of Samuel.* 2nd ed. Oxford: Clarendon Press, 1913.

Eggerichs, E. *Love & Respect.* Nashville: Integrity Publishers, 2004.

Eschelbach, Michael A. "Has Joab Foiled David? A Literary Study of the Importance of Joab's Character in Relation to David." *Studies in Biblical Literature 76,* New York: Peter Lang Publishing, 2005.

Evans, M. J. *The Message of Samuel.* Leicester: Inter-Varsity Press, 2004.

Exum, J. Cheryl. "Bathsheba, Plotted, Shot, and Painted." *Semeia* 74, 1996, 47-73.

_____. "Rizpah." *Word & World,* vol. XVII/3, 1997, 260-268.

Fensham, F.C. "The Battle Between the Men of Joab and Abner as a Possible Ordeal By Battle." *VT* 20/3, 1970, 356-357.

Fewell, Danna Nolan and Gunn, David M. *Gender, Power, and Promise: The Subject of the Bible's First Story.* Nashville: Abingdon, 1993.

Firth, David G. "1&2 Samuel," *AOTC.* Downers Grove: InterVaristy Press, 2009.

Fokkelman, J.P. *Narrative Art and Poetry in the Books of Samuel,* Vol. I: *King David (II Sam. 9–20 and I Kings 1–2).* Assen/Maastricht & Dover: Van Gorcum, 1981.

_____. *Narrative Art and Poetry in the Books of Samuel,* Vol. II: *The Crossing Fates (I Sam. 13–31 and II Sam. 1).* Assen/Maastricht & Dover: Van Gorcum, 1986.

_____. *Narrative Art and Poetry in the Books of Samuel,* Vol. III: *Throne and City (II Sam. 2–8 and 21–24).* Assen/Maastricht & Dover: Van Gorcum, 1990.

_____. *Narrative Art and Poetry in the Books of Samuel,* Vol. IV: *Vow and Desire (I Sam. 1–12).* Assen/Maastricht & Dover: Van Gorcum, 1993.

Fontaine, Carole. "The Bearing of Wisdom on the Shape of 2 Samuel 11–12 and 1 King 3." *JSOT* 34, 1986, 61-77.

Freedman, David Noel. "Dinah and Shechem Tamar and Amnon." *Austin Seminary Bulletin* 105, 1990, 51-63.

Fretheim, T. "First and Second Kings." *Westminster Bible Companion.* Louisville: Westminster John Knox Press, 1999.

Frymer-Kensky, Tikva. *Reading the Women of the Bible.* New York: Schocken Books, 2002

Garsiel, Moshe. "The Story of David and Bathsheba: A Different Approach." *CBQ* 55/2, 1993, 244-262.

Geyer, Marcia L. "Stopping the Juggernaut: A Close Reading of 2 Samuel 20:13–22." *USQR* 41, 1986, 33-42.

Gordon, Robert P. *I&II Samuel.* Exeter: Paternoster Press, 1986.

Gray, John. "I&II Kings." *OTL.* London: SCM Press, 1964.

Gray, Mark. "Amnon: A Chip Off the Old Block? Rhetorical Strategy in 2 Samuel 13:7–15: The Rape of Tamar and the Humiliation of the Poor." *JSOT* 77, 1998, 39-54.

Greenberg, Moshe. "Job." *The Literary Guide to the Bible.* eds. Robert Alter & Frank Kermode. Cambridge: Harvard University Press, 1987.

Gros Louis, K. R.R. "King David of Israel." *Literary Interpretations of Biblical Narratives.* Vol. II. ed. Kenneth R.R. Gros Louis. Nashville: Abingdon, 1982, 204-219.

Gunn, David M. "David and the Gift of the Kingdom." *Semeia* 3, 1975, 14-45.

_____. "Traditional Composition in the 'Succession Narrative.' " *VT* 26/2, 1976, 214-229.

_____. "The Story of King David: Genre and Interpretation," *JSOT,* Supp. 6, Sheffield: JSOT Press, 1978.

_____. "The Fate of King Saul: An Interpretation of a Biblical Story," *JSOT,* Supp. 14, Sheffield: JSOT Press, 1980.

Guzik, D. "Verse by Verse Commentary: 2 Samuel," *EWCS.* Redlands: Enduring WordMedia, 2004.

Hamilton, G. J. "New Evidence for the Authenticity of *bšt* in Hebrew Personal Names and for Its Use as a Divine Epithet in Biblical Texts." *CBQ* 60/2, 1998, 228-250.

Hamilton, V. P. *Handbook on the Historical Books*. Grand Rapids: Baker Academic, 2001.

Hauer, C. E. "Who Was Zadok?" *JBL* 82, 1963, 89-94.

Henry, Caleb. "Joab: A Biblical Critique of Machiavellian Tactics." *WTJ* 69, 2007, 327-343.

Hertzberg, H. W. "I & II Samuel." *OTL* Philadelphia: Westminster Press, 1964.

Ho, C.Y.S. "The Stories of the Family Troubles of Judah and David: A Study of Their Literary Links." *VT* 49/4, 1999, 514-531.

Hoftijzer, Jacob. "David and the Tekoite Woman." *VT* 20/4, 1970, 419-444.

Holloway, Steven W. "Distaff, Crutch or Chain Gang: The Curse of the House of Joab in 2 Samuel III 29." *VT* 38/3, 1987, 370-375.

Homan, Michael M. "Booths or Succoth? A Response to Yigael Yadin." *JBL* 118/4, 1999, 691-697.

House, Paul R. "1, 2 Kings." *NAC*. Nashville: Broadman & Holman, 1995.

Howard, David M. Jr., *An Introduction to the Old Testament Historical Books*. Chicago: Moody Press, 1993.

_____. "Joshua." *NAC*. Nashville: Broadman & Holman Publishers, 1998.

Jacobson, H. "Genesis iv 8." *VT* 55/4, 2005, 564-565.

Jensen, Hans, J. L. "Desire, Rivalry, and Collective Violence in the 'Succession Narrative.' " *JSOT* 55, 1992, 39-59.

Jobling, D. "1 Samuel." *Berit Olam: Studies in Hebrew Narrative & Poetry*. Collegeville: The Liturgical Press, 1998.

_____. *The Sense of Biblical Narrative, Jonathan: A Structural Study in 1 Samuel*. Sheffield: JSOT, 1978.

Kessler, John. "Sexuality and politics: the motif of the displaced husband in the Books of Samuel." *CBQ* 62/3, 2000, 409-423.

Kim, Uriah (Yong-Hwan). "Uriah the Hittite: A (Con)Text of Struggle for Identity." *Semeia* 90-91, 2002, 69-85.

Klein, R. W. "1 Samuel." *WBC*. Waco: Word Books, 1983.

Koopmans, W.T. "The Testament of David in 1 Kings 2:1–10." *VT* 41/4, 1991, 429-449.

Leithart, Peter J. "A Son to Me: An Exposition of 1&2 Samuel." Moscow: Canon Press, 2003.

_____. "1&2 Kings." *BTCB*. Grand Rapids: Brazos Press, 2006.

Levenson, Jon D. and Halpern, Baruch. "The Political Import of David's Marriages." *JBL* 99/4, 1980, 507-518.

Levenson, Jon D. "I Samuel 25 as Literature and as History." *Literary Interpretations of Biblical Narratives*, Vol. II. ed. Kenneth R.R. Gros Louis. Nashville: Abingdon, 1982, 220-242.

Long, Burke O. "A Darkness Between Brothers: Solomon and Adonijah." *JSOT* 19, 1981, 79-94.

Long, V. Phillips. *The Reign and Rejection of King Saul.* Atlanta: Scholars Press, 1989.

Macwilliam, Stuart. "Ideologies of Male Beauty and the Hebrew Bible." *BibInt.* 17/3, 2009, 265-287.

Malina, B. J. *The New Testament World: Insights from Cultural Anthropology.* Louisville & London: John Knox Press, 3rd edition, 2001.

_____. *Windows on the World of Jesus.* Louisville: Westminster/John Knox Press, 1993.

Mazar, Eilat. "Did I Find King David's Palace?" *BAR* 32:01, 2006.

McCarter, P. K. "1 Samuel." *AB.* Garden City: Doubleday & Company, Inc., 1980.

_____. "2 Samuel." *AB.* Garden City: Doubleday & Company, Inc., 1984.

McCarthy, D.J. *Old Testament Covenant: A Survey of Current Opinions.* Richmond: John Knox Press, 1972.

McEvenue, Sean E. "The Basis of Empire, A Study of the Succession Narrative." *Ex auditu* 2, 1986, 34-45.

McKane, W. "I&II Samuel." *TBC.* London: SCM Press, 1963.

Miscall, P. D. *1 Samuel: A Literary Reading.* Bloomington: Indiana University Press, 1986.

Murphy, Francesca Aran. "1 Samuel." *BTCB.* Grand Rapids: Brazos Press, 2010.

Nelson, Richard. "First and Second Kings." *IBC.* Atlanta: John Knox Press, 1987.

Nicol, George G. "The Alleged Rape of Bathsheba: Some Observations on Ambiguity in Biblical Narrative." *JSOT* 73, 1997, 43-54.

Niditch, Susan. *'My Brother Esau is a Hairy Man': Hair and Identity in Ancient Israel.* Oxford: Oxford University Press, 2008.

Noth, M. "The Deuteronomistic History." *JSOT* Supp. 15, Sheffield: JSOT Press, 1981.

Olyan, Saul M. "Zadok's Origins and the Tribal Politics of David." *JBL* 101/2, 1982, 177-193.

_____. "Honor, Shame, and Covenant Relations in Ancient Israel and Its Environment." *JBL* 115/2, 1996, 201-218.

Omanson, R. L. & Ellington, J. *A handbook on the Second Book of Samuel.* UBS Handbook Series. New York: United Bible Societies, 2001.

O'Rourke Boyle, Marjorie. "The Law of the Heart: The Death of a Fool (1 Samuel 25)." *JBL* 120/3, 2001, 401-427.

Park, Song-Mi Suzie. "The Frustration of Wisdom: Wisdom, Counsel, and Divine Will in 2 Samuel 17:1–23." *JBL* 128/3, 2009, 453-467.

Peleg, Yaron. "Love at First Sight? David, Jonathan, and the Biblical Politics of Gender." *JSOT* 30.2, 2005, 171-189.

Perdue, L.G. " 'Is There Anyone Left of the House of Saul...?' Ambiguity and the Characterization of David in the Succession Narrative." *JSOT* 30, 1984, 67-84.

Phillips, Anthony. "NEBALAH—a term for serious disorderly and unruly conduct." *VT* 25/2, 1975, 237-242.

Pigott, Susan M. "Wives, Witches and Wise Women: Prophetic Heralds of Kingship in 1 and 2 Samuel." *Review & Expositor*, 99/**2**, 2002, 145-173.

Polzin, Robert. *David and the Deuteronomist: A Literary Study of the Deuteronomic History, Part Three: 2 Samuel*. Bloomington & Indianapolis: Indiana University Press, 1993.

_____. *Samuel and the Deuteronomist*. Bloomington: Indiana University Press, 1989.

Propp, William H. "Kinship in 2 Samuel 13," *CBQ* 55/1, 1993, 39-53.

Provan, Iain W. "1 and 2 Kings." *NIBC*. Peabody: Hendrickson Publishers, Inc., 1995.

_____. "Why Barzillai of Gilead (1 Kings 2:7)? Narrative Art and the Hermeneutics of Suspicion in 1 Kings 1–2." *TynB*, 46/1, 1995, 103-116.

Provan, I., Long, V. P., and Longman III, T. *A Biblical History of Israel*. Louisville: Westminster John Knox Press, 2003.

Redpath, Alan. *The Making of a Man of God: Studies in the Life of David*. Grand Rapids: Fleming H. Revell, 1962.

Reinhartz, Adele. "Anonymity and Character in the Books of Samuel." *Semeia* 63, 1993, 117-141.

Reis, P. T. "What Cain said: A Note on Genesis 4.8." *JSOT* 27/1, 2002, 107-113.

Rendsburg, G. A. "David and His Circle in Genesis xxxviii." *VT* 36/4, 1986, 438-446.

Rowe, Jonathan. "Is Jonathan Really David's 'Wife'? A Response to Yaron Peleg." *JSOT* 34.2, 2009, 183-193.

Rowley, H. H. "Zadok and Nehustan." *JBL* 58, 1939, 113-141.

Rosenberg, Joel. *King and Kin: Political Allegory in the Hebrew Bible*. Bloomington & Indianapolis: Indiana University Press, 1986.

_____. "The Institutional Matrix of Treachery in Second Samuel 11." *Semeia* 46, 1989, 103-116.

Rost, L. *The Succession to the Throne of David*. Sheffield: Almond Press, 1982.

Ryken, L. and Longman III, T. eds. *A Complete Literary Guide to the Bible*. Grand Rapids: Zondervan, 1993.

Schipper, J. "Reconsidering the Imagery of Disability in 2 Samuel 5:8b." *CBQ* 67/3, 2005, 422-434.

_____. " 'Why do you still speak of your affairs?': Polyphony in Mephibosheth's Exchanges with David in Samuel." *VT* 54/3, 2004, 344-351.

Schwartz, Regina M. "Adultery in the House of David: The Metanarrative of Biblical Scholarship and the Narratives of the Bible." *Semeia* 54, 1991, 35-55.

Scott, R.B.Y. *The Way of Wisdom in the Old Testament.* New York & London: MacMillan Publishers, 1971.

Sheriffs, Deryck. "The Human Need for Continuity, Some ANE and OT Perspectives." *TynB* 55/1, 2004, 1-16.

Silva, Moises. *God, Language and Scripture: Reading the Bible in the Light of General Linguistics.* Grand Rapids: Zondervan Publishing House, 1990.

Smith, M. J. "The Failure of the Family in Judges, Part 1: Jephthah." *BSac.* 162/647, 2005, 279-298.

_____. "The Failure of the Family in Judges, Part 2: Samson." *BSac.* 162/648, 2005, 424-436.

Soggin, J.A. "The Reign of Eshba'al, Son of Saul." *Old Testament and Oriental Studies* Rome: Pontifical Biblical Institute, 1975.

Stansell, Gary. "Honor and Shame in the David Narratives." *Semeia* 68, 1994, 55-79.

Sternberg, M. *The Poetics of Biblical Narrative: Ideological Literature and the Drama of Reading.* Bloomington: Indiana University Press, 1987.

Swindoll, C. R. *A Man of Passion & Destiny: David.* Dallas: Word Publishing, 1997.

Trible, Phyllis. *Texts of Terror: Literary-Feminist Readings of Biblical Narratives.* Philadelphia: Fortress Press, 1984.

Tsevat, M. "Ishbosheth and Congeners: The Names and Their Study." *HUCA* 46, 1975, 71-87.

Tsumura, D. T. "The First Book of Samuel." *NICOT.* Grand Rapids: Wm. B. Eerdmans, 2007.

Vanderkam, J. "Davidic Complicity in the Deaths of Abner and Eshbaal: A Historical and Redactional Study." *JBL* 99/4, 1980, 521-539.

Vannoy, J. Robert. "1–2 Samuel." *Cornerstone Biblical Commentary.* Carol Stream Tyndale House Publishers, Inc., 2009.

Vasholz, Robert I. "The Wisdom of Bathsheba in 1 Kings 2:13–25." *Presbyterion* 33, 2007, 49.

Wenham, Gordon J. "*B^ETÛLAH* 'A GIRL OF MARRIAGEABLE AGE.' " *VT* 22/3, 1972, 326-348.

_____. "The Book of Leviticus." *NICOT.* Grand Rapids: Wm. B. Eerdmans, 1979.

_____. *Story as Torah.* Grand Rapids: Baker Academic, 2000.

Wesselius, J. W. "Joab's Death and the Central Theme of the Succession Narrative (2 Samuel IX–1 Kings II)." *VT* 40/3 (1990), 336-351.

Wharton, James, A. "A Plausible Tale: Story and Theology in II Samuel 9—20, I Kings 1—2." *Int.* 35/4, 1981, 341-354.

Whybray, R. N. *The Succession Narrative: A Study of II Sam. 9–20 and 1 Kings 1 and 2*. London: SCM Press, Ltd., 1968.

Wiersbe, W. W. *The Bible Exposition Commentary: Old Testament History, 1 Samuel.* Colorado Springs: Victor, 2003.

Willis, J. T. "An Anti-Elide Narrative Tradition from a Prophetic Circle at the Ramah Sanctuary." *JBL* 90/3, 1971, 288-308.

_____. "First and Second Samuel." *LWC.* Austin: Sweet Publishing Company, 1982.

_____. "The Function of Comprehensive Anticipatory Redactional Joints in I Samuel 16–18." *ZAW* 85, 1973, 294-314.

Wiseman, Donald J. "1 and 2 Kings." *TOTC.* Leicester: IVP, 1993.

Wong, Gregory T.K. "Ehud and Joab: Separated at Birth?" *VT*, 56/3 2006, 399-412.

Woudstra, Martin H. "The Book of Joshua." *NICOT.* Grand Rapids: Wm. B. Eerdmans, 1981.

Yee, Gale A. "Fraught with Background: Literary Ambiguity in II Samuel 11." *Int.* 42, 1988, 240-253.

Youngblood, R. F. "1, 2 Samuel." *EBC*, vol. 3. Grand Rapids: Zondervan. 1992.

Zehnder, M. "Observations on the relationship between David and Jonathan and the debate on homosexuality." *WTJ* 69, 2007, 127-174.

Index of Authors

A

Ackerman, 172, 358, 382, 399
Ackroyd, 2, 133, 146, 151, 154, 177, 189, 191, 223, 287, 399
Alter, 7, 10, 28, 78, 89, 120, 123, 143, 166, 170, 186, 192, 207, 212, 218, 223, 232, 235, 247, 248, 264, 274, 276, 283, 287, 288, 296, 303, 307, 313, 314, 317, 345, 365, 367, 385, 391, 399, 402
Amit, 351, 399
Anderson, A. A, 142, 170, 234, 270, 282, 307, 313, 316, 320, 343, 358, 359, 360, 365, 399
Anderson, Joel, 296, 399
Arnold, Bill T, and H.G.M. Williamson 199, 399
Auld, 22, 189, 267, 270, 274, 281, 283, 298, 399
Avioz, 364, 366, 399

B

Bach, 215, 216, 219, 399
Baldwin, 51, 52, 175, 180, 224, 262, 271, 286, 322, 399
Bar-Efrat, 7, 10, 31, 110, 287, 295, 307, 320, 321, 325, 331, 332, 339, 341, 342, 367, 369, 373, 375, 379, 382, 386, 387, 399
Battenhouse, 382, 399
Bergen, 67, 71, 85, 112, 113, 114, 124, 138, 143, 144, 161, 166, 170, 177, 179, 185, 212, 213, 215, 218, 221, 262, 306, 307, 320, 333, 337, 365, 370, 399
Berlin, 7, 10, 239, 248, 253, 399
Biddle, 214, 225, 226, 400
Birch, 1, 28, 30, 34, 76, 207, 212, 218, 231, 232, 233, 275, 307, 315, 400
Bodner, 204, 205, 207, 208, 209, 272, 276, 400
Bridge, 281, 400
Brueggemann, 5, 100, 140, 146, 174, 185, 204, 266, 268, 277, 282, 286, 303, 304, 305, 314, 343, 400
Burnside, 296, 400

C

Camp, 290, 400
Čapek, 260, 400
Carlson, 133, 183, 353, 400
Carson, 247, 400
Ceresko, 180, 400
Chankin-Gould, J. D'ror and Hutchinson, Derek and Jackson, David Hilton, 235, 400
Chisholm, 8, 11, 12, 13, 14, 159, 176, 400
Clines, 11, 13, 14, 125, 126, 130, 268, 400
Clines, and Eskenazi, 11, 126, 400
Coats, 169, 360, 401
Conroy, 179, 283, 285, 331, 335, 341, 356, 359, 376, 378, 382, 401
Cotter, 11, 16
Cooper-White, 351, 401
Corney, 51, 89
Cotterell, 171
Cryer, 258, 401

D

Dalglish, 167
Daube, 338, 373, 401
Davis, 14, 276, 277, 317, 344, 358, 361, 401
de Vaux, 34, 327, 401
DeSilva, 25, 61, 401
Dilday, 91, 245, 253, 401
Dillard, and Longman III, 3, 8, 46, 401
Driver, vi, 274, 401

E

Eggerichs, 134, 401
Eschelbach, 14, 263, 265, 268, 270, 282, 401
Evans, 1, 26, 27, 95, 108, 121, 141, 147, 170, 272, 276, 363, 401
Exum, 160, 161, 231, 232, 235, 401

F

Fensham, 142, 401
Fewell, and Gunn, 119, 401

Firth, 8, 138, 149, 162, 176, 224, 225, 261,
    269, 292, 302, 307, 315, 316, 320, 339,
    349, 360, 363, 364, 401
Fokkelman, 4, 23, 30, 84, 85, 86, 90, 91,
    96, 109, 110, 115, 116, 119, 124, 127,
    130, 131, 132, 138, 143, 146, 147, 148,
    153, 156, 159, 161, 162, 166, 169, 177,
    179, 180, 183, 184, 192, 201, 222, 223,
    236, 242, 245, 247, 250, 251, 253, 265,
    269, 272, 273, 274, 279, 285, 286, 287,
    289, 302, 304, 308, 310, 311, 315, 321,
    322, 324, 331, 343, 344, 356, 358, 359,
    360, 362, 367, 369, 371, 373, 375, 379,
    382, 387, 392, 401-402
Fontaine, 240, 241, 402
Freedman, 336, 402
Fretheim, 188, 402
Frymer-Kensky, 217, 219, 339, 341, 342,
    402

G

Garsiel, 231, 233, 246, 402
Gesenius, vii, 233
Geyer, 290, 318, 402
Gordon, 130, 137, 145, 161, 174, 179,
    198, 265, 274, 322, 402
Gray, John, 96, 390, 391, 402
Gray, Mark, 332, 335, 350, 402
Greenberg, 307, 402
Gros Louis, 6, 209, 213, 402, 403
Gunn, 6, 100, 119, 211, 212, 216, 221,
    228, 246, 315, 317, 356, 391, 393, 401,
    402
Guzik, 181, 402

H

Hamilton, G, 152, 167, 174, 402
Hamilton, V. P., 43, 180, 186, 190, 192,
    196, 217, 249, 276, 277, 357, 362, 373,
    375, 386, 403
Harvey, 127, 258, 259, 403
Hauer, 93, 403
Henry, 264, 269, 282, 298, 299, 403
Hertzberg, 80, 121, 151, 156, 169, 170,
    176, 263, 275, 313, 316, 403
Ho, C.Y.S, 346, 403
Hoftijzer, 216, 361, 403
Holloway, 265, 403
Homan, 270, 403
House, Paul, 8, 188, 252, 403

Howard, 46, 112, 215, 403

J

Jacobson, 113, 403
Jensen, 254, 265, 363, 371, 403
Jobling, 5, 9, 103, 105, 114, 115, 119, 121,
    200, 403

K

Kessler, 243, 403
Kim, 234, 403
Klein, 30, 67, 81, 302, 403
Koopmans, 188, 403

L

Latoundji, 90, 403
Leithart, 11, 68, 191, 193, 289, 292, 371,
    389, 391, 392, 403
Levenson, Jon D, 213, 217, 220, 223, 403
Levenson, and Halpern, 225, 403
Long, Burke, 386, 403
Long, V. Phillips, 7, 10, 14, 103, 104, 404

M

Macwilliam, 366, 404
Malina, 27, 41, 61, 62, 333, 345, 404
Mazar, 233, 404
McCarter, 2, 28, 42, 77, 78, 137, 138, 144,
    151, 152, 154, 185, 218, 232, 234, 267,
    270, 274, 280, 284, 290, 303, 304, 306,
    312, 313, 314, 316, 320, 327, 335, 338,
    342, 358, 359, 365, 365, 404
McCarthy, 107, 404
McEvenue, 256, 361, 363, 404
McKane, 72, 91, 237, 404
Merrill, 7, 404
Miscall, 80, 103, 216, 224, 404
Murphy, 38, 40, 213, 404

N

Nelson, 189, 248, 295, 296, 387, 390, 393,
    404
Nicol, 231, 235, 248, 404
Niditch, 364, 378, 404
Noth, 8, 404

O

O'Rourke, 223, 404
Olivier, 190, 404
Olyan, 61, 93, 287, 404
Omanson, R. L. & Ellington, J, 284, 404

P

Park, 241, 375, 404
Peleg, 107, 108, 120, 122, 404, 405
Perdue, 10, 405
Phillips, 337, 405
Pigott, 132, 219, 277, 405
Polzin, 26, 34, 43, 44, 51, 100, 112, 131,
    137, 148, 156, 166, 175, 180, 205, 207,
    214, 310, 317, 318, 330, 344, 347, 358,
    370, 377, 405
Propp, 332, 339, 360, 405
Provan, 295, 387, 389, 390, 405
Provan, Long, and Longman III, 7, 405

R

Redpath, 172, 405
Reinhartz, 78, 405
Reis, 113, 405
Rendsburg, 346, 405
Rice, 40, 405
Rosenberg, 5, 15, 231, 232, 233, 239, 260,
    269, 280, 322, 328, 333, 339, 350, 405
Rost, 15, 232, 256, 356, 405
Rowe, 107, 108, 405
Rowley, 93, 405
Ryken, and Longman III, 9, 16, 405

S

Schipper, 169, 177, 180, 405
Schumacher, 80, 406
Scott, 320, 406
Sheriffs, 380, 406
Silva, 12, 406
Smith, D. D. and Michael W, 114, 406
Smith, M. J, 6, 406
Soggin, 140, 141, 406

Stansell, 61, 115, 133, 213, 217, 332, 333,
    406
Sternberg, 7, 9, 13, 25, 100, 198, 231, 273,
    274, 275, 406
Swindoll, 171, 172, 406

T

Trible, 321, 331, 334, 335, 340, 341, 342,
    406
Tsevat, 151, 152, 167, 406
Tsumura, 8, 19, 21, 23, 51, 52, 104, 138,
    141, 198, 201, 218, 220, 406

V

Vanderkam, 184, 265, 266, 406
Vannoy, 143, 147, 220, 222, 233, 287, 306,
    314, 348, 358, 406
Vasholz, 252, 406

W

Wenham, 9, 15, 31, 332, 333, 374, 406
Wesselius, 234, 407
Wharton, 372, 407
Whybray, 240, 253, 270, 286, 320, 322,
    326, 353, 354, 355, 368, 389, 407
Wiersbe, 106, 145, 147, 314, 407
Willis, ix, 42, 52, 73, 81, 138, 141, 156,
    175, 220, 269, 272, 315, 327, 407
Wiseman, 296, 407
Wong, 263, 264, 289, 295, 407
Woudstra, 247, 407

Y

Yee, 231, 236, 407
Youngblood, 21, 95, 119, 123, 145, 156,
    183, 186, 215, 225, 237, 268, 281, 284,
    306, 307, 310, 313, 335, 344, 407

Z

Zehnder, 107, 108, 119, 120, 407

Subject Index

351, 356, 360, 361, 368, 382, 386, 396, 397

G

H

I

J

K

L

M

Y

Yahweh, 19, 51, 80, 108, 114, 126, 133, 135, 151, 152, 162, 183, 186, 207, 218, 224, 271, 291, 304, 365, 388
YHWH, 108, 120, 219, 297

Z

Zadok, 51, 73, 80, 91, 92, 93, 94, 96, 183, 281, 284, 294, 380, 389, 390
Zedekiah, 78

Zeruiah, sons of, 258, 259, 260, 263, 266, 267, 268, 269, 276, 280, 301, 302, 303, 304, 305, 306, 309, 311, 313, 314, 359
Ziba, iv, 3, 101, 165, 166, 168, 169, 170, 171, 173, 174, 175, 176, 177, 178, 179, 181, 183, 186
Ziphites, 100
Zoheleth, 390
Zophim, 9, 21, 22
Zuph, 22, 25

434

386 — David's imgafn
388 — not sen oh
389

394 compad A vd
+ Ab.

Made in the USA
Lexington, KY
23 May 2014